REAL WORLD
ADOBE®
ILLUSTRATOR® CS2

MORDY GOLDING

Peachpit
Press

Adobe

REAL WORLD ADOBE® ILLUSTRATOR® CS2
Mordy Golding

Peachpit Press
1249 Eighth Street
Berkeley, CA 94710
510/524-2178
800/283-9444
510/524-2221 (fax)

Find us on the World Wide Web at: www.peachpit.com
To report errors, please send a note to errata@peachpit.com
Peachpit Press is a division of Pearson Education
Real World Adobe Illustrator CS2 is published in association with Adobe Press.

Editor: Karyn Johnson
Production Editor: Becky Winter
Copy Editor: Rebecca Rider
Proofreader: Corbin Collins
Compositor: Chris Gillespie, Happenstance Type-O-Rama
Indexer: Joy Dean Lee
Cover Illustrator: Ron Chan
Cover Design: Aren Howell
Cover Art Direction: Charlene Charles-Will
Cover Production: Ellen Reilly

ISBN 0-321-33702-6

9 8 7 6 5 4 3 2 1

Printed and bound in the United States of America

This book is dedicated to my wife and kids, who have waited patiently for it to be finished so that they could have their husband and father back.

ACKNOWLEDGMENTS

There are two people who I need to thank first, even though words can't really describe the gratitude I owe for their sincere friendship. Sharon Steuer and Sandee Cohen helped me to establish myself in the Illustrator community, and for that I am eternally grateful. Sharon has also been extremely generous in allowing me to feature an excerpt from her award-winning book, *The Adobe Illustrator CS2 Wow! Book.*

I've written books before and when I was approached to write this title, I thought it would be an easy task. Months later, I look back and realize how much work has gone into this book, and I have a new appreciation for the team at Peachpit Press. Thanks to Kelly Ryer, Marjorie Baer, Nancy Ruenzel, Nancy Davis, Rebecca Ross, Rachel Tiley, and the folks at Adobe Press. I want to personally thank Rebecca Rider for copyediting this book, Corbin Collins for his proofreading edits, Becky Winter for her work in production, and David Karlins for ensuring that everything I wrote was technically accurate. Most of all, I want to thank my superb editor, Karyn Johnson, for her awesome ideas, endless patience, and demand for excellence. In addition, I'd like to give thanks to James Talmage—affectionately known to many as "JET,"—for writing the FreeHand appendix, for being a great friend, and for sharing his passion for excellence.

If you think publishing a book is a huge undertaking, I can assure you that producing an application like Adobe Illustrator is an even greater task. Special thanks go to the entire Illustrator team for their concerted efforts, and specifically to Lydia Varmazis, Leon Brown, Phil Guindi, Teri Pettit, Dave MacLachlan, and Shane Tracy for their personal assistance and advice. I also want to mention a special note of thanks to my friends Ted Alspach and Dave Burkett who brought me into the Adobe family. Thanks also to Thomas Phinney, John Nack, Will Eisley, Lynn Grillo, Julieanne Kost, and the always-entertaining Russell Brown for their continued friendship.

I'm lucky enough to count a number of professional authors and educators among my friends. Thanks to David Blatner, Chris and Jennifer Smith, Ben Willmore, Deke McClelland, Luanne Cohen, Claudia McCue, and Matthew Richmond who continue to share advice, support, and funny anecdotes over the occasional drink.

Thanks to *Wow!* artists Bert Monroy, Conrad Chavez, Ivan Torres, Yukio Miyamoto, Scott Crouse, Alan James Weimer, Brad Neal, and Steven Gordon for allowing me to feature their spectacular artwork in the color section of this book.

Even though he's a die-hard SF Giants fan (I'm a NY Mets fan), I reserve a personal note of appreciation for my friend Ron Chan who created the wonderful illustration that appears on the cover of this book.

You can't write a book unless you have a clear mind, and nothing clears the mind like the smell of fresh cut grass and the sound of your golf ball dropping into the bottom of a cup early in the morning. Thanks to Jeremy, Eli, and Shimmy for putting up with my writing schedule and for getting me out onto the course. Bethpage Black next week?

Finally, I want to thank my entire family for their encouraging words of support. I appreciate everything that you do for me and hope that I make all of you proud.

TABLE OF CONTENTS

INTRODUCTION

Because I've been the product manager of Adobe Illustrator, people frequently approach me who, prior to attending a demo or workshop on Illustrator, either thought they had no need for the program or were under the impression that it is only used for designing logos.

The truth is, Illustrator is essential to a broad range of professionals and hobbyists, and it has an incredible number of uses—so many that it's hard to define exactly what Illustrator does. Features like transparency, 3D, Live Trace, Live Paint, gradient mesh, Live Effects, professional typography, Flash animation, and SVG support have all redefined how people use Illustrator every day. It's certainly not the same program that it was ten years ago.

My goal with this book is three-fold: to teach new users how to take advantage of the technology, to help experienced users learn about things that have changed, and to give power users the understanding they need to push the envelope and produce reliable files. I love showing people all the cool and productive things you can do with the product, and nothing makes me happier than seeing a designer crank out a totally awesome design using Illustrator. Throughout this book, I share my thoughts, experiences, and knowledge about Illustrator so that you can have fun with it, sharpen your skills, and make it work for you.

THE MANY USES OF ILLUSTRATOR

Look all around you.

Billboard signs along the side of the highway, packages of cereal and groceries at the supermarket, navigation icons on a Web site, posters announcing an exhibit at a museum, advertisements throughout magazines and newspapers, logos and artwork on t-shirts and sportswear, animated cartoons and feature films, user interfaces on your computer and cell phones . . . all of these—and more—are created with the help of Adobe Illustrator.

Illustrator is used by creative individuals who want to express their creativity in print, on the Web, in video, and on wireless devices. The program itself is distributed in many different languages, and you can find millions of Illustrator users across the globe. Of course, with such a diverse user base, Illustrator itself is used and applied in many ways. To get an idea of what I mean, take a look at how some creative professionals use Illustrator and how this book can help them.

 The Adobe Illustrator CS2 WOW! Book, by Sharon Steuer (Peachpit Press, 2006), contains numerous examples of how some of the world's most talented artists are using Illustrator today. Refer to the color insert of this book to see an excerpt from it.

Creative Genius: The World of Graphic Design

It's difficult to define a graphic designer because the title itself encompasses so many different types of design. For the most part, graphic designers specialize in a particular field of design like corporate, advertising, direct mail, or even typography. Graphic designers work on a variety of projects and usually have experience with several programs including Photoshop and InDesign or QuarkXPress.

For these kinds of users, Illustrator serves as a creative springboard for designs such as logos and type treatments, ad storyboards and campaigns, spot illustrations, maps, charts, and general design elements.

If you're a graphic designer, you'll find the following chapters most helpful as you read through this book:

- Chapter 3: *Objects, Groups, and Layers* (page 69)

- Chapter 4: *Advanced Vectors* (page 99)

- Chapter 6: *Typography* (page 181)

- Chapter 7: *3D and Other Live Effects* (page 211)

- Chapter 8: *Mixing It Up: Working with Vectors and Pixels* (page 285)

- Chapter 9: *Graphs, Distortion, and Blends* (page 323)

Telling a Story: Illustration and Animation

To an animator or an illustrator, Adobe Illustrator is an empty canvas waiting to come alive. In a world of animated feature films and TV shows, it's easy to understand the benefits of drawing characters and animations directly on a computer. Its ability to repurpose art for almost any need makes Illustrator the perfect environment for creating animations and illustrations.

Adobe didn't name their product Illustrator without reason. Artists create illustrations for children's books, magazine covers and articles, packages, and a variety of other products, and they use Illustrator to take advantage of the high quality and precision available in the program. A variety of tools like gradient meshes, blends, and even 3D, allow illustrators to translate the images they see in their mind into reality.

If you're an animator or an illustrator, you'll find the following chapters most helpful as you read through this book:

- Chapter 2: *Vectors 101* (page 31)

- Chapter 3: *Objects, Groups, and Layers* (page 69)

- Chapter 4: *Advanced Vectors (*page 99)

- Chapter 5: *Brushes, Symbols, and Masks* (page 147)

- Chapter 7: *3D and Other Live Effects* (page 211)

- Chapter 8: *Mixing It Up: Working with Vectors and Pixels* (page 285)

- Chapter 10: *Illustrator and the Web* (page 361)

- Chapter 12: *Saving and Exporting Files* (page 417)

Interactive Experience: Interface and Web Design

Web designers have a language all their own, which includes acronyms like HTML, XML, SVG, SWF, GIF, JPEG, PNG, and CSS. Illustrator supports these and other Web-specific technologies, giving Web designers access to the formats in which they need to deliver their designs. Taking advantage of Illustrator's object-based design environment, Web designers can lay out precise navigation elements, buttons, and entire pages.

In today's fast-paced world, everyone needs a presence on the Web. However, businesses find that they also need to provide content in print format. By creating art in Illustrator, Web designers can easily use that art for both Web and print layouts, thus reducing the need to re-create art for each medium.

If you're a Web designer, you'll find the following chapters most helpful as you read through this book:

- Chapter 5: *Brushes, Symbols, and Masks* (page 147)

- Chapter 7: *3D and Other Live Effects* (page 211)

- Chapter 8: *Mixing It Up: Working with Vectors and Pixels* (page 285)

- Chapter 10: *Illustrator and the Web* (page 361)

- Chapter 12: *Saving and Exporting Files* (page 417)

- Appendix A: *Automation with Illustrator* (page 457)

Tomorrow's Trends: Fashion and Apparel Design

If you're thinking about bathing suits while it's snowing outside, you're either dreaming about going on vacation or you're a fashion designer. What type of clothes you design may directly correlate to the seasons of the year, but designing apparel is also a highly creative field that demands the most of a designer. Illustrator's object-based approach to design makes it easier to work with body shapes, apparel guidelines, and product labels.

Fashion designers can create symbol libraries of repeating objects like motifs, buttons, buckles, and zippers. Illustrator can also create pattern fills and simulate shading and realism using transparency effects.

If you're a fashion designer, you'll find the following chapters most helpful as you read through this book:

- Chapter 2: *Vectors 101* (page 31)

- Chapter 3: *Objects, Groups, and Layers* (page 69)

- Chapter 4: *Advanced Vectors* (page 99)

- Chapter 5: *Brushes, Symbols, and Masks* (page 147)

- Chapter 8: *Mixing It Up: Working with Vectors and Pixels* (page 285)

Thinking Outside the Box: Package Design

If you're good at reading upside-down text, you just might be a package designer. That's because most package designs are created flat on one sheet, with different panels facing different directions. Once printed, the entire package is folded up so that it appears visually correct. Package designers use Illustrator to define spot colors, place images from Photoshop, and apply trapping settings—all in an effort to grab a potential buyer's attention.

Due to production requirements, package designers often need to be able to make minute adjustments to colors and artwork. By building files in Illustrator, these designers can control nearly every aspect of the file and meet their deadlines.

If you're a package designer, you'll find the following chapters most helpful as you read through this book:

- Chapter 3: *Objects, Groups, and Layers* (page 69)

- Chapter 4: *Advanced Vectors* (page 99)

- Chapter 5: *Brushes, Symbols, and Masks* (page 147)

- Chapter 6: *Typography* (page 181)

- Chapter 7: *3D and Other Live Effects* (page 211)

- Chapter 11: *Prepress and Printing* (page 387)

The Science of Design: Art and Print Production

Production artists are a separate breed (I would know—I'm one of the them); to them, everything in a file matters. Illustrator is a tool that allows production artists to dig deep into graphics files and make the edits and changes that are necessary to print a file correctly. Whether for producing or using spot colors, overprint commands, transparency flattening, or generally cleaning up paths and shapes, production artists have come to rely on Illustrator. Because it can be used to open and edit generic EPS and PDF files (and many other file formats), Illustrator has become a utility that is a required tool for art production.

If you cringe at the thought of an RGB file with overprints, transparencies, and spot colors, then you're certainly a production artist. You might not care much about how to create nice brush strokes, but you care about simplifying paths so that they print faster.

If you're a production artist, you'll find the following chapters most helpful as you read through this book:

- Chapter 3: *Objects, Groups, and Layers* (page 69)

- Chapter 5: *Brushes, Symbols, and Masks* (page 147)

- Chapter 8: *Mixing It Up: Working with Vectors and Pixels* (page 285)

- Chapter 10: *Illustrator and the Web* (page 361)

- Chapter 11: *Prepress and Printing* (page 387)

- Chapter 12: *Saving and Exporting Files* (page 417)

- Appendix A: *Automation with Illustrator* (page 457)

The Melting Pot of Design: Creativity for Everyone

If you didn't identify with any of the titles I've listed so far, that's perfectly okay. In fact, it's nearly impossible to list all of the kinds of people who use Illustrator every day. Because Illustrator has so many uses, the people who use it are very diverse. They may include doctors, lawyers, architects, signage and environmental designers, video and film specialists—even a restaurant owner who is designing a menu cover.

The important thing to realize is that Illustrator is for everyone who wants to express their creativity, and that makes for one big happy family!

Where Did Illustrator Come From?

Our past is what helps define our future. Whether you're new to Illustrator or a veteran who has been using it for years, it helps to better understand the history behind a product that helped redefine the graphics industry.

In the 1980s, during a time when the personal computer was beginning to take the world by storm, Apple Computer introduced the Macintosh with an "affordable" laser printer called the Apple LaserWriter. What made the LaserWriter so remarkable wasn't so much the price (around $7,000 at that time), as the technology that was hidden inside of it—Adobe PostScript, a computer language that enabled the LaserWriter to print beautiful graphics.

John Warnock, one of the founders of Adobe Systems, invented PostScript and was trying to find a way to make more money selling it. Although PostScript was cool, graphics still had to be created by entering line after line of computer code. John needed a way to have people create PostScript files visually, and that's how Illustrator was born. In early 1987, using the Bézier curve as the basis for vector graphics, Illustrator 1.1 was introduced with much success. Now, nearly 20 years later, Adobe Illustrator continues to thrive and help those in the design community innovate.

WHEN SHOULD YOU USE ILLUSTRATOR?

Good designers have many different tools at their disposal. Especially in an environment where most designers have other powerful graphics applications, it can be difficult to choose which one to use for a particular task. For example, a designer can apply soft drop shadows in Photoshop, Illustrator, and InDesign—is one application any better than the other for this?

How does one know when to use Illustrator? To answer the question directly, use Illustrator when it's the right tool for the job.

In reality, using the right tool for the job is what this book is all about. When you understand the strengths (and weaknesses) of each program, you also understand when it's best to use (or not to use) a particular application. As would be expected, every design or production task that you are called upon to do will require a different technique, method, or feature. When you are comfortable with Illustrator, you'll easily be able to look at any project and know how to go about implementing it.

HOW THIS BOOK IS ORGANIZED

Unlike most other books on Illustrator, this text isn't formatted to systematically cover each menu, tool, palette, and feature. Rather, it is organized based on my years of personal experience teaching Illustrator. Concepts like appearances and groups are covered long before discussions on text or brushes. Loading and saving libraries comes before discussions about fills or strokes. In this way, you understand the important aspects behind the features before you actually use them. The way I see it, it's like taking a class on skydiving—you spend a few hours on the ground learning all about the physics of the jump and then you get on the plane. Once you've already jumped, it's a bit too late to start learning.

Most chapters in this book contain a "Featured Match-Up" sidebar that discusses conceptual or physical differences between Illustrator's features and technologies. These are meant to give you a deeper understanding of the tools you have at hand and will assist you in choosing the right tools for the right tasks. Tips and Notes appear throughout the book as well and offer bite-sized nuggets of information and resources where appropriate. When keyboard shortcuts are included for Illustrator commands, I've listed the Macintosh shortcut first, followed by the Windows shortcut.

You'll also find three appendixes at the end of this book covering automation, FreeHand conversion, and application preferences. The appendix on automation should serve as food for thought on how you can begin using actions and scripts to have Illustrator handle more of your work while you find more important things to do. The appendix on application preferences is a great reference in case you ever need to know what a particular preference setting is. In light of the merger between Adobe and Macromedia, of most importance is the appendix on FreeHand conversion. This appendix is a wonderful guide that will assist users who are making the move from FreeHand to Illustrator. It shows feature-by-feature comparisons between FreeHand and Illustrator, discusses differences in terminology between the two, and offers general advice on making the switch.

Overall, this book serves as a great resource, no matter what your experience level is with Illustrator. My hope is that you learn something about Illustrator that you never knew before—that would make me a very happy person. So read on, and enjoy!

CHAPTER 1

The Illustrator Environment

Adobe Illustrator, like most other Adobe applications, contains many different tools, palettes, windows, menus, and commands that enable you to get your work done. Adobe calls this environment your *workspace*, and you can think of it as being similar to the surface of your desk.

At any time, you can open individual documents into your workspace and work on those files. Illustrator documents are separate entities and although you can open multiple files at once, you can't work on those files as if they were in one document together. That's okay though because Illustrator files are easily exported into InDesign, QuarkXPress, and other programs if your project requires it. And although Illustrator documents contain a single page, you can specify that a single large page be split into smaller pieces, called *page tiles*, to simulate multiple pages. But, we're getting ahead of ourselves. You will learn about these capabilities and a whole lot more later in the book. For now, let's explore the Illustrator environment.

THE WELCOME SCREEN

Upon launching Adobe Illustrator CS2 for the first time, you are greeted with a Welcome screen (**Figure 1.1**) that offers several options.

Figure 1.1 The Adobe Illustrator CS2 Welcome screen gives you several options for exploring this new environment, including opening a new document and launching a new features Web page at Adobe.com.

- **Tell Me What's New.** Takes you to the Adobe Illustrator CS2 feature page on Adobe.com where you can download a PDF of new features and view a short Flash movie that covers features new to Illustrator CS2.

- **Show Me What's New.** Launches a mini application called Demonstrator, which lets you pick an Illustrator feature or a topic; then you can sit back and watch as the feature is demonstrated on your computer screen, right inside Illustrator. It's as if a teacher has taken control of your screen, and it's pretty cool. Check Adobe Studio (http://studio.adobe.com) for additional demos that you can download.

- **Browse Cool Extras.** Launches Adobe Bridge (Adobe's next-generation file browser, new in CS2) and automatically navigates to the Illustrator Sample Files and Templates folder so that you can browse through the free content that Illustrator CS2 includes.

- **New Document.** Brings up the New Document dialog (discussed later in this chapter) to create a new Illustrator document.

- **New From Template.** Brings up the Open dialog and enables you to choose an existing Illustrator template to use as a base to create a new Illustrator file.

- **Open Document.** Brings up the Open dialog and enables you to choose an existing file to open.

Unchecking the Show this dialog at startup check box keeps the Welcome screen from popping up each time you launch Illustrator. At any time, you can access the Welcome screen from the Help menu.

CREATING NEW DOCUMENTS

Clicking the New Document icon creates a new Illustrator document, and Illustrator presents you with the New Document dialog (**Figure 1.2**), allowing you to specify certain settings for the document you're about to create. You can change any of the settings in the New Document dialog later.

 Press Command-Option-N (Ctrl-Alt-N) to create a new document while bypassing the New Document dialog. The new file uses the same settings as the last document you created.

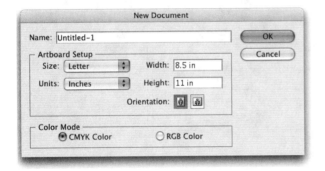

Figure 1.2 The New Document dialog gives you options for selecting the color mode and the layout of your document.

Depending on the kind of project you're working on, the document height and width aren't that important. For the most part, Illustrator is used in two ways: to create art that is printed from Illustrator itself (such as a single-page advertisement), or for art that is placed into another application (such as a logo or masthead). By default, when you place Illustrator art into other applications, the art's bounding box is what determines the dimensions of the file, not the page or artboard size that you specify in the Illustrator document.

 The New Document dialog is sticky, which means that it remembers the last settings you used. So if you create an RGB file to create a Web graphic, the next time you create a new document, the dialog is set to RGB.

Anatomy of a Bounding Box

Every Illustrator file has several different regions, or *boxes,* that determine how the portions of a file are displayed (**Figure 1.3**):

- **Art box.** Also called the bounding box, this area is defined by the art that appears in the document.

- **Trim box.** This area is defined by the Illustrator artboard and is the size you specify when creating a new document.

- **Crop box.** This area is defined by using the Object > Crop Area > Make command in Illustrator.

- **Bleed box.** This area is defined by the Bleed setting you define in Illustrator and extends beyond the trim box area.

- **Media box.** This area is defined by the size of the page on which you choose to print your file.

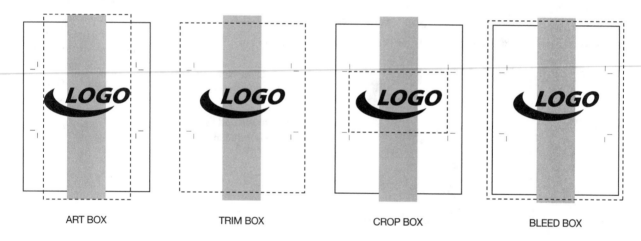

ART BOX   TRIM BOX   CROP BOX   BLEED BOX

Figure 1.3 The dotted line outlines the different boxes that are used to define the boundaries of a file.

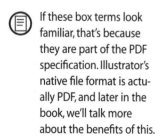

If these box terms look familiar, that's because they are part of the PDF specification. Illustrator's native file format is actually PDF, and later in the book, we'll talk more about the benefits of this.

Most applications, when placing a file saved from Illustrator, honor the art box so that you can easily align the Illustrator art with other elements in your layout. Some applications, like Adobe Acrobat Professional, InDesign, and Photoshop, allow you to choose between the different boxes.

Choosing a Color Mode

When creating a new document in Illustrator, you can choose between two color modes in the New Document dialog: CMYK and RGB. Although it isn't necessary to take a course in color theory to learn these two color modes, it does help to get a basic understanding of what they are so that you know when it's best to use them.

Since version 9, all Illustrator documents are restricted to either RGB or CMYK, and you can't have both in the same file. Even though Illustrator lets you specify an RGB color in a CMYK file, as soon as you apply that color to an object in the document, that color is converted to CMYK. If you ever select an object and see that the CMYK breakdown contains odd decimal values (like C=59.43, for example), you may be working in an RGB document.

When opening some older files, you might see a dialog telling you that the file contains mixed color spaces (**Figure 1.4**). You can choose what color mode to convert to when opening the file. Illustrator conveniently indicates the document's color mode in the Document title bar. You can convert files between the two color modes at any time by choosing File > Document Color Mode. Remember that each time a color conversion is applied, information is lost and color shifts can occur.

 If a monitor uses RGB to display color, how do you see CMYK colors on a computer screen? That's a good question; the answer is that a computer simulates what CMYK looks like. Remember that RGB has a significantly larger gamut than CMYK does, so an RGB device is able to display just about any CMYK colors.

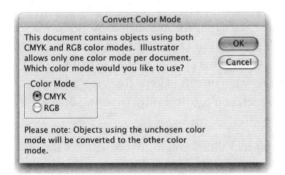

Figure 1.4 Illustrator alerts you when opening a file that contains mixed color spaces and asks you to choose which color mode you want to convert the file to.

If you plan to use the artwork that you're creating for both print and Web applications, it's recommended that you use RGB, which gives you brighter colors for your screen presentations and more options (certain filters or effects are only available in RGB). You can then convert to CMYK as you need to.

 It *is* possible to have both RGB and CMYK data in the same document by place-linking an external file. See Chapter 8, *Mixing It Up: Working with Vectors and Pixels* for more information.

Featured Match-Up: CMYK vs. RGB

CMYK stands for cyan, magenta, yellow, and black (called K because printers some-times refer to the black plate as the *key* plate). Mixing these colors creates a *gamut* (range) of colors. It's easier to think of colors in CMYK because the mode seems to follow the rules that we all learned in preschool. Mixing cyan and magenta (blue and red) makes purple, mixing yellow and magenta makes orange, and so on. Today's printing presses use the four CMYK inks to produce printed material in color. For jobs that you want physically printed, you should choose the CMYK color mode.

RGB stands for red, green, and blue and is used to display color on TV screens, com-puter monitors, and other electronic devices like digital cameras. Unlike CMYK where you start out with a white sheet of paper and then add colors to get to black, RGB works in reverse. For instance, when your TV screen is off, it's dark, and when you turn it on and add red, green, and blue, the cumulative effect is white. The RGB color mode has a significantly larger gamut of colors than CMYK does, especially in the area of bright fluorescent colors. For jobs that you want displayed on the Web or video, RGB is the color mode you should choose.

Document Setup

There was a time when the Document Setup dialog was accessed quite frequently, but since a lot of the page and printing settings were moved to the Print dialog, you don't have to go to Document Setup nearly as often. However, it's helpful to know what options you have that you may want to set when you create a new document. There are three panels to the Document Setup dialog, which you can access by choosing File > Document Setup.

- **The Artboard panel.** This panel allows you to change some of the set-tings that you saw in the New Document dialog, like artboard size and orientation (**Figure 1.5**). Additionally, there's a setting for how raster-based images appear when you're in the Outline view mode. By default, images only appear as an empty box in Outline mode for performance reasons, but with the Show Images In Outline Mode option activated, raster images are visible (in black and white) in Outline mode.

- **The Type panel.** There are several important settings for how text is used in Illustrator found in this panel (**Figure 1.6**). You can choose to have Illustrator highlight substituted fonts or glyphs, which can be helpful when opening files that other designers created. With these options activated, Illustrator highlights missing fonts in pink and missing glyphs in yellow so that you can quickly find where these problem areas are in a file.

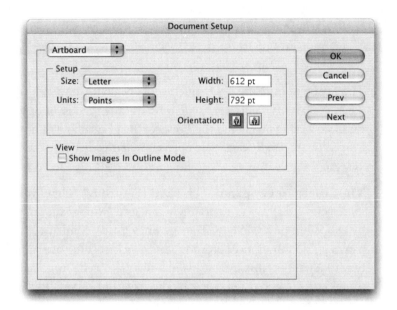

Figure 1.5 The Artboard panel in the Document Setup dialog lets you specify the physical dimensions of your artboard.

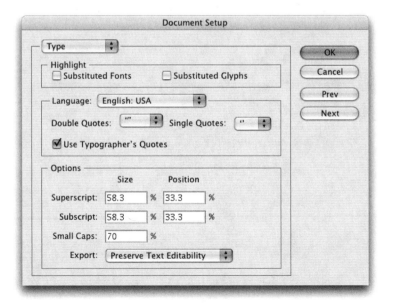

Figure 1.6 The Type panel in the Document Setup dialog is where you can specify how legacy text is exported when saving to legacy Illustrator and EPS formats.

Additionally, you can specify the language for the file and how double and single quote marks should appear when you type them in your document. There's also an option to use typographer's quotes, which means the correct curly quotes are automatically used instead of straight marks. Illustrator also allows you to define the size and position percentages for creating superscript, subscript, and small caps characters. However, if you're using OpenType fonts, you can take advantage of the built-in support for these specific features, which we'll cover extensively in Chapter 6, *Typography*.

The final option in the Type panel is for specifying how text is exported when you are saving to legacy file formats (any version prior to Illustrator CS). When you choose the Preserve Text Editability option, text is broken up into individual type objects. When you choose the Preserve Text Appearance option, all type objects are converted to vector outlines.

- **The Transparency panel**. This panel (**Figure 1.7**) allows you to specify settings for Illustrator's transparency grid (which you can turn on by choosing View > Show Transparency Grid). Similar to the transparency grid found in Photoshop, this checkerboard pattern makes it easy to identify transparent areas in a file. If your file is going to be printed on colored paper, you can also have Illustrator simulate that color onscreen by using the Simulate Colored Paper option.

Figure 1.7 The Transparency panel in the Document Setup dialog allows you to specify a paper color to simulate what your file might look like on colored paper.

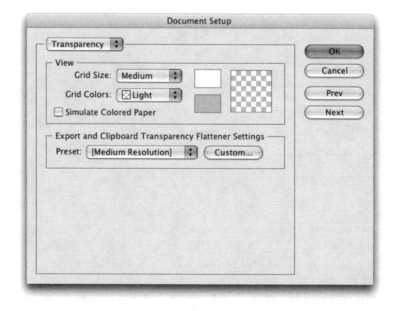

In Chapter 11, *Prepress and Printing*, we'll pick apart transparency and understand how it prints. For now, it's important to know that a process called *flattening* has to occur to correctly process artwork with transparency in it. This flattening process has many different options and you choose from different presets to specify how flattening should occur. Specifying a preset in the Export and Clipboard Transparency Flattener Settings area sets a default preset that you use when copying art with transparency to the clipboard or when exporting files to formats that don't support transparency.

LIVING IN YOUR WORKSPACE

Whether you use Illustrator an hour a week, an hour a day, or all day long, you have to feel comfortable using it. Adobe applications in general are customizable to the point that you can really arrange your work area, or workspace, to address your particular needs. In order to know what works best for you, get to know the various menus and tools well and learn how to best utilize them for your particular workflow or project. We'll offer some suggestions in this book where a customized workspace can improve workflow; Appendix C at the end of the book lists preferences in one handy resource.

Working with Tools and Palettes

As with most Adobe applications, Illustrator is loaded to the gills with tools and palettes. Each palette is designed to perform a specific function, and some of them are used all the time (like the Color palette or the Layers palette), while others aren't used nearly as often (such as the SVG Interactivity palette). Palettes can be hidden or shown as needed and all appear listed in alphabetical order in the Window menu. A check mark next to a palette's name indicates that the palette is open on your screen.

Adobe calls these palettes *floating palettes* because they sit above your Illustrator artboard and are always accessible (**Figure 1.8**, next page). At the same time, because these palettes float above your workspace, they can get in the way of your ability to see and work with your design. Depending on the size and resolution of your screen, organizing the palettes is important so that you can work efficiently. It's with good reason that Adobe has designed Illustrator palettes so that they can be easily rearranged.

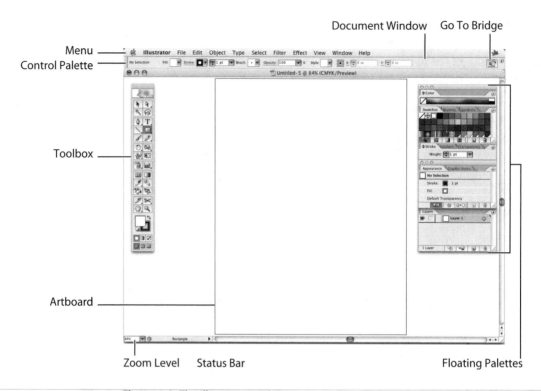

Figure 1.8 The Illustrator workspace.

Everything you see here about palettes applies not just to Illustrator, but to Adobe Photoshop, InDesign, and GoLive as well. With the exception of some small nuances, the functionality is consistent across the applications.

Pressing the Tab key on your keyboard will instantly hide all of your palettes. Pressing Tab a second time will bring them back.

You can reposition a palette by clicking and dragging its tab (where the name of the palette appears). You can create a cluster of palettes by dragging one palette into another existing one (**Figure 1.9**). You can also dock one palette to another by dragging a palette to the bottom edge of an existing palette (**Figure 1.10**). Some of Illustrator's palettes have multiple states or views to allow you to use them in different ways. For example, the Transparency palette contains a state that shows just the Blend Mode pop-up menu and the Opacity slider. Clicking the little up and down arrows that appear to the left of the name of the palette toggles these different states. Alternatively, you can double-click a palette's tab to toggle between states.

By arranging the palettes you use most on your screen, you can set up a work area that you're comfortable with and where you can easily find the functions or settings you need. Of course, you can always access the palettes you use less frequently by opening and closing them as needed.

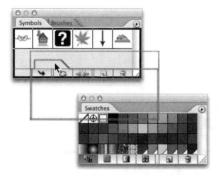

Figure 1.9 Dragging the Swatches palette into the Symbols palette results in the palettes being clustered. Notice that a heavy outline appears around the Symbols palette.

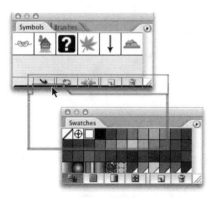

Figure 1.10 Dragging the Swatches palette to touch just the bottom of the Symbols palette results in the two palettes being docked. Notice that a heavy outline appears only at the base of the Symbols palette.

The Control Palette

The Control palette is a context-sensitive bar that contains often-used settings from different palettes. Unlike Photoshop's Tool Options bar, which is tool-centric, the Control palette in Illustrator is selection-centric, meaning it changes based on what objects are selected. Also, with the Control palette open on your screen, you can keep more palettes closed to free up more screen real estate. This is possible because of some cool features you'll find on the Control palette. First of all, you can dock the Control palette to the top or the bottom of your screen, or you can have it float, just like any other palette. You can also control what is displayed in the Control palette by choosing options from the Control palette menu (**Figure 1.11**, next page).

Figure 1.11 You can choose what information is displayed in the Control palette, which is especially useful on smaller resolution screens that don't have as much space.

At the far left of the Control palette, you'll see notification of what your targeted selection is (**Figure 1.12**). Additionally, you'll notice that some items are pop-up menus or text fields, and some labels are shown as underlined blue text. The blue underlines indicate links, and clicking them brings up their respective palettes. For example, you can set the opacity of an object by entering a value in the Opacity field in the Control palette. However, if you want to apply a blend mode to an object, that option doesn't appear in the Control palette. If you click the word Opacity (which has a blue line under it), the entire Transparency palette appears temporarily and you can choose a blend mode; then the palette disappears (**Figure 1.13**). This behavior really alleviates the need for you to ever have the Transparency palette open.

Figure 1.12 The active targeted selection is highlighted in the Control palette, acting as a reminder when you are applying certain effects and masks.

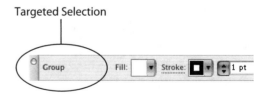

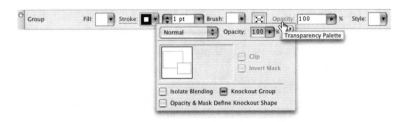

Figure 1.13 Accessing the full Transparency palette from the Control palette means you can open it when you need it, and it doesn't take up valuable screen space.

The Control palette not only saves screen real estate by relieving the need to keep certain palettes open all the time, but it also helps reduce keystrokes and mouse clicks by making certain menu items accessible. For example, when you select a raster-based image in Illustrator, you can apply a Live Trace preset directly from the Control palette instead of digging into the Object menu.

Custom Workspaces

As we explored in the Introduction, there are many different kinds of Illustrator users. Depending on the kind of work that you do, you may need to access certain tools or palettes more often than others. Experienced users carefully arrange the palettes on their screen so they have access to the features they use most often. Many designers perform a variety of tasks on a daily basis and use a wide range of features. This means that they are constantly opening and closing numerous palettes and arranging them on the screen, which often leads to confusion or loss of productivity because they are trying to find where a particular palette is. Although big monitors may help users keep more palettes open, it also takes users longer to scan such screens to find the right palette. If only there was a way to manage all of these palettes.

Thankfully, there is, and it's called Workspaces—this feature is identical to that found in Photoshop, InDesign, and GoLive. As mentioned earlier, the setup of your screen, which includes a listing of which palettes are open and their location on your screen, is what Adobe calls your workspace. Illustrator allows you to save a workspace and then return to it at any time by selecting Window > Workspace, and the name of the saved workspace. For example, you may arrange your screen for troubleshooting files, where you'll have just the Control, Appearance, Layers, and Flattener Preview palettes open. You would then choose Window > Workspace > Save Workspace to name and create a new workspace. You could create additional workspaces for other kinds of tasks as well. Each time you need to perform a different task, just switch to the workspace you've already defined and the palettes that you need will appear just as you've specified (**Figure 1.14**).

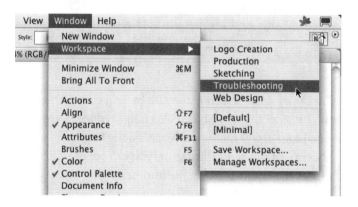

Figure 1.14 Choosing between several saved workspaces. Even having just one or two saved workspaces can save you a tremendous amount of time, especially if you're working in an environment where you share your computer with others.

Keyboard Shortcuts

Ever have someone ask you for a phone number and you can't remember it? Do you walk over to a phone and watch as your fingers automatically dial the number to remember what it is? The same phenomenon happens to many computer users whose fingers seem to know what to press without much thought. Although the mouse was a nice invention, you can get things done a lot faster by pressing the keys on your keyboard.

Workspaces are saved in the Adobe Illustrator CS2 Settings folder found in your user Preferences folder.

Illustrator keyboard shortcut sets are stored in the Adobe Illustrator CS > Presets > Keyboard Shortcuts folder.

One of the benefits of using Adobe products is that many of them share similar keyboard shortcuts, so there are fewer to remember. However, as you can imagine, there are tons of commands and tools in Illustrator and it's impossible to assign keyboard shortcuts to all of them. So Adobe assigns keyboard shortcuts to the commands they believe most people will use most often. As an individual user, however, you know what commands you use most often, so it's comforting to know that you don't have to live by what Adobe considers an often-used feature. That's because you can customize your keyboard shortcuts and tailor them to the needs of your fingers.

For example, if you're an animator and use the Blend feature a lot, you might need to access the Blend Options setting frequently. Out of the box, Illustrator doesn't have a keyboard shortcut assigned to that function, but you can choose Edit > Keyboard Shortcuts to assign your own keyboard shortcut for that command. If you try to assign a keyboard shortcut that's already taken by another feature, Illustrator conveniently alerts you to the fact, asking if you're sure you want to give up the other keyboard shortcut (**Figure 1.15**). You can save different sets of shortcuts if you'd like, which can be helpful if you share your computer with other users.

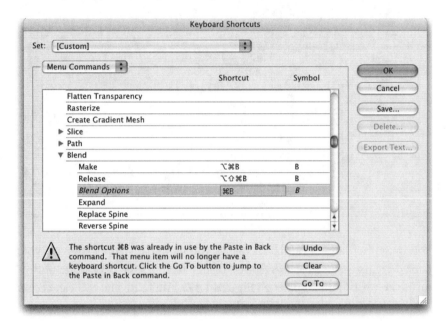

Figure 1.15 Illustrator alerts you if you try to reassign an already-used keyboard shortcut, keeping you from accidentally overwriting other keyboard shortcuts.

ADOBE BRIDGE

In today's world where hard drives and servers are filled with digital files serving different purposes, it becomes increasingly difficult to find the files that you need. In Illustrator's recent history, finding the right file to work on wasn't always a simple task because there hadn't been an easy way to visually browse through files. Enter Adobe Bridge. Adobe took the File Browser feature that appeared in previous versions of Photoshop and turned it into a full-blown application. Adobe Bridge allows you to visually preview all kinds of files including Illustrator, Photoshop, and InDesign files. In fact, Bridge can preview the individual pages *within* multiple-page PDF files—even movie and sound files (**Figure 1.16**, next page).

Figure 1.16 Viewing the individual pages of a multipage PDF file in Adobe Bridge keeps you from having to open a file just to see what's inside.

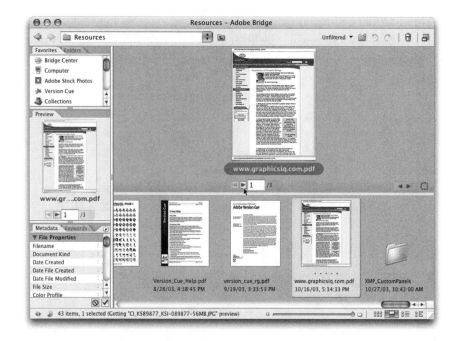

You can either launch Adobe Bridge as you would any application on your hard drive, or you can access Adobe Bridge from the Go to Bridge button in Illustrator's Control palette (**Figure 1.17**). Alternatively, you can access Adobe Bridge by choosing File > Browse.

Figure 1.17 The Go to Bridge icon in the Control palette allows you to quickly jump to the Bridge right from Illustrator or any Adobe CS2 application.

Previewing Files

The primary function of Adobe Bridge is to preview files so that you can find the right file quickly. (It isn't much fun copying a large file from a server and waiting several minutes for it to open only to find out that it isn't the file you were looking for.) The interface in Bridge is made up of different sections, called *panes*, and each is resizable. At the bottom of the Bridge window is a slider that allows you to enlarge or reduce the size of the thumbnails that appear in the main Bridge pane. There are also buttons to preview the files in different ways. The Thumbnail view mode allows you to see rows of images (**Figure 1.18**). Pressing Command-T (Ctrl-T) hides the file names and shows just the images. The Filmstrip view mode lets you quickly scroll through files while seeing a large preview as you click each one (**Figure 1.19**). The Details view mode gives you thumbnail previews with additional information about the file (**Figure 1.20**, next page).

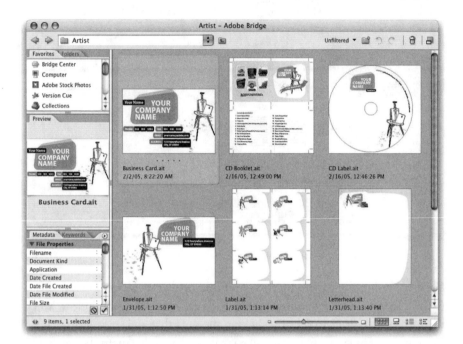

Figure 1.18 Previewing files using the Thumbnails view in Bridge gives you a clear snapshot of the different files you have in a folder.

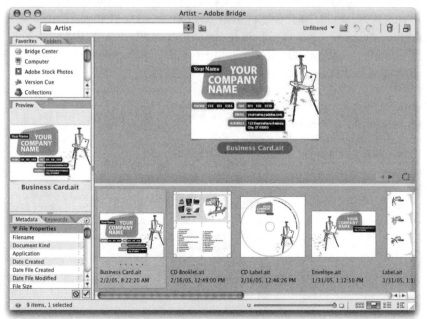

Figure 1.19 Previewing files using the Filmstrip view in Bridge makes it easy to quickly preview an entire folder of files.

Figure 1.20 Previewing files using the Details view in Bridge provides extra text-based information and metadata.

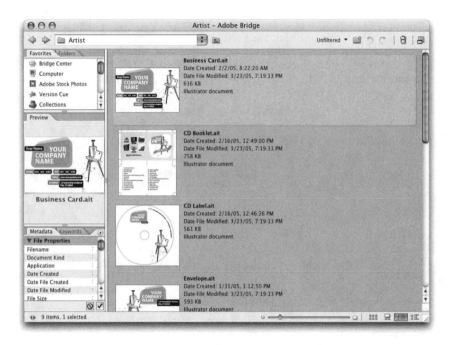

 The Versions and Alternates view is specifically for viewing files when you're using the Version Cue file manager that comes with Adobe Creative Suite.

While browsing files, you can open multiple Bridge windows to view different folders or files by choosing File > Open New Bridge Window. You can also apply ratings to files by clicking the dots that appear beneath each thumbnail. Rating your files can make it easier to organize them. For example, you might design 30 logos for a client and rate them so that you can easily find the ones you like best. Clicking the Unfiltered button at the top right of the Bridge window allows you to instruct Bridge to only display files with a specified rating (**Figure 1.21**).

Figure 1.21 Once you've rated or labeled your files, you can instruct Bridge to display only certain files, making it easier to focus on the task at hand.

Additionally, you can choose View > Slideshow to have an entire collection of images appear sequentially in full-screen mode. As each image appears on your screen, you can rate it. Press H on your keyboard during a slideshow to view the different options available.

Placing Files from Adobe Bridge

You can use Adobe Bridge for more than just opening Illustrator files. You can also use Bridge to place files into an open Illustrator document. You can do this simply by dragging files from Bridge directly into your Illustrator document. However, even on the largest of monitors, you may have trouble trying to make room for your Illustrator document, all of your palettes, and Bridge so that you can access the files. This is why Bridge has a button in its upper right corner that puts Bridge into Compact mode (**Figure 1.22**). In Compact mode, the Bridge window shrinks to be smaller and acts as a floating palette (it sits above your document window). Using Compact mode, you can easily drag files from Bridge right into your document.

Figure 1.22 When Bridge is in Compact mode, it acts much like a floating palette and enables you to easily drag files between Bridge and Illustrator or other Adobe applications.

If you still think that Bridge takes up too much space, you can click another button in the upper right corner of the Bridge window to activate Ultra-Compact mode where Bridge basically becomes a floating title bar (**Figure 1.23**). If you're placing a lot of content, you might find that toggling between Compact and Ultra-Compact modes is rather convenient.

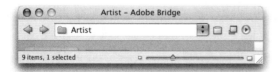

Figure 1.23 To save precious space on your screen, you can put Bridge into Ultra-Compact mode.

Searching Files

If you go to a popular stock photo Web site, you can enter a keyword or a description of the kind of image you're looking for and instantly see a list of images that match your criteria. Have you ever wondered how this works? How does a search engine know what the contents of a photograph are? The answer is metadata.

Metadata is information about a file, and it can be just about anything. The creation date, author, creation application, keywords, and copyright information are all examples of metadata. Adobe applications use an XML-based standard called XMP (Extensible Metadata Platform) to store this metadata inside of files. The metadata resides in an XML header at the top of each file, and this data can be read by Adobe applications.

You can add metadata to a file in several ways. From within Illustrator, you can open a document and choose File > File Info. This opens the File Info dialog where you can enter a variety of metadata for your file (**Figure 1.24**). When you save the file, the metadata is embedded within the file. Using Adobe Bridge, you can even add metadata to a file without having to open the file itself. Simply highlight a file in Adobe Bridge and choose File > File Info. You can add metadata to multiple files simultaneously by highlighting several different files and then choosing File > File Info.

Figure 1.24 The File Info panel in Illustrator stores keywords and other metadata using the XML-based XMP standard.

Additional Bridge Functionality

Because Adobe Bridge is a full application on its own, it has many features that are beyond the scope of this book. Some features of Bridge are only available if you purchase the Adobe Creative Suite. Here's a quick list of what else Adobe Bridge has to offer.

- **Adobe Stock Photos.** Adobe now offers the ability to search for and buy royalty-free stock photo images. Adobe doesn't own images, but they've partnered with some of the larger stock image libraries like Photodisc by Getty Images, Comstock, Digital Vision, and others. The service allows you to search all of the partner libraries simultaneously and download watermark-free comps that you can then integrate into your designs. Adobe Stock Photos is available whether you purchase Illustrator CS2 individually or you purchase Adobe Creative Suite 2.

- **Bridge Center.** Bridge Center is a section of Bridge that contains the ability to create groups of files, access previously opened files, view live RSS news feeds, and get tips and tricks on all Adobe applications. Bridge Center is installed only as a part of Adobe Creative Suite 2.

- **Workflow scripts.** Bridge acts as a connection between each of the Adobe applications. Because all Adobe applications are scriptable, Adobe has included a variety of scripts that allow you to perform functions across multiple applications. Illustrator CS2 includes a script that allows for batch processing of files with the Live Trace feature. Other scripts are available as a part of Adobe Creative Suite 2.

- **Version Cue access.** Adobe Bridge provides convenient access to Version Cue projects. Version Cue is an asset-management database that ships with Adobe Creative Suite 2.

- **Color-Management consistency.** Adobe Bridge has the capability to synchronize your color-management settings across all Adobe applications. In this way, you can easily ensure that colors appear consistent between your CS2 applications. This feature is only available as a part of Adobe Creative Suite 2.

Metadata is what makes the search function in Bridge so powerful. If you add a keyword to your files about what client a file is for, you can easily search for all files that were created for a particular client. From Bridge, choose Edit > Find, and then specify your search criteria; at this point, Bridge creates a new window to display your search results. You can click the Save As Collection button to save the search criteria you used in your search (**Figure 1.25**, next page). At any time, you can choose Collections from the Favorites pane to perform your search again.

Figure 1.25 Instead of having to repeat a search multiple times, you can save a collection in Bridge. A collection isn't a static search but rather runs the search criteria again and can display new results if items have changed.

VIEWING DOCUMENTS

As you're working in Illustrator, you can choose to view your artwork in different ways, each offering different benefits. The most common view mode, Preview mode, allows you to create and edit art while seeing a close representation of what your art will look like when printed (**Figure 1.26**). In Outline mode, Illustrator hides all of the pretty colors and shows you just the geometry of the shapes in your document. Although it may be difficult to visualize what your file is going to look like when printed, Outline mode gives you the ability to easily see if shapes are aligned correctly and it gives you a better idea of the structure of the file (**Figure 1.27**). Think of Outline mode as an X-ray film that a doctor reads. Although just black and white, an X-ray reveals what's going on behind the scenes. Just like a doctor reads an X-ray, an experienced Illustrator user can sometimes get a better idea of how an Illustrator file is constructed when in Outline mode. You can toggle between Preview and Outline mode by pressing Command-Y (Ctrl-Y).

Figure 1.26 When viewing artwork in Preview mode, you can get a really good idea of what your file will look like when printed.

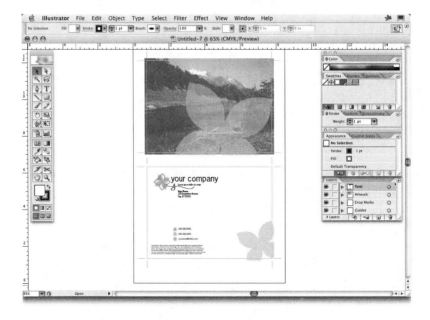

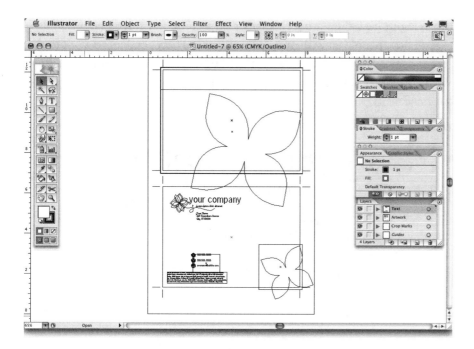

Figure 1.27 Viewing a file in Outline mode can make it easier to select objects and to identify the underlying structure of a file.

For those in the print business, Illustrator has a special preview mode called Overprint Preview, which you can access by choosing View > Overprint Preview. Overprinting is a process you use when creating color separations to control how certain colors interact with each other (we'll cover overprinting in detail in Chapter 11). Because overprinting is an attribute only applied in the print process, designers traditionally struggled with proofing files that specified overprints. Illustrator's Overprint Preview mode simulates overprints so that you can see how they will print (**Figure 1.28**, next page). In truth, Overprint Preview is far more accurate than Illustrator's regular Preview mode, especially when your file uses spot colors. However, Overprint Preview is noticeably slower than normal Preview in redraw performance.

Not to leave Web designers in the cold, Illustrator has yet another preview mode called Pixel Preview, which you can also access via the View menu. Illustrator, as a vector-based application, produces art that is resolution-independent. Most of today's printers have high-resolution settings and modern image setters use resolutions upwards of 2500 dots per inch (dpi). For that reason, print designers aren't worried about how good their artwork looks on their screen, because they know that when output at high resolution, everything will be perfect. Web designers, however, care very much about how their artwork appears on a computer screen because that's exactly how people view their designs. Pixel Preview renders artwork to the screen as pixels and shows how anti-aliasing affects the art (**Figure 1.29**). We'll cover Pixel Preview and these Web-specific issues in Chapter 10, *Illustrator and the Web*.

Figure 1.28 In the top example, the vector shape's fill is set to Overprint, as shown in the Appearance palette. In the lower example, with Overprint Preview turned on, you can see the effects of the overprint.

Figure 1.29 In Pixel Preview mode, Illustrator displays artwork as it would display in a browser. Zooming in on your artwork reveals the actual pixels and the effects of anti-aliasing.

Rulers and Guides

Even though you can scale Illustrator artwork to virtually any size, it's still important to be able to create artwork using exact and precise measurements. Package designers and technical illustrators are always careful about creating artwork to scale, and even designers need to know what size a logo or an illustration has to be.

Choose View > Show Rulers to display vertical and horizontal rulers along the left and top edge of your document window. You can Ctrl-click (right-click) a ruler to change its measurement system (**Figure 1.30**). Although the rulers can help identify the coordinates of objects that appear in a document, rulers also serve another function. You can click a ruler and drag a guide out onto your artboard. A *guide* is a line that's visible on your screen but not on your printed or exported art. Guides have "magnetic personalities" and objects that are moved or drawn near them stick to them, helping align objects and create consistent art and layouts.

By default, once you drag out a guide, it is locked and you can't reposition it. However, you can choose View > Guides > Lock Guides to toggle the editability of guides. Guides that aren't locked can be easily edited and positioned anywhere on your screen. To position guides precisely, use the Control palette to specify exact coordinates.

 In reality, guides in Illustrator are vector objects. You can select any vector shape in Illustrator and choose View > Guides > Make Guides to turn that object into a guide.

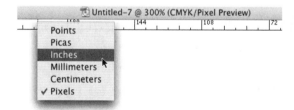

Figure 1.30 The Ruler contextual menu allows you to specify any of the measurement systems that Illustrator supports.

USING LIBRARIES (SHHHH!)

Illustrator files can contain all kinds of attributes including colors, gradients, patterns, symbols, brushes, and graphic styles. Throughout the book, we'll cover each of these in detail, but it's important to know that these attributes can be saved as libraries so that they may be shared between Illustrator documents.

Libraries are actually just Illustrator files that contain content that can be loaded into a palette. For example, to create a symbols library, you would create an Illustrator file, define several symbols in it, and then save the file.

There are four kinds of library files that Illustrator supports:

- **Swatches.** Swatches can contain solid colors (process or spot), gradients, and patterns.

- **Symbols.** Symbols are master art items that can be used repeatedly in a file. Symbols are also used for defining custom bevels for use with Illustrator's 3D Extrude & Bevel effect. In addition, the 3D artwork mapping feature requires the use of symbols as well.

- **Brushes.** Illustrator supports four different kinds of brushes: Calligraphic, Scatter, Art, and Pattern.

- **Graphic Styles.** Graphic Styles are saved appearances and allow you to easily style art objects.

Illustrator makes the process of managing libraries easy by incorporating some features directly into the actual palettes themselves. From the Swatches, Symbols, Brushes, or Graphic Styles palettes, you can choose Open Library from the palette menu. You'll see a list of libraries to choose from or you can choose Other Library to manually select another Illustrator file. The libraries that you see in the list all reside inside the Adobe Illustrator CS2 Presets folder. You can create your own library files by choosing Save Library from the palette menu of the palettes just mentioned, and you'll notice those files are saved directly into the Presets folder. The next time you launch Illustrator, your custom library appears in the Open Library list (Illustrator scans the Presets folder and populates the palette menus at launch time).

If you want a custom library to appear on your screen each time you launch Illustrator, open the library and choose Persistent from that library's palette menu (**Figure 1.31**).

Illustrator CS2 Swatch libraries are special in that they can be shared between Photoshop CS2 and InDesign CS2. To do so, create your swatches as normal and then choose Save Swatches for Exchange from the Swatches palette menu. This saves the file in the Adobe Swatch Exchange (ASE) format, which can be loaded into both Photoshop CS2 and InDesign CS2 (**Figure 1.32**). Because InDesign and Photoshop don't have the same support for Illustrator's gradient and pattern swatches, the exchange format only supports solid colors at this time.

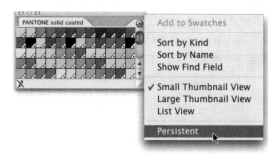

Figure 1.31 Choosing the Persistent option from any loaded custom palette will keep the palette open and on your screen even after you quit and relaunch Illustrator.

Figure 1.32 Saving swatches as Adobe Swatch Exchange (ASE) files allow you to share solid colors between the CS2 versions of Illustrator, InDesign, Photoshop, and even GoLive.

MORE TEMPLATES, PLEASE

For repetitive work, use templates, which allow you to set up a file with certain settings and attributes—even actual artwork and layers—to create more consistent files in less time. Illustrator templates are really just regular Illustrator files with one difference—you can't save them. You can only perform a Save As function with them (so you don't overwrite the template).

In order to create a template file, you start by creating a new Illustrator document. When you're ready to save your template, choose File > Save As and specify the Illustrator Template format (AIT) in the dialog. Template files contain a flag in them so that when they are reopened in Illustrator, they open as Untitled documents.

If you're a professional designer, you might not wish to use any of Illustrator's prefab templates, but it's helpful to open the files and explore them to see how they were created. One of the best ways to learn is by reverse engineering what someone else has done. One of the things you'll learn in this book is how to pick apart an Illustrator file; Illustrator's template files are perfect for this because they employ many different features and techniques.

Illustrator actually ships with hundreds of professionally designed templates, which you can access by choosing File > New from Template. Illustrator's templates are stored in the Adobe Illustrator CS2 > Cool Stuff > Templates folder. You can also browse the template files using Adobe Bridge so that you can see previews of what the templates contain. Before you wrinkle your nose about using "clip art," you'll be happy to know that Illustrator also includes an entire folder of blank templates as well. These blank templates contain trim marks and can be used to create print-ready work.

Featured Match-Up: Startup Files vs. Templates

When you create a new Illustrator file, you'll notice that several swatches, symbols, brushes, and graphic styles are already present in the file. How did they get there? Illustrator has something called a *startup file*, which is basically a master Illustrator file that all new files are made from. Illustrator actually has two startup files: one for CMYK files and one for RGB files. You can find these files in your Adobe Illustrator CS2 > Plugins folder (they are called Adobe Illustrator Startup_CMYK.ai and Adobe Illustrator Startup_RGB.ai respectively). Any content that exists in the startup file is automatically added to every new file that you create.

This means that if there are certain swatches or symbols that you use frequently, you can simply edit these startup files and you never have to load another library again. Although this is true, the more content that you have in your startup file, the more content you have in every file that you create, making for larger files.

Templates on the other hand, can also contain content, and you can have as many templates as you please, maybe for several different kinds of work that you do. It may be more efficient to keep a small startup file but have a set of rich templates that you can open at any time to get a running start on your design work. Additionally, template files are really full Illustrator files that can contain paragraph and character styles, artwork on the artboard, crop marks, layers, and more—something startup files can't do.

If you ever do edit your startup file and realize you messed it up, you can just delete the file. Illustrator automatically creates a clean, new startup file in the Plugins folder if it doesn't find one at launch.

How to Find Help

Up until now, Adobe's documentation always left much to be desired, usually offering information that was difficult to find or that didn't offer enough detail. However, Illustrator CS2 includes the new Adobe Help Center, which you can launch by choosing Help > Illustrator Help. Alternatively, you can launch the Adobe Help Center from Bridge. The Adobe Help Center lets you search across all Adobe applications, save bookmarks to easily come back to topics you've searched for, and even keep a list of all of your personal contacts you go to for help.

Another extremely valuable resource is Adobe's own user-to-user forums (**Figure 1.33**), which you can find at www.adobeforums.com.

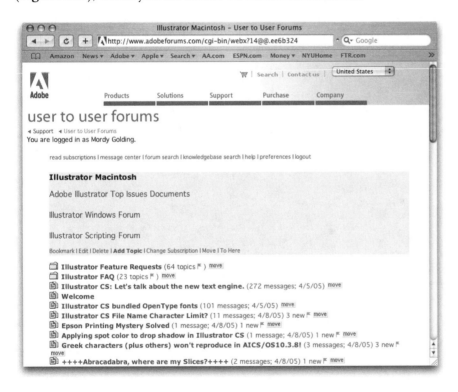

Figure 1.33 The Adobe Illustrator user to user forum on Adobe.com is a wonderful online community where you can get answers to all kinds of questions, learn cool tips and tricks from others, and even get a good laugh.

CHAPTER 2

Vectors 101

You've heard people describe Adobe Illustrator as a vector graphics application, but what does that really mean? How do graphics created using vectors behave differently than, say, graphics that are made from Adobe Photoshop? When does it make sense to use Illustrator to perform a task instead of another program like Photoshop? Answers to these questions will become apparent in this chapter. More importantly, you'll learn how to create vector graphics and understand their attributes.

In addition to learning how to draw basic shapes using a variety of drawing tools, this chapter will also introduce you to the different types of fill and stroke attributes you can apply to objects. You'll learn how to create two kinds of type objects (called point text and area text) as well. To round out your introduction to the world of vector graphics, the chapter concludes with a task you'll be doing quite often in Illustrator—selecting objects. Are you ready?

WHAT ARE VECTOR GRAPHICS?

What would the world be like if we didn't have both vanilla and chocolate ice cream? We'd probably all be a few inches smaller around the waist, right? Seriously though, just as there are two main flavors of ice cream, there are also two main flavors of computer graphics. One is *pixel-based* (these graphics are also referred to as *rasters* or *bitmaps*) and the other is *vector-based* (also referred to as *object-based*). Pixel-based graphics and vector-based graphics are different conceptually and each have its own strengths and weaknesses. For example, Photoshop is a program that is primarily geared to working with pixel-based images and is great for photographic content. Illustrator, on the other hand, is primarily a vector-based drawing application and excels in creating illustrations.

In addition, just like a vanilla-and-chocolate-swirl ice cream cone, an image can contain a mixture of both pixel- and vector-based information. In Illustrator, you can draw a shape, which is a vector, and then apply a soft drop shadow, which is a raster. In fact, you'll find that more and more today, graphics files contain a mixture of both vector and raster content (**Figure 2.1**).

Figure 2.1 An example of a file that contains both vectors and pixels. In this case, the text is a vector, but the soft drop shadow is a raster.

Once you've learned how these two graphic types differ in makeup (see the sidebar, "Featured Match-Up: Vectors vs. Pixels"), you can begin to understand how to use them and what their benefits are. High-resolution raster images can produce photorealistic paintings and actual photographs. Control over each and every pixel in the image gives the creative professional complete freedom to change even the smallest of details. However, pixel-based images have a finite level of detail, defined by the pixels per inch (ppi) or resolution of the file. Enlarging a raster-based file is akin to viewing a sheet of graph paper with a magnifying glass—the squares simply get bigger.

In contrast, vector graphics, which are defined by plotted anchor points, can be scaled to any size with no loss in detail or quality. As the image is resized, the computer does the math and plots the points at new coordinates and then redraws the Bézier path that connects them (**Figure 2.2**). Instead of storing millions of pixels in a file, a computer only needs to keep track of the coordinates of these anchor points and information on how to fill and stroke the paths that connect them. Vector graphics are also easier to edit because you have distinct shapes to work with, not miniscule pixels. Keep in mind, however, that this object-based approach translates to less control because you have no access to individual pixels.

As you go through the remainder of this book, you'll get a better understanding of how vectors and pixels work and you'll see real-world examples of how they are used.

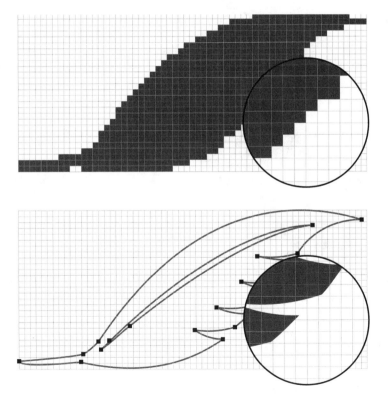

Figure 2.2 The image on top is a raster file with a section shown enlarged to 200 percent. The result is the same image with larger pixels. The image on the bottom is a vector file with a section shown enlarged to 200 percent as well, but the quality of the image remains intact.

Featured Match-Up: Vectors vs. Pixels

You may not be a huge fan of mathematics but math has a lot to do with how computer graphics work. Raster images are made up of a matrix of dots called *pixels*. If you imagine a sheet of graph paper, each square represents a single pixel. By turning pixels on or off (filling in different squares), you can create a shape. Because the squares on the graph paper are so big, the results are block-like (**Figure 2.3**). However, if you had a sheet with much smaller squares, you'd have more control over the detail of your shape.

Pixel-based images are usually measured in pixels per inch (ppi). A higher ppi number means the size of the pixels are smaller and the level of detail in the image can be higher. Higher ppi comes at a price though—file size. As you increase the number of pixels in your image, your computer has to store that much more information in the file. Color adds to file size as well because instead of each pixel being either black or white, each pixel must store additional colors. *Bit depth* is the term used to describe how many colors a file can contain. An image with a high ppi setting (referred to as the *resolution* of a file) and a high bit depth can result in large file sizes. However, because of the tiny pixels and the capability to apply different colors to each of those pixels individually, raster-based images can produce images that are photographic in nature.

Let's go back to the sheet of graph paper. Instead of coloring in squares to create a shape, map coordinates on the grid to create boundaries for the shape. Then, just as you did when you were a youngster, connect the dots to create the shape (**Figure 2.4**). This is the vector-based method of creating graphics. Instead of a collection of pixels, vector shapes are actually objects, hence the term object-based graphics.

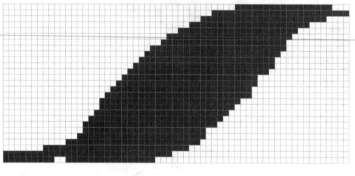

Figure 2.3 The level of detail in a pixel-based image is tied directly to the number of pixels it contains. Larger pixels result in less detail.

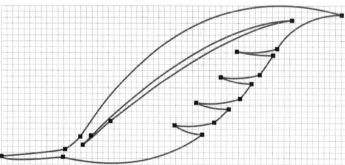

Figure 2.4 A vector-based image connects the dots to create a high level of detail without relying on pixels.

By truly understanding the benefits of these formats—and their limitations—you'll be able to achieve any look or design in the most efficient manner. For more information on this hybrid of graphics files, see Chapter 8, *Mixing It Up: Working with Vectors and Pixels*.

ANATOMY OF A VECTOR OBJECT

Now that you understand the differences between rasters and vectors, you can dissect vectors and find out what makes them tick. We mentioned that vectors are defined by plotted anchor points, and the coordinates of these points are what define the actual shape. You'll start with a simple path—a straight line—to see exactly what that means. A straight line is made up of two anchor points. The first anchor point defines where the path begins, and the second anchor point defines where the path ends (**Figure 2.5**). Once the two points are plotted, Illustrator connects them with a straight line.

OK, you can create two anchor points to create a line, so logic dictates that you need four anchor points to create a rectangle (**Figure 2.6**, next page). Again, focus on the four points and remember that Illustrator connects them all with straight lines.

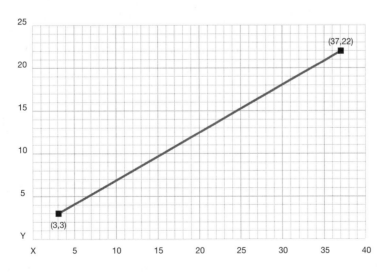

Figure 2.5 A straight vector path has two anchor points. The numbers in parentheses are the coordinates of the anchor points.

Figure 2.6 A vector rectangle has four anchor points; straight lines makes them all connect.

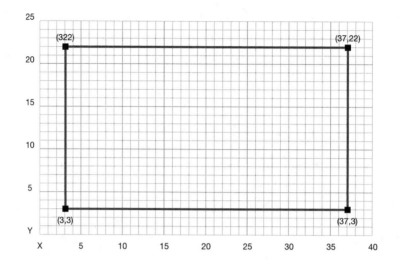

It's important to think of the line as two points, not as a drawn line, because when working in Illustrator, you often create the points, not the path itself. For example, imagine that you are the artist creating a children's connect-the-dots coloring book. You create the dots, but someone else actually connects the lines. When you think of vectors in this way, it becomes a lot easier to grasp.

By creating both a straight line and a rectangle, you've created the two kinds of vector paths you can draw. A straight line is an *open path*, because the path that connects the dots starts at one anchor point and ends at another. The rectangle, however, has a path that begins at one anchor point and then returns to that same anchor point, creating a *closed path*.

This all seems easy because we've been talking about straight lines. However, the line that Illustrator draws to connect two anchor points doesn't have to be straight—it can be curved. Anchor points connected by straight lines are called *corner anchor points*. Anchor points that are connected to each other by curved lines are called *smooth anchor points* and they have some additional attributes.

A smooth anchor point has two *direction handles* (aka control points), which specify how the curved line is drawn. The smooth anchor point becomes a tangent to the drawn path itself and the position of the direction handles defines the curve (**Figure 2.7**). For example, to draw an oval, you need to create four smooth anchor points; each anchor point has to have two control handles that define how the curved lines should be drawn (**Figure 2.8**).

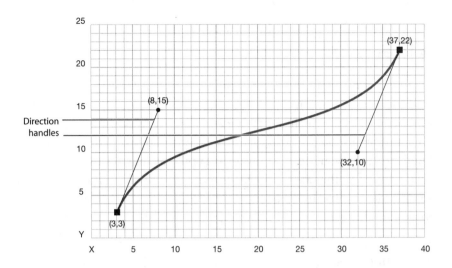

Figure 2.7 A vector path that is curved contains direction handles that define the slope of the path that connects the two anchor points.

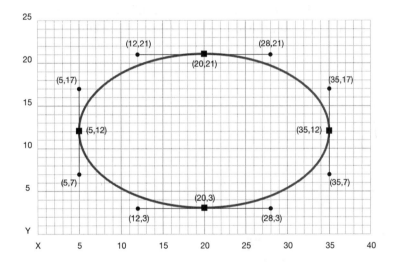

Figure 2.8 A vector ellipse, like a rectangle, has four anchor points. However, the additional direction handles define a curved path that is drawn between each anchor point.

The good news is that Illustrator's primitive drawing tools allow you to create simple shapes without having to worry about anchor points or direction handles. You won't be creating individual anchor points at this stage (we'll cover that in Chapter 4, *Advanced Vectors*), but for now, you'll be able to use what you know to start drawing.

 Anchor points and direction handles don't actually print. They just appear on your screen so that you can edit vector paths. When you print a file, only the lines that connect the anchor points print.

DRAWING PRIMITIVE VECTOR SHAPES

Illustrator contains a healthy set of primitive vector drawing tools. In this case, primitive doesn't mean "something simple" as much as it means "acting as a basis from which something else is derived." Artists are taught to sketch using primitive shapes, like rectangles and ovals, so that they can build structure; you can certainly apply similar techniques to drawing with vector shapes in Illustrator. Instead of trying to draw complex shapes, try to visualize how you can combine simple shapes in a variety of ways to create more complex ones.

A simple example involves drawing a crescent shape. Rather than trying to draw it from scratch, it's far easier to create two overlapping circles and then remove the parts that you don't need, which leaves you with the crescent shape (**Figure 2.9**). In Chapter 4, you'll find out how Illustrator's Pathfinder functions make it easy to add or subtract parts of paths, but for now, we'll explore how to create these primitive shapes.

Figure 2.9 By creating two circles and offsetting them, you can define the geometry you need to create a crescent shape. The Pathfinder palette, covered later in the book, makes it easy to create single shapes from multiple objects.

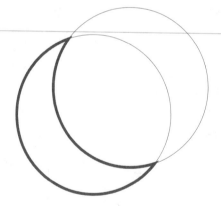

Illustrator's primitive drawing tools are split up between those that create closed path vector objects and those that create open path vector objects. Additionally, these tools are interactive in that you can specify or control certain settings while drawing shapes. To take advantage of this functionality, you choose a tool and begin drawing. As you hold down the mouse button, you're able to make changes to the shape you're creating, but once you release the mouse button, you commit the shape. Let's explore how this works.

Closed Path Shape Tools

The closed path tools in Illustrator comprise the Rectangle, Rounded Rectangle, Ellipse, Polygon, and Star tools, and are all grouped together in the Toolbox (**Figure 2.10**). To create any of these shapes, choose the desired tool, click the artboard, and drag outward. While dragging the mouse, you can add commands to interactively adjust the shape. See **Table 2.1** for a list of these interactive commands.

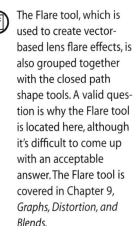 The Flare tool, which is used to create vector-based lens flare effects, is also grouped together with the closed path shape tools. A valid question is why the Flare tool is located here, although it's difficult to come up with an acceptable answer. The Flare tool is covered in Chapter 9, *Graphs, Distortion, and Blends.*

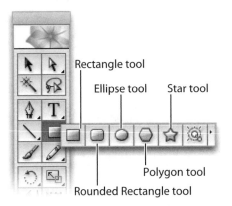

Rectangle tool
Ellipse tool   Star tool
Polygon tool
Rounded Rectangle tool

Figure 2.10 The closed path shape tools are all grouped together with the Rectangle tool in the Toolbox.

Table 2.1 Drawing with Closed Path Shape Tools

Interactive Command	Rectangle Tool	Rounded Rectangle Tool	Ellipse Tool	Polygon Tool	Star Tool
Keyboard Shortcut	M	N/A	L	N/A	N/A
Shift	*Shift* constrains all sides to be equal, resulting in a perfect square.	*Shift* constrains all sides to be equal, resulting in a perfect square with rounded corners.	*Shift* constrains all arc segments to be equal, resulting in a perfect circle.	*Shift* constrains the bottom side to be parallel to the constrain angle.	*Shift* constrains the bottom two points to be parallel to the constrain angle.
Option (Alt)	*Option (Alt)* draws the shape out from its center point instead of its corner.	*Option (Alt)* draws the shape out from its center point instead of its corner.	*Option (Alt)* draws the shape out from its center point instead of its corner.	N/A	N/A
Command (Control)	N/A	N/A	N/A	N/A	*Command (Control)* adjusts the inner radius of the shape.

(continues)

Table 2.1 Drawing with Closed Path Shape Tools *(continued)*

Interactive Command	Rectangle Tool	Rounded Rectangle Tool	Ellipse Tool	Polygon Tool	Star Tool
Spacebar	*Spacebar* allows you to reposition the shape on the artboard.	*Spacebar* allows you to reposition the shape on the artboard.	*Spacebar* allows you to reposition the shape on the artboard.	*Spacebar* allows you to reposition the shape on the artboard.	*Spacebar* allows you to reposition the shape on the artboard.
Tilde	*Tilde* creates multiple copies of the shape.	*Tilde* creates multiple copies of the shape.	*Tilde* creates multiple copies of the shape.	*Tilde* creates multiple copies of the shape.	*Tilde* creates multiple copies of the shape.
Up Arrow	N/A	*Up Arrow* increases the corner radius value.	N/A	*Up Arrow* increases the number of sides.	*Up Arrow* increases the number of points.
Down Arrow	N/A	*Down Arrow* decreases the corner radius value.	N/A	*Down Arrow* decreases the number of sides.	*Down Arrow* decreases the number of points.
Right Arrow	N/A	*Right Arrow* turns on the rounded corners.	N/A	N/A	N/A
Left Arrow	N/A	*Left Arrow* turns off the rounded corners.	N/A	N/A	N/A
Moving the Mouse	N/A	N/A	N/A	*Moving the Mouse* in a circular motion rotates the shape.	*Moving the Mouse* in a circular motion rotates the shape.

Open Path Shape Tools

 Even though they are grouped with the open path tools, the Rectangular Grid and the Polar Grid tools create a combination of both open and closed paths.

The open path tools in Illustrator comprise the Line Segment, Arc, Spiral, Rectangular Grid, and Polar Grid tools, and they are all grouped together in the Toolbox (**Figure 2.11**). To create any of these shapes, choose the desired tool, click the artboard, and drag outward. While dragging the mouse, you can add commands to interactively adjust the shape. See **Table 2.2** for a list of these interactive commands.

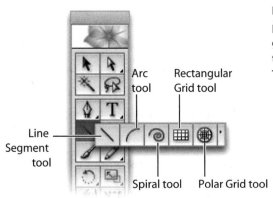

Figure 2.11 The open path shape tools are all grouped together with the Line tool in the Toolbox.

Line Segment tool

Arc tool

Rectangular Grid tool

Spiral tool   Polar Grid tool

Table 2.2 Drawing with Open Path Shape Tools

Interactive Command	Line Segment Tool	Arc Tool	Spiral Tool	Rectangular Grid Tool	Polar Grid Tool
Keyboard Shortcut	\ (backslash)	N/A	N/A	N/A	N/A
Shift	*Shift* constrains the path to angles in 45-degree increments.	*Shift* constrains the X and Y axis, creating a perfect quarter circle.	*Shift* constrains the path to angles in 45-degree increments.	*Shift* constrains the grid to a perfect square.	*Shift* constrains the grid to a perfect circle.
Option (Alt)	N/A	*Option (Alt)* draws the arc out from its center point instead of its corner.	*Option (Alt)* increases the length of the path.	*Option (Alt)* draws the grid out from its center instead of its corner.	*Option (Alt)* draws the grid out from its center instead of its corner.
Command (Control)	N/A	N/A	*Command (Control)* adjusts the decay of the path (making the winds of the spiral more drastic).	N/A	N/A
Spacebar	*Spacebar* allows you to reposition the path on the artboard.	*Spacebar* allows you to reposition the path on the artboard.	*Spacebar* allows you to reposition the path on the artboard.	*Spacebar* allows you to reposition the path on the artboard.	*Spacebar* allows you to reposition the path on the artboard.
Tilde	*Tilde* creates multiple copies of the path.	*Tilde* creates multiple copies of the path.	*Tilde* creates multiple copies of the path.	*Tilde* creates multiple copies of the path.	*Tilde* creates multiple copies of the path.

(continues)

Table 2.2 Drawing with Open Path Shape Tools *(continued)*

Interactive Command	Line Segment Tool	Arc Tool	Spiral Tool	Rectangular Grid Tool	Polar Grid Tool
Up Arrow	N/A	**Up Arrow** increases the slope of the curve to make it more convex.	**Up Arrow** increases the number of segments in the spiral.	**Up Arrow** increases the number of rows in the grid.	**Up Arrow** increases the number of concentric dividers.
Down Arrow	N/A	**Down Arrow** decreases the slope of the curve to make it more concave.	**Down Arrow** decreases the number of segments in the spiral.	**Down Arrow** decreases the number of rows in the grid.	**Down Arrow** decreases the number of concentric dividers.
Right Arrow	N/A	N/A	N/A	**Right Arrow** increases the number of columns in the grid.	**Right Arrow** increases the number of radial dividers.
Left Arrow	N/A	N/A	N/A	**Left Arrow** decreases the number of columns in the grid.	**Left Arrow** decreases the number of radial dividers.
Moving the Mouse	N/A	N/A	**Moving the Mouse** in a circular motion rotates the path.	N/A	N/A
C	N/A	**C** draws the arc as a closed shape instead of an open path.	N/A	**C, X** skews the columns in the grid to the left or the right.	**C, X** skews the concentric dividers toward or away from the center.
F	N/A	**F** flips the X and Y axis of the path.	N/A	**F, V** skews the rows in the grid to the top or the bottom.	**F, V** skews the radial dividers toward the left or right.
V	N/A	N/A	N/A	**F, V** skews the rows in the grid to the top or the bottom.	**F, V** skews the radial dividers toward the left or right.
X	N/A	N/A	N/A	**C, X** skews the columns in the grid to the left or the right.	**C, X** skews the concentric dividers toward or away from the center.

Drawing by Numbers

For aspiring artists, you can buy a sheet of paper that uses numbers to indicate where colors are supposed to go, taking the guesswork out of the design process. Although being free to create is certainly a good thing, you don't want to be guessing when you've been asked to create a shape to an exact size. The methods of drawing that we've discussed to this point are purely for those in a creative state of mind. As you create each shape, your mind is saying, "Yeah, that's about right." However, there are times when you are required to specify exact dimensions for shapes, and Illustrator can be precise up to four decimal places.

To create any shape numerically, select the tool you need, click once on the artboard, and immediately release the mouse. A dialog appears, letting you specify exact values for the shape or path you want to create (**Figure 2.12**). For most shapes, this action uses the point where you clicked the artboard as the upper left corner of the shape. To draw a shape out from its center point from the place that you click, press the Option (Alt) key while clicking with the mouse.

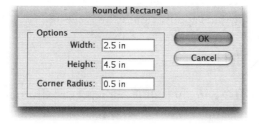

Figure 2.12 Clicking a blank area on the artboard with a shape tool allows you to specify numeric values and create a shape precisely.

In Chapter 4, we'll discuss how you can use the Control palette or the Transform palette to change an existing object's dimensions numerically as well.

APPLYING FILLS AND STROKES

As we mentioned earlier in this chapter, vector shapes comprise anchor points, which control how the paths that connect them are drawn. The anchor points and direction handles make up the physical structure of a vector object, which is further made up of two attributes: a fill and a stroke. The *fill* of a vector object is the appearance of the area that is enclosed by its path. If the shape isn't a closed path, the fill is defined by the existing path and is closed with a straight line connecting the start and end points (**Figure 2.13**). The *stroke* of an object is the appearance of the vector path itself. These paths are referred to as *Bézier curves* and, because of their nature, they result in objects or shapes that have clean smooth edges.

Figure 2.13 Open paths can have a fill attribute applied, and Illustrator stops the fill by creating a boundary (no physical path is created).

Fills and strokes can have a variety of appearances and vector objects can also contain multiple fill and stroke attributes—something we'll cover in Chapter 3, *Objects, Groups, and Layers*. Additionally, a vector object can have an attribute of *none* applied to its fill or stroke. Fills or strokes with a none attribute applied appear invisible and completely transparent.

To quickly specify an attribute of none to an object, press the / (slash) key on your keyboard.

Fills

There are three different types of fill attributes: solid colors, gradients, and patterns (**Figure 2.14**). Each of these fill types is stored in the Swatches palette. The buttons along the bottom of the Swatches palette determine if the palette displays all kinds of swatches, or just solid color, gradient, or pattern swatches individually. You can also use the Swatches palette menu to have the swatches listed by name or with larger thumbnails.

Figure 2.14 Three objects, are shown each containing a different kind of fill: solid color, gradient, and pattern.

Illustrator's Control palette makes applying color to objects easier than in previous versions. With any object selected, you can specify a fill and a stroke color directly from the Control palette (**Figure 2.15**). To apply a color using the Color palette or the Swatches palette, you have to choose between applying that color to the fill or to the stroke of your object.

Figure 2.15 When applying attributes from the Control palette, you don't have to target the fill or stroke of an object first. Instead, you can choose directly from the two separate pop-ups.

The Toolbox, Color palette, and Swatches palette all contain two square icons that overlap each other: the fill and stroke indicators (**Figure 2.16**). Pressing the X key on your keyboard toggles the focus between the fill and stroke.

Figure 2.16 The fill and stroke indicators in the Toolbox allow you to specify whether you want to apply an attribute to the fill or stroke of a selected object. Double-clicking the indicators opens the Color Picker.

You can create a new color swatch by either specifying a color in the Color palette and then dragging the color into the Swatches palette, or by holding down the Option (Alt) key while clicking the New Swatch icon at the bottom of the Swatches palette. The Swatches palette always has two swatches: one for None, and one for Registration (color that separates at 100 percent on every plate).

If you thought Gradient Mesh was a fill attribute, think again. Gradient Mesh is actually a special kind of an object that Illustrator refers to as a mesh object. Mesh objects are treated differently and don't act like normal vector paths. We'll talk more about Gradient Mesh in Chapter 5, *Building Better Files*.

When you're using the sliders to specify colors in the Color palette, hold the Shift key while you drag one slider to get lighter or darker shades of your color.

Solid Fills

 Because it's easy to forget whether the fill or stroke is in focus, it's recommended that you always keep the focus on the fill, and if you need to toggle to the stroke, try toggling back to fill immediately when you're done. Otherwise, there are just too many times where you click a color to fill an object and nothing happens to the fill. This occurs when the focus is on the stroke and the color is applied to the stroke in error.

A solid color fill applies a single color to the appearance of the fill of a vector shape. Ordinarily that would be a simple concept, but Illustrator can actually create three different kinds of solid colors. Each of them serves specific purposes and it's important to understand when each should be used.

Process Colors. A *process color* is one that is defined by a mixture of either CMYK or RGB values. For color print work that is separated and printed using a four-color process (CMYK), for output to a color printer, or for Web design and video work, you want to define your swatches as process color swatches. Creating process color swatches allows you to easily apply set colors to art that you create in your document, but updating colors on existing objects is difficult. As you'll see shortly, you'll often want to look into using global process colors instead.

Global Process Colors. A *global process color* is the same as a process color with one main difference: the swatch is global in that if you ever update the swatch, all objects in the document that have that swatch applied update as well. Most production artists request that designers use global swatches because they are easier to manage in an entire document. To create a global process color swatch, check the Global option in the New Swatch or Swatch Options dialog (**Figure 2.17**). In the Swatches palette, global process colors display with a small white triangle in their lower right corner (**Figure 2.18**).

Figure 2.17 Double-clicking an existing solid color swatch opens the Swatch Options dialog where you can specify the values for a color and create a global swatch.

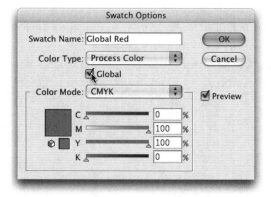

Global process colors act much like spot colors in that you can specify tint values for a global color (*Figure 2.19*). Regular process colors cannot have tint values assigned.

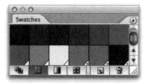

Figure 2.18 Swatches with white triangles are global process colors. Swatches with black dots in addition to the triangles are spot colors.

Figure 2.19 You can use the Color palette to specify a tint value of a global process color—something that is not possible with a process color.

Spot Colors. A *spot color* is a named color that appears on a custom plate during the color-separation process. Instead of a printer breaking a color into cyan, magenta, yellow, or black, a spot color is a specific custom color ink that the printer creates for your print job. You might have a variety of reasons for using a spot color in a document.

- **To get a specific color.** Not every color can be reproduced using CMYK, which in reality has a small gamut. A custom color can be a bright fluorescent color, a color with a metallic sheen, or even one that involves specialized inks, like the magnetic inks used on bank checks.

- **To get consistent color.** Because process colors are made up of a mixture of other colors, they can shift and appear differently, even on the same print job. When you're dealing with a company's corporate colors, you want to make sure that color is consistent across all print jobs.

- **To get a solid color.** Process colors are formed by mixing inks in various percentages. Not only does this require perfect registration on press (where all plates hit the exact same place on each sheet of paper), the process can also reveal odd patterns in reproduction in some cases (called moiré patterns). Spot color inks don't exhibit these issues and present a solid clean appearance.

- **To get cheaper color.** When you are performing a process color job, you're printing with four different color inks. But if you are creating a business card with black text and a red logo, it's cheaper to print using black ink and a single red spot color instead. Sometimes working with two or three spot colors gives your design the color it needs while keeping the printing costs down.

Because many designers are familiar with spot colors, often they specify Pantone colors for work that will be separated as process colors. Chapter 11, *Prepress and Printing* discusses how to convert spot colors to process colors, and the pitfalls to avoid.

- **To specify something other than a color.** Print designs can be extremely creative, using processes like foil stamping, die cutting, spot varnishing, or embossing. Even though these special effects don't print in ink, they still need to be specified to a printer. Spot colors allow you to easily define areas of color that will ultimately be regions of an emboss effect, a die stamp, and so on.

You can either define your own custom color (by choosing the Spot Color option in the Color Type pop-up menu), or you can choose a spot color from an existing library. Pantone libraries are examples of the most common of these; these were created to help printers and designers standardize on colors by using a numbering system. To apply a color from a Pantone library, choose Open Swatch Library from the Swatches palette menu and choose from the list of Pantone libraries.

Gradient Fills

Although a solid color fill is made up of just one color, a *gradient fill* is made up of solid colors that blend into each other. A gradient can contain as few as one color and as many as—well let's just say we stopped counting at 300. *Linear* gradients start with a color on one side that gradually blends into a color on the other side. *Radial* gradients start with a color at the center and gradually blend into a color, radiating outward (**Figure 2.20**). A gradient has four attributes:

- **Type.** Either linear or radial, as just described.

- **Color Stop.** The point at which a new color is added to a gradient.

- **Midpoint.** The point at which two adjacent colors meet at exactly 50 percent of each color.

- **Angle.** The direction of the gradient (only for linear gradients).

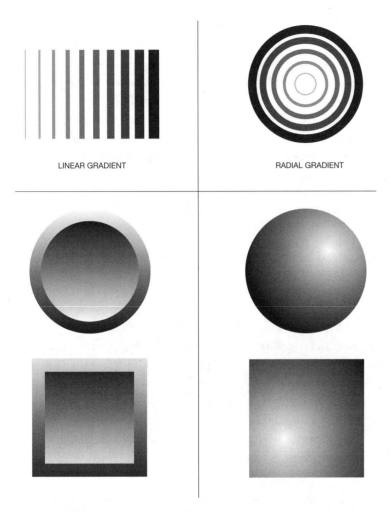

You can create gradients using a combination of the Color, Swatches, and Gradient palettes. The Gradient palette can be expanded to show the gradient slider and the angle and location fields. To define a gradient, drag colors from the Color or Swatches palette directly onto the gradient slider.

To replace an existing gradient, hold the Option (Alt) key while you drag the preview icon from the Gradient palette over the existing gradient swatch in the Swatches palette. The swatch appears with a thick black outline to indicate that it will be replaced with the new one.

The little icons that appear beneath the slider are color stops. You can drag colors directly onto an existing color stop to change its color. To remove a color stop from a gradient, simply drag it down, away from the gradient slider. The diamond-shaped icon that appears above the gradient slider indicates the midpoint between two colors. Drag the midpoint to the left or right to adjust how quickly one color blends into the other. Once you've defined a gradient, you can drag the preview icon (in the upper left of the Gradient palette) into the Swatches palette (**Figure 2.21**).

Figure 2.21 Moving a color stop shifts where color appears in the gradient. Dragging one color stop on top of another while holding the Option (Alt) key swaps the colors.

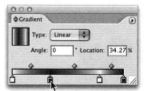

To modify how a gradient fill is applied to an object, you can use the Gradient tool. Start by selecting an object and filling it with a gradient of your choice. Then, select the Gradient tool and click and drag to define the start point of the gradient. The direction in which you drag the cursor determines the angle of the gradient. The point where you release the mouse defines the end point of the gradient. When you're using radial gradients, the first click determines the center point of the gradient and the release point determines the outside of the gradient (**Figure 2.22**).

Figure 2.22 The Gradient tool makes it easy to apply gradients at an angle.

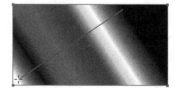

What makes the Gradient tool so powerful is that you can begin or end a gradient anywhere, even outside the boundaries of the object you have selected (**Figure 2.23**). Additionally, you can select multiple objects and apply a single gradient across all of them using the Gradient tool.

Figure 2.23 A gradient fills the distance from where you first clicked to where you release the mouse, even if those locations are beyond the boundaries of your selection.

Pattern Fills

A *pattern fill* uses a repeating art element to fill the boundaries of a path or object (**Figure 2.24**). To define a pattern, create just about any kind of art on your artboard (including raster images and text objects) and drag them into your Swatches palette. You can apply pattern fills to objects the same way you apply solid color fills—by targeting the fill or stroke of a selection and choosing a pattern swatch from the Swatches palette.

 Be sure to check out Alan James Weimer's Intricate Patterns side-by-side tutorial in the color insert.

Figure 2.24 Three examples of vector objects with pattern fills. Good patterns have no visible seams.

In Chapter 4, we'll talk about transformations (such as scaling and rotating objects). When objects are filled with patterns, you can choose to rotate the patterns with the objects, or you can have Illustrator rotate just the objects but not the pattern fill.

The Art of Pattern Making

In reality, an entire book could be written on creating patterns, which is an art form in and of itself. Creating perfect, repeating patterns that tile seamlessly can take a bit of advance planning, as well as trial and error.

When you drag artwork into the Swatches palette to create a pattern swatch, Illustrator uses the bounding area of the artwork that you selected as the boundary of the repeat area. In many cases however, this default bounding box does not create a seamless pattern. In order to create a seamless pattern, you may have to position objects well inside the repeat area, or even have artwork extend beyond the repeat area. To define a repeat area for a pattern, draw a rectangle and send the rectangle to the bottom of the stacking order. Even if there are objects that extend outside the rectangle, Illustrator will use that rectangle to define the repeat area (**Figure 2.25**).

Sometimes, the best way to learn is to reverse-engineer existing artwork. To get a better feel for how repeats are designed, take a look at some of the patterns that Illustrator CS2 ships with. Choose Open Swatch Library > Other Library from the Swatches palette menu, and navigate to the Adobe Illustrator CS2, Presets > Patterns folder. To access the art that was used to define any pattern swatch, simply drag a swatch from the Swatches palette out onto the artboard.

Figure 2.25 Creating a rectangle as the bottom-most shape in your pattern art defines a repeat area, thus helping to create a seamless pattern.

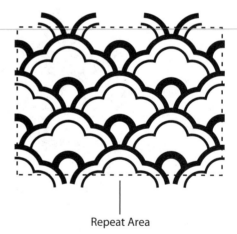

Repeat Area

Strokes

As you learned earlier, a *stroke* is the appearance of the vector path itself. You can specify a stroke color by choosing one from the Stroke pop-up in the Control palette or by targeting the stroke using the fill/stroke indicator and then choosing a color from either the Color or Swatches palette. You can choose between several different settings to control the appearance of a stroke, all of which are available in the Stroke palette:

- **Weight.** The thickness of a stroke is referred to as the *stroke weight*, and it is traditionally specified in points (pt). Specifying a stroke weight of less than .25 pt might be problematic for most printing presses.

- **Miter limit.** A stroke's *miter limit* specifies the appearance of corners that have very acute angles. If you find that the corner of a stroke appears clipped, you can increase the miter limit to correct the appearance (**Figure 2.26**).

Figure 2.26 The object on the left has an 18-point stroke applied with a miter limit of 2, whereas the object on the right has an 18-point stroke applied with a miter limit of 4.

- **Cap.** The *cap* setting is an attribute that affects the appearance of the start and end points of a stroke. Obviously, this setting applies to open paths only. You can choose between a Butt, Round, or Projecting cap (**Figure 2.27**).

Figure 2.27 The cap setting defines how the start and end of a stroke appears. From the top, Butt, Round, and Projecting caps can also add to the length of a stroke.

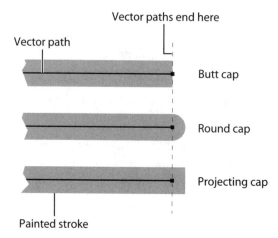

- **Join.** A join attribute determines the appearance of a stroke as it passes through an anchor point. Miter, Round, and Bevel are the different options that you can choose from (**Figure 2.28**).

Figure 2.28 The join setting defines the appearance of connecting straight anchor points. From left to right are examples of stroked paths with Miter, Round, and Beveled joins.

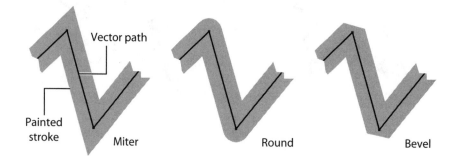

The Control palette, Transform palette, and Info palettes all provide exact feedback on coordinates, positioning, sizing, and more. By default, these palettes use the actual vector path to determine these numbers, not the visual boundaries of the object. For example, you may have a shape that has a thick stroke applied to it, which is not represented in the value you see in the Transform palette. With the Use Preview Bounds option activated in Illustrator's General Preferences, all palettes use the visual boundary of a path as the dimensions value, not the underlying vector path.

Aligning Strokes

By default, Illustrator paints a stroke on the center of a path. For example, if you specify a 10-point stroke for an object, the result is 5 points appearing on the outside of the path and 5 points appearing on the inside of the path. In the Stroke palette, you can specify whether you want the entire stroke painted on the inside or the outside of the vector path (**Figure 2.29**).

Figure 2.29 Use the Align Stroke options in the Stroke palette to specify if a stroke should be painted on the center, inside, or outside of the path.

Dashed Strokes

Strokes don't have to be solid lines. They can have a broken appearance resulting in dashed lines. The nice thing is, rather than just choose a preset dashed line, you can specify exactly how the dashes should appear along a stroked path.

When specifying the appearance of a dash, you can specify the length of the dash, and the length of the gap—the space that appears after the dash. The Stroke palette contains three sets of dash and gap settings. If you specify a dash without specifying a gap, Illustrator creates a gap equal to the size of the dash. For most standard dashed strokes, you will only use the first dash and gap setting. However, you can use all three to create a sequence of dashes and gaps (**Figure 2.30**). When you specify the Round cap option for the stroke, a dash value of 0 results in a perfect circle, allowing you to create dotted lines.

Figure 2.30 Illustrator's ability to set custom dashes on a stroke allows you to create a plethora of dashed strokes, which you can use for a variety of tasks.

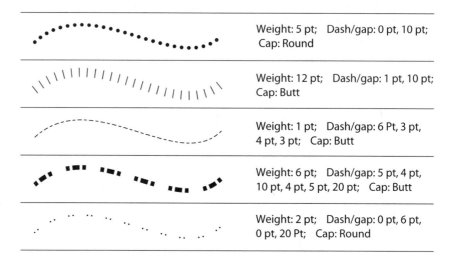

	Weight: 5 pt; Dash/gap: 0 pt, 10 pt; Cap: Round
	Weight: 12 pt; Dash/gap: 1 pt, 10 pt; Cap: Butt
	Weight: 1 pt; Dash/gap: 6 Pt, 3 pt, 4 pt, 3 pt; Cap: Butt
	Weight: 6 pt; Dash/gap: 5 pt, 4 pt, 10 pt, 4 pt, 5 pt, 20 pt; Cap: Butt
	Weight: 2 pt; Dash/gap: 0 pt, 6 pt, 0 pt, 20 Pt; Cap: Round

One shortcoming of Illustrator is its inability to ensure that dashes set on strokes match up evenly on the corners of an object (**Figure 2.31**). This is because you can only specify absolute dash and gap settings, and those settings don't always match up exactly with the object that you've drawn. It's interesting to note that Adobe InDesign does have the ability to stretch or adjust dashes and gaps to display consistent corners.

Figure 2.31 Because Illustrator uses absolute values for dashes, it's nearly impossible to get dashes to line up perfectly at the corners of a path.

In Illustrator, there is a way to get consistent dashes to appear around a shape—by using the versatile Pattern brush feature, which we'll discuss in Chapter 5, *Brushes, Symbols, and Masks*.

TEXT OBJECTS

They say that a picture speaks a thousand words, but you still need to type words every once in a while. Illustrator has very powerful typography features, which we'll cover in detail in Chapter 6, *Typography*. For now, it's sufficient for you to learn about the two kinds of type objects that Illustrator can create: point text and area text. Naturally, each has its own benefits.

Point Text

The simplest form of text in Illustrator is *point text* (or *point type*), which you can create by choosing the Type tool and clicking any blank area on your artboard. Once you've defined a point at which to start typing, you can enter text onto the artboard. Point text doesn't have defined boundaries, so text never wraps automatically (although you can use Enter or Return characters to manually type on a new line). When you use point text, the paragraph alignment settings (left, right, and center) use the single point that you created when you first clicked with the Type tool (**Figure 2.32**).

Point Text

Point Text

Point Text

If adjusting dashes along a path is something you need to do often, you might want to check out a shareware ($15) plugin created by Rick Johnson called Nudge Palette. You can find Nudge Palette at http://rj-graffix. com. This plug-in allows you to easily shift dashes along a path to get the most optimal appearance.

There's really a third kind of type object called path text, where you can specify text to follow along a vector path. We'll talk more about path text in Chapter 6.

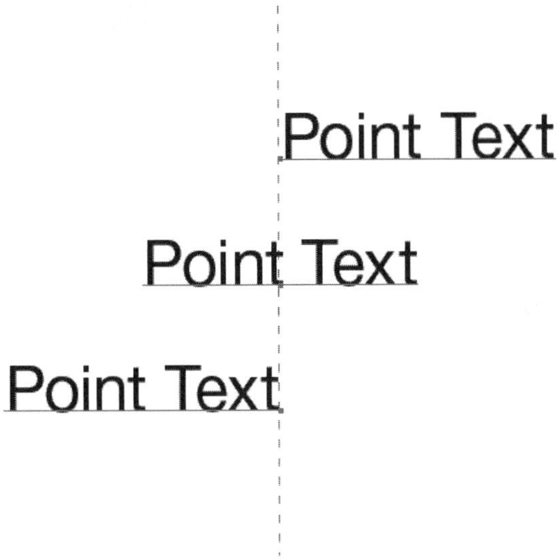

Figure 2.32 Text in a Point Type object aligns differently depending on the paragraph alignment options you set for the text.

Although point text is easy to create, many of the powerful text features that Illustrator has, including the paragraph composer, text threading, and the ability to set text in columns, are not available. However, if you want to place text in numerous areas of an illustration (like callouts, maps, graphs, etc.), point text is the way to go.

Area Text

As with most page-layout applications, you can also place text within a frame, although with Illustrator, any vector object can serve as a text frame. *Area text* (or *area type*) is type that is enclosed within the confines of a vector shape (**Figure 2.33**). To create an Area Type object, you can either use the Area Type tool to click an existing vector shape, or you can use the Type tool to click inside any closed vector shape (**Figure 2.34**). Alternatively, you can click and drag a blank area of the artboard with the Type tool to create an Area Type object.

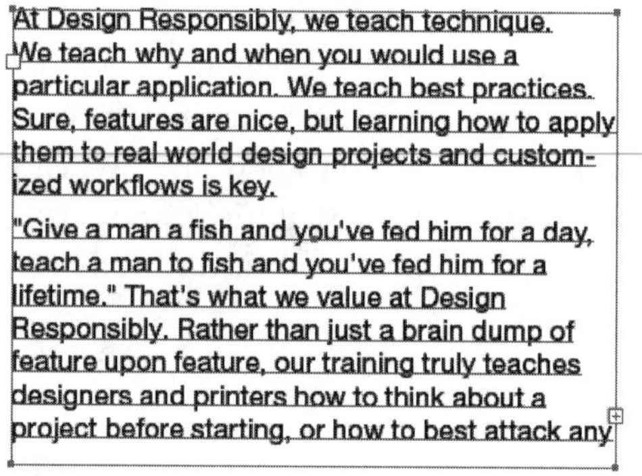

Figure 2.33 An example of an Area Type object. Any vector object in Illustrator can serve as a text frame.

> At Design Responsibly, we teach technique. We teach why and when you would use a particular application. We teach best practices. Sure, features are nice, but learning how to apply them to real world design projects and customized workflows is key.
>
> "Give a man a fish and you've fed him for a day, teach a man to fish and you've fed him for a lifetime." That's what we value at Design Responsibly. Rather than just a brain dump of feature upon feature, our training truly teaches designers and printers how to think about a project before starting, or how to best attack any

Figure 2.34 As you drag the Type tool over an object that can become a text frame, Illustrator displays the place text icon in parentheses.

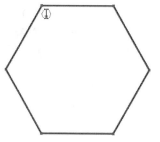

Multiple Area Type objects can be linked to have a single story flow across them called a *thread of text*. Text flows from line to line automatically within an Area Type object, and more advanced paragraph settings like columns, composition, hyphenation, and indents are available. We'll cover text threading and the advanced text features that are available when we get to Chapter 6.

Area text may take an extra click or two to create, but for uniform layouts and longer runs of copy, you'll want to use it.

Converting Text to Editable Vectors

Earlier in the chapter, you learned about Illustrator's primary shape tools. The characters in both Point and Area Type objects are vector shapes too, but they can't be edited as regular vector shapes can because you can't access their anchor points or direction handles. In essence, text is a special kind of vector object. Fonts have specific information built into them, called *hinting*, which modifies character shapes slightly based on the size in which text is printed. For example, a lowercase "e" character has a small hole in the middle, and at really small point sizes, that hole may appear to close up or fill in when printed. Font hinting adjusts the size of that hole to be slightly larger at smaller point sizes.

You can select any text object and choose Type > Create Outlines to convert text into regular, editable vector shapes. Doing so allows you to perform edits on the actual shapes of the characters (for example, extending an ascender or removing the dot from an "i") but results in the loss of any font hinting, because the shape is no longer a text object (**Figure 2.35**).

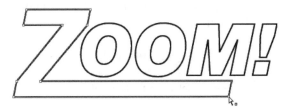

Figure 2.35 Converting text to outlines gives you unlimited freedom to edit the vector paths.

 Older versions of Illustrator required text to be converted to outlines if the text was going to be used with certain features such as gradients, patterns, and masks. The next-generation text engine introduced in Illustrator CS allows you to use text with just about any feature while allowing it to remain completely editable. Other than the reasons given earlier for converting text to outlines, you can take advantage of using editable text in all of your design workflows.

Where possible, it's always best to leave text in an editable state and avoid converting it to outlines. In this way, you'll be able to make edits easily and you'll preserve font information. However, there are times when it's a good idea to convert text to outlines, like when you've created artwork that will be distributed or used in many different places (logos are good examples). In this way, you don't need to worry about passing font files around as well (which has legal ramifications anyway—something we'll discuss later in the book).

SELECTING OBJECTS

 In reality, the selection tools mentioned here do more than just select objects. You can use them to move selected objects as well. Moving an object in Illustrator is actually considered a transform function, so we'll be talking about the Selection and Direct Selection tools in Chapter 4 as well.

By far, the tools you will employ most often when using Illustrator on a day-to-day basis are the selection tools. The power of Illustrator lies not just in creating graphics, but more so in manipulating them. In order to perform just about any function in Illustrator (or nearly any computer graphics program for that matter), you need to select something first. Without selections, Illustrator has no idea which of the objects in your document you want to modify.

If you've used Illustrator before, you're familiar with the twins: the *Selection tool* and the *Direct Selection tool* (**Figure 2.36**). These tools have been given a variety of alternative names over the years (some of which can't be printed in this book), including the black and white arrows or the solid and hollow arrows. In reality, there's a third tool called the *Group Selection tool*, although it doesn't get much exposure due to a certain keyboard shortcut that we'll talk about shortly.

Figure 2.36 The dynamic duo, the Selection and Direct Selection tools, are also referred to as the black and white arrow tools.

Making Selections

Before we talk about the tools themselves, the reason why there are two different selection tools, and when to use one over the other, let's first see how you can make a selection in Illustrator.

- **The click method.** To select an object, just click it with any of the selection tools. To select multiple objects, you can click a second object while holding the Shift key to add the second object to your selection. Shift-clicking an object that is *already* selected will *deselect* it.

- **The marquee method.** Another way to create selections is by creating a *marquee*, which is similar to drawing a rectangle, only with a selection tool instead of a shape tool. You start by clicking and dragging the mouse to specify a rectangular area, called a marquee. When you release the mouse, any objects that fall within the boundaries of the marquee become selected (**Figure 2.37**).

Figure 2.37 Selecting multiple objects using the marquee method keeps you from having to Shift-click multiple shapes to select all of them.

Keep in mind that you can use a combination of both methods to make more efficient selections. For example, say you want to select all of the objects in a certain area except for one. You can use the marquee method to first select all of the objects, and then Shift-click the object that you don't want in order to deselect just that object.

Illustrator does have a contextual menu to select objects that appear underneath others. With an object selected, right-click (Control-click on Macs with a one-button mouse) and choose Select > Next Object Below from the contextual menu that appears (**Figure 2.38**).

The keyboard shortcut to quickly select all objects is Command-A (Control-A) and the shortcut to deselect all is Command-Shift-A (Control-Shift-A).

Sometimes, you don't want to be able to select an object at all. Especially in complex files with many overlapping objects, it can be easy to accidentally select objects without realizing what you've done (until it's too late, of course). Illustrator allows you to select an object and choose Object > Lock > Selection, which makes the object unavailable for editing. Unfortunately, it can be difficult to select objects that overlap each other (there's no easy way to click through the stacking order of objects like Adobe InDesign can), so locking and unlocking objects becomes a frequent endeavor. Learning the keyboard shortcuts to lock (Command-2 or Control-2) and unlock (Command-Option-2 or Control-Alt-2) is a good idea.

Figure 2.38 Use the contextual menu to select objects that appear beneath others. You'll find the contextual menus helpful throughout Illustrator.

The Direct Selection Tool

If there's one thing that confuses people most about Illustrator, it's the fact that there are two selection tools (the Pen tool doesn't *confuse* people nearly as much is it *frustrates* them). Fear not, though, there's a method to the madness—and once you understand it, you'll breathe easier. The good news is that whatever you learn here will apply to InDesign and Photoshop as well, because they use the same selection tools.

Featured Match-Up: Selection Tool vs. Direct Selection Tool

At the most simple level, the Selection tool (the black, or solid arrow) is used to select entire objects and groups. The Direct Selection tool, on the other hand, is used to select parts of objects, or individual objects within a group. For example, if you draw a star shape and click it with the Selection tool, the entire star becomes selected. In contrast, if you click one of the points of the star with the Direct Selection tool, only that point becomes selected (**Figure 2.39**).

Figure 2.39 The object on the left is being selected with the Selection tool. The object on the right is being selected with the Direct Selection tool.

At first, it sounds like life in Illustrator is all about the constant switching between these two tools. To make things a bit easier, when you have one selection tool active, you can press the Command (Control) key to temporarily switch to the other selection tool. To make life even easier than that, you can learn how power users use modifier keys with the Direct Selection tool efficiently; this practice practically negates the need for both the Selection tool and the Group Selection tool.

When you are using the Direct Selection tool, clicking the fill area of an object selects the entire object (unless the object is filled with None, or Object Selection by Path Only is turned on in Preferences). Clicking the vector path itself either selects a segment of the path (if you click between two anchor points), or it selects the anchor point that you click. If you hold the Option (Alt) key while clicking either the fill or the path of an object with the Direct Selection tool, it selects the entire object—just as the Selection tool does. So with a single keyboard shortcut, you can make the Direct

Selection tool "act" like its twin. If you are working with a group of objects, Option (Alt) clicking once on an object's path with the Direct Selection tool selects the entire object. Option (Alt) clicking a second time selects all of the objects in the group. If there are nested groups (groups within other groups), each additional Option (Alt) click results in the next level up in the hierarchy of the group being selected. If you ever want to select an entire group with one click, press the Command (Control) key to temporarily switch to the Selection tool.

Once you master this method of using the Direct Selection tool while using the keyboard shortcuts, you'll never think twice about the two selection tools again.

 By default, the Object Selection by Path Only setting in Preferences is turned off, which allows you to select an object by clicking its path, or anywhere within its fill area (if it has a fill attribute applied). Although this is convenient, there are times, especially when you are working with complex artwork, when this behavior makes it difficult to select objects. Turning this preference on allows you to select objects only by clicking their vector paths, not their fill areas.

The Group Selection Tool

In reality, there are *three* selection tools: the Selection tool, the Direct Selection tool, and the Group Selection tool. The Group Selection tool is useful for selecting groups of objects. As you will learn in Chapter 3, groups can be nested (meaning you can have groups within groups). Using the Group Selection tool, clicking once on an object selects the object itself. Clicking a second time on that same object selects the entire group that the object belongs to. Each successive click will select the next nested group in the hierarchy.

Earlier we referred to Illustrator as having two selection tools because the Group Selection tool is rarely chosen. Why? Because of the keyboard shortcut that was mentioned. When you have the Direct Selection tool chosen, pressing the Option (Alt) key toggles to the Group Selection tool, which is why you can then select entire objects.

Alternative Selection Techniques

Although most of the selection that you make will incorporate the use of the Selection tool or the Direct Selection tool, there are times when you may need a more specialized selection tool. Illustrator can offer a helping hand in a variety of ways.

The Lasso and Magic Wand Tools

Two selection tools first appeared in Photoshop but both have made their way into Illustrator's toolset: the Lasso tool and the Magic Wand tool. Although similar in concept to those found in Photoshop, remember that Illustrator is an object-based program, so these tools select objects, not pixels.

The Lasso tool in Illustrator acts much like the Direct Selection tool in that it can select individual anchor points, but you can only use it with the marquee method of making selections. Whereas a marquee is always limited to a rectangular shape, the specialty of the Lasso tool is that you can draw a marquee in any freeform shape. Where you have many objects in close proximity to each other, the Lasso tool allows you to draw a custom marquee shape to select just the objects—or anchor points—that you need (**Figure 2.40**).

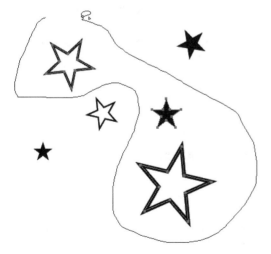

Figure 2.40 Drawing a freeform marquee with the Lasso tool can be helpful when you are trying to make complex selections with art that is in close proximity to other art.

Unlike the Selection and Direct Selection tools, the Lasso and Magic Wand tools can't move objects, they can only select them.

If you have several similarly styled objects in your document and you need to select them all, it can be tedious to manually select them using the click method. If they are scattered throughout the document, the marquee method won't work for you either. In such cases, the Magic Wand tool allows you to click one object; when you do, any other objects in your file that have the same attributes as the object you clicked become selected as well. Not bad for one click, right? If you double-click the Magic Wand tool in the Toolbox, the Magic Wand palette appears; here you can specify which specific attributes you want the Magic Wand tool to pay attention to (**Figure 2.41**). The true power of the Magic Wand tool is that you can set a tolerance for each attribute. So if your document contains several objects colored a variety of shades of yellow, you can still select them all with the Magic Wand tool by clicking a single yellow object.

Figure 2.41 You can use the Magic Wand palette to specify tolerance levels for different attributes.

 If you're a production artist, the Magic Wand tool is invaluable. By setting a tolerance of .25 point for Stroke Weight and clicking a path with a .25 point stroke on your artboard, you can select all paths in your document with a stroke weight between 0 and .5 points, making it easy to set consistent hairline stroke widths.

Selecting Similar Objects

Illustrator has a Select menu in the menu bar, which contains a variety of selection-based functions. Some of the most useful ones are found in the Select > Same and Select > Object submenus. To use the *Same* functions, first make a selection on the artboard with any of Illustrator's selection tools. Then, choose from the list of attributes to select objects based on that attribute (**Figure 2.42**). At any time, you can use the *Object* functions to select a certain kind of object in your file.

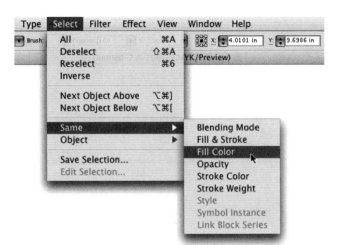

Figure 2.42 Illustrator offers powerful selection features, allowing you to make complex selections more easily, like the Select > Same functions.

Saving Selections

Making complex selections can take time and it can be tedious having to constantly make selections to objects as you are working on a design. To make life just a tad easier, you can save your selections and retrieve them later. Once you have made a selection using any of the methods mentioned earlier, choose Selection > Save and give your selection a name. That selection then appears at the bottom of the Select menu, which you can access, or *load* at any time. Because selections in Illustrator are object based, a saved selection remembers objects even after they've been moved or modified.

CHAPTER 3

Objects, Groups, and Layers

Some people have clean, organized desks, whereas others have desks that are quite messy. Likewise, some designers organize their Illustrator files using groups and layers, while many do not. And just as there are benefits to keeping an orderly desk, there are advantages to using groups and layers for adding structure to your files. In Adobe Illustrator CS2, groups and layers not only offer a convenient way to manage objects in a file (as they did in earlier versions of Illustrator), but now they can also control the appearance of your file. For example, applying a drop shadow to several objects that are grouped looks different than a drop shadow that is applied to those very same objects if they aren't grouped. You may even find that using groups and layers is necessary to create the art you need.

UNDERSTANDING APPEARANCES

As we discussed in the previous chapter, a vector path can have certain attributes applied, which can define the appearance of that path. When you print a file, you aren't seeing the vector path, you're seeing the appearance that was specified for that path. An example of an attribute might be a particular fill or stroke setting. As we'll learn later in this chapter, attributes can also be effects like drop shadows or 3D effects.

Smart Targeting

The *target* is simply the chosen entity to which attributes are applied. For the most part, targeting happens by itself. Illustrator employs a feature called Smart Targeting, which anticipates your actions and targets everything automatically. Although it may sound scary to know that Illustrator is trying to stay one step ahead of you, Illustrator actually does a great job of targeting for you. When you select a path, that path is automatically targeted. When you select a group, Illustrator assumes you want any attributes that you apply to be applied at the group level, rather than at the object level, and so Illustrator targets the group. See the Featured Match-Up sidebar "Selecting vs. Targeting" on the next page for more on targeting.

Of course, it's possible to manually target things on your own, and we'll discuss how to do that when we talk about layers, later in this chapter.

The Appearance Palette

When you specify attributes, they appear listed in the Appearance palette. We know this sounds like an advertisement for a movie, but if you keep only one Illustrator palette open on your screen while you're working, make it the Appearance palette. In fact, the Appearance palette is probably the most important palette in Illustrator—ever.

Like X-ray vision, the Appearance palette enables you to look at the underlying objects in your file and see how they were built or created. This palette also gives you access to every attribute of an object. But before we get ahead of ourselves, let's start with the basics.

Basic Appearances

Draw a rectangle with the default white fill and a 10-point black stroke and take a look at the Appearance palette. When the rectangle is selected, the

Featured Match-Up: Selecting vs. Targeting

At first glance, it can appear that selecting and targeting are one and the same. They appear this way because of Illustrator's Smart Targeting feature, where Illustrator does most of the targeting for you automatically, but selecting and targeting are really two different things.

For the most part, *selecting* is an action that is used to define a set of criteria that will be used for performing transformations. As we'll see in Chapter 4, *Advanced Vectors,* transformations consist of moving, scaling, rotating, skewing, or mirroring objects. You select objects because you want to move them from one side of your document to another, because you want to delete them, and so on.

Targeting on the other hand, is an action that is used to define a set of criteria specifically to apply an attribute such as a stroke, a fill, a transparency, or a live effect. When you select a path with the Selection tool, Illustrator automatically targets that path so that you can apply attributes to it. However, there may be times when you want to specifically target an entity. For example, you can target a layer and then add a stroke attribute to it (**Figure 3.1**). This gives every object on the layer a Stroke attribute (we'll discuss this concept in detail later in this chapter). Selecting the layer simply selects all of the objects on that layer. Applying a Stroke attribute at this point results in the individual paths getting the stroke. Targeting the layer results in the layer itself getting the Stroke attribute (the layer is a container, much like a group is a container for its contents).

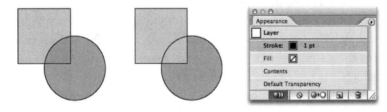

Figure 3.1 When you add a stroke to a layer, it is added to the top of the stacking order. All objects on that layer appear with a stroke. Because the stroke applies to the entire layer, even objects that are overlapping each other are stroked.

Appearance palette displays a thumbnail icon and the word "Path," which is the targeted item. (When we discuss Groups later in the chapter, we'll discuss what the target is.) The palette also lists the target's stroke (with the weight beside it), the fill, and the transparency (**Figure 3.2**). The order in which the listed items appear is important, because they define the final appearance of the object.

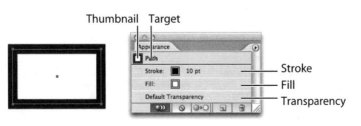

Figure 3.2 The Appearance palette displays the attributes for the targeted item.

Let's expand on what you learned in the previous chapter about fills and strokes. By default, a fill is painted first; the stroke is then painted on top of the fill. This is why you can see the entire weight of a stroke that is painted on the centerline of a path. However, you can click the Stroke attribute that is listed in the Appearance palette and drag it so that it appears listed beneath the Fill attribute (**Figure 3.3**). This ability to change the stacking order of attributes in an object's painting order becomes even more important when we talk about groups and layers later in the chapter.

Figure 3.3 The Appearance palette gives you the ability to change the stacking order of attributes. Here, the stroke attribute appears beneath the path's fill.

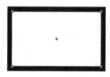 

You can also use the Appearance palette to target individual attributes by simply clicking them to highlight them. For example, when you click an object to select it, you can apply an opacity setting to that object via the Transparency palette. This opacity setting is applied to both the Fill and the Stroke attribute of the selected object (**Figure 3.4**). However, if you first target the fill by clicking it in the Appearance palette (**Figure 3.5**) and then changing the opacity setting, you'll notice that the setting is applied to the fill only and not to the stroke. This is indicated in the Appearance palette by a disclosure triangle just to the left of the Fill entry: The Opacity setting appears indented immediately underneath the fill's Color setting (**Figure 3.6**).

Figure 3.4 The Appearance palette displays the object's transparency setting. Here, an Opacity value of 48 percent is applied to the entire object.

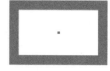 

Figure 3.5 Clicking the Fill or Stroke setting in the Appearance palette targets the attribute, allowing it to be adjusted independently of other attributes in the object.

Figure 3.6 When a setting is applied to an attribute individually, it appears indented beneath the attribute.

 You can't change an object's transparency settings from the Appearance palette, but double-clicking on the transparency listing in the Appearance palette will open the Transparency palette, where you can make changes. Note that this action will always edit the entire object's transparency. To apply transparency to individual strokes and fills, highlight them in the Appearance palette and then make a change using the Transparency palette directly.

Complex Appearances

Objects that have a Fill and a Stroke attribute are referred to as having a *basic appearance*. However, vector objects aren't limited to just one fill and one stroke and can contain multiple attributes. An object with more than just one fill or stroke is referred to as having a *complex appearance*.

To add an attribute to an object, choose Add New Fill or Add New Stroke from the Appearance palette menu (**Figure 3.7**). You'll see the new attribute appear in the Appearance palette, where you can change its place in the stacking order. Alternatively, you can drag a Fill or a Stroke attribute to the duplicate icon at the bottom of the Appearance palette. Dragging an attribute to the trash icon removes the attribute from the object.

Figure 3.7 Choosing to add a new stroke from the Appearance palette menu. There's no limit to how many fills or strokes you can add to a single object.

You may be wondering what good two fills or two strokes do in an object, because one always covers the one beneath it. Earlier, we discussed the ability to target a specific attribute so that you can apply settings to each individually. By first targeting the lower fill and specifying one color and then targeting the second fill, choosing a different color, and setting that fill to overprint, or by giving it an opacity setting or a blend mode, you've combined two inks in a single object (**Figure 3.8,** next page). Adding multiple strokes, each with different widths, colors, and dash patterns, can result in useful

 Be sure to check out Steven Gordon's use of multiple fills in the color insert.

borders or even stitch lines (**Figure 3.9**). There are numerous reasons for adding multiple attributes, and there's no limit to how many fills or strokes you can add to an object. Another benefit of numerous fills and strokes is that you can create a complex appearance yet edit just a single path. We'll discuss more ways in which this feature can be useful when we talk about Live Effects, later in this chapter.

Figure 3.8 Combining two fills in a single object allows you to create interesting effects. Here, a pattern fill and a gradient fill are combined using a transparency blend mode.

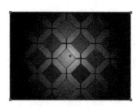

Figure 3.9 Combining two strokes in a single path gives you the ability to create complex strokes and still edit a single path.

The Appearance palette also gives you control over the behavior of appearances. At the bottom of the palette are several buttons (**Figure 3.10**):

Figure 3.10 The Appearance palette contains several functions to control the appearances of objects.

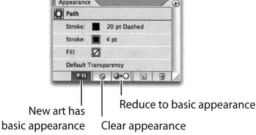
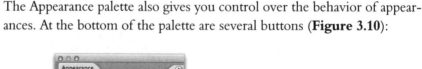

New art has basic appearance

Clear appearance

Reduce to basic appearance

- **New Art Has Basic Appearance.** This toggle, on by default, means that each new object you draw will have a basic appearance—a single fill and a single stroke. Normally, Illustrator styles a newly drawn object based on the last object that is selected. For example, if you click an object with a black stroke and a yellow fill, the next object you draw has a black stroke and a yellow fill as well. However, if you select an object with a complex appearance and then create a new shape, you may not want that new shape to be drawn with multiple attributes. When this is toggled off, all new objects pick up the complex appearances of any object previously selected.

- **Clear appearance.** This function reduces any appearance to a single fill and a single stroke, both with an attribute of None. This is a great way to select a shape and start from scratch.

- **Reduce to Basic Appearance.** This function reduces any complex appearance to a basic appearance by removing all fills and strokes except for the topmost fill and the topmost stroke.

Expanding Appearances

You'll notice that you can't select a specific attribute of an object from the artboard—the only place to access this functionality is via the Appearance palette. This makes the Appearance palette infinitely important, but it may make you wonder how an object with a complex appearance will print. After all, how does the printer or export format know to draw these multiple attributes on a single path?

The answer is that Illustrator breaks these complex appearances down into multiple overlapping paths—each path contains a basic appearance. This process, called *expanding*, doesn't happen on your artboard—it happens in the print stream or the export stream.

There are times when you may want to manually expand your appearances to access the multiple attributes on the artboard. To do so, choose Object > Expand Appearance. Remember that once you've expanded an appearance, you are dealing with a group of multiple objects, not a single object anymore. Each of those individual objects has a basic appearance, and unless you've created a graphic style (covered later in this chapter), you have no way to return to the original complex appearance.

 Although some people don't trust Illustrator and expand all appearances before sending final files off to print, we don't condone such behavior. There is no risk in printing files with appearances—they print just fine. Additionally, expanding your appearances limits your options if you have to make a last-minute edit or if your printer has to adjust your file.

ENHANCING APPEARANCES WITH LIVE EFFECTS

Illustrator has two entire menus dedicated to manipulating art and applying cool effects (like 3D and warp distortions): the Filter menu and the Effect menu. The Effect menu differs from the Filter menu in several ways (see the sidebar "Featured Match-Up: Filters vs. Effects"), but one of the most important is how effects are used in concert with the Appearance palette.

Illustrator refers to effects as *Live Effects*. There are several reasons for this. First of all—and most importantly—any effect that you apply from the Effect menu is added as an attribute in the Appearance palette. Secondly, all effects can be edited at any time, even after the file has been closed and reopened at another date. Finally, when an object's path is edited, any effects that are applied to that object are updated as well. Because these effects are non-destructive, they are considered as "live" and are always editable.

The way that Illustrator accomplishes this live behavior is by keeping the underlying vector object intact, while changing just the appearance of the object by adding the effect. Think of those 3D glasses that you get at a movie theater. Without the glasses, the movie appears like any other, but once you don the glasses, the movie appears to be 3D. You can think of the Appearance palette as a pair of 3D glasses in this sense—once you add an effect, the object changes in appearance, but the original untouched vector paths remain beneath the hood (**Figure 3.11**).

Figure 3.11 After a Warp effect has been applied, a vector shape appears distorted (left). When viewed in Outline mode, you can see the underlying vector shape still exists, unscathed (right).

Just as adding a second fill or stroke categorizes an object as having a complex appearance; adding a live effect to an object also produces an object with a complex appearance.

You can choose from many different Live Effects in Illustrator, including those that are vector-based (like Scribble) as well as those that are raster-based (like Gaussian Blur). For the purposes of understanding how these effects work and how they interact with the Appearance palette, we'll discuss what is arguably the most commonly used live effect—Drop Shadow—in this chapter. The remainder of the Live Effects are covered in Chapter 7, *3D and Other Live Effects*.

Featured Match-Up: Filters vs. Effects

You'll notice that Illustrator has both a Filter menu and an Effect menu. At first glance, the contents of these menus seem very similar and many of the items listed in the Filter menu appear to be identical to those in the Effect menu. In truth, there's a big difference between filters and effects in Illustrator.

As we mentioned, effects in Illustrator are referred to as Live Effects, and as they are applied, they appear in the Appearance palette. As you update your objects, any applied effects update accordingly. You can remove or edit these nondestructive effects at any time. In contrast, once you apply a filter, the actual vector object is changed and the filter can't be edited or removed. For this reason, you can refer to filters as "dead effects" because they are applied to objects in a destructive fashion.

Although you will most likely use effects for the majority of your work, there are certain times when it makes sense to use filters instead. For example, there may be times when you need to apply a filter and edit the vector paths right away. Rather than having to apply an effect and then expand it, you can just apply the filter, which is already expanded.

Additionally, some items in the Filter menu do not appear in the Effect menu—namely, those that appear in the Filter > Color and Filter > Create submenus. These filters (for example, converting color objects to grayscale or creating trim marks) are usually applied once and aren't edited afterward.

Applying a Live Effect

Applying a Live Effect is easy. To apply a soft drop shadow, select an object and choose Effect > Stylize > Drop Shadow. The Drop Shadow dialog appears, where you can specify the exact settings for your drop shadow including blend mode, opacity, offset (the distance between the object and its shadow), and the blur amount, which is the softness of the shadow. Additionally, you can choose a color or darkness value for your drop shadow (**Figure 3.12**, next page).

Figure 3.12 The Drop Shadow live effect gives you the ability to control all of the specifics to create a soft drop shadow.

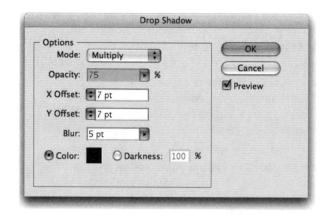

To choose a spot color for your drop shadow, you must first define the desired color as a swatch using the methods described in the previous chapter. Click the color swatch in the Drop Shadow dialog and then click the Color Swatches button, where you'll find your custom color in the list of swatches.

Note that the dialog has a Preview option, which, when checked, allows you to see your shadow update as you make changes to the settings. This is a useful feature and you'll find that nearly all Live Effects have a Preview option (yet another difference between filters and effects). Once you're happy with the appearance of your drop shadow, click OK to apply it.

Now, let's take a look at the Appearance palette. Note that the path is listed as the target and then examine the attributes in the object itself. Reading from the bottom up (the order in which the attributes are drawn), you have default transparency, the drop shadow effect that you've just applied, the fill, and then finally, the stroke of the object (**Figure 3.13**). The drop shadow appears beneath the fill and the stroke of the object because it wouldn't be much of a drop shadow if it were painted above the fill and stroke, would it?

Figure 3.13 Live Effects, once they are applied, appear listed in the Appearance palette.

The truth is, you can use the Appearance palette to control exactly how and where your drop shadow—and any live effect—is painted. Using the method we discussed earlier to apply opacity settings to fills and strokes independently, you can click the Fill or Stroke attribute in the Appearance palette and then add the drop shadow. In this way, you can add a live effect to just the fill or just the stroke of an object (**Figure 3.14**). If your object contains multiple fills or strokes, you can apply Live Effects to each of them individually. Once you've already applied a live effect, you can drag it within the Appearance palette to change its place in the painting order and to have it applied to a specific Fill or Stroke attribute.

Figure 3.14 Live Effects can be applied to fills or strokes of objects individually. Here, the drop shadow is applied just to the stroke of an object.

Editing a Live Effect

One of the important benefits of Live Effects is that you can edit them at any time. Double-clicking an effect that is listed in the Appearance palette opens the dialog for that effect, where you can view the current settings and change them at will. Many people make the mistake of going to the Effect menu to edit an effect. For example, if an object has a drop shadow applied to it, some might select the object and choose Effect > Stylize > Drop Shadow in order to change the settings of the effect. Doing so actually adds a *second* drop shadow effect to the selected object (**Figure 3.15**). Illustrator allows you to apply an effect to an object as many times as you'd like, and in Chapter 7 we will explore when that might be beneficial. The important thing to remember is that when you want to add a new effect to an object, you choose it from the Effect menu. To edit an effect that already exists, you double-click it in the Appearance palette.

Figure 3.15 If you try to edit an existing effect by choosing it from the Effect menu, Illustrator informs you that you must edit existing effects though the Appearance palette.

To duplicate an effect that you've applied, highlight it in the Appearance palette and click the Duplicate icon in the palette. You can also drag effects to the Duplicate icon. To delete an effect from an object, highlight it in the Appearance palette and click the trash icon in the palette. You can drag effects directly to the trash icon as well.

USING GRAPHIC STYLES

You probably already have a sense of how powerful appearances and Live Effects are. However, if you have several objects in your file to which you need to apply the same appearance, it can be inefficient to do this manually using Live Effects. Additionally, if you ever need to update the appearance you applied, you would need to do so for each object individually. Graphic Styles can help.

A *graphic style* is a saved set of attributes, much like a swatch. When you apply a style to an object, that object takes on the attributes that are defined in the style. At any time, you can redefine the attributes of a particular style, and when you do, any objects in your file that already have that style applied are updated as well. The best part about Graphic Styles is how easy they are to use. And you'll never guess which palette plays an integral part in creating graphic styles—that's right, the Appearance palette.

Defining a Graphic Style

As we mentioned earlier, a graphic style is a saved set of attributes. You know that the Appearance palette lists all attributes, so you already understand the first step in creating a graphic style—specifying the attributes you want defined in the style. Once you've specified stroke and fill settings and added Live Effects, click the New Graphic Style button in the Graphic Styles palette (**Figure 3.16**). Alternatively, you can drag the target thumbnail from the Appearance palette and drop it into the Graphic Styles palette. Double-click a style in the Graphic Styles palette to give it a name (which is always helpful). If you Option-click (Alt-click) the New Graphic Style button, you can define a new style and give it a unique name in a single step.

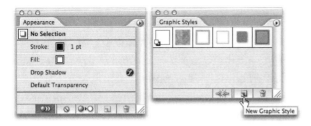

Figure 3.16 Once you've specified your attributes in the Appearance palette, you can use the Graphic Styles palette to create a new graphic style.

Notice that when you apply a graphic style to an object in your file, the Appearance palette identifies the target and the style that is applied. This makes it easy to quickly see which style is applied to an object (**Figure 3.17**).

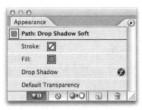

Figure 3.17 When a graphic style is applied, the Appearance palette helps you easily identify the target and the applied style.

Sometimes designers need to combine two inks to create a certain effect. For example, package designers often want to mix black ink with a spot color ink. Although you can't create a swatch that contains two inks, you can create a graphic style that contains two fills. The lower fill is the spot color, the other fill is a percentage of black, set to Overprint (**Figure 3.18**). You can then apply the style to any object with a single click.

Figure 3.18 To simulate a multi-ink color, combine two fills and use the Overprint command. The result is a single editable path that contains two colors.

Editing a Graphic Style

Editing a graphic style is an exercise that involves both the Appearance palette and the Graphic Styles palette, so it makes sense to position them side by side. You don't need to have an object selected in order to modify an existing graphic style, but if you do have an object selected, you'll be able to preview the changes you're making to the style.

In the Graphic Styles palette, click the style that you want to edit. The Appearance palette lists all of the attributes for the selected style. You can modify the style by either adding additional attributes, deleting existing ones, or by changing the paint order by dragging attributes in the Appearance palette. Once you're happy with the modifications, choose Redefine Graphic Style from the Appearance palette menu to update the style (**Figure 3.19**).

Figure 3.19 Once you've modified the attributes, you can update the style, which updates all other objects that have the style applied.

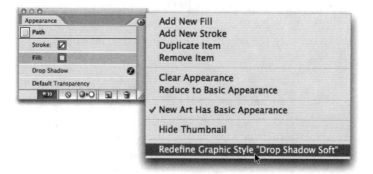

Any objects in your file that have that particular style applied then immediately update to reflect the modifications. Alternatively, you can Option-drag (Alt-drag) the target thumbnail on top of the existing style in the Graphic Styles palette. A heavy black outline appears around the style in the palette to indicate that the style will be updated (**Figure 3.20**).

Figure 3.20 Dragging the thumbnail from the Appearance palette on top of an existing graphic style while holding the Option (Alt) key redefines the style.

 As we mentioned back in Chapter 1, Illustrator ships with many libraries, including a variety of graphic styles. It's a good idea to load some of these and use the Appearance palette to see how they were created. Not only does this give you some ideas on the kinds of styles you can create, it allows you to better understand how powerful both appearances and Graphic Styles can be.

Loading Attributes with the Eyedropper Tool

You can use Illustrator's Eyedropper tool to load the attributes of existing objects quickly. This can be useful in two ways. First, if you already have an object selected when you click another object with the Eyedropper tool, your selected object changes to match the object you clicked. Second, you can click once with the Eyedropper to sample the attributes of an object, and you can then Option-click (Alt-click) to apply those attributes to other objects in your file without actually having to select them.

You can configure the Eyedropper tool to sample just the basic appearance of an object (the topmost fill and stroke) or complete complex appearances. To control what the Eyedropper tool can sample, double-click the tool in the Toolbox (**Figure 3.21**).

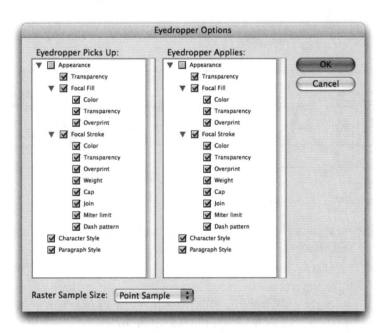

Figure 3.21 Double-click the Eyedropper tool in the Toolbox to control what specific attributes the tool uses for sampling.

Shift-click with the Eyedropper tool to sample colors from the pixels of raster images. In this way, the Eyedropper tool works much like the one found in Photoshop.

WORKING WITH GROUPS

As we mentioned in the beginning of this chapter, creating groups is a way to organize the elements in a file. Most importantly, groups allow you to easily select or work with several objects that may belong to a single design element. You can also nest groups, meaning that you can have groups within other groups. For example, you might have a logo that's made up of an icon and a type treatment that has been converted to outlines. You can group together the objects that make up the icon, and you can make the items that make up the type treatment a separate group as well. Both groups can then be grouped, resulting in a single group (the logo) that contains two groups (the icon and the type treatment) within it (**Figure 3.22**).

Figure 3.22 An example of a nested group, where two groups are nested within a third group.

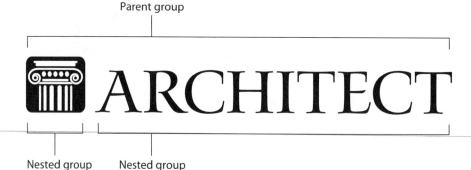

Parent group

Nested group   Nested group

When you think of groups in this way, it's simply a matter of labeling certain objects that belong together. But now that we have appearances in Illustrator, it's more than just a concept—a group is actually an entity itself. Illustrator refers to a group as a *container*—something that contains the grouped objects within it. This introduces two important concepts: the container itself can have attributes applied to it; and the container can affect the way the grouped objects interact with each other and other art elements in your file. Let's take a look at a simple example using the Drop Shadow effect you just learned about in the previous section.

Adding a Soft Drop Shadow to a Group

Draw two overlapping shapes, a circle and a square, each a different color. Now create an exact copy of those two shapes, only in the copied version, group the two objects together by selecting them and choosing Object > Group. So now you're looking at two design elements, each identical in appearance, only one is made up of two separate objects, and one is made of two objects that are grouped together (**Figure 3.23**). Select the first set of objects and choose Effect > Stylize > Drop Shadow and apply the default settings. Now select the grouped objects and apply the same drop shadow. Observe the results (**Figure 3.24**).

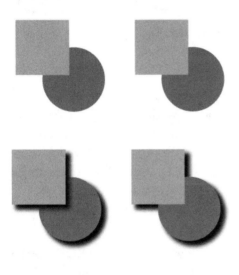

Figure 3.23 The design elements shown here are identical except for one fact: the element on the right has been grouped.

Figure 3.24 Applying a drop shadow to individual objects (left) appears different than the same drop shadow applied to a group of objects (right).

The first design element appears to have drop shadows applied to each object individually. The second design element—the group—has a single drop shadow applied to it, as if the two separate shapes were really one shape. This difference in appearance occurred because in the second design element, Illustrator applied the drop shadow not to the actual objects themselves, but to the container that has the two objects inside of it—the group. Now, select the group and choose Object > Ungroup, and the drop shadow disappears! By removing the container (ungrouping), you've removed the effect that was applied to that container.

Adjusting Opacity to a Group

Let's look at another example using the same two design elements—one of which is grouped. Select the first set of objects and change the opacity value in the Transparency palette to 50 percent. Now select the group and make the same change to the opacity value. Observe the results (**Figure 3.25**).

Figure 3.25 When applying an opacity setting to individual overlapping objects, you can see one object through the other (left), but when the opacity is applied to a group, the entire group takes on the attribute, giving it a different appearance (right).

The first design element has the opacity value applied to each object individually, and each object interacts with the other, enabling you to see through one object to the one underneath it. The grouped objects have the same opacity applied, but you don't see the objects overlapping with each other. Again, this appearance is due to the fact that Illustrator is applying the opacity setting to the container, not to the objects themselves. As in the previous example with the drop shadow, simply ungrouping the two objects removes the opacity setting as well.

These two examples clearly illustrate how groups can have attributes applied to them, or how they can control how grouped objects interact with each other. In this context, you begin to see that grouping objects is more than just making files easier to manage. Creating groups can have a significant impact on the appearance of your art. In fact, simply ungrouping art can alter the appearance of your file completely.

The obvious questions you should be asking are, "How do I know when I'm applying an attribute to an object versus a group?" and "How can I tell if ungrouping something will alter the appearance of my file?" The answers lie in the all-important Appearance palette, which tells you what is targeted. If you think back to the grouping examples we discussed earlier, you'll recall that when you selected the group, the drop shadow was applied to the group because it was targeted. Had the individual paths been targeted, the drop shadow would have been applied to the paths themselves.

 The current target is also displayed on the far left side of the Control palette.

Text as a Group

Text is a special kind of object in Illustrator—it's actually a group. The type object itself is the container, and the actual text characters are like the objects inside a group. You can see this by looking at—that's right—the Appearance palette. Select a point text object with the Selection tool and the Appearance palette shows "Type" as the target. Switch to the Type tool and select the text and the Appearance palette shows "Characters" as the target.

When you select a text object with a selection tool, Illustrator's Smart Targeting automatically targets the Type container. You can see Characters listed in the Appearance palette, and double-clicking the Characters listing automatically switches to the Type tool and highlights the text on your artboard (**Figure 3.26**). The target is now Characters and you can see the Fill and the Stroke attributes.

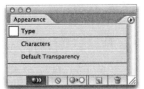

Figure 3.26 When a Type object is selected, the Appearance palette shows the Type as the container and the characters within it.

Group Isolation

Sometimes you'll want to draw a new object and add it to an existing group. For example, say your client requests that you add the Registered Trademark symbol to a logo, which is already grouped. One way to accomplish this is to use the Type tool to add the Registered Trademark symbol to your document. Then you select the logo, ungroup it, and then select the logo and the new trademark symbol and group the objects together.

 Group Isolation Mode is especially useful when you're using the Live Paint feature in Illustrator CS2, which we'll cover in detail in Chapter 4, *Advanced Vectors*.

Illustrator CS2 introduces an easier way to add objects to existing groups using a feature called Group Isolation Mode. Using the logo example we just discussed, you would use the following method to add the trademark symbol. Using the Selection tool, double-click any object in the logo. A gray border appears around the perimeter of the group, indicating that the group is now isolated (**Figure 3.27**, next page). When a group is isolated, any new shapes or objects that are created become part of the group. Select the Type tool and create a text object with the trademark symbol to automatically add the symbol to the logo group. To exit isolation mode, either click any object that's outside the group, or double-click the artboard, at which time the gray border disappears.

Figure 3.27 Double-clicking any object in a group puts the group into Group Isolation Mode, making it easy to add new objects directly into the group.

When you have a group selected, the Control palette has a button that also allows you to enter isolation mode (**Figure 3.28**). You can use the same button to exit isolation mode as well.

Figure 3.28 You can also enter Group Isolation Mode by clicking an icon in the context-sensitive Control palette when a group is selected.

WORKING WITH LAYERS

Layers are nearly identical to groups in concept, but they offer more flexibility and functionality. Whereas groups are used to combine design elements in a file, layers also allow you to organize and combine elements within a file. Just as groups can be nested within each other, so can layers. And just as groups are containers that hold contents within them, layers are containers as well. In addition, layers, just like groups, can also have attributes applied to them. As we explore the power of layers in Illustrator, all of these concepts will come to light.

The Layers Palette

You'll start learning to use layers by taking a look at the Layers palette and learning some of its simple functions. Then you'll put together everything that you've learned in this chapter to take full advantage of the power found in the Layers palette.

The Significance of Layers

Don't be fooled into thinking that layers are just for making files neat and organized. Quite the contrary, a file that takes advantage of using layers can benefit
from many other features as well.

- **Layer clipping masks.** Illustrator has the ability to make the topmost object in
  a layer a mask for all items within that layer.

- **PDF layers.** Illustrator can export PDF files with layers intact, allowing users in
  Adobe Acrobat or Adobe Reader to interactively turn on and off those layers.
  Additionally, InDesign CS2 has the capability to control the visibility of PDF
  layers.

- **Photoshop export.** When exporting an Illustrator file to a PSD file, you can
  choose to have layers preserved, thus making your file easier to edit when you
  bring it into Photoshop.

- **Transparency.** There are times when artwork with transparency can result in
  files that look less than perfect when printed on a high-resolution press—*if*
  the file is built in a certain way. Using layers can significantly reduce the number of issues you might encounter when using transparency features.

- **Animation.** When creating art for frame-based animations, like those used in
  GIF and SWF (Flash) animations, Illustrator layers serve as frames. Layers are
  also integral when you are creating art that will be animated in programs like
  Adobe After Effects.

- **CSS (Cascading Style Sheets).** Illustrator layers can be exported as CSS Layers
  when you're creating web layouts and SVG graphics, allowing for greater flexibility and better support for browser standards.

- **SVG (Scalable Vector Graphics).** Illustrator layers serve as basic building
  blocks when you're creating files that are going to be saved as SVG. Providing
  structure for SVG files can help make it easier to animate and edit the SVG files
  in a web or wireless environment.

- **Variables.** Illustrator's XML-based variables feature relies on the organization
  of layers in your document. Object visibility and naming conventions are all
  done through the Layers palette.

There are plenty of other good reasons to use layers in Illustrator, and you're sure
to find yourself using layers more and more.

By default, all Illustrator documents are created with a single existing layer,
called Layer 1. The buttons across the bottom of the palette are used to activate clipping masks (which we'll cover in detail in Chapter 5, *Brushes, Symbols, and Masks*), create new layers and new sublayers, and to delete layers.

To the left of each layer are two boxes—the box on the far left controls layer visibility, whereas the other box enables locking (**Figure 3.29**). The Layers palette menu contains duplicates of these functions, as well as some other functions that we'll cover when we talk about animation in Chapter 10, *Illustrator and the Web*.

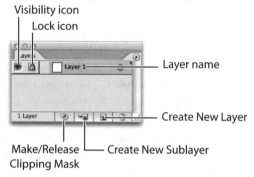

Figure 3.29 All files are created with a blank layer in the Layers palette.

Double-clicking a layer enables you to specify several settings for that layer (**Figure 3.30**):

Figure 3.30 The Layer Options dialog allows you to specify settings for each layer—most notably, the name of the layer.

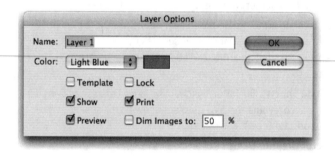

Option-click (Alt-click) the visibility icon of a Layer to hide all other layers with one click. Option-click (Alt-click) once more to show all layers again. The same shortcut applies to the lock icon as well. To change layer visibility for multiple layers, you can click and drag across several layers.

- **Name.** Every layer can have its own distinct name. Layer names are important when you're creating SVG files and generally make files easier to work with. Naming layers is especially important when you're designing templates. A file littered with layers named Layer 1, Layer 2, Layer 3, can make editing a challenging task.

- **Color.** This setting is a bit deceiving because it doesn't add a fill color to the layer but instead defines the selection color used for the layer. When you select an object in Illustrator, the path of that object is highlighted so that you see what is selected. By assigning different colors to each layer, you can tell what objects belong to which layer by selecting the object and observing the highlight color. Setting a layer color to black or really light colors generally isn't a good idea because you won't be able to differentiate a selection from a regular path.

- **Template.** This setting is used specifically when you want to manually trace placed images. Setting a layer as a Template automatically locks the layer and sets the Dim Images setting to 50 percent. Although this makes it easier to see and draw over placed images, the new Live Trace feature makes this option less important.

- **Show.** This setting controls layer visibility (whether the art on a layer is shown or hidden) and performs the same function as clicking the show/hide icon in the Layers palette.

- **Preview.** This setting controls the preview setting for the chosen layer. By default, Illustrator's Preview mode is turned on, but unchecking this option displays the layer in Outline mode.

- **Lock.** This setting controls layer locking and performs the same function as clicking the lock/unlock icon in the Layers palette itself. Locking a layer effectively prevents you from selecting any object on that layer.

- **Print.** By default, all layers in a file will print. However, Illustrator allows you to uncheck this option to create a nonprinting layer. This can be useful when you want to add instructions to a template file or to explain how a file should be folded or printed, but you don't want those instructions to print. Layers that have the Print option turned off appear italicized in the Layers palette.

- **Dim Images to.** This option allows you to define an opacity setting for placed images. By making placed images dim, you can make it easier to manually trace them. This feature is often used in tandem with the Template function.

Object Hierarchy

When a layer contains artwork, a disclosure triangle appears just to the left of the layer. Clicking this triangle reveals the contents of the layer within the Layers palette (**Figure 3.31**, next page). Every object that appears in a n Illustrator document appears listed in the Layers palette. The order in which items appear has significance—it indicates the stacking order, or object hierarchy of the file. Objects that appear at the bottom of the Layers palette are drawn first, and therefore they appear at the bottom of the object stacking order.

In the Layers palette, layers and sublayers appear with shaded backgrounds, and objects appear with white backgrounds.

You can drag items listed in the Layers palette to adjust where they sit in the stacking order. Dragging an object from the bottom of the Layers palette to the top of the palette places that object at the top of the stacking order. It's important to note that each layer and each group also maintain their own stacking order. The Layers palette basically represents the stacking order of the entire file.

Figure 3.31 Clicking a disclosure triangle reveals the raw power of the Layers palette—the ability to view the entire object hierarchy of a file.

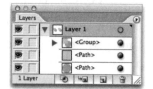

Configuring the Layers Palette

If you find that the level of detail offered by the Layers palette is beyond the needs of your simple design tasks, you can set the behavior of the Layers palette to match the functionality that existed prior to Illustrator 9. Choose Palette Options from the Layers palette menu and check the Show Layers Only button (**Figure 3.32**). This hides all objects from the Layers palette. Additionally, you can turn off layer thumbnails (which will significantly enhance performance). For documents that have lots of layers (like maps, for example), you might also choose the Small option for Row Size (**Figure 3.33**). One caveat to these options is that they are document-specific, which means that you need to change these settings for each document.

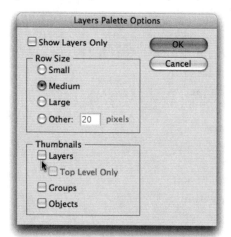

Figure 3.32 Turning off layer thumbnail previews in the Palette Options dialog significantly enhances performance in large files.

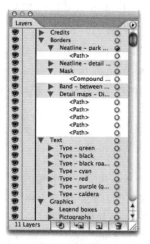

Figure 3.33 Choosing the Small option for Row Size in the Palette Options dialog can give you the ability to see far more layers on screen at once and reduce the need to scroll as often.

You can create nested layers by dragging one layer into another layer (**Figure 3.34**). You can do the same with groups as well, which makes it easy to organize your artwork even after the art is created. In fact, this method of dragging items within the Layers palette makes it possible to move objects from one group and place them into another group. As you learned earlier in this chapter, groups can have attributes applied to them; this becomes significant because when you're moving an object into a group that has an attribute applied to it, that object takes on the attributes of the group. The reverse applies as well, so simply moving an object from one layer to another, or into or out of a group can change the appearance of the art in your file.

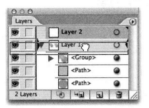

Figure 3.34 When you're dragging layers in the Layers palette, black arrows on the left and right indicate that you're moving a layer into another layer rather than above or below it.

Layers and Appearances

If you take another look at the Layers palette, you'll notice that to the right of every item listed is a small circle, called the target indicator (**Figure 3.35**). If you remember, we spoke earlier about how the target controls where attributes are applied. If you take the same examples we used earlier, the ones of identical design elements of which one is grouped and one is not, you can clearly see how targeting works.

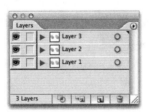

Figure 3.35 The little circles that appear on the right side of each layer are target indicators.

In the Layers palette, the ungrouped design element appears listed as separate paths, whereas the grouped design element appears as objects nested inside a group (**Figure 3.36**). When you select the first design element, a double circle appears on each of the individual paths, indicating that those paths are targeted (**Figure 3.37**). Now select the grouped design element and you'll see that although the objects are *selected*, the group is *targeted* (**Figure 3.38**).

Figure 3.36 A quick look at the Layers palette reveals the hierarchy of the file. Layer 1 contains two path objects and a group. The group contains two path objects.

Figure 3.37 Selecting the path objects also targets the two individual paths. The large squares to the right indicate the objects are selected and the small square to the right of the layer indicates that some objects on the layer are selected, but not all of them.

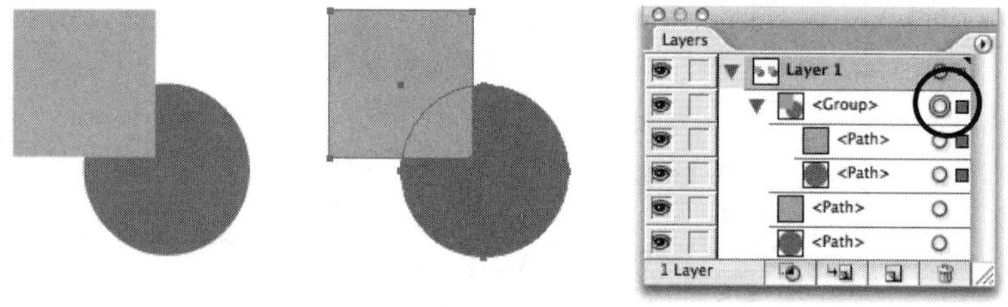

Figure 3.38 When selecting the group, Illustrator's Smart Targeting feature targets the group, not the objects themselves. Notice the double circle target indicator appears only on the group, not the objects.

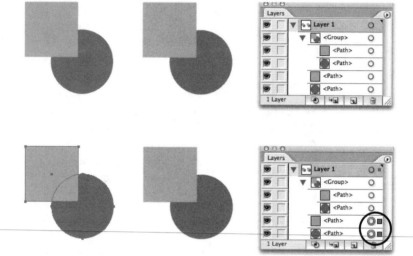

Now you'll add a drop shadow to each of the design elements. A quick glance at the Layers palette now shows that some of the target indicators are shaded or filled, whereas some of the target indicators are hollow (**Figure 3.39**). Hollow circles indicate that the item listed has a basic appearance, whereas filled circles indicate that a complex appearance exists on that object (Adobe engineers refer to these filled circles as *meatballs*). Just by looking at the Layers palette, you can tell that the second design element has some kind of effect applied to the group. This is your first indication that ungrouping such a group will result in a change in appearance.

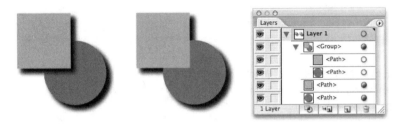

Figure 3.39 Shaded target indicators—meatballs—show where complex appearances exist.

You can manually target groups or layers by clicking the target indicator for that object. For example, you can target a layer and then use the Appearance palette to add a new stroke. The Appearance palette lists the attributes for the targeted layer, and if you look at the contents of the palette, you'll see that the stroke appears above the contents of the layer. Dragging the stroke underneath the contents of the layer causes the stroke to be drawn behind each of the objects on that layer (**Figure 3.40**). When you drag a shape into such a layer the object automatically appears to have a stroked appearance, and when you drag any objects out of that layer, that stroked appearance disappears.

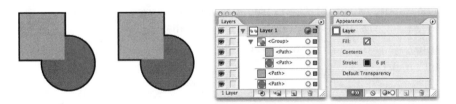

Figure 3.40 With a layer targeted, you can add appearances directly to the layer. Here, a stroke has been added to the layer, and the stroke has been moved to appear below the contents of the layer, adding an interesting outlining effect.

 Dragging a meatball from one layer or object to another effectively copies the complex appearance and applies it to the object you are dragging it to.

The important concept to remember is that taking a quick look at the Layers palette and scanning for meatballs helps you find complex appearances that appear in the file. In this way, you won't accidentally change a file's appearance just by grouping or ungrouping objects.

The Appearance palette is also useful in helping you understand how files are built because if you select an object that is part of a group or layer that has an appearance applied, the Appearance palette lists the group or layer above the target (**Figure 3.41**).

Figure 3.41 When you select an object that is part of a group or layer that has a complex appearance, the Appearance palette alerts you to this by displaying multiple targets.

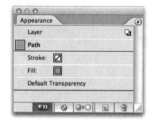

PUTTING IT ALL TOGETHER

The importance of the Appearance palette is obvious. Without it, you have no way to edit multiple attributes applied to an object; you have no way to edit attributes that are applied to groups or layers; and you have no way to edit the properties of a live effect.

The importance of the Layers palette is equally apparent. Without it, you have no way to understand the hierarchy of a file and you have no warning as to when a simple action like grouping or ungrouping will change a file's appearance.

But it's deeper than that. The Appearance palette is like the Matrix—you can look at it and see the underlying makeup of any Illustrator file. By using the Layers and Appearance palettes together, you can quickly and efficiently reverse engineer any file that you receive (**Figure 3.42**). If you're a production artist who needs to know every detail about a file, or if you're trying to troubleshoot a particular file, these two palettes will be your best friends.

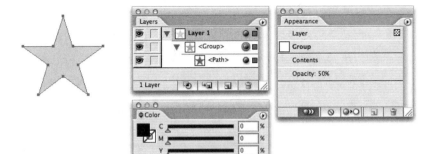

Figure 3.42 Don't trust everything you see on the artboard. It's easy to create a single object, group it by itself, and then apply a 50-percent opacity setting to the object, the group, and the layer. The result is an object that prints at 12.5-percent opacity. The meatballs in the Layers palette should be an indicator that you need to take a closer look.

Throughout the remaining chapters of this book, you'll learn how features like clipping and opacity masks, envelope distortions, and placed images are all easily identified in the Layers palette. You'll also learn the importance of using layers when you're creating Flash animations or SVG files for the Web.

 In complex files, it can be hard to locate certain objects either on your artboard or in your Layers palette. Using the Layers palette to select objects can make it easier to find and select objects on the artboard, and selecting objects on the artboard can also quickly identify where those objects appear in the Layers palette.

CHAPTER 4

Advanced Vectors

Drawing rectangles, ovals, and stars is nice, but that's not why you use Adobe Illustrator. The true power of Illustrator is that you can use it to create custom shapes as you need them—this allows you to tweak a design to perfection. Illustrator comes with a variety of tools and functions, each with its own strengths and uses. Whether it's the mystifying Pen tool, the new Live Paint feature that allows you to edit and color vector objects more freely, or the dependable Pathfinder and path functions that have helped make Illustrator so powerful over the years, this chapter reveals the true art of the vector path.

DRAWING AND EDITING FREEFORM VECTORS

Strip away the cool effects. Forget all the fancy tools. Ignore the endless range of gradients and colors. Look past the veneer of both print and Web graphics. What you're left with is the basis of all things vector—the anchor point. You can learn to master every shape tool in Illustrator, but if you don't have the ability to create and edit individual anchor points, you'll find it difficult to design freely.

Illustrator contains a range of tools that you can use to fine-tune paths and edit anchor points. At first, it might seem like these all do the same thing, but upon closer inspection, you'll find that each has its use.

A Pen Tool for Everyone

Just the mention of the Pen tool sends shivers down the spines of designers throughout the world. Traditionally, Illustrator's Pen tool has frustrated many users who have tried their hand at creating vector paths. In fact, when the Pen tool was introduced in the first version of Illustrator back in 1987, word had it that John Warnock, the brainchild and developer behind Illustrator, was the only one who really knew how to use it. In truth, the Pen tool feels more like an engineer's tool rather than an artist's tool.

But don't let this prevent you from learning to use it.

Learning how to use the Pen tool reaps numerous rewards. Although the Pen tool first appeared in Illustrator, you'll now find it in both Adobe Photoshop and Adobe InDesign; since you can use it in Illustrator, you can use it in the other applications as well. You can use the Pen tool to tweak any vector path to create the exact shape you need, at any time. Additionally, if you give yourself a chance, you'll see that there's a method to the madness. After learning a few simple concepts, you'll quickly realize that anyone can use the Pen tool.

Mastering the Pen Tool

Usually, when new users select the Pen tool and try to draw with it, they click and drag it the same way they might use a normal pen on paper. They are surprised when a path does not appear on screen; instead, several handles appear. At this point, they click again and drag; now a path appears but it is totally not where they expect it to appear. This experience is sort of like grabbing a hammer by its head and trying to drive a nail by whacking it with the handle—it's the right tool, but it's being used in the wrong way.

While we're discussing hammers, let's consider their function in producing string art. When you go to create a piece of string art, you first start with a piece of wood and then you hammer nails part of the way into it, leaving each nail sticking out a bit. Then you take colored thread and wrap it around the exposed nail heads, thus creating your art. The design that you create is made of up the strands of colored thread, but the thread is held and shaped by the nails. In fact, you can say that the nails are like anchors for the threads.

When you're using the Pen tool in Illustrator, imagine you're hammering those little nails into the wood. In this situation, you aren't drawing the shape itself; instead, you're creating the anchors for the shape—the Bézier anchor points. Illustrator draws the thread—the path itself—for you. If you think about drawing in this way, using the Pen tool isn't complicated at all. The hard part is just figuring out where you need to position the anchors to get the shape you need. Learning to position the anchors correctly comes with experience, but you can get started by learning how to draw simple shapes.

Drawing Objects with Straight Paths

Follow these steps to use the Pen tool to draw a straight path.

1. Select the Pen tool and click once on the artboard—do not click and drag with the mouse.

    Clicking once with the Pen tool creates a *corner anchor point*. This anchor point that you create is the beginning or start point of your path.

2. Now, move your cursor to where you want the end point of your path (**Figure 4.1**); click again to define a second corner anchor point.

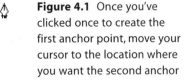

Figure 4.1 Once you've clicked once to create the first anchor point, move your cursor to the location where you want the second anchor point.

When drawing new paths with the Pen tool, it's best to set your fill attribute to None and your stroke attribute to black. Otherwise, Illustrator will fill the path as you create it, making it difficult to see your work.

Once you create this second point, Illustrator automatically connects the two anchor points with a straight path, completing the line (**Figure 4.2**).

Figure 4.2 Clicking a second time creates the path between the two anchor points. No clicking and dragging is necessary.

For now, the first concept becomes clear: When you're using the Pen tool, clicking—not dragging—is what defines a corner anchor point.

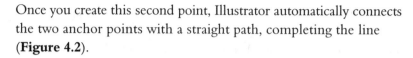

Holding the Shift key while you click with the Pen tool constrains paths to 45-degree increments. Additionally, you can choose View > Smart Guides to have Illustrator display helpful guides and hints as you move the cursor (see Appendix C, *Application Preferences* for more information).

At this point, with your Pen tool still selected, Illustrator assumes that you want to add additional points to your path. By clicking the artboard, you can create a third corner anchor point, and if you do, Illustrator draws a path to connect the second anchor point to the newly created one (**Figure 4.3**).

Figure 4.3 Each successive click with the Pen tool continues to create additional path segments.

Admittedly, this behavior may prove confusing because you may have been expecting to start a new path rather than add to the existing one. To start a new path, you first have to deselect the current path. The easiest way to do this is to click a blank area on the artboard while pressing the Command (Ctrl) key, which temporarily changes your tool to the Selection tool. Once you've deselected the path, you can click with the Pen tool to start drawing a new path.

So now you understand a second concept: When drawing an open path with the Pen tool, each click of the mouse adds another anchor point to the path until you deselect the path, which is how you indicate to Illustrator that you've finished that path.

There is another way to indicate that you've finished drawing a path—by drawing a closed path. Until now, you've been creating open paths, but now you can try to create a closed shape—in this case, a triangle.

1. With nothing selected, choose the Pen tool and click once to define the first anchor point of the triangle.

2. Move the cursor to another part of the artboard and click again to define the second point.

3. Now move the cursor once more and click to define a third anchor point (**Figure 4.4**).

   A triangle has three sides, so you have all of the anchor points you need, but at the moment, the object you've drawn is an open path.

4. To complete the shape, move the cursor so that it rests directly on the first anchor point that you defined and click once to close the path (**Figure 4.5**).

   At this point, if you click again elsewhere on the artboard, the Pen tool starts drawing a new path.

Figure 4.4 A triangle needs three anchor points; the third click creates two path segments.

Figure 4.5 Clicking the first anchor point completes the shape. The screenshot shows the shape after it has been closed.

This brings us to a third concept: When you create a closed path, the next click with the Pen tool starts a new path.

If this sounds confusing, try it once or twice, that should help—especially if you pay attention to your Pen tool cursor. When you're using the Pen tool, the cursor changes as you draw, helping you understand the three concepts you've just learned. When the Pen tool is going to start creating a new path, a small "X" appears at the lower right of the icon; when the Pen tool is going to add anchor points to an existing selected open path, no icon appears next to it; and when the Pen tool is going to close a path, a small "O" appears at the lower right of the icon (**Figure 4.6**).

Figure 4.6 The Pen tool shows subtle indications in its icon that let you know the function it will perform.

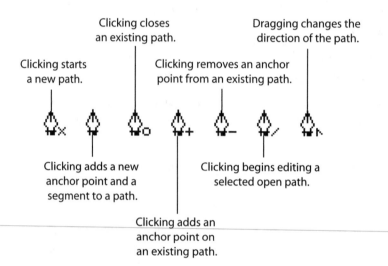

Clicking closes an existing path.

Dragging changes the direction of the path.

Clicking starts a new path.

Clicking removes an anchor point from an existing path.

Clicking adds a new anchor point and a segment to a path.

Clicking begins editing a selected open path.

Clicking adds an anchor point on an existing path.

Drawing Objects with Curved Paths

By now, you should be able to understand the statement we made earlier about how drawing the path is the easy part of using the Pen tool. The hard part is trying to figure out where to place the anchor points to get the path you want.

The paths that you've drawn up until this point were all made up of corner anchor points, which are connected with straight lines. Of course, you'll also need to create paths with curved lines; this section explains what you need to know.

In Chapter 2, *Vectors 101*, you learned that curves are defined with *direction handles*, which control how the paths between anchor points are drawn. When you want to draw a curved path, you follow the same basic concepts you learned for creating straight paths, with one additional step that defines direction handles.

1. To draw a curved path, choose the Pen tool and make sure an existing path isn't selected. Position your cursor where you want to begin your path and then click and drag the mouse outward before releasing the button (**Figure 4.7**).

This action creates a *smooth anchor point* where you first clicked with the mouse and defines direction handles at the point where you released the mouse.

Figure 4.7 Clicking and dragging with the Pen tool defines the smooth anchor point and, at the same time, allows you to position the direction handles.

2. Now position your cursor where you want the next anchor point to be and click and drag once again (**Figure 4.8**).

    Using the direction handles as guidance, Illustrator draws a curved path connecting the two smooth anchor points.

Figure 4.8 Clicking and dragging a second time completes a curved path between the first two anchor points and defines the next curve that will be drawn.

3. Move your cursor to another location on your artboard and click and drag to create a third smooth anchor point.

4. Click and drag on the first anchor point to close the path (**Figure 4.9**).

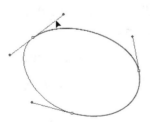

Figure 4.9 Clicking and dragging on the first anchor point completes the curved shape.

We can now define a fourth concept: Clicking and dragging with the Pen tool creates a smooth anchor point and defines its direction handles.

Learning to anticipate how the placement of direction handles creates the path you want takes time, but there's no reason why you have to get it right the first time. Once you create a smooth anchor point, you can switch to the Direct Selection tool and click and drag on the anchor point to reposition it (**Figure 4.10**). Additionally, when you select a smooth anchor point at any time, the direction handles become visible for that anchor point, and you can use the Direct Selection tool to reposition those as well.

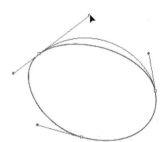

Figure 4.10 Using the Direct Selection tool, you can change the position of anchor points and direction handles to adjust a curved path.

Drawing Objects with Both Straight and Curved Paths

 Even the most experienced Illustrator artists need to switch to the Direct Selection tool to tweak the curves they create, which can be time consuming. To get around this time suck, you can press the Command (Ctrl) key while the Pen tool is active to temporarily access the last-used Selection tool. While the Selection tool is active, click and drag on the anchor points or direction handles to make adjustments to the path, then release the key to continue creating more points with the Pen tool.

In the real design world, shapes are made up of both straight and curved lines. You can use the knowledge you've gained up until this point to create paths that contain a mixture of both corner and smooth anchor points. Basically, you know that clicking with the Pen tool produces a corner anchor point and a straight line, and dragging with the Pen tool produces a smooth anchor point and a curved line.

Try drawing a path with both types of anchor points.

1. Choose the Pen tool and make sure you don't have an existing path selected (look for the small "X" icon on the Pen tool cursor). Click once to create a corner anchor point.

2. Move your cursor and click again to create a straight line (**Figure 4.11**).

3. Move your cursor and click and drag to create a smooth anchor point.

Figure 4.11 You can begin a new path by creating two corner anchor points to make a straight line.

You now have a single path that is made up of both a straight line and a curve (**Figure 4.12**).

You can use Illustrator's Convert Anchor Point tool to convert a corner anchor point to a smooth anchor point, and vice versa. To do so, choose the Convert Anchor Point tool (which is grouped with the Pen tool) and apply the same concepts that you've learned. Click once on an existing anchor point to convert it to a corner anchor point and then click and drag on an existing anchor point to pull out direction handles and convert it to a smooth anchor point.

Figure 4.12 Adding a smooth anchor point creates a single path with both straight and curved paths.

Changing Direction on a Path

As you were creating smooth anchor points, you may have noticed that when you are creating or editing direction handles, a mirror effect occurs. On a smooth anchor point, the direction points are always opposite each other, and editing one seems to affect the other. Remember that the direction handles control how the path passes through the anchor point, so the direction handles are always tangential to the curve (**Figure 4.13**).

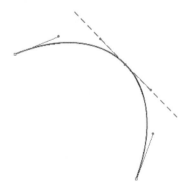

Figure 4.13 With a smooth anchor point, the direction handles are always tangential to the curve of the path.

You can, however, change the direction of a path as it passes through an anchor point.

1.   Use the Direct Selection tool to select a smooth anchor point.

2.   Switch to the Convert Anchor Point tool and click and drag on one of the *direction handles* (not the anchor point).

      In essence, this creates a combination point, which you can then continue to edit with the Direct Selection tool (**Figure 4.14**).

Figure 4.14 Clicking and dragging a direction handle with the Convert Anchor Point tool creates a combination anchor point.

To make life easier, you can create combination points as you draw with the Pen tool.

1.   Start by clicking once to create a corner anchor point.

2.   Move your cursor to a different position and click again to create another corner anchor point, and hence, a straight path.

3.   Now, position your cursor directly on the second anchor point that you just created. You'll notice that the Pen tool icon now shows a small inverted "V" in its icon.

4.   Click and drag on the anchor point while holding the Option (Alt) key to drag out a single direction handle (**Figure 4.15**).

5.   Move your cursor to another location and click again and you'll see that you've created a combination point.

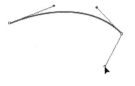

Figure 4.15 As you're drawing a path with the Pen tool, you can create a combination point by clicking and dragging on the last anchor point of the path while holding the Option (Alt) key.

A Final Thought Regarding the Pen Tool

Overall, using the Pen tool takes some getting used to, and if you're going to use Illustrator often, it's best to practice. While practicing, you might find it useful to convert some type to outlines (Type > Create Outlines) to see how the anchor points are positioned in those shapes (**Figure 4.16**). Try to re-create them on your own and get a feel for when you need a corner anchor point and when you need a smooth anchor point. The more you use the Pen tool, the easier it will be to use.

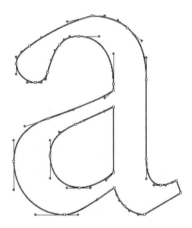

Figure 4.16 When you're learning to use the Pen tool, it can be helpful to convert some type characters to outlines so you can study the placement of the anchor points and direction handles. Choose Select > Object > Direction Handles to see the direction handles for an entire shape at once.

Adding and Deleting Anchor Points

Because anchor points are used to define paths, you must add and delete points from a path to achieve the shapes you need. You may think you can select an anchor point with the Direct Selection tool and simply press the

Delete key on your keyboard, but doing this deletes a portion of the path (**Figure 4.17**). Although this may be useful at times, what you really want is to keep the path but remove the anchor point.

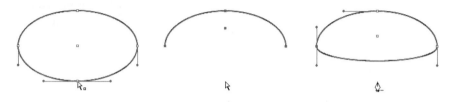

Figure 4.17 Using the Direct Selection tool to select and delete an anchor point (left) also deletes the connecting path segments (center). The Delete Anchor Point tool keeps the path closed but removes the anchor point (right).

To delete an anchor point from a path, without deleting the path itself, choose the Delete Anchor Point tool and click once on the anchor point that you want removed from the path. Likewise, you can switch to the Add Anchor Point tool and click anywhere on a selected path to add a new anchor point to the path (**Figure 4.18**).

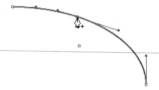

Figure 4.18 The Add Anchor Point tool enables you to add new anchor points to an existing path.

Illustrator tries its best to help you get your work done, but sometimes its overzealousness gets in the way. By default, when you move your cursor over an existing path with the Pen tool, Illustrator, thinking you want to add a point to the existing path, conveniently switches to the Add Anchor Point tool. Likewise, when you mouse over an existing anchor point, Illustrator switches to the Delete Anchor Point tool, thinking you want to remove that anchor point. This is great, unless you wanted to start drawing a new path with the Pen tool on top of an existing selected path. You can turn this feature off by checking the Disable Auto Add/Delete option in General Preferences, which politely tells Illustrator, "Thanks, but no thanks."

Drawing with the Pencil Tool

To draw with the Pencil tool, simply click and drag on the artboard. As you drag the mouse, you'll see a light path trail the movement of your cursor (**Figure 4.19**). After you release the mouse button, Illustrator creates the anchor points necessary and creates a vector path for you (**Figure 4.20**).

Figure 4.19 As you drag with the Pencil tool, a faint line traces the path of your cursor.

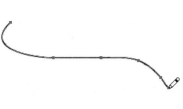

Figure 4.20 After you release the mouse button, Illustrator creates anchor points as necessary and displays the drawn path. Depending on your mouse control, the path may have a jittery appearance.

Because drawing with the Pencil tool relies on how steadily you handle your mouse or tablet pen, there are several tools and settings that you can employ to help create better-looking paths.

The Smooth tool, which you'll find grouped with the Pencil tool in the Toolbox, is a tool that you can use to iron out the wrinkles of any selected vector path. Select any vector path and click and drag over it with the Smooth tool. Doing this repeatedly makes the vector path more and more smooth. The angles in the path become smoother and the path itself modifies to match the contour of the direction in which you drag with the Smooth tool (**Figure 4.21**).

Figure 4.21 Using the Smooth tool repeatedly on a path can enhance its appearance.

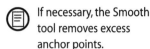 If necessary, the Smooth tool removes excess anchor points.

Double-clicking the Pencil tool or the Smooth tool opens the Pencil Tool Preferences dialog, allowing you to specify that tool's behavior (**Figure 4.22**):

Figure 4.22 Choosing the Edit Selected Paths option allows you to easily reshape or adjust existing paths.

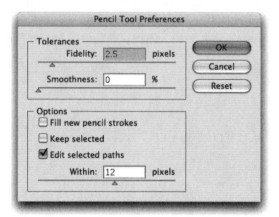

- **Fidelity, Smoothness.** Available for both the Pencil and Smooth tools, the Fidelity setting determines how close the vector path is drawn in relation to the movement of your mouse or input pen. A lower Fidelity setting results in a path that more closely matches the exact movement of your mouse. A higher Fidelity setting results in a path that is smoother and less jittery, but which may not match your stroke exactly. If you're good with handling the mouse or are using an input pen, you might go with a lower setting. Those of you who have trouble controlling the mouse or pen precisely might benefit from a higher Fidelity setting. The Smoothness setting refers to how much smoothing Illustrator applies to paths as you draw them. The higher the Smoothness setting, the fewer anchor points you'll see on your paths. If you're looking for more fluid strokes, increasing the Smoothness setting will help.

- **Fill new pencil strokes.** By default, Illustrator creates paths drawn with the Pencil tool as paths with a stroke, but no fill. Back in Chapter 2, you learned that even open paths can have fill attributes and that checking this option gives you the ability to choose a fill color and create filled paths as you draw them with the Pencil tool. This setting is available for the Pencil tool only, not for the Smooth tool.

- **Keep selected, Edit selected paths.** With Illustrator's default behavior, when you draw a path with the Pencil tool, the path becomes selected as soon as you complete it. You can change this behavior by unchecking the box marked Keep selected. When the Edit selected paths option is checked and if your cursor is within the specified number of pixels from an existing selected path, Illustrator allows you to modify the selected path by simply drawing over it with the Pencil tool. This can be helpful because it allows you to tweak a path to perfection as you are drawing it, almost as if you were using the Smooth tool. Where this gets in the way, however, is when you intend to draw a new path but inadvertently end up editing a path that is selected instead. This can happen very often if you have the Keep selected option turned on. Many designers prefer to turn off the Keep selected option, but leave on the Edit selected paths option. This way, if they do need to edit a path, they can Command-click (Ctrl-click) a path to select it; at this point, the Edit selected paths feature lets them draw over it.

 Featured Match-Up: The Pen Tool vs. the Pencil Tool

In contrast to the Pen tool, the process of drawing with the Pencil tool mimics that of drawing with a real pen on paper. In reality, the Pencil tool is the exact opposite of the Pen tool. With the Pen tool, you define the anchor points and Illustrator completes the paths. With the Pencil tool, you draw the path and Illustrator creates the anchor points for you.

If using the Pencil tool to draw paths sounds a lot easier than creating anchor points with the Pen tool, remember that the mouse isn't the easiest tool to control when you're trying to draw. Although the Pencil tool is easier to use to create paths, it's not as easy to create exact or precise paths with it. However, if you have a pressure-sensitive tablet available, the Pencil tool is a bit easier to control.

For technical drawing and precise illustration work, including logo creation and letterforms, you'll most likely find that the Pen tool offers the fine control you need. You'll find the Pencil tool useful when you're working with creative illustrations, cartoons, and projects that require a more natural feel. As you'll see later in this chapter, the Pencil tool proves valuable when you're utilizing the new Live Paint feature.

 The preferences for the Pencil and Smooth tools are saved when you quit Illustrator so that you don't have to set these for each new file that you create or each time that you launch Illustrator. If you trash your preferences file, however, you'll need to reset these preferences to your liking.

You can also use the Erase tool to remove parts of a vector path. It's important to realize that the Erase tool is not akin to the Erase tool found in paint programs, which you can use to just erase pixels at will (although such a tool would be welcome in Illustrator). In Illustrator, you use the Erase tool specifically to erase portions of a selected vector path. As you trace over an existing selected path with the Erase tool, a light path appears to trail the movement of your cursor. When you release the mouse button, Illustrator deletes the portion of the path that you've traced.

Using the Reshape Tool

Remember that the Smooth and Erase tools can be used on any vector path in Illustrator—even those that were not created with the Pencil tool.

Using the Direct Selection tool to select individual points on a path results in some anchor points moving, while others remain stationary. In most kinds of path editing, this is the desired behavior, although it can result in paths that appear distorted (**Figure 4.23**). At times, you may want to stretch a path by moving selected points, but you may also want other points to move as necessary to maintain a non-distorted path appearance. The Reshape tool is perfect for this task.

Figure 4.23 Although you can always select individual points on a path and move them, you may not get acceptable results.

1.   Select a path using the Selection tool and then choose the Reshape tool.

2.   Click an anchor point or a part of a path that you want to act as a focus point when you stretch the path. This way, you'll have the most control over how this focused point is moved.

     You can also hold the Shift key and select additional focus points (as well as drag to marquee-select additional anchor points).

3. Once you've selected your focus points, click and drag one of the focus points to reshape the path.

   You'll notice that as the points that are in focus move, other points in the path move as well, to keep the general proportion of the path (**Figure 4.24**).

You can also use the Reshape tool across multiple selected paths.

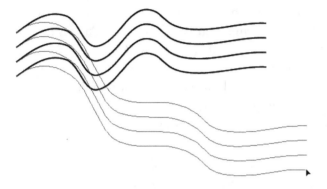

Figure 4.24 Using the Reshape tool, you can stretch paths and reshape them without telltale distortion.

Cutting Paths with the Scissors and Knife Tools

When editing paths, you might find that you need to cut or split a path at a certain point. With the Scissors tool selected, you can click any topmost vector path (selected or not) to cut the path. In essence, you create two anchor points by doing this. The Scissors tool can only cut one path at a time.

The Knife tool is much like the Scissors tool only you cut or split a path by dragging the cursor across a path instead of clicking it. Whereas using the Scissors tool results in an open path, using the Knife tool results in at least two closed paths (**Figure 4.25**). The Knife tool cuts through multiple paths, but if you hold the Shift key while you're using it, the Knife tool only cuts through the objects that are selected (even if those selected objects appear beneath other objects).

If you find that you need to cut through multiple paths at once, you should look into Rick Johnson's Hatchet tool plugin (http://rj-graffix.com).

Holding the Option (Alt) key while dragging with the Knife tool constrains the tool so that it uses straight lines only.

Figure 4.25 Using the Knife tool to slice a single object results in two separate closed paths.

CREATING COMPOUND PATHS

A *compound path* is a single path that is made up of more than one path. Sounds like an oxymoron, no? Think of the letter "O" in the alphabet. It appears to be a large circle with a smaller circle cut out from its center. How is such a shape created with Illustrator? The answer is by drawing two circles and combining them to become a single compound path. You do this by choosing Object > Compound Path > Create. The result is a shape with a hole cut out of the middle (**Figure 4.26**). Compound paths are treated as one entity and therefore, both paths that make up this compound path take on the attributes of the bottom-most path. If your compound path is made up of multiple shapes, Illustrator does its best to figure out which paths become hollow and which appear solid.

Figure 4.26 An example of a compound path. The hole in the center is actually cut out from the path and objects that appear beneath the compound shape are visible through the hole.

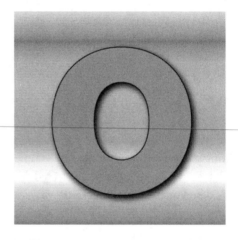

 When a path reverses direction in a shape such as in a figure eight, it can never be all clockwise or all counterclockwise. In such a case, the direction of the region(s) with largest total area is what defines the results.

Illustrator uses one of two methods to decide which paths of a compound shape are hollow and which are solid. The default method is called the *Non-Zero Winding Fill Rule*; Illustrator can also use another method, the *Even-Odd Fill Rule*. You'll find both of these methods in the Attributes palette and you can choose them when a compound path is selected on the artboard (**Figure 4.27**). By default, Illustrator uses the Non-Zero Winding Fill Rule and makes the bottom-most path clockwise and all the other selected paths counterclockwise.

When you create a compound path and choose the Non-Zero Winding Fill Rule, you can manually reverse the path direction to control whether a shape is hollow or solid. Use the Direct Selection tool to select the path you need and click the appropriate button in the Attributes palette (**Figure 4.28**).

Use the Even-Odd Fill Rule. ⎯⎯⎯⎯
Use the Non-Zero Winding Fill Rule. ⎯⎯⎯

Figure 4.27 You can use the Attributes palette to choose one of the two supported compound path methods for determining hollow and solid areas.

 For more on this, refer to the sidebar, "Featured Match-Up: Non-Zero Winding Fill Rule vs. Even-Odd Fill Rule," on the next page.

Figure 4.28 Using the Attributes palette to manually reverse the direction of a path, you can specify whether a part of a compound path using the Non-Zero Winding Fill Rule is hollow or solid.

ADVANCED PATH EDITING

Editing paths by hand can be tedious, but it doesn't always have to be. Many times, you'll need to perform certain edits on vector paths, such as removing extra anchor points from a complex path or splitting larger shapes into smaller ones of equal size. Other times, you may need to create outlines of strokes, create duplicate paths at larger or smaller sizes, or simply clean up loose paths and objects in your file. The good news is that Illustrator has a variety of useful path functions that you can use to perform these kinds of tasks.

The functions found in this section can all be found in the Object > Path submenu.

Featured Match-Up: Non-Zero Winding Fill Rule vs. Even-Odd Fill Rule

More math! When you compare them to each other, the Even-Odd Fill Rule seems more intuitive and it is easier to predict which areas will be filled and which areas will be hollow. Although you have more flexibility with the Non-Zero Winding Fill Rule—you can manually control the result—this rule is more difficult to understand and the result is harder to predict.

With the Even-Odd Fill Rule, every area that is inside of an even number of enclosed areas becomes hollow, and every region that is inside an odd number of enclosed areas becomes solid (**Figure 4.29**). An enclosed area refers to an area enclosed by another path (or the loop of a path in a self-intersecting shape). The outermost enclosed area is always numbered 1, and therefore a regular path is filled (it is enclosed by a single area, which is an odd number).

In contrast, the Non-Zero Winding Fill Rule takes into account the direction of a path: an area enclosed by a clockwise loop counts as +1; and an area enclosed by a counterclockwise loop counts as –1. When the sum of these counts is zero, that area becomes hollow. When it is anything else, that area becomes solid (**Figure 4.30**). Because you can manipulate the path direction to get different results from the same shapes, the Non-Zero Winding Fill Rule is more flexible, but it's an exercise of trial and error since you can't see the direction of a path on the artboard.

Although the results in most cases are the same whether you use the Non-Zero Winding Fill Rule or the Even-Odd Fill Rule, there are several cases where the result is different (**Figure 4.31**). —*Special thanks to Teri Pettit of the Adobe Illustrator team for helping explain these rules.*

Figure 4.29 When you're using the Even-Odd Fill Rule, Illustrator labels areas using odd and even numbers to determine hollow and solid areas.

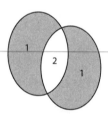 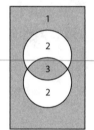

Figure 4.30 When you're using the Non-Zero Winding Fill Rule, Illustrator takes into account the direction of the path when it determines the hollow and solid areas of a compound path. The arrows indicate path direction.

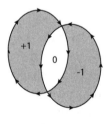 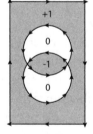 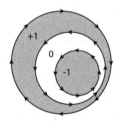

Figure 4.31 Some compound shapes appear different, depending on the fill rule specified, especially with self-intersecting paths.

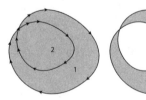

Working with the Join and Average Commands

When you have two anchor points, you can use the Join command to connect the two points with a straight path. Although this sounds simple, certain requirements must be met in order for the Join command to work:

- Only two anchor points can be selected. If you have three or more anchor points selected, the Join command will not work. Unless . . .

- All of the anchor points on an open path are selected. In this case, the Join command draws a straight line between the start and end anchor points to close the shape.

- The selected anchor points cannot belong to different groups.

- The selected anchor points cannot be part of a graph object.

If the two anchor points overlap each other exactly, Illustrator combines the two anchor points and gives you the option of converting the resulting single point to a smooth point or a corner point (**Figure 4.32**).

Figure 4.32 When you are trying to join two overlapping anchor points, Illustrator offers you the option of creating a corner anchor point or a smooth anchor point.

The Average function allows you to select at least two anchor points and reposition them by evenly dividing the space between them. You can average anchor points horizontally, vertically, or both horizontally and vertically. There is no limit to how many anchor points you can average at once (**Figure 4.33**, next page).

You can also select two anchor points and press Command-Opt-Shift-J (Ctrl-Alt-Shift-J) to perform a combined Average and Join function in one step.

 Older versions of Illustrator allow you to use the Average command to easily align point text objects. Unfortunately, that functionality is not present in Illustrator CS2.

 Illustrator's Join command can only connect two anchor points at a time. If you need to join several paths at once, you should take a look at Rick Johnson's Concatenate plug-in (http://rj-graffix.com/software/plugins.html).

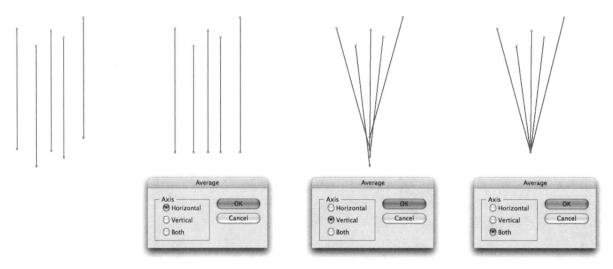

Figure 4.33 The Average command makes it easy to quickly align multiple anchor points.

Using the Outline Stroke Command

The stroke of a path adds thickness to the appearance of the path, but it's an attribute that you can't physically select and manipulate on the artboard. However, you can select a path with a stroke attribute and choose Object > Path > Outline Stroke; when you do, the stroke of that path expands to become a filled shape that you can then edit with the Pen tool. This allows you to tweak the path to make it appear as if the "stroke" is thinner and thicker in different places.

There are also times when you might want to convert a stroke to an outline for production reasons. If you have a final version of a logo, converting all strokes to filled paths assures that it will scale properly under all circumstances, because users may forget to turn on the Scale Strokes & Effects setting.

Similar to what happens with patterns, when you apply transformations to objects that have strokes or effects applied, the default behavior is that only the shape is transformed, not the strokes or the effects (**Figure 4.34**). Turning on the Scale Strokes & Effects option in General Preferences changes the default behavior so that strokes and effects are transformed as well. You can also find this setting in the Scale tool dialog.

Figure 4.34 If you forget to turn on the Scale Strokes & Effects setting, you can run into problems when scaling artwork. In this example, the text of the logo was reduced, as was the path, but the stroke weight was not scaled. Outlining strokes prevents these kinds of accidents.

Exploring the Offset Path Function

One of the most useful path functions that exists in Illustrator is Offset Path. When used, this function creates a new vector path that is offset a user-specified amount from the selected object(s). The original selected path is not affected. If you think about it, it's like a scaling function—you can offset paths to be larger or smaller. But if you've ever tried to scale an object like an oval, you'll know that doing so creates an oval of a different proportion. If you want to create an object that is exactly the same but that has its edges enlarged evenly across the entire object, choose Object > Path > Offset Path (**Figure 4.35**).

Using the Outline Stroke command on a stroke with a dash attribute applied results in the dash being ignored. To get the expected result, choose Object > Flatten Transparency and make sure the Convert All Strokes to Outlines option is checked. If you need to do this often, you may consider creating a keyboard shortcut for this command.

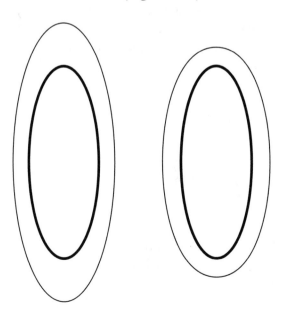

Figure 4.35 Scaling an oval shape results in a distorted shape (left). Using the Offset Path function results in a non-distorted result (right).

You can use Offset Path with negative values as well, which allows you to create paths that are offset inside of existing paths.

Offset Path works a bit differently depending on the kind of path you have selected. On a closed path, it seems to work as expected, by creating the new path at the offset that you specify. On an open path, however, the Offset Path command creates a new closed path, appearing on both the inside and the outside of the original path (**Figure 4.36**). Depending on the task, this might mean you need to take an extra step to delete the part of the path that is not needed.

Figure 4.36 The Offset Path function, applied to an open path, results in a new closed path. You have to delete a portion of the resulting path if you want an open path.

Simplifying Vector Paths

Earlier in this chapter, you learned how to use the Remove Anchor Point tool to delete existing anchor points from a path. Although that tool is useful for removing a point or two from a path here or there, it's quite another story when you're trying to remove a lot of anchor points from a path.

You may find that some vector paths contain unnecessary anchor points. By unnecessary, we mean that you might be able to create the same path with fewer anchor points. Too many unnecessary anchor points on a path translates into more complex files that take longer to print and that are more difficult to edit (**Figure 4.37**).

Figure 4.37 Paths with numerous unnecessary anchor points are harder to edit and take longer to print.

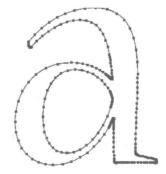

You'll often come across this problem when you're importing files from CAD applications, or when you're using vector tracing programs such as Adobe Streamline (the Live Trace feature in Illustrator CS2, covered in Chapter 8, *Mixing It Up: Working with Vectors and Pixels*, does not suffer from this problem).

To reduce the number of anchor points on a path, select the path and choose Object > Path > Simplify. You can use the Preview option to see the results as you change the settings. The Simplify dialog also gives you real-time feedback on the number of anchor points on the original path and the number of points using the current Simplify settings (**Figure 4.38**). The dialog also offers the following settings:

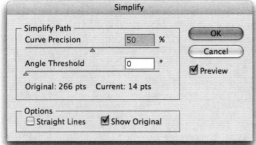

Figure 4.38 When using the Simplify function, you can see real-time feedback on the number of reduced anchor points and the integrity of the shape of the path.

- **Curve Precision.** This controls how closely the simplified path matches the curves of the original selected path. A higher Curve Precision setting results in a path that more closely matches the original, but one that has fewer reduced anchor points.

- **Angle Threshold.** The Angle Threshold setting determines the smoothness of corners. If the angle of a corner point is less than the Angle Threshold, the corner point is not changed to a smooth anchor point.

- **Straight Lines.** This setting forces the simplified path to only use corner anchor points, resulting in a path that is far less complex. Of course, the path may not match the original that well, but this option may be useful in a creative mindset.

- **Show Original.** With the Show Original option checked, Illustrator displays both the original path and the simplified result, allowing you to preview the difference between the two.

Using the Split Into Grid Feature

The Split Into Grid feature is wonderful for creating layout grids and for creating columns that you might use for text threads or even tables.

The Rectangular Grid tool is great for creating quick grids for illustration purposes, but with it you lack fine control, especially if you want to create gutters—space that appears between columns and rows. Illustrator's Split Into Grid feature takes an existing shape and splits it into a specified number of equal-sized rectangles.

With any vector object selected, choose Object > Path > Split Into Grid to bring up the dialog. Check the Preview button so that you can see the results as you enter the values. Add rows and columns as needed, and also specify a value for the gutter. Illustrator automatically calculates the width and height values for you as you change the other values. At the bottom of the dialog is a check box to Add Guides, which draws guides at the borders of the rows and the columns (**Figure 4.39**).

Figure 4.39 Using the Split Into Grid feature can make it easy to set up layout grids.

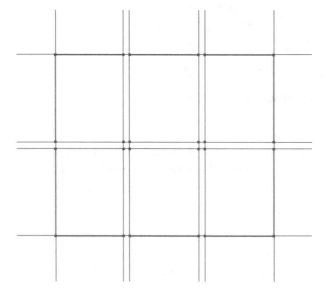

Removing Unnecessary Elements with the Clean Up Feature

While working on revision after revision of a file, your document may become littered with stray anchor points, empty text objects, or unpainted objects (those that have neither a fill nor a stroke attribute applied). Having these objects present in a file can be problematic for a variety of reasons. Empty text objects may contain references to fonts, and you, thinking that those fonts aren't there, may forget to include them when you send source files to prepress. Additionally, stray points in a file can cause files to export with unexpected size boundaries (refer to Chapter 1, *The Illustrator Environment*, where we spoke about bounding boxes), and could lead to corrupt files.

Choose Object > Path > Clean Up and choose which of these elements you want to automatically remove from a file (**Figure 4.40**). Beware that to Illustrator, a stray point is a single anchor point with no path. Some designers use Scatter brush art by using the paintbrush to click just once to place a single instance of a brush. Running the Clean Up command to delete stray points deletes these scatter brush objects from a file as well. In reality, it's better to use Symbols rather than Scatter brushes for these designer tasks, something we'll discuss in Chapter 5, *Brushes, Symbols, and Masks*.

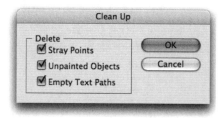

Figure 4.40 Illustrator's Clean Up feature makes it easy to remove excess elements from a document.

INTRODUCING THE LIVE PAINT FEATURE

Although you can appreciate the power that vector graphics have to offer, you should also appreciate how easy it is to use pixel-based paint programs like Adobe Photoshop or Corel Painter to easily apply color to artwork. In a paint program, you can perform flood fills, in which you choose a color and use a paint bucket–like tool to fill areas of the illustration with color. When working with vectors, you know that you have to create distinct paths and shapes in order to apply a fill attribute to add color. This need to create distinct objects can make drawing in Illustrator seem nonintuitive, or time-consuming at best.

New to Illustrator CS2, Live Paint is a feature that introduces a new concept of working with vector paths, where you can colorize vectors and edit them without having to follow the traditional vector rules that we've been covering up to this point. This new feature makes it a lot easier to draw in Illustrator. Let's take a closer look.

Using Live Paint to Color Paths

First, you'll create something using Live Paint to get a feel for what the feature is all about. Then we'll discuss how the feature works and at that point, you'll better understand how to use it in a meaningful way. Choose the Line Segment tool and draw two parallel vertical lines and two parallel horizontal lines to create a tic-tac-toe board. Don't worry if the lines or spacing aren't perfect—for this exercise, you just want to make sure the lines cross each other (**Figure 4.41**).

Figure 4.41 Using the Line Segment tool, you can create a simple tic-tac-toe graphic.

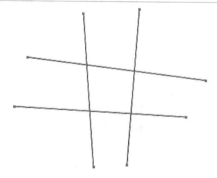

Select the four lines and choose the Live Paint Bucket tool. As you move your cursor over the four paths, the paths become highlighted (**Figure 4.42**). Click once to create a *Live Paint group*. Now, choose a fill color (a solid color, gradient, or pattern) from the Control palette and move your cursor over the center area of the tic-tac-toe board. The enclosed area in the middle becomes highlighted in red, which indicates an area that you can fill with color (**Figure 4.43**). Click once with the Live Paint Bucket tool to fill the highlighted area (**Figure 4.44**).

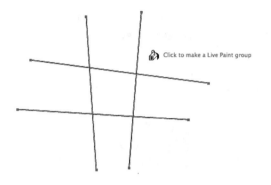

Figure 4.42 If you have the Live Paint Bucket tool selected, Illustrator shows a tool tip to create a Live Paint group when your cursor passes over a valid selection.

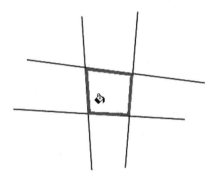

Figure 4.43 Illustrator's Live Paint Bucket tool highlights areas that can be filled as you mouse over them, even if the Live Paint groups aren't selected.

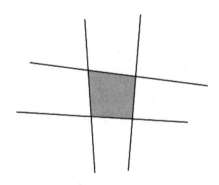

Figure 4.44 With one click of the Live Paint Bucket tool, you can fill areas that appear to be enclosed, even though there is an actual vector object there.

The resulting behavior is very Photoshopesque—you've filled an area that is enclosed on all sides, but you didn't fill an actual object. Choose the Direct Selection tool, select one of the paths, and move it just a bit. Notice that the color in the area updates to fill the center (**Figure 4.45**, next page). If you move one of the paths far enough to the side so that it no longer touches the other paths, you'll find that the fill color disappears, because there is no longer an enclosed area to fill (**Figure 4.46**).

Figure 4.45 The fill areas in a Live Paint group update automatically when you're moving the paths with the Direct Selection tool.

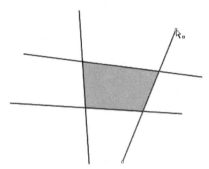

Figure 4.46 When editing the paths in a Live Paint group, creating an opened area results in the loss of the fill attribute.

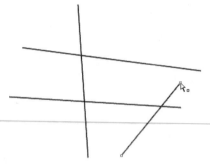

Understanding Live Paint Groups

If you move a path so that an enclosed painted area becomes unpainted, Illustrator doesn't remember that the region was filled with a color prior to the edit. Moving the path back to its original position will not bring back the fill; you'll need to reapply the fill color.

Let's take a moment to understand how Live Paint works. When you select several overlapping paths or shapes and click on them with the Live Paint Bucket tool, you are creating a *Live Paint group*. This is a special kind of group in which object stacking order is thrown out the window. All objects in a Live Paint group are seemingly combined onto a single flat world, and any enclosed area acts as a closed shape, which can be filled with color.

Although clicking several selected paths is the easiest way to create a Live Paint group, you can also select several paths and choose Object > Live Paint > Make to create a Live Paint group. Once you've created a Live Paint group however, you may find that you want to add additional paths or shapes to the group. To do so, draw the new paths and use the Selection tool to select the existing Live Paint group and the new paths. Then choose Object > Live Paint > Add Paths. The new paths will become part of the group and any intersecting areas will act as individual areas that you can fill with color.

Live Paint groups can also utilize the Group Isolation Mode feature that enables you to draw objects directly into existing groups. Using the Selection tool, double-click an existing Live Paint group to enter Group Isolation Mode. Now switch to any shape or path tool to add paths directly into the Live Paint group (**Figure 4.47**). This ability to add paths directly into a Live Paint group is extremely powerful because it allows you to define regions for color in just a few quick steps. Using Pathfinder filters to create multiple overlapping shapes is no longer required for such tasks.

 You can use the Live Paint Bucket tool to color multiple regions with a single color in one step by clicking in one region and dragging the mouse across additional contiguous regions.

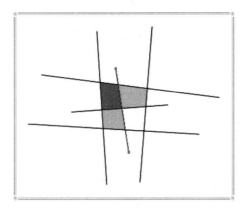

Figure 4.47 In Group Isolation Mode, you can draw new paths into an existing Live Paint group to instantly create additional regions that can be filled with color.

In the Toolbox, double click the Live Paint Bucket tool to change its behavior. By default, the Live Paint Bucket tool only affects the fill of a path, but you can also set the tool to apply color to strokes as well (**Figure 4.48**). Additionally, you can specify the color that the Live Paint tool uses to highlight closed regions.

 The gray box that indicates Group Isolation Mode displays with stars at its corners when a Live Paint group is selected.

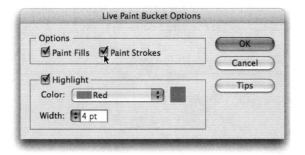

Figure 4.48 You can set the Live Paint Bucket tool to apply color to stroke attributes in a Live Paint group as well.

Gap Detection

Until now, all of the regions that you were filling with color were completely closed. But what happens if your paths don't exactly meet each other? That's where the Illustrator Gap Detection feature can really make a difference. You need to choose Object > Live Paint > Gap Options to control the settings for this feature (**Figure 4.49**). If you don't have any Live Paint groups selected when you choose this option, the settings you choose becomes the default settings for all new Live Paint groups. You can specify different Gap Options for each selected Live Paint group in a document as well.

Figure 4.49 The Gap Options dialog makes it possible to fill areas in a Live Paint group even if they aren't completely enclosed.

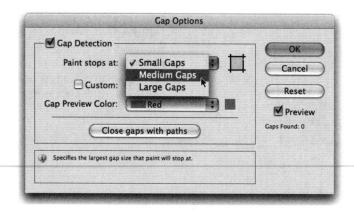

Gap Options

With Gap Detection turned on (**Figure 4.50**), you can specify that paint will fill areas that contain small, medium, or large gaps. Additionally, you can specify an exact amount for how big a gap can be before Live Paint considers it an open area instead of a closed one. Illustrator previews gaps in the selected color, and you can also choose to have Illustrator fill any gaps in an object with physical paths (Illustrator always uses straight paths to do so).

Figure 4.50 With a Live Paint group selection, you can choose to open the Gap Options dialog from the Control palette.

Releasing and Expanding Live Paint Groups

Live Paint groups can be expanded, at which time they behave like ordinary vector paths. The appearance of an expanded Live Paint group remains identical to the original, but it is split into multiple objects for both fills and strokes. This is similar in concept to expanding Live Effects. To expand a selected Live Paint group, either click the Expand button in the Control palette or choose Object > Live Paint > Expand.

From a production standpoint, there's no need to expand Live Paint groups in order to prepare a file for print. Live Paint groups print perfectly, because Illustrator performs the necessary expanding of paths at print time (similar to Live Effects).

Additionally, you can choose Object > Live Paint > Release to return a Live Paint group to the original paths that were used to create it. Where expanding a Live Paint group results in objects being broken up in order to preserve appearance, releasing such a group preserves the geometry of the original paths, but the appearance or colors are lost.

 With Live Paint groups that are made up of many complex paths, Gap Detection impedes performance. You will experience better performance by splitting very large Live Paint groups into several smaller ones.

Using Live Paint to Edit Paths

If you think about it, Live Paint allows you to apply attributes—like fills and strokes—to paths based on their appearance as opposed to their actual makeup. It would be even nicer if you could actually edit your paths based on appearance as well, don't you think? Adobe was apparently reading your mind (a scary thought) and added another tool to the mix—the Live Paint Selection tool—which enables you to select portions of objects based on their appearance.

Let's take a look at an example. Use the Line Segment tool to draw two perpendicular lines, creating an X. Select both paths and press Command-Opt-X (Ctrl-Alt-X) or choose Object > Live Paint > Make to convert the two paths into a Live Paint group. Now, choose the Live Paint Selection tool and click one of paths. You'll notice that each segment of the line can be selected individually. What were two paths before are now four line segments (**Figure 4.51**, next page). With one segment selected, press the Delete key to remove that segment from the path. Select another segment and change its stroke attribute (**Figure 4.52**, next page). You can also click one segment and then drag to select other segments in one step.

Figure 4.51 Using the Live Paint Selection tool, you can select visual segments of a path.

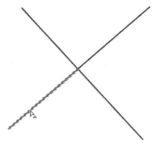

Figure 4.52 In a Live Paint group, you can easily apply different stroke attributes to the segments of a path.

The Live Paint Selection tool can also select the fills of Live Paint areas. If you have two overlapping shapes in a Live Paint group, you can select the overlap and delete it (**Figure 4.53**).

Figure 4.53 The Live Paint Selection tool enables you to select any area of a Live Paint group.

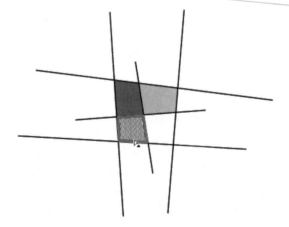

At the end of the day, Live Paint adds a more flexible way to color and edit paths, and it also adds more value to the Pencil tool, because complete closed paths aren't required. The important thing to remember is that a

Live Paint group is a group, and anything that you can do with a group in Illustrator you can do with Live Paint groups as well. For example, you can add attributes like strokes to the Live Paint group for interesting effects (**Figure 4.54**). Experimenting with the Live Paint feature certainly helps you when you're editing paths, and the good news is that it's a fun feature to use.

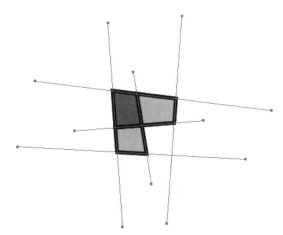

Figure 4.54 Adding a stroke to a Live Paint group at the group level makes it possible to apply stroke attributes that appear only around areas that are filled.

Exploring the Pathfinder Palette

In Chapter 2, we learned about using the basic drawing tools like the Rectangle tool and the Ellipse tool. Those tools are great on their own, but you'll often need to create shapes that are a bit more complex. Although you can use a variety of the tools we've mentioned so far in this chapter to create and edit paths of any shape, there are many times when it's far easier to combine simple shapes to create more complex ones. It can also be easier to edit existing shapes using other shapes rather than trying to adjust the anchor points of individual paths.

Illustrator's Pathfinder palette, which you can open by choosing Window > Pathfinder, contains a wellspring of functions that you can perform with at least two selected paths.

Combining Shapes with Shape Modes

The top row of the Pathfinder palette contains four functions, called *shape modes*, which are used to combine multiple selected shapes in different ways. Once a shape mode is applied, the resulting shape is referred to as a *compound shape*.

When you create a compound shape from multiple selected objects, the resulting shape appears as a single object and takes on the attributes of the topmost object (**Figure 4.55**). Using the Direct Selection tool, you can select the individual objects in the compound shape and edit them. See the sidebar entitled "Illustrator Shape Modes and Photoshop Shape Layers" for additional functionality that you can take advantage of when using compound shapes.

Figure 4.55 Here are some examples of the different possible shape modes you can apply.

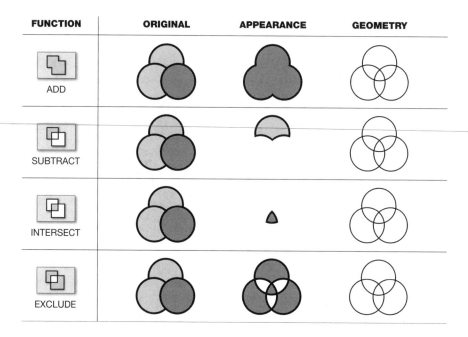

The following are the four different shape modes that you can choose from in the Pathfinder palette:

- **Add.** The Add shape mode combines all of the selected shapes and gives the appearance as if they were all joined together. This function replaces the Unite pathfinder, which you can find in older versions of Illustrator.

- **Subtract.** The Subtract shape mode combines all of the selected shapes and takes the top objects and removes them from the bottom-most object. This function replaces the Minus Front pathfinder, which was found in older versions of Illustrator.

- **Intersect.** The Intersect shape mode combines all of the selected shapes and displays only the areas in which all of the objects overlap with each other.

- **Exclude.** The Exclude shape mode combines all of the selected shapes and removes the areas in which the objects overlap with each other.

It is certainly useful to be able to select the individual objects of a compound shape, but many times you just want to create a new shape that combines all of the selected shapes. To do so, you can expand a compound shape by clicking the Expand button in the Pathfinder palette. If, when you're creating a compound shape, you know that you want to expand it, you can hold the Option (Alt) key while clicking the Add, Subtract, Intersect, or Exclude buttons. This applies the function and expands the shape in one step.

 In reality, using any of the Shape modes can give you similar results to creating compound paths. Compound Shapes utilize the Even-Odd File Rule.

Additionally, you can release a compound shape by choosing Release Compound Shape from the Pathfinder palette menu. Releasing compound shapes returns the objects to their individual states and appearances.

Illustrator Shape Modes and Photoshop Shape Layers

If you've used Adobe Photoshop before, you might be familiar with vector shape layers, which allow you to create vector-based masks. Although Photoshop is primarily a pixel-based program, these shape layers, as Photoshop refers to them, allow you to create vector shapes within your Photoshop document. Upon close inspection, you'll find that to help you create more complex shapes, Photoshop's shape layers can be created using a variety of modes, including Add, Subtract, Intersect, and Exclude—the exact same functions found in Illustrator's Pathfinder palette.

These objects are interchangeable between the applications and they retain their shape mode settings in the process as well. Create a compound shape in Illustrator, copy and paste it into Photoshop, and the compound shape becomes an editable vector shape layer. The same applies in reverse (**Figure 4.56**).

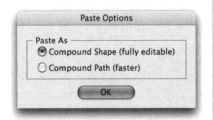

Figure 4.56 When you are pasting a shape layer from Photoshop, Illustrator asks if you want to have it pasted as a compound shape.

Changing Paths with Pathfinders

The functions in the second row of the Pathfinder palette are called pathfinders, and unlike with compound shapes, when you use pathfinders, they do not retain the original objects. Once you apply a pathfinder function, the paths are changed permanently (**Figure 4.57**). The following are the six pathfinder functions in the Pathfinder palette:

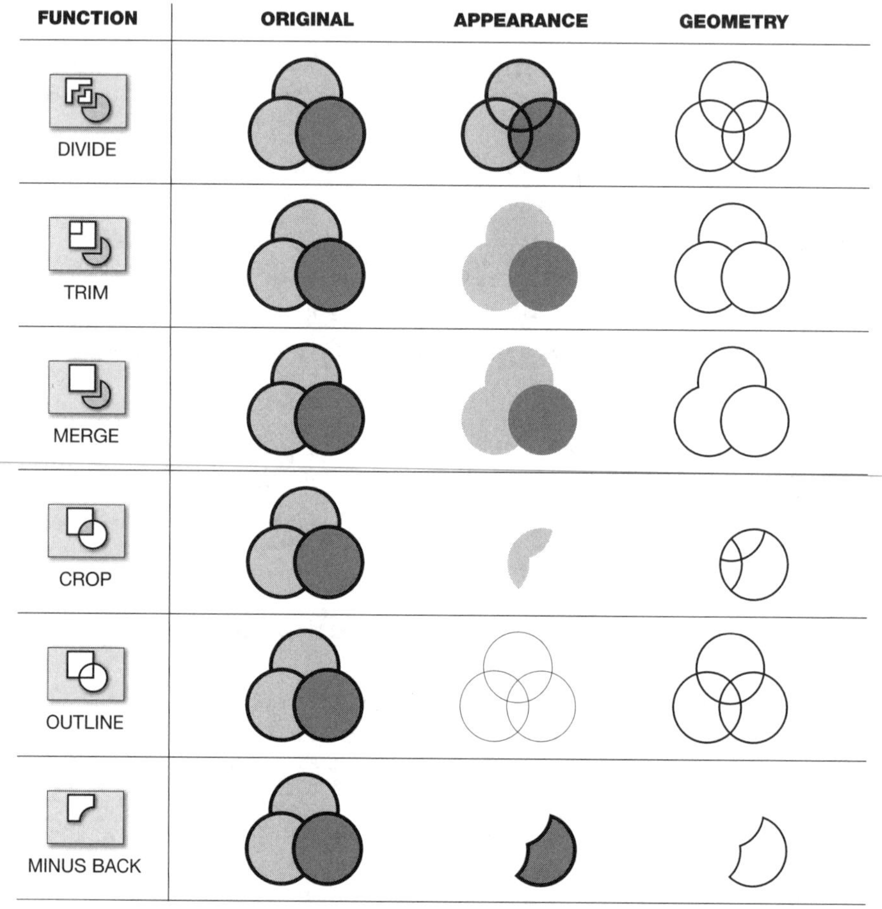

Figure 4.57 Here are some examples of the different possible pathfinder functions that you can apply.

FUNCTION	ORIGINAL	APPEARANCE	GEOMETRY
DIVIDE			
TRIM			
MERGE			
CROP			
OUTLINE			
MINUS BACK			

- **Divide.** One of the most often-used pathfinders, Divide takes all selected objects and breaks them apart into individual shapes based on their overlapping parts. Open paths act like knives and slice paths that intersect with them.

- **Trim.** The Trim pathfinder removes all overlapping areas from the selected paths.

- **Merge.** The Merge pathfinder removes all overlapping areas from the selected paths and joins all areas of the same color.

- **Crop.** The Crop pathfinder takes the topmost selected object and removes all objects and areas beneath it that fall outside of its path. Unfortunately, this pathfinder works on vector objects only and you can't use it to crop a raster image (you'll need Photoshop for that). This function ignores strokes on objects, so it's best to perform an Outline Paths function before applying the Crop pathfinder.

- **Outline.** The Outline pathfinder converts the selected shapes to outlines and divides the lines where they intersect.

- **Minus Back.** The Minus Back pathfinder is similar to the Subtract shape mode, only instead of using the top object to define the subtracted area, the function uses the bottom object.

Once you've applied a pathfinder function, you can choose Repeat Pathfinder from the Pathfinder palette menu to apply the same effect again. In reality, it takes longer to access the palette menu than it does to just click the actual icon in the palette, but by having this function available, you can assign a keyboard shortcut to it in the Keyboard Shortcuts dialog if you find that you use these functions often.

From the Pathfinder palette menu, you can also choose Pathfinder Options, where you can set the level of precision to use when applying pathfinder functions (lower numbers may result in more complex paths). You can also specify that Illustrator should remove redundant points (always a good idea) and should remove unpainted artwork when performing Divide or Outline functions.

ALIGNING AND DISTRIBUTING OBJECTS

When working with a range of objects, you will often want to align them evenly or distribute them across a specified distance. Rather than being forced to figure out the math on your own and then manually move each object, you can apply the variety of functions that Illustrator's Align palette contains to a range of objects in order to both align and distribute objects precisely. The Align palette can be opened by choosing Window > Align.

To align a range of objects, select them and click one of the Align icons in the Align palette. Admittedly, these small icons can be hard to decipher, but if you let your mouse pointer hover over them for a second, a tool tip pops up identifying the name of the function (**Figure 4.58**).

Figure 4.58 The icons in the Align palette can be a bit difficult to decipher, so it's a good idea to watch for the tool tips that pop up.

The align functions consider a group of objects to be a single object, so performing an align function on a group won't do anything (you're basically aligning a single object to itself). However, you can select multiple groups and align them as if each group were a single object.

Unfortunately, the align functions only work on complete paths. You cannot apply align functions to the individual points of a path. For aligning specific anchor points, you are pretty much limited to using the Average command, covered earlier in this chapter.

Aligning Objects to a Specific Object

You'll notice that when you align several objects, all of the objects move. However, there are times when you have the position of one object set perfectly, and you want to be able to align all of your selected objects to that specific object. You can do this by defining what Illustrator calls a *key object*.

To define a key object, select all of the objects that you want to align, and then, using the Selection tool, click once on the object to which you want all other the objects to align.

Additionally, you can choose to align objects to the document artboard. This can be helpful if you want to easily center objects on a page. From the Align palette menu, choose Align to Artboard (**Figure 4.59**). This setting is a toggle and it stays on until you turn it off.

Figure 4.59 Choosing the Align to Artboard setting from the Align palette menu makes it easy to align objects to the artboard.

You can use the distribute functions that appear in the bottom half of the Align palette to space multiple objects evenly. Illustrator takes the objects at the two extremes of your selection and uses those as the boundaries of the distribution. All objects that appear between those two shapes are distributed evenly between them, based on the specific distribute function that you choose (**Figure 4.60**).

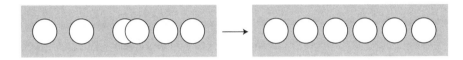

Figure 4.60 When you're distributing objects, the objects at the opposite extremes define the boundary and all objects are distributed evenly between them.

If you choose Show Options from the Align palette menu, you can also perform distribute commands based on spacing. You can specify a numeric value and then distribute the selected objects vertically or horizontally.

MAKING TRANSFORMATIONS

Drawing objects in Illustrator is only part of the design process. Once art is created, you can manipulate it in a multitude of ways. In Illustrator, the process of changing or manipulating a path is called a transformation, and transformations can include anything from simply moving an object to changing its size or rotation.

When you move a file, its x,y coordinates change, and Illustrator considers that a transformation. You can also move selected objects precisely by changing the x,y coordinates in the Control panel. Alternatively, double-click the Selection tool to bring up the Move dialog, where you can specify values numerically as well (**Figure 4.61**). Clicking the Copy button in the Move dialog leaves the original shape in place and moves a copy of it.

Of course, you can use the Selection tool to click and drag an object to reposition it manually. If you press and hold the Option (Alt) key while dragging, Illustrator creates a copy. Pressing and holding the tilde key moves pattern tiles within the fill of an object without moving the object itself.

Figure 4.61 Double-clicking the Selection tool in the Toolbox brings up the Move dialog where you can specify move functions numerically.

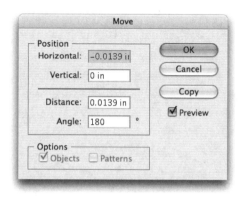

Using the Bounding Box

The bounding box allows you to perform several common transform functions; you can do this by simply clicking an object and using just the Selection tool. Once you've made a selection, you can click an object to move it, or you can click any of the eight *handles* that appear on the perimeter of the bounding box to scale or resize the selection (**Figure 4.62**). Holding the Shift key while resizing constrains proportion. If you place your cursor just outside the edge of a handle, you can rotate your selection (**Figure 4.63**). If you hold the Shift key while you're rotating, you constrain rotation angles to increments of 45 degrees.

Figure 4.62 With the bounding box active, you can scale objects by dragging one of the eight handles.

Figure 4.63 Positioning your cursor just outside a handle, you can use the bounding box to rotate a selection.

By default, Illustrator has the bounding box setting turned on. To turn it off, choose View > Hide Bounding Box.

The bounding box only appears when you select objects with the Selection tool. Although the bounding box is certainly useful, it can get in the way as well. Illustrator has a feature called *snap to point*, where you can drag an object by an anchor point and easily align it to an anchor point in a different object. As your mouse approaches an anchor point, the object you are dragging snaps to it. When the bounding box is turned on, you can't always grab an object by the anchor point because doing so allows you to scale the object instead. Your alternative is to either turn off the bounding box or use the Direct Selection tool (which many Illustrator users do anyway).

If you do turn off the bounding box function, you can still access similar functionality by using the Free Transform tool.

Living by the Numbers with the Transform Palette

The Transform palette, which you can access by choosing Window > Transform, is a production artist's best friend. In reality, it's a palette that can be helpful to anyone. The Transform palette provides numeric feedback on the exact specifications of a selection. This includes x,y coordinates, width and height measurements, and rotate and shear values. You can also use the palette to make numeric changes to selected objects.

Values can be entered using any measurement system, and you can even specify math functions. For example, you can change the x coordinate of an object by adding a +.125 in at the end of the value and pressing Enter or Tab. You can even mix different measurement systems, like subtracting points from millimeters. Use the asterisk for multiplication functions and the slash for division. If you press the Option (Alt) key while pressing Enter for a value, a copy is created.

At the far left of the palette is a 9-point proxy that corresponds to the 8 points of an object's bounding box and its center (**Figure 4.64**, next page). The point you click is extremely important—not only for the Transform palette, but for all transform functions. If you click the center point, the x,y coordinates you see in the Transform palette refer to the center point of your selection. Clicking a different point reveals the coordinates for that point of the selection. When specifying transformations like width or height settings or rotation or skew values, the point you choose becomes the *origin point*—the point from which the transformation originates.

 To lock the proportion of width and height values, click the link icon at the far right of the Transform palette. This allows you to specify just the height or the width of a selected object, and Illustrator scales the other value proportionally.

Rotating an object from its lower left corner yields very different results from that same rotation applied from its center point.

Figure 4.64 The 9-point proxy in the Transform palette enables you to set an origin point for a transformation. You can find the proxy in numerous transform dialogs and in the Control palette as well.

9-point proxy

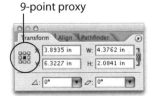

In many cases though, you'll also want to transform the strokes and effects. If this is the case, choose the Scale Strokes & Effects option from the Transform palette menu, which stays on until you turn it off. From the same palette menu, you can also choose to flip objects on their horizontal or vertical axis.

Using Preview Bounds

One of the benefits of using Illustrator is that you can be extremely precise when drawing objects. Illustrator's Control, Transform, and Info palettes all provide exact feedback on coordinates, positioning, sizing, and more. By default, these palettes use the actual vector path to determine these numbers, not the visual boundaries of the object. For example, you may have a shape that has a thick stroke or a scale effect applied to it that is not represented in the value you see in the Transform palette. When the Use Preview Bounds preference is activated in General Preferences, all palettes use the visual boundary of a file as the value, not the underlying vector path.

Working with the Transformation Tools

Illustrator contains specific tools for performing scale, rotation, reflection (mirroring), and shearing (skewing). These specific tools allow you to perform transformation with precision and with more power than the bounding box or even the Control palette.

The four transformation tools—the Scale, Rotate, Reflect, and Shear tools—all work the same way. Here, we'll discuss the Rotate tool specifically; you can apply the same techniques to the other tools.

To rotate an object, select it and choose the Rotate tool. Take a look at the selection on your screen and you'll see a special icon that appears at its center. This icon, which looks like a small crosshairs, is your origin point (**Figure 4.65**). To perform a rotation, position your cursor a fair amount of space away from the origin point and click and drag. You don't have to click the object itself to perform the rotation. If you click too close to the origin point, you'll find that it is difficult to control the rotation. The further away you move your cursor from the origin point before dragging, the more leverage and control you have (**Figure 4.66**).

Figure 4.65 The crosshairs icon indicates the precise location of the transformation origin point.

Figure 4.66 When using the Rotate tool, clicking away from the origin point gives you better leverage for rotating your selection.

While dragging with the Rotate tool, press the Shift key to constrain rotation to 45 degree increments, press the Option (Alt) key to create a copy, and press the tilde key if your object is filled with a pattern and you want to rotate just the pattern.

The powerful part of using a transformation tool is that you have control over the exact placement of the origin point. For example, if you select an object and then switch to the Rotate tool, you'll see the origin point, as we discussed earlier. At that time, you can click once anywhere on your screen to redefine that point elsewhere. If you then click and drag, Illustrator uses the repositioned origin point for the rotation. Alternatively, you can simply click and drag the origin point itself to any location on your screen.

The ability to reposition the origin point arbitrarily means that you can specify an origin point that's outside the boundaries of your object. When using the Transform palette, you can only choose from one of the nine pre-set options using the 9-point proxy.

You can also specify transformations numerically with any of the four transformation tools listed here by making a selection and double-clicking the desired transformation tool. One of the powerful things about bringing up the dialog for a specific transformation tool is that when you enter a value, the next time you open the dialog, that same value remains. Additionally, the dialogs for each transformation tool record the last transformation you performed with the tool. For example, if you use the Scale tool to manually resize an object, you can then open the Scale tool dialog to see the exact percentage that you scaled the object to.

Transforming Multiple Objects at Once

When you select several objects, Illustrator performs all transformations based on a single origin point. This behavior is certainly fine for some needs, but there will be times when you want to have transformations applied to a range of objects, and you want those transformations to be applied using individual origin points. For example, if you have several shapes selected and you want them each to rotate 45 degrees, you want each selected shape to rotate around its own center (**Figure 4.67**).

Figure 4.67 When you have several individual shapes (left), selecting them all and rotating them forces all objects to share a single origin point (center). With the Transform Each function, you can rotate multiple objects around their own individual origin points (right).

The Transform Each function was designed specifically for applying transformations across a range of objects, where each object maintains its own origin point. As an added bonus, the feature also contains something no other transformation tool has—a randomize function.

To use this feature, select a range of objects—even grouped objects—and choose Object > Transform > Transform Each to open the dialog. Clicking the Preview button allows you to see the effects of the transformation before you apply it. Specify Scale, Move, Rotate, and Reflect settings and if you'd like, click the Random button so that each object gets a slight variation of the settings you specify.

By far, the most important thing you need to specify in the Transform Each dialog is the origin point. Choose a point from the 9-point proxy to define the origin point for each selected object. Click OK to apply the transformations or click the Copy button to create copies.

Exploring the Power of the Transform Again Feature

Here's a feature that builds on the power of the transformation tools you've learned in this chapter. Illustrator always remembers the last transformation that you applied, so choosing Object > Transform > Transform Again simply reapplies that transformation, even if you've selected a different object. The keyboard shortcut for this feature is Command-D (Ctrl-D); it's a good idea to memorize it, because you'll use it often.

This example illustrates the power of this feature. Draw a rectangle on your artboard. Choose the Selection tool and drag the rectangle to the right while holding the Option (Alt) key, which creates a copy of the rectangle beside the original. Now apply the Transform Again command. Illustrator now repeats the last transformation, leaving you with three rectangles, evenly spaced.

The Transform Each dialog allows you to apply multiple transformations in one step. Applying a Transform Again command after applying a Transform Each function simply duplicates those settings. The power to transform is now within you. Use it wisely.

 Even though the Transform Each function was created for applying transformations to multiple objects at once, it's a great tool to use on single objects as well. This is especially true since the Transform Each dialog allows you to specify multiple transformations in one step.

CHAPTER 5

Brushes, Symbols, and Masks

Take a moment and think about the true strength of what a computer offers to a designer. Is it fancy drawing tools? Is it cool special effects? Is it the speed at which you can create art? Maybe. But that's all on the surface. In truth, you may find that a designer can draw something with a pencil and paper in half the time it would take to draw it using a computer. The real benefit of using a computer to a designer is that once they have created a design on a computer, they can edit it at will. When you're working with a deadline, it's far easier to make a small edit to a file than to have to redraw the whole design from scratch.

As you build files in Illustrator, you'll find that there are always several ways to accomplish a particular task. Your job is to find the most efficient way to create the art you need, which doesn't necessarily always mean the fastest way. You might be able to create two identical Illustrator files: in one, the file is huge, takes a long time to print, and is difficult to edit or update; the other is created using different features or techniques and results in a leaner, cleaner, and more editable file.

You already know about groups, layers, live effects and graphic styles—all of which you can use to build more efficient objects. In this chapter, you learn to take advantage of other features like brushes, symbols, and masks. By using these features, you will make your files more efficient and easier to update, which can mean the difference between being home in time for dinner with the family or another all-nighter at the office when a deadline is near.

UNLEASHING THE POWER OF BRUSHES

Each version of Adobe Illustrator brings new features and tools to the hands of designers. Some are cool effects, and some add useful functionality. And every once in a while, a feature is introduced that is so unique and powerful, that it changes everything. The brushes feature in Illustrator is such a feature.

The concept is simple: instead of drawing a predictable and boring line using the Pencil tool, the Paintbrush tool can create flourishes, lines with tapered ends, and artsy elements that mimic the strokes you can create with Speedball or calligraphic pens. More powerful than you might think, brushes support pressure-sensitive tablets and can even distribute art and patterns along a drawn path. By using brushes, you can streamline your work by creating complex artwork with just a few paths. Brushes are also easy to modify.

Under the hood, the Paintbrush tool functions exactly like the Pencil tool and allows you to click and drag to create a vector path. The difference is in the appearance of the path that it creates. The Paintbrush tool applies predefined vector artwork to the paths that you draw. When using a pressure-sensitive tablet, you can also control how the artwork is applied to the vector paths.

Stop! Before you start a new file or project, take a few moments to think about the art you will use and how you plan on creating the file. A few minutes of careful planning allow you to understand the kinds of features you need to use, and this planning can save you a significant amount time should you need to make changes to the file at a later date.

Illustrator's Brush Quartet

Illustrator has four different kinds of brushes; each offers a different kind of behavior in which art is applied to a path:

- **Calligraphic brush.** The Calligraphic brush allows you to define a nib, or tip, of a pen. The art that is drawn with a Calligraphic brush takes into account the angle and shape of the nib, resulting in natural thick and thins and variable thickness (**Figure 5.1**).

Figure 5.1 With the help of a pressure-sensitive tablet, the Calligraphic brush can create strokes with natural thicks and thins to achieve a hand-drawn look and feel.

- **Scatter brush.** The Scatter brush allows you to define any vector art as a brush (except the ones listed in the sidebar "What's in a Brush?"). The art that is drawn with a Scatter brush is made up of copies of the art, scattered across the vector path. You can control the way that art is scattered in each brush's settings (**Figure 5.2**).

Figure 5.2 You can use a Scatter brush to create consistent borders or to quickly fill a page with what appears to be random art.

- **Art brush.** The Art brush allows you to define any vector art as a brush (except the ones listed in the sidebar "What's in a Brush?"). The art that is drawn with an Art brush is stretched across the entire length of the path, resulting in the controlled distortion of art along a vector path (**Figure 5.3**).

Figure 5.3 You can use an Art brush to apply artistic brush strokes or to create interesting variations of art.

- **Pattern brush.** The Pattern brush allows you to specify up to five already-defined patterns as a brush. The art that is drawn with a Pattern brush is distributed along a vector path based on the brush's settings, resulting in perfect corners and art that is contoured to the vector path (**Figure 5.4**, next page).

Figure 5.4 A Pattern brush can bend art to match the curve of a path and can also contain a variety of settings that change based on the makeup of the path.

What's in a Brush?

When you're creating artwork that will be used to define a brush, be aware that brushes cannot understand all kinds of vector objects. Brushes cannot contain gradients, blends, other brush strokes, mesh objects, bitmap images, graphs, placed files, or masks. For Art and Pattern brushes specifically, the artwork also cannot contain editable type objects. If you want to include these kinds of objects, you either need to expand them or convert them to outlines first.

Applying Brush Strokes

To paint with a brush, choose the Paintbrush tool from the Toolbox and then choose a brush from the Brushes palette. You create brush strokes the same way you create paths with the Pencil tool, so once you've selected a brush to use, click and drag on the artboard to define a path. When you release the mouse, Illustrator applies the brush stroke to the newly created vector path (**Figure 5.5**). Illustrator also indicates the applied brush stroke in the Appearance palette, making it easy to identify when a particular brush as been used (**Figure 5.6**).

Figure 5.5 When you create a brush stroke, a single vector path is defined, and the appearance of that path displays the brush.

Figure 5.6 By identifying the brush applied to a path, the Appearance palette gives yet another reason for why it should always be opened on your screen.

You don't have to use the Paintbrush tool to apply a brush stroke to a vector path. Simply selecting a vector path and clicking a brush in the Brushes palette applies the brush to the selected path. The only benefit you gain by using the Paintbrush tool is the ability to define a brush shape using a pressure-sensitive tablet (see the Sidebar, "Can You Handle the Pressure?").

 If you double-click the Paintbrush tool, you'll find that the preferences are identical to those of the Pencil tool.

Can You Handle the Pressure?

Illustrator has full support for pressure-sensitive pen tablets like the line of Wacom tablets. You can set Calligraphic or Scatter brushes to use variable settings based on pressure, thus enabling you to easily draw lines of varying thickness or to apply different scatter settings.

The natural lines you can achieve with a Calligraphic brush and a Wacom tablet are perfect for sketching or drawing in Illustrator. It would seem that the next logical step after creating a sketch with the Paintbrush tool is to convert the art to a Live Paint group to quickly colorize the art. Unfortunately, the Live Paint feature doesn't support brushes and converting a brushed path to a Live Paint group results in the loss of the appearance of the brush. Hopefully, future versions of Illustrator will address this.

When using either the Calligraphic or Scatter brushes, Illustrator CS2 also supports Wacom's new 6D pen. You can find a library of these brushes that is already filled with 18 Calligraphic and 6 Scatter brushes in the Illustrator CS2 Goodies folder on the application installation CD. If you purchased Illustrator as a component of the Creative Suite, you'll find this library on the CS2 Standard Content CD.

Defining a Calligraphic Brush

To define a new Calligraphic brush, click the New Brush icon in the Brushes palette or select New Brush from the Brushes palette menu. Choose New Calligraphic Brush from the New Brush dialog and click OK to open the Calligraphic Brush Options dialog (**Figure 5.7**).

Figure 5.7 The Calligraphic Brush Options dialog allows you to click and drag on the nib shape in the preview area to define its settings.

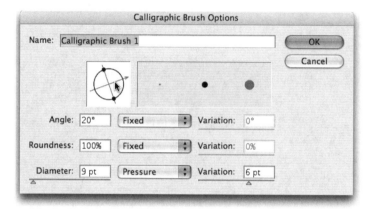

The Calligraphic Brush Options dialog allows you to specify the shape and behavior of the nib using three different settings:

- **Angle.** The angle of a Calligraphic brush can be set to a fixed angle or to a random number. When the roundness setting is at 100%, the angle setting does not produce any noticeable change in the shape of the brush. With pressure-sensitive tablets, you can set the angle to change based on pressure, stylus wheel, tilt, bearing, or rotation. When you're not using the fixed option, the Variation slider allows you to specify a range that the angle can change, which you can also see in the preview area of the dialog.

- **Roundness.** The roundness of a calligraphic brush can be set to a fixed or a random number. When the roundness is set closer to 100%, the tip of the nib becomes circular in shape (like a traditional ink pen). When the roundness is set closer to 0%, the tip of the nib becomes flat (like a traditional calligraphy pen). With pressure-sensitive tablets, you can set the roundness to change based on pressure, stylus wheel, tilt, bearing, or rotation. When you're not using the fixed option, the Variation slider allows you to specify a range that the roundness can change, which you can also see in the preview area of the dialog.

- **Diameter.** You can set the diameter, or size, of a Calligraphic brush to a fixed or a random number. With pressure-sensitive tablets, you can set the diameter to change based on pressure, stylus wheel, tilt, bearing, or rotation. When you're not using the fixed option, the Variation slider allows you to specify a range that the diameter can change, which you can also see in the preview area of the dialog.

 When you're using a pressure-sensitive tablet, giving the diameter setting a variation based on pressure enables you to create strokes that appear thicker as you press harder. If you have Wacom's 6D Art Pen, it makes sense to set the angle to the pen's rotation attribute.

Defining a Scatter Brush

To define a new Scatter brush, start by creating the art for the brush on the artboard. Once it is complete, drag the artwork directly into the Brushes palette. Alternatively, you can select the art and click the New Brush icon in the Brushes palette or select New Brush from the Brushes palette menu. Choose New Scatter Brush from the New Brush dialog and click OK to open the Scatter Brush Options dialog (**Figure 5.8**).

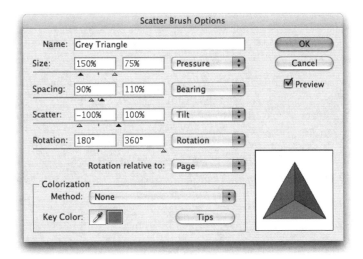

Figure 5.8 The Scatter Brush Options dialog presents a plethora of settings that you can use to create a wide variety of results.

- **Size.** The Size setting can be a fixed or random number; this setting determines how big or small the art is drawn on the path, relative to the actual size of the art that was used to define the brush. For example, if you create a design that is 1 inch tall and use it to define a Scatter brush, a size setting of 50% result in a Scatter brush that creates designs that are .5 inches tall. With pressure-sensitive tablets, you can set the size to change based on pressure, stylus wheel, tilt, bearing, or rotation. When you are not using the fixed option, the two values determine the range that the size can change.

- **Spacing.** The Spacing setting can be a fixed or random number and determines the amount of space that appears between each instance of art that is drawn on the path. Higher values add more space between each copy of the art, and lower values make the copies of art appear closer together. With pressure-sensitive tablets, you can set the spacing to change based on pressure, stylus wheel, tilt, bearing, or rotation. When you're not using the fixed option, the two values determine the range that the spacing can change.

- **Scatter.** The Scatter setting can be a fixed or random number and determines how far away each instance of art that is drawn deviates from the path. Negative values shift art lower and to the left of the path; positive values shift art higher and to the right of the path. With pressure-sensitive tablets, you can set the scatter to change based on pressure, stylus wheel, tilt, bearing, or rotation. When you're not using the fixed option, the two values determine the range that the scatter can change.

- **Rotation.** The Rotation setting can be a fixed or random number and determines the angle that each instance of art is drawn on the path. With pressure-sensitive tablets, you can set the rotation to change based on pressure, stylus wheel, tilt, bearing, or rotation. When you're not using the fixed option, the two values determine the range that the rotation can change.

- **Rotation relative to.** You can set the rotation so that it is relative to the page, in which case all instances of the art appear consistent, or to the path, in which case all instances of the art rotate in accordance with the direction of the path (**Figure 5.9**).

Figure 5.9 Depending on your desired result, you can specify art to rotate in relation to the page, where all of the triangles are rotated in the same way (left) or to the path, where all of the triangles are rotated to match the curved path (right).

- **Colorization.** The Colorization option lets you choose from one of four different settings. If you choose the None setting, the Scatter brush creates art in the same color that is used to define it. If you choose the Tints setting, the Scatter brush creates art in varying tints of the current stroke color. If you choose the Tints and Shades setting, the Scatter brush creates art in varying tints of the current stroke color while preserving black colored objects. If you choose the Hue Shift setting, the Scatter brush creates art and changes the key color of the art to the current stroke color. To define a key color, click the Eyedropper icon in the dialog and click on a part of the art in the preview area.

Defining an Art Brush

To define a new Art brush, start by creating the art for the brush on the artboard. Once it's complete, drag the artwork directly into the Brushes palette. Alternatively, you can select the art and click the New Brush icon in the Brushes palette or select New Brush from the Brushes palette menu. Choose New Art Brush from the New Brush dialog and click OK to open the Art Brush Options dialog (**Figure 5.10**).

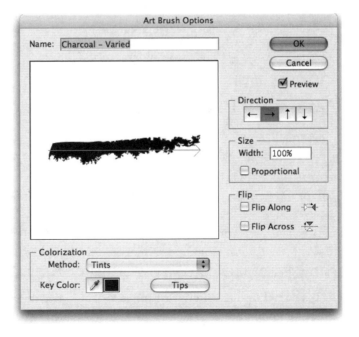

Figure 5.10 The Art Brush Options dialog gives you a visual preview of the direction that the art will appear in relation to the path.

- **Direction.** The Direction setting determines the orientation of the art with respect to the path to which the brush is applied. A blue arrow appears in the preview area allowing you to visually understand how the art will be drawn on a path.

- **Size.** The Size setting determines how big or small the art is drawn on the path relative to the actual size of the art that was used to define the brush. For example, if you create a design that is 1 inch tall and use it to define an art brush, a size setting of 50% results in an art brush that creates designs that are .5 inches tall. When specifying width values, you can also choose to keep the artwork scaled in proportion.

- **Flip.** The Flip Along and Flip Across settings enable you to reflect the artwork on both the horizontal and vertical axis.

- **Colorization.** The Colorization option lets you choose from one of four different settings. When you choose the None setting, the art brush creates art in the same color that is used to define it. If you choose the Tints setting, the Art brush creates art in varying tints of the current stroke color. If you choose the Tints and Shades setting, the Art brush creates art in varying tints of the current stroke color while preserving black colored objects. If you choose the Hue Shift setting, the Art brush creates art and changes the key color of the art to the current stroke color. To define a key color, click the Eyedropper icon in the dialog and click a part of the art in the preview area.

Defining a Pattern Brush

To define a new Pattern brush, you must first define the pattern swatches that will be used in the brush, using the methods you learned in Chapter 2, *Vectors 101*. A Pattern brush can contain up to five different pattern tiles, used for different parts of a path (see the Pattern Tiles bullet below). Once you've defined the necessary pattern swatches, click the New Brush icon in the Brushes palette or select New Brush from the Brushes palette menu. Choose New Pattern Brush from the New Brush dialog and click OK to open the Pattern Brush Options dialog (**Figure 5.11**).

- **Pattern Tiles.** A Pattern brush can use up to five different pattern tiles for the different parts of a drawn path. The side tile is used along the middle of the path, the outer and inner corner tiles are used whenever the path encounters a corner anchor point at 90 degrees, and the start and end tiles are used at the beginning and end of an open path (**Figure 5.12**). To set a tile, click the preview box above each tile and choose from the list of defined pattern swatches. Only pattern swatches from the current document appear in the list. It is not necessary to assign a pattern swatch to every tile in order to define a Pattern brush. For example, some Pattern brushes do not have start or end tiles defined.

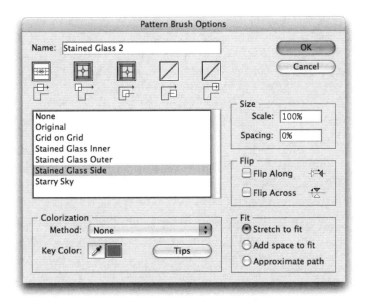

Figure 5.11 Though it might appear complicated at first, the Pattern Brush Options dialog makes it easy to define powerful Pattern brushes.

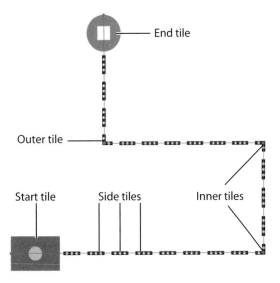

Figure 5.12 A Pattern brush can contain up to five different pattern tiles, which apply to side, outer and inner, and start and end points of a path.

- **Scale.** The Scale setting determines how big or small the pattern swatch is drawn on the path, relative to the actual size of the art that was used to define the pattern (by default, a Pattern brush applies art at the size the art was originally created). For example, if you create art that is 1 inch tall and use it to define a pattern swatch, a size setting of 50% results in a Pattern brush that creates tiles that are .5 inches tall.

To create a dashed line on a rectangle that will always have perfect corners, create two pattern swatches, one for a dash and one for a corner. Then create a pattern brush that uses the dash pattern as a side and the corner pattern as an outer corner tile and choose the Add space to fit option.

- **Spacing.** The Spacing setting determines the amount of space that appears between each pattern tile that is drawn on the path. By default, all pattern tiles touch each other, and specifying higher values adds more space between them.

- **Flip.** The Flip Along and Flip Across settings enable you to reflect the pattern tiles on both the horizontal and vertical axis.

- **Fit.** The Fit setting, arguably one of most powerful settings among all of the brushes, allows you to specify how pattern tiles are drawn on a path. The Stretch to fit option modifies the brush's Scale setting to ensure a perfect fit across the entire path, with no spaces between tiles. The Add space to fit option modifies the brush's spacing setting to ensure the tiles fit evenly across an entire path. The Approximate path option actually changes the size of the path so that it fits to the size of the pattern tiles.

Be sure to check out Bert Monroy's Pattern brush example in the color insert.

- **Colorization.** The Colorization option lets you choose from one of four different settings. When you choose the None setting, the Pattern brush creates tiles in the exact same color that it is used when the pattern swatches are defined. If you choose the Tints setting, the Pattern brush creates tiles in varying tints of the current stroke color. If you choose the Tints and Shades setting, the Pattern brush creates tiles in varying tints of the current stroke color while preserving black colored objects. When you choose the Hue Shift setting, the Pattern brush creates tiles and changes the key color of the tiles to the current stroke color. To define a key color, click the Eyedropper icon in the dialog and click a part of the tile in the preview area (which is extremely difficult considering how small the previews for each tile are).

Modifying Brush Strokes

Double-click any brush in the Brushes palette to specify or change its settings. Alternatively, you can hold the Option (Alt) key while dragging vector art from the artboard onto an existing Art or Scatter brush to modify or replace the brush. When you do, a thick black line appears around the brush icon indicating that you are about to modify it.

When you're about to modify a brush, Illustrator checks to see if the existing brush has already been applied to objects in your document. If it finds such objects, Illustrator asks if you want the existing paths to now take on the appearance of the modified brush, or if you want to leave them intact. If you want to leave them intact, Illustrator makes a copy of the modified brush rather than replace the existing one (**Figure 5.13**).

You can delete brushes from a document by dragging them to the trash icon in the Brushes palette. If you try deleting a brush that is already applied to an object in your file, Illustrator prompts you asking if you want to either expand the path, remove the brush appearance from the path altogether, or cancel.

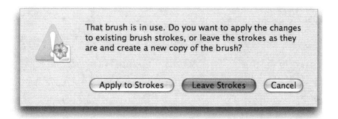

That brush is in use. Do you want to apply the changes to existing brush strokes, or leave the strokes as they are and create a new copy of the brush?

Apply to Strokes   Leave Strokes   Cancel

Figure 5.13 Always watching what you're doing, Illustrator alerts you if your edits will affect objects that have already been drawn.

Expanding Brush Art

When you apply a brush stroke to a path, only the vector path itself is editable. The art that makes up the brush stroke cannot be edited or otherwise tinkered with. However, you can easily reduce any brush stroke to editable vector art by choosing Object > Expand Appearance. Doing so removes the link to the brush and the path no longer updates if the brush swatch is updated.

Additionally, you can always access the original art that was used to create an Art, Scatter, or Pattern brush by dragging the brush out of the Brushes palette and onto a blank area on the artboard.

 Like swatches, brushes travel with a file, so you don't need to expand a brush just because you're sending the file to someone else. When you define and use brushes, those brushes are saved in the file and are there until you manually delete them.

Saving Space and Time with Symbols

Sometimes, a project calls for a range of repeating design elements. For example, when creating a map of a park, you might use icons to indicate restrooms or picnic areas. And when designing an item of clothing, you might draw the same button in several different places. Illustrator has a feature that was created specifically to manage repeating graphics in a file, called *symbols*.

You can think of a symbol as a master art item, which is defined once per Illustrator document. Once created, you can place multiple *instances* of a symbol within a document. Each instance is simply an alias or a placeholder that points back to the original defined symbol. Using symbols in a document offers several benefits. First, if you edit or modify a symbol, all instances of that symbol are automatically updated as well. Second, because Illustrator only stores a single copy of a symbol per document, you can take advantage of smaller file sizes. Smaller file sizes translate to faster open and save times, faster print times, and faster server transfer times.

Designers who create certain kinds of Web graphics can also take advantage of using symbols. In Chapter 10, *Illustrator and the Web*, we'll discuss how symbols can be used to generate smaller file sizes when creating SWF (Flash) and SVG files.

Working with Symbols and Instances

Defining a symbol is quick and easy. Select any artwork on your artboard and drag it into the Symbols palette. Double-click a symbol in the Symbols palette to give it a unique name. Unlike brushes, which are limited in the kinds of artwork they can contain, you can use any kind of artwork to define a symbol with the exception of placed-linked images (for more information on linked images, see Chapter 8, *Mixing It Up: Working with Vectors and Pixels*). Objects with live effects applied, and even editable text, can be stored inside a symbol in Illustrator. Once you've defined a symbol in the Symbols palette, you can delete the artwork that you used to create it if you'd like—a complete copy of the artwork is stored inside of the file.

Dragging a symbol from the Symbols palette out onto the artboard creates a symbol instance. Alternatively, you can select a symbol in the Symbols palette and click on the Place Symbol Instance icon to create a symbol instance at the center of the document (**Figure 5.14**). Once on the artboard, you'll notice that a symbol instance cannot be edited, even when you're using the Direct Selection tool. A symbol instance doesn't give you access to the actual artwork because it is simply a placeholder (**Figure 5.15**). However, you can use any of Illustrator's transformation tools and functions with symbol instances. For example, you can scale or rotate a symbol instance as necessary. Additionally, you can specify transparency features and even apply live effects to symbol instances. You can place as many symbol instances in a document as you desire and each instance can be scaled or transformed differently. You can copy and paste symbols between documents as well.

 Pressing Command-Shift (Ctrl-Shift) while dragging artwork into the Symbols palette defines a symbol and at the same time turns the art on the artboard into a symbol instance.

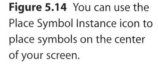

Place Symbol Instance

Figure 5.14 You can use the Place Symbol Instance icon to place symbols on the center of your screen.

Figure 5.15 Even though a symbol may be made up of vectors, you can't edit symbol instances on the artboard.

Replacing Symbols

 Although you can't include linked images in a symbol, you can include embedded images. Because you can use symbols many times in a document with no adverse effect on file size, it makes sense to think about creating symbols from an embedded image if you need to use them often in a file.

If you think about it, a symbol instance is really an empty box, which references real artwork that resides in the Symbols palette. With this fundamental understanding, it should be possible to take a symbol instance that references one symbol, and change it so that it references a different symbol that you've defined. In Illustrator, the ability to switch an instance to point to a different symbol is called *replacing symbols*.

To replace a symbol instance, select it on the artboard and then click the symbol in the Symbols palette that you want to replace it with. With both the symbol instance and the new symbol selected, click the Replace Symbol icon in the Symbols palette or choose Replace Symbol from the Symbols palette menu. The selected symbol instance updates accordingly. When replacing symbol instances, any transformations or effects that you've applied to any individual instances will remain intact.

Modifying Symbols and Instances

At any time, you can click the Break Link to Symbol icon in the Symbols palette to "expand" the instance. Doing so gives you access to the individual objects that were used to define the symbol (**Figure 5.16**). Once you've broken a link to a symbol, the artwork is no longer tied back to the symbol and any benefits of using symbols no longer apply to that art. Updating or modifying the symbol does not update the art.

Figure 5.16 Once a symbol instance has broken its link, the paths and objects are available to edit.

Modifying a symbol is much like modifying a swatch or a brush. Select both the new artwork on the artboard and the symbol in the Symbols palette that you want to modify. Hold the Option (Alt) key down and drag the artwork onto the symbol in the Symbols palette. When you do, a black border appears around the symbol indicating that you are about to modify it. Alternatively, you can select both the art and the symbol and choose Redefine Symbol from the Symbols palette.

When a symbol is redefined, all instances on the artboard that reference the symbol are updated to reflect the change. Any attributes or transformations that were applied to the instances are preserved.

When you redefine a symbol in one document, it does not update other files that may use the same symbol. The change is local to just the document that is open and being worked on.

Uses for Symbols

When you take a moment to think about your project before you start working on it, you might be able to determine whether using symbols would benefit you. Here is a list of several ways symbols can be used to help build better files:

- Although Illustrator's doesn't have master pages, symbols can act like miniature "master art elements" in a file. For example, when creating several different ideas for a packaging concept, use symbols as the base for each design, (i.e., ingredients, nutrition info, weight, etc.). Updating a symbol then instantly updates all of the design comps in the file at once.

- Create symbol libraries to store commonly used logos and icons. (Back in Chapter 1, *The Illustrator Environment*, you learned how to save and load libraries.)

- Create symbol libraries to store collections of fashion elements like buttons, zippers, or labels, or other specific art elements, like architectural elements or cartography symbols.

- The use of symbols is required in order to perform certain features in Illustrator, including the ability to create custom 3D bevels and artwork mapped onto the surfaces of 3D objects. This functionality is covered in Chapter 7, *3D and Other Live Effects*.

Be sure to check out Ivan Torres's Symbols example in the color insert.

Of course, there are plenty of other ways you can use symbols in Illustrator. The next section deals with some special tools created specifically for working with symbols: the Symbolism tools.

Having Fun with the Symbolism Tools

So you've been reading along and totally get the benefits of using symbols where possible to create more efficient files. Say, for example, that you are going to create a night sky for an illustration and need to fill the sky with stars. So you create a symbol of a nice star with a cool glow effect and define it as a symbol. One by one, you drag out symbol instances and scale and rotate each star to achieve a more natural look (**Figure 5.17**). As you drag out yet another symbol instance, you think, there's got to be a better way to do this. The good news is, there is. The great news is, the better way is extremely fun!

In the Toolbox, you'll find the Symbol Sprayer tool. Hidden beneath it, you'll find seven more tools; together, these tools are referred to as the Symbolism tools (**Figure 5.18**). The reason for the name is that these tools all work using symbols, and not by any coincidence, the tools all begin with the letter "s" (See? Adobe actually *does* pay attention to detail).

Figure 5.17 Dragging out and editing individual symbol instances can be tedious.

Figure 5.18 The Symbolism tools all appear grouped in the Toolbox with the Symbol Sprayer tool.

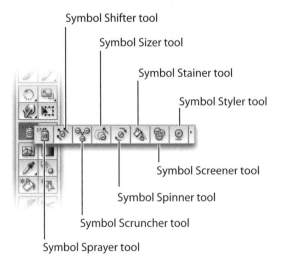

Symbol Shifter tool

Symbol Sizer tool

Symbol Stainer tool

Symbol Styler tool

Symbol Screener tool

Symbol Spinner tool

Symbol Scruncher tool

Symbol Sprayer tool

Creating a Symbol Set

The Symbol Sprayer tool was created to easily add multiple symbol instances to a document. Choose the Symbol Sprayer tool from the Toolbox and then click any symbol in the Symbols palette. Because the Symbol Sprayer tool only works with symbols, it's important to first select a symbol to work with—otherwise the Symbol Sprayer won't work. Click and drag on the artboard while holding the mouse button, and you'll begin to see the Symbol Sprayer adding symbols to your page (**Figure 5.19**). When you release the mouse button, a single outline appears around the perimeter of the symbols. What you have actually created is a *symbol set*, which is a collection of symbol instances (**Figure 5.20**). If you switch to the Selection tool, you'll find that you can't select the individual symbol instances, but you can move the entire symbol set as a whole.

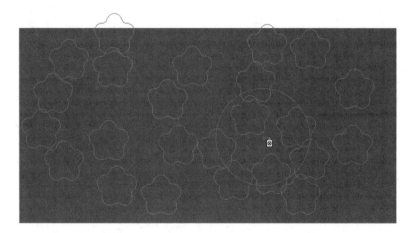

Figure 5.19 As you click and drag with the Symbol Sprayer tool, instances appear to flow onto your artboard.

Figure 5.20 Once you release the mouse, the symbol instances appear united in a single symbol set.

Although it may seem silly that you can't select individual instances within a symbol set, that notion quickly changes when you realize that the Symbol Sprayer tool is interactive. Select the symbol set and switch back to the Symbol Sprayer tool. If you click and drag, the Symbol Sprayer tool adds more symbol instances to the set. If you press the Option (Alt) key while dragging, you remove symbols from the set. In addition, the Symbol Sprayer tool has support for pressure-sensitive tablets, so the harder you press, the faster the instances appear.

It's certainly fun to spray symbols all over your document, but there is a way that you can control the individual symbols that appear inside of a symbol set. To do this, you need to employ the Symbolism tools.

Using the Specialized Symbolism Tools

You can add different symbols to the same symbol set. Once you've created a symbol set using one symbol, choose another symbol from the Symbols palette and add more symbols to your symbol set. You can add as many different kinds of symbols as you want to a symbol set.

Once you've created a symbol set with the Symbol Sprayer tool, you can switch to any of the other Symbolism tools to adjust the symbols within the set. It's important to realize that symbol sets are intended to create a natural collection of symbol instances. You'll find that you can't position symbol instances precisely with the Symbolism tools. On the contrary, the Symbolism tools are meant to offer Illustrator users a more free-flowing style, and it almost feels as if you are suggesting a particular movement or behavior to symbol instances rather than performing a definitive action to them. As you try each of these tools, you'll get a better feel for how they function, and for how you might be able to use them for your projects.

For each of these tools, you'll notice that a circle appears, which indicates the diameter of the tool's area of influence (**Figure 5.21**). You can make this area larger or smaller by pressing the bracket keys ([/]) on your keyboard (similar to Photoshop's keyboard shortcut for changing brush size).

Although the Symbolism tools aren't meant to work on just one symbol instance at a time, you can make your area of influence small enough so that you can affect a much smaller area, or even individual symbols.

- **Symbol Shifter tool.** The Symbol Shifter tool moves symbol instances around. Clicking and dragging this tool pushes symbols in the direction of your cursor (**Figure 5.22**). If you hold the Shift key while dragging, Illustrator brings the symbol instances from the back of the symbol set's stacking order to the front.

- **Symbol Scruncher tool.** The Symbol Scruncher tool moves symbol instances closer together, making the appearance more dense. Clicking and dragging with the Symbol Scruncher tool causes instances to become attracted to your cursor and to slowly gravitate toward it. If you hold the Option (Alt) key while dragging, the reverse effect applies, and instances move further away from your cursor.

Figure 5.21 You can resize the circle area, which indicates the tool's area of influence, to be bigger or smaller.

Figure 5.22 The Symbol Shifter tool allows you to reposition the symbol instances within a symbol set.

- **Symbol Sizer tool.** The Symbol Sizer tool scales symbol instances within a symbol set. Clicking and dragging with the Symbol Sizer tool causes instances to become larger. If you hold the Option (Alt) key while dragging, the reverse effect applies, and instances become smaller.

- **Symbol Spinner tool.** The Symbol Spinner tool rotates symbol instances. Clicking and dragging with the Symbol Sizer tool causes instances to rotate toward the direction of your cursor. As you drag, arrows appear that indicate the direction in which the instances will rotate (**Figure 5.23**, next page). Instances that appear closer to the center of the area of influence rotate at a lesser rate than objects toward the edges of the area of influence.

Figure 5.23 When dragging with the Symbol Spinner tool, arrows appear, helping you get an idea of how the instances will rotate.

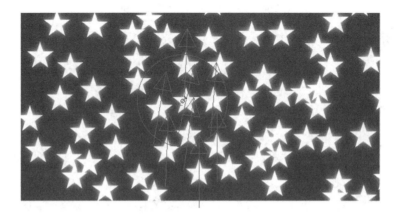

When using the Symbolism tools, you'll often find yourself jumping from one Symbolism tool to another. You can either tear off all of the Symbolism tools to access them easier, or you can use a special context-sensitive menu. If you're on a Mac, with any of the Symbolism tools selected, press Control-Option and click with the mouse. If you're on Windows, press Alt and right-click with the mouse to access a circular contextual menu that contains all of the Symbolism tools (**Figure 5.24**). Mouse over the tool you want and release the keys to switch to the Symbolism tool you have chosen.

Figure 5.24 The Symbolism contextual menu makes it easy to switch between the tools.

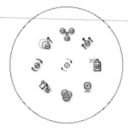

- **Symbol Stainer tool.** The Symbol Stainer tool applies color tints to symbol instances. To use the Symbol Stainer tool, you must first select a color from either the Control, Swatches, or Color palettes. Once a color is selected, clicking and dragging with the Symbol Stainer tool gradually tints the symbol instances. If you hold the Option (Alt) key while dragging, the reverse effect applies, and the instances will gradually return to their original color.

- **Symbol Screener tool.** The Symbol Screener tool applies opacity to symbol instances. Clicking and dragging with the Symbol Screener tool causes instances to become transparent. If you hold the Option (Alt) key while dragging, the reverse effect applies, and instances become more opaque.

- **Symbol Styler tool.** The Symbol Styler tool applies graphic styles to symbol instances. To use the Symbol Styler tool, you must first select a graphic style from the Graphic Styles palette. Once you've selected a style, click and drag with the Symbol Styler tool to gradually add appearances from the style to the symbol instances. If you hold the Option (Alt) key while dragging, the reverse effect applies, and the instances gradually return to their original appearance. Note that using this particular tool can result in extremely slow performance, especially with complex symbols.

Double-click any of the Symbolism tools to see the options for the entire Symbolism toolset (**Figure 5.25**). The Intensity setting controls how quickly the Symbolism tools work, and choosing Pressure for the Intensity setting if you have a pressure-sensitive tablet makes it easier to control the flow of symbols and the edits you make to them.

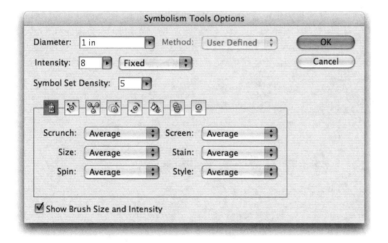

Figure 5.25 In one dialog, you can set the behavior and view options for all of the Symbolism tools.

Expanding a Symbol Set

You can reduce a symbol set to a group of individual symbol instances by selecting the symbol set and choosing Object > Expand. Although the Symbol Sprayer only works with symbol sets, the remaining Symbolism tools work on individual symbol instances. You can also select several symbol instances and use a Symbolism tool to adjust them all at once. Still, you'll find that most times, you'll be using the regular Scale and Rotate tools to adjust individual symbol instances, and the Symbolism tools for when you're working with symbol sets.

If you add multiple symbols to a single symbol set, using any of the Symbolism tools only affects the symbol that is currently selected in the Symbols palette.

Featured Match-Up: Scatter Brush vs. Symbol Sprayer Tool

You may be wondering why there's a Symbol Sprayer tool in Illustrator, since you know that earlier in the chapter, we discussed the Scatter Brush, which allows you to distribute graphics along a path.

Although the concept of creating multiple copies of art is common between the two, the differences end there. A Scatter Brush is limited by what can be defined as a brush, whereas there are far fewer limitations when you are defining symbols. Additionally, using a Scatter Brush to add many shapes to a file increases file size and adds complexity to the file. The Symbol Sprayer tool can spray hundreds of symbols onto a page without you having to worry about files getting too big or too complex to print.

Of course, you can adjust symbol sets that are created with the Symbol Sprayer tool using a range of Symbolism tools. This allows you to tweak and massage a design until you're happy with the results. In contrast, when using a Scatter Brush, you've already specified the settings of the brush before you've created the path. However, a Scatter Brush can follow a specific path, whereas the Symbol Sprayer tool is harder to control if you need art placed at specific intervals.

ACHIEVING PHOTOREALISM WITH GRADIENT MESH

As you learned back in Chapter 2, *Vectors 101*, gradients allow you to fill an object with gradations of color that blend into each other. Although these gradients are certainly useful, they are limited from a creative standpoint because they can only be used in linear or radial forms. In Illustrator 8, Adobe introduced a radical new feature called Gradient Mesh: an incredible tool that allows you to create gradients in any shape. The results are painterly effects that look as if they had come right out of Photoshop—yet they are all in vector form using the gradient mesh feature. And if you can achieve the appearance you're looking for while keeping your file in vector form, you can keep your art completely scalable and editable throughout the design process. For example, changing one color in a gradient mesh is far easier than trying to replace a color that's used in a Photoshop file.

However, the Gradient Mesh tool isn't the easiest feature to understand. Many people would like to use the feature, but they can't figure out any consistent way to explain its behavior. Hopefully, this section will help you understand what a gradient mesh is and how it works.

Before you learn how gradients are applied, let's talk about what a mesh is. A *mesh* is a grid made up of multiple anchor points, called *mesh points* (**Figure 5.26**). You can pull or adjust each of these anchor points to control the shape of the mesh. A mesh is really a special kind of construct or object in Illustrator, and it does not act like a regular path does. Mesh objects do not have normal Fill or Stroke attributes and can't display certain kinds of Live Effects. Rather, you use mesh objects to contain two kinds of attributes in Illustrator: Gradients and Envelopes. We'll talk more about Envelopes in Chapter 9, *Graphs, Distortion, and Blends*. When you're using a mesh to define a gradient, each mesh point determines a color stop and the way in which that color blends into other colors.

 Be sure to check out Yukio Miyamoto's examples using the Gradient Mesh tool in the color insert.

Mesh points

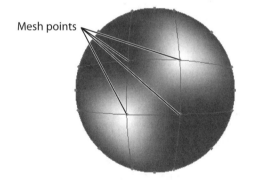

Figure 5.26 A mesh is a grid that is made up of paths and mesh points.

Creating and Editing a Gradient Mesh Object

To create a Gradient Mesh object, choose the Mesh tool from the Toolbox and click any vector path in your document. You don't draw Gradient Mesh objects from scratch in Illustrator; you convert existing vector shapes to mesh objects. Each click with the Mesh tool adds additional mesh points to the mesh object. You'll also notice that as you add mesh points to an object, the paths that connect the mesh points match the contours of the object (**Figure 5.27**, next page).

Once you have mesh points defined, you can switch to the Direct Selection tool and select each individual mesh point to adjust its position and its direction handles (**Figure 5.28**). With a mesh point selected, you can choose a color from the Control, Swatches, or Color palette to define the color for that point. Each mesh point can contain only one color. Each mesh point's direction handles and paths define how its color blends with other colors from other mesh points (**Figure 5.29**). As needed, you can switch back to the Mesh tool and click to add additional mesh points.

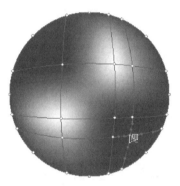

Figure 5.27 In this example of using a circle, notice how the mesh points that are added create curved paths, not straight ones.

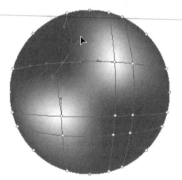

Figure 5.28 Editing a mesh point is no different than editing an anchor point.

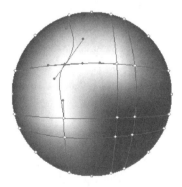

Figure 5.29 The paths that connect the mesh points define how colors blend and the shapes and contours of the gradient.

You can also create a gradient mesh from an existing vector object. With the object selected, choose Object > Create Gradient Mesh. You can then choose how many rows or columns you want in the mesh, and if the object is filled with a color, you can specify a highlight towards the center or the edge of the object. Once the gradient mesh is created, you can continue to tweak it using the methods mentioned previously.

 If you converted a path to a mesh object and then want to get the path back, you can select the mesh object and use the Offset Path function with a setting of 0. This creates a new path that you can edit and color as you wish.

LOOKING BEHIND THE MASK

When we refer to masks, we're not talking about the kind you wear to Mardi Gras. *Masking* in Illustrator is a way to define parts of your artwork as being hidden from view. Rather than having to delete unwanted parts of your art, you can use a vector shape to define an area that acts like a window: Anything that appears within the borders of the shape is visible, and anything that falls outside its boundaries is not visible. The main benefit derived from using masks is that you aren't deleting anything from your file, and once a mask is created, it's possible to change the mask or the artwork behind it, as well as reposition the mask to show or hide different parts of your artwork.

When you use masks in a file and are required to make changes, you'll never have to re-create art that you've already deleted. Instead, everything that you create is always in the file, and you simply choose what is or isn't visible. Additionally, a mask allows you to instantly clip parts of an image or an object. By using a mask, you can do with one click what might take tens of clicks if you use pathfinder functions to chop up and delete parts of objects.

There are three different kinds of masks that you can create in Illustrator, each with its own benefits. A *clipping mask* allows you to specify a certain vector shape as a mask for other individual or grouped objects. A *layer clipping mask* allows you to specify a certain vector shape as a mask for all the objects within the same layer. An *opacity mask* allows you to use the luminance value of any object to create a mask for other individual or grouped objects. As you will see, this last type of mask—one of the most well hidden features of Illustrator—is also the most powerful.

Creating Clipping Masks

A clipping mask can be made up of any vector object, including editable text. To create a clipping mask, you select both the path that will be the mask and the art that you want to appear inside of the mask. The path that you want to use as the mask must be the topmost object in your selection. Choose Object > Clipping Mask > Make, and only art that falls within the boundaries of the mask object will remain visible (**Figure 5.30**).

Figure 5.30 Before creating a clipping mask, the objects are all selected (left), and once the mask is applied, the topmost object defines what is or is not visible for the remainder of the selected objects (right).

 A clipping mask uses the vector path as the boundary for the mask, even if the object has an appearance applied to it.

When Illustrator creates a clipping mask, the mask and the art are grouped together, making it easy to move them around as a single unit when you're using the Selection tool. However, you can use the Direct Selection tool to select and edit just the mask, or just the artwork independently.

In truth, because the masked art is still selectable, it can make life difficult when you have a lot of masks in a file, because you can easily select masked artwork when you don't intend to do so. At the same time, this behavior does make it easy to edit artwork within masks. Getting into the habit of using the Layers palette to lock the art that you aren't working with for a particular task helps avoid this.

Organized Masking with Layer Clipping Masks

A layer clipping mask is very similar to a clipping mask, with one main difference: instead of masking another selected object or group of objects, it masks entire layers. In reality, layer clipping masks are far easier to control and work with because you aren't constantly selecting and deselecting objects to define what is or what isn't in a particular mask. Instead, you use the Layers palette, which you use to organize your artwork anyway, to create these kinds of masks.

To create a layer clipping mask, place the vector object that will be your mask at the top of the layer's stacking order. Click once on the layer name in the Layers palette, which selects the layer (you don't want to target the layer, just select it in the palette). Then, click the Make/Release Clipping Mask icon at the bottom of the Layers palette (**Figure 5.31**). The topmost object in your layer now becomes a mask for all objects in that layer. The mask appears listed in the Layers palette with an underline, giving you a visual indication of its behavior (**Figure 5.32**).

With layer clipping masks, you can easily drag items into a masked layer to have them affected by the mask, and vice versa. To release a layer clipping mask, select the layer and click the Make/Release Clipping Mask button.

Figure 5.31 To create a layer clipping mask, select the layer first, and then define the mask.

Figure 5.32 If you see something listed in the Layers palette with an underline, you know that object is a clipping mask.

Seeing Through Objects with Opacity Masks

When you're creating clipping and layer clipping masks, the vector path of the mask is what defines the boundary of what is visible and what is not. Additionally, anything that falls inside the mask area is completely visible and anything that falls outside that area is completely hidden. Opacity masks bring a whole new level of functionality to Illustrator because in addition to using the vector path itself as the mask, the visual appearance of the mask is what defines what is shown and what is hidden.

If you've used Photoshop before, you're familiar with something called an alpha channel. In reality, an alpha channel in Photoshop is just like a mask, where the color black represents areas of the image that are visible and the color white represents areas of the image that are hidden. With an alpha channel, however, you can also specify a color of gray, which translates to part of an image that's partially visible. In fact, alpha channels support up to 256 levels of gray, which translate to up to 256 levels of visibility in such a mask. Because of this functionality, users can specify masks with soft edges and fades when they use Photoshop. Each pixel of the mask can represent a different opacity value. Opacity masks in Illustrator can take advantage of that same functionality.

When you use an object as an opacity mask, the vector path is not the only thing that determines what it shown and what is hidden—the visual makeup of the object is what determines the mask as well. Opacity masks support 256 levels of gray, meaning that you can create a soft-edged mask in Illustrator. Let's see how this works by using a gradient as an opacity mask.

Creating an Opacity Mask

For this exercise, imagine you want to create a gradient that fades from 100-percent color to none (which is not currently possible as you can't assign the None attribute to a color stop in a gradient). Begin by creating a rectangle and fill it with a solid color. Next, select the rectangle and copy it by pressing Command-C (Ctrl-C). Now paste it in front of the first rectangle by pressing Command-F (Ctrl-F). Fill the second rectangle with a regular black to white linear gradient. You now have two objects, stacked on top of each other, with the gradient visible on top (**Figure 5.33**).

Figure 5.33 Two rectangles stacked on top of each other, and only the one filled with the gradient is visible.

Use the Selection tool to select both objects and open your Transparency palette. In order to create an Opacity mask, you have to expand the palette to show all of its options, so click the triangles to the left of the Palette tab or choose Show Options from the palette menu. You will see a thumbnail of your selection in the Transparency palette (**Figure 5.34**). Finally, choose Make Opacity Mask from the Transparency palette menu. The result is a mask that uses the values of the gradient to define what parts of the object are visible below it—an object that effectively fades from 100-percent color to transparent (feel free to create an object that appears beneath the rectangle if you don't believe me).

Figure 5.34 A thumbnail of your selected art is visible in the Transparency palette.

Editing an Opacity Mask

Once you've created the opacity mask, you can use the thumbnails in the Transparency palette to work with both the mask and the artwork beneath it. Instead of one thumbnail as you saw before, there are now two thumbnails: the one on the left is the artwork, the one on the right is the mask. To edit the artwork, click the left thumbnail. If you look at your Appearance palette, you'll notice that the object you have selected is a normal path that has a solid fill attributed to it. The name of the path displays with a dashed underline in both the Appearance palette and the Layers palette, indicating that it has an opacity mask applied (**Figure 5.35**). At this point, the mask itself is not editable, nor can it even be selected.

Figure 5.35 A target with a dashed underline quickly identifies an object that has an opacity mask applied to it.

 Clicking the Invert Mask button reverses a mask and, rather than having the color black appear as transparent, the color black represents areas that are opaque. The Transparency palette menu also has an option to set all new masks to be created so that they are inverted.

Clicking the right thumbnail selects the mask, allowing you to edit its attributes (**Figure 5.36**). Take a look at the Layers palette; doing so reveals something very interesting. Instead of displaying all of the layers and objects in your file, when you click the mask thumbnail, the Layers palette switches to display just the opacity mask (**Figure 5.37**). The title bar of your document also indicates that you are editing the opacity mask and not the art. These visual indications help you easily identify when you are editing art and when you are editing an opacity mask. To return to artwork editing mode, simply click again on the left thumbnail icon.

Figure 5.36 Clicking a thumbnail in the Transparency palette tells Illustrator what you want to edit. A black outline around the thumbnail indicates which one is selected.

Figure 5.37 The Layers palette offers a visual cue to indicate when you are editing an opacity mask.

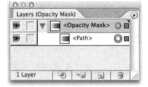

When you are editing either the artwork or the opacity mask itself, using the selection tool to move items will result in both the artwork and the mask moving together. The reason for this is that by default, a mask and its artwork are linked with each other, indicated in the Transparency palette by a link icon that appears between the two thumbnail icons (**Figure 5.38**).

Clicking the link icon allows you to move the mask and artwork independently of each other, and clicking between the thumbnails toggles the link behavior.

Figure 5.38 Clicking the link icon between the thumbnails allows you to move the art and the mask independently.

 Featured Match-Up: Clipping Masks vs. Opacity Masks

When do you use an opacity mask instead of a clipping mask? One certainly doesn't replace the other, because each mask has specific benefits. A clipping mask uses the actual path of the vector object to define the clipping area. This means a clipping mask always has a hard vector edge. In contrast, an opacity mask uses the actual appearance of a shape as the mask, meaning that you can create masks with soft edges or different levels of opacity. Additionally, opacity masks are controlled via the Transparency palette, making it easier to choose when you want to work with the mask or the artwork behind the mask. Of course, using an opacity mask means that you're using transparency in your file, which requires flattening. When you're creating files for certain workflows that become complicated when you use transparency effects, using a clipping mask is beneficial. For more information on transparency and flattening, see Chapter 11: *Prepress and Printing*.

Taking Opacity Masks to the Next Level

Because opacity masks are "hidden" deep within the Transparency palette, they are a feature that doesn't get much publicity. However, they are really one of the most sophisticated features you'll find that offers a wide range of functionality. If you truly understand that opacity masks are just levels of gray that determine visibility, you can use these to achieve effects that you once thought were only possible in Photoshop.

Take photographs for example. By using a vector object with a Feather live effect applied to it, you can create a soft-edged vignette for a placed photograph right in Illustrator (the Feather live effect is covered Chapter 7). Additionally, you can use placed images themselves as an opacity mask, which opens the door to creating Photoshop effects like mezzotints and halos (**Figure 5.39**).

Figure 5.39 In this example, a mezzotint effect was applied to an object that was then used as an opacity mask for some type. The result is fully editable type that has a roughened appearance.

Trace Techniques

Using Live Trace for Auto & Hand-Tracing

Advanced Technique

Overview: *Use the same image as a foundation for both a background created using Live Trace and a hand-traced foreground.*

1

Swatches palette before and after removing unused swatches

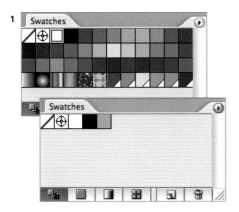

The original photograph Crouse used as the starting point for both the Live Trace background and hand-traced foreground

Scott Crouse drew this portrait of George Jenkins, the founder of Publix Markets, as part of a series of exterior murals for the Publix grocery store chain. To communicate the warm, friendly personality of "Mr. George," Crouse applied his personal illustration style as he hand-traced the portrait from a photograph. The background image did not need to be as distinctive, so Crouse saved time by using the Live Trace feature to create it from the same photograph. For easier hand-tracing, Crouse simplifies images by limiting tonal levels and removing distracting stray bits; in many cases Live Trace can replace Photoshop for this preparatory task.

1 Preparing the document. Crouse chose Select All Unused from the Swatches palette menu, and then he clicked the trash can icon in the Swatches palette to delete the selected swatches. Removing all unused swatches from the document made it easier to see the swatches that will be created later by Live Trace.

Crouse chose File > Place to select the original photograph of Mr. George and add the photo to the page.

2 Copying the image layer. To separate the foreground and background images, you can duplicate them while keeping them aligned. Drag the original layer (not just the image) to the New Layer icon in the Layers palette, then double-click the name to rename it.

To prevent changes to layers other than the one you're editing, click the lock column to lock any layers not in use. The background is edited in the next step, so lock the foreground layer at this time.

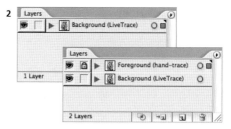

Layers palette before (top) and after (bottom) duplicating the image layer and locking the foreground layer

3 Tracing the background. Crouse selected the photo and chose Object > Live Trace > Tracing Options. You can produce results similar to Crouse's by applying settings like these: For Mode, choose Grayscale; for Max Colors, enter 3 (some images need more levels); and select Output to Swatches. Leave other options at their default settings. Click Trace to commit the settings. The tracing is live, so you can change the settings at any time by choosing Object > Live Trace > Tracing Options.

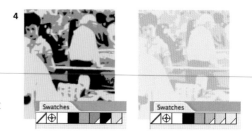

Tracing Options dialog box

4 Adjusting the background graphic's colors. To keep the viewer's focus on the subject, Crouse gave the background a light, low-contrast appearance. Selecting Output to Swatches in Step 3 added colors to the Swatches palette as global swatches applied to the Live Trace object. This is valuable because editing a global swatch updates all of its applied instances. To edit any of the new global swatches created by Live Trace, double-click them. In this case, the gray tones were changed to colors and lightened overall.

Before (left) and after (right) editing swatches output by Live Trace; white corners signify global swatches

Tracing Options button on the Control Palette, located to the right of the Preset pop-up menu

5 Simplifying the foreground copy for hand-tracing. In the Layers palette, lock the background layer and unlock the foreground. Select the foreground image and click the Tracing Options button on the Control Palette to edit the Live Trace settings for the selected image. Here, Max Colors was changed to 7, Blur to 1 px, Resample to 150 dpi, Path Fitting to 1 px, and Minimum Area to 10 px. The optimal values depend on the resolution of the image, so try different settings until you see what you want.

Detail of original image (left) and after adjusting for hand-tracing using Live Trace (right)

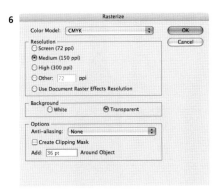

The Rasterize dialog box

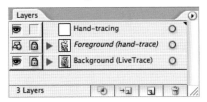

The Layers palette with the foreground tracing image layer set up as a template, and a new layer added to contain the hand-tracing

Completed tracing over the dimmed template (top), and with the template hidden to reveal the actual background (bottom)

6 Rasterizing the hand-tracing template. The Live Trace object contains many vector objects which could slow redraw. Converting it to a raster object simplifies the object and speeds screen redraw during hand-tracing. To rasterize the Live Trace object, select it and choose Object > Rasterize. Medium Resolution is a good compromise between a decent display speed and the ability to trace at high magnifications.

In the Layers palette, double-click the layer containing the foreground tracing image, select Template, and click OK. This locks and dims the layer, putting it in an ideal state for hand-tracing. Click the New Layer button to provide a layer to contain the paths that will be hand-traced.

7 Hand-tracing the foreground. Crouse used the Pen tool to hand-trace the template image, resulting in the foreground portrait. The goal of hand-tracing is to produce a personal interpretation of the original image, so Crouse didn't follow the template exactly; he added, edited, or removed paths as needed. Through his linework, Crouse enhanced and advanced the desired mood and feeling of the illustration and the physical and facial expressions of the subject.

When he was satisfied with his hand-tracing, Crouse used Save As to save a copy of his working file. With the original version saved, in this final copy of the file he deleted the hand-tracing template layer, leaving his hand-traced foreground over the Live Trace background.

Pre-processing a tracing image in Photoshop

Live Trace works by creating paths along significant changes in contrast. In some photos, the areas you want Live Trace to trace may not contain enough contrast. To address this, open the image in Photoshop and apply a Curves adjustment layer to increase or decrease image contrast or make other changes as needed. After you edit a placed image outside of Illustrator, use the Links palette in Illustrator to update the image link and the Live Trace object will also update.

Molding Mesh

Forming Bottles Using Gradient Mesh

Advanced Technique

Overview: *Create a basic rectangle; add mesh lines; use the Scale tool to move points in tandem; use the Direct Selection tool to edit paths; color the mesh; add finishing details.*

Yukio Miyamoto is one of the world's experts in creating objects using the Gradient Mesh tool. This wonderful collection of bottles was created for the book and CD that he and his wife Nabuko Miyamoto write and produce; published in Japan, the *Adobe Illustrator CS* book is an amazing compendium of Illustrator techniques.

Making a basic rectangle, adding mesh points where the shape will be contoured, using the Scale tool to move groups of points inward.

1 Creating mesh from rectangles. To create his complex mesh objects, Miyamoto begins with a colored rectangle. Then using the Gradient Mesh tool, he clicks on the rectangle to create basic horizontal mesh lines where he intends to modify the exterior shape of the object.

To narrow the bottle neck, Miyamoto then used the Direct Selection tool to select the anchor points at the top of the bottle. With these points selected he switched to the Scale tool. By default the Scale tool is centered on the object, so he grabbed one of the selected points and holding the Shift key, dragged towards the center of the bottle, narrowing the neck symmetrically. He also selected the bottom two points and dragged the points inward.

Using the Direct Selection tool to round curves, and adding new grid lines by clicking with the Gradient Mesh tool

2 Shaping mesh objects. To continue to transform your rectangle into a rounded bottle, you'll next modify the corner points along the edge into curves. Using the Convert Anchor Point tool (hidden under the Pen tool) and the Direct Selection tool, select anchor points, smooth anchor points and modify the corners to rounded curves.

Miyamoto smoothed curves at the bottom of the bottle, holding Shift to constrain the path curves.

With the new shape contour established, Miyamoto used the Gradient Mesh tool to click within the bottle to establish vertical mesh lines, aligned with the new curve at the bottom of the bottle.

3 Modifying the mesh lines to create distortion, shadows and highlights. Light reflects and refracts on glass bottles. Once the basic inner and outer topography of the bottle is in place, Miyamoto uses the Direct Selection tool to modify the mesh lines within the bottle to mimic the affects of light. Using the Direct Selection tool, select points and groups of points to adjust their position. Click on anchor points to activate their direction handles so you can modify the length and angle of the curves.

Once your mesh lines are in place, you can select individual or groups of points, or click in areas between points and adjust colors using the Color palette sliders. You can also click on a color swatch in the Swatches palette, or pick up colors from another object by clicking in on the color you want with the Eyedropper tool. Miyamoto used a photographic reference to help him decide where to place lights and darks.

4 Creating finishing details. Although Gradient Mesh objects are an astoundingly flexible and powerful drawing tool, sometimes it's necessary to create details in layers above the mesh object. To make selections and isolated viewings of the various objects easier, create new layers for your detail objects above your mesh objects. For the blue bottle (in a layer above the mesh), Miyamoto created a few punctuations of color and light using objects drawn with the Pen tool, and filled with solid colors or custom gradients. For his beer bottle Miyamoto created type shapes, for the small milk bottle he added additional rim colors, and for the green wine bottle he added more reflections and a raised inner bottom.

3

Coloring the bottle

The finished blue bottle mesh in outline, hidden, and in Preview with details on a layer above

4

The final bottles shown with the mesh layer in Outline mode, and the finishing details (mostly gradient-filled objects) in Preview mode

Intricate Patterns
Designing Complex Repeating Patterns

Advanced Technique

Overview: *Design a rough composition; define a confining pattern boundary and place behind all layers; use the box to generate crop marks; copy and position elements using crop marks for alignment; define and use the pattern.*

WEIMER

Top, arranging pattern elements into a basic design; bottom, adding the pattern tile rectangle behind the pattern elements

Creating crop marks based on selection of the pattern tile rectangle

Included with Illustrator are many wonderful patterns for you to use and customize, and *Illustrator Help* does a good job of explaining pattern-making basics. But what if you want to create a more complex pattern?

A simple trick with crop marks can help to simplify a tedious process of trial and error. With some help from author and consultant Sandee Cohen, Alan James Weimer used the following technique to design an intricate tile that prints seamlessly as a repeating pattern.

1 Designing your basic pattern, drawing a confining rectangle, then creating crop marks for registration. Create a design that will allow for some rearrangement of artwork elements. **Hint:** *Pattern tiles cannot contain linked images—to include a linked image in a pattern, select it and click Embed Image in the Control palette.*

Use the Rectangle tool to draw a box around the part of the image you would like to repeat. This rectangle defines the boundary of the pattern tile. Send the rectangle to the bottom of the Layers palette or to the bottom of your drawing layer (Object > Arrange > Send to Back). This boundary rectangle, which controls how your pattern repeats, must be an unstroked, unfilled, nonrotated, nonsheared object. Make certain this rectangle is selected, and select Filter >Create >Crop Marks. Last, Ungroup these marks (in the next step, you'll use the crop marks to align elements that extend past the pattern tile).

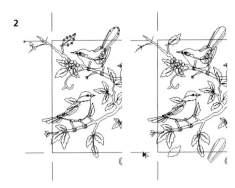

2 **Developing the repeating elements.** If your pattern has an element that extends beyond the edge of the pattern tile, you must copy that element and place it on the opposite side of the tile. For example, if a flower blossom extends below the tile, you must place a copy of the remainder of the blossom at the top of the tile, ensuring that the whole flower is visible when the pattern repeats. To do this, select an element that overlaps above or below the tile and then Shift-select the nearest horizontal crop mark (position the cursor on an endpoint of the crop mark). While pressing the Shift-Option or Shift-Alt keys (the Option/Alt keys copy the selections and the Shift key constrains dragging to vertical and horizontal directions), drag the element and crop mark upward until the cursor snaps to the endpoint of the upper horizontal crop mark. (For any element that overlaps the left or right side of the tile, select the element and the vertical crop mark and hold down Shift-Option/Shift-Alt as you drag them into position.)

Left, selecting the flower blossom and horizontal crop mark; right, after dragging a copy of the flower blossom and crop mark into position at the top of the pattern tile artwork

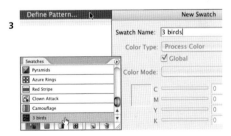

Finished artwork for the pattern tile, before turning into a pattern swatch in the Swatches palette

3 **Testing and optimizing your pattern.** To test your pattern, select your pattern elements (including the bounding rectangle), and either choose Edit >Define Pattern to name your pattern, or drag your selection to the Swatches palette (then double-click the swatch to customize its name). Create a new rectangle and select the pattern as your fill from the Swatches palette. Illustrator will fill the rectangle with your repeating pattern. If you redesign the pattern tile and then wish to update the pattern swatch, select your pattern elements again, but this time Option-drag/Alt-drag the elements onto the pattern swatch you made before.

Optimize your pattern for printing by deleting excess anchor points. Select pattern elements and use the Simplify command (Object >Path >Simplify).

Making a new swatch using Edit >Define Pattern

Speeding redraw with patterns

After filling an object with a pattern, speed up screen redraw by setting View to Outline mode, or by rasterizing a copy of the object (keep the original object unfilled in case you need to use it later).

Color Insert, *Page 7.* From *The Adobe Illustrator CS2 Wow! Book,* by Sharon Steuer.

Pattern Brushes

Creating Details with the Pattern Brush

MONROY

Overview: *Create interlocking chain links by drawing and cutting duplicate curve sections; select the link artwork and create a new Pattern brush; draw a path and paint it with the new brush.*

1

At the left, the ring drawn with the Ellipse tool and given a thick stroke; in the middle, the ellipse cut into four curve sections shown in Outline view (sections are separated to show them better); on the right, the four curve sections shown in Outline view, after using the Object > Path > Outline Stroke command

On the left, the two left curve sections copied and pasted, and colors changed to light brown in the middle; on the right, the two sections are slid to the right to form the right half link

On the left, the half-link selected and reflected using the Reflect tool (the X in the middle of the guide ellipse served as the axis); on the right, both half-links in position

One look at a Bert Monroy image and you will immediately recognize the intricacy and rich realism of his style of illustration. When crafting an image like the Rendezvous Cafe, Monroy travels between Illustrator and Photoshop, stopping long enough in Illustrator to construct the intricate shapes and details that turn his scenes into slices of life in Photoshop. The easel chain is one such detail that Monroy created in Illustrator using a custom-made Pattern brush.

1 Drawing, cutting, copying, and reflecting curves. To build a chain-link Pattern brush, Monroy first created one link that was interconnected with half-links on either side (the half-links would connect with other half-links to form the chain once the Pattern brush was applied to a path). To create the pattern unit with the Ellipse tool, begin the center link by drawing an ellipse with a thick stroke. Copy the ellipse, Paste in Back; then turn the ellipse into a guide (View > Guides > Make Guides). You'll use this guide later when making the half-links. Now select the original ellipse and use the Scissors tool to cut the ellipse near each of the four control points (choose View > Outline to better see the points). Shift-select the four curved paths with the Direct Selection tool and select Object > Path > Outline Stroke. Illustrator automatically constructs four closed-curve objects.

To make the right half-link, select the left two curve objects and duplicate them to make the right half-link by dragging the two objects to the right while holding down the Opt/Alt key; then change the color of the copies. For the left half-link, select the two curves you just dragged and colored, choose the Reflect tool, hold down the Opt/Alt key and click in the center of the ellipse guide (the center point is an **X**). In the Reflect dialog box, click the Vertical Axis button and click Copy to create a mirror-image of the right half-link for the left half-link.

Note: *The center link must be aligned exactly in-between the two half-links, so that the half-links join when applied to a path as a Pattern brush.*

2 Finishing the link. The two adjoining half-links should look like they're entwined with the link. Monroy selected the top objects of both the left and right half-links and moved them behind the center link (Object > Arrange > Send to Back). You can create a different look by selecting the top of the left half-link, and the bottom of the right half-link, and moving them to the back.

3 Making and using a Pattern brush. To make the brush, select the artwork and drag it into the Brushes palette. Choose New Pattern Brush in the New Brush dialog box; in the next dialog box, name the brush and click OK (leave the default settings as you find them). You can now apply the chain pattern to a path by selecting the path and clicking on the brush in the Brushes palette.

Depending on the size of your original links artwork, you may need to reduce the size of the brush artwork to fit the path better. You can do this by reducing the original artwork with the Scale tool and making a new brush, or by double-clicking the brush in the Brushes palette and editing the value in the Scale field of the dialog box.

2

Finished link artwork; at the left, the links as Monroy created them; at the right, an alternative version of the interconnected links

3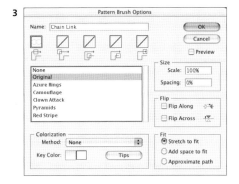

The Pattern Brush Options dialog box showing default settings

Original path on top; below, path painted with Chain Link Pattern brush

Drop Shadows

Even if your artwork is destined for Photoshop, you can make a drop shadow for it in Illustrator. Select the artwork, then choose Effect > Stylize > Drop Shadow. Copy the object (which automatically copies all of its appearances) and paste in Photoshop (Edit > Paste > Paste as Pixels).

Tinting a Scan

Adding a Color to a Grayscale Image

Advanced Technique

Overview: *Prepare a grayscale image; import the image into Illustrator; colorize the image; trim the artwork to the required shape; add a vignette.*

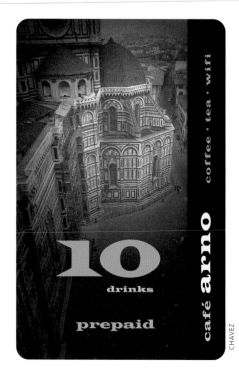

The original scanned image

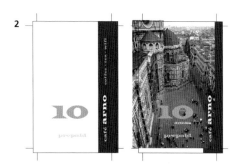

The layout (left) and the image placed in the layout, initially on top of the design (right)

Conrad Chavez created this concept for a prepaid coffee card that can use different background photographs. To preserve design flexibility, Chavez imported a grayscale version of the image and added color in Illustrator so that he could change the image color at any time.

1 Scanning and preparing the image. Chavez started by scanning a photograph and saving it as a grayscale image. Save the image in a format Illustrator can place, such as a TIFF or Photoshop file. If your original image is in color, you must first convert the image to grayscale in a program like Photoshop. Color images can't be tinted in Illustrator.

2 Importing the image. Chavez chose File > Place to import the image. In the Place dialog box, he disabled the Template and Replace checkboxes. He then positioned the image on the layout.

You can also use Adobe Bridge to browse a folder of images, then import the images you want by dragging them from Bridge to the Illustrator document window.

3 Colorizing the image. Chavez selected the image, clicked the Fill box in the toolbox, and then clicked a solid color swatch in the Swatches palette to tint the image. He had already applied the dark brown swatch to other elements in the design, unifying the composition.

If applying a color doesn't change the image, make sure the Fill box is active and that the image was saved as a true grayscale image, not as an RGB or CMYK image.

Colorizing the image (left) by selecting it and then clicking the dark brown solid color swatch on the Swatches palette (right)

4 Visualizing a trim. To preview the composition as it would appear after trimming, Chavez drew a rounded-corner rectangle at the trim size. With the rectangle in front of both the background image and the dark vertical rectangle, he selected all three objects and chose Object > Clipping Mask > Make, which created a clipping group.

Rounded-corner rectangle indicating final trim (left) and after clipping artwork to it (right)

5 Adding a vignette. Chavez created a vignette to better distinguish the foreground and background. He drew a new rectangle the size of the Artboard and used the Gradient palette to apply a radial gradient. He changed the gradient's default black slider to the same dark color swatch applied to the image. In the Control palette, he clicked Opacity and then chose Multiply from the pop-up menu to blend the gradient with the image under it.

The vignette needed to be behind all objects except the scan. In the Layers palette, Chavez not only dragged the vignette farther back in the stack but also into the clipping group, so that the vignette could be visualized within the temporary clipping group.

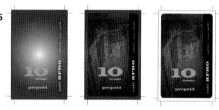

Applying a radial gradient to the new rectangle (left), applying the Multiply blending mode to the rectangle (right), and after dragging the vignette path into the clipping group (right)

Layers palette before (left) and after (right) dragging the vignette into the clipping group

6 Editing the vignette. Chavez decided to refine the composition by editing the vignette. He selected the vignette in the Layers palette and clicked the Gradient tool over the building to reposition the gradient center there. He dragged the Gradient palette sliders to widen both the light center and the dark edge of the gradient. Finally, to restore the bleed required for the press, Chavez selected the clipping group and chose Object > Clipping Mask > Release, and then he deleted his temporary clipping path.

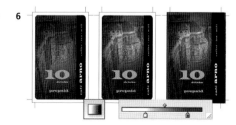

Before (top left) and after (top right) gradient edits: moving the radial gradient center with the Gradient tool (bottom left) and editing the Gradient palette's slider positions (bottom right); ready for prepress with mask deleted (top right)

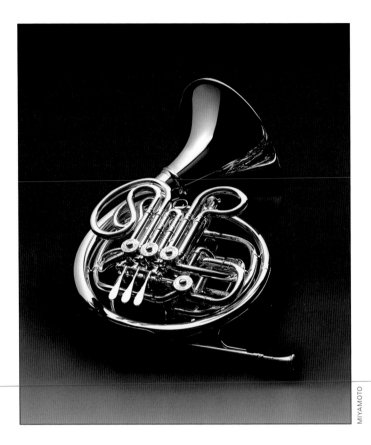

MIYAMOTO

Yukio Miyamoto

As with most of his mesh art, Yukio Miyamoto began this illustration of a Yamaha French horn by manually tracing over a photo with the Pen tool, then filling the objects with solid fills. In layers above the basic tracing, Miyamoto drew the reflections and details of the tubular structure and filled them with linear gradients. He used the Mesh tool to define several reflections within the horn, with the most obvious on the horn's bell. He then created other areas of reflection with clusters of solid and gradient-filled objects (as on the bell and the valves). Miyamoto made the background out of a large, rectangular, gradient mesh. Within this mesh,

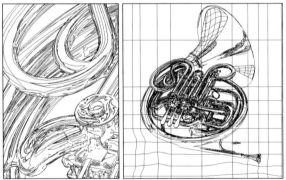

he created the horn's shadow. The magnificent level of detail is evident even when the image is viewed in Outline mode (a detail is shown directly above left; the full image in Outline is above right).

Color Insert, *Page 12*. From *The Adobe Illustrator CS2 Wow! Book*, by Sharon Steuer.

Brad Neal

Brad Neal combined an attention to detail with Illustrator's wide range of drawing and rendering tools to create this photo-realistic image of a Ford Taurus stock car. Beginning with a contour shape filled with a flat color, Neal overlaid a series of custom blends to replicate the subtle modeling of the car's surface. Neal simulated the grill work at the front of the car by overlaying a series of four dashed stroked paths. The racing logos on the side of the car were drawn by hand, grouped, and positioned using the Shear tool. The Taurus, Valvoline, and Goodyear logos were fitted to the contour of the body with the help of the Envelope Distort tool. To achieve the realistic look of the front right wheel, Neal created custom blends with outer edges that blended smoothly into the flat color of the underlying shapes. Neal created a drop shadow for the car using a carefully controlled blend. This blend had an inner path that contained a solid black fill that blended to white as it approached the outer edge.

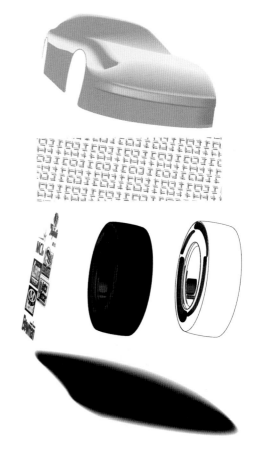

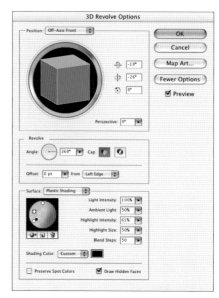

Mordy Golding

To demonstrate the 3D effect of Illustrator CS for Adobe Systems, Inc., Mordy Golding created a wine label and then dragged the label to the Symbols palette (so he could use it next to create the 3D rendering). He drew a half-bottle shape and selected Effect > 3D > Revolve. In the 3D Revolve Options dialog box, Golding clicked the Preview checkbox and then clicked on the Map Art button. From the Map Art dialog box's Symbol menu, he selected the wine label symbol he had created previously. Back in the 3D Revolve Options dialog box, Golding adjusted the preview cube, changing the rotation angles until he was satisfied with the look of the bottle. He finished the effect by adding lights, using the New Light icon in the Surface panel of the dialog box; this created the cascading highlights on the bottle. After creating the cork, using the same technique as he used for the bottle, Golding selected the bottle, moved it above the cork, and changed its opacity to 94% in the Transparency palette.

GOLDING / ADOBE SYSTEMS, INC.

Color Insert, *Page 14*. From *The Adobe Illustrator CS2 Wow! Book*, by Sharon Steuer.

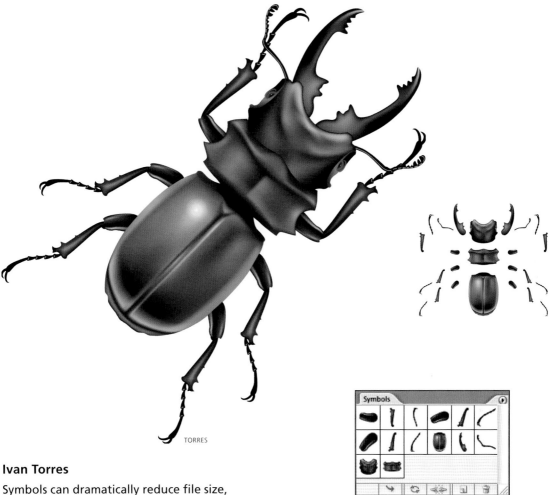

TORRES

Ivan Torres

Symbols can dramatically reduce file size, especially in art destined for the Web. Artist Ivan Torres began this beetle by first creating individual body parts, many of which were complex gradient meshes. Then he converted the parts into symbols by dragging and dropping each onto the Symbols palette. To assemble the beetle from body part symbols, Torres dragged the parts from the Symbols palette and dropped them on the Artboard, creating instances of the symbols. To create the body parts with mirrored twins on opposite sides of the beetle body, he used the Reflect tool, chose Vertical and clicked Copy. When he had completed the illustration, Torres chose File > Save for Web and selected SWF from the format pop-up, and AI File to SWF File from the pop-up below that. After opening Flash (SWF), Torres imported the Illustrator Flash file (File > Import) and then used Flash's tools to manipulate the body part symbols to create an interactive animation.

Color Insert, *Page 15.* From *The Adobe Illustrator CS2 Wow! Book*, by Sharon Steuer.

Steven Gordon / Cartagram

When you mix Illustrator's brushes with live effects, you can transform the lettering of a font into art that looks hand-rendered with traditional pens and brushes. To begin this map title, Steven Gordon typed "Yakima" and then chose a calligraphic font, Zapfino, at 72 points. In the Character palette, he adjusted kerning to tighten the space between several pairs of letter characters. With the text object selected and the Appearance palette open, Gordon chose Add New Fill from the palette's Options menu and gave the new fill a dark magenta color. He duplicated the fill by clicking on the Duplicate Selected Item icon at the bottom of the palette, and then gave the duplicate a pale blue color. Lastly, he clicked on a brush in the Brushes palette and chose the Dry Ink brush.

He selected a dark blue color for the brush. Because the brush strokes were too large for the lettering effect he wanted, Gordon double-clicked the brush name in the Appearance palette, resized its width to 60% of the default size, and clicked to apply it to existing objects. To further customize the title, Gordon selected the pale blue fill in the Appearance palette, offset the fill and distorted the fill's edges using the Transform and Roughen commands from the Effect > Distort and Transform menu. He also reduced opacity by moving the Opacity slider in the Transparency palette to 35%. To finish, Gordon selected the bottom fill and applied the Roughen command from the Effect > Distort and Transform menu to tightly erode the fill's edges.

CHAPTER 6

Typography

Adobe Illustrator is a top-notch illustration tool, but it is also capable of setting professional-level type—its typography features are on par with those found in the award-winning Adobe InDesign.

In truth, prior to Illustrator CS, setting type in Illustrator was something you did only if you really had to. Things like setting columns of type, creating lists with tab leaders, or creating text wraps were either impossible or extremely difficult to do and control. With the release of Illustrator CS, however, Adobe has replaced an aging text engine with a modern, powerful one that offers features like paragraph style sheets, optical kerning, and OpenType support. Even more important, this new text engine brings a level of global technology to Illustrator that enables seamless integration across multiple systems and languages.

In this chapter, we'll explore some of these important technologies, like Unicode compliance, as well as some of the new typography features found in Illustrator. Toward the end of the chapter, we'll discuss a very important side effect of all of this new technology—backward compatibility with previous versions of Illustrator.

GLOBAL TEXT SUPPORT WITH UNICODE

For more information on the Unicode standard, visit www.unicode.org.

When you use your keyboard to type words on your computer, each character that you type is stored on your computer by a number. Every font also has a number assigned to each of its characters. This method of mapping characters to numbers is called *character encoding*. The idea is that when you type an "a," your computer matches up its code with the code in the selected font, and an "a" shows up on your screen. Simple, right?

Besides Unicode support, Illustrator also has fantastic support for Asian languages and type features such as Mojikumi, Kinsoku, and Composite Fonts. To activate these extended features in the English language version of Illustrator, check the Show Asian Options option in the Type preferences panel.

The problem is that not every computer uses the same encoding system. For example, Mac and Windows use different character encodings. Operating systems in different languages and countries around the world also use a variety of different encodings. Conflicts also exist in that one system may encode a certain character with a number, whereas another system may have a completely different character encoded for that same number. Because there are so many different ways of encoding characters, you can run into a situation where you create a file on one computer, and simply opening that same file on a different computer results in words not appearing correctly. If you've ever typed something on Windows and transferred it to a Mac and noticed that certain characters appear as question marks or disappear completely, you can now understand why that happened.

In 1991, a standard was formed called Unicode, which, as its name implies, is a single encoding that can be used to describe every single character, in any language, on any computer platform. The new text engine that was introduced in Illustrator CS uses Unicode, and if you use Unicode-compliant fonts to create your documents, you can pass your documents across the world and have them display correctly on any computer.

THE WAY OF THE FONT

Have you heard about the latest reality show? Ten designers have to create a logo, but first they have to get their fonts to work on their computers.

Seriously though, you'd think that in a day and age where we can put men on the moon and do just about anything wirelessly, we would have figured out the whole font thing by now. As you will soon learn, there are different font formats that are available, and each offers different capabilities. In addition, Illustrator is specifically sensitive to corrupt fonts and although a bad font may work in other applications, it can still cause problems with Illustrator. Several different font-management utilities are available, including Suitcase, Font Reserve, and Font Agent, and each of these has components to help you identify and repair problematic fonts.

More importantly, different font formats are available. As a designer, you may be familiar with PostScript Type 1 fonts, TrueType fonts, or Multiple Master fonts. Adobe reduced support for Multiple Master fonts with the release of Illustrator CS, and although those fonts might still work in Illustrator CS2, there's no way to take advantage of the extended technology that they were meant to bring. TrueType fonts aren't used as much in print workflows because when they were first introduced, they weren't as reliable as PostScript Type 1 fonts (although nowadays, those problems no longer exist). Because of this, PostScript Type 1 fonts have always been perceived as being higher quality fonts.

 If you find that Illustrator is crashing frequently, the cause might be a corrupt font. By turning off all fonts and activating them one by one, you can help troubleshoot these issues and locate a problematic font.

Another font type, called OpenType, has introduced a new era in working with fonts, bringing extended functionality and even higher quality to the desktop.

What's Your Type?

I once had a bumper sticker that declared, "Whoever dies with the most fonts, wins." There's nothing a designer loves more than a unique font that no one else has. At the same time, with so many fonts out there, you want to make sure that you're using high-quality fonts. These days, fonts come in several different formats:

- **PostScript Type 1.** Originally developed by Adobe, PostScript Type 1 fonts consist of a printer or outline font, a screen or bitmap font, and usually a font metrics file (an .afm file). Type 1 fonts have been considered the high-quality standard over the years, although OpenType is changing that.

- **TrueType.** Originally developed by Apple and Microsoft, the intent of TrueType was to overtake the Type 1 font standard. A TrueType font consists of a single file. TrueType fonts have traditionally been prevalent on Windows computers.

- **Multiple Master.** Originally developed by Adobe, Multiple Master fonts were intended to give the designer creative freedom to scale fonts to custom widths and weights. They are actually a flavor of Type 1 fonts. Some Multiple Master fonts also allows designers to scale serifs as well. Adobe has since dropped development and support for this format.

- **OpenType.** Originally developed by Adobe and Microsoft, the intent of OpenType is to create a universal font format that includes the benefits of Type 1 and TrueType font technologies. In fact, an OpenType font can contain either Type 1 or TrueType outlines. An OpenType font is Unicode-compliant, cross-platform, and consists of a single font file.

Introducing OpenType

 At one time, Adobe offered certain fonts in "expert" collections; these were created because the type designer wanted to create additional glyphs and characters but ran out of space. Creating an expert version of the font gave the designer another 256 glyphs to work with.

Although PostScript Type 1 fonts are great, they have some issues and limitations, which make them difficult to use. For one, Type 1 fonts are not Unicode-compliant. Second, Type 1 fonts are platform dependent, which means that if you have the Mac version of a font, you can only use that font on a Mac. You need to purchase a Windows version of a Type 1 font to use it on a Windows computer. Additionally, a Type 1 font is made up two different files: a screen font and a printer font, both of which you must have to correctly print a file. If you forget to send either of these files to a printer, the file won't print. Finally, a Type 1 font is limited to 256 glyphs per font. A *glyph* is a specific graphical representation of a character. For a given character, there may be a default glyph, and then alternates. For example, a ligature is a glyph that represents multiple characters. Although the English language doesn't normally require that many glyphs, some languages, like Japanese, Chinese, and Korean, are severely affected by this limitation.

OpenType fonts address all of these limitations and offer extended functionality. OpenType fonts are Unicode compliant, are platform independent (you can use the same font file on both Windows and Mac), and consist of a single font file (both printer and screen fonts are embedded into a single file). In addition, OpenType can contain over 65,000 glyphs in a single font. With the 256 glyph limit gone, type designers can create fonts with extended character sets that include real small caps, fractions, swash characters, and anything else they dream up.

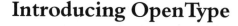 OpenType fonts work with applications that don't support OpenType, but those apps only see the first 256 glyphs in that font.

The good news is that you already have OpenType fonts! Illustrator (whether you bought it separately or as a part of the Adobe Creative Suite) automatically installs 100 OpenType fonts on your computer. You can quickly identify OpenType fonts in two ways: a green "O" icon appears to the left of their font names when you're scrolling through the font menu (**Figure 6.1**); or they end in the letters *Std* (standard) or *Pro*. OpenType Pro fonts contain extended character sets.

OpenType + Illustrator = Intelligent Fonts

Although the technological benefits of OpenType fonts are nice, they are just half the story. From a design perspective, OpenType fonts also offer superior typographical functionality through something called *automatic glyph replacement*.

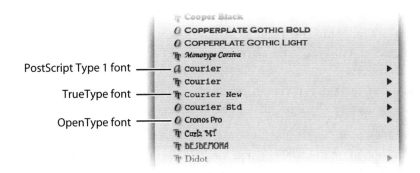

PostScript Type 1 font

TrueType font

OpenType font

Figure 6.1 Illustrator's WYSIWYG font menu not only displays a preview of the font, but also displays icons to identify the font type—this is especially helpful when you have multiple versions of a font.

To best describe what automatic glyph replacement is, we'll use ligatures as an example. A ligature is a special combination of characters that don't ordinarily look that great when they appear together. For example, common ligatures include fi or fl where the lowercase f collides or overlaps the following i or l character. So type designers create a new glyph, called a ligature, which somehow connects the two letters and makes them aesthetically pleasing (**Figure 6.2**).

finish finish

Figure 6.2 An f and an i character as they appear together in a word (left) and appearing combined as a ligature in the same word (right).

The way ligatures are traditionally applied, a designer locates two characters that appear together, and if the font has a ligature for that character pair, he or she manually deletes the two characters and replaces them with the ligature character. Besides the extra time it takes to make this switch, there are two issues with this method. First of all, a spell check tool will find errors when ligatures are used, because the spell check sees a ligature character and not two separate letters. Second, if you change the font of your text to a typeface that doesn't have a ligature character, you end up with a garbage character where the ligature was.

Automatic glyph replacement is when Illustrator automatically inserts a ligature for you, as you type, when you're using an OpenType font. Illustrator watches as you enter text and if it finds a ligature in the font you are using for the characters you type, it automatically swaps the individual characters for the ligature. But that isn't even the cool part. Even though the ligature appears on your screen and prints, Illustrator still sees it as two separate characters (you can even place your cursor between the two characters). That means if you run spell check, you won't get a spelling error, nor will you run into issues if you change fonts. If the font you switch to doesn't have a ligature character, the individual characters are displayed.

What's astounding is that if you take into account that each OpenType font can contain up to 65,000 glyphs, you'll realize that this functionality goes way beyond simple ligatures. Many OpenType fonts can also automatically replace fractions, ordinals, swash characters, real small caps, discretionary ligatures, contextual alternates, and more. Of course, the beauty of this functionality is that it happens automatically, so you don't have to even search through a font to find these special characters.

Using the OpenType Palette

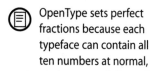

OpenType sets perfect fractions because each typeface can contain all ten numbers at normal, numerator, and denominator sizes.

Although automatic glyph replacement is nice, giving a computer program total control over how your text appears is something that should only exist in the movies. In real life, a designer has complete control over a project. Choose Window > Type > OpenType to bring up the OpenType palette where you can specify exactly where and how Illustrator replaces glyphs. When text that is styled with an OpenType font is chosen, you can use the eight icons at the bottom of the palette to turn on and off the automatic glyph replacement for each kind of feature (**Figure 6.3**). If icons appear grayed out, that indicates the font you have chosen doesn't contain those kinds of glyphs.

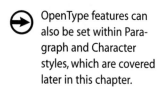

OpenType features can also be set within Paragraph and Character styles, which are covered later in this chapter.

The nice thing about using the OpenType palette is that you can experiment with different type treatments simply by toggling a few of the palette icons. You can still use Type 1 and TrueType fonts with Illustrator of course, and you can even mix them within the same document, but the OpenType palette only works with OpenType fonts.

Figure 6.3 With text selected, clicking the different icons in the OpenType palette gives you instant feedback on the different glyphs available in a particular OpenType font.

Finding Glyphs and Fonts

If you are trying to find a specific glyph in a font, it is usually a tiresome game of trying to find the right keystroke combination. If you've ever run your fingers across the keyboard, typing every key just to find where the square box is in the Zapf Dingbats typeface (lowercase "n" by the way), you know what we mean.

The reality is, because there can be up to 65,000 glyphs in a font, it can be almost impossible to find the glyph you need. More to the point, how do you even know what glyphs are in a font to begin with? The answer is that you use the Glyphs palette.

The Glyphs Palette

You can see a graphic representation of all of the glyphs in any font installed on your computer by opening the Glyphs palette. To do so, choose Type > Glyphs.

You can resize the Glyphs palette by dragging from the lower right corner. By clicking on the two icons at the bottom right side of the palette, you can make the previews bigger and smaller. You can choose any font (even non-OpenType ones) from the pop-up at the bottom of the palette, and you can use the pop-up menu at the top of the palette to show only specific kinds of characters in a chosen font. If your text cursor is in a text object on your artboard, double-clicking any icon in the Glyphs palette places that glyph within your text. If an icon contains a small black arrow in its lower right corner, that indicates alternate glyphs for that character (**Figure 6.4**).

Figure 6.4 OpenType fonts can contain a variety of glyphs for each character, including small caps, old style, numerator, and denominator versions.

The Find Font Dialog

Knowing what fonts are used in your document is important when you're sending files out for others to use, especially printers. There are also times when it might be necessary to switch fonts, either when you want to replace a Type 1 font with an OpenType version, or if you are missing fonts and want to substitute them for ones that you have installed on your computer.

Choose Type > Find Font to open the Find Font dialog where you can see a list of all fonts used in an open document. An icon at the far right of each listing identifies the type of font. The bottom portion of the dialog allows you to replace fonts with those that already exist in the document or with those that are installed on your computer (**Figure 6.5**). You can also use the check boxes to filter the kinds of fonts that you want to see listed.

Figure 6.5 The Find Font dialog is great for replacing fonts, but even better for quickly seeing all the fonts used in a document.

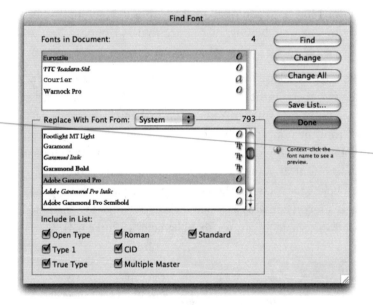

SPECIFYING CHARACTER AND PARAGRAPH OPTIONS

Just about all of the text settings you would expect to find in a page layout program are present in Illustrator. You can find these settings in the Control palette when you select the Type tool, or in the Character and Paragraph palettes, both of which you can find in the Window > Type submenu.

The Character Palette

The Character palette allows you to specify font family and font style (italic, bold, etc.) as well as the settings for type size and leading (pronounced *ledding*, which controls the vertical distance from one baseline to the next). You can also specify kerning, which is the amount of space that appears between individual text characters (see the sidebar entitled "Optical Kerning"), and the tracking, which is the amount of space that appears between characters over a range of text (entire words, paragraphs, etc.).

Horizontal and vertical scaling can make type appear more narrower or wider, although most designers avoid these settings because they can distort text. Use the condensed or extended versions of fonts instead, if they are available. You can apply the baseline shift setting to individual characters and use it to adjust where the selected text sits relative to the baseline of the type object. The character rotation setting allows you to rotate individual characters within a text string, although you should be aware that you'll most likely need to perform manual kerning when you use this setting. You can specify whether you want selected text underlined or crossed out (the strikethrough feature), and you can also choose from the language pop-up menu to indicate to Illustrator what language the selected text is (**Figure 6.6**). This is helpful for hyphenation and spelling dictionaries (discussed later in this chapter).

Figure 6.6 When creating multilingual documents, choosing a language for text tells Illustrator which spelling and hyphenation dictionaries to use.

Optical Kerning

Getting just the right kerning is critical when you're working with logos and headlines; it can often mean the difference between text that is easy to read or difficult to understand. Kerning is usually set in a typeface automatically and described in a metrics file that identifies the amount of space that each letter has. Some font designers also include kerning pairs, which are letters that have natural white space between them when set side by side (the letters V and A are the most commonly used example of this).

Illustrator has a setting in the Kerning field of the Character palette called Optical, which performs kerning automatically. Rather than using metrics tables to define the space between letters, Illustrator looks at the actual glyph shapes and kerns the characters as they appear to the eye (**Figure 6.7**). There are two immediate benefits of using optical kerning.

Figure 6.7 The word on the top is set to Auto kerning and is using metrics to determine kerning. Notice the open space between the "m" and the "u" and how the "u" almost touches the base of the "s." The word on the bottom is set to Optical kerning. Notice how the letters appear evenly spaced.

$$\text{mustard}$$
$$\text{mustard}$$

First, you can apply optical kerning to any text in your file—even body copy or the 4-point legal text that appears at the bottom of an advertisement. Although designers spend time kerning logos and headlines, it's too time consuming to kern all of the text in your file. With optical kerning, you can kern all of the text in your document with a single click. Optical kerning can even be specified in a character or paragraph style.

Second, kerning applied by hand is only good for the typeface you've chosen. Once you change your text to use a different typeface, you need to redo the kerning. When using optical kerning, Illustrator automatically makes adjustments because it is always using the visual appearance of the text to do the kerning.

Of course, you can always override or make additional adjustments to optically kerned text. Once you've specified optical kerning to text, you can kern that text as you would normally. Generally, for well-designed fonts, metrics kerning is superior to optical. But optical kerning is very useful for poorly made fonts (almost every shareware font, for instance). It's also handy for specific pairs that the type designer may have missed.

There is one case where optical kerning can work against you, and that's when you're using the underscore character to create fields when you're designing forms. With optical kerning turned on, the underscore characters won't touch each other; the result is what appears to be a dashed line. However, you can select the underscore characters and change the kerning to the Auto setting to get the appearance of a solid line (**Figure 6.8**).

Figure 6.8 The word on top is set to Auto kerning, and the underscore characters appear as one line. The word on the bottom is set to Optical kerning and the underscores appear as a dashed line.

Account:_____

Account:_____

The Paragraph Palette

The Paragraph palette allows you to choose between seven different ways to align your text. You can also specify left, right, and first line indents and add space before or after paragraphs. There's also a check box to enable/disable hyphenation for the selected paragraph(s).

Through the Paragraph palette flyout menu, you can also choose to use the Adobe Single-line or the Adobe Every-line composer to determine how line breaks are specified in a paragraph of text (see the following Featured Match-Up sidebar).

Setting Tabs

To create tab settings in Illustrator, select a Path Type or Area Type object and choose Window > Type > Tabs. Clicking the magnet icon at the far right of the palette aligns the palette with your selected text. Choose between one of the four kinds of tabs (left, center, right, and decimal) and click the ruler to add a tab. As you drag a tab on the ruler, a vertical line appears on screen to help you visualize where the tab stop will be (**Figure 6.9**). You can add up to 99 tabs on a single line (if you can find a page big enough), and to delete a tab, simply drag it off the ruler. Clicking a tab selects it and you can specify an exact coordinate for it if you don't have a steady hand. Additionally, you can specify any character as a leader; doing so fills up the space between tabs with the specified character.

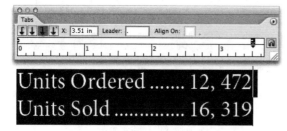

Figure 6.9 Setting tabs in previous versions of Illustrator was never fun. Now, it's easy to align tabs perfectly.

Featured Match-Up: Adobe Single-Line Composer vs. Adobe Every-Line Composer

When good designers talk about setting a nice paragraph of text, they refer to something called the color of the type. In this case, they aren't referring to black, blue, or yellow. Rather, they are talking about how readable the text is, which is heavily influenced by the spacing that appears between letters and words, and how text is broken from line to line. It is especially common to see *rivers* in justified text, which are areas of white space that seem to connect from line to line so that the eye sees these when you are looking at the paragraph.

Using a technology that first appeared in InDesign, Illustrator has two "engines" that you can use to compose a paragraph of text. The Adobe Single-line composer looks at each line as it flows text into an Area Type object. Based on hyphenation and justification settings, as well as on font and point size, the Single-line composer determines how many words can fit on each line. It does so by looking at the first line, flowing the text, then moving on to the next line, and so on. Once a line of text has been set, it's as if Illustrator isn't even aware of its existence. Sometimes, the result is a line that doesn't fit right. As a designer, you may look at such a line and manually break it differently by adding a forced line break somewhere in the paragraph in an attempt to create better spacing.

In contrast, the Adobe Every-line composer looks at the entire paragraph as it flows text into an Area Type object. As it composes type, Illustrator analyzes the previous lines and sees if it can get better spacing, fewer hyphens, etc. The result is a paragraph of text that has superior color and that requires less manual work from the designer (**Figure 6.10**).

One thing to keep in mind is that with the Every-line composer, adding a manual line break may result in text reflowing above your cursor, not just after it. This happens because Illustrator is relentless in trying to set the perfect paragraph of text; by making a forced line break, you've changed the layout of the paragraph. If you are manually breaking lines in a paragraph of text, you should consider using the Adobe Single-line composer.

Figure 6.10 The paragraph on the left was set using the Single-line composer and the paragraph on the right, which has fewer spacing problems and a more even look, was set using the Every-line composer.

At its Worldwide Developer Conference today, Apple® announced plans to deliver models of its Macintosh® computers using Intel® microprocessors by this time next year, and to transition all of its Macs to using Intel microprocessors by the end of 2007. Apple previewed a version of its critically acclaimed operating system, Mac OS® X Tiger, running on an Intel-based Mac® to the over 3,800 developers attending CEO Steve Jobs' keynote address. Apple also announced the availability of a Developer Transition Kit, consisting of an Intel-based Mac development system along with preview versions of Apple's software, which will allow developers to prepare versions of their applications which will run on both PowerPC and Intel-based Macs.

At its Worldwide Developer Conference today, Apple® announced plans to deliver models of its Macintosh® computers using Intel® microprocessors by this time next year, and to transition all of its Macs to using Intel microprocessors by the end of 2007. Apple previewed a version of its critically acclaimed operating system, Mac OS® X Tiger, running on an Intel-based Mac® to the over 3,800 developers attending CEO Steve Jobs' keynote address. Apple also announced the availability of a Developer Transition Kit, consisting of an Intel-based Mac development system along with preview versions of Apple's software, which will allow developers to prepare versions of their applications which will run on both PowerPC and Intel-based Macs.

DEFINING TEXT STYLES

Sure, there are lots of text settings, and having to constantly choose between them can make design work boring and time consuming. Have no fear, though, paragraph and characters styles can get you back to having fun designing in no time. Similar to page layout applications, you can define a style that stores paragraph- and character-based settings, which you can apply to selected text with the click of a button. In Chapter 3, *Objects, Groups, and Layers*, you learned how to create Graphic Styles, which is similar in concept.

To define a paragraph or character style, you can use one of two methods. The first is what some call the "show me" way, where you style text on your artboard in the usual way. Once you've got your text styled the way you want, you select the text and click the New Style button in either the Paragraph Styles or Characters Styles palette. This way is more visual and allows you to experiment with ideas before committing to creating a particular style. The second way is referred to as the "flying blind" method, where you create a new style and then double-click the style name in the palette to define the settings for that style (**Figure 6.11**). This second way is useful when you already have a pretty good idea of what settings you want to define in the style.

Everything that we've discussed in this chapter with regards to styling text can be stored as an attribute in a paragraph or character style. Once a style is defined, you can apply the style to selected text just by clicking the style name in the Character Styles or Paragraph Styles palette. To modify a style, double-click its name, and when you've made changes, any text that has that style applied in your document is updated with the changes.

 Some people who use page layout programs refer to paragraph styles as text style sheets.

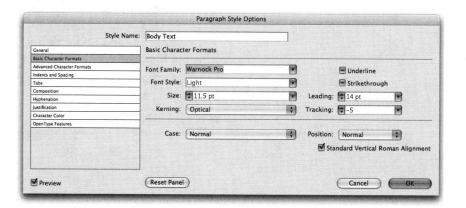

Figure 6.11 When flying blind, you can quickly specify font style settings in the Paragraph Style Options dialog.

WORKING WITH AREA TYPE

If a style appears with a plus sign after its name, that indicates that the selected text contains an override, or a setting that doesn't match the style. Pressing the Option (Alt) button while clicking the style name clears the override.

In Chapter 2, *Vectors 101*, you learned the differences between point type and area type (or point text and area text). Because area type has more structure than point type, you will find that area type has many features that you would expect to find in a page layout application. For example, an Area Type object can contain multiple columns of text within a single frame and can flow text from one frame to another, which is called *text threading*.

Creating and Editing Text Threads

Text that flows across multiple type objects is called a *text thread*. In previous versions of Illustrator, this was called *linking text boxes* and was difficult to work with. Taking a note from its sister application InDesign, Illustrator CS2 now makes it possible to easily manage text threads.

An Area Type object always displays two boxes on its path, one located at the upper left of the object, called the *in port*, and one located at the lower right, referred to as the *out port* (**Figure 6.12**). Text flows into an Area Type object through the in port and exits the object via the out port. The ports themselves are also used to control text threads.

Figure 6.12 Every Area Type object in Illustrator has an in port and an out port.

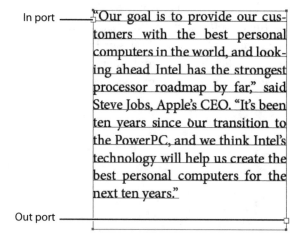

To create a new text thread, you must first have an existing text object to work with.

1. First, either use the Type tool to drag out an Area Type object, or click any closed vector path with the Type tool to convert the shape to an Area Type object.

2. Switch to the Selection tool and select the Area Type object.

    With the object selected, you'll see the in and out ports, of which both will be empty (colored white). An empty in port indicates the beginning of the story and an empty out port indicates the end of a story.

3. Using the Selection tool, click the Area Type object's out port and you'll notice your cursor changes to the place text icon.

4. At this point, you can either click an existing closed vector path or you can click and drag on an empty area on the artboard to create a second Area Type object. The two objects are now linked together.

You can see that the objects are linked because the out port of the first object and the in port of the second object are filled with a blue arrow. A line connects the two ports so that you can easily identify the direction of a thread when the Area Type objects are selected (**Figure 6.13**). To turn this preview off, choose View > Hide Text Threads.

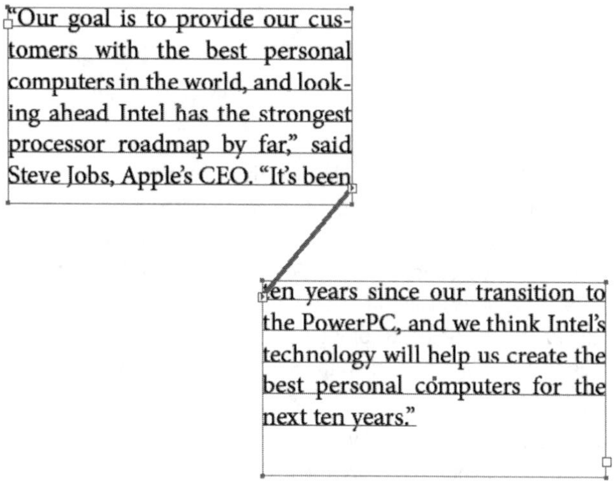

"Our goal is to provide our customers with the best personal computers in the world, and looking ahead Intel has the strongest processor roadmap by far," said Steve Jobs, Apple's CEO. "It's been

ten years since our transition to the PowerPC, and we think Intel's technology will help us create the best personal computers for the next ten years."

Figure 6.13 A blue arrow and a connecting line help identify the direction of a text thread.

You can also extend a text thread from the beginning of a story by clicking the empty in port and then drawing a new Area Type object.

You can add as many objects to a text thread as you'd like. To remove an object from a text thread, simply select it and press the Delete key on your keyboard. Illustrator automatically updates the thread with the remaining objects for you. To add a new Area Type object in the middle of an existing thread, you can always click the out port (even though it has a blue arrow in it), and drag out a new text object, which will be inserted into the thread.

Because Area Type objects are enclosed areas, there is a finite amount of text that can fit within them. *Overset text* is what happens when you have an Area Type object that has more text than it can handle and doesn't have another text object to link to. An object's out port displays a red plus sign to indicate where overset text exists (**Figure 6.14**). When working with objects that contain overset text, you can either edit the text so that there are fewer words, enlarge the Area Type object to allow for more text, or create a thread and link the object with other text objects.

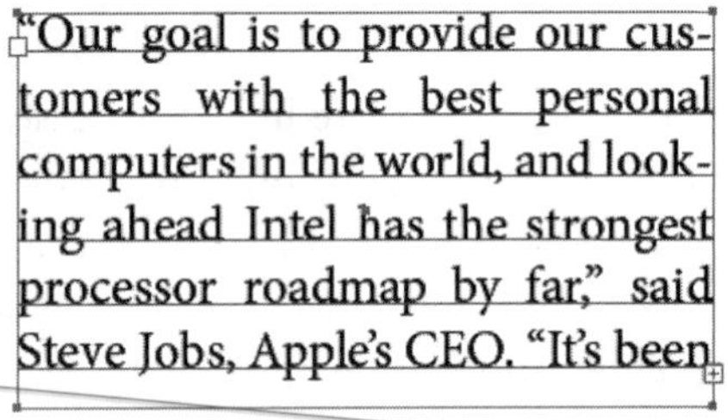

Figure 6.14 A production artist never wants to see one of these. The plus sign in the out port indicates that there is overset text and it could mean text reflow has occurred.

"Our goal is to provide our customers with the best personal computers in the world, and looking ahead Intel has the strongest processor roadmap by far," said Steve Jobs, Apple's CEO. "It's been

Transforming Type

When you have the bounding box option turn on (View > Show Bounding Box), you can use the Selection tool to resize text objects, but there's a difference between transforming Point Type and Area Type objects in this way. When you are working with a Point Type object, the bounding box that appears around the text gives the illusion of an Area Type object (sans in and out ports). When you use the Selection tool to scale the Point Type object by dragging on any of the eight handles, the text scales in size as well. If you don't hold the Shift key while scaling, the text will not scale in proportion.

In contrast, when you select an Area Type object with the Selection tool, you can click and drag on any of the eight handles to resize the text frame, but the text itself that resides inside the Area Type object will not be scaled.

Area Type Options

One of the benefits of working with area type is that you can easily define the area in which the text will be contained. You can also specify many different settings as to how text will fill this defined area, which you can access by selecting an Area Type object and choosing Type > Area Type Options.

In the Area Type Options dialog, you can adjust the overall width and height of the Area Type object, as well as specify both rows and columns. The *Gutter value* determines the amount of space that appears between each row or column. The *Inset Spacing setting* determines the amount of space that appears between the border of the actual Area Type object and where the text itself begins. You can think of it like margins that are specific to this Area Type object. You can also choose from a variety of settings of where the first baseline is calculated. By specifying a text flow, you can also control if text flows from column to column or row to row. Check the Preview button so that you can preview the changes you make before you apply them.

Achieving Perfect Alignment

As designers, we are extremely particular about the appearance of the art we create. Setting type can present a designer with a variety of challenges because each character of each font is different. Even though a column of text is set to be justified, that doesn't mean that from a visual perspective, it will appear so. Punctuation and special characters can present optical illusions and make text appear as though it is set incorrectly, although mathematically, it is set correctly. Because of these issues, a designer may struggle to align text so that punctuation marks sit just outside the actual margin of text to ensure a clear line that the human eye can follow.

However, this sort of struggling is no longer necessary because Illustrator has two features that take care of these optical issues. With an Area Type object selected, you can choose Type > Optical Margin Alignment to have Illustrator make sure that margins on both sides of an Area Type object are visually straight from a design perspective (not a mathematical one). Additionally, you can select an Area Type object and choose Window > Type > Paragraph to open the Paragraph palette. Then, choose Roman Hanging Punctuation from the Paragraph palette menu to force all punctuation marks like commas, periods, and quote marks to appear outside the margin of the text at the beginning and end of a line (**Figure 6.15**, next page).

Figure 6.15 The Roman Hanging Punctuation setting makes setting great-looking text almost too easy.

"Our goal is to provide our customers with the best personal computers in the world, and looking ahead Intel has the strongest processor roadmap by far," said Steve Jobs, Apple's CEO. "It's been ten years since our transition to the PowerPC, and we think Intel's technology will help us create the best personal computers for the next ten years."

Putting Type on a Path

Having text follow along a path is nothing new to Illustrator users. However, if you've used Illustrator before, you'll find that since Illustrator CS, type on a path is implemented quite differently than in previous versions—to the point where it might even seem like a new feature.

To make it easier to learn how to use this feature, you will start by creating type on an open path. After you've done this, you will understand how to perform the same function on a closed path.

Everything you're learning about type on a path here can be applied to InDesign as well, because the functionality is identical to Illustrator.

1. Using your tool of choice, create an open path, or you can select an open path that already exists on your artboard.

2. Choose the Type tool and move your cursor so that it touches the path and changes to the Type on a Path tool icon, with a line through the icon.

3. Click the path to create a Path Type object.

   This action removes any Stroke attributes from the path, but you can apply them to the path again later if you wish. At this point, you'll see the blinking text insertion icon and you can enter or copy text onto the path.

4. Now switch to the Selection tool and select the path with the text on it (you can click either on the path, or on the text itself).

   As you look at the selection, you'll notice a vertical line with a small white box on the left, a line at the center, and a small white box and a line on the far right (**Figure 6.16**).

The small boxes should look familiar to you—they are in and out ports. The ports are there because Illustrator treats type on a path like area type. The two vertical lines that appear on either end define the boundary, or the start and end points, of the text. The line in the center determines the center point between the start and end points and allows you to specify which side of the path the text sits on.

You can use the in and out ports to thread text across multiple Path Type objects, and you can even create a thread of text that includes both Path Type and Area Type objects (très cool). By dragging the start and end points, you can define the area of the path that can contain text. For example, you can have a long path, but have text appear on just a small portion of that path (**Figure 6.17**). If you think about it, adjusting the start and end points on a Path Type object is akin to adjusting the width of an Area Type object. You can also drag the middle line to either side of the path to flip the text.

 Prior to Illustrator CS, Type on a Path objects behaved similarly to Point Type objects.

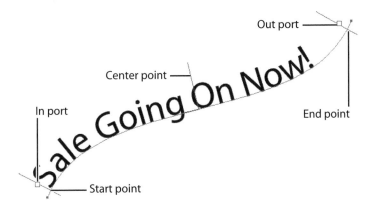

Figure 6.16 A Path Type object is similar to an Area Type object in many ways.

Figure 6.17 By moving the position of the start and end points, you can control the portion of the path that can contain text.

Path Type with Closed Paths

 To convert a closed path to a Path Type object, you have to hold the Option (Alt) key while clicking the path with the Type tool. Or you can simply use the Type on a Path tool.

Now that you understand how path type works, you're ready to learn how to work with path type on a closed path. When you convert a path to a Path Type object, the point at which you click the path becomes the start point. On an open path, you can easily see the start and end points because they are on opposite sides of the path. However, when you are working with a closed path, the point that you click becomes the start *and* the end point (a closed path is continuous).

If, for example, you want to place text on a circle, click the top of the circle to create the start point and the end point; if you center your text, it actually aligns to the bottom of the path (**Figure 6.18**). To get text to align to the top center of a circle, either click at the bottom of the circle when you're creating the Path Type object, or adjust the start and end points so that the center of the text rests at the top of the circle (**Figure 6.19**).

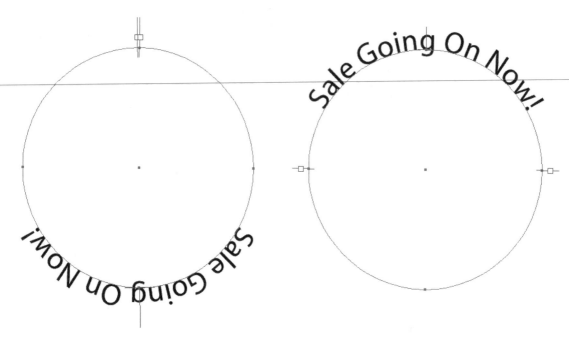

Figure 6.18 At first placing text on a circle seems non-intuitive—clicking at the top of a circle centers your text at the bottom of the circle.

Figure 6.19 Changing the position of the start and end points can make it easier to center text at the top curve of a circle.

Path Text Options

Positioning text on a path—especially a curved path—can be difficult because the spacing can look irregular. However, you can adjust these and other settings by selecting the Path Type object and choosing Type > Type on a Path > Type on a Path Options. The following settings are available in the Type on a Path Options dialog:

- **Effect.** The Effect setting controls the orientation of the text relative to the path. Prior to Illustrator CS, all Type on Path objects used the Rainbow setting, which rotated each character to be tangent to the path. Illustrator now allows you to also choose from Skew, 3D Ribbon, Stair Step, and Gravity (**Figure 6.20**, next page).

- **Align to Path.** The Align to Path setting determines which part of the text actually lines up with and touches the path. You can choose from Baseline (the default), Ascender, Descender, and Center (**Figure 6.21**, next page).

- **Spacing.** You can use the Spacing setting to help get consistent spacing between characters on curved paths (the setting doesn't do much on straight paths). Where paths make sharp curves, the spacing between characters could appear at odd angles or with inconsistent spacing. Specifying a higher spacing value brings characters closer to each other and corrects the spacing issues.

- **Flip.** The Flip setting allows you to control the side of the path on which the text appears.

If you want to apply an appearance to the path itself on a Path Type object, click just the path with the Direct Selection tool (it might be easier to do this while you are in the Outline view mode). You can then apply attributes to the path as you would normally. To offset text from the path itself, use the Baseline Shift setting, although if you're working with wavy or curved paths, using one of the Align to Path settings offers better results because it takes advantage of the Spacing setting.

Figure 6.20 Listed here are the five different effect settings you can use with path type.

Sale Going On Now! — Rainbow

Sale Going On Now! — Skew

Sale Going On Now! — 3D Ribbon

Sale Going On Now! — Stair Step

Sale Going On Now! — Gravity

Figure 6.21 Listed here are the four different align settings you can use with path type.

Sale Going On Now! — Baseline

Sale Going On Now! — Ascender

Sale Going On Now! — Descender

Sale Going On Now! — Center

WRAPPING TEXT AROUND OBJECTS

Graphic layouts sometimes call for text wrapping around the perimeter of other objects. Because the wrap is an attribute of the object, not the text, you'll find the text wrap feature listed under the Object menu. You can specify text wraps for individual objects, or for groups as well. Similar to what you learned about groups in Chapter 3: *Objects, Groups, and Layers*, applying a text wrap to an entire group allows you to specify one text wrap setting for the entire group. Choosing several objects and then applying a text wrap simply applies an individual text wrap to each selected object. Once you've made a selection, choose Object > Text Wrap > Make.

Unlike layout applications such as InDesign, Illustrator's text wrap feature doesn't allow you to edit the text wrap in the form of a path. The only thing that you can specify is the offset value, which you can access by selecting the object with the wrap and choosing Object > Text Wrap > Text Wrap Options.

Once a text wrap has been applied to an object, any area text that appears below it in the stacking order will wrap around the object (**Figure 6.22**). Point type is not affected at all by text wraps. To remove a text wrap, select an object that has an existing text wrap already applied and choose Object > Text Wrap > Release.

 Older versions of Illustrator required that you apply a text wrap by selecting both the text and the object. Doing this in Illustrator CS2 creates a wrap around both the text and the object, so make sure you have just the object selected.

 A text wrap's boundary is defined by the object's appearance, not its vector path. If you have live effects applied to an object, a text wrap that is applied to that object will follow the appearance.

"Our goal is to provide our customers with the best personal computers in the world, and looking ahead Intel has the strongest processor roadmap by far," said Steve Jobs, Apple's CEO. "It's been ten years since our transition to the PowerPC, and we think Intel's technology will help us create the best personal computers for the next ten years."

Figure 6.22 The spell check feature in Illustrator can prove to be helpful, although it's amusing to note that InDesign isn't in the dictionary.

EDITING TEXT

There's a saying that goes, "The written word is forever." but obviously that saying was meant to be applied *after* the client had already reviewed the job. As a designer, making text edits is a part of life. Illustrator does have several features that make AA's (author's alterations) a bit easier to digest, including a powerful find and replace function and a spectacular spell check feature.

Using Find and Replace

Illustrator may be a single-page-per-document application, but a find and replace feature can still be helpful when you're making specific edits across large amounts of text. Choose Edit > Find and Replace to search across all text within a single Illustrator document. The arrows at the end of both the Find and Replace With fields allow you to specify special characters including Tab characters and non-breaking hyphens (**Figure 6.23**).

Figure 6.23 You don't have to remember special codes to find special characters. Illustrator provides you with a list of common characters for search and replace functions.

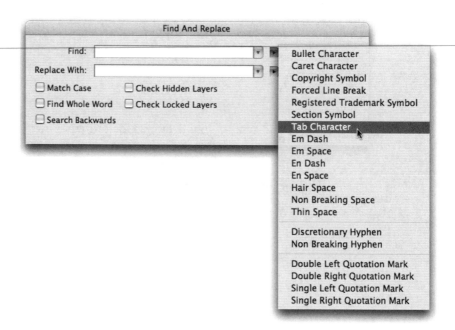

Displaying Invisible Characters

When performing text edits, it can be helpful to identify where non-visible characters appear. Spaces, tabs, soft and hard returns, and end of story markers can all be made visible by choosing Type > Show Hidden Characters. When visible, these characters display in blue-colored icons.

Checking Spelling

We're sure that you've never sent a job off for print or uploaded a Web page with a typo in it. But just in case, it never hurts to learn how to check your spelling. Especially since Illustrator's spell check feature is quite the linguist—it speaks many different languages—23 in all!

You can specify what language a selected string of text is by choosing from the pop-up menu that appears at the bottom of the Character palette. You can also specify the language within a character or a paragraph style sheet. When Illustrator's spell check feature encounters text that is specified as Spanish, it uses its Spanish dictionary to check the spelling, and it does the same for any other language that you've specified.

To run the spell check feature on your document, choose Edit > Check Spelling and click the Start button. Illustrator starts suggesting corrections for misspelled words; you can also choose to ignore them or add a word to Illustrator's dictionary (**Figure 6.24**).

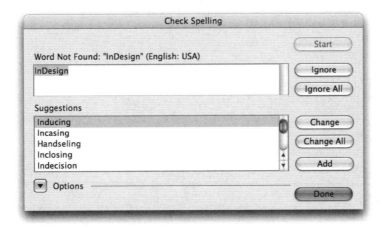

Figure 6.24 The spell check feature in Illustrator can prove to be helpful, although it is amusing to note that InDesign isn't in the dictionary.

LEGACY TEXT AND BACKWARD COMPATIBILITY

After reading through this chapter, it's obvious that the text features that appear in Illustrator's next-generation text engine are a powerful set of tools that bring a professional level of typography into the hands of users such as yourself. Beyond that, the advanced technology that enables Unicode and OpenType support and features like optical kerning means that you can rely on consistent type today and in the future.

All of this functionality comes at a price, though, when you consider backward compatibility with versions of Illustrator that use the older text engine. At the end of the day, the text engine that appeared in Illustrator CS wasn't just an enhancement—it was a brand new feature.

When you have a particular feature in a new version—say symbols in Illustrator 10—you can use this feature in that version, but you can't export that file to an older version and expect to edit it, right? For example, you can't create a symbol in Illustrator 10, save the file as an Illustrator 8 file, open it in Illustrator 8, and expect to edit the symbol. This is because the symbol feature doesn't exist in version 8. The visual appearance is correct, but the art isn't editable as a symbol anymore.

Because of the huge advancement in technology of the new text engine in Illustrator CS, text isn't compatible with previous versions of Illustrator. You can think of this as a line drawn in the sand, with Illustrator CS2 and CS on one side, and all older versions (Adobe calls these "legacy" versions) on the other.

Opening Legacy Illustrator Files in Illustrator CS2

Let's take a common design scenario. You launch Illustrator CS2 and open a file that contains text, which was created in a legacy version of Illustrator (say Illustrator 10). When you open the file, you're presented with a warning dialog that states that following: *"This file contains text that was created in a previous version of Illustrator. This Legacy text must be updated before you can edit it.*" The dialog presents you with three options:

- **Update.** Clicking the Update button converts all of the legacy text in your file so it is compatible with the new text engine in Illustrator CS2. This process may result in some of your text reflowing and displaying different line breaks and kerning. However, sometimes no reflow occurs at all. Because this happens as you open the file, you won't see the reflow or kerning changes happen if they do, and so if text place-ment is critical, you should avoid choosing this option (you'll see shortly how you can update the text manually later). The only time it makes sense to choose Update is when you know you will be changing or deleting the text anyway.

- **Cancel.** In essence, clicking Cancel is like saying, "I always wanted to be a welder anyway." Cancel simply closes the file and Illustrator for-gets this little incident ever happened.

- **OK.** If you click OK, the file opens and none of the legacy text is affected at all—the file opens just as it did in Illustrator 10. The catch is, you can't edit the legacy text, which appears in the document much like a placed file—in a box with an "X" through it. You can print the file perfectly and make edits to other art in the file, but Illustrator treats the text as a *foreign object*, which cannot be edited. However, you can convert individual legacy text objects to the new text engine as you need to, as you will soon learn.

Basically, if you are opening a file where you know you will be changing or deleting the text, choosing Update is the best way to go because you don't care if the text reflows. If, however, you just want to open a file so that you can print it, or if text placement is important (which it usually is), choosing the OK option is the smart choice.

Updating Legacy Text in an Open Document

If you choose to open a legacy Illustrator file by clicking OK, the file opens, but each text object is not editable until you convert it to the new text engine (**Figure 6.25**, next page). You can do so on an object-by-object basis by selecting the Type tool and clicking a legacy text object, at which time Illustrator presents you with another dialog that offers three options (**Figure 6.26**):

- **Copy Text Object.** Choosing the Copy Text Object option converts the legacy type to the new text engine, and therefore the text is editable. Some reflow may occur in the conversion, but Illustrator creates a copy of the legacy text on a locked and dimmed layer beneath the new converted text. If the new text did actually reflow, you can see the difference between the new text and old text, which is on the layer beneath it. You can then adjust the new text to perfectly match the legacy text.

- **Cancel.** Choosing Cancel leaves the legacy text as a foreign object—it can be printed, but not edited.

- **Update.** Choosing Update converts the text to the new text engine so that you can edit it. However, a copy of the legacy text is not created, so if the text does reflow, you may not be able to tell.

Figure 6.25 A legacy text object is not editable, and it appears much like an image does, although the text is vector.

Figure 6.26 Trying to edit legacy text with the Type tool results in another dialog.

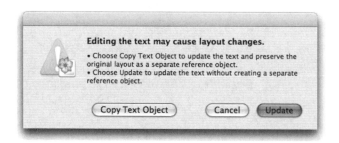

For converting taglines, logotype, and other sensitive type treatments, choosing the Copy Text Object option is obviously the best. However, if you have a lot of text objects to convert, it can take a long time to ensure that all of the text matches the legacy document (although depending on the task, you may not have a choice). The Update option can be useful if you just want to make an edit to a few lines of text and the reflow there won't make a difference anyway.

You may find that when you're updating text, no significant reflow occurs. If, after updating several text objects, you decide to convert all of the legacy text at once, you can choose Type > Legacy Text > Update All Legacy Text. Additionally, you can select several legacy text objects on your artboard and choose Type > Legacy Text > Update Selected Legacy Text. Both of these options perform the same function as choosing the Update option, but to multiple legacy text objects at once.

If you did choose the Copy Text Object option so that you can see if there was text reflow, remember that the copy of the legacy text that was created will still print. Once you have matched the new text to the legacy text, you must delete the legacy text copy by either removing it manually from the Layers palette, or by choosing Type > Legacy Text > Delete Copies.

Saving Illustrator CS2 Files to Illustrator Legacy Versions

It's said that sticking your hand into a thorn bush isn't painful, because the thorns are shaped facing in toward the center of the bush. It's pulling your hand out of the thorn bush that causes the wound. With Illustrator, moving text from legacy versions to the CS versions is a straightforward transition. However, trying to move text from the CS versions of Illustrator so that it is compatible with legacy versions can be painful.

Based on a preference in your Document Setup dialog, text is either broken up into individual Point Type objects (the default setting) or the text is converted to outlines. You can change this setting by choosing File > Document Setup, navigating to the Type panel, and choosing Preserve Text Editability or Preserve Text Appearance, respectively. In Chapter 12, *Save and Export*, you will learn how to create files that are compatible with legacy versions of Illustrator.

Basically, there isn't much you can do to avoid this issue. There are scripts that are available (such as Rick Johnson's most excellent Concat Text script, which you can find at http://rj-graffix.com/software/scripts.html) that allow you to select broken up text and combine it into a single string of editable text. While these scripts will help, they certainly aren't a solution. If you're creating a file that must have editable text that you can use in a legacy version of Illustrator, you might consider creating your file in Illustrator CS2, but saving it in Illustrator 10 format and adding the text using version 10.

 When opening files that were created in previous versions of Illustrator (what Illustrator refers to as legacy files), you may have to adjust text objects. In order to prevent you from accidentally overwriting your original files, Illustrator tacks on the word [converted] to your file name when it opens legacy files. You can disable this behavior in Illustrator's General Preferences, although we don't suggest it.

CHAPTER 7

3D and Other Live Effects

So far, we've only scratched the surface with the kinds of effects that Adobe Illustrator has to offer. Soft drop shadows (such as those we discussed in Chapter 3, *Objects, Groups, and Layers*) are certainly cool, but they are only a small sampling of Illustrator's Live Effects options, which include 3D effects, warp distortions, and a wide range of pixel-based Photoshop effects. In fact, the 3D effects in Illustrator are quite significant, as you will see later in this chapter.

As you read through this chapter, remember that Live Effects can be applied to fills and strokes individually, as well as to objects, groups, and layers. All Live Effects are applied via the Effect menu, and once applied, Live Effects are listed in the Appearance palette and can be edited or deleted at any time. Additionally, you can apply multiple Live Effects to a single target.

It's also important to realize that you can apply Live Effects to type without needing to convert to outlines. As you make changes to the text, the applied effect updates. This makes it easy to apply warp and 3D effects to text, and more importantly, it allows you to work with editable text.

Combining Features and Effects

New features aren't added haphazardly in Illustrator. Rather, each new feature is carefully thought out in regard to how it might interact with other existing features in Illustrator. One of the most powerful things that you can do with Live Effects in Illustrator is apply several of them to a single object, or even better, use effects in combination with other features, like transparency and blends (**Figure 7.1**).

Figure 7.1 You don't have to be a high roller to see the benefits of combining features in Illustrator. This example uses the 3D effect with artwork mapping, transparency, and blends.

When using Illustrator, you should always be asking yourself "what if. . ." questions. For example, you know that you can apply transparency to objects in Illustrator, so what if you applied transparency to a 3D effect? Would you be able to see through the 3D object? (We'll discuss how to do this later in the chapter.) Experimenting in Illustrator is a great way to discover new techniques and creative ideas. The worst thing that can possibly happen is that you get something that doesn't look that great; the Undo function serves nicely at this point.

The effects are listed in this chapter in the order in which they appear in Illustrator's Effect menu.

Throughout this chapter, we ask "what if" questions and explore the ways that Live Effects integrate with other Illustrator features. These questions are answered with advice on how to get the most out of Illustrator. More importantly, the "what if" scenarios will open your eyes to the power of Illustrator's Live Effects.

Deconstructing the Effect Menu

The Effect menu is basically split into four main sections. At the very top are two settings: Apply Last Effect and Last Effect. The former allows you to duplicate the last effect you applied, including all of its settings; the latter opens the dialog for the last effect that you applied so that you can choose different settings. The next section of the Effect menu is something called Document Raster Effects Resolution, which we'll get to in a moment. The remaining two sections are Illustrator Effects and Photoshop Effects; each section contains a collection of effects that fall into those two categories. For the most part, Illustrator Effects are Illustrator-specific features, whereas Photoshop Effects are a collection of filters that were taken from Photoshop (see "Featured Match-Up: Illustrator Effects vs. Photoshop Effects," later in this chapter).

Is It Vector, or Is It Raster?

You already know that a Live Effect is simply an appearance that is added to an object, meaning that the underlying vector object exists in your document in its original state. As you change the underlying object, the appearance updates to reflect that change. If you want to lock in an appearance, you need to choose Object > Expand Appearance to alter the actual vector paths, at which point the effect is no longer live, and can't be edited.

Some effects, such as Drop Shadow, are raster-based. Even though this effect appears grouped under the Illustrator Effects section, when the appearance is expanded, the drop shadow becomes a raster image (**Figure 7.2**). The same applies when you print a file, because all effects are expanded when they are sent to the printer (your file remains in an unexpanded state however, allowing further editing).

 Refer to Chapter 11, *Prepress and Printing*, for more information on what happens when you print Illustrator files.

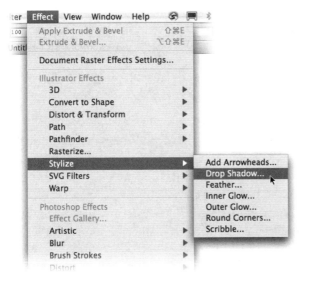

Figure 7.2 Many of the Stylize effects, including Drop Shadow, produce raster-based results, even though they are listed within the Illustrator Effects section of the Effect menu.

The following is a list of features that appear in the Illustrator Effects section of the Effect menu; these produce raster images when output or expanded:

- 3D Extrude & Bevel and 3D Revolve, when raster images or gradients are present in mapped artwork (see "Specifying Mapped Artwork," later in this chapter).

- Rasterize.

- Stylize > Drop Shadow.

- Stylize > Feather.

- Stylize > Inner Glow.

- Stylize > Outer Glow.

Each of these is covered in detail, later in this chapter.

Massaging Pixels in Illustrator

 When you choose to save a file as EPS, all effects are expanded and any raster-based effects are rasterized. This means that Illustrator EPS files can contain raster content and can't be scaled infinitely when placed into other applications. See Chapter 12, *Saving and Exporting Files,* for information.

If it is true that some effects in Illustrator produce a rasterized result, who determines the resolution of those rasters? When you work in Photoshop, you can't even create a new file without first defining its resolution. But with Illustrator, which is vector-based, you don't think much about resolution. So the question is, what determines the resolution of these raster-based effects? To find the answer, choose Effect > Document Raster Effects Settings.

The Document Raster Effects Settings dialog is where you can specify the resolution for raster-based effects. In fact, the dialog offers all the necessary settings for determining how raster-based effects eventually print (**Figure 7.3**).

- **Color Model.** Depending on the document color mode setting to which your file is set, you'll either see CMYK, Grayscale, and Bitmap listed here, or RGB, Grayscale, and Bitmap. This is because a document cannot contain both CMYK and RGB elements. This setting can be extremely useful, because it allows you to change the color model of an object (even an image) as a Live Effect, which can always be edited. For example, you can turn a colored object into grayscale as an effect.

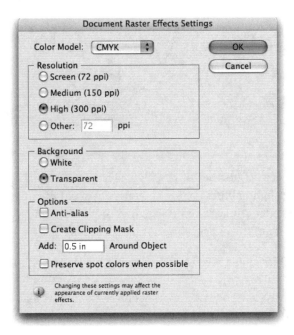

Figure 7.3 When using Live Effects, choosing the right settings in the Document Raster Effects Settings dialog is key to achieving the best results from your files.

- **Resolution.** Illustrator's default resolution setting is 72 ppi (screen resolution). Contrary to popular belief, Adobe did not choose this setting as the default to make web designers happy. Rather, the resolution setting has a direct bearing on the performance of Illustrator (Adobe doesn't want you to think Illustrator is slow). Just as in Photoshop, working at higher resolutions means more number crunching for your computer and more time for you to stare at your screen watching the progress bars slowly creep along. If your file is destined for print, however, you'll want your effects to print at a much higher resolution. This is an extremely important setting and should not be overlooked. See the sidebar "Featured Match-Up: Illustrator Effects vs. Photoshop Effects," later in this chapter for details on whether you need to change this setting before or after you create your file.

- **Background.** You can choose whether the resulting raster has a transparent background or a white background. If your effect overlaps other objects, you probably want to use the Transparent setting (**Figure 7.4**), although remember that the file still needs to be flattened (see Chapter 11 for more information on transparency flattening).

 All of the settings in the Document Raster Effects Settings dialog are *sticky*, meaning that once you change the settings, the next document you create takes on those new settings.

Figure 7.4 In this example, the artwork on the left used the White Background setting, whereas the artwork on the right used the Transparent Background setting.

- **Anti-alias.** You can define whether or not the raster image is anti-aliased. Anti-aliasing slightly blurs color boundaries to avoid the appearance of jagged edges. For more information on anti-aliasing, refer to Chapter 10, *Illustrator and the Web*.

- **Create Clipping Mask.** This setting creates a clipping mask around the area of a shape so that you can have it blend into a background (raster images are always rectangular and may block out objects that appear behind them). This setting won't work very well for objects that have Drop Shadow, Feather, or Glow effects applied, because clipping masks have hard edges. You don't need this setting if you specify the Transparent option for the background.

- **Add Space Around Object.** This is a very important setting. When certain effects, like Feather or Gaussian Blur, are applied, the resulting raster image has a soft edge. In order to ensure that this soft edge fades into the background correctly, you must make the bounding box of the raster image larger than the actual object. If you don't, the fade stops abruptly and you see a visible line where it ends. By default, Illustrator adds 36 points (.5 inch) of space around an object, but if you have a large blur setting, you may need to increase this amount (**Figure 7.5**).

Figure 7.5 On the left is a circle with a 60-pixel Gaussian Blur applied. With the default Add .5 in Around Object setting, the blur is visibly clipped. On the right, that same blur appears correctly with the Add Space Around Object setting increased to 1.5 inches.

- **Preserve spot colors when possible.** If your artwork contains spot colors and you want to prevent those from being converted to process colors, this setting instructs Illustrator to preserve those spot colors, employing overprinting where possible. Refer to Chapter 11 for more information on overprinting.

Any Live Effects that you apply in your document will use the settings in the Document Raster Effects Settings dialog, and you can't have different settings for different effects. Well, you can, sort of. Not in any way that Adobe intended though. All Live Effects update when you make a change to the Document Raster Effects Settings, but once you expand a Live Effect, that object no longer updates when you change the settings. So if you need to use different settings for different objects, apply an effect to one object, then use the Object > Expand Appearance function to expand the effect, lock in the Document Raster Effects Setting for that effect, and then apply a different setting to another object. Of course, once you expand an effect, you have no way to go back and perform edits to it.

3D: A Whole New World

Few features in Illustrator are as fun to use as the 3D effect. You might want to clear your calendar for a few days so that you have time to explore all of the cool functionality you're about to discover.

However, before you tie a bungee cord to your ankles and jump into the spectacular world of 3D, it's important to realize just what the 3D effect in Illustrator is capable of and what its limitations are. In this way, you'll get a better idea of what you can realistically expect from the 3D effect.

- **The 3D effect in Illustrator is real 3D.** Unlike 3D plug-ins or other vector-based applications that have 3D features (like Macromedia FreeHand or CorelDRAW), the 3D effect in Illustrator isn't some cheesy feature. Rather, Illustrator does real 3D rendering in a true 3D environment. Although the artwork that appears on the artboard is 2D, within the Effect dialog, the artwork exists in a 3D space where you can rotate and view it from any angle (**Figure 7.6**).

- **The 3D effect in Illustrator is vector based.** Illustrator applies 3D effects to vector objects and the result is a vector object. Lighting and shading are done through the use of blends (more detail on this later). Illustrator does not use ray tracing (a pixel-based rendering technique that can create shading and lighting with reflections and refractions).

 It's important to set your resolution before you start designing a file, because the appearance of some effects can change if the resolution is changed later. See the sidebar on page 281 for more information.

Be sure to check out Mordy Golding's 3D example in the color insert.

Figure 7.6 Once you've applied a 3D effect to a shape, you can choose to view it from any angle.

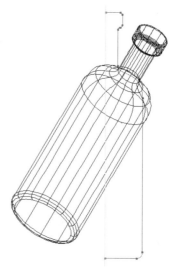

 Because Illustrator does real 3D rendering, performance is commensurate with system resources. Illustrator's 3D effect is optimized for Apple's G5 processor.

- **The 3D effect in Illustrator supports artwork mapping.** Illustrator's 3D effect has the ability to map 2D artwork onto the surface of 3D objects. Artwork that will be mapped onto a 3D surface must first be defined as an Illustrator symbol.

- **The 3D effect in Illustrator is self-contained.** Because 3D in Illustrator is an effect, it applies to particular objects that you have selected. Each object is treated as a separate entity and lives in its own individual 3D world. This means that separate 3D objects cannot interact with or intersect each other (for example, a rod that pierces a sphere). Additionally, each object maintains its own vanishing point. This limitation makes it difficult to create 3D compositions in which multiple objects share the same vanishing point (although using groups can make a difference).

- **The 3D effect in Illustrator is proprietary.** The 3D effect is an internal feature and is only applicable within the Illustrator application. You cannot export 3D geometry from Illustrator (although you can export the 2D representation of that artwork), nor can you import 3D geometry from CAD or 3D modeling applications (like Maya or Strata).

- **The 3D effect in Illustrator is a Live Effect.** As a Live Effect, the 3D features in Illustrator abide by the same rules as other effects. This means you can apply 3D effects to groups (which is important, as we'll see later), you can save them as Graphic Styles, you can edit them easily, and you can expand them.

There's another side effect to applying a 3D effect to an object with a stroke applied that pertains to artwork mapping. You already know that artwork mapping allows you to apply 2D art to the surface of any 3D object. We'll discuss exactly how artwork mapping is applied later in the chapter, but one of the main things you'll need to do with artwork mapping is choose on which surface of a 3D object you want your mapped artwork to appear (you can apply artwork to multiple surfaces as you will learn later).

When you apply an Extrude effect to a rectangle with just a fill, the result is a 3D object that has six surfaces. However, if you apply a stroke to that rectangle, the result is a 3D object with 24 surfaces. This is because Illustrator counts all of the surfaces generated by the fill as well as those generated by the stroke (the surfaces that appear along the inside of the stroke, even though they are not visible, are still counted as surfaces). Because of this, it can be difficult to choose from the numerous surfaces to figure out which one you want the artwork mapped onto.

Of course, there are times when you will want to apply a stroke to an object with a 3D effect, such as with extruded text. By adding a stroke to your Text object, you can create text that is filled with one color but that is extruded using a different color (**Figure 7.16**). Chances are good that you won't be mapping artwork onto your text, so this example is a good use of a stroke on a 3D object.

In review, feel free to use strokes on your objects if you need them to get the look you are trying to achieve. However, be aware that adding strokes slows performance and makes artwork mapping a confusing process because of all of the extra surfaces.

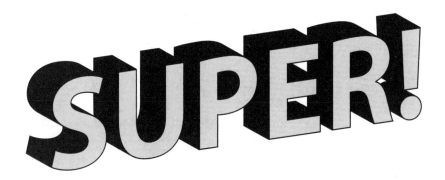

Figure 7.16 When extruding text, adding a stroke allows you to create a powerful contrast to the extruded effect.

Editing a 3D Effect

Because 3D is a Live Effect in Illustrator, you can make edits to the original vector shape on the artboard and the 3D effect updates accordingly. You can also change the color of the object and the 3D effect automatically updates as well, including the shading of the object.

You know that you can double-click an effect listed in the Appearance palette to edit 3D effects that have already been applied to artwork. However, it's important to remember that the artwork that appears on your artboard after you've applied a 3D effect is 2D. If you want to rotate a 3D object, don't do it on the artboard using the usual transformation tools. Rather, double-click the 3D effect in the Appearance palette and rotate the object in the 3D Options dialog. Changing the artwork on the artboard produces undesirable results (**Figure 7.17**). For more information on transforming artwork that has Live Effects applied, see the sidebar, "Transforming Objects with Effects," later in this chapter.

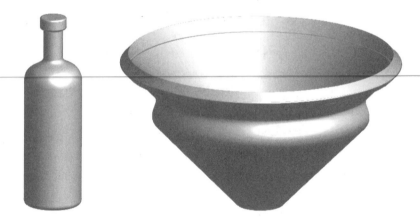

Figure 7.17 What started out a wine bottle (left) may not appear the same when you rotate it on the artboard (right). To rotate the bottle in 3D, you have to edit the 3D effect.

Applying the 3D Extrude & Bevel Effect

Now that you generally understand how the 3D effect works in Illustrator, you will learn how to apply the effect, determine all of its settings, and perhaps most importantly, study a few practical examples of how you might use such an effect.

As we defined earlier, the Extrude & Bevel effect adds depth to an object. To apply this effect, select a vector object on the artboard and choose Effect > 3D > Extrude & Bevel to open the Extrude & Bevel Options dialog. First, check the Preview button in the dialog so that you can see what the 3D effect looks like as you adjust the settings. If you don't have a large screen, it helps to position your artwork on one side of the screen before you apply the effect, and place the Extrude & Bevel options dialog (when it opens) to the other side so that you can see the preview on the artboard (**Figure 7.18**).

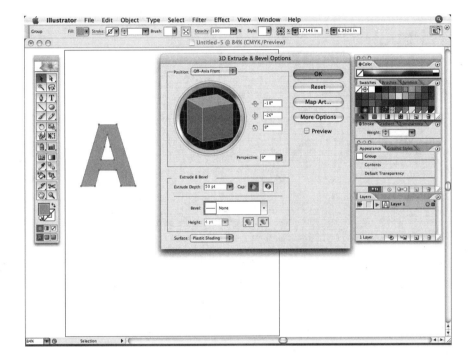

Figure 7.18 Especially on smaller screens, it helps to keep your art positioned on the left side of the screen so that you have room to preview the art while you make adjustments in the 3D Extrude & Bevel Options dialog.

At this point, you are ready to begin experimenting with the different settings found in the dialog. To make the feature more approachable, Adobe splits the dialog into two parts. By default, only half of the settings appear in the dialog. By clicking the More Options button, you can expand the dialog to show all of the settings that we will be talking about here (**Figure 7.19**, next page).

 You'll always have to check the Preview button when you open the dialog. Adobe chose this behavior for performance reasons.

Figure 7.19 By clicking the More Options button, you can expand the 3D Extrude & Bevel Options dialog to see all of the available settings.

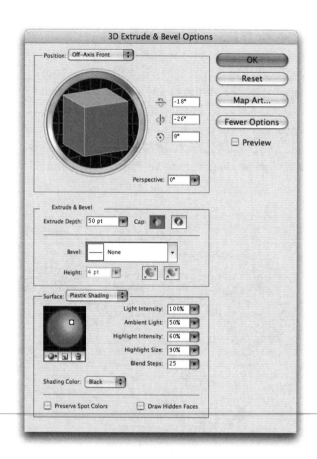

 Most 3D applications allow you change the position of the objects and the camera in a scene. Because each 3D effect lives within its own 3D world, Illustrator's camera is always stationary and you are adjusting the position of the object only.

The 3D Extrude & Bevel Options dialog is divided into three sections—Position, Extrude & Bevel, and Surface—each covering a different aspect of 3D.

Specifying the Position Settings

The Position section of the 3D Extrude & Bevel Options dialog allows you to rotate your object within a 3D space (on its X, Y, and Z axes) in order to control the view of your object. In 3D applications, the term *camera* is used to define the view of the object (as if you were seeing the object through the lens of a camera; **Figure 7.20**).

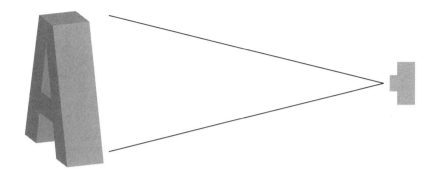

Figure 7.20 The Position setting allows you to rotate the view of an object, as if you were looking at the object through the lens of a camera.

The most distinctive element in the 3D Extrude and Bevel Options dialog is what Adobe engineers affectionately call the "track cube"—a visual representation of the position of your 3D object. The track cube acts much like a trackball, only it isn't round (hence, the name). To adjust the position of your 3D object, simply click and drag on the track cube. As you adjust the position, a wireframe preview appears on your screen, indicating how the object will appear (**Figure 7.21**). When you release the mouse, a full preview, with shading, appears.

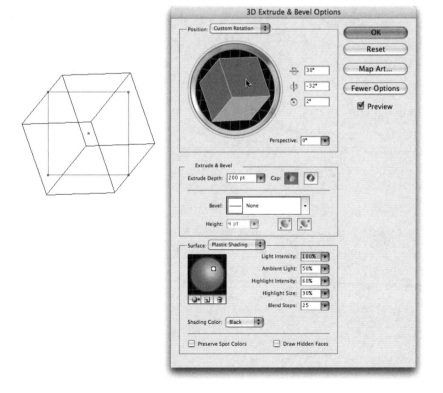

Figure 7.21 As you adjust the track cube, a wireframe preview shows you what your art will look like.

Illustrator utilizes a track cube instead of a track-ball because it is difficult to differentiate between the multiple sides (front, back, etc.) of the 3D object using a sphere as a reference.

The track cube is more than just fun to play with—it also has some pretty cool functionality. The sides of the cube are shaded in different colors to help you easily identify the position of your object: the front side is shaded blue and the back is a very dark gray; the top and bottom are light gray; and the left and right sides are a neutral gray.

In addition, as you move your mouse over the edges of each side, you'll notice the edges highlight in red, green, and blue (**Figure 7.22**). Clicking and dragging on these highlighted edges constrains the object to rotate only along one axis, making it easier to control the position of your object. Holding the Shift key while dragging the track cube simulates a rotation of the floor beneath the object, and dragging on the outer ring of the track cube constrains the rotation in the other direction.

Figure 7.22 Moving your mouse over the edges of the track cube allows you to make adjustments to one axis at a time.

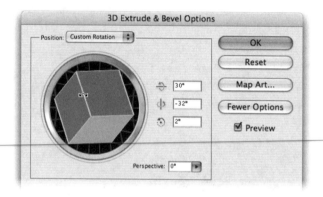

 While the Extrude & Bevel Options dialog is open, press the Option (Alt) key and the Cancel button turns into a Reset button. Clicking the Reset button resets the values in the dialog so that you can start fresh.

Along the right side of the track cube are three values that represent the three axes that a 3D object needs. Each axis can have a value of –180 to 180 degrees (for a total of 360). You'll notice that the highlighted colored track cube edges match the color shown for the icon in each of these three axes.

Appearing directly above the track cube is a pop-up menu that contains a list of preset positions from which you can choose. Choosing one of these presets positions your object in a variety of different views. Unfortunately, you cannot define your own presets here, but they can make it easy to apply consistent views throughout your artwork (**Figure 7.23**).

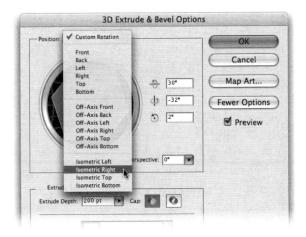

Figure 7.23 Choosing one of Illustrator's preset position settings can make it easy to position several objects with the same view, such as when you are creating isometric art.

Last, you can add perspective to your object by dragging the Perspective slider. This setting mimics the natural lens distortion that occurs if you move your object closer to the lens of the camera (**Figure 7.24**). If you hold the Shift key while adjusting the slider, you will see your preview update in real time (system performance permitting).

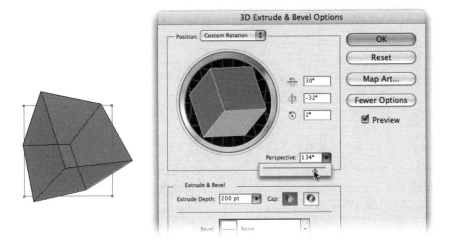

Figure 7.24 Adjusting the Perspective slider can add natural distortion to your object.

You will notice that as you increase the Perspective value, your 3D object becomes darker. Think about it: as you move an object closer to the lens of a camera, less light is available to reflect off the object and the object becomes darker. Soon we'll talk about surface and lighting options, which we can use to adjust the lighting of the object.

Specifying the Extrude & Bevel Settings

The Extrude & Bevel section of the 3D Extrude & Bevel Options dialog allows you to define the depth of your object as well as how the edges of your 3D object appear, also known as the bevel.

To adjust the depth of your object, enter a numeric value, click and drag the Extrude Depth slider, or enter a value in the field. If you hold the Shift key while adjusting the slider, you can preview the extrude depth setting in real time. The values used for the extrude depth settings are shown in points, although you can specify values in inches or any other format, and Illustrator will do the conversion for you. You can specify an extrude depth up to 2000 points (a tad more than 27.75 inches). Speaking of measurements, when you're trying to create package mockups, it's always a good idea to work at actual size or in scale to ensure that your 3D object is proportioned correctly.

By default, Illustrator creates closed extruded objects from filled paths. However, you can also specify the extrude setting you want to use so it shows only the extrusion and not the actual face or back of the shape. Toggling between the two cap settings allows you to control whether your objects have a solid or a hollow appearance (**Figure 7.25**).

Figure 7.25 The Cap setting appears as two icons. The shaded icon indicates the selected setting.

 When you specify a bevel, there are times when you might see rendering errors caused by self-intersecting paths. You can usually alleviate the problem by specifying a smaller bevel size, using a less complex bevel, or adjusting the position or perspective settings.

When you extrude an object, you can almost think of copying your object, offsetting the copy from the original, and then connecting the two with straight lines (**Figure 7.26**). A bevel is defined when you connect the two shapes with a line that is not straight, and therefore, the extrusion follows the direction of the line (**Figure 7.27**).

Illustrator provides a list of ten different bevels, which you can choose from the Bevel pop-up menu (see the sidebar, "Defining Your Own

Bevels"). The Height setting controls the size of the bevel. You can also choose whether you want the bevel to be subtracted from the size of the original shape, or if you want it added to the shape (**Figure 7.28**).

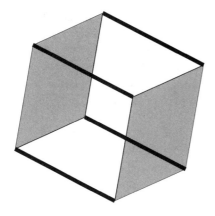

Figure 7.26 A normal extrude is created by connecting the front and back faces of an object with a straight line.

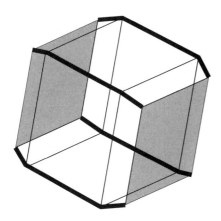

Figure 7.27 An extrude with a bevel is created by connecting the front and back faces of an object with a line that is not straight.

Figure 7.28 Toggling between the Bevel Extent In and Bevel Extent Out options can have an effect on the overall size of your object.

Defining Your Own Bevels

Illustrator ships with a collection of ten different bevel shapes, some simple and straightforward, others more complex. However, you may find that you want to create your own bevel shapes. The good news is that you can create just about any bevel you can dream up. The not-so-good news is that it takes a few steps to create a custom bevel, and you'll need to quit and restart Illustrator before you can use your bevel.

Bevels are actually regular open-ended paths that are defined as symbols. These symbols live in a file called Bevels.ai, which you will find in your Illustrator Plug-ins folder. Simply open the file and follow the directions that appear on the artboard of the file (the directions are clear and straightforward).

Be careful not to delete any of the existing bevels in the file, otherwise you'll lose them forever. It might be a good idea to create a backup of your Bevels.ai file before you modify it on your own. If the file is locked, you may need administrator rights to edit it.

Specifying the Surface Settings

The first two settings, Position and Extrude & Bevel, define the actual geometry of the shape. The Surface section of the 3D Extrude & Bevel Options dialog enables you to control the appearance of the surface of your object. This includes the type of shading used, as well as indicating how light will interact with the object. If you talk to a photographer, he will tell you that above all, lighting is of utmost importance. As you'll find out, the same is true with 3D.

You may have noticed that when you first checked the Preview button to see what your 3D effect looks like on the artboard, the object changed somewhat in color. For example, if your original object was filled with a bright yellow color, the object might now show a darker muddy yellow color instead. By default, 3D objects in Illustrator are rendered with a single light source from the upper right and are shaded by adding black to the original fill color, giving that darker appearance.

From the Surface pop-up menu, you can choose from one of four different options to specify the type of surface you want your 3D object to have. The surface type that you choose also defines what other surface settings are available for your object, and ultimately how you see the final 3D object (**Figure 7.29**). The four surface settings are as follows:

- **Plastic Shading.** You use the Plastic Shading setting when you want your object to have a highly reflective surface, such as glass or metal. This shading option enables you to adjust and control a lighting highlight on the object.

- **Diffuse Shading.** You use the Diffuse Shading setting when you want your object to have a matte surface, such as paper or wood. This shading option does not have a highlight setting.

- **No Shading.** The No Shading option disables shading completely and renders each side of your object using the solid color defined for the object. Granted, this option doesn't leave your object with a 3D appearance, but if your intent is to expand the 3D effect so that you can edit the geometry of the shape, this setting could be helpful.

- **Wireframe.** The Wireframe surface setting removes all filled areas, or "walls," from your object and displays the object's 3D wireframes. The result is technical and rather cool and it is useful for creating design elements. The rules that make up the wireframe are set to .25 point in width and cannot be changed without first expanding the 3D effect.

Figure 7.29 From left to right, this art demonstrates examples of Plastic Shading, Diffuse Shading, No Shading, and Wireframe.

On the left side of the Surface section of the dialog is a lighting sphere, which is used to control how light is directed at your 3D object. A small white circle indicates the light source, and you can drag it to control the direction of the light (**Figure 7.30**). As you move the light source, you can hold the Shift key to see the shading preview in real time. To add additional lights (you can add up to 30 of them), click the New Light icon that appears directly beneath the sphere, and to delete a selected light, click the Delete Light icon. You can also send lights behind an object by clicking the Move selected light to back of object icon.

Figure 7.30 You can drag lights across the sphere to adjust the shading of the 3D object.

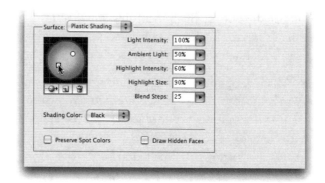

To the right of the lighting sphere, there are five settings that define how the surface and the lighting interact with each other. Depending on the Surface option that you select, you may see all or only some of these options:

- **Light Intensity.** The Light Intensity setting controls the strength, or brightness, of the selected light. Think of this setting as a dimmer switch—the closer the value is to 100, the brighter the light, the closer the value is to 0, the dimmer the light. You can use this setting to apply different intensity values for each selected light.

- **Ambient Light.** The Ambient Light setting is a general lighting setting that affects the entire surface of the object. By default, this is set it 50%, which is a neutral setting. Think of this setting as a global lightness/darkness setting for the object itself, not of the individual lights.

- **Highlight Intensity.** The Highlight Intensity setting controls the contrast or transition between the surface and the highlight. Higher values produce sharper highlights, indicating a more reflective surface, such as glass. This highlight setting is applied globally to all highlights on the object (you can't set this differently for different lights). This setting is only available when you choose the Plastic Shading option.

- **Highlight Size.** The Highlight Size setting controls the size of the highlights on a 3D object. This highlight setting is applied globally to all highlights on the object (you can't set this differently for different lights). This setting is only available when you choose the Plastic Shading option.

- **Blend Steps.** The Blend Steps setting is an extremely important setting, and therefore, it's difficult to understand why it appears listed at the bottom of the dialog, grouped with other lighting settings, seemingly hidden. Illustrator uses blends to create shading, not gradients (blends are covered in depth later in Chapter 9, *Graphs, Distortions, and Blends*). A blend is made up of a start and an end object, with multiple "steps" in between. If there are too few steps in a blend, you can see the individual steps, which results in shading that appears posterized and not smooth (**Figure 7.31**). By default, Illustrator specifies 25 blend steps, which is fine for viewing art on a computer screen, or for printing smaller 3D shapes, but for the best results in a high-resolution print workflow, a blend step setting of 200 or more is necessary. The reason why Illustrator's default setting is set to 25 is strictly for performance reasons. A higher Blend Steps setting results in much slower 3D performance, so it's a good idea to work with the default setting and then increase it right before you send your final file off to the printer.

Figure 7.31 Without enough steps in a blend, you can see "stair-stepping" side effects (also referred to as banding) rather than a smooth transition of color.

If you want to use gradients to do your own shading (which decreases file size when you're exporting art to Flash), choose the No Shading option, expand the appearance of the object, and then manually fill the shapes with gradients.

Illustrator also offers a pop-up menu from which you can choose a shading color. By default, Illustrator adds black to your object to simulate shading; however, you can choose Other and pick any color from the color picker or from existing swatches in your document to use as a shading color instead. If you use colors other than black for shading, the result will be as if you were casting a colored light on your object.

Using Spot Colors in 3D Objects

If your object is filled with a spot color, and if you use black or a spot color as your shade color, choosing the Preserve Spot Colors option causes the overprint function to be utilized when you're creating blends for shading. The result is an object that prints and separates correctly using the spot colors. You may have to view your file with Overprint Preview turned on if you want to preview the art correctly on your screen.

Illustrator and 3D Geometry

Although it's true that the 3D feature in Illustrator is doing real 3D rendering in a 3D world, that's only true while the 3D effect dialog is open on your screen. Once you click OK, Illustrator creates a 2D representation of that graphic and displays it on your artboard (Illustrator's artboard is only 2D). If you want to view your object differently, you can always edit the effect by double-clicking it in the Appearance palette, at which time the dialog opens. At this point, you're in the 3D world again, where you can rotate the object in space and then press OK to create the 2D representation that is displayed on the artboard.

Because Illustrator knows that the end result will be a 2D drawing, it saves processing time by only calculating and drawing the visible sides of an object. For example, if you were to create a rectangle and extrude it to create a cube, at any one time, you would only be able to view three of the six surfaces. You can see this for yourself by following a few quick steps to expand the appearance of a 3D object.

1. Using the Rectangle tool, draw a 2-inch square.

2. Give the square a fill of 25K and a stroke of None.

3. Choose Effect > 3D > Extrude & Bevel.

4. Leave the position set to Off-Axis Front, set the Extrude Depth to 2 inches, and click OK to apply the effect.

5. Choose Object > Expand Appearance to expand the 3D effect.

6. Deselect the object so that nothing is selected.

7. Switch to the Direct Selection tool and move each panel of the cube. You'll see that only the visible surfaces of the cube are there (**Figure 7.32**).

Figure 7.32 A regular square (left), with an Extrude applied (center), and then expanded, with the front face removed (right).

There are times however, when you might want the full geometry of the 3D object rendered. For example, if you wanted to expand the cube you created to modify the 3D object on your own, you might want all of the surfaces to be available. For this reason, Illustrator includes an option called Draw Hidden Faces, which forces Illustrator to render the entire object, even the surfaces that aren't visible. Again, you can easily see the difference by following a few short steps using the Draw Hidden Faces option.

1. Using the Rectangle tool, draw a 2-inch square.

2. Give the square a fill of 25K and a stroke of None.

3. Choose Effect > 3D > Extrude & Bevel.

4. Leave the position set to Off-Axis Front, and set the Extrude Depth to 2 inches.

5. Click the More Options button in the 3D Extrude & Bevel Options dialog and check the Draw Hidden Faces option.

6. Click OK to apply the 3D effect.

7. Choose Object > Expand Appearance to expand the 3D effect.

8. Deselect the object so that nothing is selected.

9. Switch to the Direct Selection tool and move each panel of the cube. You'll see that all of the surfaces of the cube are there, even those that are hidden from view (**Figure 7.33**, next page).

As you learn more about the 3D effect, you'll find that there are other uses for the Draw Hidden Faces option as well.

Figure 7.33 A regular square (left) with an Extrude applied with Draw Hidden Faces turned on (center), and then expanded, with the front face removed (right).

 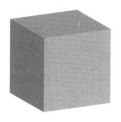 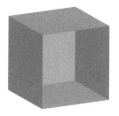

Creating a Photorealistic Button

Now that you've learned the different settings for the 3D Extrude & Bevel effect, it's time to put that knowledge to good use. In this exercise, you will create a realistic button (the kind you would find sewn to a shirt), but don't worry—you don't need to know how to draw. Illustrator's 3D effect allows you to create this button easily by drawing simple shapes.

1. Using the Ellipse tool, create a .25 inch circle.

2. Give the circle a fill of 25K and a stroke of None.

3. With the circle selected, double-click the Selection tool in the Toolbox to bring up the Move dialog.

4. Specify a Horizontal value of .375 inches and a Vertical value of 0, and click the Copy button. This gives you two buttons.

5. Now, select both circles and double-click the Selection tool to bring up the Move dialog again.

6. This time, specify a Horizontal value of 0 and a Vertical value of .375 inches and click the Copy button. You now have four circles (**Figure 7.34**).

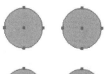

Figure 7.34 Once you've created the duplicates, you should see four stacked circles.

7. Select all four circles and click the Add to Shape Area button in the Pathfinder palette. This combines the four circles into a single compound shape.

8. Using the Ellipse tool, create a 2-inch circle.

9. Give the circle a fill of 25K and a stroke of None.

10. With the circle selected, choose Object > Arrange > Send to Back.

11. Using the Selection tool, select all five circles and open the Align Palette.

12. Click once on the Horizontal Align Center button and once on the Vertical Align Center button. Because you combined the four smaller circles with the Add to Shape Area function, they are centered nicely within the larger circle (**Figure 7.35**).

13. With all five circles still selected, open the Pathfinder palette and click the Subtract from Shape Area button. This "cuts" the smaller circles out from the larger one, allowing you to see through the button. This action also combines all five circles into a single object, allowing you to apply a single 3D effect to all of the circles at once (**Figure 7.36**).

14. With the button selected, choose Effect > 3D > Extrude & Bevel, and check the Preview checkbox.

Figure 7.35 All of the circles, centered, now make up the shape of a button.

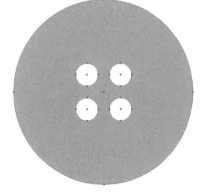

Figure 7.36 Once you've subtracted the smaller circles from the larger one, you're left with the art that you will use to create a button.

15. Set the Extrude Depth to .25 inches and set the bevel to Rounded.

16. Adjust the position to your liking, and click OK to apply the effect (**Figure 7.37**).

Figure 7.37 A wireframe preview allows you to position your 3D object with precision.

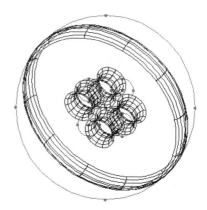

Because 3D is applied as a Live Effect, you can change the color of the button simply by applying a different fill color to the shape. Additionally, you can double-click the effect in the Appearance palette to edit the effect and change the position of the button so that you can view it from virtually any angle (**Figure 7.38**). This is a great example of how you can use the 3D Extrude & Bevel effect in a creative way, allowing you to easily create design elements that might otherwise be difficult to draw.

Figure 7.38 Once you've created the button in 3D, you can change its position so that you can view it from any angle.

Applying the 3D Revolve Effect

As we briefly discussed earlier, the Revolve effect adds dimension to an object by rotating a 2D shape around an axis. To apply this effect, select a vector object on the artboard and choose Effect > 3D > Revolve to open the 3D Revolve Options dialog. First, check the Preview button in the dialog so that you can see what the 3D effect looks like as you adjust the settings. If you don't have a large screen, it helps to position your artwork on one side of the screen before you apply the effect, and to position the Revolve options dialog, when it opens, to the other side so that you can see the preview on the artboard.

At this point, you are ready to begin experimenting with the different settings found in the dialog. As with the 3D Extrude & Bevel dialog, the 3D Revolve dialog has a More Options button, which expands the dialog to reveal all of the settings for the feature (**Figure 7.39**).

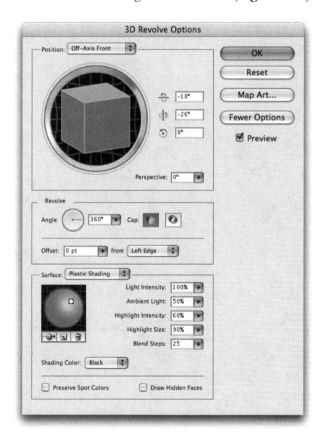

Figure 7.39 Similar to the 3D Extrude & Bevel Options dialog, you can expand the 3D Revolve Options dialog to reveal more options as well.

The fully expanded 3D Revolve Options dialog is divided into three sections: Position, Revolve, and Surface. The Position and Surface sections are identical to those found in the 3D Extrude & Bevel Options dialog, so we will focus on just the Revolve section here.

Specifying the Revolve Settings

The Revolve section of the 3D Revolve Options dialog allows you to define exactly how your object will appear when revolved around an axis. Before we discuss the settings themselves, it's important that you first understand how the 3D Revolve effect in Illustrator works. By default, the left-most point of the selected object becomes a vertical axis for the effect. An object can only have one axis and the axis is always vertical. Unfortunately, Illustrator doesn't preview or show you this axis onscreen, so think of it as an imaginary axis (**Figure 7.40**).

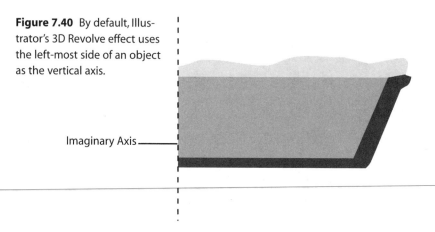

Figure 7.40 By default, Illustrator's 3D Revolve effect uses the left-most side of an object as the vertical axis.

Imaginary Axis

Now that you understand how revolve works, you can learn how to use the remaining settings in the Revolve section of the dialog:

- **Angle.** The Angle setting determines how far around the axis the artwork travels. By default, the angle is set to 360, which creates a shape that goes completely around the axis, resulting in a closed shape. Smaller values result in an object that seems to have a piece missing (**Figure 7.41**). You may find the angle setting useful when you want to create a cutaway view to the inside of an object or when you want to display just a portion of an object, like a single slice of pie (**Figure 7.42**).

- **Cap.** Similar to the Cap setting found in the 3D Extrude & Bevel Options dialog, here you can toggle between objects that have either a solid or hollow appearance.

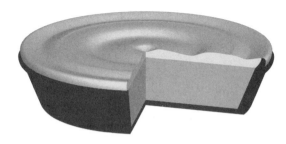

Figure 7.41 Using a large Angle setting can leave you with almost an entire pie …

Figure 7.42 … or you can be left with just a small slice of pie with a small Angle setting.

- **Offset.** The Offset setting is specific to the invisible axis. An offset value repositions the axis and effectively allows you to revolve an object from a point other than its left-most edge. The result is an object that is hollow (**Figure 7.43**). In addition, you can specify whether the axis is offset from the left or the right side of the object.

Figure 7.43 Adding an offset value to the 3D pie results in a pie that resembles a Danish with a hollow center.

Drawing a Sphere

Now that you've learned how the 3D Revolve effect works, you can learn how to create a simple object—a sphere (**Figure 7.44**).

1. Using the Ellipse tool, draw a 2-inch circle.

2. Give the circle a fill of 25K and a stroke of None.

3. Choose the Direct Selection tool and deselect the circle.

4. Then select just the left anchor point of the circle by clicking it once.

5. Once the anchor point is selected, press the Delete key on your keyboard to remove the selected anchor point and the paths that are connected to it. You will be left with half of a circle.

6. With the semicircle selected, choose Effect > 3D > Revolve. The default settings are fine for this exercise.

7. Click OK to apply the effect.

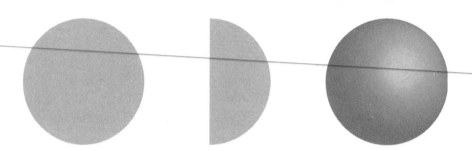

Figure 7.44 From left to right: creating a circle; deleting an anchor point to create a semicircle; and applying a 3D Revolve effect to create a sphere.

The most important part of this exercise was deleting half of the circle. As we mentioned earlier, the left side of the object is what defines the invisible axis on which the object revolves. If you were to apply a 3D Revolve effect to a full circle, the result would be quite different (**Figure 7.45**). In fact, applying the 3D Revolve effect with an offset value specified would produce a donut shape, which is nice, but not what you intended (**Figure 7.46**). Getting hungry?

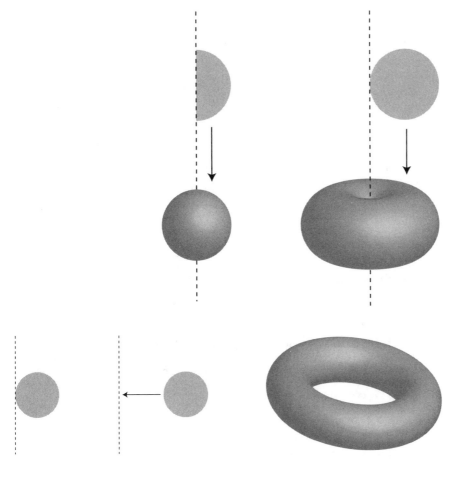

Figure 7.45 It's important to pay attention to where the vertical axis is. With a semi-circle (left), the vertical axis is positioned to create a sphere. With a full circle (right), though, the vertical axis is positioned to create a donut shape.

Figure 7.46 Starting with a full circle (left) and specifying an offset for the axis (center) results in a donut shape (right).

Drawing an Exercise Barbell

To get your mind off of food for a while, here's a little mental exercise that uses the 3D Revolve effect and incorporates the use of groups—an extremely important aspect of creating complex 3D shapes (see sidebar titled "The Importance of Applying 3D Effects to Groups" later in this chapter). In this example, you will create a group of shapes that will result in a great-looking barbell. Again, you don't want to focus on drawing a barbell as much as trying to build the shapes that will eventually help Illustrator's 3D feature draw it for you (it's always preferable to let the computer do all the hard work while you relax and rack up the billable hours).

To create the barbell, perform the following steps:

1. Choose View > Show Rulers and drag out a vertical guide (anywhere on your screen is fine).

   Although creating a guide isn't necessary, you will find that this vertical guide will help you visualize where the invisible axis will be. In addition, the guide will help you align the objects so that they are all aligned to the same left edge.

   Remember when you used ordinary circles to create a button using the extrude effect? Well this time, you're going to use ordinary rectangles to create your barbell.

2. Use the Rectangle tool to create a rectangle with a width of .25 inches and a height of 3.25 inches.

3. Give the rectangle a fill of 60K and a stroke of None. This shape will be the handle for your barbell.

4. Position the rectangle so that its left edge touches the vertical guide that you created in the previous step (**Figure 7.47**).

5. Create a second rectangle with a width of 1.25 inches and a height of .25 inches.

Figure 7.47 Aligning the rectangle to a guide will help you visualize where the vertical axis will be.

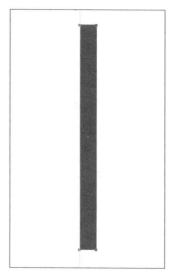

6. Give the rectangle a fill of 25K and a stroke of None. This shape will be one of the weights that appear on your barbell.

7. Choose the Selection tool and select both rectangles.

8. Then, click once on the larger rectangle and open the Align palette.

9. Click once on the Horizontal Align Left button and once on the Vertical Align Bottom button.

10. Then select just the smaller rectangle and double-click the Selection tool in the Toolbox to bring up the Move dialog.

11. Specify a value of 0 for Horizontal and .25 inch for Vertical and click OK (**Figure 7.48**).

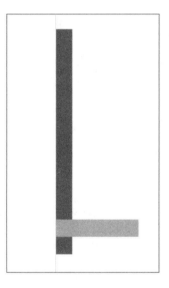

Figure 7.48 The first two rectangles are in position. Notice how they both are aligned to where the vertical axis will be.

12. Select the small rectangle and double-click the Selection tool to bring up the Move dialog.

13. Specify a value of 0 for Horizontal and .375 inch for Vertical and click the Copy button. You will now see two stacked rectangles. These will be the weights that appear on one side of the barbell.

14. To create the weights that will appear on the opposite side of the barbell, select both small rectangles and bring up the Move dialog once again.

15. Enter a value of 0 for Horizontal and 2.125 inches for Vertical, and click the Copy button. You now have all of the shapes necessary to create your 3D shape (**Figure 7.49**).

Figure 7.49 All of the necessary shapes are now created and aligned correctly.

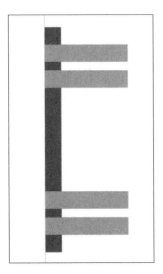

16. Use the Selection tool to select all of the objects and choose Object > Group. This will allow the 3D effect to treat all of the objects as one unit so that they all share a single vertical axis.

17. With the group selected, choose Effect > 3D > Revolve and turn on the preview.

18. Edit the position of the object to your liking using the track cube and then click OK to apply the effect (**Figure 7.50**).

Figure 7.50 Adding a Perspective setting can add a touch of realism to your barbell as well.

The most important part of this exercise is to try and visualize where the invisible axis is. When you think of a barbell, you may think of it as you normally see it—lying on the ground, in a horizontal format. Because Illustrator's Revolve effect always uses a vertical axis, you had to think of the barbell as standing on its side. Once it's created, you can use the track cube to rotate it into any position or orientation that you need.

The Importance of Applying 3D Effects to Groups

When applying any 3D effect, it's important that you understand its limitations so that you can figure out how to make it do what you want it to. Previously in this chapter, we stated that there are two main limitations with Illustrator's 3D effects: 3D objects cannot intersect each other, and each 3D object lives in its own 3D world. Hence, each object maintains its own individual vanishing point or invisible axis. Basically, multiple objects in your document cannot share a single vanishing point, share the same perspective, or revolve around the same axis.

If you were paying attention back in Chapter 3, you remember that effects produce a different appearance when applied at the group or layer level instead of at the object level. Because 3D is a Live Effect, the same rules for how groups work apply here as well. If you apply a 3D effect at the group level, all objects inside that group can share the same vanishing point or perspective.

In the example of the barbell that you just created, you were able to create a single axis that all of the objects shared by grouping all of the objects together before applying the 3D effect. Had you selected the objects in the file and applied the 3D Revolve effect without first creating a group, the result would be different, and not what you would expect (**Figure 7.51**).

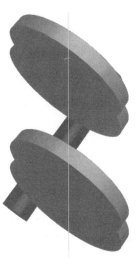

Figure 7.51 If you take the same barbell example, but skip the step that collects all of the shapes within a single group, the result is quite different.

Hopefully, these examples that you've tried so far will help fuel your creativity and give you the information you need to create complex 3D objects on your own.

Applying the 3D Rotate Effect

The Revolve effect doesn't add dimension to an object. Rather, the effect allows you to position a 2D object in a 3D space. Basically, the 3D Rotate effect does the same as the 3D Extrude effect without adding any depth. To apply this effect, select a vector object on the artboard and choose Effect > 3D Rotate to open the 3D Rotate Options dialog. The settings found with this 3D effect are identical to those we've already discussed, although take note that the 3D Rotate effect is limited to far fewer options (**Figure 7.52**). Most notably, you can only specify the Diffuse Shading or No Shading option, there are no bevels, and there is no support for artwork mapping (which we'll cover next).

Figure 7.52 Although there is a More Options button in the 3D Rotate Options dialog, you'll find it doesn't really offer that much.

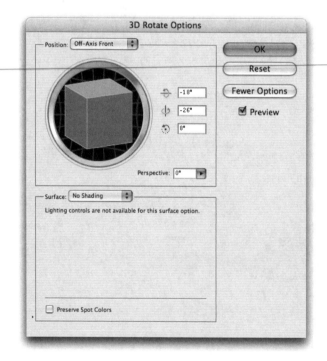

The 3D Rotate effect can be useful for applying distortion to artwork, such as making artwork look as if it's mounted on a billboard. It also enables you to add perspective to your artwork as well.

Mapping Artwork to 3D Surfaces

One of the things that really sets Illustrator's 3D effect apart from the 3D features found in other vector applications is the ability to map 2D artwork onto the surface of a 3D object. This method of combining 2D and 3D graphics is called *artwork mapping*.

So that you understand what artwork mapping really is, let's take a closer look at a 3D cube. As we discussed earlier in the chapter, a 3D cube has six surfaces. Each of these surfaces is treated as a separate entity, and artwork mapping is the process of placing artwork onto these surfaces (**Figure 7.53**).

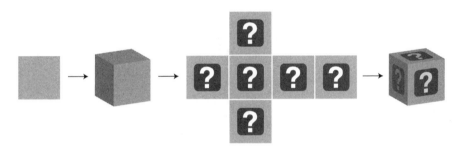

Figure 7.53 Starting with a normal square, a 3D Extrude effect produces a cube with six surfaces. When 2D artwork is placed onto these surfaces, the result is a 3D object with artwork mapping.

There are a few things you have to know before you get started with artwork mapping:

- Artwork must first be defined as a symbol before it can be mapped to a 3D surface. This is actually pretty cool because as you modify a symbol, you will see it automatically update on any 3D surfaces. Refer to Chapter 5, *Brushes, Symbols, and Masks*, for detailed information on how to create and modify symbols.

- You can't map a single symbol across multiple surfaces of a 3D object. If your 3D object has multiple surfaces, you can map symbols to each side individually (**Figure 7.54**).

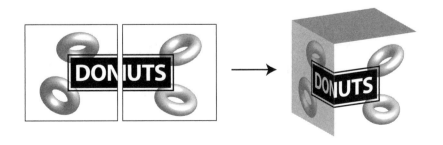

Figure 7.54 In order to create the appearance of artwork that wraps around multiple sides of an object, you have to create multiple symbols and map each section separately.

- When rendering a 3D object, Illustrator uses corner anchor points to define a new surface. Smooth anchor points will not define a new surface. When drawing your art, carefully specifying where corner or smooth anchor points appear on your path gives you greater control over how many surfaces are created and where they appear (**Figure 7.55**).

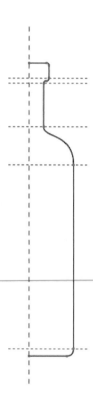

Figure 7.55 By using corner anchor points at certain points on the path of this profile of a wine bottle, you can specify several surface areas to which you can map art.

- Stroked objects make things more complicated. As you learned earlier in the chapter, objects with fills and strokes applied result in an object that has many more surfaces, which makes it difficult to work with. When you're creating a 3D object that will have artwork mapped to it, it's best to avoid using stroked paths.

- Although the 3D effect in Illustrator produces vector results, there are certain times when the 3D effect has to rasterize mapped artwork. If your mapped artwork contains gradients or raster images (such as those placed from Photoshop), Illustrator renders them at the resolution that is set in the Document Raster Effects Settings dialog. Even if your mapped art contains a high-resolution Photoshop file, Illustrator resamples it to match the resolution set in the Document Raster Effects Settings dialog. For best results, make sure the resolution setting in this dialog is high enough for your output needs. Refer to the beginning of this chapter for more information about the settings in this dialog.

Specifying Mapped Artwork

In order to map artwork onto the surface of a 3D object, you must first apply a 3D effect to an object. Then, from either the 3D Extrude & Bevel Options dialog or the 3D Revolve Options dialog, click the Map Art button to bring up the Map Art dialog (**Figure 7.56**). If the Preview option in the resulting Map Art dialog isn't checked, go ahead and turn it on so that you can see what your mapped artwork will look like as you make adjustments to it.

Figure 7.56 The Map Art button appears directly below the Cancel button in the 3D Revolve or 3D Extrude & Bevel Options dialog.

Before you can map art onto your object, you have to choose onto which surface of the object you want to place your artwork. At the top of the Map Art dialog, there are buttons with arrows that allow you to navigate or step through each of the surfaces of your object. As you step through each surface, Illustrator displays the selected surface in the center of the Map Art dialog. In addition, Illustrator tries to help you identify the selected surface by highlighting it with a red outline on the artboard (**Figure 7.57**, next page). Depending on the color of your object, this red outline could be helpful, or it could be barely visible.

Figure 7.57 Illustrator tries to help you identify each of the surfaces, although the alignment of the red outlines isn't always perfect on the artboard.

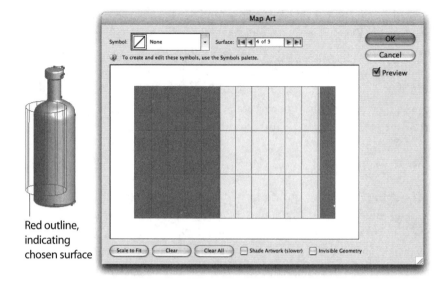

Red outline, indicating chosen surface

The surface that appears in the Map Art dialog is shaped as if it is laid flat. You'll notice as you step through the different surfaces on your object that some show a light gray background whereas others show a dark gray background. Some surfaces may even show a background that is dark gray only in certain areas. This is Illustrator's way of letting you know which surfaces, or which parts of a surface, are not visible, or are hidden from view (**Figure 7.58**). As you would expect, if you choose to use the track cube to view your object from a different perspective, the shaded surface areas in the Map Art dialog updates accordingly.

Figure 7.58 This surface, which is the section that connects the body and neck of the wine bottle, has both shaded and non-shaded sections.

Once you've chosen the surface you want to map art onto, use the Symbol pop-up menu to choose a symbol. The selected symbol appears on the surface area in the Map Art dialog with a bounding box. You can drag the symbol to position it to your liking on the surface, and you can also drag on the handles to resize it (**Figure 7.59**). As you adjust the position of the symbol, you will see the preview update on the actual 3D object on the artboard. Alternatively, you can use the Scale to Fit button at the bottom of the Map Art dialog to have Illustrator resize your symbol to fit to the surface, although it does so non-proportionally.

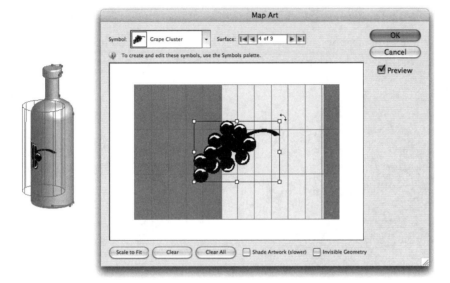

Figure 7.59 You can move and rotate a symbol so that it appears as you need it to on the surface of the object.

Once you're happy with the size and position of your symbol on the selected surface, use the arrows at the top of the dialog to navigate to another side to map additional symbols, as needed. At any time, you can click the Clear button to remove a symbol from a selected surface, or you can click the Clear All button to remove symbols from all surfaces at once.

By default, Illustrator only calculates shading and lighting for the actual surface of a 3D object, and not artwork that is mapped to a 3D surface. Illustrator does this purely for performance reasons. We mentioned earlier that Illustrator uses blends to calculate shading, and breaking down intricately mapped artwork and shading each element with blends takes quite a bit of processing. However, in order to get a realistic appearance, most likely you will want your mapped artwork to be shaded, even if it takes a bit longer to do so. Checking the Shade Artwork (slower) check box forces Illustrator to shade both the surface of your object and the mapped artwork as well. This setting applies to the entire object, and you don't need to turn it on for each individual surface.

It's easier if you create your symbols at the correct size before you map them to a surface; this way, you won't have to worry about getting just the right size or position in the Map Art dialog.

A surface can contain only one symbol. If you want multiple art items to appear on a single surface, you have to define a single symbol with all of the elements in it.

The last setting in the Map Art dialog is a check box marked Invisible Geometry, which is a slightly technical term. When this option is turned on, Illustrator hides the actual 3D object on your artboard and displays just the mapped artwork. The result is a symbol that appears to float in space. A good example of when this setting might be useful is when you want to make text appear as if it were wrapped around a sphere (**Figure 7.60**).

When you're happy with your artwork mapping settings, click OK to accept the settings in the Map Art dialog and then click OK to close the 3D dialog.

Figure 7.60 You can map artwork around a sphere (left), and by using the Invisible Geometry option in the Map Art dialog, you can hide the sphere leaving just the artwork (right).

What If . . . You Add Transparency to 3D?

Throughout this entire book, you've seen how transparency is integrated into Illustrator's feature set with features like soft drop shadows and opacity masks. You might ask yourself, "What if I added transparency to a 3D object?" After all, wouldn't it be cool to make a 3D object that was also transparent so that you could see right through to the back of the object?

Have no fear—as if the 3D effect wasn't cool enough, you can also create transparent 3D objects—but there are two things that you'll have to do in order to get transparency and 3D to work together.

- As we learned earlier in the chapter, before Illustrator applies a 3D effect to an object, it breaks the object down into its components (fills and strokes). In that process, transparency attributes are tossed out and just the appearance remains. For example, if you set an object to 50%

opacity, the 3D effect sets the object to a 50% tint of that color, but you won't be able to see through to what's behind the object. The trick is that you have to sneak transparency into the 3D effect without letting the effect know about it. You can accomplish this in one of two ways. If you have a single object that you're working with, you can target just the fill of the object in the Appearance palette and then change the Opacity value (**Figure 7.61**). Alternatively you can create a group (you can create a group of one object, if you'd like). If transparency is applied to any object within a group, that transparency makes it through the 3D effect unscathed.

Figure 7.61 When you're using the Appearance palette, targeting the fill allows you to apply transparency to just the fill and not the entire object.

- Another useful nugget of information that we learned earlier was that by default, Illustrator only renders the parts of a 3D object that are visible. To speed up the rendering process, Illustrator doesn't bother drawing the sides of a 3D object that are hidden from view. Well, this presents a problem if you're creating an object that is transparent and you expect to see through the front of the object to the back side that's behind it. After all, if Illustrator isn't drawing the hidden side of an object, how does Illustrator know what the back side of the object looks like? The answer is that you have to force Illustrator to draw the hidden sides—you do this by turning on the Draw Hidden Faces option in the 3D Extrude & Bevel Options or 3D Revolve Options dialog.

Once you've addressed these two issues, you'll end up with a 3D object that is truly transparent (**Figure 7.62**, next page). Adding transparency to 3D objects opens new doors to creativity, like creating transparent glass bottles and vases. And don't forget to throw some artwork mapping in there as well. If you map art to a transparent 3D object, you'll be able to see through to the art on the other side. Now you've got to admit, that's pretty freakin' cool, no?

Figure 7.62 This martini glass is transparent, allowing you to see what is inside.

What If . . . You Blend 3D Objects?

In Illustrator, you can select two objects and use the Object > Blend > Make feature to morph one vector shape into another. This technique, as we'll discover in Chapter 9, *Graphs, Distortions, and Blends*, can be useful for a variety of tasks including shading, special effects, and object distribution. However, what if you created a blend using two 3D objects? Would the 3D effect morph as well, along with the blend?

The answer is, yes, it will! If you apply a 3D effect to an object and then duplicate that object (so you have two identical objects), you can create a blend between them. Because 3D is a Live Effect, you can edit the 3D effect of one of the objects and change the position so that you're viewing the object from a completely different angle. The blend will then update—and generate the intermediate steps (**Figure 7.63**).

Not impressed? Well, in Chapter 10, we'll learn how to use blends to create instant Flash animations that you can put on your Web site. That means you can create a box and have it rotate in space. Hey, wait—don't go running off to Chapter 10 yet—we still have plenty of cool stuff to cover in here.

Figure 7.63 By creating a blend between spheres with mapped artwork, you can create the illusion of the sphere rotating.

What If . . . You Apply a 3D Effect to a Graph?

We haven't covered graphs yet (we'll get to that in Chapter 9), but a graph is made up of a group of objects. And because a 3D effect applied at the group level results in all the objects in that group sharing the same effect, what happens if you apply a 3D Extrude effect to a graph? The answer is that you get a powerful way to present numbers in an eye-catching manner (**Figure 7.64**). And if you add transparency to a 3D graph—well, you can see where that might lead.

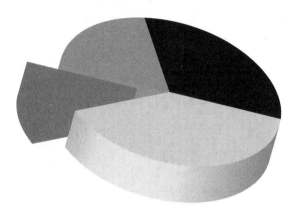

Figure 7.64 Adding 3D effects to just about anything, like graphs, for example, can turn something ordinary into something unique and atten-tion-grabbing.

Can't Find Your Object? Get Smart (Guides)

When you apply a Live Effect to an object, the underlying object remains and only the appear-ance changes. With effects like 3D, there could be a large difference between how the object appears on your artboard and the actual shape itself. When you need to select the vector object to edit it, you might have a hard time trying to locate its exact position. Some users will tell you to switch to the Outline preview mode for such editing, but don't listen to them. Instead, turn on Smart Guides by choosing View > Smart Guides. There are actu-ally many different kinds of Smart Guides (all covered in Appendix C, *Application Pref-erences*), but one in particular—Object Highlighting—can make it easier to find the objects you're looking for.

The Object highlighting attribute of Smart Guides identifies the underlying origi-nal artwork when you mouse over artwork that has had effects or Envelopes applied to it (**Figure 7.65**).

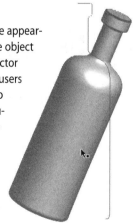

Figure 7.65 When moving the mouse over this 3D object, the Object Highlighting setting of Smart Guides identifies the vector artwork that was used to define the shape.

CONVERT TO SHAPE: CHANGE IS GOOD

The Convert to Shape effect takes the fill of your targeted selection and converts it to a rectangle, a rounded rectangle, or an ellipse. When you first see this effect, you might scratch your head thoughtfully and ask yourself, "Well, if I had wanted a rectangle, wouldn't I have drawn the shape that way in the first place?" It's a good question if your object only has one fill, but if you've added multiple fills, you'll realize that you can apply the Convert to Shape effect on just one of them, which means you can have a single shape with fills that have different shapes. This effect is particularly useful for text objects and for groups and layers as well.

Applying the Convert to Shape Effect

To apply any of the three Convert to Shape effects, target the fill of an object, group, or layer, and choose Effect > Convert to Shape > Rectangle. Although you can choose between the Rectangle, Rounded Rectangle, and Ellipse options, it doesn't matter which one you choose because the ensuing Shape Options dialog allows you to easily switch between the three different shapes via a pop-up menu at the top of the dialog (**Figure 7.66**).

Figure 7.66 It doesn't make a difference which shape you choose from the Convert to Shape submenu, because you get a chance to change your mind in the Shape Options dialog.

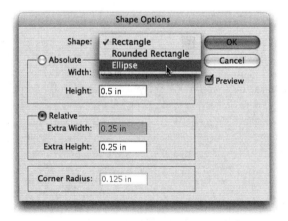

The Shape Options dialog gives you two options for specifying the size of the targeted fill:

- **Absolute.** The Absolute setting allows you to define a specific width and height for the fill shape, which can be completely different than the size of the object's actual path.

- **Relative.** The Relative setting allows you to define a specific amount that is added to the object's actual size. For example, if the object's actual path is 4?4 inches, if you use a relative setting with the Extra Width and Extra Height setting set to .5 inch, the shape effect produces a shape that is 4.5?4.5 inches. The Relative setting is useful when you want to create a shape that changes when the original object changes (see the following "What If . . . You Apply the Convert to Shape Effect to Text?" example).

When the Rounded Rectangle setting is chosen from the Shape pop-up menu, you can also specify a corner radius for the fill shape.

What If . . . You Apply the Convert to Shape Effect to Text?

A practical use for the Convert to Shape effect is to create a background for an object that dynamically adjusts itself as you change the object itself. A good example is when you want to create a button that has text inside of it. Using the Convert to Shape effect, you can have Illustrator automatically resize the button as you change the text within it. Here are the steps required to create this dynamic shape:

1. Choose the Type tool and click a blank area on the artboard to create a Point Type object.

2. Using your keyboard, type the word **Dynamic**.

3. Set your text to 36-point Myriad Roman.

4. Switch to the Selection tool and select the Type object.

5. Then, open the Appearance palette, and from the palette menu, choose Add New Fill.

6. In the Appearance palette, drag the fill you just created so that it appears listed beneath the characters in your Type object (**Figure 7.67**).

Figure 7.67 The fill that you created should be moved so it appears below the characters in the Type object.

7. With the new fill highlighted in the Appearance palette, choose a color from either the Control palette, the Color palette, or the Swatches palette.

   At this stage, you won't see the color change into your text, because the fill you are coloring appears beneath the characters in the Type object.

8. With the colored fill still highlighted in the Appearance palette, choose Effect > Convert to Shape > Rounded Rectangle.

9. In the Shape Options dialog that appears, choose the Relative options and specify .125 inch for both the Extra Width and the Extra Height fields.

10. For the Corner Radius, specify a value of .25 inch, and click OK to apply the effect (**Figure 7.68**).

11. Switch to the Type tool and edit the text.

    You will notice that as you change the text, the colored background expands or contracts as necessary to match the text.

Figure 7.68 The second fill that you created now acts like a background for the text.

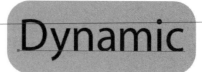

As always, a little bit of experimenting not only gets you more comfortable with these kinds of effects, but it helps you think of ways you can get your work done faster and more efficiently (which is a good thing).

DISTORT & TRANSFORM: THE POWER OF CHANGE

Throughout your design process, you are constantly making changes to your artwork. Sometimes, you need to alter paths by distorting them and other times you need to transform them using functions like Scale or Rotate. Illustrator features a variety of these functions as Live Effects, which make it easy to go back and perform tweaks or changes to these settings as necessary.

Distortion Effects

Illustrator features six different distortion effects, each providing a different type of look and feel. Distortion effects in particular are useful when applied to strokes or fills individually, and this is especially so when you're building complex appearances that contain multiple fills and strokes. You can find each of the effects listed here by first choosing Effect > Distort & Transform and then by choosing one of the following distortion effects:

- **Free Distort.** The Free Distort effect displays your art with a rectangular bounding box. You can drag any of the four corners to stretch or apply a distortion (**Figure 7.69**). This is useful if you want to add perspective to make art appear as if it has a vanishing point, although the 3D Rotate effect offers similar functionality in that regard.

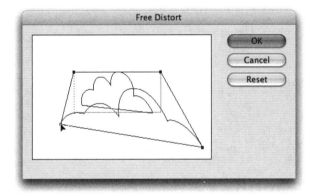

Figure 7.69 The Free Distort effect lets you stretch artwork to apply perspective or distortion.

- **Pucker & Bloat.** The Pucker & Bloat effect offers a slider that applies distortion to your objects by spiking paths. When you're looking for a really funky shape, this distortion effect probably fits the bill.

- **Roughen.** The Roughen effect allows you to take straight paths and make them appear as if they just experienced an earthquake (**Figure 7.70**). The Roughen dialog offers the ability to adjust size and detail; you can also specify whether you want the result to have smooth (rounded) or corner (straight) path segments.

Figure 7.70 You can use the Roughen effect to create torn paper effects, or simply to apply an uneven look to vector art.

- **Tweak.** At first, the Tweak effect appears to be similar to the Pucker & Bloat distortion, but the Tweak effect adjusts control points in addition to anchor points on paths. The result is a path that is far less predictable.

- **Twist.** The Twist effect allows you to twist art from its center using a specified angle.

- **Zig Zag.** The Zig Zag effect is similar to the Roughen effect, but it creates methodical zigzag patterns on selected objects.

Illustrator also has other distortion tools and effects. The Warp effect, covered later in this chapter, provides a way to stretch art using predefined warp styles. Other distortion features like Envelopes and the Liquefy set of tools are covered in Chapter 9.

Transform Effect

If you want to rotate or scale an object on your artboard, using the Transform effect is overkill. Rather, the Transform effect is useful when you want to apply transformations to parts of an object. For example, you might scale two different fills within the same object so they are different sizes. To do so, apply the Transform effect, choose Effect > Distort & Transform > Transform.

The Transform Effect dialog is actually identical to the one that appears when you use the Transform Each function (which we covered back in Chapter 4, *Advanced Vectors*). There is, however, one huge addition in the Transform Effect dialog—the ability to specify copies (**Figure 7.71**).

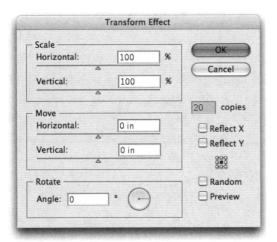

Figure 7.71 The Transform Effect dialog mimics the Transform Each dialog and it includes the ability to set the number of copies you want transformed.

Transforming Objects with Effects

Because we're on the topic of transformations, there are a few things you should be aware of when performing standard transformations on the artboard—specifically when scaling or rotating objects that have Live Effects applied to them.

By default, when you scale an object on the artboard, Illustrator does not scale the values that you may have specified for any Live Effects applied to that object. For example, if you specify a 30-pixel Gaussian Blur effect and then scale that object 200 percent, the Gaussian Blur is still set to 30 pixels. In order to scale an object's Live Effect attributes, you must turn on the Scale Strokes & Effects setting, which you can find in Illustrator's General Preferences panel or by double-clicking the Scale tool in the Toolbox.

It's also important to realize that the values of certain effects have limits. For example, you can't set a Gaussian Blur to anything higher than 250 pixels. Even if you have Scale Strokes & Effects turned on, you can only scale your artwork up until the limit, at which point Illustrator just uses the maximum value it allows. If you need to scale objects to extremely large sizes (for creating signs or banners, for instance), you first have to expand the effect and then scale it as you would any object.

Finally, the values that are specified in the dialogs of Live Effects are relative to the rulers of your document. In many cases, modifying your object may cause unexpected results. For example, say you apply a drop shadow to an object and specify an offset that sets the shadow down and to the right. If you rotate the object 180 degrees on your artboard (effectively turning it upside down), the drop shadow still displays at the lower right of the object. In order to get the correct appearance, you need to edit the drop shadow effect and set the offset so that the drop shadow now falls up and to the left. Alternatively, you can expand the effect before you perform the rotation. This issue requires special attention from printers who often impose files or create work and turn layouts for their presses. It should be noted that InDesign's drop shadows suffer from the same symptoms.

PATHS: DRAWING OUTSIDE THE LINES

At some point, editing vector paths is something that just about every Illustrator user has to come to terms with. However, there are times when performing some of these edits make sense as a Live Effect, which allows the paths to be updated easily. Specifically, three path functions—Offset Path, Outline Object, and Outline Stroke—are available as Live Effects. You can find all of these effects by choosing Effect > Path and by then choosing the required function.

For the most part, these effects are useful when you apply them to Type objects. The Outline Object effect is particularly useful for using text in a way that normally requires the text to be outlined into vector paths. In addition, the Offset Path effect can be helpful when you're trying to create type effects in tandem with the Pathfinder effects, as described later in this chapter (see "What If . . . You Combine Offset Path and Pathfinder Effects on a Text Object?").

PATHFINDER: COMPLEX SHAPES

The Pathfinder effects are identical to those found in the Pathfinder palette (covered in Chapter 4), only here they are applied as Live Effects. Before you question the reason for making these available as Live Effects, remember that you can apply Live Effects to groups and layers. Applying these effects to type may also prove useful.

The following Pathfinder commands are available as Live Effects: Add, Intersect, Exclude, Subtract, Minus Back, Divide, Trim, Merge, Crop, Outline, Hard Mix, Soft Mix, and Trap. Refer to Chapter 4 for details on each of these functions.

To apply any of the Pathfinder effects, make a selection, choose Effect > Pathfinder, and choose the Pathfinder function you need.

What If . . . You Combine Offset Path and Pathfinder Effects on a Text Object?

A design may sometimes call for a word or sentence of text to be outlined with a single line that encompasses all of the letters. The Offset Path filter is perfect for this, but the effect outlines each individual letter that appears in the text. The result is a mess of paths that overlap, making the text difficult—if not impossible—to read. If you were to expand the appearance of the overlapping paths, you might use the Pathfinder Add function to create a single unified shape, but if you do, the text can no longer be edited. This is where a Pathfinder effect can be really helpful:

Follow these steps to learn how you can apply both the Offset Path and Pathfinder effects to text:

1. Choose the Type tool and click a blank area on the artboard to create a Point Type object.

2. Using your keyboard, type the word **Outline**.

3. Set your text to 36-point Myriad Bold.

4. Switch to the Selection tool and select the Type object.

5. Then, open the Appearance palette, and from the palette menu, choose Add New Stroke.

6. With the new stroke highlighted in the Appearance palette, choose Effect > Path > Offset Path.

7. In the Offset Path dialog that appears, specify a value of .0625 inch for the Offset and click OK to apply the effect (**Figure 7.72**).

Figure 7.72 Adding an Offset Path effect to the new stroke that you created adds an outline around the text.

8. With the new stroke still highlighted in the Appearance palette, choose Effect > Pathfinder > Add. The effect is applied immediately (**Figure 7.73**).

9. Switch to the Type tool and edit the text. You will notice that as you change the text, the outline updates accordingly.

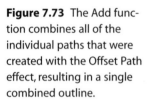

Figure 7.73 The Add function combines all of the individual paths that were created with the Offset Path effect, resulting in a single combined outline.

RASTERIZE: VECTORS THAT ACT LIKE PIXELS

Illustrator has a Rasterize command in the Object menu that gives you the ability to rasterize any object in Illustrator. The Rasterize effect in the Effect menu gives you the exact same functionality—but as a Live Effect. When you think about it, the result of applying this effect is a bit of an oxymoron: the object is a vector, yet it appears and acts like a raster image.

To apply the Rasterize effect, select an object and choose Effect > Rasterize. The options that appear in the Rasterize dialog are similar to those found in the Document Raster Effects Settings dialog and you can even choose to have the Rasterize dialog pick up the resolution settings from that dialog by selected the Use Document Raster Effects Resolution radio button (**Figure 7.74**).

There are several reasons why you might want to use the Rasterize effect. For example, you might want to disable anti-aliasing on small text so that it appears easier to read when displayed on a Web site (more information on this can be found in Chapter 10). In addition, you can use the Rasterize effect to change the Color Model of selected artwork (see the following "What If . . . You Apply the Rasterize Effect to a Raster Image?" example).

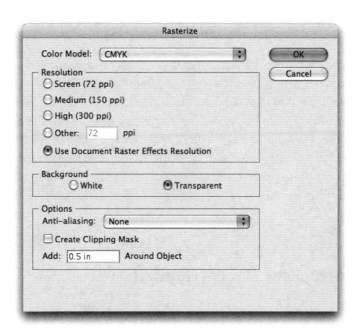

Figure 7.74 To ensure a consistent overall appearance, you might want to have the Rasterize effect share the same resolution setting as in the Document Raster Effects Settings dialog.

What If . . . You Apply the Rasterize Effect to a Raster Image?

It doesn't take a whole lot to realize that the Rasterize effect can turn vector elements into raster elements, but have you ever thought about the possibility of applying the Rasterize effect to a placed raster image in Illustrator? Not only is it possible, it's extremely useful as well. Besides the obvious ability to temporarily downsample high-resolution files to a lower resolution for faster processing, the Rasterize effect has the ability to change color modes. That means you can place a full color photo into a layout, but use the Rasterize effect to change the image to grayscale. Of course, since it's a Live Effect, you can always switch it back to color at any time.

In addition, you can use this method of converting images to grayscale for when you want to convert an entire file to grayscale—including both raster and vector objects. In such a case, you may find it easier to apply the Rasterize effect at the layer level, where all items on a layer can be converted to grayscale.

STYLIZE: NOW YOU'RE STYLIN'!

 The Scribble effect looks simple at first glance, but refer to "What If … You Apply the Scribble Effect to Multiple Fills?" later in this chapter to see how powerful the effect can be.

The group of Stylize Live Effects gets a bit more visibility than other effects for one main reason: the celebrity factor. Among the different effects you'll find in the Stylize submenu is the rock star of all Live Effects, the Drop Shadow. Although there's nothing that special about the Drop Shadow effect per se, it seems designers these days are trying to find untold ways to add drop shadows to their artwork. We don't discriminate between different Live Effects (we're an equal opportunity educator), and the reality is, plenty of other useful effects appear in the Stylize submenu including Add Arrowheads, Feather, Inner and Outer Glow, Round Corners, and the sleeper Live Effect of the year—Scribble.

The Add Arrowheads Effect

 The Drop Shadow Live Effect is covered in Chapter 3.

If you need to add arrowheads to the end of paths for creating diagrams or callouts, the Add Arrowheads Live Effect is just for you. With any path selected, choose Effect > Stylize > Add Arrowheads. From the Add Arrowheads dialog, you can specify 27 different types of arrowheads for both the start and/or end of your path (**Figure 7.75**). A helpful Preview check box makes it easy to see the results of the effect on your artboard as you experiment with different arrowhead styles.

Figure 7.75 The Add Arrowheads dialog offers a variety of styles, although unfortunately, there's no way to define or create your own.

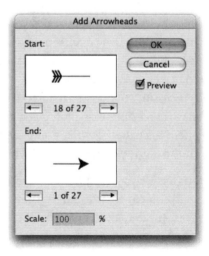

Illustrator uses the stroke width of your path to determine the size of the arrowhead, but you can adjust the size to perfection by using the Scale setting at the bottom of the dialog. You'll also notice that the arrowheads always match the orientation of the path, so if you adjust the path after you've added the effect, the arrowhead updates accordingly.

The Feather Effect

Vector paths are known for their clean, crisp edges, but at times, you want a softer edge to your objects. That's where the Feather effect can be of help. Choose Effect > Stylize > Feather and specify an amount to determine how soft of an edge you want your shape to have. You can even apply a Feather effect directly to a placed photograph (**Figure 7.76**).

Another way to add an arrowhead to a stroke is to define and use a custom Pattern brush. Refer to Chapter 5 for more information on Pattern brushes.

It's interesting to note that the Add Arrowheads effect works on both open and closed paths. The filter is also a great way to quickly figure out the direction of a path.

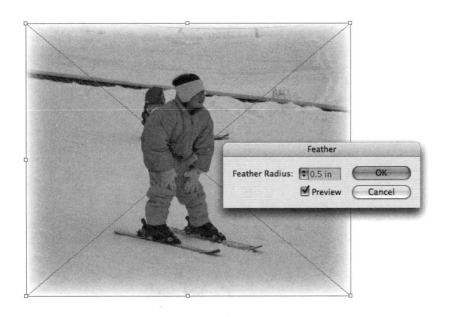

Figure 7.76 With a placed image selected, you can apply a Feather effect as you would to any vector object.

The Inner Glow and Outer Glow Effects

As a variation to the Drop Shadow effect, Illustrator also offers an Inner Glow and an Outer Glow effect. You can find both of these effects in the Effect > Stylize submenu.

Try using a Feather on an object that you're using as an opacity mask; this allows you to create a mask with soft edges.

The Inner Glow effect adds a soft glow to the inside area of an object. From the Inner Glow dialog, you can choose the Center option, which starts the glow from the center of the object and extends it toward the edges, or you can choose the Edge option, which begins the glow in the opposite direction—from the edge toward the center of the shape (**Figure 7.77**). The Outer Glow effect adds a soft glow to the outside edges of an object.

Figure 7.77 Depending on the desired effect, you can specify an Inner Glow effect to start from the center (left), or the edge (right).

The Round Corners Effect

 Glow effects can sometimes appear too soft for your needs. To beef up a glow effect, try applying two or three glow effects to the same object.

Illustrator's Rounded Rectangle tool is so year 2000. Welcome to today's fast-paced world where you can add rounded corners to any object, no matter how many corners the object has (**Figure 7.78**). When you select an object and choose Effect > Stylize > Round Corners, you can use the Preview check box to experiment with different Radius settings until you get just the look you need. Of course, you can always change the Radius setting because it's a Live Effect.

Figure 7.78 The usefulness of the Round Corners effect becomes apparent when you apply it to objects with many corners.

Unfortunately, you can't specify which corners of your object will get rounded—the Round Corners effect rounds all corners. If you only want some corners to be rounded in your object, you need to apply the Round Corners effect, and then expand the effect so that you can manually adjust each corner as necessary.

For an interesting effect, try applying the Round Corners effect to type.

The Scribble Effect

If there's one thing that you can count on with vector graphics, it's clean sharp edges. However, sometimes a design calls for something a little bit less technical and more natural. The Scribble effect in Illustrator is perfect for this task. And, as you will see, the power of the Scribble effect lies in its ability to randomize individual attributes, giving the effect a truly natural and hand-drawn appearance. One of the nicest things about the Scribble effect is that it has the ability to draw outside the lines. In fact, what the Scribble effect really does is convert your object into one long stroke (**Figure 7.79**).

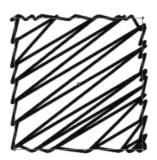

Figure 7.79 Here, using one of the many settings in the Scribble effect, we illustrate how the object's appearance is converted to one lone stroke.

To apply the Scribble effect, select an object and choose Effect > Stylize > Scribble to bring up the Scribble Options dialog. The dialog contains five main settings that control the overall appearance of the Scribble effect. Some of the settings also have a Variation slider, allowing the scribble appearance to vary throughout your object.

As you will quickly find out, making even small adjustments to the Scribble effect settings can have a large impact on the appearance of the object. Using a combination of different settings, you can also achieve a variety of different styles for your Scribble. To illustrate this, Adobe added a pop-up menu at the top of the dialog that contains different presets (**Figure 7.80**). Switch between the different presets to see the ways you might use the Scribble effect. Unfortunately, you cannot define your own presets. However, you can always save your Scribble setting as a Graphic Style once you've applied it to an object.

Figure 7.80 A variety of presets help you quickly learn the different types of styles you can achieve with the Scribble effect.

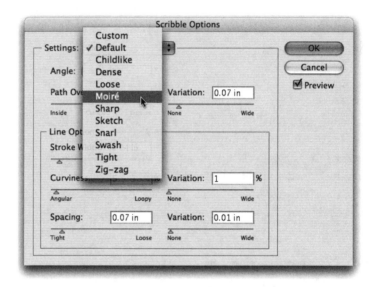

Although it may seem a bit daunting at first, the different settings in the Scribble Options dialog are rather straightforward:

- **Angle.** The Angle setting defines which direction the stroke will travel. Click and drag the dial to adjust the setting or enter a value manually in the field.

- **Path Overlap.** The Path Overlap setting defines how far the stroke overlaps the edge of the object's path. This setting can also be set to a negative value, which effectively defines how close the stroke can come to the edge of an object's path. You can also set a variation, which allows the Path Overlap setting to randomly change throughout the object within the value that you define (**Figure 7.81**).

- **Stroke Width.** The Stroke Width setting defines the thickness of the stroke that Illustrator uses to create your Scribble effect. Unfortunately, this setting does not have a variation slider.

- **Curviness.** The Curviness setting defines how much a stroke loops when it changes direction. A very small number produces more of a straight zigzag effect with pointy ends, while a larger number produce loose changes in direction with loopy ends (**Figure 7.82**). You can also define a Variation value so that this setting appears differently throughout the object.

- **Spacing.** The Spacing setting defines how dense the strokes appear. Again, this setting has a Variation slider, which allows the Scribble effect to vary the spacing throughout the object.

Figure 7.81 Adding a Variation to the Path Overlap setting allows the Scribble effect to draw outside the lines using a natural technique.

Figure 7.82 Smaller Curviness settings create sharp lines (left) while higher values create a more freestyle appearance (right).

What If . . . You Apply the Scribble Effect to Multiple Fills?

Adding a Scribble effect to an object can certainly give it a hand-drawn look and feel, but there are times when you need something more than just strokes traveling in the same direction. Combining multiple fills—each with a different Scribble effect setting—can produce cross-hatching effects that produce wonderful patterns, textures, and edges. Here's how it is done:

1. Using the Ellipse tool, draw a circle that is 4 inches in diameter.

2. Give the circle a fill of Black with a stroke of None.

3. With the circle selected, open the Appearance palette and target the fill by clicking it.

4. Choose Effect > Stylize > Scribble to open the Scribble Options dialog.

5. Choose Default from the Setting pop-up menu and make the following adjustments: set the Stroke Width to .01 inches; set the Curviness to 2%; and set the Spacing to .03 inches.

6. Leave all of the remaining settings and click OK to apply the effect (**Figure 7.83**).

Figure 7.83 Applying the Scribble effect to the circle gives it an interesting appearance.

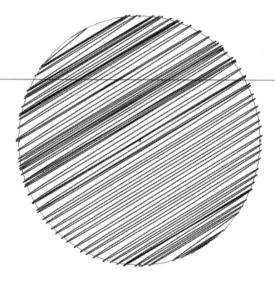

7. With the fill still highlighted in the Appearance palette, choose Duplicate Item from the palette menu to create a second fill with the same attributes as the first.

8. Double-click one of the Scribble effects listed in the Appearance palette (it doesn't matter which one), to edit the effect.

9. Change the Angle setting to 130 degrees and click OK to apply the edit (**Figure 7.84**).

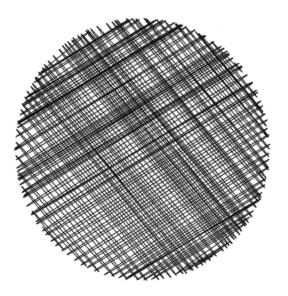

Figure 7.84 Adding a second fill with another Scribble effect gives the circle a lattice-like appearance. Notice the crosshatch effects around the edges of the shape as well.

SVG FILTERS: TECHNICAL EFFECTS

SVG (Scalable Vector Graphics) is a vector-based file format that can be used for displaying graphics on the Web and handheld devices. We discuss SVG graphics in detail in both Chapter 10 and Chapter 12, but there are certain effects that can be applied to graphics that are saved in the SVG format. These effects, called SVG filter effects, are really XML-based instructions that are applied when the SVG graphic is rendered in a Web browser or viewer. As a result, these effects are only useful when applied to graphics that will eventually be saved as SVG.

Illustrator ships with a collection of 18 SVG filter effects, although if you know how to code them yourself, you can also write your own. To apply an SVG filter effect, select an object and choose Effect > SVG Filters > Apply SVG Filter. Once the Apply SVG Filter dialog is open, you can click a filter from the list and click OK. Alternatively, you can highlight a filter and click the Edit SVG Filter button to modify the selected filter effect, or you can click the New SVG Filter button to create a new SVG filter effect from scratch. Additionally, you can delete selected filters by using the trash icon in the Apply SVG Filter dialog.

 For information on how to create your own SVG filter effects (and download existing code), visit www.w3.org/TR/SVG/filters.html.

 SVG Effects should be the last effects applied in the stacking order when multiple effects are being specified, otherwise the SVG Effect will end up being rasterized.

Illustrator can also import SVG filters. To do so, choose Effect > SVG Filters > Import SVG Filter. In the ensuing dialog, open an SVG file with a filter effect in it; when you do, Illustrator will import that filter into your current file.

Warp: Controlled Distortion

Refer to Chapter 9 for detailed information on Illustrator's other distortion features, as well as a featured match-up sidebar of those features as they compare to the Warp effect.

The Warp effect is one of several distortion functions in Illustrator's arsenal. You can use Warp to apply any of 15 different preset distortions to any object, group, or layer.

To apply a Warp effect, make a selection and choose Effect > Warp > Arc. Even though all 15 warp styles are listed in the submenu, you don't have to worry about choosing the right one just yet—the Warp Options dialog lets you choose from any of the preset warp styles.

When the Warp Options dialog appears, turn on the Preview check box so that you can preview your warp on your artboard as you adjust the settings. Click the Style pop-up menu to choose from the list of warp styles, which comprise Arc, Arc Lower, Arc Upper, Arch, Bulge, Shell Lower, Shell Upper, Flag, Wave, Fish, Rise, Fisheye, Inflate, Squeeze, and Twist. Little icons appear to the left of each warp style to help you visualize what each one does, although trial and error work better in our opinion (**Figure 7.85**).

Figure 7.85 The little icons that appear to the left of each Warp effect help you understand what each option actually does.

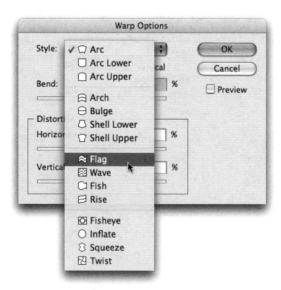

Once you've chosen a warp style, you can specify whether the warp is applied horizontally or vertically, and you can adjust how slight or extreme the warp is applied by adjusting the Bend slider. Additionally, you can use the Horizontal and Vertical Distortion sliders to apply additional distortion to your selection.

Warp effects are particularly useful when applied at the group or layer level, where you might often add or remove elements from the group. For example, you might apply a Warp effect to a logo to show movement or excitement. If you applied the Warp effect at the group level, adding new art to the group will automatically cause the new art to take on the same Warp effect as well.

What If . . . You Apply the Warp Effect to 3D Text?

A powerful way to accentuate a logo or a headline is to add a 3D Extrude effect to text. Because 3D is a Live Effect, there is no need to first convert text to outlines. Adding a Warp effect to 3D text can take things to the next level and opens a world of possibilities. Try it:

1. Choose the Type tool and click a blank area on the artboard to create a Point Type object.

2. Using your keyboard, type the word **SPECTACULAR**.

3. Set your text to 36-point Myriad Bold, and specify a fill of 25K and a stroke of 60K.

4. Using the Selection tool, select the text and choose Effect > 3D > Extrude & Bevel.

5. The default settings are fine for this exercise, so click the OK button to apply the effect (**Figure 7.86**).

Figure 7.86 When you've applied the 3D effect, you'll notice that the extrude color is the darker stroke color that you specified earlier.

6. With the text still selected, choose Effect > Warp > Arc.

7. Specify a Bend value of 30% and click OK to apply the effect (**Figure 7.87**).

Figure 7.87 Applying a Warp effect to the 3D text combines the two effects for a truly spectacular result.

Of course, you can use the Type tool to edit the text as needed—both the 3D and the Warp effects update accordingly. Turning on Smart Guides makes it easier to select the text on the artboard.

APPLYING PHOTOSHOP EFFECTS

The effects that we have discussed to this point are considered Illustrator effects, and for the most part, they are vector in nature and make adjustments to vector paths (with the obvious exception of the Rasterize effect and most of the Stylize effects).

However, Illustrator also has the ability to apply a variety of purely pixel-based effects to any object, group, or layer. These effects are grouped together under the Photoshop Effects section of the Effect menu. The same rules as to how effects are applied through the Effect menu and edited via the Appearance palette apply to these effects as well.

In truth, the Photoshop effects that are found at the bottom portion of the Effect menu are really Photoshop filters. You can copy Photoshop filters and plugins into the Illustrator Plug-ins folder (found in the same folder in which the Illustrator application file appears), and those appear listed in the Effect menu as well.

At first, it may seem unnatural to find that you can apply a Gaussian Blur or an Unsharp Mask in Illustrator, but you'll quickly find that you can achieve wonderful designs and cool effects by employing Photoshop filters like

Crystallize and Mezzotint. Some of the Graphic Styles libraries that ship with Illustrator employ a variety of these effects, and by reverse engineering them, you can learn how to use them.

 ## Featured Match-Up: Illustrator Effects vs. Photoshop Effects

At first glance, it may appear that the Illustrator effects are purely vector in nature and the Photoshop effects are raster-based ones, but this isn't true. Effects like Feather and Drop Shadow, which appear in the Stylize submenu, are listed as Illustrator effects and they produce raster content. So what then is the distinction between Illustrator and Photoshop effects?

The difference is relatively simple, yet absolutely critical: resolution.

At the beginning of the chapter, we learned how the Document Raster Effects Settings dialog determines the resolution at which effects are rasterized when the document is either flattened or printed. But the setting is also important for determining the appearance of some effects. Let's take a look at an example.

1. Open the Document Raster Effects Settings dialog and set the resolution to 72 ppi and Click OK.

2. Draw two identical circles.

3. Apply a Feather effect to one circle (an Illustrator effect) and a Gaussian Blur effect to the other (a Photoshop effect) and then observe the results (**Figure 7.88**).

4. Now open the Document Raster Effects Settings dialog, change the resolution to 300 ppi, and click OK. Observe the results of the effects (**Figure 7.89**).

You'll notice that the appearance of the Gaussian Blur effect has changed, but the Feather effect remained the same. This happens because the Gaussian Blur effect (and all Photoshop effects, for that matter) uses absolute measurements to calculate the effect. You'll notice the Gaussian Blur effect dialog specifies the blur value in pixels (**Figure 7.90**, next page). Changing the resolution—the number of pixels in your file—changes the appearance of your effect. In contrast, the Feather effect—and all Illustrator effects—uses relative units to calculate the effect (**Figure 7.91**, next page). The Feather dialog specifies the feather value in inches (or whatever measurement system you've chosen in preferences), so when you change the resolution setting, Illustrator simply adjusts the number of pixels it uses in the effect, as needed.

Figure 7.88 Shown is a circle with a Feather effect applied (left), and a circle with a Gaussian Blur effect applied (right). Both appear similar.

Figure 7.89 The circle with the Feather (left) remains unchanged in appearance, but the circle with the Gaussian Blur (right) now displays differently than it did before the change in resolution.

continues on next page

Featured Match-Up: Illustrator Effects vs. Photoshop Effects *(continued)*

Overall, we refer to Photoshop effects as below-the-line effects because they appear below the divider line in the Effect menu (**Figure 7.92**). When using below-the-line effects, it's best to ensure that your Document Raster Effects Setting is correct before you begin working on your design. Otherwise, the appearance of your artwork will change when you adjust it later (or if your printer adjusts it). If you use above-the-line effects (Illustrator effects), you can get better performance by leaving the Document Raster Effects Setting at a lower resolution until you are about the send the file out for high-end output.

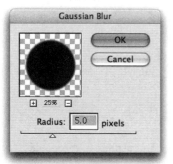

Figure 7.90 The Gaussian Blur effect uses pixels to calculate the effect.

Figure 7.91 The Feather effect uses relative units (in this case, inches) to calculate the effect.

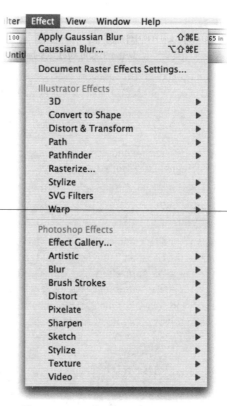

Figure 7.92 All effects that appear below the line are considered Photoshop Effects and are resolution dependent.

A Gallery of Effects

Going through each Photoshop Effect listed in the Effect menu is beyond the scope of this book, but one feature that really makes it easy to experiment with a wide range of Photoshop effects is the Effects Gallery. If you're familiar with Photoshop's Filter Gallery feature, you'll find that the Effects Gallery is the same. To use this feature, you have to be in an RGB document (see "CMYK Need Not Apply," on the next page). Once you've targeted an object, group, or layer, choose Effect > Effects Gallery, which opens the Filter Gallery dialog. The dialog is split into three main sections: a preview on the left; a list of the different effects that you can apply in the center; and the parameters for the selected effect on the right (**Figure 7.93**).

 Be aware that copying objects with below-the-line effects from one document to another may cause the appearance to change if the two files have different resolution settings.

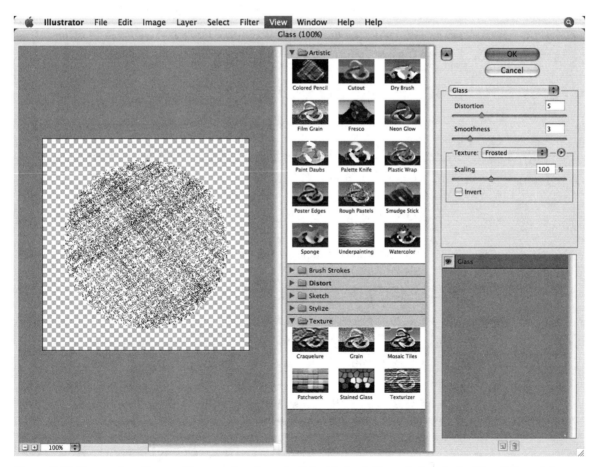

Figure 7.93 You can literally spend hours going through all the kinds of effects that are in the Filter Gallery dialog.

To preview different effects, click an effect in the center area (expand the folders to see the individual effects), and adjust the settings at the upper right of the dialog. Once you've found the effect you like, click the OK button to apply it.

CMYK Need Not Apply

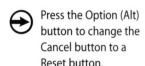

Press the Option (Alt) button to change the Cancel button to a Reset button.

Don't freak out if you find that many of the Photoshop effects are grayed out in your menu. Many of the Photoshop effects are only available when your document color mode is set to RGB. This is because these effects, which come from Photoshop, are designed to work only in RGB mode, and the algorithms used for these effects do not work in four channels (they are usually grayed out in CMYK Photoshop files as well).

If you're working in a CMYK document but want to apply a Photoshop effect that only works in RGB mode, you can do the following:

1. Choose File > Document Color Mode > RGB Color to change the color mode of the document from CMYK to RGB.

2. Apply the desired Photoshop effect from the Effect menu.

3. Select the object and choose Object > Expand Appearance.

    This step is necessary because if you leave the effect as a Live Effect, when you switch the document back to CMYK, the appearance of the effect disappears (it will still be listed in the Appearance palette for that object, but the effect won't be visible and won't print). By expanding the appearance, you are rasterizing the effect so that it effectively becomes an embedded image that can be converted back to CMYK.

4. Choose File > Document Color Mode > CMYK Color to change the color mode of the document back to CMYK.

It's important to note that this method can result in colors shifting or changing in value, but if you really want to apply a certain effect that only works in RGB mode, this is a way to accomplish that. If there are many other objects in your file, you might consider performing the color conversion in a separate file and simply copying the converted art back into your original file when you are done.

Additionally, because you've expanded the effect, the effect is no longer live and any editing would require you to rebuild the object and to repeat the steps outlined here.

CHAPTER 8

Mixing It Up: Working with Vectors and Pixels

There's no velvet rope barring entry to Adobe Illustrator's exclusive vector graphics club. Pixels are always welcomed inside. In fact, in the last chapter, we learned how certain Live Effects use pixels to produce their appearance. In Illustrator, there is indeed a peaceful coexistence between vectors and pixels, and as we discussed back in Chapter 2, *Vectors 101*, there are benefits to combining both vectors and pixels (such as adding a soft drop shadow to text). There's no reason why you should feel that you have to choose only one graphic type or the other.

Although Illustrator does have the ability to support pixels in some ways (as we'll see throughout this chapter), it in no way replaces the need for applications like Adobe Photoshop. Quite the contrary, in this chapter we'll see how you can bring pixel-based images from Photoshop into Illustrator documents. You will also learn how both Photoshop and Illustrator can work together by enabling you to share editable content between them. You can then focus on producing the kinds of graphics that you need by relying on the strengths of each of these powerful applications.

So turn up the music and feel the pulsing beat of vectors dancing with pixels, because this chapter will also cover Illustrator CS2's ability to assimilate pixels and convert them into vector paths using a feature called Live Trace.

PLACING RASTER-BASED FILES

When creating designs and layouts in Illustrator, at times you will need to incorporate raster-based content, such as photographs. Naturally, these images are neither created nor edited in Illustrator—raster-based application programs such as Photoshop take care of things like that. However, you can *place* raster-based content into your Illustrator file. In fact, Illustrator works very much like a page layout application in this way.

When an image is placed, Illustrator can incorporate that image in the file in two different ways. In the first method, Illustrator places a preview of the image on your artboard, but the image file itself is not incorporated into the Illustrator file. The image file exists as an external reference, separate from the Illustrator file. This first method is referred to as *place-linking* because the image file is linked to the Illustrator document. If you were to misplace the linked file, Illustrator would not be able to print the image.

In the second method, Illustrator places the actual image file within the Illustrator document and incorporates the image into the Illustrator file. This second method is referred to as *place-embedding*, where the image becomes a part of the Illustrator file.

You can choose which of these two methods you want to use when you physically place the file. For a detailed explanation of the numerous benefits and caveats of using each method, refer to the sidebar, "Featured Match-Up: Place-Linked Files vs. Place-Embedded Files."

Ways to Place an Image

You can place a raster file into an Illustrator document in several ways. You can either place a file, open it directly, or drag it right onto your artboard. Each method has its own benefits; your task is to determine which one you will use.

Method One: Placing a File

When you already have a file open and you need to place an image into your document, this method offers the most options and is one of the most commonly used ways to place a file.

1. From an open document, choose File > Place and navigate to a raster file on your hard drive or server.

2. At the bottom of the Place dialog are three check boxes (**Figure 8.1**): check the Link box to place-link the file (unchecking the Link box place-embeds the file); check the Template box to have the image automatically placed on a Template layer; and check the Replace box to have the image replace one that is already selected on the artboard.

3. Once you've selected the file and checked the options you need, click the Place button to place the file into your document.

Figure 8.1 When placing a file, you can control whether an image is place-linked by checking the Link check box in the Place dialog.

 See "Manual Tracing with Template Layers," later in this chapter, for more information on creating a template layer.

Method Two: Opening a File

Choose File > Open, and then navigate to choose a raster file on your hard drive or server and click the Open button. Illustrator creates a new document and places the image in it. When you're opening a raster file in this way, the image is always place-embedded within your Illustrator document.

Method Three: Dragging a File

From Adobe Bridge, the Finder on Mac OS, or from any Windows Explorer window, drag a raster file right onto your Illustrator artboard. You can also select multiple files and place them all at once (**Figure 8.2**). Using this method, Illustrator place-links the files. To place-embed images while dragging them into your document, hold the Shift key while dragging the images.

 It is notably easier to drag files into your document when Bridge is in Compact mode.

Figure 8.2 When you're dragging several images at once from Bridge, an icon indicates the placement of multiple files into your Illustrator document.

Featured Match-Up: Place-Linked Files vs. Place-Embedded Files

When placing an image into Illustrator, you can choose to have the image linked to your document or embedded within it. Each method has its own benefits, and which you choose depends on your needs and your workflow.

When you link an image, a preview of the image appears in your layout, but the actual image exists in a completely separate file. At all times, Illustrator needs to know where this file is. Otherwise, Illustrator won't be able to print the file correctly. In fact, if you were to save your Illustrator file and send it off to someone else (like a service provider for example), you would have to send the external linked image along with the file. If you have several linked images in your document, you have to keep track of many different files. In contrast, an embedded file exists within your Illustrator document, and therefore, the original external image that you placed is no longer required. When you send the document to another user, the image travels along with the single Illustrator file.

Images—especially high-resolution ones—feature hefty file sizes. When you choose to embed a placed image, the file size of the image is added to the size of your Illustrator file. For example, if your Illustrator file is 1 MB in size and you place-embed a 30 MB image into your document, the size of your Illustrator document grows to 31 MB. When you place-link an image however, the file is never added to your document, so the Illustrator file stays at 1 MB.

Although managing multiple files and file size are issues that will affect your decision to link or embed image files, one of the main reasons you will choose to link a file rather than embed it is so you can easily update the image when necessary. When you place-link a file, the image that you see in your layout is a preview of the file that really exists elsewhere. Anytime you make an adjustment to the original image (i.e., in Photoshop), the preview in your layout updates to reflect those changes. Illustrator even has a feature called Edit Original that assists in this process of updating linked images (see "Managing Placed Images," later in this chapter). However, if you place-embed an image, you can no longer update that image easily.

Placing Native Photoshop Files (PSD)

Typically, the interchange file formats for images that are used in print design layouts are TIFF or EPS, but Illustrator allows you to place native Photoshop files (PSD) as well.

Generally, placing a native Photoshop file isn't any different than placing any other file. Illustrator enjoys a wonderful relationship with Photoshop, however, and you can take advantage of extended functionality when placing Photoshop files.

If the PSD file that you are placing contains Photoshop Layer Comps, Illustrator presents you with the Photoshop Import Options dialog, where you can choose which Layer Comp will be visible in the file from the Layer Comp pop-up menu (**Figure 8.3**). Check the Show Preview box to see what the Layer Comp looks like before you place the file. You can also choose whether Illustrator or Photoshop controls how layer visibility is updated by choosing from the When Updating Link pop-up menu. The Photoshop Import Options dialog offers additional options, which are covered later in this chapter in "Working with Adobe Photoshop."

The Layer Comps feature in Photoshop allows you to create named sets of visible layers. For more information on Layer Comps, refer to Photoshop's Online Help or *Real World Adobe Photoshop CS2*, by David Blatner and Bruce Fraser (Peachpit Press, 2005).

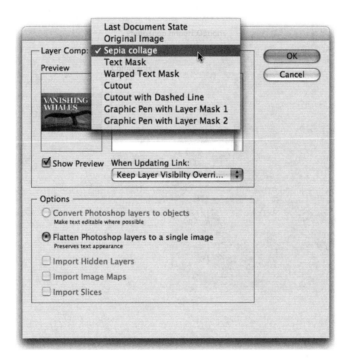

Figure 8.3 The Photoshop Import Options dialog allows you to control the appearance of your Photoshop file before you place it into your document.

Unfortunately, once an image is placed into an Illustrator document, there is no way to access the Photoshop Import Options dialog to change to a different Layer Comp. To work around this apparent oversight, you can use the Relink function, which effectively places the file again and brings up the dialog (see "Managing Placed Images" for information on relinking files).

For a detailed description of the different file formats and their benefits and roles in a design workflow, refer to Chapter 12, *Saving and Exporting Files*.

WORKING WITH PLACED IMAGES

Once you've placed an image into an Illustrator document, the image acts like a single rectangular shape that can be transformed (scaled, rotated, skewed, and mirrored). You can apply opacity and blend mode values from the Transparency palette, and you can also apply many different Live Effects to a placed image, including Feather and Drop Shadow.

Sometimes a design calls for showing only a portion of a placed image. Programs like Photoshop (which can crop images) and page layout applications such as InDesign (which use picture frames) are able to display only portions of an image. Illustrator however, has no such tool or functionality. To have only a portion of an image display on your artboard, you have to create a mask (**Figure 8.4**). (Creating masks is covered in detail in Chapter 5, *Brushes, Symbols, and Masks*).

Figure 8.4 Using a clipping mask, you can display just a portion of a placed image.

 Be sure to check out Conrad Chavez's example of colorizing images in the color insert.

You can also apply color to certain kinds of placed images. Illustrator allows you to apply either a solid process or spot color to a 1-bit TIFF image, or any image that uses the grayscale color model. Simply select the image on the artboard and choose a fill color from the Swatches palette or the Color palette.

Manual Tracing with Template Layers

There may be times when you want to place an image into Illustrator—
not as a design *element*, but rather as a design *guide*. For example, you might
sketch out an idea for a design on paper and then scan that sketch into your
computer. Then, you would place that scan into your Illustrator document
as a guide for drawing final shapes with Illustrator's vector tools. Alternatively, you may place a map into Illustrator so that you can create your own
customized directions to an event.

In these cases, you may not actually want to trace the scan exactly as it
appears (using Illustrator CS2's Live Trace feature, covered later in this
chapter, might be a better choice for such a task), but rather, you just
want the image to act as a reference. To prevent the image from getting in
the way of your design, you might want to adjust the opacity of the
image. Additionally, you may want to lock the image so that you don't
move it accidentally.

Rather than going through the process of adjusting and locking images,
Illustrator has a way to manage this process in a more dignified manner—
using a template layer. Once a template layer has been created, the image on
that layer automatically becomes locked and the opacity level of the image
is set to 50% (**Figure 8.5**, left). You can either check the Template option at
the bottom of the Place dialog when placing an image to have the image
automatically appear on a template layer, or you can double-click any layer
and check the Template option (**Figure 8.5**, right).

 Template layers are not
to be confused with
Illustrator templates,
which are actual Illustrator files that contain
elements already inside
of them. Illustrator
templates are covered in
Chapter 1, *The Illustrator
Environment.*

Figure 8.5 Drawing on top of
an image at full strength may
be difficult (left). Placing an
image on a dimmed template
layer allows you to trace over
the image with ease (right).

Figure 8.6 The Template option appears in the Layer Options dialog and applies to a single layer.

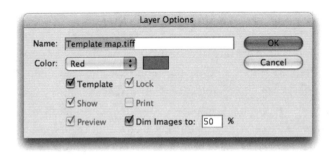

MANAGING PLACED IMAGES

Whether the images that you place in a file are linked or embedded, it's important to be able to track where those images came from and to access additional information about the images themselves. To manage all of the placed images in your document, choose Window > Links to open the Links palette.

By default, the Links palette lists all of the images in your document. However, from the Links palette menu, you can specify that the Links palette only display missing, modified, or embedded images (**Figure 8.7**). In addition, you can choose to have the Links palette list images sorted by name (filename), kind (file type), or status (up to date, or modified).

Figure 8.7 Icons in the Layers palette indicate additional information about the images that are placed in your document. No icon indicates a place-linked file.

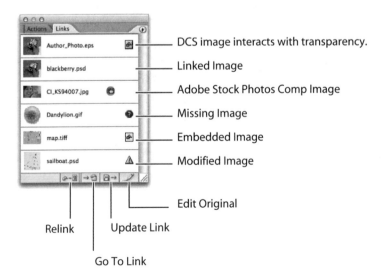

Double-clicking any file listed in the Links palette opens a Link Information dialog, offering additional information about the image. Besides listing the file size of the image, the Link Information dialog also gives you the location of the image (the file path), and detailed scaling and rotation information (**Figure 8.8**).

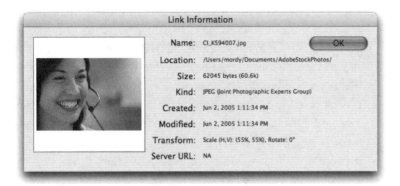

Figure 8.8 Double-clicking a listing in the Links palette brings up Link Information, a dialog containing useful information.

Along the bottom of the Links palette are four buttons (refer back to Figure 8.7) that allow you to perform certain functions with the images in your document. To use these functions, first highlight an image in the Links palette, and then click the desired button.

- **Relink.** The Relink button allows you to replace one image with a different one. When you click the Relink button, the Place dialog appears, allowing you to choose another file, which replaces the selected image. You can use Relink to either swap high-resolution files for low-resolution ones, or to replace FPO (For Position Only) placeholder images with final copies. Additionally, you can use the Relink function and choose to replace your file with the same image (replacing it with itself), which allows you to access different Place settings or to replace an embedded image that was updated.

- **Go To Link.** The Go To Link button adjusts the view setting of your document window so that the highlighted image in the Links palette is centered on your screen. In addition, the image becomes selected. This makes it easy to quickly find an image and it is especially useful in documents that contain many placed images.

- **Update Link.** The Update Link button is used to update place-linked images when Illustrator detects that external files have been modified outside of Illustrator. Images that have been modified appear with a yellow warning icon in the Links palette. The Update Link button is dim when an embedded image is chosen.

 Refer to Appendix C, *Application Preferences,* for information on the Update Links setting in the File Handling & Clipboard preference panel, which controls whether Illustrator updates modified files automatically or manually.

- **Edit Original.** The Edit Original button is used when you want to modify a place-linked image in the image's creator application. When you highlight an image in the Links palette and choose Edit Original, Illustrator launches the application that was used to create the file (or that is set to open files of that type on your system) and then opens the file for you. Once you perform any necessary edits on the file, simply save and close it and return to Illustrator, where the image updates accordingly. The Edit Original button is dim when an embedded image is chosen.

Additional Links Palette Functionality

In addition to the functions in the Links palette that we've already discussed, you can take advantage of several other settings through the use of the Links palette, which you'll find listed in the palette menu (**Figure 8.9**).

Figure 8.9 The Links palette menu grants you access to additional features for working with placed images.

- **Link File Info.** Images and files can contain metadata (refer to Chapter 1 for more information), and at times, you may need to view the metadata of images that you've placed into your document. For example, you may want to know if you have rights to reproduce the image, or whom you need to credit for using an image. The Link File Info option in the Links palette menu allows you to view the placed image's metadata (you won't be able to edit it, however).

- **Placement Options.** When you relink or replace a file, you can use the Placement Options setting to define how an image appears once it has been placed into your document. By default, Illustrator preserves any transforms that you've applied to the image that you're replacing, but you can also choose from four other settings. A helpful illustration within the Placement Options dialog explains what each setting does (**Figure 8.10**).

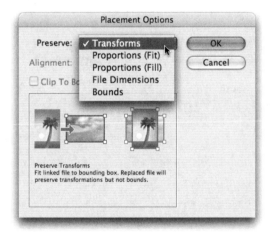

Figure 8.10 Each setting in the Placement Options dialog offers an illustration and a description for what it does.

- **Purchase This Image.** When placing a comp that you've downloaded using the Adobe Stock Photos service, Illustrator displays a special icon that indicates that the image is an Adobe Stock Photos comp image (the Adobe Stock Photos service can be found in Adobe Bridge). After the client approves the use of an image, you can choose the Purchase This Image option in the Links palette menu, at which point you are led through the process of purchasing the image through the Adobe Stock Photos service.

- **Embed Image.** If you have a placed-linked image in your document, you can select the image in the Links palette and choose the Embed Image option from the Links palette menu to embed that image in your file.

- **Palette Options.** Always trying to accommodate, Illustrator allows you to customize the Links palette somewhat by choosing Palette Options from the Links palette menu. You can choose a thumbnail size, or if you prefer, you can eliminate thumbnails altogether (**Figure 8.11**; useful when you have many placed images in your document). Additionally, you can choose the Show DCS Transparency Interactions option to have Illustrator alert you when placed DCS (Desktop Color Separations) files interact with transparency in your document. This setting results in slower performance though.

Figure 8.11 With thumbnails turned off, the Links palette in Illustrator looks just like the one in InDesign.

Faster Access to Image Settings with the Control Palette

 During the transparency flattening process, Illustrator cannot process linked DCS files, so when using transparency, it is best to avoid using DCS files. Use PSD or EPS files instead.

Although the Links palette offers a single location from which to track information about your placed images, you can also use the Control palette to quickly access certain settings and features that pertain to a selected image. The Control palette displays the file name, the color mode, and the resolution of a selected image. In addition, for linked images, the Control palette offers options to embed or edit the file via the Edit Original feature, which was discussed earlier in the chapter. You can also click the image's file name in the Control palette to access additional features that are found in the Links palette (**Figure 8.12**).

Figure 8.12 Clicking the file name of a linked image in the Control palette offers a shortcut to several often-used functions.

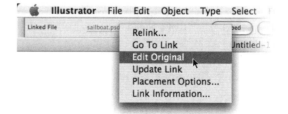

Using the Document Info Palette

The Links palette isn't the only place where you'll find information about place-linked and place-embedded images. You can choose Window > Document Info to open the Document Info palette, which offers information on a lot more than just images. In fact, the Document Info palette can prove quite useful for providing document information on a variety of attributes and settings (**Figure 8.13**).

By default, the Document Info palette only shows information on objects that are selected on the artboard. To find out information about all of the objects in a file, choose Select > All, or you can uncheck the Selection Only option in the Document Info palette menu.

To find out information about certain aspects of an Illustrator document, choose from one of these settings in the Document Info palette menu:

- **Document.** The Document setting displays the color mode for your document along with a listing of other important document settings like text editability and color profile.

- **Objects.** This setting displays the total number of objects in your file, broken down by object type. This setting offers a quick way to find out how many linked or embedded images you have in your document, how many objects are colored with spot colors, or how many transparent objects there are.

- **Graphic Styles.** To see a list of all the Graphic Styles that are used in your document, as well as how many objects each style is applied to, choose this setting.

- **Brushes.** The Brushes option lists all brushes that are used in your document.

- **Spot Color Objects.** This setting provides a list of spot colors that are used in your document.

- **Pattern Objects.** The Pattern Objects option lists all of the patterns that are used in your document. This is especially helpful because it includes patterns that are used inside of complex appearances and Pattern brushes.

- **Gradient Objects.** This setting lists all of the gradients that are used in your document.

- **Fonts.** The Fonts option provides a list of the all of the fonts used in your document.

- **Linked Images.** The Linked Images option lists all of the linked images that appear in your document, along with information about each image.

- **Embedded Images.** The Embedded Images setting provides a list of all the embedded images that appear in your document, along with information about each image.

- **Font Details.** The Font Details option lists information about the fonts that are used in your document. This is helpful when you want to quickly find out if you are using OpenType, TrueType, or PostScript fonts in your document.

You can save all of the information listed in the Document Info palette by choosing Save from the Document Info palette menu. A text file is created that contains the information for all of the items just outlined.

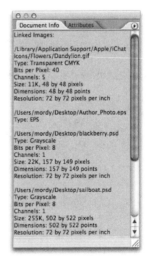

Figure 8.13 The Document Info palette provides detailed information on just about anything you could ask for about your file, including linked images.

LIVE TRACE: CONVERTING RASTERS TO VECTORS

Certain Illustrator features, like Pathfinder, are incredibly useful and as a result, are used many times a day. Features like 3D are also extremely cool, but they aren't used as often. Every once in a while, a feature comes along in Illustrator that is cool and fun to use, but that is also practical enough that you use it on a regular basis. Illustrator's Live Trace is such a feature.

The concept is simple enough: take a raster-based image and convert it into a vector-based image. You would want to do this to get around the limitations of a raster-based file. For example, if you want to scale artwork up in size, or if you want to edit the artwork easily and use spot colors, you want to work with a vector-based file.

There are separate applications (like Adobe Streamline) and Illustrator plug-ins (like Free Soft's Silhouette) that have the ability to convert raster content into vectors, but Illustrator CS2's Live Trace is a far step above and beyond what those tools are capable of. One of the main reasons for this is because of how Live Trace works.

Be sure to check out Scott Crouse's Live Trace example in the color insert.

Live Trace uses a two-step process when converting rasters to vectors. In the first step, Live Trace *conditions* the raster image for optimal tracing. This means that Illustrator makes adjustments to the raster image, like adjusting contrast or blurring jagged edges. In the second step, Live Trace draws vector paths, creating highly accurate vector art (**Figure 8.14**). Although the tracing is theoretically done at that point, Illustrator retains a link to the original raster image so that you can make adjustments to the tracing settings. As you update the different raster conditioning and vector tracing settings, you can preview the results immediately. This makes it easy to get just the right tracing result that suits your needs best.

Tracing an Image

Tracing an image is simple. Select any raster image in your Illustrator document and click the Live Trace button in the Control palette. Alternatively, you can choose Object > Live Trace > Make. This action traces the image using Illustrator's default trace preset. Illustrator actually ships with 13 different tracing presets, each optimized for different kinds of images and desired result. Once the image is traced, it maintains a live link to the

ORIGINAL SCAN

ORIGINAL SCAN ENLARGED 300%

Figure 8.14 Illustrator's Live Trace feature starts with the original raster image (top), conditions the image (center), and then converts it to clean vectors (bottom). The first two examples in this 3-page spread use the Black and White setting for tracing, whereas the third shows the Grayscale tracing setting.

CONDITIONED IMAGE

CONDITIONED IMAGE ENLARGED 300%

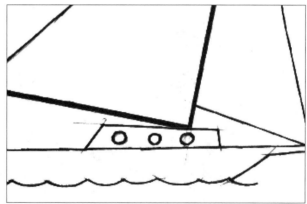

TRACED RESULT

TRACED RESULT ENLARGED 300%

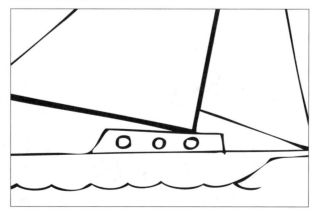

ORIGINAL IMAGE

ORIGINAL IMAGE ENLARGED 300%

CONDITIONED IMAGE

CONDITIONED IMAGE ENLARGED 300%

TRACED RESULT

TRACED RESULT ENLARGED 300%

ORIGINAL IMAGE

ORIGINAL IMAGE ENLARGED 300%

TRACED RESULT

TRACED RESULT ENLARGED 300%

CONDITIONED IMAGE

CONDITIONED IMAGE ENLARGED 300%

raster image and you can customize the tracing settings. For example, once the image is traced, the Control palette changes to reflect different settings, including a Preset pop-up menu (**Figure 8.15**). Choose from any of Illustrator's thirteen different presets to see a different traced result on your screen.

Figure 8.15 The Preset pop-up menu in the Control palette lets you quickly experiment with different tracing presets.

If you know which tracing preset you want to use before you trace your image, you can select it directly by clicking the upside-down triangle that appears just to the right side of the Live Trace button and choosing it from the list that pops up (**Figure 8.16**).

Figure 8.16 It doesn't look like a pop-up menu, but it is. Clicking the upside-down triangle allows you to apply a specific tracing preset when you first choose to trace an image.

 If you're happy with the traced results, there's no need to expand the object at all. Illustrator can print the vector paths just fine (it expands the paths in the print stream).

As long as Illustrator maintains a live link to the raster image, you won't be able to edit the actual vector paths that were created during the tracing process. In order to do so, you either have to expand the traced object or convert it to a Live Paint group. We discuss both of these options later, but for now, we're going to focus on how to customize the tracing settings so that you can get the bests results from the Live Trace feature.

Exploring the Live Trace Preview Options

Once you've traced an image, Illustrator displays the traced result on your artboard so that you can see the results. However, Illustrator offers a variety of different settings that you can use to control how both the raster image and the traced vector result appear on your artboard.

When a traced image is selected on the artboard, the Control palette updates to contain two icons that, at first glance, look like triangles. Upon closer inspection, you'll notice that one icon features a jagged edge; this icon is used to control how the raster image is previewed. The icon on the right, which has a smooth edge, is used to control how the traced vector result is previewed (**Figure 8.17**). Each of these settings is separate and can be chosen independently of the other.

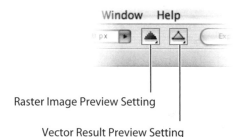

Raster Image Preview Setting

Vector Result Preview Setting

Figure 8.17 Once you've traced an image, you can use the two icons in the Control palette to control how the artwork appears on the artboard.

Previewing the Original Raster Image

In the Control palette, the jagged triangle on the left controls how the raster image is viewed. Click once on the icon and choose from one of the four available settings **(Figure 8.18)**.

- **No Image.** This setting completely hides the raster image from the screen (and is the default setting).

- **Original Image.** This setting displays the original raster image in your document, which can be useful when you're comparing the original image to the traced result.

- **Adjusted Image.** This setting displays the raster image as it appears after Live Trace has applied the raster conditioning adjustments. This preview mode is great for seeing how Live Trace works and it makes it easier to preview any adjustments that you make to the raster image settings.

- **Transparent Image.** This setting displays a dimmed preview of the bitmap image beneath the traced result, letting you see the traced results as compared to the original raster image.

Figure 8.18 You can preview the raster image with the Original Image setting (left), the Adjusted Image setting (center), or the Transparent Image setting (right). The No Image option is not shown for obvious reasons.

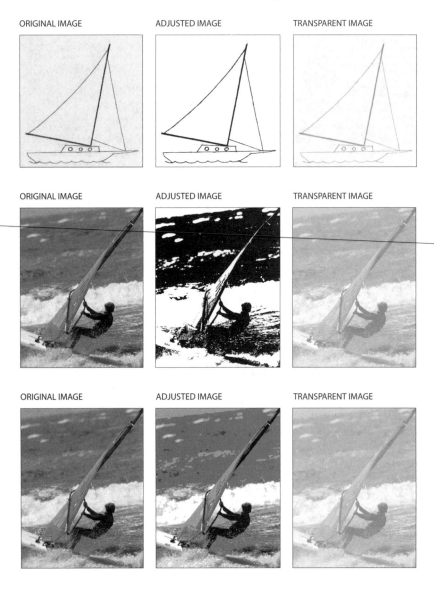

Previewing the Traced Vector Result

In the Control palette, the smooth triangle on the right controls how the traced vector result is viewed. Click once on the icon and choose from one of the four available settings (**Figure 8.19**).

- **No Tracing Result.** This setting hides the traced vector objects from the screen.

- **Tracing Result.** This setting displays the vector result of the tracing (and is the default setting).

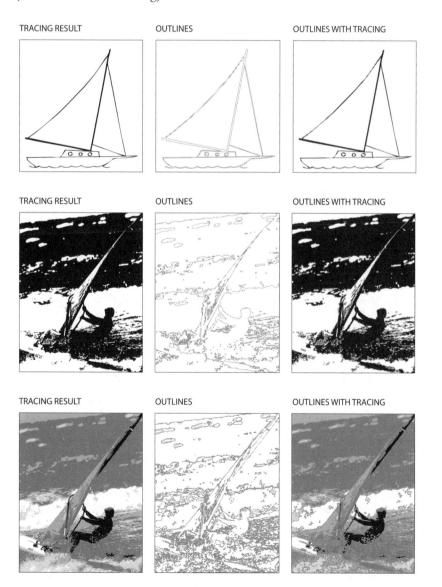

Figure 8.19 You can preview the vector result with the Tracing Result setting (left), the Outlines setting (center), and the Outlines With Tracing setting (right). The No Tracing Result option is not shown.

- **Outlines.** This setting highlights the actual Bézier paths that were created when the image was traced.

- **Outlines With Tracing.** This setting highlights the Bézier paths as semi-transparent, enabling you to compare filled areas of the traced vector result with the original bitmap image. The color of the outlines will match the color specified for guides in the Guides & Grid preferences panel.

Tweaking to Get the Perfect Trace

What makes the Live Trace feature a joy to use is the ability to make adjustments to the settings while you see the results update on your screen. Aside from the different presets that you can apply, Illustrator contains a dialog box chock full of settings that you can use to ensure that you get the results you need from the Live Trace feature.

To access these settings, select a Live Trace object and click the Tracing Options dialog button in the Control palette. Alternatively, you can choose Object > Live Trace > Tracing Options. Once the Tracing Options dialog appears on your screen, you'll notice that it's split into several different sections (**Figure 8.20**).

Figure 8.20 The Tracing Options dialog offers a smorgasbord of settings to achieve the perfect trace.

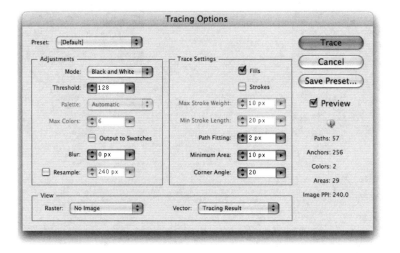

First of all, a Preview check box appears on the far right of the dialog, which allows you to see results update as you make changes to the different settings. Directly underneath the Preview check box is a list of important details about your traced object. The values for the number of paths, anchor points, colors, distinct closed areas, and image resolution update as you make adjustments to the settings in the dialog. Keeping an eye on these values helps you make decisions as you edit your trace settings. At the top of the dialog is a Preset pop-up menu, similar to what you see in the Control palette when a Live Trace object is selected. Stepping through the different presets in the Tracing Options dialog allows you to see the settings for each of the presets.

The rest of the Tracing Options dialog is separated into three sections called Adjustments, Trace Settings, and View. The View section allows you to specify how the traced object appears on your artboard, as discussed in the earlier section, "Exploring the Live Trace Preview Options."

The following "Modifying the Raster Adjustments" and "Adjusting the Vector Trace Settings" sections will help you clearly understand the two-step process that the Live Trace feature performs when converting raster images into vector form.

Modifying the Raster Adjustments

The Adjustments settings found on the left side of the Tracing Options dialog apply to the raster conditioning that occurs before the image is traced.

- **Mode.** Live Trace converts a bitmap image to either 1-bit black and white, 8-bit grayscale, or 8-bit color, which you can choose from the Mode pop-up menu.

- **Threshold.** The Threshold setting determines the boundaries between pixels when using the Black and White trace setting. For example, in a gray bitmap, a high threshold setting results in more gray pixels becoming black vector objects, and thus a heavier appearance. In that same image, a low Threshold setting results in more gray pixels ignored, making for more white-colored objects and an overall lighter or more delicate appearance (**Figure 8.21**). Too low of a Threshold setting may also result in a loss of image detail. The Threshold setting is also available in the Control palette when a Black and White Live Trace object is selected.

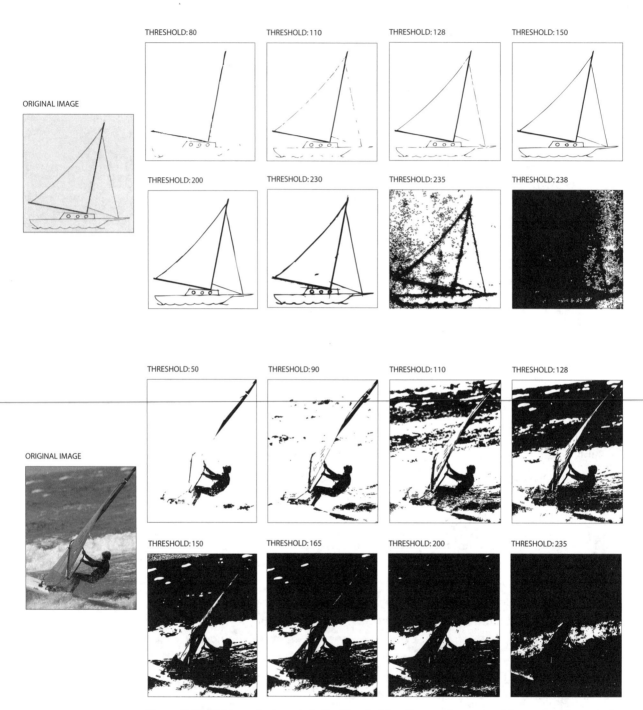

Figure 8.21 Making adjustments to the Threshold setting can have a large impact on the overall appearance of the traced result. Here are examples of an image with a variety of different Threshold settings.

- **Palette.** By default, Illustrator uses the selective color reduction method to choose the best colors to fit the image (based on the Max Colors value). However, you can choose specific colors that Illustrator should use when tracing your image. To do so, you must first load a custom swatch library (refer to Chapter 1 for instruction on how to define a custom swatch library). When a custom swatch library is opened in your document, the Palette pop-up menu displays all of the available palettes (**Figure 8.22**). Live Trace then only uses the colors that appear within the custom swatch library that you choose.

Figure 8.22 Loading several different custom libraries allows you to quickly experiment with a variety of different color schemes.

- **Max Colors.** The Max Colors setting determines the maximum number of colors that can be used in the final traced result. This setting is not available for the Black and White Mode setting. Live Trace uses the selective color reduction method to reduce the number of colors in the raster image to match this setting during the conditioning process. The Threshold setting is also available in the Control palette when a Grayscale or Color Live Trace object is selected.

- **Blur.** The Blur setting applies a Gaussian Blur to the image, which helps remove noise from the raster image. This reduces the number of anchor points in the tracing result, especially when you are tracing photographic images.

 Check the Output to Swatches option to have Illustrator add each color that is used during the tracing process as a global process color in your Swatches palette.

- **Resample.** The Resample setting lets you change the resolution of the bitmap image to help obtain a better traced result. Resampling a high-resolution image to a lower resolution greatly enhances the speed performance of Live Trace.

Adjusting the Vector Trace Settings

The Trace Settings found on the right side of the Tracing Options dialog apply to the actual tracing of the image and determine how the final vector paths are drawn.

- **Fills.** When you have Fills selected, Live Trace creates closed and filled vector paths for all resulting vector objects. Fill tracing produces results that more closely match the original image, including variable-width lines that are common in marker or ink renderings (**Figure 8.23**). Fill tracing also results in more complex vectors because it needs more anchor points.

Figure 8.23 When you choose the Fills setting, the traced paths appear with thick and thin edges, closely matching the original image.

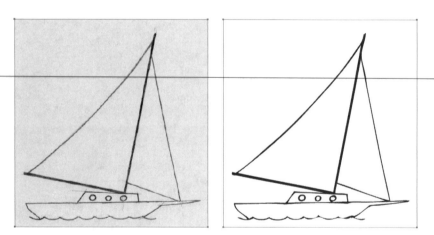

- **Strokes.** With the Strokes setting selected, Live Trace creates stroked open paths for all areas that fall within the Max Stroke Weight setting. Areas that exceed this setting result in unfilled areas outlined with a 1-point stroke. Stroke tracing results in paths with fewer anchor points (**Figure 8.24**).

Figure 8.24 When you choose the Strokes setting, the traced paths appear consistent and results in a less complex traced image overall.

- **Max Stroke Weight.** The Max Stroke Weight setting determines the heaviest stroke weight Live Trace can use when tracing the image. This setting is only available when the Strokes trace setting is used.

- **Min Stroke Length.** The Min Stroke Length setting determines the shortest path that Live Trace can use when tracing the image. This setting is only available when the Strokes trace setting is used.

- **Path Fitting.** Path Fitting determines how closely Live Trace follows the shape of the original raster image. A lower Path Fitting setting results in paths that closely match the original raster image, yet might also reveal imperfections or irregular paths that aren't smooth. A higher setting produces smoother paths with fewer anchor points but might not match the raster image as closely (**Figure 8.25**, next page).

- **Minimum Area.** The Minimum Area setting sets a threshold for how large a section of the raster image has to be in order to traced into a vector object. By setting a minimum area, you can have Live Trace only trace areas of pixels that meet a minimum size. For example, if the Minimum Area is set to 9 pixels, Live Trace ignores regions of pixels that are less than 3 by 3 pixels in size.

 The Minimum Area setting is also available in the Control palette when a Live Trace object is selected.

- **Corner Angle.** The Corner Angle setting defines the sharpness of the angles used in the resulting vector objects. This setting is measured in degrees, not pixels. If you think of 0 degrees as perfectly flat and 180 degrees as a hard corner (rather than a rounded one), anything sharper than the Corner Angle setting (the default is 20) is converted to a corner anchor point rather than a smooth anchor point.

Figure 8.25 This figure shows examples of a variety of path fitting settings for the same image. Notice how the paths get smoother as the number is increased but that the result doesn't match the original sketch as much.

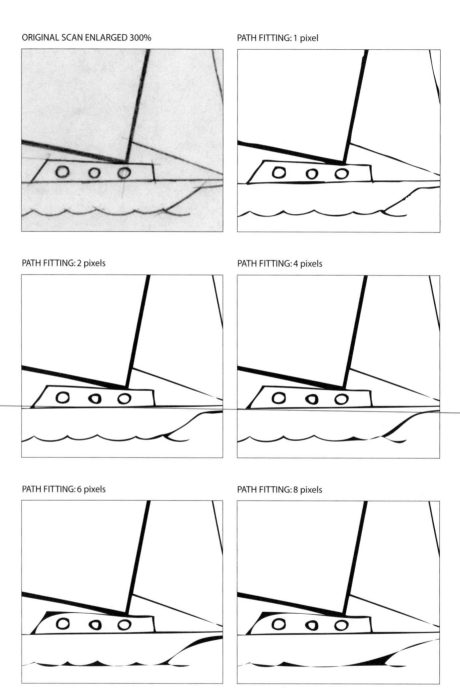

ORIGINAL SCAN ENLARGED 300%

PATH FITTING: 1 pixel

PATH FITTING: 2 pixels

PATH FITTING: 4 pixels

PATH FITTING: 6 pixels

PATH FITTING: 8 pixels

Editing Live Trace Paths

Once you've achieved a trace result that you're satisfied with, you might want to edit the Bézier paths, either to delete portions of the image, or to apply your own colors, gradients, or patterns. In order to edit the vector paths of the traced object, you will need to either expand the trace, or convert the traced object to a Live Paint group.

 Once you've specified your settings in the Tracing Options dialog, you can click the Save Preset button to define your own tracing presets.

Expanding a Live Trace Object

With a Live Trace object selected, click the Expand button in the Control palette. Alternatively, you can choose Object > Live Trace > Expand. You can then use the Direct Selection tool to edit anchor points and Bézier paths (**Figure 8.26**). At this point, the traced object is no longer linked to the original raster image, and the traced result can no longer be adjusted using any of the Live Trace options.

 If you select both the Fills and the Strokes options, Live Trace converts the raster to a vector using a combination of both stroked and filled paths.

Figure 8.26 Once you've expanded a Live Trace object, you can edit the paths as you would with any vector object.

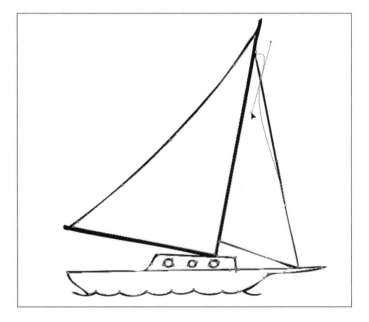

Converting Traced Images to Live Paint Groups

In Chapter 4, *Advanced Vectors,* you learned about Illustrator's new Live Paint feature, which allows you to apply fill attributes to areas, even if they aren't fully enclosed shapes. If you've traced an image because you want to fill

 For performance reasons, Gap Detection is turned off for Live Paint groups that are created directly from a Live Trace object. You can either turn Gap Detection on manually, or you can create smaller Live Paint groups to get better performance.

regions of the image with color, converting the Live Trace object to a Live Paint group makes a lot of sense.

With a Live Trace object selected on the artboard, click the Live Paint button that appears in the Control palette. This action expands the traced object and converts all of the resulting vector objects into a Live Paint group in a single step. You can then use the Live Paint Bucket tool to fill your art with color without any additional steps (**Figure 8.27**). For more information on Live Paint groups, refer to Chapter 4.

You can press Option (Alt) while clicking the Live Trace button or when choosing a Live Trace preset from the Control palette to both trace and expand an image in one step.

Figure 8.27 What started out as a pencil sketch quickly turns into final art when you combine the Live Trace and the Live Paint features in Illustrator.

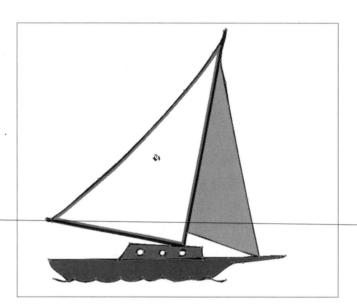

Rasterize: Turning Vectors into Rasters

It's easy to see the benefits of converting raster images into vector-based artwork to allow for better scaling and editing. Interestingly enough, Illustrator can also perform the transition in reverse—converting vector-based artwork into rasterized art. Sometimes this is done to achieve a special effect where you might want to see a pixilated image (**Figure 8.28**). Alternatively, you might start with a gradient mesh object, which you then rasterize and then convert back to vectors using Live Trace to achieve a posterized graphic effect (**Figure 8.29**).

- **Slices.** If you create web slices in your Illustrator file, those slices appear when the file is opened in Photoshop. Additionally, any optimization settings that you've applied to your slices, including settings that you've applied from the Save for Web dialog, are preserved and can be edited once the file is opened in Photoshop.

- **Image Maps.** If you've used the Attributes palette in Illustrator to assign URLs to an object, that information can be retained when the file is opened in Photoshop. Additionally, if you assign a URL to a web slice, that URL is also preserved.

Illustrator does its best to keep elements editable during the export process. However, if you find that certain elements are not being preserved, the cause may be that preserving editability would change the appearance of the artwork. Try rearranging the layers in Illustrator to avoid issues where artwork appearance is dependent upon the interaction of multiple layers.

Honoring Crop Marks in a File—Illustrator's Export Function

To ensure that you export a file using the exact dimensions that you require, or to ensure proper positioning of your art, it's best to draw a rectangle of the size you need and position it on the page. Then, choose Object > Crop Area > Make to specify the crop area (**Figure 8.31**).

Figure 8.31 When you set crop marks before exporting your file, Illustrator sets the bounding box where you set the crop marks. If art extends beyond the crop area, that art is still preserved in the file, thus allowing you to reposition the artwork in Photoshop as needed.

Copying and Pasting Between Illustrator and Photoshop

Copying and pasting art between Illustrator and Photoshop works extremely well. You can copy text freely between the two applications, and when you paste art from Illustrator into Photoshop, you can paste the art as a Photoshop Smart Object, which preserves editability within Photoshop. In fact, when you paste art from Illustrator in Photoshop, you are presented with a dialog asking if you want the art to be pasted as pixels, a path, a shape layer, or a smart object (**Figure 8.32**).

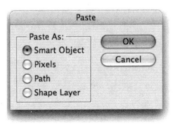

Figure 8.32 Photoshop offers you several options when pasting artwork from Illustrator. Pasting art as a smart object allows you to edit the pasted artwork back in Illustrator if needed.

Going from Photoshop to Illustrator

When you open a native Photoshop file, or place-embed one into an existing document, Illustrator prompts you with the Photoshop Import Options dialog asking how you want the Photoshop file to be placed (refer to Figure 8.3, earlier in this chapter). You can either choose the Flatten Photoshop layers to a single image option, or you can choose the Convert Photoshop layers to objects option, in which case Illustrator tries to keep as much of the elements in the Photoshop editable as possible.

The following is a list of the attributes that can be preserved when Illustrator embeds a native Photoshop file using the Convert Photoshop layers to objects option in the Photoshop Import Options dialog:

- **Layers.** Any layers that you've created, and the names of those layers, are preserved when the file is opened in Illustrator. If you've created groups of layers in Photoshop, those groups show up in Illustrator as sublayers, thus preserving the hierarchy of the file.

- **Vectors.** If you've created vector shape layers in Photoshop, those layers are converted into editable compound shapes when the file is opened in Illustrator.

- **Text.** Text objects that appear in the file are editable when the file is opened in Illustrator.

- **Transparency.** If you've applied opacity values or blend modes from the Layers palette, those values are preserved when the file is opened in Illustrator as well. Because Photoshop applies these settings at the Layer level, you may find that these transparency settings are applied to the layer that an object is on rather than to the object itself.

- **Masks.** If you create layer masks in your Photoshop file, those masks are preserved and show up in Illustrator as opacity masks. Additionally, the boundaries of the file become a layer-clipping mask, acting almost like crop marks.

- **Slices.** If you create web slices in your Photoshop file, those slices appear when the file is opened in Illustrator. Additionally, any optimization settings that you've applied to your slices, including settings that you've applied from the Save for Web dialog, are preserved and can be edited once the file is opened in Illustrator.

- **Image Maps.** If you've assigned a URL to a web slice, that URL is also preserved when the file is opened in Illustrator.

Illustrator does its best to keep elements editable during the embedding process. For example, if you have a text object with a drop shadow that overlaps a background, Illustrator keeps the text editable, and also places the drop shadow on a separate layer, allowing you to position the text and the drop shadow without affecting the background beneath it. If you find that certain elements are not being preserved, the cause may be that preserving editability would change the appearance of the artwork. Try rearranging the layers in Photoshop to avoid issues where appearance is dependent upon the interaction of multiple layers.

CHAPTER 9

Graphs, Distortion, and Blends

In case you haven't figured it out by now, the underlying theme of this book is learning to combine the features in Illustrator with each other, rather than just focusing on each feature on its own. This chapter is certainly no exception.

You may be asking yourself what it is that graphs, distortions, and blends have in common so that they deserve to share space within the same chapter. The answer is that for the most part, these seemingly disparate features firmly drive home the notion that using a combination of features can reap big rewards.

After all, graphs on their own can be pretty boring, but with a few Live Effects applied, such as 3D or Drop Shadow, you can end up with a graph that seemingly pops off the page and demands a reader's attention. Not only do tools and effects in Illustrator CS2 help to make for more interesting-looking graphs, but they also help to make for more effective graphs. The Liquify distortion tools can turn a gradient mesh into something special, and the Envelope distortion features can add just the right look to text. As for blends, combining them with features like Symbols and SWF Export can turn static Web art into fantastic animations.

To finish the chapter off on a bright note, we'll even talk about the innovative vector Flare tool for creating cool lens flares.

PUTTING THE "ART" IN CHART

We are bombarded with information on a daily basis. Whether it is from newspapers, the Internet, BlackBerrys, magazines, outdoor advertising, television, or radio, we can absorb only a limited amount. At the same time, certain bits of information require a degree of focus and attention in order for us to process and really understand them.

Aware of the challenges, designers often turn to graphs or charts to present complicated information in a simpler manner. Also known as an *infographic,* a well-designed graph presents key data points in a visually stimulating way that quickly conveys a message to the reader (**Figure 9.1**). Graphs are often used in annual reports, business or sales presentations, and magazine or newspaper articles.

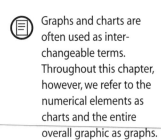 Graphs and charts are often used as interchangeable terms. Throughout this chapter, however, we refer to the numerical elements as charts and the entire overall graphic as graphs.

The use of graphs is a great way to communicate numeric information in a visual and graphical manner; when you use such a way to represent your data, you can turn a jumble of numbers into compelling data points. The important thing is to remember that a graph is meant to communicate information. As we'll see in this chapter, Illustrator offers many ways to control a graph's appearance, and it can be easy to get caught up in making a graph look so pretty that the reader misses its entire point.

Figure 9.1 In today's fast-paced work, graphs help people visualize and digest numerical data. In this example, the percentage of teens interested in golf is highlighted. A salesperson for golf equipment might use this to bring attention to growth in that segment.

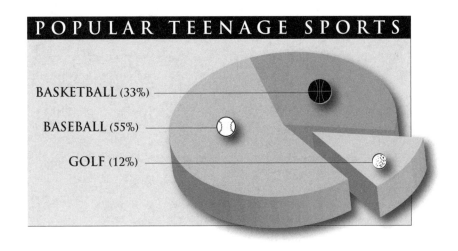

POPULAR TEENAGE SPORTS

BASKETBALL (33%)

BASEBALL (55%)

GOLF (12%)

The Anatomy of a Graph

Before we get into the specifics of creating and editing graphs, let's first explore how Illustrator constructs them.

A graph itself can be made up of several different elements, including the chart itself, a value and category axis, and a legend. These elements are each created as individual groups so that they can be managed easily. A graph in Illustrator is a special kind of parent group that comprises the individual groups shown in **Figure 9.2**. Depending on the settings that you use, a graph can have all or just some of these groups.

As long as the elements are contained by the special parent group, you can make edits to the graph data or the settings of the graph itself, and Illustrator updates the graph accordingly. However, if you remove the parent group (by choosing Object > Ungroup), the individual elements act like regular vector objects, and you can no longer edit the graph data. (See the section "Ungrouping a Graph," later in the chapter, where we discuss under what circumstances you would want to ungroup a graph.)

 Because a graph is a group, all that you've learned so far about how groups work and how you can apply effects to groups apply to graphs as well.

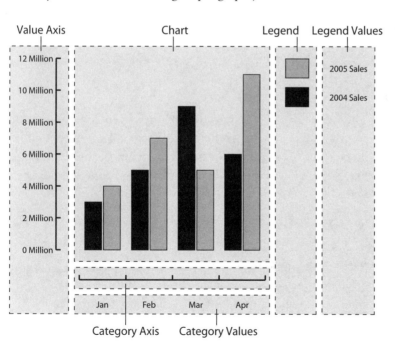

Figure 9.2 A graph in Illustrator is made up of many different parts.

Creating a Graph in Illustrator

Creating a graph in Illustrator is a two-step process. First, you specify a size for your graph (much like drawing a rectangle), and second, you specify the data for the graph.

1.   To create a graph, choose one of the nine Graph tools in the Toolbox (**Figure 9.3**) and click once on your artboard. This brings up the Graph dialog where you must first specify the size for the graph and then click OK. Alternatively, you can click and drag with the Graph tool on the artboard to generate a size for the graph on the fly.

Figure 9.3 The nine different Graph tools are grouped together in the Toolbox.

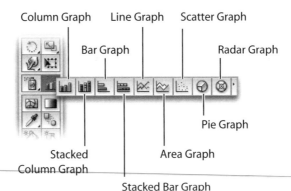

The size that you specify is the area that is enclosed within the value and the category axis (or the X and Y axis). This size won't necessarily be the final size of all of the elements in the graph because items like values and legends will appear outside of the boundaries of the two axes.

 If you aren't sure which type of graph you want to use, you can choose any type in which to enter your data. You can always change between types after you've created the graph.

2.   Once you've specified the size of your graph, Illustrator opens the Graph Data window, in which you can enter the data for your graph.

Refer to the options in the "Specifying Graph Data" section for detailed information about the different settings in the Graph Data window and the different ways you can format your data.

3.   When you're done, click the Apply button and close the Graph Data window.

Choosing a Graph Type

Creating a graph in Illustrator is much like following a recipe. You take a few numbers here, a few values there, toss them together, and Illustrator produces a functional visual representation of your data. In the world of graphs, there are many different ways to present data. Illustrator has nine different ways; each of these is called a graph type.

- **Column graph.** A column graph presents a single group of data as a series of vertical columns. This common graph type is often used to compare a range of values (**Figure 9.4**).

- **Stacked column graph.** A stacked column graph presents multiple groups of data as a series of vertical columns. Multiple values are accumulated and stacked on top of each other. Stacked column graphs are used to compare a range of values and also to indicate how individual data points may have contributed to the overall totals (**Figure 9.5**, next page).

- **Bar graph.** A bar graph presents a single group of data as a series of horizontal bars. The bar graph type is identical to the column graph type, only it is in a horizontal format (**Figure 9.6**, next page).

- **Stacked bar graph.** A stacked bar graph presents multiple groups of data as a series of horizontal bars. Multiple values are cumulated and added to the ends of the bars. The stacked bar graph is identical to the bar graph type, only in a horizontal format (**Figure 9.7**, next page).

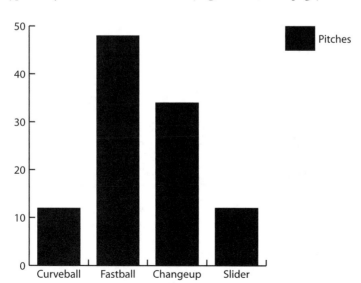

Figure 9.4 This column graph displays how many of each kind of pitch were thrown in a baseball game.

Figure 9.5 This stacked column graph displays the same information as in the previous graph, only now you can also view how many of each kind of pitch were thrown for a ball or a strike.

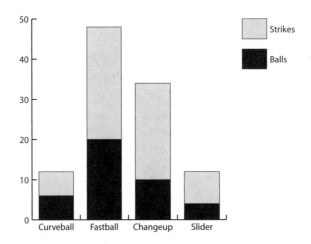

Figure 9.6 This bar graph also displays how many of each kind of pitch were thrown in a baseball game.

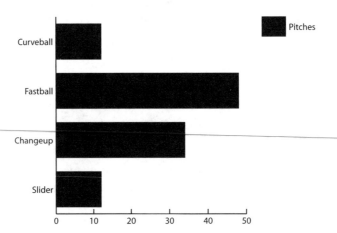

Figure 9.7 This stacked bar graph displays the same information as in the bar graph, only now you can also view how many of each kind of pitch were thrown for a ball or a strike.

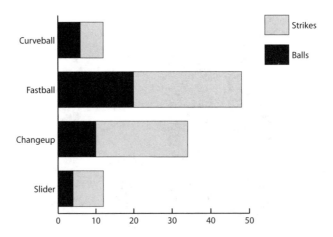

- **Line graph.** A line graph presents multiple groups of data as a series of connected lines. Line graphs are often used to show continuous measurements or trends over time (**Figure 9.8**).

- **Area graph.** An area graph is similar to a line graph, only the areas created by the lines are filled in, thus offering a visual representation of volume. This presents a cumulative value of the areas as well (**Figure 9.9**).

- **Scatter graph.** A scatter graph maps multiple data points as individual dots, which makes it possible to chart trends and compare non-linear data points (**Figure 9.10**, next page).

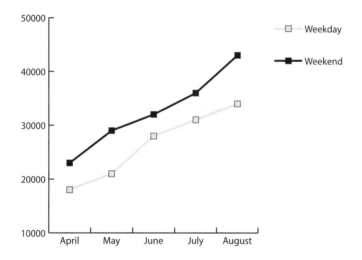

Figure 9.8 This line graph displays ticket sales across a range of several months. The graph shows growth in ticket sales over time, and the weekend games draw larger crowds.

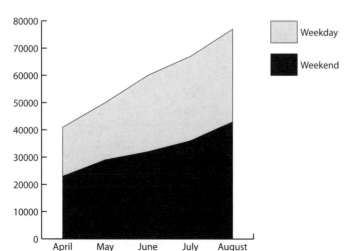

Figure 9.9 This area graph displays the same data as in the previous line graph, only here you can see a total cumulative attendance of both weekday and weekend ticket sales.

- **Pie graph.** A pie graph presents a single group of data points as slices or wedges of a circle. Pie charts are generally used to show percentages or how a whole is broken up into individual parts (**Figure 9.11**).

- **Radar graph.** A radar graph, also called a web or polar graph, plots data points in a circular pattern, which reveals values with overlapping areas (**Figure 9.12**).

Figure 9.10 This scatter graph compares the age of hitters with the number of home runs they hit. The chart shows data for three different decades, and the data reveals a peak in home runs hit by hitters between the ages of 30 and 35.

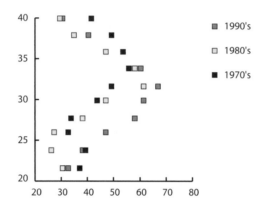

Figure 9.11 This pie graph breaks down the type of tickets that are sold at a baseball game. You can clearly see that the majority of tickets sold are from advanced sales.

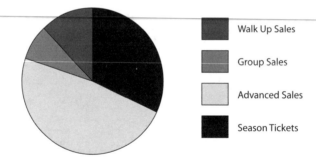

Figure 9.12 This radar graph compares the sales of beer and soda over the course of a nine-inning baseball game. The graph reveals that beer sales spike between the third and fifth innings, whereas soda sales peak between the seventh and ninth innings.

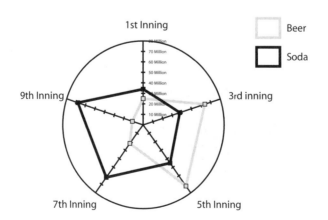

Specifying Graph Data

When you create a graph in Illustrator, you are presented with the Graph Data window, which is the life and soul of a graph (**Figure 9.13**). After all, without any data, Illustrator can't draw a meaningful graph. If you've ever seen a spreadsheet before (like in Lotus 1-2-3 or Microsoft Excel), you'll recognize the vertical columns and horizontal rows of cells where you can specify data. You can click and drag the vertical lines to adjust the width of each row. This won't have any effect on the appearance of your graph, but it will allow you to view all of your data if they extend beyond the boundary of each cell.

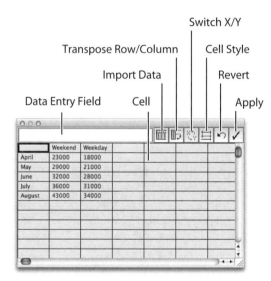

Figure 9.13 The Graph Data window contains the values that determine how a graph is drawn.

If you've already created a graph and you've closed the Graph Data window, you can always reopen this window for further data editing. To do so, with a graph selected on your artboard, just choose Object > Graph > Graph Data; the Graph Data window will appear.

Across the top of the Graph Data window are several items. A field where you can enter data for a selected cell (to select a cell, simply click it) appears along the entire top left side. Along the top right of the window are the following six icons, which offer additional functionality:

- **Import Data.** Illustrator allows you to import data from an external file by clicking the Import Data icon. Illustrator presents you with a system dialog box that allows you to choose a file to use. The file that you choose must be a tab-delimited text (TXT) file. Unfortunately, Illustrator does not allow you to import Excel files directly. If you have data that already exists in an Excel file, you can save the Excel file as a tab-delimited text file, which you can then import into Illustrator.

- **Transpose Row/Column.** When you click the Transpose Row/Column icon, the data that is already entered in the Graph Data window is swapped so that rows become columns and columns become rows. This is useful for when you either enter data incorrectly, or you want to experiment with a different graph result.

- **Switch X/Y.** When editing graph data for a scatter graph, the Switch X/Y icon allows you to swap the X and Y axis. The icon is disabled for all other graph types.

- **Cell Style.** By default, each cell in the Graph Data window is wide enough to display 7 digits, and each value is shown with two decimal places. By clicking the Cell Style icon, you can change both the column width and the number of decimals. This setting applies to all of the cells in the Graph Data window (you can't apply different settings to individual cells).

- **Revert.** Clicking the Revert icon returns the graph data to the values specified when you last clicked the Apply button.

- **Apply.** The Apply button takes the values specified in the Graph Data window and generates or updates your selected Graph.

Formatting Data Within the Graph Data Window

Almost as important as the data itself is the way that you actually enter it into the Graph Data window. The graph type that you choose and the way in which you format the values within the cells of the Graph Data window are the two items that most impact how Illustrator draws your graph.

For example, if you just specify numeric values in the Graph Data window, Illustrator draws the graph correctly, but people who read your graph may not understand its significance. In order for a graph to be effective, a reader needs to understand what the values stand for. One way to help a reader make sense of a graph is by adding labels, which identify what a particular axis or data point represents.

In the Graph Data window, you can specify labels simply by entering the text of the labels within the cells. If Illustrator sees a value that contains

A nasty bug in the shipping version of Illustrator CS2 causes text that is pasted into the Graph Data window to become garbled, making it impossible to copy data (i.e., from an Excel spreadsheet or an email message) and paste it into the Graph Data window. A free patch—Illustrator 12.01—is available from Adobe that fixes this problem. To get the patch, open Illustrator CS2 and choose Help > Updates.

letters instead of numbers, it assumes the cell contains a label, and not a numerical value that affects the graph itself (**Figure 9.14**). In order to specify a number as a numerical value, you must enclose it in quotation marks.

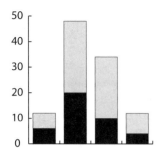 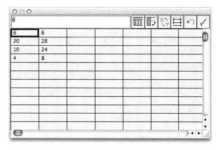

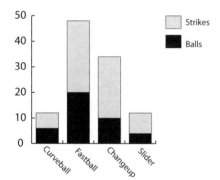 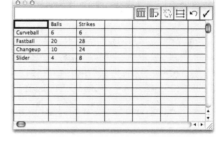

Figure 9.14 These two graphs represent the same data, but the bottom one has legend and category labels added to make the meaning of the graph immediately apparent.

Customizing Graphs

Once you've created a graph, you can edit it and customize it to fit your needs. At any time, you can select a graph and open the Graph Data window where you can change the data. When you check the Apply button, your graph updates to reflect the new data.

However, there can be more to a graph than just the data itself. For example, a graph has a category axis, a value axis, a legend, and other elements. To make adjustments to these settings, select a graph on the artboard and choose Object > Graph > Type to open the Graph Type dialog. Depending on the type of graph that you have chosen, the Graph Type dialog offers several panels with specific options (**Figure 9.15**, next page).

Working with data and labels can get confusing at times, but there's no need to get frustrated. Keep your Graph Data window open and use the Apply button to quickly see the results of how Illustrator draws your graph. You can then make quick adjustments to the data as needed.

Figure 9.15 Illustrator offers additional settings for how graphs appear through the Graph Type dialog. Each graph type maintains options specific to its type of graph.

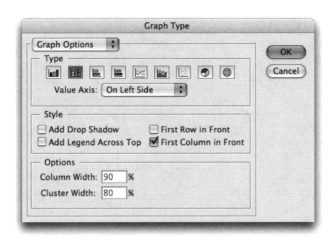

Utilizing Graph Designs

Purely from a numbers point of view, bars, lines, and squares get the point across when you're creating a graph. However, there's plenty of room for creativity when you're drawing graphs as well. Sometimes, a graphic can add a really nice touch to the overall appearance of a graph, and it can even make it easier to pick up on key data points.

In Illustrator, custom art that is used instead of bars to display values in a graph is called a *graph design*. For the most part, graph designs behave much like patterns do. First, you define a graph design. Once defined, you can apply the graph design to a graph in your document. There are two kinds of graph designs in Illustrator: a Column graph design, which is used for drawing columns in column graphs; and a Marker graph design, which is used for drawing markers in line or scatter graphs.

 The Graph Data window must be closed in order to define or apply graph designs.

Here are the steps that you need to follow to create a graph design:

1. Select the art on your artboard that you'd like to use as a graph design. Most Illustrator objects can be used in a graph design, with the exception of editable text or placed images—although you can use symbols.

2. Choose Object > Graph > Design to bring up the Graph Design dialog.

3. Click the New Design button and then click the Rename button so that you can give your graph design a unique and recognizable name. Click OK (**Figure 9.16**).

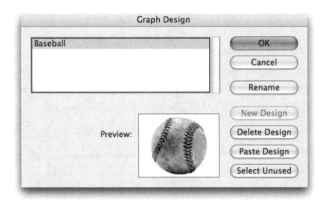

Figure 9.16 Here we've defined a Graph Design using a baseball that we traced and expanded.

Now that you've created a graph design, here are the steps you need to follow in order to apply the graph style to your graph:

1. Select the graph object on the artboard.

2. If you're working with a column graph, choose Object > Graph > Column. From the Graph Column dialog, choose a column design and a column type (**Figure 9.17**).

3. If you're working with a line or scatter graph, choose Object > Graph > Marker. From the Graph Marker dialog, choose a marker and click OK.

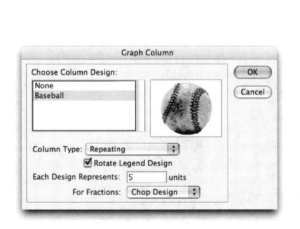

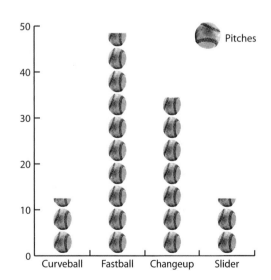

Figure 9.17 On the left is the Graph Column dialog where we used the Baseball design for the columns of the graph. On the right is the finished graph.

Ungrouping a Graph

At any time, you can decide to ungroup your graph, although if you do so, the graph is reduced to regular vector objects and is no longer editable as a graph object. Designers may ungroup a graph once they know the numbers won't change anymore. Once ungrouped, a designer can edit the objects freely.

Raising the Bar with Graphs

In the Adobe Illustrator CS2 > Cool Extras > Sample Files > Graph Designs folder, you'll find four files that contain predefined graph designs and samples of different graphs.

You can take advantage of the graph feature in Illustrator in numerous ways. Once you've created a graph, you can use the Direct Selection tool to select individual parts of a graph and apply different fill or stroke attributes (by default, Illustrator generates graphs using different shades of gray). You can also apply other Illustrator features, such as Live Effects (like 3D or Scribble) or transparency. You can even use graph elements as masks for photographs.

In addition, you can use an Illustrator graph as a guide for more customized artwork. For example, you may want to create an intricate infographic using customized shapes. By creating a simple graph with real data, you can draw artwork in scale to depict numeric data in a visual way (**Figure 9.18**).

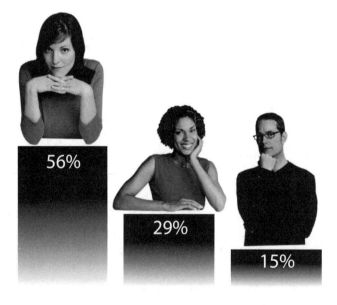

Figure 9.18 Graphs don't have to be boring. Use Illustrator's feature set and your creativity to create graphs that demand attention.

If bringing data into Illustrator isn't your cup of tea, you can use Excel to generate a graph, which you can then save as PDF from Excel (if you have Acrobat installed on your computer, you should have a utility called PDF-Maker available from within Microsoft Office). Once you've created the PDF, open it in Illustrator, where you can customize it as needed (you won't be able to edit the graph data however).

WORKING WITH TOOLS OF MASS DISTORTION

Illustrator has a plethora of tools that can help you create crisp, clean paths with extreme precision. But there are times when a design calls for something less perfect, and when it is also appropriate to bend or stretch artwork to achieve a distorted effect. That's where the distortion tools come into play.

You have already caught a glimpse of Illustrator's Warp effect, which was discussed in Chapter 7, *3D and Other Live Effects*. In addition, Illustrator contains a suite of distortion tools, dubbed the Liquify tools, and a feature called *Enveloping*, which allows you to squeeze artwork into a customized shape. Let's take a closer look at these two additional distortion techniques.

Painting with Distortion: The Liquify Tools

In your average box of classic toys, you'd surely find an Etch A Sketch, a Slinky, a collection of Tinkertoy parts, and undoubtedly, a plastic egg filled with Silly Putty. For those not familiar with the popular toy, Silly Putty is this gooey plastic substance that looks much like a wad of chewing gum. Once you've flattened the plastic out, you can press it firmly on newsprint (we always used the comics section) to transfer the images or text to the plastic surface. Then the fun begins; you can pull and twist and stretch the plastic to distort the pictures or comics.

If you've missed out on all of the fun over the years, fear not, you can perform the same distortion to your artwork using Illustrator's suite of Liquify distortion tools (although your hands won't smell of Silly Putty afterward). The Liquify toolset includes the Warp, Twirl, Pucker, Bloat, Scallop, Crystallize, and Wrinkle tools (**Figure 9.19**, next page). Each of these tools allows you to "paint" with distortion effects by simply clicking and dragging over vector art. The tools feature a brush size, which helps determine how large of an area is distorted (**Figure 9.20**). You can change the brush size for any of the Liquify tools interactively by holding the Option (Alt) key while dragging with the tool. Adding the Shift key while dragging constrains the brush size to a perfect circle.

Figure 9.19 The Liquify tools appear grouped together in the Toolbox and offer a wide range of distortion effects.

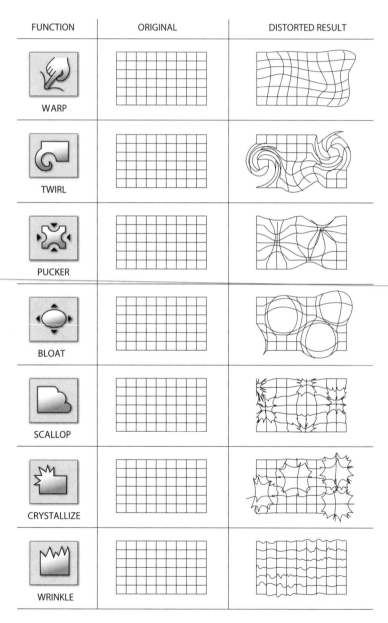

FUNCTION	ORIGINAL	DISTORTED RESULT
WARP		
TWIRL		
PUCKER		
BLOAT		
SCALLOP		
CRYSTALLIZE		
WRINKLE		

Figure 9.20 Changing the size of a Liquify brush allows you to control how much a selection becomes distorted with each drag of the mouse.

You'll have to be careful when using the Liquify tools, because they exhibit different behavior based on your selection. If you have artwork selected before you start dragging with a Liquify tool, only the selected art becomes distorted. However, if you have not made a selection, clicking and dragging with a Liquify tool distorts any path that you touch.

The Liquify tools don't work on live text (you'll need to convert text to outlines first), but the tools do work on embedded images. As you drag a Liquify tool over an embedded image, Illustrator creates a mesh that is used to distort the image beneath it (**Figure 9.21**). In fact, if you've created a gradient mesh object, using the Liquify tools on the mesh object produces interesting effects as well.

Figure 9.21 Although you can't change actual pixels in Illustrator, you can apply Liquify distortions to embedded images.

Controlling the Behavior of the Liquify Tools

Double-clicking any of the Liquify tools in the Toolbox brings up a dialog offering a variety of settings. The top half of the dialog features Global Brush Dimensions settings, which control the size (width and height), angle, and intensity of the tools. In addition, if you are using a pressure-sensitive tablet, you can choose to control the intensity with pen pressure by checking the Use Pressure Pen check box. Any changes you make to the Global Brush Dimensions settings are applied to all of the Liquify tools (**Figure 9.22**).

Figure 9.22 If you have a pressure-sensitive tablet, you can achieve greater control over the Liquify tools.

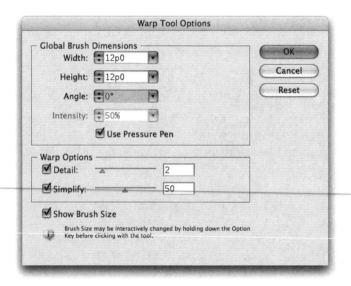

The bottom half of the dialog offers options for the specific tool that you double-clicked. Most tools offer Detail and Simplify settings, although the Wrinkle tool offers many additional options as well. The changes you make to each of these tool-specific settings only affect the tool you double-clicked.

Getting into Shape: Envelope Distortion

Ever see those cartoons where one of the characters gets his head stuck in a glass jar? And when he pulls his head out of the jar, his head is in the shape of the jar? Wouldn't it be cool if you could do the same thing with your artwork? Well, you can, using Illustrator's enveloping features.

An *envelope* is a regular vector shape that can contain other artwork. And any artwork that is contained inside the envelope becomes distorted to take on the shape of the envelope itself. As you will soon learn, envelopes use Illustrator's mesh technology to distort artwork. In fact, these envelope meshes, as they are called, are identical to the gradient meshes you created back in Chapter 5, *Brushes, Symbols, and Masks*.

There are actually three different ways to create an envelope distortion in Illustrator, and naturally, each offers a slightly different approach and warrants its own benefits. As you learn about these three different types of envelopes, you will understand when it's best to use them for a specific project or desired result. These three methods are found in the Object > Envelope Distort submenu and are named Make with Top Object, Make with Mesh, and Make with Warp.

Method One: Make with Top Object

A commonly used Envelope distortion technique in Illustrator is the Make with Top Object method. Creating an Envelope distortion using the Make with Top Object method is similar to creating a mask. A regular vector shape at the top of the stacking order acts as the envelope, and all selected artwork that appears beneath the envelope becomes distorted to fit within the envelope shape. Here are the steps you'll need to follow to perform this technique:

1. Select the shape that you will be using as the Envelope. Any vector object consisting of a single path can be used as an envelope.

2. Choose Object > Arrange > Bring to Front. This ensures that the envelope is at the top of the stacking order.

3. Select both the artwork that you want to distort and the vector shape that will become the envelope.

4. Choose Object > Envelope Distort > Make with Top Object (**Figure 9.23**, next page).

Figure 9.23 On the left, the envelope shape and the art-work appear selected. On the right, after the envelope has been applied, the artwork appears distorted within the envelope shape.

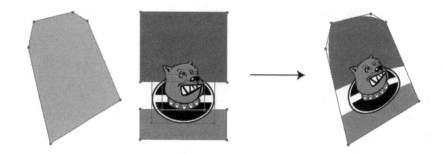

Once you've created an Envelope distortion, you can edit the envelope shape using your direct selection tool—just as you'd do with any other vector shape. As you adjust the shape of the envelope, the distorted artwork updates to match the edited shape (**Figure 9.24**). Pay close attention to the position of the control handles that appear on the anchor points of your envelope path, because they also have an effect on how art within the envelope shape is distorted (**Figure 9.25**).

Figure 9.24 Changing the shape of the envelope after you've applied the distortion makes it easy to tweak your distortion to perfection.

Figure 9.25 When you drag one of the control handles higher on the shape, you can see that the Envelope distortion also pulls the artwork up higher near that point.

Using a distinct custom shape as a distortion envelope is useful for times when you need artwork to fit within the confines of a specific shape. However, you'll notice that although you can easily adjust the outside path to change the overall shape of the distortion, you have little control over how the artwork inside the envelope is distorted. To control distortion across the entire object, not just the edges, you need to employ one of the next two methods: Make with Mesh, or Make with Warp.

Method Two: Make with Mesh

When using the Make with Mesh method, Illustrator creates the envelope shape for you, so you don't need to create a shape first. The shape that Illustrator creates is a rectangle, so no immediate distortion is visible when you apply this kind of envelope. Once the envelope is created, you can edit the mesh points to control how the distortion affects the artwork. Editing an envelope mesh is identical to editing a gradient mesh.

To create an Envelope distortion using the Make with Mesh method, perform the following steps:

1. Select any artwork on your artboard. You can select multiple objects, and although you aren't required to group them, you may want to do so to ensure easier editing later on.

2. Choose Object > Envelope Distort > Make with Mesh.

3. In the Envelope Mesh dialog, specify how many rows and columns you want the mesh to be initially created with (**Figure 9.26**). It doesn't matter if you aren't sure of the exact number of rows and columns at this point, because you are able to add mesh points later on as needed. Click OK to apply the Envelope distortion.

4. Using the Mesh tool or the Direct Selection tool, move the individual mesh points and their control handles to apply distortion to your artwork (**Figure 9.27**, next page).

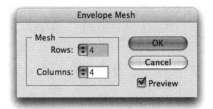

Figure 9.26 The Envelope Mesh dialog gives you the ability to set how many mesh points appear initially in the envelope. Creating more rows and columns gives you additional control over the amount of distortion you can apply.

Figure 9.27 Similar to working with a gradient mesh, adjusting the position and control handles of mesh points in an envelope mesh controls the distortion of the artwork.

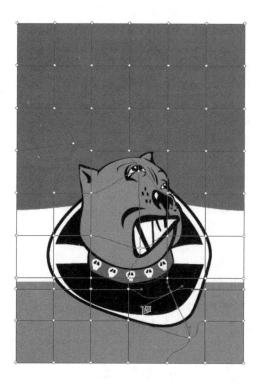

If you want to add mesh points to your envelope, select the Mesh tool and click anywhere within the selected envelope. Hold down the Option (Alt) key while clicking with the Mesh tool to remove mesh points.

You can also use the Mesh tool to add mesh points to envelopes that you created using the Make with Top Object method.

Although you start out with a rectangle mesh shape, moving the individual mesh points on the envelope gives you control over not just the outer edge of the distortion, but also any points within the envelope shape. However, this method is harder to use only because you aren't starting with a distorted shape, just a grid of mesh points.

Method Three: Make with Warp

The Make with Warp method of applying envelope distortion is nearly identical to the Make with Mesh method—only with a twist (sorry, couldn't resist). Instead of starting with a rectangular shaped mesh, Illustrator gives you the option of choosing from several different preset shapes. Actually, they are the same presets as those found in the Warp effect.

Follow these steps to apply an Envelope distortion using the Make with Warp method:

1. Select any artwork on your artboard. You can select multiple objects, and although you aren't required to group them, you may want to do so to ensure easier editing later on.

2. Choose Object > Envelope Distort > Make with Warp.

3. In the Warp Options dialog that appears, choose a Warp style and adjust the settings as necessary. Click OK to apply the Envelope distortion (**Figure 9.28**).

4. Using the Mesh tool or the Direct Selection tool, move the individual mesh points and their control handles to apply distortion to your artwork (**Figure 9.29**).

Figure 9.28 Starting an Envelope distortion with a warp gives you a head start in getting the look you need.

Figure 9.29 Although the envelope starts out as a warp, you can add mesh points as needed to adjust the distortion to your needs.

Overall, this third method of creating an envelope mesh is a combination of the first two. You start with an initial distortion using a warp, then you complete the distortion by editing the envelope as a mesh object. This method is useful for times when you want to use a warp shape but need the ability to tweak the distortion a bit—something that isn't possible with the Warp effect. Refer to "Featured Match-Up: Envelopes vs. the Warp Effect" for an in-depth comparison of the Envelope and Warp effect distortion features.

 Featured Match-Up: Envelopes vs. the Warp Effect

After learning how to apply some of the Envelope distortion features—especially the Make with Warp method—you may wonder how these kinds of distortions differ from the Warp effect distortions that you learned about in Chapter 7.

Although it's true that both the Warp effect and Envelope distortions are live in that you can edit them after they've been applied, they don't behave the same way. The Warp effect, which appears in the Effect menu, exhibits the same behavior as any other live effect. That means you can apply the Warp effect to any object, any group, or even to an entire layer. Because Live Effects appear listed in the Appearance palette, you can apply warps to individual parts of an object (i.e., just to the Stroke attribute). In addition, a warp can be saved in a graphic style to be easily applied to other objects.

On the other hand, Envelope distortions give you complete control of the shape of your overall distortion, and using mesh points, you can even control how the interior artwork itself is distorted. Overall, envelopes offer a level of control that is simply not possible with the Warp effect. After all, the Warp effect only contains 15 different shapes to choose from, and these cannot address every design need. Generally, the Warp effects are great for quick adjustments to artwork, whereas envelopes excel at distortions that require individual attention.

Adjusting Envelope Distortion Settings

By default, Illustrator tries to create Envelope distortions as quickly as possible. Artwork that takes longer to distort, like Live Effects, gradients, or patterns, are not distorted at all, and images or other complex artwork may not fit perfectly within the envelope shape. Don't assume that Illustrator's Envelope distortion is below par; rather, select your envelope and choose

Object > Envelope Distort > Envelope Options. This opens the Envelope Options dialog where you can adjust the settings that Illustrator uses to create Envelope distortions (**Figure 9.30**).

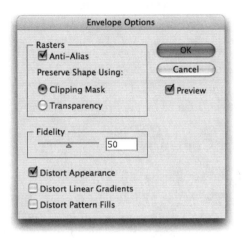

Figure 9.30 The Envelope Options dialog gives you greater control over how Illustrator distorts artwork within envelopes.

- **Rasters.** If your envelope contains a raster image, you can choose to turn antialiasing on or off. With antialiasing turned on, Illustrator produces smoother and nicer looking art, at the expense of longer calculations and render times. When nonrectangular shapes are used as an envelope (as is usually the case), you can choose to have any raster art enclosed by a clipping mask or a transparency alpha channel.

- **Fidelity.** When Illustrator performs an Envelope distortion, it has to stretch or squeeze artwork to fit within another shape. During this process, Illustrator may make small adjustments to the art so that it doesn't become overly complex. A higher fidelity setting forces Illustrator to preserve the integrity of the artwork as much as possible, which may produce more anchor points, but results in final distorted art that closely matches the original. A lower fidelity setting gives Illustrator more wiggle room to create files that print and save faster.

- **Distort Appearance.** If the artwork that you're placing into an envelope contains Live Effects or multiple Fill or Stroke attributes, those appearances do not become distorted by the envelope shape by default. You must check the Distort Appearance option if you want the appearance to be affected by the Envelope distortion.

- **Distort Linear Gradients.** If the artwork that you're placing into an envelope contains linear gradients, the gradient itself does not become distorted by the envelope shape by default. You must check the Distort Linear Gradients option if you want the gradient fill to be affected by the Envelope distortion.

- **Distort Pattern Fills.** If the artwork that you're placing into an envelope contains a pattern fill, that fill does not become distorted by the envelope shape by default. You must check the Distort Pattern Fills option if you want the pattern to be affected by the Envelope distortion.

Editing Envelopes and Their Contents

It is certainly no coincidence that many of Illustrator's features exhibit live functionality, thus allowing you to perform edits without having to re-create art. Live Effects, symbols, Live Trace, Live Paint, and Compound Shape modes are all examples of effects that are live and can be edited at any stage of the workflow. Envelope distortion is no exception. Once you apply an Envelope distortion using any of the three methods described earlier, you can continue to make adjustments to either the envelope itself, or to the artwork that it contains.

Illustrator manages the process of editing envelopes and their contents by giving you two distinct modes in which to work. At any one time, you can either work with the envelope shape itself, or you can change modes and edit the contents of the envelope. Unfortunately, Illustrator doesn't clearly identify the difference between these two modes so we'll take a closer look at how you can edit Envelope distortions and the artwork within them.

When you first create a new Envelope distortion, Illustrator is in the Edit Envelope mode. In this mode, you can select and edit the shape of the envelope, but you have no way to access the art that is distorted within the envelope. If you look at the Layers palette, you'll notice an object named Envelope, but you won't find the distorted artwork listed anywhere (**Figure 9.31**).

In order to edit the contents of an envelope, select it on your artboard and choose Object > Envelope Distort > Edit Contents, or press Command-Shift-V (Ctrl-Shift-V). Doing so puts Illustrator into the Edit Contents

Figure 9.31 The Layers palette lists only one object on Layer 1—the envelope. The artwork that appears distorted within the envelope doesn't appear listed in the Layers palette at all.

mode, where you can select the artwork and edit it as normal. In the Edit Contents mode, you cannot adjust, or even select, the envelope. If you look at the Layers palette, you'll see that the Envelope object now contains a triangle to the left of its name, which you can click to reveal the objects contained within the envelope (**Figure 9.32**). This triangle is your only clue in figuring out what mode you are in. If you see the disclosure triangle, you're in Edit Contents mode, and if you don't, then you are in Edit Envelope mode. If you are in Edit Contents mode and want to return to Edit Envelope mode, use the same keyboard shortcut mentioned earlier, or choose Object > Envelope Distort > Edit Envelope.

Keep in mind that Illustrator maintains each Envelope distortion in your file as a separate entity. Therefore, it's entirely possible to have one envelope in Edit Envelope mode and have another envelope in Edit Contents mode.

 When you're editing the contents of an envelope, you might find it easier to make edits to your art with Smart Guides turned on. The Object Highlighting feature of Smart Guides allows you to quickly find and see the art that you are editing.

Figure 9.32 When you're in Edit Contents mode, Illustrator reveals the artwork within the envelope on Layer 1.

Releasing and Expanding Envelopes

At any time, you can select an existing envelope and choose Object > Envelope Distort > Release, which returns the artwork to an undistorted state. In addition, you can choose Object > Envelope Distort > Expand, which applies the Envelope distortion to the artwork itself. You can then edit the distorted paths freely (**Figure 9.33**) although you won't be able to edit or change the Envelope distortion itself after this point.

Figure 9.33 When you expand an envelope, the distortion is applied permanently to the artwork, as seen here, in Artwork Preview mode.

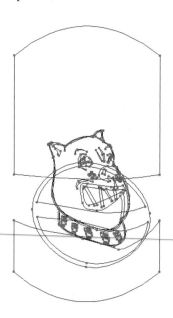

CREATING TRANSITIONS WITH BLENDS

By definition, a *blend* is the result of two or more items that are combined. In Illustrator, a blend is a set of at least two objects that morph into each other. In an example where you are blending two objects, Illustrator generates new shapes that appear between the two objects, making it seem like one of the objects is turning into the other. The iterations that are created between the two main objects (also referred to as *key objects*) are called *steps*, and as you'll learn shortly, Illustrator gives you control over how many steps make up each blend (**Figure 9.34**).

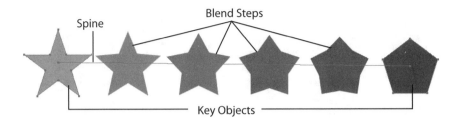

Figure 9.34 A blend in Illustrator is made up of key objects and blend steps. A straight line, called the spine, connects the key objects.

Although at first glance it may seem like creating blends is something reserved for highly specialized tasks, the reality is that you can use blends for many different reasons. In fact, back in the day, before gradients were introduced to Illustrator, blends were the only way you could create color gradations. Here's a list of some other common uses for blends in Illustrator:

- **Creating shading effects.** You can use blends to create photorealistic shading effects. Because blends can be created using any vector shape, you can create customized gradations not only in color, but in shape as well (**Figure 9.35**). This gives using blends a distinct advantage over using gradients.

- **Creating animations.** When creating animations in Illustrator, you can use a blend to *tween* steps between objects, saving you from having to create the necessary keyframes yourself (**Figure 9.36**). Tweening is a term used in animation to define the steps that appear when showing movement or one object morphing into another. In Chapter 10, *Illustrator and the Web,* you will learn how to export animated SWF (Flash) files directly right from Illustrator.

Be sure to check out Brad Neal's gallery in the color insert for examples of how blends can be used.

Figure 9.35 By blending two crescent shapes, you can get realistic shading in a way that is not possible with linear or radial gradients.

Figure 9.36 By blending two symbols with different opacity levels, Illustrator creates the necessary steps to create an animation.

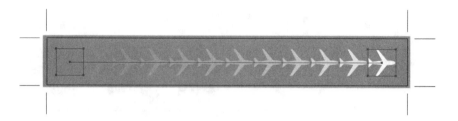

- **Distributing objects.** If you need to repeat art across an area or along the curve of a path, you can use a blend to evenly distribute a specific number of steps (**Figure 9.37**).

Figure 9.37 If you are creating a blend between identical stars, you can have it follow a specific path. This technique is covered later in the chapter, "Replacing the Spine of a Blend".

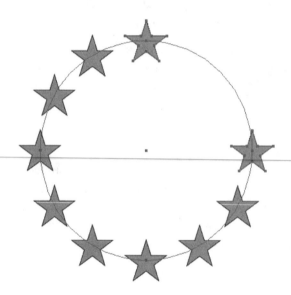

In case you're ever playing something like the Adobe edition of Trivial Pursuit, you'll find this info helpful: The 3D effect in Illustrator uses blends to create lighting and shading effects.

You can't blend images or area text objects, but you can blend just about anything else—including symbols and groups. In fact, as we discussed briefly in Chapter 7, you can blend between objects that have different effect settings; Illustrator blends the settings of those effects as well. Blends are pretty powerful, but don't worry, they are easy to work with.

Creating a Blend

If there were always just one way to perform a particular function in Illustrator, there would be less of a need for books like this one. But as we've seen up to this point in this book, Illustrator offers a variety of ways to perform tasks, each of which offers specific benefits. In the case of blends, Illustrator allows you to generate a blend from a menu item, or you can achieve finer control over the result of your blend using the Blend tool.

Method One: Using the Blend Submenu

Creating a blend using the Make command is the quickest way. You simply select at least two objects and choose Object > Blend > Make. Using this method, Illustrator takes the bottom-most object in your selection and creates a blend with the next object up in the stacking order.

Method Two: Using the Blend Tool

Creating a blend using the Blend tool takes a few extra clicks of the mouse but gives you the ability to control the blend in ways that the menu command can't. You begin by selecting the objects that you want to blend, and then you choose the Blend tool from the Toolbox. Then, click once on an anchor point in the first object to define where you want the blend to start, and click an anchor point in the second object where you want the blend to end. If you have more than two objects to blend, keep selecting an anchor point from each object until the blend is created.

Unlike the first method where Illustrator created the blend based on stacking order, this method allows you to control in which order key objects appear in the blend. Additionally, if you click an anchor point near the top of one object and then choose an anchor point toward the bottom of the next key object, Illustrator rotates and modifies the intermediate steps of the blend to match the orientation of the anchor points (**Figure 9.38**).

First click

Second click

Figure 9.38 When you click with the Blend tool to blend specific points (instead of the entire object), Illustrator twists and rotates the blend steps accordingly.

Editing a Blend

Once you've created a blend, you can edit it in a variety of ways. It should come as no surprise to you at this point to learn that blends are live in Illustrator, meaning you can adjust them even after the blend is applied. To do so, using the Direct Selection tool, click a key object and change its color, shape, position, attributes—whatever—when you do, Illustrator simply redraws the blend to incorporate the change.

You will notice that you can't select or edit the intermediate steps that Illustrator creates to form the blend. This is an attribute of the live functionality of the blend—you can only access the steps by expanding the blend (see "Releasing and Expanding Blends," later in the chapter). However, you can control how Illustrator draws blend steps by selecting a blend and choosing Object > Blend > Blend Options.

In the Blend Options dialog, you have two general settings: Spacing and Orientation:

- **Spacing.** The Spacing setting determines the number of blend steps that are created. When Smooth Color is chosen, Illustrator creates as many steps as are necessary to display a smooth and gradual transition between key objects (**Figure 9.39**). The Specified Steps setting allows you to define exactly how many blend steps Illustrator creates. Using a higher number of steps results in a smoother transition, whereas a lower number allows you to see the individual steps in the blend (**Figure 9.40**). The Specified Distance allows you to specify how far apart each step appears from the next.

- **Orientation.** The Orientation setting controls the baseline angle of each step in your blend. With the Align to Page setting, each blend step aligns parallel to the bottom of the page, even if the path is curved or diagonal. With this setting, all blends steps share the same orientation. In contrast, the Align to Path setting aligns the baseline of each blend step to the angle of the path itself. With this setting, you'll see that each blend step has a different orientation (**Figure 9.41**).

Figure 9.39 When you want to create shading techniques using blends, the Smooth Color option provides the best results.

Figure 9.40 By specifying a particular number of blend steps, you can control how visible the individual steps of the blend are.

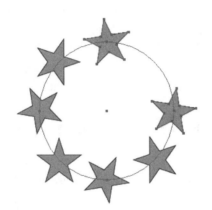

Figure 9.41 On the left, the blend is set to the Align to Page option. The blend on the right is set to the Align to Path orientation option.

Replacing the Spine of a Blend

As we briefly mentioned earlier, you'll notice a straight path that connects the key objects in a blend. This path is referred to as the *spine* of the blend. The individual steps that are created in a blend follow along the spine as they connect the two outer objects. The spine is an editable path, and you can use the Pen tool and the Direct Selection tool to edit the path if you want to alter the direction of the blend steps. In fact, the position of the control handles on a spine can control how the individual steps are distributed along the spine.

Additionally, you can perform a delicate operation—a spine transplant. You can draw any vector path, open or closed, and use it as the spine for an existing blend. To perform this surgery, select both the blend and the path

 Illustrator can have a maximum of 256 steps in a blend. The number of steps that appear in a blend has a direct impact on screen redraw speed, print performance, and file size.

you've created, and then choose Object > Blend > Replace Spine. Illustrator then uses the path you created as the spine for the blend, allowing you to customize how blend steps appear.

Reversing Blends

With a blend selected, you can choose Object > Blend > Reverse Spine, to reverse the order of the key objects in your blend. This function is helpful for when you want to flip the blend so that it travels in the opposite direction.

Additionally, you can reverse the stacking order of the key objects in a blend by selecting the blend and choosing Object > Blend > Reverse Front to Back. This setting is especially useful for when you are using blends to create animations, which always travel in one direction. To have your animation play in reverse, you use this feature.

Releasing and Expanding Blends

As with Envelope distortions, you can select an existing blend and choose Object > Blend > Release, which removes the blend steps and returns the artwork to its original state (just the two original objects). In addition, you can choose Object > Blend > Expand, which applies the blend to the artwork itself, leaving the individual blend steps visible and available for editing. Once a blend has been expanded, it is no longer updated when the original two objects are edited.

Releasing a Blend to Layers

There is yet another way to release a blend that is useful, especially when you're creating frames for animations that will either be exported directly from Illustrator as SWF (Flash) files, or that will be imported into a video package like Adobe After Effects and Premiere Pro, or Apple Final Cut Pro. This method actually expands the blend into its individual steps and then places each step on its own layer. To release a blend in this way, you must follow these steps:

1. If it isn't already open, choose Window > Layers to open your Layers palette.

2. In the Layers palette, highlight the blend object that you want to release by clicking once on it (**Figure 9.42**).

3. From the Layers palette menu (**Figure 9.43**), choose Release to Layers (Sequence) or choose Release to Layers (Build).

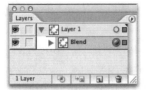

Figure 9.42 The Release to Layers command is a feature of the Layers palette, so selecting the blend on the artboard won't help. You have to highlight the blend in the Layers palette.

Figure 9.43 Illustrator supports the ability to release artwork to layers using the Sequence or the Build method.

You should use the Sequence option when you want each layer to contain only one step, and the Build option when you want to produce layers that add steps cumulatively to each layer that is created.

Adding Pizzazz with the Flare Tool

You may ask yourself, what is the Flare tool doing in a chapter about distortion and blends and graphs? It seems as if it's out of place. In reality, the Flare tool is unlike any of the other tools in Illustrator, and so it seems out of place in general.

The Flare tool is really something spectacular, although it's a one trick pony. The tool is present in Illustrator to create fantastic lens flares of the likes you would normally create in programs like Adobe Photoshop or After Effects. However, the Flare tool creates these effects using only vector objects, not rasters, and Illustrator keeps them in an editable state, which makes them easy to adjust.

Creating a Vector Lens Flare

Drawing a flare with the Flare tool is basically a two-step process. First, you define where the highlight will go, and then you define the angle of the light. In reality though, there are many more little steps that need to happen in between. To apply a lens flare with the Flare tool, follow these instructions:

1. Select the Flare tool, which you'll find grouped with the closed path shape tools (don't ask why it's there, just accept it; **Figure 9.44**).

Figure 9.44 The Flare tool is grouped with the closed path shape tools.

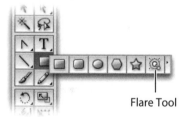

Flare Tool

2. Click and drag from the point where you want the center of the highlight to be (**Figure 9.45**). Do not release the mouse button yet.

3. Press the up and down arrows to add and remove the number of rays in the lens flare.

4. Release the mouse.

5. Click and drag to define the lighting direction of the Flare. Do not release the mouse button yet (**Figure 9.46**).

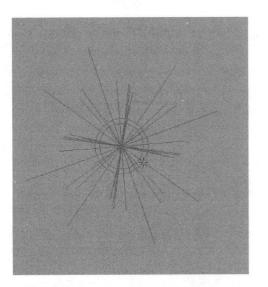

Figure 9.45 Clicking and dragging with the Flare tool is the first step in creating a vector flare.

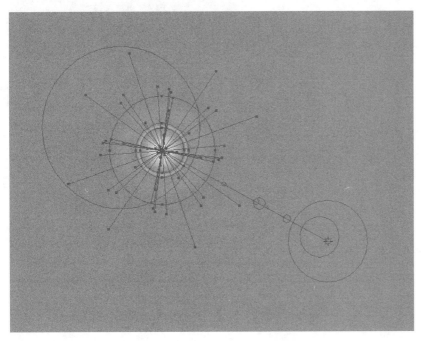

Figure 9.46 The second click and drag with the Flare tool defines additional options.

6. Press the up and down arrows to add and remove the number of rings in the lens flare.

7. Release the mouse to complete the lens flare (**Figure 9.47**).

Figure 9.47 The Flare creates cool effects, although you should refer to Chapter 11, *Prepress and Printing*, for important information on printing documents with transparency effects.

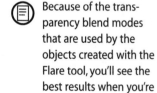
Because of the transparency blend modes that are used by the objects created with the Flare tool, you'll see the best results when you're creating flares over colored backgrounds.

Even though it isn't a Live Effect, once a flare has been applied, it can still be edited—although not via the Appearance palette. To edit a flare, select it with the Selection tool and double-click the Flare tool in the Toolbox. This opens the Flare Tool Options dialog, where you specify any changes to the appearance of the flare. When you check the Preview button you will be able to see the changes happening to the flare as you adjust the settings.

CHAPTER 10

Illustrator and the Web

There's no question that Adobe Illustrator suffers from schizophrenia. One moment it's a print-based application with spot colors and crop marks, and the next, it's a Web-based application with Web-safe color palettes and slices. And that's okay, because as designers living in the 21st century, we all suffer from the same schizophrenia. This is because we are called upon to create art that will be used in many different ways—most notably in print and on the Web. Even if you are living in a print- or Web-centric world, others may use and repurpose the art that you create. That's where Illustrator excels— in repurposing artwork for a variety of uses.

In this chapter, we focus on Web technologies and understanding how the Web and Web browsers display graphics. We then discuss how you can use your favorite design application—Illustrator—to create quality Web graphics with ease.

Illustrator's Role in Web Design

Before we dive into the world of Web design, it's important to realize where Illustrator fits in when it comes to creating Web graphics. There's certainly more to creating a Website than drawing pretty pictures. Programs are dedicated specifically to creating and maintaining Web sites, such as Adobe GoLive and Macromedia Dreamweaver, and in no way does Illustrator compete with or replace those programs.

You can use Illustrator to design how a Web page looks (by creating a composition), but you wouldn't normally use Illustrator to create an actual HTML-based Web page. Similarly, you wouldn't use Illustrator to manage a multipage Website, as Illustrator lacks the toolset to do so.

Illustrator's strength is in designing Web interfaces or the navigation bars, buttons, individual Web graphics, and general artwork that appear within a Web page. You can place elements like this that you design in Illustrator into GoLive, Dreamweaver, or any other program you use to create your Web pages.

DESIGN CONSIDERATIONS FOR THE WEB

Throughout this entire book, you have been learning how to create vector-based artwork. You've even learned how to use Illustrator's Live Trace feature, which converts pixel-based images into Bézier paths. So it's with a large spoonful of irony that we inform you how important pixels are in the world of Web graphics.

Unlike printed artwork that is produced with image setters or digital presses that are capable of resolutions upward of 3000 dots per inch (dpi), artwork that is created for the Web is always viewed on a computer screen, usually at 72 pixels per inch (ppi). Things that a print designer might be used to, like working with high-resolution images, choosing spot colors, or carefully calculating where fold lines or trim lines will be, are of no concern to someone who is designing a Website.

However, don't be fooled into thinking that Web designers have it easier than print designers. There are plenty of challenges that a Web designer faces—things that never cross the minds of print designers. For example, because people view Websites on a computer screen, a designer has no way of knowing what size a viewer's screen is. Especially now, where you have WebTV, Internet kiosks, and Web-capable cell phones, it is important for Web designers to create their art so that it can be displayed on virtually any device.

Although print and Web technologies are different, it's important not to lose sight of your goal as a designer—to communicate a message in an effective manner. The same rules of design that apply to the print world also apply to artwork destined for the Web. If you keep this at the forefront of your mind, and if you follow the advice and techniques revealed throughout the rest of this chapter, you're sure to create effective and compelling Web graphics.

THE ATTRIBUTES OF WEB GRAPHICS—COLOR, QUALITY, AND FILE SIZE

In the business world, there's a saying that goes "we offer excellent service, exceptional quality, and cheap prices—pick any two out of the three." You can apply a similar saying to Web graphics; it would sound something like "there's color, quality, and file size—pick any two out of the three." Allow us to explain.

With Web graphics, there's a delicate balance between the way an image looks when viewed on a computer screen and the time it takes to download the image so that you can view it. No matter how good the image looks, if viewers have to wait too long for a graphic to appear on their screen, their patience runs out and they click to some other Website in the blink of an eye. In general, there is a direct correlation between the detail and number of colors in an image and the size of the file. A file with many colors may have a large file size, but an image with a small file size may not have enough colors or detail to look good. As a designer, your job is to find a happy medium—an image that looks good and is small enough that it downloads quickly. Luckily, you have Illustrator CS2 on your side, which has the tools you'll need to get results.

Understanding and Using Web-Safe Colors

Although the argument can be made that file size isn't that important anymore because of the growing population of broadband internet installations, remember that many people still have slower dialup connections (especially outside of the United States). In addition, handheld wireless devices and Web-based cell phones are becoming increasingly popular, and those devices have much slower download capabilities.

Most designers have a swatch book by their side—such as a Pantone book—that helps them choose colors to use in a design. And even though color management technologies have been getting better over the years, most people still don't trust the color they see on their computer screens. If you're designing Web graphics though, you don't have much of a choice because the computer screen is the delivery medium for your artwork. Therefore, it's entirely possible that you can choose a nice yellow color on your screen, but when someone views your Website on a different computer, that color might appear green or orange. So what's a designer to do?

With a little bit of information and some simple math, it's possible to narrow the number of colors that you might use to ensure that your color looks decent on someone else's computer screen. Although there are all types of computers and graphics cards out there, the minimum number of colors that a system supports is 256 (also referred to as VGA). However, not all computer systems use the same set of 256 colors. In fact, Windows-based computers use a different system-set of colors than Mac-based computers (not surprising). The good news is that of these two mainstream systems, only 40 colors are different, which leaves 216 common colors. This means that if a designer were to use one of these 216 colors, referred to as *Web-safe colors*, they would be assured that their artwork would display properly on just about any computer.

Illustrator can help you choose from these Web-safe colors in several ways. First, you can load a custom palette that contains all 216 Web-safe colors by choosing Window > Swatch Libraries > Web (**Figure 10.1**). Illustrator also features a color palette called VisiBone2, which displays Web-safe colors in a more intuitive way (**Figure 10.2**). Alternatively, you can choose Web Safe RGB from the Color palette menu, which allows you to choose Web-safe colors using the color ramp, the RGB sliders, or by directly entering their hexadecimal values. If you are using the regular RGB sliders in the Color palette, Illustrator lets you know when a color is not a Web-safe color by displaying a small cube under the color icon. If you click the cube, Illustrator chooses the closest Web-safe color for you (**Figure 10.3**).

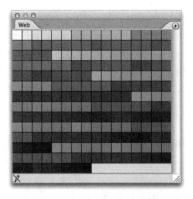

Figure 10.1 Illustrator's Web palette displays all 216 Web-safe colors.

Figure 10.2 When the palette is resized correctly so that there are white swatches in each of the four corners, the VisiBone2 palette displays the 216 Web-safe colors in a way that closely matches a color wheel, making it easier to use when designing.

Cube ——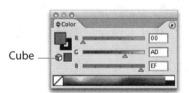

Figure 10.3 A small cube in the Color palette indicates when a chosen color is not a Web-safe color. You can have Illustrator snap to the closest Web-safe color by clicking the cube.

Maximizing Image Quality on the Web

Overall, there are two things that affect the appearance of Web graphics—
dithering, and *anti-aliasing*. We mentioned earlier how computers display
different colors. Higher-end graphics cards allow computers to display
many millions of colors, whereas lower-end cards restrict the display to

a far smaller number of colors. Therefore, the following question arises: "If you create multicolored artwork on a high-end machine (which most designers use), what happens when that graphic is displayed on a low-end machine that can't display all of those colors?"

Dithering

The answer is dithering—a process in which a computer simulates a color that it doesn't have by mixing colors that it does have. For example, if you have a set of paints, you might only have a few colors, but you can create more colors by mixing the paints. Although the dithering concept is nice in theory, the results are not always great. The problem is that a computer can't mix colors within a single pixel, and so the dithering process creates a pattern of different-colored pixels in an effort to appear as another color. Many times, this pattern is visible and can give an odd appearance to a graphic (**Figure 10.4**). In fact, the entire concept of using a Web-safe color is to ensure that you'll be using a color that won't dither. As we'll see later in the chapter, Illustrator contains certain settings that can control how dithering is applied to a graphic.

Figure 10.4 The gradient on the left has been enlarged to show the effects of dithering. Notice the pattern of pixels that are visible where colors blend into one another. The same gradient on the right however, exhibits no dithering.

Anti-aliasing

Another issue that arises with screen-rendered graphics has to do with the low resolution that a monitor uses—in most cases, 72 ppi. At such a low resolution, the eye actually sees pixels, and curved edges display with jagged edges (often referred to as "jaggies"). To make graphics look better onscreen, computers use a method called anti-aliasing to slightly blur the edges of boundaries between colors. The result is an image that looks smooth instead of jagged (**Figure 10.5**).

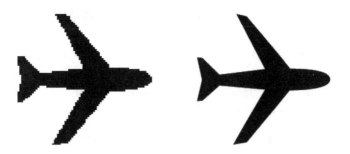

Figure 10.5 Pictured here are identical vector objects. The object on the right has anti-aliasing turned on, resulting in a smoother appearance onscreen.

Using Pixel Preview mode

When you save or convert your vector graphic to a raster format, Illustrator can apply anti-aliasing (it does by default). However, when you're viewing your graphic on the Illustrator artboard, you might also want to see what your graphic looks like with anti-aliasing applied. To do so, choose View > Pixel Preview, which is a special preview mode where your graphics display on your artboard as they would when viewed in a Web browser. You can work and edit graphics in Pixel Preview mode, and you should do so when you're designing graphics for the Web.

Working in Pixel Preview mode is important because anti-aliasing can cause slight adjustments in the appearance of your graphics, like thin black lines becoming fat gray lines, or text appearing chunky or blurry (see the sidebar entitled "Disabling Anti-aliasing"). With Pixel Preview on, you can position your artwork and see results instantly.

Using Compression to Reduce File Size

The last—and possibly the most important—attribute of a Web graphic is its file size. Anyone can create great-looking graphics with large, high-resolution images, but a Web designer has to deliver the best possible graphics using low-resolution images that download fast.

For the most part, Web designers can save files in a variety of different file formats, each of which utilizes compression techniques to help reduce file size. For the most part, file formats use one of the following two types of compression: *lossless,* and *lossy*. Lossless compression reduces file size without any loss in image quality or image detail. In contrast, lossy compression reduces file size by sacrificing image data, resulting in images that have less detail. As with just about anything else in life, a designer is faced with making decisions based on what attributes are most important on an image-by-image basis. In the next section, you'll learn about all of the different file types Illustrator can utilize and the compression techniques these file types use.

Disabling Anti-aliasing

Although anti-aliasing is generally a good thing, sometimes it can work against you. The side effect of blurring edges of color is that sometimes doing so makes your graphics unsightly or your text illegible. This is especially true when your design contains small text or thin lines. Using Pixel Preview helps you see these issues before you export these graphics (**Figure 10.6**).

You may find that for some artwork, it is even beneficial to turn off anti-aliasing altogether. To do so, make your selection and choose Effect > Rasterize. Choose 72 ppi for the Resolution setting, choose None for the Anti-aliasing setting, and click OK. With Pixel Preview turned on, you will clearly see the difference between objects that do and do not have anti-aliasing disabled (**Figure 10.7**).

Figure 10.6 Although you may have specified a 1-point black stroke for an object, Pixel Preview mode may reveal that anti-aliasing has produced a 2-point gray stroke instead.

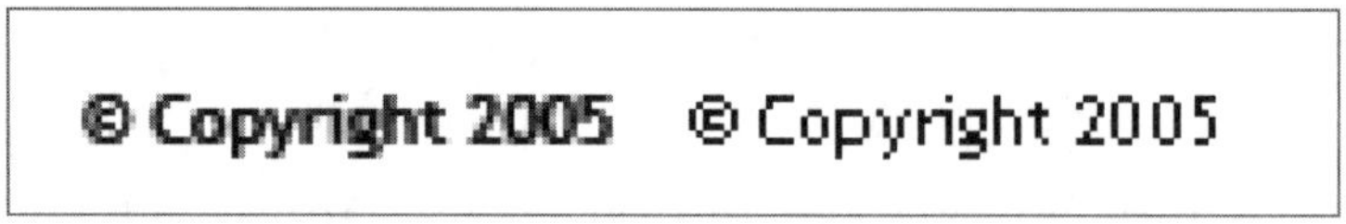

Figure 10.7 Legibility can suffer on small text when anti-aliasing is used. The text on the right has anti-aliasing disabled. Although it doesn't look as pretty, at least you can read it.

OPTIMIZING WEB GRAPHICS

The process of preparing graphics for display on the Web is called *optimization*. This process entails choosing how artwork is exported from Illustrator, what file formats are being used, and what settings are being used for each file type. Illustrator offers several features, such as Web slicing and Save for Web, which helps you create the best-looking Web graphics.

Creating Web Slices

One way to optimize Web graphics is to use a technique called *Web slicing*. In simple terms, Web slicing is the process of cutting a large image into several smaller images, which is desirable for various reasons.

First of all, there's user perception. If you try to load a Web page that has a single large image on it, you sit there impatiently waiting for it to download and appear on the page. But when an image is sliced into smaller parts, each smaller image loads faster, and as a result, it feels like the image itself is loading faster.

On that same note, you can use different file formats for each image slice, which can save some valuable file size space, resulting in a faster-loading graphic overall. As you'll see when we discuss the Save for Web feature, these settings directly impact the final file size (read: download time) of your total image.

Slicing is also helpful if parts of a graphic need to be updated often. Instead of always creating larger images, you can update just a part of the image. Swapping out a slice or two can be more efficient than having to work with one large, bulky file all the time.

Finally, because each slice is its own image, you can assign a link (a URL) to it, effectively making it a button. When someone clicks a sliced part of an image, they are linked to another Web page. Of course, you can specify other functionality for such a button as well.

Any Way You Slice It...

Illustrator offers two ways to create Web slices. The more traditional way is to draw them yourself, but Illustrator can also create slices from objects automatically using a feature called *object-based slicing*. Let's explore both methods.

Once your artwork is created, you can choose the Slice tool from the Toolbox and click and drag in your document window. When you do, Illustrator draws rectangular regions—slices—and each appears with a number that identifies it (**Figure 10.8**). As you create slices, other dimmed slices might appear automatically in the document. These are called *auto slices*. Slices that you create are called *user slices*. Because the overall image has to be rectangular (for an explanation, see the sidebar "Web Slices = HTML Tables"), and all of the slices must be rectangles as well, Illustrator creates slices as necessary (**Figure 10.9**). As you continue to create slices, Illustrator updates the auto slices accordingly.

Figure 10.8 Create slices where it makes sense to do so to allow for interactivity or future editing.

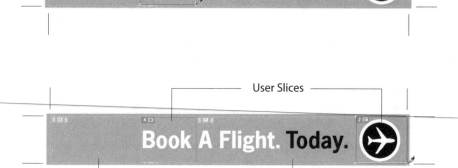

Figure 10.9 As you draw slices with the Slice tool, Illustrator creates other slices to fill out the rest of the document.

Web Slices = HTML Tables

So what exactly happens when you create a slice? Illustrator splits a single graphic into multiple images. An HTML table is created, with each cell of the table containing one of these slices, or pieces of the image. In this way, when you display the Web page in a browser, all the sliced-up images appear together, almost like a puzzle. This is an important concept to keep in mind because you can create only rectangular slices.

When you draw a slice with the Slice tool, Illustrator is really drawing a rectangle with no fill and no stroke and making it a slice (**Figure 10.10**). When you want to edit the slice, you can use the Slice Select tool to change the boundaries of the slice.

Figure 10.10 Slices that you create with the Slice tool appear listed in the Layers palette. They are special rectangles that have their Fill and Stroke attributes set to None.

However, Illustrator also has a different kind of slice. Instead of creating graphics and drawing slices over them, you can apply a slice as an attribute to a selection—something that Illustrator calls an object-based slice. To apply this kind of slice, make a selection and then choose Object > Slice > Make. Illustrator uses the bounds of your selected artwork as the area for the object-based slice. Using this method, if you make an edit to your graphic, the slice updates automatically along with it.

If you want to hide all the little squares and numbers that indicate slices on your screen, you can do so by choosing View > Hide Slices.

Editing Slice Attributes

You can specify certain attributes for a slice. Remember that a slice is really a cell in an HTML table. So, for example, a slice can have its own background color or URL link. Once a slice has been defined using either of the two methods described earlier, you can select it with the Slice Select tool. To edit the attributes of a slice, select a slice and choose Object > Slice > Slice Options to specify settings such as URL and ALT text (**Figure 10.11**). When you specify text as an object-based slice, you can also set the slice to be an HTML slice (rather than an image slice). In that case, Illustrator exports the text as editable HTML instead of as a graphic.

 When exporting files in the Photoshop file format, you can preserve slices defined in Illustrator. Refer to Chapter 12, *Saving and Exporting Files*, for more details.

Figure 10.11 The Slice Options dialog gives you the ability to assign specific URLs and additional information for each slice in your document.

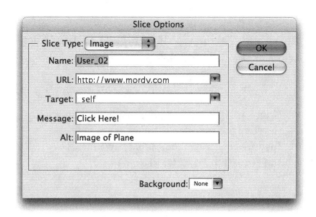

HTML text slices might not format exactly as you see them in Illustrator. Although bold or character attributes are preserved, exact fonts and sizing depend on the browser used. Other text features, such as kerning and baseline shift, are ignored.

Once you have created all of your slices, you can choose individual file formats and additional settings by using the Save for Web feature, which we discuss in detail right about . . . now.

Using the Save for Web Feature

At one time, saving a graphic for use on the Web was a difficult task that involved saving an image, opening it in a Web browser, and then repeating that process again and again. Illustrator's Save for Web feature—which is also found in Photoshop and GoLive—is actually a component of Adobe ImageReady and allows you to speed up the process of optimizing and saving Web graphics.

Once you're ready to export a final version of your Web graphic, choose File > Save for Web to open the Save for Web dialog. The dialog, which fills up most of your screen, is split into several different sections (**Figure 10.12**). Along the far left are several tools that you can use within the Save for Web dialog. In the center, a preview pane allows you to view up to four different versions of your art. The upper right side offers a variety of different export formats and their settings and the lower right side offers a trio of palettes that control color, image size, and layer settings. Along the bottom of the dialog are zoom controls, color information, and a Preview in Browser button.

Save for Web Toolbox   Preview Pane   Export Formats and Settings

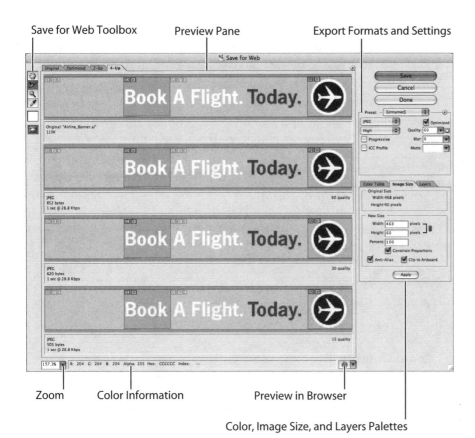

Figure 10.12 The Save for
Web dialog is almost an entire
application within itself.

Zoom   Color Information   Preview in Browser

Color, Image Size, and Layers Palettes

Let's take a closer look at each of the individual sections of the Save for
Web dialog.

- **Save for Web Toolbox.** The Save for Web dialog has its own Toolbox,
  which is the first indication that this feature is above and beyond just a
  simple dialog. The Hand tool is used to pan the view of your artwork;
  it is especially useful when you are viewing your art at higher zoom
  levels. The Slice Select tool enables you to select a particular slice with
  which to work. The Zoom tool allows you to change the zoom setting
  of your artwork, and the Eyedropper tool can be used to sample color
  from an image that appears in the preview pane. In addition to the icon
  that indicates the eyedropper color (you can click it to get the Color
  Picker), there's also a button that toggles slice visibility on and off.

- **Preview Pane.** The preview pane is the main feature of the Save for Web dialog. By clicking any of the four tabs, you can choose to view your original art (as it appears on the Illustrator artboard), an optimized version of your art (based on the current file settings chosen), and 2-Up and 4-Up versions of your art. Using the 2-Up and 4-Up tabs, you can easily compare different file settings, or how an optimized file looks compared to its original version. Illustrator displays useful information below each preview, including file size and estimated download times, making it easy to find just the right file type for your image (**Figure 10.13**).

Figure 10.13 Besides being able to preview the results of different file and compression settings, you can also view file size and estimated download times.

- **Zoom Control.** The zoom control allows you to easily choose from a preset zoom level to view your artwork. Alternatively, you can enter any number in the zoom field.

- **Color Information.** As you move your mouse over artwork in the preview pane, the Save for Web dialog provides feedback for colors in real time. This is helpful if you want to confirm color information or if you want to sample a specific color from an image.

- **Preview in Browser.** The preview in browser function is a huge timesaver. Although you get a beautiful preview of your artwork in the preview pane of the Save for Web dialog, it can be useful at times to see what your artwork looks like in an actual Web browser. This is especially useful for when you want to preview SWF animations, because those do not preview in the Save for Web dialog. Clicking the icon previews the selected artwork in your computer's default Web browser. Clicking the arrow pops up a list of installed browsers that you can choose from (**Figure 10.14**), or you can edit the list of browsers to customize it to your needs.

Figure 10.14 The Preview in Browser feature makes it easy to quickly see what your art will look like when rendered in your favorite Web browser.

The two remaining sections, which feature the group of three palettes and the ability to choose from different file types are covered individually, in the following sections.

Choosing the Right Image File Type

Overall, the main benefit of using the Save for Web feature is the ability to compare the final results of multiple file formats, and choosing the one that fits best for a particular use. To make the right decision, you have to understand the differences between each of these file formats, and what their strengths and weaknesses are. Let's take a closer look.

Choosing the GIF File Format

A common image file format used on the Web, the GIF format (Graphics Interchange Format) was developed by the people at CompuServe, one of the pioneers of the Internet and the Web, though you hardly hear their name mentioned today (amazing how fast things change). Recognizing the need to send graphics files across modem connections (which in those days, were quite slow), they developed the GIF file format, which can contain a maximum of 256 colors and which uses a lossless method of compression. A GIF tries to save space by looking for large areas of contiguous solid color; this makes the format perfect for logos, backgrounds, text headlines, and the like. However, the 256-color limit and the limited compression for images with a lot of detail make the GIF format a bad choice for photographic content.

The GIF format supports other features, including the ability to control the exact number of colors present in the file and the ability to specify a single color of the file as being transparent.

 To get an exact image size when you're exporting via the Save for Web dialog, draw a rectangle around your artwork and choose Object > Crop Area > Make. The Save for Web feature honors Illustrator's crop area setting when you're exporting graphics. Any artwork that appears outside of the crop area is not exported.

When you choose the GIF file format in the Save for Web dialog, you have the following settings available:

GIF files can also contain multiple images or frames, creating an animation, although Illustrator doesn't support the creation of animated GIF files.

- **Color Settings.** The color table settings enable to you to specify exactly how many colors the GIF will contain. Lower numbers of colors result in smaller file sizes but could also result in lower quality images. Because a GIF can contain a maximum of 256 colors, you can choose from several color-reduction algorithms, including the restrictive option, which chooses only Web-safe colors.

- **Dithering.** The dither settings control what method of dithering is used when the image calls for a color that isn't available in the reduced set of colors, or when the image is displayed on a computer screen that doesn't support enough colors to display the image.

- **Transparency.** The transparency setting enables to you to define a single color that will display as transparent in a browser. For example, if you want to place a logo on a colored background, you can specify the background color of the GIF to be transparent; doing so causes the background color in the browser to show through those transparent areas. The edges where color meets the transparent edge are usually white when displayed in a browser, and specifying a matte color that matches the background ensures that the edges of your art blend seamlessly into the background (**Figure 10.15**).

Figure 10.15 The image on the left was saved with a Matte setting that matched the background on which the art would eventually appear. The image on the right used the default Matte setting of white.

- **Interlacing.** An interlaced image loads gradually in a Web browser. First, in a low resolution, and then in a higher resolution in a second and third pass. This allows the image to appear in the browser immediately so that viewers can get an idea of what the page will look like, and then after a few seconds, the higher quality image appears. Turning interlacing off means the image won't display on a Web page until the entire image has been downloaded.

- **Web Snap.** By specifying a value in the Web snap field, you can have Illustrator ensure that a certain percentage of the colors used in the graphic are actually Web-safe colors.

Choosing the JPEG File Format

JPEG (pronounced jay-peg) stands for Joint Photographic Experts Group, and it was created to allow photographers to share images using a standard file format. JPEG files can contain millions of colors and use a lossy compression method. Digital images usually contain more color information than the human eye can see or detect, and by throwing out some of that extra information, JPEG images can achieve amazing file size savings. For example, a 10 MB photograph can easily be compressed into a JPEG that's less than 1 MB.

Because the JPEG format supports millions of colors (as opposed to only 256 in a GIF), it's the perfect format to use for photographs or images with complex colors and gradient fills. However, JPEG files do not support transparency as GIF files do.

When you choose the JPEG file format in the Save for Web dialog, you can choose from the following settings:

- **Compression/Quality.** The Quality settings enable you to specify how much information is thrown out of a file when the file is compressed. The settings are actually a bit confusing in the way they are presented in the dialog. You might think that a setting of Maximum would mean the highest compression with a smaller resulting file size, but that's incorrect. To prevent confusion, it's best to think of these settings as quality settings. A setting of Maximum means the best quality of an image, meaning less information is being tossed from the image (**Figure 10.16**). The result is a better-looking image that is larger in file size. Alternatively, you can specify numerical values in the Quality field. A setting of 100 is the same as choosing the Maximum setting.

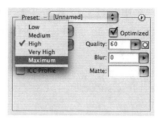

Figure 10.16 Don't be confused by the different settings for JPEG compression. For the best quality, choose Maximum. For the smallest file size, choose Low.

- **Blur.** One of the most noticeable side effects of compression in a JPEG file is artifacts or stray pixels that appear in the image. Specifying a blur amount can help cover up those artifacts.

- **Matte.** The matte setting enables you to specify a color for the edge of the graphic, thus allowing it to blend smoothly into colored backgrounds.

- **Progressive.** The progressive setting allows a JPEG image to load gradually in a browser, similar to the interlacing setting we discussed, which is available for GIF images.

Choosing the PNG File Format

The PNG (pronounced ping) format was developed mainly as an alternative to the GIF format. Shortly after the GIF format became popular on the Web, the Unisys corporation, which developed the actual compression algorithm used in the GIF format, tried to collect royalties on its technology from those who used the GIF format. To get around the legal issues, an open standard called PNG (Portable Network Graphic) was developed. The PNG format utilizes lossless compression and can support millions of colors. Instead of allowing you to specify a single color as being transparent, the PNG format also supports 256 levels of transparency, similar to alpha channels inside Photoshop.

Older Web browsers require a special plug-in to view PNG files, although most newer browsers can display them natively. PNG files also might not be compatible with some PDA devices and cell phones. PNG files come in two varieties, 8 bit and 24 bit. The different optimization settings for PNG-8 are identical to those found for the GIF format, mentioned previously.

Choosing the SWF File Format

SWF (Shockwave Flash) is a popular Web-based file format that supports both vectors and rasters. This Flash file format has become extremely popular because of its capability to contain interactive or animated content. You can use Illustrator to generate a SWF file that you want to upload directly to a Website or to create art for import into Macromedia Flash for further editing.

When you choose the SWF file format in the Save for Web dialog, you can choose from the following settings:

- **File Options.** You can create SWF files in one of two ways: AI File to SWF File, which creates a single SWF file that contains all of your Illustrator artwork; and AI Layers to SWF Frames, where each layer is converted into a keyframe, resulting in a single animated SWF file. Additionally, you can choose the Protect File option to prevent others from opening the resulting SWF file. The Text as Outlines options converts all text to outlines (so no font files are necessary) and you can make the file size smaller by choosing the Compressed option. The Curve Quality setting controls the fidelity of curved paths.

- **Appearance.** When using transparency or other special effects in Illustrator, you can choose to Preserve Appearance, which flattens any effects as necessary, or you can choose the Preserve Editability Where Possible option if you plan on opening the file in Macromedia Flash in order to edit it. This way you can make additional tweaks to the artwork if you need to.

- **Animation Settings.** If you choose the AI Layers to SWF Frames option, all layers in your Illustrator file become keyframes and play as an animation when the SWF file is viewed in a Web browser. The Frame Rate setting controls the speed at which the animation plays (you can't control the timing of individual frames like you can in a GIF animation), and the Looping option forces the animation to repeat continuously. More information on creating animated SWF files is covered later in this chapter.

The Macromedia Flash (SWF) export dialog offers additional options for creating SWF files that are not present in the Save for Web dialog. For detailed information about the Flash format and these additional settings, see Chapter 12.

Illustrator uses Apple QuickTime to preview SWF files within the Save for Web dialog. If you don't have QuickTime installed, you won't be able to preview SWF files and will have to use the Preview in Browser feature to do so.

Choosing the SVG File Format

SVG (Scalable Vector Graphics) is an XML-based file format that is used primarily on the Web and has recently become more popular in creating content for cell phones and handheld wireless devices.

Most Web browsers require a special plugin to view SVG files, although some of the newer versions of browsers, including Firefox and Apple's Safari are beginning to support SVG files natively. Because SVG files are text-based, they can be edited easily, even after they have been exported and uploaded to a Web server. Because of this ability, SVG files are used in data-driven server-based workflows where customized content is a necessity.

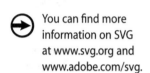 You can find more information on SVG at www.svg.org and www.adobe.com/svg.

When you choose the SVG file format in the Save for Web dialog, you can choose from the following settings:

- **DTD.** The DTD (Document Type Definition) setting is akin to the version of SVG with which your file is compatible. Because SVG is an open standard, additional specifications are revised and approved. If you save an SVG file with a particular DTD, it means that your file will be compatible with any device that supports that DTD. Newer specifications usually support more functionality than the older ones did. SVG Tiny (also referred to as SVG-t) is a subset of SVG used for displaying content on SVG-enabled cell phones. SVG Basic is another subset used for displaying content on PDAs.

- **Fonts.** When text is present in your file, you can specify the Adobe CEF type, which results in better-looking text when your file is viewed with the Adobe SVG Viewer, but which may not be supported with other SVG viewers. The SVG creates more compatible text, but this text may not be as readable at smaller font sizes. Alternatively, you can convert all text to outlines, which increases file size.

- **Images.** When you save a file in SVG, you have the ability to embed any images within the SVG file (making for larger, but self-sufficient files), or you can choose to create smaller SVG files by using the Link option.

- **CSS Properties.** There are a variety of ways to format SVG code, and the CSS Properties settings allows you to determine how object attributes are coded within the file. For the most part, this setting affects the performance of your file when viewed.

- **Decimal Places.** Illustrator allows you to specify how precisely vector paths are drawn. You may choose a value from 1 to 7, where higher numbers result in better-looking paths at the expense of file size and performance.

- **Encoding.** When you save an SVG file that contains text, you can specify a character encoding, including ISO-8859-1 (suitable for European languages), and 8- or 16-bit Unicode (suitable for more complex languages).

- **Optimize for Adobe SVG Viewer.** If people will be using the Adobe SVG Viewer to view your SVG files, you can check this option, which takes advantage of proprietary optimizations that exist in the Adobe SVG Viewer, including faster rendering of SVG Filter Effects.

Choosing the WBMP File Format

The WBMP file format, which stands for Wireless Bitmap, is a format that is optimized for wireless devices that have slow connections and limited display capabilities. These devices are quickly fading because newer phones are being introduced constantly and cell phones are the largest-selling consumer electronic devices worldwide. WBMP files are black-and-white images (color isn't supported) and are optimized via a dithering setting.

Specifying Additional Image Settings

In addition to choosing a file format, Illustrator's Save for Web allows you to control how colors, image sizes, and layers are treated when saving your files. These settings are found within the three palettes that appear at the lower right side of the Save for Web dialog.

Color Table

The Color Table palette displays a complete list of all of the colors that are contained within the selected slice. Colors that appear with little diamond icons are Web-safe colors (**Figure 10.17**). Using the Eyedropper tool to sample colors, you can click the Maps selected colors to transparent icon beneath the palette to specify a color that will appear as transparent.

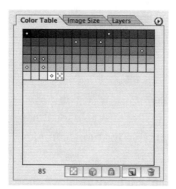

Figure 10.17 Illustrator indicates Web-safe colors in a color table with tiny diamond-shaped icons.

Image Size

The Image Size palette gives you feedback on the actual size of the selected slice, and it also allows you to specify new sizes, although it's always better to make changes to image size on the Illustrator artboard, before launching the Save for Web dialog. Of importance are the Anti-Alias button and Clip to Artboard check boxes. By default, Illustrator anti-aliases artwork that is exported from the Save for Web dialog and exports artwork based on the art's bounding box or your crop area setting. To have the Save for Web dialog honor the artboard size, you can check the Clip to Artboard setting.

Layers

If you specified layers in your Illustrator document, you have the option of exporting those layers as CSS Layers by checking the Export as CSS Layers option in the Layers palette found in the Save for Web dialog. CSS, which stands for Cascading Style Sheets, allows you to take advantage of absolute positioning and overlapping objects within a Web page. Although the technical aspects of CSS are outside the scope of this book, it's important to realize that CSS has become a standard, especially when you're generating content that will be displayed on a wide range of devices.

 For more information on CSS, refer to *Stylin' with CSS: A Designer's Guide* by Charles Wyke-Smith (New Riders, 2005).

If you choose to export Illustrator layers as CSS layers, you can choose whether each top-level layer in your document should be exported as being visible, or hidden (**Figure 10.18**). Alternatively, you can specify that certain layers aren't exported at all.

Figure 10.18 CSS Layers that are exported as hidden can be activated via scripts on the server using Dynamic HTML.

 Featured Match-Up: Web Slicing vs. CSS Layers

If you think about it, no matter whether you choose to export Web graphics as a group of slices or as CSS layers, you end up with a single graphic that is broken down into several parts. But there's a big difference between these two approaches. In fact, you can almost categorize Web slicing as yesterday's technology and CSS Layers as the way of the future.

As we mentioned earlier, Web slicing is a process of taking a single image and converting it into an HTML table. Each cell in the table contains a different portion of the image, and when the entire table is rendered within a browser, you can see the entire graphic. Although this method of slicing is widespread, HTML tables were never intended to be used in this way. As a result, when these tables are displayed on handheld devices or different browsers, the results can vary. Sometimes, the images may not appear as intended at all. In addition, a limitation in HTML is that images cannot overlap each other, which makes designing with slices an exercise in careful planning.

In contrast, CSS layers are an open standard built on the premise that Web graphics will be displayed on a variety of different devices. When CSS layers are used, there's a good chance your artwork will appear as intended even on smaller devices. In addition, CSS layers support overlapping graphics, and each layer can be programmed with interactivity, meaning you can have layers animate independently and also appear and disappear based on user-defined parameters. To take full advantage of CSS though, Illustrator alone won't be enough and you'll want to add functionality on your own through the use of applications like GoLive or Dreamweaver.

Efficient Web Design

Above and beyond the Web-specific features that we've discussed in this chapter, like using Web-safe colors and the Pixel Preview mode, there are other features and strategies that you can employ to achieve more efficient Web design.

When you're designing Web graphics that will eventually be exported as PSD files to be edited in Photoshop or ImageReady, be sure to use layers to organize your artwork in a meaningful way. Because layers can be preserved when exporting to Photoshop, you will be able to perform edits and add functionality easily when different elements of your design are easily accessible. Pixel-based applications like Photoshop rely heavily on the organization of layers and functions like assigning rollovers or other interactivity and are based on layers as well. Refer to Chapters 8 *Mixing It Up: Working with Vectors and Pixels*, and 12, *Saving and Exporting Files,* for more information on exporting Illustrator files in the PSD file format.

 Using layers is extremely important when created SVG graphics as the format relies heavily on object hierarchy.

By using symbols, you can achieve tremendous file size savings when you are creating Web graphics for export in the SWF and SVG file formats. When you use symbols in your artwork, you can repeat a graph many times, but only one original copy of that artwork is stored within the file. When designing maps, creating animations, or using other designs that incorporate repeating graphics, it's well worth the effort to find excuses to use symbols. Refer to Chapter 5, *Brushes, Symbols, and Masks,* for more information on how to create, use, and edit symbols in your artwork.

Adding Interactivity and Creating Animations

Although it's nice to admire graphics on a Web page, nothing is quite like a graphic that invokes action on the viewer's part. It is images that move with animation or that contain clickable hotspots that can take a viewer to additional content that make the Web such an exciting medium. Although Illustrator is no replacement for an application like Macromedia Flash, you can still create Web graphics that come to life using your favorite vector graphics application.

Creating Image Maps

On the Web, a designer's job is far more than just to create a pretty graphic. Rather, a graphic must draw a viewer to action. The action could be as simple as switching to a different page, or as significant as generating a sale. In Illustrator, you can assign a URL to an object, which results in an *image map*. An image map is a region or portion of a graphic on which a viewer can click.

To create an image map, follow these steps:

1. Select an object on your artboard and choose Window > Attributes to open your Attributes palette.

2. Once the palette is open, choose Rectangle or Polygon from the Image Map pop-up menu (**Figure 10.19**). For objects that are rectangular, choose the Rectangle option. For images that fit any other shape, choose the Polygon option.

3. Once you've chosen an Image Map type, enter a URL in the field below the pop-up menu. For best results, it's best to enter the complete URL, including the http://.

   Illustrator keeps track of all of the URLs that you enter, so if you're applying the same URL to multiple objects in your document, you can choose the correct URL from the URL pop-up (**Figure 10.20**). To test a URL to see if it is correct, click the Browser button; when you do, Illustrator launches your system's default browser and navigates to the chosen URL.

Figure 10.19 Older browsers only supported rectangular image maps, but just about all of today's browsers support polygonal image maps.

Figure 10.20 Once you've entered a URL into the Attributes palette, Illustrator remembers it so that you can easily apply it to other objects in your document.

Animation: Making It Move

 Animation in SVG is not directly supported within Illustrator. In order to add animation to SVG files, you can either add the code by hand once you've exported the SVG from Illustrator, or you can use an SVG animation application, like Ikivo's Animator (www.ikivo.com).

There's no question that adding motion to Web graphics enhances their appearance and ability to garner the attention of viewers. Illustrator can build frame-based animations quite easily, although if you're looking for a high-end animation tool, you'd best look elsewhere. The techniques we discuss here are indicative of the simple animations you can create quickly and easily with Illustrator. You might still want to keep Macromedia Flash and Adobe After Effects on hand for more complex work.

The key to creating great animations in Illustrator is through the careful use of layers. There is no animation palette or timeline in Illustrator. Rather, Illustrator treats each top-level layer in your document as a frame in your animation. As you build your animation with each new layer, keep in mind the advice you learned throughout this chapter, especially with regard to using symbols (**Figure 10.21**). Illustrator allows you to create blends between symbols, and even objects with Live Effects applied. Refer to Chapter 9, *Graphs, Distortion, and Blends*, for detailed information on creating blends.

 Illustrator can only generate SWF animations. If you want to create animations using SVG, GIF, or other formats, you'll have to export your Illustrator artwork into other applications.

Once you've created the art for your animation, choose File > Export and choose the Macromedia Flash (SWF) file format. When you choose the AI Layers to Flash Frames setting, your resulting SWF file plays through each layer sequentially. Setting the animation to loop causes the animation to repeat endlessly (always fun). Refer to Chapter 12 for detailed information on the settings found in the Macromedia Flash (SWF) Export dialog.

Figure 10.21 In this illustration, the airplane was defined as a symbol and then used in a blend across the width of the banner. The symbol on the far left was then set to 0% Opacity, resulting in a blend that makes the plane appear to fade in as it moves from left to right.

CHAPTER 11

Prepress and Printing

Nothing is more frustrating than spending hours designing the perfect piece of art, only to have it come back from the printer not looking the way you expected it to. Many times, we take printing for granted and assume that whatever we design will reproduce in print the exact way we see it on our computer screen. Achieving consistent color across multiple devices is one challenge (which good color management strategies can help control). Even more of a challenge are features like transparency, Live Effects, and overprint settings; these can turn what seems like an ordinary print job into a weekend-long nightmare.

In reality, you need to think about printing when you first start working on a design. If you work with a printer, they will help you figure out things in advance, including spot colors, page settings, folds, and a host of other issues. Although there are certainly times when you don't have the luxury of knowing who the printer is before a job gets started, you can still spend a few moments at the onset of a project carefully reviewing the details; this alone can make a huge difference. Every job has its own specific requirements and you should always feel comfortable asking an experienced printer or production artist for advice.

Whether you're a designer or a printer, this chapter is for you. This chapter teaches you everything you need to know about printing files, using transparency, and overprints—and it leads you to expect the best results every time.

Printing from Illustrator

Printing a file should be a straightforward experience, but it wasn't always that way in Adobe Illustrator. Prior to Illustrator CS, getting a file to print correctly often meant opening the Page Setup dialog, the Document Setup dialog, and the Print dialog. With the release of Illustrator CS, however, Adobe updated Illustrator's printing engine and interface and modeled them after the Print dialog found in Adobe InDesign. Now, you can go directly to the Print dialog and control all of your print specifications in one place.

Because every print job is different and has specific requirements, we've organized the contents of this chapter to match the order in which print features appear in the Print dialog. In this way, you can read the chapter and use it as a handy reference as well.

The General Print Panel

As you're designing a job, printing quick and accurate proofs to your laser or inkjet printer is just as important as printing final output to an image setter. For this reason, you'll find that Adobe put many often-used settings in the General panel of the Print dialog (**Figure 11.1**). This way you can

Figure 11.1 The General panel in the Print dialog contains the most often-used print settings.

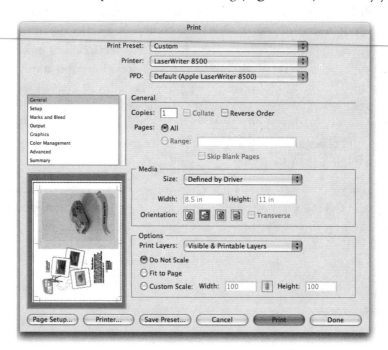

quickly print consistent and accurate files from Illustrator without having to dance between multiple dialogs or settings panels. At the top of the Print dialog you'll find a pop-up to choose from predefined Print Presets (more on Print Presets later in this chapter), a pop-up to choose which printer you want to print to (extremely useful for those of you who have several different printers at your disposal), and a pop-up to choose a PPD (PostScript Printer Definition) file.

A PPD file contains specific information about a printer, including media dimensions, color information, and printer-specific settings like resolution. Illustrator makes an educated guess to select the right PPD file for your selected printer, although you can override it and choose your own if you need to. You can choose a PPD only when a PostScript device is selected as your printer.

Along the left side of the Print dialog is a list of all of the different panels you can choose from to specify a range of print options. Beneath the list of panels is a print preview, which gives you a better idea of what will print. But this is no ordinary print preview—it's interactive. You can click and drag the artwork around in the preview to determine which part of the paper the art will print on (**Figure 11.2**). Hold the Shift key while dragging to constrain movement to the X or Y axis and double-click anywhere on the preview to reset the positioning to the default. As you specify changes in the Print dialog, like adding trim marks, you'll see those appear in the preview as well.

 One of the options available in the Printer list is Adobe PostScript File, which allows you to print your document as a PostScript file that can then be downloaded directly to a printer, or converted to PDF using Acrobat Distiller.

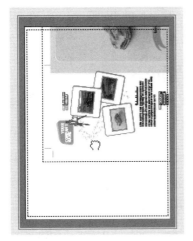

Figure 11.2 If you're an experienced Illustrator user, you may have used the Page tool to print different parts of a page; you can now do this directly from the Print dialog by moving the artwork within the interactive print preview.

Basic Print Options

 The items that we've discussed to this point, which appear across the top and along the left side of the Print dialog, are always visible no matter which panel of the dialog is active.

As in just about any other program, in the Print dialog, you can specify the number of copies as well as the range of pages that you want to print. Although it's true that Illustrator doesn't have multiple pages, when you're using the Page Tiling option (which we'll cover shortly), each tile is assigned a page number, which allows you to specify exactly what will print. When you specify a range of pages, use a comma as a separation device and a hyphen to indicate a continuous string of pages. For example, you can specify a range of 1-3, 6, which will print pages 1, 2, 3, and 6.

In the Media section of the dialog, you can specify the size of the paper on which you want to print. The items that appear in this pop-up are defined by the PPD file that is chosen for your printer. If your printer supports it, you'll also have the ability to define custom media sizes; being able to do so is extremely useful for those of you who have large-format inkjet printers, or for those of you who are printing to image setters or plate setters. Additionally, you can choose an orientation to flip a page on its side. Changing the orientation can be extremely important when printers want to choose which side of a sheet the press will grip from.

You can use the Print Layers pop-up menu to specify what kinds of layers will or won't print: Visible & Printable Layers, Visible Layers, or All Layers. Additionally, you can set a custom scale size at which to print your file. The Do Not Scale option prints your file at actual size, the Fit to Page option reduces or enlarges your artwork so that it fills the entire size of the output media, and the Custom Scale settings allow you to specify any scale size for the height and/or the width.

The Setup Print Panel

When you print a file, you can specify which parts of the artwork will print by choosing from the three different Crop Artwork settings (**Figure 11.3**):

- **Artboard.** The Artboard setting uses the boundaries of the artboard as the printable area and is the default setting. When you choose this setting, only artwork that appears on the artboard prints.

- **Artwork Bounding Box.** The Artwork Bounding Box setting uses the boundaries of the artwork that appears in the document, no matter whether the artwork appears on or off the artboard. This setting is useful when you use it with the Fit to Page option to print a piece of art that fills an entire page.

- **Crop Area.** The Crop Area setting uses a user-defined area for the boundaries of the printable area. To define a crop area, you can draw a rectangle around any portion of your file and choose Object > Crop Area > Make. If no crop area is manually defined, Illustrator uses the artboard size as the crop area.

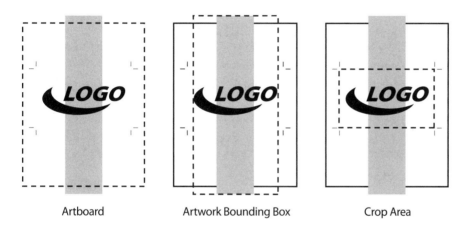

Artboard   Artwork Bounding Box   Crop Area

Figure 11.3 Using the different Crop Artwork settings can make it easy to print the parts of a file that you want.

Using Page Tiling

Page Tiling is a feature that was initially added to Illustrator to enable users to print a single large file across several smaller pages. This would allow a designer to assemble a large document at actual size using a printer with smaller media sizes. However, over the years, designers learned to use this feature to create a single large artboard, using the tiled areas as a substitute for multiple pages. For example, setting up a document at 11 x 17 inches with Page Tiling would result in two 8½ x 11 pages.

There are three Page Tiling settings that you can choose from (**Figure 11.4**):

- **Single Full Page.** The Single Full Page option turns tiling off and treats the entire artboard as a single page.

- **Tile Full Pages.** The Tile Full Pages option divides a single artboard into multiple sections, or tiles. Each tile matches the media size you choose in the General panel, and Illustrator creates as many of those tiles as necessary to cover the entire document.

- **Tile Imageable Areas.** The Tile Imageable Areas option divides a single artboard into multiple sections, or tiles. Tiles match the media size you choose in the General panel where possible, and Illustrator creates custom-sized tiles as necessary to tile the entire document.

Figure 11.4 You can simulate a multiple page document by setting up a large page with one of the tiling settings.

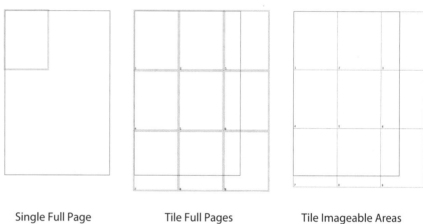

Single Full Page   Tile Full Pages   Tile Imageable Areas

 When you're using Tile Full Pages or Tile Imageable Areas, each tile is assigned a number, and you can specify which tiles you want to print by entering a tile number in the Page Range field in the General panel.

Because tiling is something you might want to set in your document before you even start working on your design, be aware of the Done button that appears at the bottom of the Print dialog. Clicking Done keeps the settings you've made in the Print dialog and returns you to the document for further editing and designing without actually printing the file. Although it may seem odd to open the Print dialog to specify tiling settings, remember that the main reason for tiling in Illustrator is specific to printing.

The Marks and Bleed Print Panel

When printing a page for final output, you need to add page marks and bleeds to help printers print the job correctly on press. *Trim marks* tell a printer where to cut the paper; *registration marks* help a printer align each separated plate correctly; *color bars* help a printer calibrate color correctly on press; and *page information* makes it possible for printers to easily identify each separated plate (**Figure 11.5**).

Page information

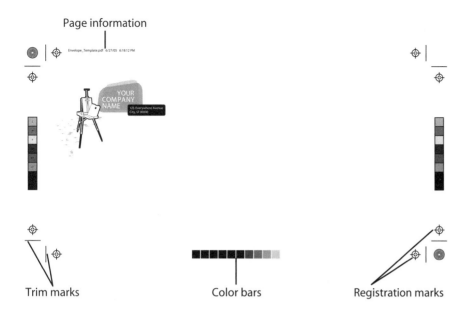

Trim marks   Color bars   Registration marks

Figure 11.5 A printer uses a variety of printer marks to help ensure that the job prints correctly.

Of course, you don't always need all of this information on each printout, so you choose them individually (for example, on a one-color job, registration marks aren't necessary). Additionally, you can choose between Roman and Japanese style trim marks (refer to Appendix C, *Illustrator Preferences*, for examples of these). The trim mark weight determines the width of the strokes used to create trim marks, and the offset determines how far from the page the trim marks will appear.

Specifying Bleed

When you have artwork that extends beyond the boundary of a page, you can specify a bleed setting to ensure that the printable area of the page includes the extra bleed area. When the bleed settings are set to zero, even if you've extended artwork beyond the boundary of the artboard, the art clips to the edge of the artboard. Additionally, if you specify a bleed setting, you'll need to print to a paper size large enough to display the page size and the bleed as well. For more information on bleeds, see the sidebar, "Take Heed: Add Bleed."

 Page marks print outside the margins of the artboard (or wherever you've defined a crop area), so you need to make sure that the media size you've chosen in the General panel is large enough to include the page marks. If you use the Fit to Page option, Illustrator scales the entire document to ensure that the trim marks print on the chosen page.

Take Heed: Add Bleed

In order to print art all the way to the edge of a sheet, a printer uses a larger sized sheet than the finish size (trim size) and after printing, they cut the paper down to size. Printers can't print all the way to the edge of a page because a certain amount of space is needed for gripper space (space for the press to "grab" the sheet of paper). Additionally, if this space wern't there, the ink could run off the sheet and onto the press causing smudging on other sheets.

When a printer trims the paper to the final size, the paper may shift while being cut, and if your image only comes up to the border of the trim size, you might end up seeing a bit of white near the edge of the paper. To avoid this, printers need bleed, or extra image space. If the artwork extends beyond the edges of the trim size, even if the cutter is off a bit, you'll still get color all the way to the edge of your sheet.

As a designer, it's important to leave enough image when you're cropping photos to allow for bleed (**Figure 11.6**). Talk to your printer if you have questions, but most printers ask for anywhere from .125 to .25 inches of bleed. If printers don't have enough image space to add bleed, they may need to trim the paper to a slightly smaller size.

Figure 11.6 If your design calls for artwork that prints to the edge of a page, make sure you add bleed before sending it off to the printer.

The Output Print Panel

The Output panel in the Print dialog is a prepress operator's dream come true. With the ability to specify color separations and control the behavior of inks, a print service provider can output Illustrator files with confidence.

Illustrator supports three different printing modes, each of which is used for a different workflow (**Figure 11.7**):

- **Composite.** When you choose the Composite setting, Illustrator sends a single composite of the artwork, with all colors appearing on the same page, to the printer or RIP (raster image processor). This is the setting you would use to create any kind of black and white or grayscale printout, as well as any color proof printout.

- **Separations (Host-Based).** When you choose the Separations (Host-Based) setting, Illustrator (the host) separates the artwork into the required number of plates (specified in the Document Ink Options settings mentioned shortly) and sends each plate to the printer or RIP as a separate page. This is the setting you use if you want to proof color-separated artwork. A prepress operator or printer also uses this setting to create final film or plates from your artwork.

- **In-RIP Separations.** When you choose the In-RIP Separations setting, Illustrator sends a single composite of the artwork to the RIP so that the RIP itself can perform the color separation instead of Illustrator. All of the Document Ink Options and separation-specific settings become available so that you can still control the inks that will print on the composite. This is the setting you use if you want to take advantage of proprietary trapping, screening, and separations software present in your RIP.

 A RIP, or raster image processor, is the software in a printer, image setter, or platesetter, that converts all art into dots so that it can be printed.

Figure 11.7 Printing a composite is perfect for proofing (left). Printing separations is required for printing colors on a printing press (right).

Specifying Color Separations

If you choose either of the two separations print modes, you can specify additional options for how the color separation will print.

You can choose to print Right Reading Emulsion Up or Down, and whether to print a Positive or Negative image. You'll notice that as you choose these settings, the interactive print preview updates to show you how the art will print. You can also choose a printer resolution setting; these settings are specific to the printer to which you've chosen to print. This information comes from the PPD file chosen for your printer or RIP.

If there are spot colors present in your file, you can choose to convert them all to separate as process colors by choosing the Convert All Spot Colors to Process option. In Illustrator CS2, this option is even available when you're printing composite proofs.

When you choose the Overprint Black option, all objects that are colored 100% K overprint. See "Understanding Overprints" later in this chapter for more information on overprinting.

In the Document Ink Options section of the Output panel, you can specify which plates are sent to the printer and what settings each plate uses (**Figure 11.8**). Colors that appear with a printer icon on the far left print. To prevent an ink from printing, click the printer icon to remove it. Inks that appear with a four-color icon separate as process colors. Inks that appear with a solid color icon print to their own plate as a spot (custom) color. Clicking a solid color icon causes just that color to separate as a process color. Additionally, you can specify custom Frequency, Angle, and Dot Shape settings for each ink individually.

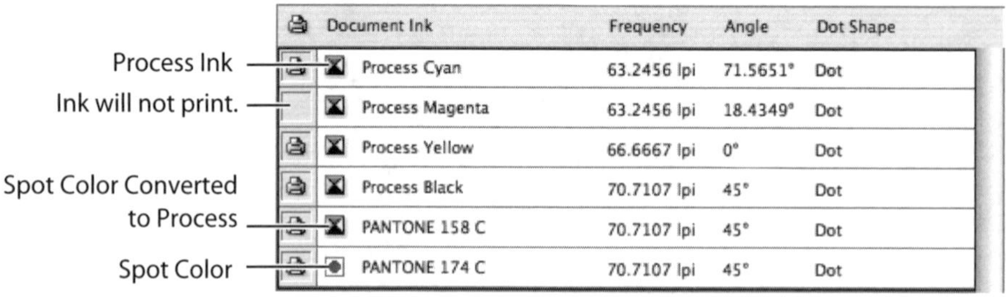

	Document Ink	Frequency	Angle	Dot Shape
	Process Cyan	63.2456 lpi	71.5651°	Dot
	Process Magenta	63.2456 lpi	18.4349°	Dot
	Process Yellow	66.6667 lpi	0°	Dot
	Process Black	70.7107 lpi	45°	Dot
	PANTONE 158 C	70.7107 lpi	45°	Dot
	PANTONE 174 C	70.7107 lpi	45°	Dot

Process Ink
Ink will not print.
Spot Color Converted to Process
Spot Color

Figure 11.8 The different icons that display in the Document Ink Options section of the Output panel indicate how the inks print.

The Graphics Print Panel

The settings in the Graphics panel in the Print dialog are mainly for specifying options for your print device.

Prior to the release of Illustrator CS, the Document Setup dialog box of Illustrator contained a setting called Object Resolution, which determined the flatness setting for Bézier paths at output time. In Illustrator CS and CS2, the flatness setting is set by default, based on information from the selected PPD file. You can override this setting and use the slider to sacrifice path quality for print performance (although we don't suggest doing so).

By default, Illustrator downloads subsets of fonts to the printer when you print a file. By *downloading a subset* we simply mean that Illustrator only sends the parts of a font that are required to print the text you have in your document. If you have the word "me" in your document, Illustrator only sends the letters "m" and "e" to the printer instead of the entire font (this practice speeds up print times). You can override this behavior and choose Complete, which forces Illustrator to download the entire font to the printer at print time. Alternatively, you can choose not to download any fonts at all. You choose this option if you have fonts installed in your printer (some printers can contain hard drives and store fonts internally).

By default, Illustrator chooses a PostScript Language Level that your selected printer will support. Language Level 3 PostScript can print certain documents with transparency more reliably, and it also contains Smooth Shading technology that helps prevent banding from appearing in gradients. Additionally, you can choose whether to send data to the printer in ASCII or the default Binary format.

As we discussed in Chapter 7, *3D and Other Live Effects*, the resolution at which Live Effects are rasterized is determined by the setting in the Document Raster Effects Resolution dialog. Here in the Graphics panel of the Print dialog, Illustrator displays the current setting in that dialog, allowing you to double check to make sure the setting is indeed correct for printing (**Figure 11.9**). Illustrator won't allow you to change the setting from the Print dialog because, as you learned in Chapter 7, changing the resolution setting may change the appearance of your artwork. To change the resolution setting, click the Done button in the Print dialog and choose Effect > Document Raster Effects Settings. You can then return to the Print dialog to print your file.

 If you have problems printing Illustrator files to older print devices, try checking the Compatible Gradient and Gradient Mesh Printing option.

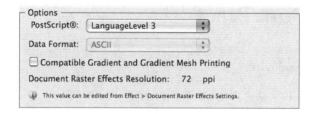

The Color Management Print Panel

The topic of color management really requires a book of its own. In fact, if you really want to learn everything there is to know about color management, you should check out *Real World Color Management, Second Edition,* by Bruce Fraser, Chris Murphy, and Fred Bunting (Peachpit Press, 2004).

Within the scope of this book (the one you are now reading), however, here are some brief explanations for the settings found in the Color Management panel of the Print dialog:

- **Document Profile.** The Document Profile displays the color profile that is currently embedded in the file. If you didn't manually choose one, the profile you see here is the profile that is chosen in the Color Settings dialog.

- **Color Handling.** The Color Handling setting allows you to determine whether Illustrator will perform any necessary color adjustments (based on the chosen printer profile), or whether your printer will handle any required conversion on its own.

- **Printer Profile.** When the Color Handling setting is set to Let Illustrator determine colors, the Printer Profile setting allows you to specify a profile for your printer. This gives Illustrator the information it needs to change colors so they look correct on your printer. If the Color Handling setting is set to Let PostScript printer determine colors, the Printer Profile setting is not applicable.

- **Rendering Intent.** If there are colors in your document that cannot be reproduced on the chosen output device, those colors are considered *out of gamut* and must be converted to colors that will reproduce on the output device. There are different methods for converting these colors, and the Rendering Intent setting determines the method used. The most commonly used method, Relative Colorimetric, moves out of gamut colors to the closest possible color that will print on the device.

It also makes adjustments to other colors so that colors appear to be accurate. The Absolute Colorimetric setting only adjusts out of gamut colors and may result in *posterization*, where many shades of similar colors are used. The Perceptual method shifts colors so that they appear correct relative to each other, but it may not represent colors as being the most accurate match to the original values. The Saturation method enhances colors and makes them more vibrant and most suitable for business presentations where bright colors are more important than accurate colors.

- **Preserve CMYK Numbers.** The Preserve CMYK Numbers setting is only active when Color Handling is set to the Let PostScript printer determine colors option. With Preserve CMYK Numbers active, color values will remain untouched in native artwork and text components of your file.

The Advanced Print Panel

The Advanced panel in the Print dialog gives you control over important settings like overprinting and transparency flattening.

If your document contains overprint settings, you can choose from one of three different settings to control overprint behavior:

- **Preserve.** The Preserve option leaves all overprints intact in your file.

- **Discard.** The Discard option strips your file of any overprint commands. Those of you who have proprietary production systems or advanced trapping software in your RIPs will find this option useful. Rather than use a designer's overprint settings, the trapping software applies and determines all overprint behavior instead.

- **Simulate.** The Simulate option, available only when printing composite proofs, simulates overprints in the printout, giving the correct appearance of the final output in the proof.

If your document contains transparency, you can choose from a list of predefined Transparency Flattener Presets. Illustrator ships with three presets called Low Resolution, Medium Resolution, and High Resolution, but you can also define your own by choosing Edit > Transparency Flattener Presets. For detailed information about what these settings are used for and what the differences between them are, see "The Truth About Transparency," later in this chapter.

The Print as Bitmap option is available for non-PostScript printers only and rasterizes all artwork in your file for printing.

See "Understanding Overprints," later in the chapter, to learn more about overprints.

Defining Print Presets

 If you delete your application preferences, you won't lose your saved Print Presets.

As you've undoubtedly seen, Illustrator's Print dialog contains a plethora of different settings, and going through each panel to make sure the settings are correct is an exercise in patience in and of itself. Print presets allow you to capture all of the settings set in the different Print dialog panels so that you can easily retrieve those settings at any time. To create a Print preset, either click the Save Preset button at the bottom of the Print dialog or choose Edit > Print Presets where you can manage your presets. Print Presets are saved in XML and are cross-platform, so you can import and export them and distribute them among others.

THE TRUTH ABOUT TRANSPARENCY

Illustrator contains several features that use transparency, including the ability to specify blend modes and opacity masks with the Transparency palette, and effects like Feather and Drop Shadow. Transparency as a feature in Illustrator (and InDesign as well) requires closer attention when it comes to printing documents. In fact, Adobe Illustrator CS2, Adobe InDesign CS2, and Adobe Acrobat 7.0 all use the same methods to print with transparency, so the concepts that you learn here apply to all of those applications as well.

Although you may have heard that printing with transparency is problematic, the reality is that a lot has changed since transparency was first introduced in Illustrator 9. Once you understand what happens to a file with transparency and you learn about a few simple settings, you won't have to worry about running into printing issues when you're using transparency features.

In truth, transparency has always been around—in raster form—in Photoshop. The only difference now is that you can apply these effects in vector form and still edit them late in your workflow. At the end of the day, these transparency effects will become rasterized, leaving you with the same result as if you had done everything in Photoshop. In any case, let's take a closer look at what transparency is and how it works.

Understanding Transparency Flattening

Let's start with a simple fact: PostScript doesn't understand transparency. As you probably know, PostScript is the language that printers and RIPs speak. Native transparency is understood only by PDF language version 1.4 or higher (present in Acrobat 5 and Illustrator 9).

In order to print objects with transparency, Illustrator must "translate" any transparent artwork into a language that PostScript understands. This translation process is called *transparency flattening*.

The process of flattening is simple, and Illustrator follows two cardinal rules when performing flattening on a file:

1. All transparency in the file must be removed.

2. In the process of performing Rule #1, the appearance of the file cannot change.

 If you've used Photoshop before, you may be familiar with the term flattening, which combines all layers in a document. Although similar in concept, transparency flattening is different.

Both of these rules are followed during the flattening process, with no exception. Obviously, all transparency has to be removed because PostScript doesn't know what transparency is. Additionally, if removing the transparency would result in your file changing in appearance, that would mean you could design something in Illustrator that couldn't be printed, which doesn't make sense either. If you think about it, if you're removing transparency from the file and you're also keeping the visual appearance of the object, something has to give, and that something is the editability of your file. Let's take a look at an example of this.

An Example of Flattening

We'll draw two different-colored circles, one overlapping the other, and we'll set the top circle to Multiply (**Figure 11.10**). The nice thing about transparency is that you can move the top circle around or change its color and any overlapping areas will simply multiply. The problem is that PostScript doesn't know what transparency is and doesn't know how to print that overlapping area, so transparency flattening is required.

Select both circles, choose Object > Flatten Transparency, and click OK (don't worry about the dialog, we'll get to that later). The file is now flattened. Does it look any different? It can't, because of Rule #2, but the file now no longer contains any transparency and can be printed on a PostScript device. The difference is that the file is no longer editable as it was before it was flattened. Upon selecting the circles, you'll find that the two transparent circles have now been broken up into three individual opaque shapes (**Figure 11.11**).

This flattening process happens every time you print something with transparency. However, the flattening happens in the print stream, not to your actual Illustrator file. When you choose to print a file, Illustrator flattens a copy of your file and sends the flattened file to the printer, while leaving your document intact. It wouldn't be good if simply printing a file rendered it uneditable. In our example, we specifically flattened the file using the Flatten Transparency function to see the results, but under normal circumstances, you would not flatten the transparency manually—Illustrator would do that for you automatically at print time.

Figure 11.10 By setting the top circle to the Multiply blend mode, you can see through it to the circle below, even with Opacity set to 100%.

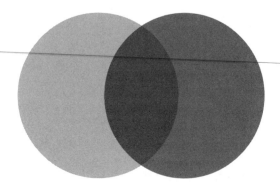

Figure 11.11 Once the objects are flattened, the artwork is split up into individual opaque pieces, called *atomic regions*.

So we can now understand that when you print a file with transparency, this flattening process occurs so that a PostScript printer can print the file correctly, and that this process happens on the way to printer, so your Illustrator file is not affected in any way.

This example of the two overlapping circles is a very simple case of flattening. However, there are other examples that can display certain side effects. Let's explore such a case.

 Flattening also happens whenever you save or export your file to a format that doesn't understand transparency. For example, EPS (which is PostScript) and PDF 1.3 do not support transparency.

Flattening with Rasterization

As in the previous example, create two overlapping circles and set the top circle to Multiply. Fill each circle with a linear gradient, but in one of the circles, apply the gradient on a 45-degree angle. The result is two circles with gradients, but the area in which these two shapes overlap appears as two gradients traveling in different directions (**Figure 11.12**).

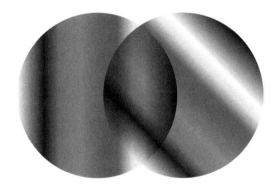

Figure 11.12 This figure shows two overlapping circles, each filled with a gradient on a different angle.

When this file is flattened, you know that the result will be three separate shapes as in the previous example; however, there's a difference. Although gradients can be preserved in vector form, there's no way to describe a crisscross gradient like you see in the overlapping area as a vector. Because of Rule #2, Illustrator is not allowed to change the appearance of your file during flattening, and so Illustrator's only course of action is to turn that overlapping area into a raster image.

Select both circles, choose Object > Flatten Transparency, and click OK. You'll find that although the file looks the same, it is now made up of two vector shapes and a raster image in the middle. Illustrator creates a vector mask for the middle shape so that the file will print correctly (raster images are always rectangular in shape). It's important to point out that Illustrator didn't raster the entire file, it only rasterized the portion of the file that could not be preserved in vector form (**Figure 11.13**).

Figure 11.13 Where appearance can't be preserved in vector form, Illustrator converts parts of a file into a raster.

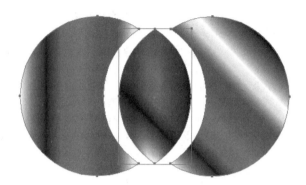

At this point, a question should be forming in your brain: If part of the file is now a raster image, what is the resolution of that raster? Patience, my young Padawan, we'll get to that soon. Here's a review of what we've learned to this point:

1. Transparency flattening is required to correctly print a file with transparency to a PostScript device.

2. Transparency flattening happens automatically, in the print stream, when you print a file with transparency from Illustrator CS2, InDesign CS2, or Acrobat or Reader 7.0.

3. Transparency flattening may cause certain parts of a vector file to become rasterized to prevent a file from changing in appearance.

Printing Files with Transparency from QuarkXPress

You can now begin to understand at a basic level why some people have problems printing files with transparency. If you save a PDF from Illustrator and place that file into QuarkXPress, there is still native transparency in that file. Although Quark can place PDF files, QuarkXPress doesn't translate the file when sending the page to the printer, and so the transparency flattening never occurs. The result is transparency commands being sent to a PostScript printer that doesn't understand them, and what shows up on the printed page is anyone's guess.

In Chapter 12, *Saving and Exporting Files*, you'll explore the different file formats that Illustrator CS2 can save with, and you'll learn to understand the correct formats to use when printing from QuarkXPress and other applications.

Two Levels of Rasterization

In the previous example, where two vector shapes resulted in a portion of that file becoming rasterized, Illustrator had no choice but to rasterize the middle region because there was simply no other way to preserve the appearance in vector form. This is one level of rasterization.

However, there is another case where a second level of rasterization may occur, even if the appearance of a file could be preserved in vector form. Before printing a file, Illustrator analyzes the entire document and looks for *complex regions* where there are many overlapping objects (which would result in a large number of atomic regions). Illustrator may then choose to rasterize those complex regions for performance reasons. Although we've been trained to think vector objects are simpler than their bitmapped counterparts, try to imagine an Illustrator graphic filled with many overlapping objects with transparency applied (**Figure 11.14**). Although it may only seem like several objects at first glance, once those objects are broken up into atomic regions, we may be looking at thousands of vector shapes, which can take a long time to process and print (**Figure 11.15**). In those cases, Illustrator can save precious RIP and processing time by rasterizing these complex regions.

Figure 11.14 Using the Symbol Sprayer tool, you can easily create a file that contains many overlapping shapes. Using the Symbol Screener tool, you can also make some of these symbols transparent.

Figure 11.15 Even though you may have started with a small number of objects, the resulting number of atomic regions due to flattening can be extremely large.

As far as the first level of rasterization goes, we really have no choice but to allow Illustrator to rasterize objects where it needs to. What we *can* do, however, is learn how to build files that work around this issue (see "Object Stacking Order and Transparency Flattening," later in this section). With regard to the second level of rasterization, we can control how liberal Illustrator is when looking for complex regions. In fact, we can even disable this second level of rasterization altogether. Finally, with either level of rasterization, Illustrator always gives us total control over *how* these areas are rasterized.

Understanding the Transparency Flattener Settings

As mentioned earlier in this chapter, Illustrator has three Transparency Flattener presets that you can choose from in the Advanced panel of the Print dialog. These settings control how files with transparency are flattened at print time. To access these settings, choose Edit > Transparency Flattener Presets and click the New button to define a new preset. Let's explore the settings in the Transparency Flattener Preset Options dialog box (**Figure 11.16**).

Figure 11.16 You can define your own custom flattener settings, or your printer or service provider can define one for you.

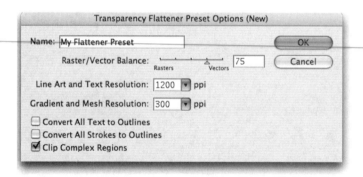

Raster/Vector Balance: This slider is what controls how liberal Illustrator is when looking for complex regions to rasterize (what we've defined above as the second level of rasterization). A number closer to zero (0) gives Illustrator more freedom to rasterize at will, resulting in faster print times. Moving the slider closer to 100 results in fewer rasterized areas, but longer print times. At the 100 setting itself, Illustrator does not rasterize *any* parts of the file for performance reasons, effectively disabling the second level of rasterization altogether. The High Resolution flattener preset uses this setting. In cases where files are taking extremely long to print (or crashing the RIP altogether), adjusting this slider to a slightly lower setting helps.

Line Art and Text Resolution: In cases where Illustrator is going to rasterize line art or text, you can specify a resolution that results in good-looking, sharp output. You'll notice that the High Resolution flattener setting specifies a resolution of 1200 ppi, ensuring that text elements and vector objects still have nice, clean, sharp edges in final output.

Gradient and Mesh Resolution: Because gradients and meshes are continuous tones in nature, they don't require a resolution as high as line art or text. In fact, anything twice your line screen is probably getting thrown out anyway. Therefore, Illustrator uses this setting to rasterize elements that can afford to be set at a lower resolution. You'll notice that the High Resolution flattener preset uses a value of 300 ppi.

Convert All Text to Outlines: In cases where text is going to be rasterized, chances are that the rasterized text looks a bit chunkier than regular vector text. To compensate for this, you can turn on this option to convert all text to outlines, giving a consistent chunkier look to all of your text. If you use the method described later in this chapter to move text onto its own layer, you'll rarely need to concern yourself with this setting.

Convert All Strokes to Outlines: Similar to the previous setting, this compensates for disparity between vector and rasterized strokes by converting all strokes to outlines.

Clip Complex Regions: We mentioned that InDesign can look for complex areas of a file and rasterize them for performance reasons. However, we know that raster images are always rectangular in shape, which means it's possible for "innocent" parts of your file to become rasterized simply because they fall into the rectangular bounding box of the area that is complex. More often than not, this results in stitching, or noticeable boxes and color shifts. The Clip Complex Regions option avoids this issue by creating a clipping mask around any rasterized complex region (so the rectangular-shaped raster is masked by the vector outline of the object). As you can probably understand, this makes for even more complex files and can result in longer print times as well. This option is turned on in the Medium Resolution flattener preset but isn't applicable at all in the High Resolution preset because no complex regions are rasterized at all with that setting (as it has a Raster/Vector Balance setting of 100).

 The two resolution settings in the flattener controls are used whenever vector objects are forced to become rasters during the flattening process. However, Live Effects, like Feather and Drop Shadow, use the Document Raster Effects Resolution setting to determine their resolution.

Object Stacking Order and Transparency Flattening

When rasterization occurs during transparency flattening, the last thing you want to see turning into a raster is text. That's because you always want text to be clean and sharp in your printouts. Even at the High Resolution setting, where text is rasterized at 1200 ppi, that resolution is still less than half of what most image setters set text with—usually upward of 2400 ppi.

Although it's true that under certain circumstances rasterization must occur in order to print a file and maintain its appearance, the way you build your files can affect how often this happens. Let's look at a simple example that clarifies this.

Draw a circle and add a drop shadow to it by choosing Effect > Stylize > Drop Shadow. As you learned in Chapter 7, the Drop Shadow effect is a raster-based effect, and when transparency is flattened, the drop shadow becomes rasterized. Switch to the Type tool, create some text, and position the text near the drop shadow (**Figure 11.17**). With the text still selected, choose Object > Arrange > Send to Back.

Figure 11.17 Placing text near an object is common, especially when you're adding captions or credit text near photographs.

Adobe
Creative Suite

Now select both the circle and the text, choose Object > Flatten Transparency, and click OK. Upon close inspection, you'll see that a portion of the text was rasterized. This happened because the text was below the drop shadow in the stacking order, and to maintain the file's appearance when the drop shadow was rasterized, Illustrator had to include part of the text in the drop shadow's bounding area (**Figure 11.18**).

Figure 11.18 In order to maintain the appearance of the file, Illustrator rasterized the text that was behind the drop shadow.

Choose Edit > Undo to go back before you applied the Flatten Transparency function and select the text object. Choose Object > Arrange > Bring to Front. Select both the circle and the text, choose Object > Flatten Transparency, and click OK. In this case, the text, which was above the drop shadow in the stacking order, was not affected at all and was not rasterized (**Figure 11.19**).

Figure 11.19 If the text appears above the shadow in the stacking order, the text is not rasterized during flattening.

When using transparency features in Illustrator, it's important to make sure that text always appears above objects with transparency to avoid unwanted rasterized text issues. Of course, some designs call for text to appear beneath transparent objects, and in those cases, you don't have much of a choice.

Does My File Contain Transparency?

Not every document needs flattening—only those with transparency in them. The tricky thing is that transparency can be introduced into an Illustrator document in any of several different ways:

- You apply a blend mode or an Opacity value other than 100% from the Transparency palette.

- You apply the Effect > Stylize > Drop Shadow feature.

- You apply the Effect > Stylize > Feather feature.

- You apply the Effect > Stylize > Outer Glow.

- You apply any "below the line" Photoshop effect from the Effect menu.

- You place a PDF file that contains transparency.

- You place a native Photoshop file that contains transparency.

Previewing Transparency Flattener Results Before You Print

It would be helpful to know if the document you're working on uses transparency or is even going to require any of the two levels of rasterization we spoke of earlier. You can use the Flattener Preview palette (Window > Flattener Preview) to tell if a document has transparency effects in it, as well as to preview areas that will become rasterized in the flattening process.

By clicking on the Refresh button in the palette, Illustrator highlights specific areas in your file in red, indicating where rasterization will occur. You can enlarge the palette to see a larger image, and you can also click with your mouse inside the preview area of the palette to zoom in closer to see more detail. From the Highlight pop-up menu, you can choose from a variety of items that Illustrator will preview. If all of the items listed in your Highlight pop-up are grayed out, that indicates that there is no transparency present in your file, and no flattening is necessary to print your file (**Figure 11.20**). For example, when you choose Transparent Objects, Illustrator shows you where all objects are on your page that use transparency—although those regions may not necessarily become rasterized. We also mentioned earlier that Illustrator looks for complex areas of a document; you can see where those areas are by choosing Rasterized Complex Regions in the pop-up (**Figure 11.21**). Additionally, the All Affected Objects option shows you all of the objects that may not be transparent themselves but that interact with transparency in some way (like the example we mentioned above with the drop shadow and the text: the text itself doesn't have transparency applied to it, but if the text appears below the drop shadow, the text must become rasterized to preserve the appearance).

Figure 11.20 If your file contains no transparency, you don't have to worry about the effects of flattening.

Figure 11.21 You can use the Flattener Preview palette to identify areas that Illustrator deems as complex regions, giving you a heads up for what areas will become rasterized.

To take advantage of all that the Flattener Preview palette can offer, adjust the different flattener settings and preview the results—making changes or adjustments where necessary—all before you actually print the file. As an aside, InDesign CS2 and Acrobat 7.0 Professional also contain a similar Flattener Preview palette and identical flattener settings (in fact, it's the same underlying code).

What Kind of RIP Are You Using?

To throw yet another variable into the mix, the kind of printer or RIP that you use can also render different results. For the most part, any Adobe PostScript Language Level 3 device should be able to handle transparency without issue. Specifically, PostScript version 3015 (which appears in the latest versions of RIPs) has enhanced functionality to process files that have been flattened. It's important to remember that flattening has to occur for any RIP to understand how to print transparency. If your RIP can process PDF files, that doesn't necessarily mean that it can process PDF files with transparency in them. If you're in doubt, check with your RIP manufacturer to find out if transparency flattening can occur inside the RIP or if you need to print files from an Adobe application to flatten them.

There are some older print devices that are confused by the effects of flattening. For example, Scitex (since acquired by Creo) RIPs look at jobs that are printing and split up the vector and raster elements onto two layers. The rasterized content prints on a CT (Continuous Tone) layer at a lower resolution (like 300 dpi), and line art prints on a separate vector layer at a much higher resolution (like 2400 dpi). Because flattening could cause a vector object to be rasterized, the RIP only sees that raster as a CT image and prints it at the lower resolution. This might cause text that is rasterized to print with noticeably jagged edges. Scitex has since updated their RIPs to address this issue, but that doesn't automatically mean that everyone who owns a Scitex RIP has installed the update (or knows that it exists).

Bottom line, the best advice in any case is to talk with your printer. For any big job, most printers will be happy to run a test file for you to make sure everything will print correctly. Taking advantage of these opportunities will surely save you headaches when press deadlines loom. Adobe also has free specialized training materials for print service providers if your printer needs more information (found online at http://partners.adobe.com/asn/programs/printserviceprovider/index.jsp).

Printing with Confidence

You can avoid accidents by learning to anticipate possible problems. Now that you're aware of how transparency works, here are a few ways to ensure that you get the results you expect when you're printing from Illustrator.

- Use the right flattener presets—Low Resolution, Medium Resolution, and High Resolution. For quick proofs to your laser printer, you can use the Low or Medium setting, but when you're printing to a high-end proofer or image setter, use the High setting. You'll find the Transparency Flattener settings in the Advanced panel of the Print dialog.

- To avoid text becoming rasterized, create a new layer in your Illustrator file and place all of your text on that layer. As long as you keep that text layer as the top layer in your document, you won't have to worry about chunky or pixilated text due to rasterization.

- A potential problem is that even if you, as a designer, are aware of transparency, there are still plenty of printers out there who aren't. If you are sending out a file and aren't sure who will be printing it or what they will be using to print it, you might consider sending the file as a PDF/X-1a file. See Chapter 12 for more information on PDF/X.

Designing with transparency allows you to create things that were previously prohibitive and difficult to implement, thus allowing you to save valuable time while being even more creative. Now that you know how transparency works and what's necessary to use it in your workflow, give it a test drive. You'll be happy you did.

UNDERSTANDING OVERPRINTS

Hang around a print shop long enough and you'll hear the term *overprint*. In the world of prepress, overprinting is a way to control how color-separated plates interact with each other. A printing press imprints each color on a piece of paper, one after the other, as it runs through the press. Because of this process, certain considerations need to be made when color separations are made.

Take an example where you design some blue text over a yellow background. When those colors are separated and printed on press, the blue and yellow mix, resulting in green text on a yellow background. Therefore, under normal conditions, when pages are separated, color that appears underneath other objects is removed so that the color on top is unaffected. In the preceding example, the blue text removes or *knocks out* the yellow background underneath it, allowing the blue to appear correctly when printed.

Overprinting, on the other hand, is a method of overriding a knockout and forcing overlapping colors to mix on press. In our example, setting the blue text to overprint means that the yellow background still appears behind it and the result on press is green text on a yellow background (**Figure 11.22**).

Figure 11.22 The text on the left, by default, knocks out the background behind it. The text on the right is set to overprint and the background behind it is unaffected.

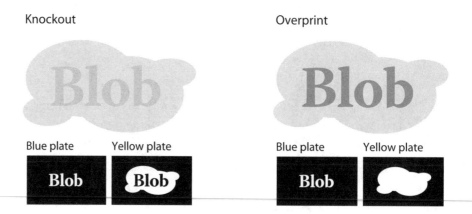

Why Overprint?

You'd want to apply an overprint when you specifically want to mix colors on press. Some designers who work with low-budget jobs that print in two or three spot colors can simulate other colors by mixing those spot colors. Before transparency rolled around, designers would also specify overprints to simulate objects being transparent; you could also simulate shadows or shading by overprinting with black over other elements.

Overprinting is also essential when you're creating plates for custom dies and varnishes. For example, if you want to create a spot varnish for a particular photo, you need to create a color called Varnish and set it to overprint, because this allows the photo that appears beneath it to print (otherwise, the varnish knocks out the photo).

You can easily specify overprinting from the Attributes palette (Window > Attributes). With an object selected, you can choose to force the fill, the stroke, or both, to overprint. Remember that Illustrator also allows you to specify whether a stroke is painted in the centerline, inside, or outside of a path, and you should be aware that if you overprint a stroke that's on the inside or the centerline of a path, the stroke also overprints the fill of that object.

Trapped into a Corner

Those who work in packaging rely on using overprints all the time for creating *traps*—colors that share borders with other colors that overlap slightly. This is because the materials that are used for many packages and the printing processes used (called *flexographic printing*, or *flexo* for short) don't always result in perfect printing. Remember that the requirements for printing 1,000 brochures and printing several million containers of milk can be quite different. The next time you see a bag of potato chips or a bottle of soda, take a close look at the label; you'll be able to see the overprint traps. These are usually created in Illustrator by setting just the stroke set to overprint.

Limitations with Overprints

Let's get technical for a moment. There are some limitations when it comes to using overprints. First of all, whereas one color plate can overprint another, an overprint cannot overprint its own plate. For example, if you have a color that contains cyan and you set it to overprint over a background that contains cyan, you won't get an overprint on the cyan plate.

Here's another issue: Sometimes users specify overprinting for objects colored white. Usually, white is always a knockout (as it lets the white paper show through), and setting a white object to overprint would kind of defeat the purpose. However, these things do happen accidentally. You might have a logo that you created that's colored black and that you've set to overprint. Then you might come upon a situation where you need a reverse (white) version of the logo, so you might just open the file, color it white, and save it with a different name, forgetting that you had set the fill to overprint. This would most likely result in the file not printing properly, because either the white overprints (making it entirely transparent) or the RIP doesn't process the file correctly.

Previewing Overprints

Because overprints are really PostScript commands that you use when you're printing color separations, you'll always have a problem with displaying overprints on screen or when you're printing composite proofs to show a client. In the past, the only real way to proof overprints was by printing separations and creating a Matchprint proof or by investing in expensive prepress plug-ins. More often than not, a designer would show a proof to a client and say, "it won't look like this when it's actually printed." If only there was a better way . . .

Illustrator offers that better way. By choosing View > Overprint Preview, you can actually see on your monitor what the effects of overprint commands are. Additionally, in the Output panel of the Print dialog, there's a Simulate Overprint option, which when activated, prints composites as they will look with overprints applied. This is perfect for showing clients exactly what they are going to get. The Simulate Overprint option is also available in the Advanced panel of the PDF dialog, so you can even show your client an accurate proof via PDF. You disable Simulate Overprint when you choose to print separations—it's only available when you're printing composites.

Although overprints are useful (and essential in some workflows), our advice is to talk to your printer before you use them, because some printers prefer to specify overprints themselves.

CHAPTER 12

Saving and Exporting Files

Saving and exporting your Adobe Illustrator files is obviously very important. Illustrator is a fantastic utility that can open a wide variety of file types, including EPS and PDF. Additionally, you can also use Illustrator to save and export files in just about any format that you need, including SWF and SVG. If you aren't familiar with these file types, that's okay, because that's what this entire chapter is about.

With so many file formats to work with, how do you know which format to use when you're saving or exporting a file? How do you know what each file format supports and what they are each used for? Throughout this chapter, you will learn the strengths and weaknesses of each file format and see examples of when to use or not use each.

SAVING FILES FROM ILLUSTRATOR

When you save a document from Illustrator using any of the file formats found in the Save or Save As dialog, you are able to reopen that file and edit it as needed. When you do, all native information, by default, is preserved in the file. For example, if you save a file as an EPS document, you can reopen the EPS file in Illustrator and make edits to the file with no loss of functionality or editablity. Adobe calls this *round-tripping* and there are many benefits to working in this way.

If you create a file in Illustrator, but you need to place it into a QuarkXPress document, you'll learn that you need to create an EPS file. Because an Illustrator EPS file is round-trippable, you can place the EPS into your QuarkXPress layout, yet you can edit that same EPS in Illustrator if you need to make changes.

As you will find out, Illustrator accomplishes this by using what engineers call *dual path* files. This means a single file contains two parts in it: one part contains the EPS data that QuarkXPress needs; the other contains the native Illustrator information that Illustrator needs. As we explore the different formats and their settings, this dual path concept will become clear.

The Native Illustrator (.ai) Format

By default, when you choose to save a new file, the Adobe Illustrator Document setting is chosen as the file format. Whenever you create documents, it's best to save them as native Illustrator files, because they will *always* contain rich and editable information.

 When creating documents that you plan to use as a base for other files, you may choose to save your file as an Illustrator Template (.ait). Details on this format appear in Chapter 1, *The Illustrator Environment.*

Up until version 8, Illustrator's native file format was PostScript (EPS), but for a variety of reasons, with the release of version 9, Adobe changed Illustrator's native file format to use the PDF language. In fact, Adobe is quick to tell you that a native Illustrator file can be opened and viewed in Adobe Acrobat or the free Adobe Reader. Adobe also advertises that you can place native Illustrator files directly into InDesign layouts. It makes sense when you think about it, because if Illustrator's native file format is using the PDF language, then placing it into InDesign is similar to placing a PDF file in InDesign.

In reality though, Illustrator's native file format is a special flavor of the PDF language—a flavor that only Illustrator can understand. There are certain constructs that exist in Illustrator but that do not exist in the PDF language, such as live blends, Live Paint, and Live Effects (these effects are all expanded when printed or translated to regular PDF). You can think of Illustrator's native file format as a superset of the PDF language. If this is the case, however, how is InDesign or Acrobat able to import and display native Illustrator files? That's where the dual path concept comes in.

When you save a native file, Illustrator embeds two files—a native Illustrator file (.ai) and a standard PDF file (**Figure 12.1**). When you place the native Illustrator file into InDesign, the application sees the PDF portion of the file and uses that for display and printing. When you reopen the file in Illustrator, the application sees the native Illustrator portion and uses that for editing. In the end, everyone is happy, and you get to work with a single file.

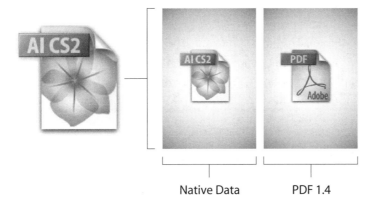

Native Data   PDF 1.4

Figure 12.1 When you save a native Illustrator file, you're really saving two files. The PDF file that is created with the native Illustrator file is PDF 1.4, which preserves transparency.

To save your file as a native Illustrator file, choose File > Save and select Adobe Illustrator Document from the pop-up menu. When you click Save, you are presented with the Illustrator Options dialog where you can specify settings for how your file should be saved. These are described in the section, "Native Illustrator File Format Settings."

 The two files within an Illustrator file print and display the same and are exactly identical except the native Illustrator version maintains more editability within the Illustrator environment.

A bug in Mac OS 10.4 (Tiger) may cause your pop-up list to display the words "Adobe PDF Document" instead of Adobe Illustrator Document. Even though the words are wrong, the file is still correctly saved as a native Illustrator document.

Using Legacy Illustrator Formats

Illustrator CS2 allows you to save your file so that it is compatible with a variety of versions of Illustrator. Obviously, the older the version you specify, the less editable your file will be. Specifically, there are two lines in the sand that you should be aware of:

- Adobe introduced a new text engine in Illustrator CS. If you save your file to any version prior to Illustrator CS, your text is either broken apart or converted to outlines. For more details, see "Saving Illustrator CS2 Files to Illustrator Legacy Versions" in Chapter 6, *Typography*.

- Adobe introduced transparency features in Illustrator 9. If you save your file to any version prior to Illustrator 9, transparency flattening will occur, resulting in a document that may be extremely difficult, or even impossible, to edit. For more details, see "The Truth About Transparency" in Chapter 11, *Prepress and Printing*.

Your file will print or display correctly when you're saving back to older versions because appearance is always maintained. However, you are limited in what kind of edits you can make in your file. For this reason, we recommend that you *always* save a native CS2 version of your file to keep on your computer or server for editing purposes. If someone else requests a file from you that is compatible with a previous version of Illustrator, send them a copy of your file.

Native Illustrator File Format Settings

A variety of settings are available in the Illustrator Options dialog (**Figure 12.2**), and depending on your needs for each particular workflow, you can make adjustments to these settings.

- **Version.** The Version pop-up menu allows you to choose which version of Illustrator you want your file to be compatible with. See "Legacy Illustrator Formats" earlier in this chapter for more information.

- **Fonts.** When you're saving a file, any fonts that you use are embedded in the PDF portion of the file. This allows other applications to print the file without requiring the fonts. However, you still need the fonts installed if you are going to reopen the file within Illustrator. This setting is disabled when the Create PDF Compatible File option is unchecked (see the following description). At the 100% setting,

Illustrator only embeds the characters of a font that are necessary to print the text in your document. Using a setting much lower (like 0%) embeds the entire font, resulting in a larger file. Fonts with permission bits turned on cannot be embedded (see the sidebar entitled "Font Embedding and Permissions," later in this chapter).

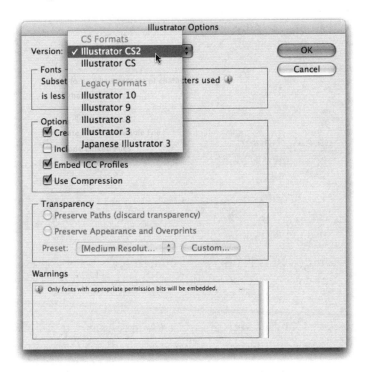

Figure 12.2 The Illustrator Options dialog allows you to specify what version of Illustrator you want your file to be compatible with, among other settings.

- **Create PDF Compatible File.** The Create PDF Compatible File option embeds a full standard PDF 1.4 file within your Illustrator document. As just mentioned, this allows applications like Acrobat or InDesign to read and place native Illustrator files. Turning this option off effectively cuts your file size in half and also reduces how long it takes to save an Illustrator file (**Figure 12.3**). If you use Illustrator for all of your work and print directly from Illustrator, you can turn this option off to enhance performance and to create smaller file sizes, but be aware that you won't be able to place your file into an InDesign layout. Even if you do turn this option off, you can always reopen the file in Illustrator and resave the file with the option turned on.

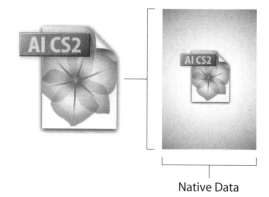

Figure 12.3 When you have the Create PDF Compatible File option unchecked, only the native Illustrator portion is saved with the file, cutting save time and file size in half. The result, however, is a native file that cannot be placed into another application.

Native Data

- **Include Linked Files.** When you choose the Include Linked Files option, any place-linked files are embedded in your document. Although this means you can send the file to someone without requiring any external links, it also means that you can't easily update linked graphics anymore. This option also increases file size because the images are now included within the file.

- **Embed ICC Profiles.** The Embed ICC Profiles option includes any color profiles (including those from placed images) within your document.

- **Use Compression.** The Use Compression option employs compression algorithms to your file to try to reduce file size.

- **Transparency.** When you're saving back to Illustrator 8 or Illustrator 3 formats, transparency flattening must occur in documents that contain transparency effects. You can choose to discard the transparency effects completely (which preserves path geometry) or you can choose to preserve the appearance of your file. You can also choose from the list of available Transparency Flattener presets. For more information on which flattener preset to use, refer to Chapter 11.

The Encapsulated PostScript (.eps) Format

When Adobe introduced PostScript to the world, it forever changed the face of design and publishing. Since desktop publishing became a buzzword, the format in which designers and printers exchanged file information was always EPS. To this day, EPS is a reliable universal format that can be used to reproduce graphics from just about any professional (and even some nonprofessional) graphics applications. You can even use EPS files with video applications like Adobe After Effects.

As you learned in Chapter 11, PostScript doesn't support transparency, so if your file contains any transparency effects, those effects are flattened when the document is saved as EPS. However, you can still reopen and edit the native transparency in Illustrator CS2 because Illustrator also uses a dual path when saving EPS files. An Illustrator CS2 EPS file has two portions within it: a native version for editing within Illustrator, and an EPS version that other applications, like QuarkXPress, use (**Figure 12.4**).

To save your file as an EPS file, choose File > Save and select Illustrator EPS from the pop-up menu. When you click Save, you are presented with the EPS Options dialog where you can specify settings for how your file should be saved, as described later in the section, "EPS File Format Settings."

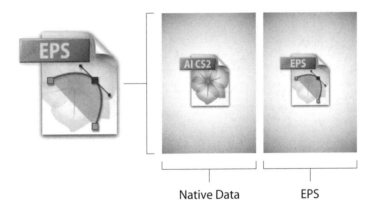

Native Data   EPS

Figure 12.4 When you save a document as an EPS file, Illustrator also embeds a native version of the file so that you can reopen and edit the file in Illustrator again with no loss in editability.

Using Legacy EPS Formats

As with native files, Illustrator CS2 allows you to save your file so that it is compatible with a variety of versions of Illustrator EPS. This setting affects both the native portion and the EPS portion of the file. When you save a file that is compatible with an older version of Illustrator, both the native data and the PostScript are written so they are compatible with that version (**Figure 12.5**, next page). Obviously, the older the version you specify, the less editable your file is.

Figure 12.5 When you save a file in Illustrator 8 EPS format, the native portion of the file is also saved in Illustrator 8 format, which doesn't support transparency. Even if you reopen the file in Illustrator CS2, any transparency that was in the file is flattened.

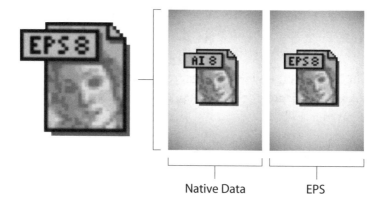

Native Data   EPS

The same rules mentioned for native Illustrator files apply here (with regard to versions that result in loss in text and transparency editability), and it always makes sense to save an Illustrator CS2 EPS for your own needs and deliver older or legacy EPS versions for others, as needed.

EPS File Format Settings

A variety of settings are available in the EPS Options dialog (**Figure 12.6**), and depending on your needs for each particular workflow, you can make adjustments to these settings.

Figure 12.6 The EPS Options dialog offers a variety of setting to choose from when you're saving an EPS file, including the type of preview that you want saved within the file.

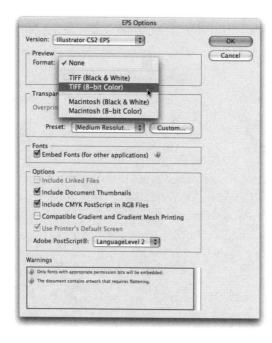

- **Version.** The Version pop-up menu allows you to choose which version of Illustrator EPS you want your file to be compatible with. See preceding section, "Legacy EPS Formats," for more information.

- **Preview.** The Preview setting lets you choose from different options for embedding a preview in your EPS file. Because most programs can't display PostScript on your computer screen, a low-resolution preview is stored along with the file so that programs like QuarkXPress or Microsoft Word can give you a visual representation of what the file will look like in your layout.

- **Transparency.** If your file contains transparency, your file must be flattened so that it can be saved in PostScript and printed from another application (remember, the version you choose determines if the native portion of the file, which Illustrator reads when it reopens the file, still contains editable unflattened data). Although you can choose from different Transparency Flattener presets from the pop-up menu, it almost always makes sense to choose the High Resolution setting, because you'll always want to get the best possible results when printing the EPS from other applications (see "File Formats and Workflow" later in this chapter).

- **Embed Fonts.** When this option is checked, any fonts used are embedded in the EPS portion of the file. This allows other applications to print the file without requiring the fonts. However, even with the setting turned on, you still need the fonts installed if you are going to reopen the file within Illustrator. Fonts with permission bits turned on can't be embedded (see the sidebar entitled "Font Embedding and Permissions" later in this chapter).

- **Include Linked Files.** Choosing the Include Linked Files option embeds any place-linked files in your document. Although this means you can send the file to someone without requiring any external links, it also means that you can't easily update linked graphics anymore. This option also increases file size because the images will now be included within the file.

- **Include Document Thumbnails.** Use this option if you want to be able to see a preview of your file in the Open and Place dialog boxes in Illustrator.

- **Include CMYK PostScript in RGB Files.** This setting allows you to maintain RGB colors in your Illustrator file, but have the EPS portion of the file converted to CMYK so other applications that don't support RGB can still print the file correctly.

- **Compatible Gradient and Gradient Mesh Printing.** If you experience problems printing EPS files saved from Illustrator on older print devices, try turning this option on.

- **Use Printer's Default Screen.** Instructs the PostScript to use the line screen of the default setting of the printer.

- **Adobe PostScript Level.** Use this pop-up menu to write the EPS file as PostScript Language Level 2 or Language Level 3. Illustrator uses Level 2 as the default setting in order to create a file that is compatible with a wider range of devices, but Level 3 PostScript offers certain benefits like SmoothShading technology to prevent banding in gradients.

The Portable Document Format (.pdf)

Walk up to just about anyone on the street these days and ask them about Adobe. Most will reply, "Oh sure, I have Adobe on my computer." What they are probably referring to is the free Adobe Reader file viewer, which enables just about anyone to view and print PDF files. Now that Adobe Reader is nearing a billion downloads worldwide, PDF files are ubiquitous and are quickly becoming a standard format used not only by designers and printers, but also by governments and enterprise corporations.

Over the past few years, PDF has become the format of choice for both printers and designers, replacing EPS and other formats. There are several reasons for this, including:

 You can instruct clients or users to download the free Adobe Reader at www.adobe.com/products/acrobat/readstep2.html. The Adobe Reader is available for Mac, Windows, Unix, and a variety of mobile platforms.

- **Smaller file sizes.** PDF supports a variety of image compression techniques, resulting in smaller file sizes. In addition, users can easily create low-resolution files to send to clients for review, and high-resolution files to send to printers for high-quality output.

- **A free universal viewer.** Adobe Reader is free and available for nearly every computer platform, including Palm-based handheld devices. This means that a designer can deliver a PDF file and be assured that anyone can view the file correctly.

- **Ability to embed fonts.** A PDF file is a single, self-contained file that includes all necessary images and fonts. This makes it easier to distribute and reduces the chance of error.

- **Easy to create.** Designers can easily create PDF files from any Adobe application. Additionally, Adobe supplies free utilities, like PDFMaker, that enable users to instantly create PDF files from Microsoft Office documents or AutoCAD files. A PDF virtual printer also enables a user to create a PDF file simply by printing a file from any application.

- **Security.** PDF files can contain multiple levels of security that can restrict functionality such as printing or editing. This ensures the integrity of a file and gives a designer the ability to protect his or her work.

By default, a PDF saved from Illustrator is also a dual-path file, containing both PDF data and native Illustrator data (**Figure 12.7**). In fact, if you think about it, saving a native Illustrator file and an Adobe PDF file is quite similar. When you save a PDF file from Illustrator though, you can control a variety of settings in the resulting PDF data of the file.

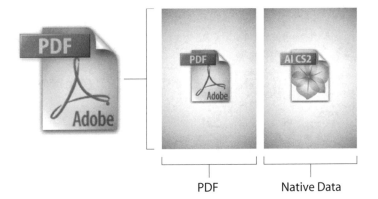

PDF   Native Data

Figure 12.7 If you've ever heard that Illustrator creates large PDF files, it's because Illustrator embeds a native version of the file along with the PDF data, resulting in a PDF file that appears twice as large.

To save your file as a PDF file, choose File > Save and select Adobe PDF from the pop-up menu. When you click Save, you are presented with the Save Adobe PDF dialog where you can specify settings for how your file should be saved.

Different Uses of PDF Files

Before we discuss all of the different options you have available when saving a PDF file, it's important to realize that there are many different uses for PDF files. For example, you might create a PDF file to send to a client so that they can approve a design, or you might create a PDF file to send to a printer for final output. Alternatively, you might even create a PDF file to upload to a Web site so that anyone can view the content. Each of these PDF files serves a different purpose and therefore each can have very different settings. Just because you create a PDF file doesn't mean that you can use it for any and all purposes.

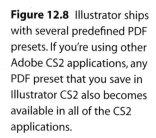

PDF presets are similar to Distiller Job Options, which are simply a captured set of PDF settings.

Instead of having to manually specify PDF settings each time you want to create a file for a specific purpose, Illustrator offers to let you create Adobe PDF presets, which capture all of the settings a PDF can have. At the top of the Save Adobe PDF dialog, there's a pop-up menu where you can choose from some presets with which Illustrator ships (**Figure 12.8**), or you can define your own by clicking the Save Preset button at the bottom left of the dialog.

Figure 12.8 Illustrator ships with several predefined PDF presets. If you're using other Adobe CS2 applications, any PDF preset that you save in Illustrator CS2 also becomes available in all of the CS2 applications.

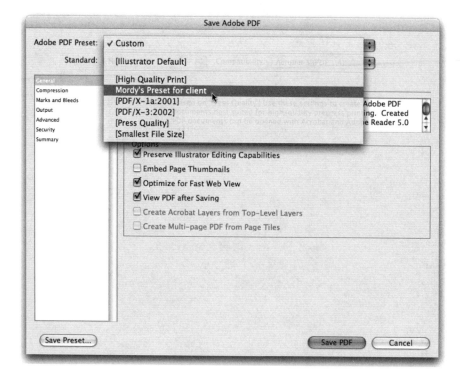

Acrobat Version Compatibility

When PDF was first introduced, it had limited support (spot colors weren't supported until version 1.2), but as each new version of Acrobat has been introduced, Adobe has updated the PDF Language specification (called PDFL for short) to include more advanced functions and to feature new capabilities.

Adobe released PDFL version 1.3 when it introduced Adobe Acrobat 4.0, which was the first mainstream version of Acrobat and the free Adobe Acrobat Reader. With each new version of Acrobat, Adobe has also revised the PDFL version (Acrobat 5 = PDF 1.4, Acrobat 6 = PDF 1.5, etc.), although trying to remember all of these different numbers can prove quite confusing. An easy way to figure it out is if you add up the numbers in the PDFL version; it equals the corresponding version of Acrobat (1+4 = 5).

In any case, when you save a PDF file from Illustrator, you can specify which version of Acrobat you want your file to be compatible with in the Save Adobe PDF dialog (**Figure 12.9**). Although saving a file using a newer version compatibility setting offers more options when saving, anyone who wants to view that PDF file needs to use a newer version of Acrobat or Reader to see and print the file correctly.

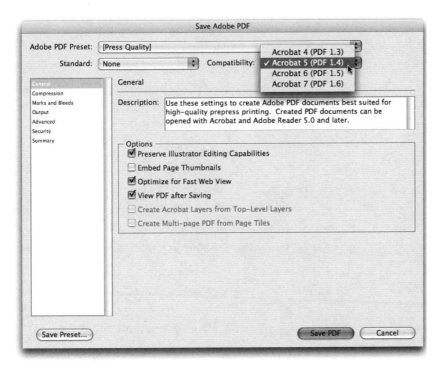

Figure 12.9 The Save Adobe PDF dialog offers a plethora of settings for creating PDF files for a wide variety of purposes. The Compatibility setting determines the version of Acrobat that the resulting PDF file needs in order to display and print correctly.

The most important point to remember is that from a print perspective, there's a line in the sand between PDF 1.3, which doesn't support transparency, and all later PDF versions, which do support live transparency (**Table 12.1**). See "File Formats and Workflow" later in this chapter to learn when to use each version.

Table 12.1 Acrobat Version Compatibility

Version of Acrobat	PDFL Version	Transparency Support	Main Features Introduced
Acrobat 4	PDF 1.3	No	Smoothshading, digital signatures
Acrobat 5	PDF 1.4	Yes	Transparency, XML tagging and metadata
Acrobat 6	PDF 1.5	Yes	Layers, JPEG2000 compression
Acrobat 7	PDF 1.6	Yes	Object-level metadata, AES encryption

The PDF/X Standard

Imagine the following scenario: A designer submits a PDF file to a printer for final printing. When the job is complete, the designer is horrified to find that the wrong fonts printed and that the colors weren't anywhere near close to those that appeared on the screen when the designer designed the job. How did this happen? After all, didn't the printer say they accept PDF files? For designers, and especially for printers, this is a scenario that unfortunately happens too often.

This happens because PDF is a "garbage in, garbage out" file format. Whatever you put into it, that's what you can expect to get out of it. If you don't embed your fonts when you create a PDF file, a printer can't print your file unless they also have your fonts. If you embed RGB images when a printer needs CMYK, you will see color shifts in your output (some devices may not print RGB images at all).

With so many other possible things that could go wrong with a PDF file, printers and publishers realized that they needed a way to ensure that a PDF file meets certain requirements before it is submitted for final printing or publication.

Understanding PDF Standards

Because there are so many different uses for PDF files, and because each workflow is different, a variety of PDF standards exists. Below is an explanation of what each standard is and what they are best used for.

- **PDF/X-1a:2001.** The PDF/X-1a standard was defined to allow for the reliable exchange of files between designers and printers or publishers. The standard, which was first defined in the year 2001 (hence the PDF/X-1a:2001 name), is based on PDF 1.3 and therefore doesn't support transparency. Hence, when you save a PDF/X-1a file from Illustrator, a Transparency Flattener preset is used to flatten the transparency in the file. A PDF/X-1a-compliant file must also have all fonts embedded within the file. If your file uses a protected font that cannot be embedded (see the sidebar, "Font Embedding and Permissions," later in this chapter), Illustrator can't create a valid PDF/X-1a file. Additionally, PDF/X-1a files are CMYK and spot only (any RGB information is converted to CMYK). For ad submission, or for sending final files to a printer for offset printing, PDF/X-1a:2001 is the preferred choice.

- **PDF/X-1a:2003.** In the year 2003, the PDF/X-1a standard was updated to support PDF 1.4. However, with this version, transparency must still be flattened because transparency is not allowed in the PDF/X-1a:2003 specification. Because Illustrator always preserves transparency when saving to PDF 1.4, you have to manually flatten the transparency in your file before you save it (by choosing Object > Flatten Transparency). For this reason, Illustrator actually saves PDF/X-1a:2003 files using PDF 1.3 compatibility. In any case, it's best to speak with your printer before using the newer PDF/X-1a:2003 standard.

- **PDF/X-3:2002.** In recent years, print service providers have been adopting color management technologies to offer better color matching. Rather than converting images to CMYK early in the process, in a color-managed workflow, you can have images remain in RGB and tag them with profiles that allow color integrity to be preserved from proof to final print. Because PDF/X-1a doesn't support RGB or embedded color profiles, PDF/X-3:2002 was created to allow for these variables. If you or your printer are using a color-management workflow, you might consider using PDF/X-3:2002.

- **PDF/X-3:2003.** In the year 2003, the PDF/X-3 standard was updated to support PDF 1.4. However, with this version, transparency must still be flattened because transparency is not allowed in the PDF/X-3:2003 specification. Because Illustrator always preserves transparency when saving to PDF 1.4, you have to manually flatten the transparency in your file before you save it (by choosing Object > Flatten Transparency). For this reason, Illustrator actually saves PDF/X-3:2003 files using PDF 1.3 compatibility. In any case, it's best to speak with your printer before using the newer PDF/X-3:2003 standard.

- **PDF/X-2:2003.** Certain workflows require images to be swapped at print time for other images. Some packaging or catalog workflows, for example, are set up so that a designer uses low-resolution images for placement, and when the file is printed, the low-resolution images are replaced with their high-resolution counterparts. These workflows aren't possible with the PDF/X-1a or PDF/X-3 formats, and so PDF/X-2:2003 has been proposed to address packaging and catalog production needs. The PDF/X-2:2003 specification is expected to become an ISO standard in the near future.

- **PDF/A.** Industries other than printing or publishing also see the value in creating standards for PDF to address specific needs and uses. Another standard on the horizon is PDF/A, which will address the needs of archiving documents. Enterprise and government organizations that require the ability to archive large amounts of documentation are interested in the PDF/A standard. Illustrator doesn't currently support the export of validated PDF/A files.

See "File Formats and Workflow," later in this chapter, for additional examples of when you would want to submit a PDF file using one the standards listed here. More information on PDF/X-1a can be found at www.pdf-x.com.

One way to do that was by providing designers with a detailed list of the settings they needed to use whenever they created a PDF file. Although this was a nice idea in concept, printers and publishers soon realized that designers use a variety of different programs, and each has a different ways of creating PDF files. They also realized that this meant that each time a new version of software was introduced, a designer would need to learn new settings.

Instead, an ISO (International Organization for Standardization) standard was created, called *PDF/X*. A PDF/X file is not a new kind of file format, but rather a regular PDF file that simply meets a list of predefined criteria. Now, when a designer submits a PDF/X file for final printing, a printer can assume that the file meets the minimum requirements to reproduce correctly.

By choosing a standard from the Standard setting pop-up menu in the Save Adobe PDF dialog, you are embedding an identifier within the PDF file that says, "I am a PDF/X-compliant file." Certain scripts and preflight utilities can read these identifiers and validate PDF/X-compliant files in a prepress or publishing workflow. See the sidebar "Understanding PDF Standards" for an explanation of the different kinds of PDF/X versions.

General PDF Settings

The General panel of the Save Adobe PDF dialog contains several important settings that determine how your PDF file is saved.

- **Preserve Illustrator Editing Capabilities.** The Preserve Illustrator Editing Capabilities option embeds a full native Illustrator file within your PDF file. This allows Illustrator to reopen and edit the file with no loss in editability. This option is turned on in the default preset, but turning this option off effectively cuts your file size in half and also reduces how long it takes to save a PDF file (**Figure 12.10**). If you want to send a file to a client for approval for example, you can turn this option off to create a smaller PDF file (which is also not as editable should they try to open it in Illustrator themselves). If you do turn this option off, make sure to always save a copy of your file, because you won't be able to reopen the smaller PDF and edit it as a fully editable file.

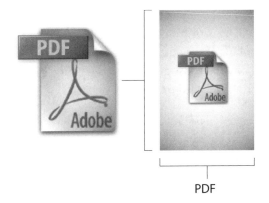

Figure 12.10 By turning off the Preserve Illustrator Editing Capabilities option, you can create a PDF file that is smaller and suitable for posting to the Web or sending via email.

PDF

- **Embed Page Thumbnails.** With the Embed Page Thumbnails option turned on, Illustrator creates thumbnails for each page. You can display these in Acrobat by choosing to view the Pages tab. Be aware that the thumbnails do increase the file size somewhat, however.

- **Optimize for Fast Web View.** Choosing the Optimize for Fast Web View option produces a smaller PDF file because all Illustrator symbols are converted to PDF symbols. Additionally, for multipage PDF files, those who view the file online can stream the PDF file, meaning they can view the first page while additional pages are still loading.

- **View PDF after Saving.** It's always a good idea to take a look at a PDF on your screen to make sure it's okay before you release it to a printer or to a client. Checking the View PDF After Saving option launches Acrobat and opens the file after the PDF file is created.

- **Create Acrobat Layers from Top-Level Layers.** If you choose to save your file with Acrobat 6 (PDF 1.5) or Acrobat 7 (PDF 1.6) compatibility, you can have Illustrator convert all top-level layers to PDF layers. You can view a document with PDF layers in either Acrobat or the free Reader, versions 6.0 and higher (**Figure 12.11**).

Figure 12.11 When a file is opened in Acrobat or Reader, a layer cake icon indicates that the document contains PDF layers.

- **Create Multi-page PDF from Page Tiles.** If you set up your document to use either the Tile Full Pages or the Tile Imageable Areas option in the Print dialog, checking this option creates a single PDF file with multiple pages. Each tile in your Illustrator document appears as a separate page in the resulting PDF file (**Figure 12.12**).

Figure 12.12 A document set up with Tile Full Pages (left) can be saved directly as a multipage PDF file (right).

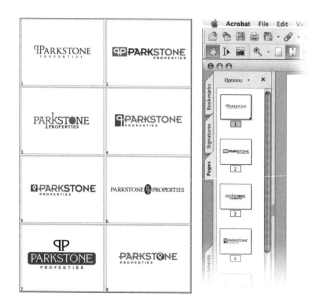

PDF Compression Settings

The Compression panel of the Save Adobe PDF dialog offers a variety of settings for compressing the images and art that appear in your file (**Figure 12.13**). One of the benefits of using the PDF format is that you can specify a variety of image settings for each need. For example, when you send a file to a client for review, you want to create a small file that transmits quickly via email and might set all images to resample at 72 ppi. However, that same file, when transmitted to the printer for final output, needs to contain high-resolution images, which you might set to at least 300 ppi.

When you create a PDF, Illustrator has the ability to resample an image. Resampling is a method used to change the resolution of a raster image. Although upsampling adds new pixels to a file, downsampling removes pixels from a file, resulting in a lower resolution and a smaller file size.

Obviously, downsampling an image results in loss in image detail and is therefore inappropriate for final output to a printer.

- **Resampling settings.** Illustrator can apply different settings to raster images that appear in your file, according to image type and resolution. You can specify these settings for color, grayscale, and monochrome bitmap images. More importantly, you can define a threshold for when images will be resampled. The Do Not Downsample option leaves images at their native resolution. Alternatively, you can choose from three different types of downsampling (Average, Bicubic, and Subsampling), which reduce the resolution of any raster images within your file according to the threshold settings. The first value is for the resolution that you want images to be downsampled to. The second value determines which images in your file get downsampled. For example, if you set the first value to 72 ppi and the second value to 150 ppi, then any image in your file that exceeds 150 ppi is downsampled to 72 ppi. However, if your file contains an image that's set to 100 ppi, that image is not downsampled and remains at 100 ppi because it falls below the threshold.

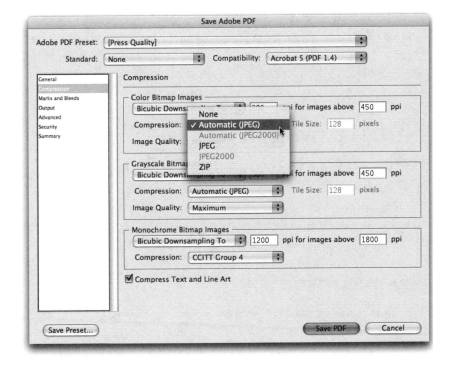

Figure 12.13 The Compression panel of the Save Adobe PDF dialog lets you determine which image types will be resampled as well as choose the compression method in which to do so.

- **Compression and Image Quality.** In addition to resampling raster images, PDF also uses compression techniques to further reduce the size of a file. Different methods are used for compression, or you can choose None to disable compression completely (see the sidebar, "Compress This").

- **Compress Text and Line Art.** To achieve smaller file sizes, check the option to compress text and line art. This uses a lossless method of compression and doesn't sacrifice quality in your file.

Compress This

Getting smaller file sizes comes at a cost. That cost is the quality of the image after it has been compressed. As we discussed in Chapter 10, *Illustrator and the Web*, there are two types of compression algorithms: lossy compression results in smaller files at the expense of image detail; and lossless compression, which doesn't make files quite as small, but loses no information in the process.

When saving PDF files from Illustrator, you can choose no compression, JPEG compression, JPEG2000 compression (both JPEG compression types are lossy), or the lossless zip compression method. When using lossy compression, you can also choose an image quality setting to control how much information or detail is lost in the compression process. The Maximum setting preserves the most information in the file, while the Minimum setting sacrifices quality for a smaller file size.

PDF Marks and Bleeds Settings

The Bleed settings that you specify here in the Marks and Bleeds panel define the bleed box value in the resulting PDF.

The Marks and Bleeds panel of the Save Adobe PDF dialog (**Figure 12.14**) is strikingly similar to the Marks and Bleeds panel that you'll find in the Print dialog. Here you can specify whether your PDF should have printer's marks and whether the document will have bleed space added. See Chapter 11 for detailed descriptions of these settings.

PDF Output Settings

The Output panel of the Save Adobe PDF dialog (**Figure 12.15**) gives you control over what color space your PDF is saved in, and whether you want to include image color management profiles within your PDF. Additionally, you can specify color-management settings for files that will be saved using one of the PDF/X standards.

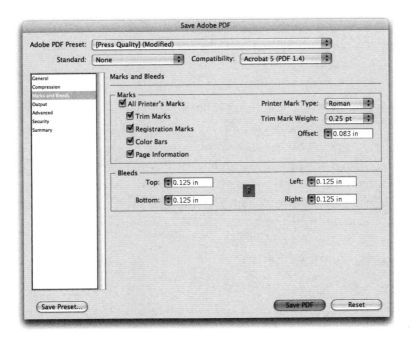

Figure 12.14 The Marks and Bleeds panel of the Save Adobe PDF dialog lets you create PDF files with crop marks automatically. Additionally, the Bleed settings makes it easy to turn bleed on or off depending on whom you are sending the PDF file to.

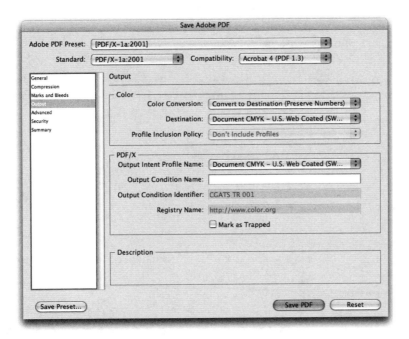

Figure 12.15 The Output panel of the Save Adobe PDF dialog gives you the ability to convert all objects to a specific color space. For example, when saving a PDF/X-1a file, any linked RGB images are converted to CMYK automatically.

- **Color.** When you create a PDF file, you can specify a color conversion for the file. In the Color Conversion pop-up, you can choose No Conversion, in which case the color values and color space will remain untouched, or you can choose Convert to Destination and choose from the Destination pop-up options to convert the color values or color space using a color profile of your choice. You can also specify when Illustrator will include color profiles in the PDF file.

- **PDF/X.** When you create a PDF/X file, you must specify a color profile intent; with PDF/X-1a, this is usually set to SWOP. You can also choose to mark the file as being already trapped, which is useful in workflows where trapping may occur in the RIP. If you trapped a file in Illustrator (either manually or via a plugin like Esko-Graphics' DeskPack), identifying the file as already trapped prevents the file from being trapped again in the RIP.

PDF Advanced Settings

The Advanced panel of the Save Adobe PDF dialog (**Figure 12.16**) allows you to specify how fonts are embedded in your PDF file and how transparency is flattened, if necessary.

Figure 12.16 The Advanced panel of the Save Adobe PDF dialog allows you to specify a Transparency Flattener preset when saving to PDF 1.3 (all other versions support live transparency).

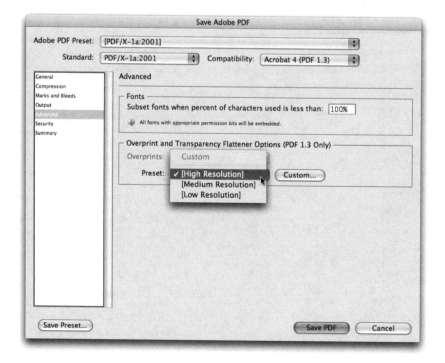

- **Fonts.** By default, Illustrator embeds subsets of fonts when saving a PDF file. A subset simply means that Illustrator only includes the parts of a font that are required to view and print the text you have in your document. If a font is protected, however, Illustrator does not embed the font. See the sidebar "Font Embedding and Permissions" for more information.

- **Overprint and Transparency Flattener Options.** If your document contains overprint settings, you can choose to preserve or discard them. Additionally, if your file contains transparency, you can choose a Transparency Flattener preset to control how the transparency is flattened. For more information on both overprinting and transparency, see Chapter 11. It's important to note that these two settings are only applicable when you're saving a PDF file with Acrobat 4 (PDF 1.3) compatibility because all other versions support transparency and don't require flattening.

Font Embedding and Permissions

Using fonts these days isn't the same as it was several years ago. Designer, meet lawyer. Lawyer, meet designer. There are some legal restrictions when it comes to using fonts, and depending on the licensing agreement that comes along with the fonts you own, you may be limited in how you can use your fonts.

Generally, a font can have two kinds of embedding permissions. *Preview and Printing* permissions give the owner of the font the rights to use the font in a design and distribute the file with the font embedded so that others may view and print the document as well. *Editing* permissions give the owner the same rights as Preview and Printing permissions, but others who receive the file with the fonts embedded may also make edits and changes to the file.

Even though most fonts posses one of these two permissions (which are specified in the font licensing agreement), they usually aren't enforced in any way. A font vendor expects a user to abide by the terms specified in its license agreement. For example, a font may have Preview and Printing permissions (the more stringent of the two settings), but you may still be able to embed that font in a PDF file. This means that someone using Acrobat Professional, or another product that can edit PDF files (including Illustrator), can make changes to the document, which would violate the license agreement.

To prevent unauthorized use, some font vendors protect their fonts by specifying that their fonts can't be embedded at all. These fonts are referred to as protected fonts. If an Adobe application encounters such a font, the application does not embed the font within a PDF file, honoring the rights of the font vendor. Obviously, if a designer is using a protected font and wants to send a PDF file with the fonts embedded to a publication, this can pose a problem. The only solution is for the designer to contact the font vendor and request an extended license, which allows the font to be embedded. Alternatively, you may be able to convert the text to outlines before saving the file.

Unfortunately, Illustrator doesn't offer any way to easily tell if a font is protected or not (InDesign does). Once you create a PDF, you can open the file in Acrobat and use the Document Properties setting to make sure your fonts are embedded.

PDF Security Settings

In today's world, security has become a priority—not only in airports, but with regard to electronic communications and documentation as well. One of the benefits of using PDF files is the ability to password-protect them so that you can control who can view or edit your file.

The Security panel of the Save Adobe PDF dialog (**Figure 12.17**) allows you to specify two kinds of passwords to protect the content of your PDF file.

Figure 12.17 The Security panel of the Save Adobe PDF dialog allows you to choose a password that will restrict how your PDF file can be viewed or printed.

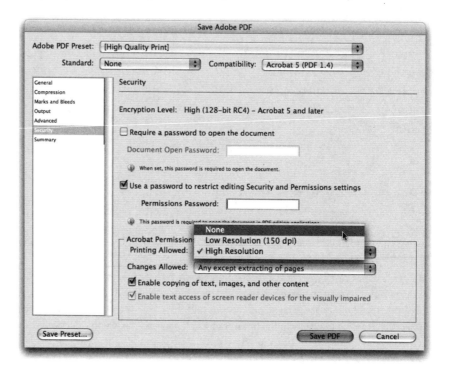

- **Document Open Password.** A document open password, also referred to as a master password, controls who can open your PDF file. If a user attempts to view the PDF, they are prompted for a password. Upon entering the password, the user is able to view the file. The file will not open if the password is incorrect.

- **Permissions Password.** A permissions password controls what a user can do with a PDF file once it is open on their screen. For example, a user who has the Professional version of Acrobat or a variety of Acrobat plugins, such as Enfocus PitStop, has the ability to edit a PDF file. Even if a file has a master password, once a user opens the file, they are free to do with the file as they please. By specifying a permissions password, you can restrict what a user can do with a file, even once they've opened the file in Acrobat Professional. For a detailed explanation of the different permissions settings, see the sidebar, "Did You Ask for Permission?"

Did You Ask for Permission?

Illustrator provides a range of permissions settings that give you control over the kinds of things a user can do with your PDF file once they've opened it. These options are found in the lower portion of the Security panel in the Save Adobe PDF dialog.

- **Printing.** Choosing None disallows the printing of your file. Users are able to view the file in its entirety on their computer screens, but their Print command is grayed out (**Figure 12.18**). Choosing High Resolution enables full printing of the file. When using a compatibility setting of Acrobat 6 or higher, you can also choose the Low Resolution setting, which forces all pages to print only as raster images at 150 dpi.

- **Changing/Editing.** Choosing None disallows all editing of your file. Users are able to view the file in its entirety on their computer screens, but all of Acrobat's editing tools are disabled. You can choose from four additional settings to restrict specific types of edits. For example, by choosing the Filling in form fields and signing setting, you allow users to fill out PDF form fields and to digitally sign the file, but this setting disables all other editing features.

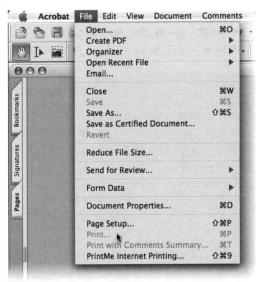

- **Copying.** If you want to prevent users from copying content from your PDF file and pasting that data into other applications, uncheck the option marked Enable copying of text, images, and other content. However, realize that by doing so, you may affect the accessibility of your document, especially for users who are visually impaired—who rely on screen readers to speak the content of files. These screen readers copy the text and paste the data into an application that reads the words to the user. When you check the option to enable text access to screen readers, Acrobat allows the copying of text if it senses that the application that's copying the data is a screen reader application. Additionally, you can enable a user to copy the metadata from a file.

Figure 12.18 If you use a permissions password to restrict printing, a user without the password is able to view the document, but is not able to print the PDF file.

The Scalable Vector Graphics (.svg, .svgz) Format

SVG is an XML-based file format that is used primarily on the Web and has recently become more popular in creating content for cell phones and handheld wireless devices. For more information about how SVG is used, refer to Chapter 10. The SVGZ format is simply SVG that is zipped (compressed).

SVG File Format Settings

A variety of settings are available in the SVG Options dialog, and depending on your needs for each particular workflow, you can make adjustments to these settings. Click the More Options button in the SVG Options dialog to see the full list of available settings (**Figure 12.19**).

- **DTD.** The DTD (Document Type Definition) setting is akin to the version of SVG that your file is compatible with. Because SVG is an open standard, additional specifications are revised and approved. If you save an SVG file with a particular DTD, it means that your file will be compatible with any device that supports that DTD. Newer specifications usually support additional functionality than the older ones did. SVG Tiny (also referred to as SVG-t) is a subset of SVG used for displaying content on SVG-enabled cell phones. SVG Basic is a subset of SVG used for displaying content on PDAs.

For more information on the SVG specification and SVG-enabled cell phones, visit www.svg.org.

- **Fonts.** When text is present in your file, you can specify Adobe CEF type, which results in better-looking text when your file is viewed with the Adobe SVG Viewer, but may not be supported with other SVG viewers. The SVG creates more compatible text, but text that may not be as readable at smaller font sizes. Alternatively, you can convert all text to outlines, which increases file size.

- **Images.** When you save a file in SVG, you have the ability to embed any images within the SVG file (making for larger, but self-sufficient files), or you can choose to create smaller SVG files by using the Link option.

- **Preserve Illustrator Editing Capabilities.** The Preserve Illustrator Editing Capabilities option embeds a full native Illustrator file within your SVG file (**Figure 12.20**). This allows Illustrator to reopen and edit the file with no loss in editability. This option is unchecked by default, but turning this option on effectively doubles your file size. If you do leave this option off, make sure to always save a copy of your file because you won't be able to reopen the SVG file and edit it as a fully editable file.

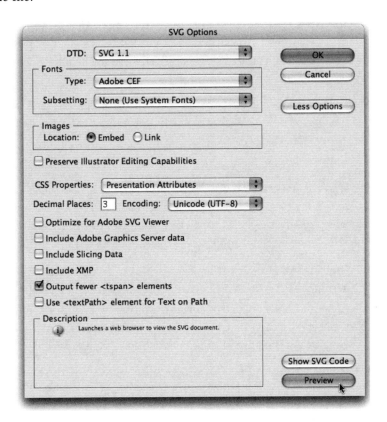

Figure 12.19 Illustrator's SVG Options dialog offers a variety of settings that allow you to fine-tune SVG files, including a Preview button that launches a web browser so that you can see the file before you save it.

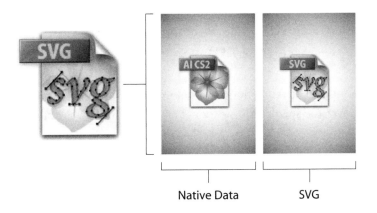

Native Data   SVG

Figure 12.20 Similar to a PDF file, Illustrator can embed a native version of the file within an SVG document to assure editability when the SVG is reopened in Illustrator.

- **CSS Properties.** There are a variety of ways to format SVG code, and the CSS Properties settings allows you to determine how object attributes are coded within the file. For the most part, this setting affects the performance of your file when viewed.

- **Decimal Places.** Illustrator allows you to specify how precisely vector paths are drawn. You may choose a value from 1 to 7, where higher numbers result in better-looking paths at the expense of file size and performance.

- **Encoding.** When you save an SVG file that contains text, you can specify a character encoding, including ISO-8859-1 (suitable for European languages), and 8- or 16-bit Unicode (suitable for more complex languages).

- **Optimize for Adobe SVG Viewer.** If people will be using the Adobe SVG Viewer to view your SVG files, you can check this option, which will take advantage of proprietary optimizations that exist in the Adobe SVG Viewer, including faster rendering of SVG Filter Effects.

- **Include Adobe Graphics Server data.** If you've defined variables within your Illustrator file (using the Variables palette), checking this option includes those variables within the file. This enables access to variable content when the SVG file is used as a template with Adobe Graphics Server, or via Java or ECMAScript otherwise.

 For more information on Adobe Graphics Server, visit www.adobe.com/ products/server/graphics/ main.html.

- **Include Slicing Data.** If you've specified web slices and optimization settings in your Illustrator document (using the Slice tool or the Object > Slice > Make function), checking this option preserves the slice information in the file, making it available to other applications, like Adobe GoLive CS2.

- **Include XMP.** Checking this option includes XMP metadata with the file, specified in the File > File Info dialog. This results in a larger file size.

- **Output fewer <tspan> elements.** This option, on by default, helps create smaller files, although at the risk of text shifting slightly. If you notice errors in the way the text is displayed in your final SVG file, try turning this option off.

- **Use <textPath> element for Text on Path.** If your document contains text on a path, you can turn this option on to use the <textPath> function in SVG to display that text. Otherwise, Illustrator writes each character as a separate <text> element in your file, making for a larger (although more precise) SVG file.

- **Show SVG Code/Preview.** Clicking either of these buttons launches a web browser and allows you to preview the code and the file itself before you save the file.

EXPORTING FILES FROM ILLUSTRATOR

Illustrator is a robust application that supports a wide range of file formats. Although Illustrator does a great job in opening just about any graphic file format, it can also export files in different file formats for a plethora of uses. To export a file from Illustrator, choose File > Export and then choose from one of the many formats listed in the pop-up in the Export dialog. Each of these formats are listed in the following pages, with descriptions of their settings as well as when you might want to use them.

Remember that when exporting, it is expected that some level of formatting or editability will be lost, so always save a native Illustrator version of your file first before you export to another format.

The Bitmap (.bmp) Format

Bitmaps are raster-based files and are often used in older computer applications. The bitmap format is also used by some applications for displaying logos or barcodes.

When exporting a bitmap, you can choose one of three different color models: RGB, Grayscale, or Bitmap, which creates a file that contains only black and white pixels (**Figure 12.21**, next page). Additionally, you can specify the resolution for your image and choose whether or not to antialias the art.

Figure 12.21 Many applications (including Illustrator and QuarkXPress) allow you to change the color of a bitmap file that uses the Bitmap color model.

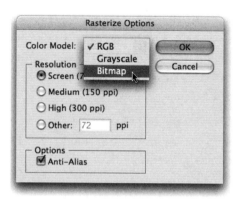

The Targa (.tga) Format

The Targa file format is a raster-based image format used mainly in video applications. For example, you might use the Targa file format to add Illustrator artwork as masks in Adobe Premiere.

When exporting a Targa file, you can choose one of two color models: RGB or Grayscale. Additionally, you can specify the resolution for your image and choose whether or not to antialias the art.

The Portable Network Graphic (.png) Format

The PNG file format (pronounced "ping") was originally formed as an open standard format to replace the need for the GIF image file format, due to legal complications with those who developed the compression technology used in the GIF format.

As you learned in Chapter 10, you can also create PNG files from Illustrator using the Save for Web feature. However, the PNG format also appears as an export format because the Save for Web feature is hard-wired at 72 ppi. To export a PNG file at any other resolution, you need to use the PNG export function.

The PNG format is a raster-based image format, and is used for web design, icon and interface design, and as a general image exchange format.

In fact, Apple's Tiger operating system (Mac OS X version 10.4) creates a PNG file when you take a screen shot. PNG files can support 24-bit color, but more importantly, the format also supports 256-level alpha channels for transparency, meaning that you can give images soft edges that fade to transparent (unlike the GIF format, which supports one-color transparency only).

When exporting a PNG file, you can specify the resolution for your image as well as the background color. You can choose a transparent background or you can choose Other to select a color from the Color Picker (**Figure 12.22**). Additionally, you can choose to turn on antialiasing and interlacing.

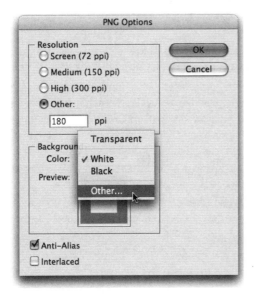

Figure 12.22 You can specify any color as a background color for a PNG file, including transparency.

The AutoCAD Drawing (.dwg) and AutoCAD Interchange File (.dxf) Formats

The DWG and the DXF file formats are both used for exchanging files with CAD applications. These formats can be especially helpful when you want to send Illustrator artwork to architects, interior designers, or industrial designers. Both formats support vector and raster elements.

 If you need some of the functionality that CAD applications have, you might look into the CAD tools plugin from Hot Door, available at www.hotdoor.com.

Exporting Art for Use in Microsoft Office Applications

One of the most difficult things to do is create artwork in a professional design application (such as Illustrator) and have that same artwork display and print reliably in a business application, such as Microsoft PowerPoint. Finding the right file format for this workflow is difficult because JPEG images don't support transparent backgrounds and EPS files don't display well on screen. In addition, EPS files require the use of a PostScript printer, which most business professionals do not have access to.

After much research, the folks on the Adobe Illustrator development team discovered that the PNG format was perfect for placing art from Illustrator into Microsoft Office documents. Because the format supports transparent backgrounds and displays beautifully on computer screens, a PNG file set to a resolution high enough to also print well results in a great way to get great-looking art in Office documents.

To save time and make it easier to quickly export a file from Illustrator to use in Microsoft Office, choosing File > Save for Microsoft Office. Illustrator saves your file as a PNG file set to 150 ppi with antialiasing turned on. Once you've created the PNG file, you can place it into any Microsoft Office application by choosing the Insert Picture function from Word, Excel, or PowerPoint (**Figure 12.23**).

Due to a bug in the Macintosh version of Microsoft Office, transparency in a PNG file does not appear correctly at the default view setting (it does appear correctly when viewed in full-screen mode and when printed). For this reason, the Save for Microsoft Office command sets the background color to white instead of transparent. If you are placing your art into Microsoft Office for Windows, you can create a PNG with a transparent background by using the PNG Export function.

Figure 12.23 To place a PNG file into a Microsoft Office document, choose Insert > Picture > From File and locate the file on your computer or server.

When exporting a DXF or a DWG file (they both use the same export dialog; **Figure 12.24**), you can specify the version of AutoCAD you want your file to be compatible with, and the number of colors in the resulting file. If there are raster elements in your file (or if vector elements need to be rasterized), you can choose to have them embedded as either bitmap or JPEG files).

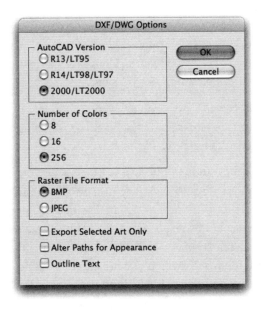

Figure 12.24 Illustrator uses the same export options dialog for both DWG and DXF formats.

Additionally, you can choose to export only the artwork that you currently have selected on the artboard. Choosing Alter Paths for Appearance modifies paths, if necessary, so that they appear when opened in a CAD application. Additionally, you can outline all text to avoid the need to send fonts.

The Windows Metafile (.wmf) and Enhanced Metafile (.emf) Formats

The Windows Metafile and Enhanced Metafile formats were developed to move graphics between applications on the Windows platform. Both formats support both vector and raster elements but are severely limited with regard to the kinds of art they can reliably display and print (EMF is slightly better). Both formats can only create straight vector lines, not curved ones. To make up for this, curved lines appear as numerous tiny straight paths, which results in large files with many anchor points. If possible, avoid using these formats for anything other than simple artwork. There are no additional options or settings that you can specify when exporting WMF or EMF files.

The Macromedia Flash (.swf) Format

SWF is a popular Web-based file format that supports both vectors and rasters. The Flash file format has become extremely popular because of its capability to contain interactive or animated content. You can use Illustrator to generate a SWF file that you want to upload directly to a Web site, or to create art for import into Macromedia Flash (the application), for further editing.

The Macromedia Flash (SWF) Format Options dialog was completely revamped for Illustrator CS2 and contains "just a few" options for creating the SWF files that are right for you (**Figure 12.25**).

- **Export As.** You can export Illustrator files in one of three ways: AI File to SWF File, which creates a single SWF file that contains all of your Illustrator artwork; AI Layers to SWF Frames, where each layer is converted into a key frame, resulting in a single animated SWF file; and AI Layers to SWF Files, where each layer in your Illustrator document is exported as a separate SWF file (useful when you are creating Flash scenes). Additionally, you can generate HTML along with your SWF file (which you can display directly or copy and paste into an existing HTML page), and you can choose to close the file so that others can't open the SWF file by choosing Protect from Import. The Clip to Artboard Size forces Illustrator to ignore the artwork bounding box and uses the size of the artboard as the size of the file. Additionally, you can convert all text to outlines (so no font files are necessary) and you can make the file size smaller by choosing the Compress File option. The Background Color setting gives you the ability to set the color that appears behind the SWF file when it displays in a Web browser (if the file is not rectangular in shape) and the Curve Quality setting controls the fidelity of curved paths.

- **Method.** When using transparency or other special effects in Illustrator, you can choose to Preserve Appearance, which flattens any effects as necessary, or you can choose the Preserve Editability Where Possible option if you plan on opening the file in Macromedia Flash in order to edit it. This way you can make additional tweaks to the artwork if you need to.

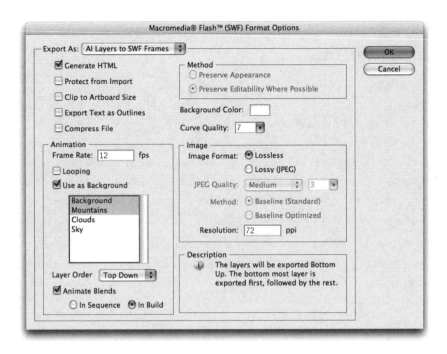

- **Animation.** If you choose the AI Layers to SWF Frames option, all layers in your Illustrator file become keyframes and play as an animation when the SWF file is viewed in a web browser. The Frame Rate setting controls the speed at which the animation plays (you can't control the timing of individual frames like you can in a GIF animation), and the Looping option forces the animation to repeat continuously. You can check the Use as Background option to choose a layer (or layers) that appears in each frame of the animation and you can choose a Top Down or Bottom Up layer order, which determines if your animation plays forward or backward. If you've defined blends in your Illustrator document, you can choose to animate those blends using the Sequence or Build options.

- **Image.** If there is raster content in your file (or if flattening requires that content becomes rasterized), you can choose how those images are stored in your SWF file—either using a lossless format or a lossy format. If you choose the lossy format, which is JPEG, you can set how the JPEGs are saved and at what resolution.

For an in-depth discussion of how you can create great SWF files, including adding interactive hotspots and animations, refer to Chapter 10.

The Joint Photographic Experts Group (.jpg) Format

An extremely popular raster-based format, JPEG files are used mainly for exchanging photographic content and artwork. Although the JPEG format is used heavily in Web design, it is also the format of choice for the electronic delivery of stock photographs and for digital cameras. One of the reasons why JPEG is used for these tasks is because the JPEG format can take advantage of compression algorithms that can dramatically reduce file size. For example, a high-resolution image that is normally 10 MB in size might be only 1 MB in size when saved as a JPEG.

However, the JPEG format utilizes a lossy compression algorithm, and sometimes a JPEG file may exhibit artifacts or loss in detail due to this compression (**Figure 12.26**). A lower compression setting enhances image detail, at the cost of a larger file size.

Figure 12.26 When saving a file as a JPEG, using the Maximum setting results in a file with fewer artifacts, but doing so also results in a larger file size.

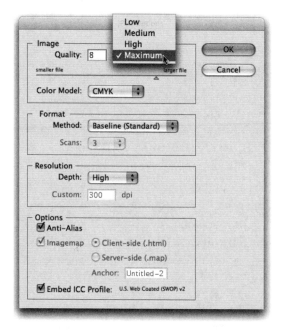

Although you can save JPEG files from Illustrator's Save for Web feature, you can only do so at 72 ppi. Using the JPEG Export function, you can specify a custom resolution for your file, which allows you to create high-resolution files.

Besides choosing an image compression level for your file, you can also specify the RGB, CMYK, or Grayscale color model. Format methods determine how the image appears when viewed in a web browser. If you choose the Baseline setting, the image loads completely and is then displayed at full resolution. The Progressive setting (similar to interlacing) allows the image to appear immediately at a lower quality setting; it then appears in full quality once the entire image is loaded (the number of scans determines how many passes are done until the final image is previewed).

Illustrator also gives you the option of antialiasing the art, embedding a color profile, or including a client-side or server-side image map. Refer to Chapter 10 for more information on how to define image maps and the differences between client- and server-side image maps.

The Macintosh PICT (.pct) Format

Much like the WMF and EMF formats, the PICT format was developed to move files between applications on the Macintosh platform. The format supports both vector and raster elements. There are no additional options that you can specify when exporting a PICT file.

The Adobe Photoshop (.psd) Format

As you learned in Chapter 8, *Mixing It Up: Working with Vectors and Pixels*, you can export an Illustrator file as a Photoshop file and preserve vital information in the file. This makes it easy to start work on a design piece in Illustrator and then bring it into Photoshop to add the finishing touches. Bringing Illustrator art into Photoshop or ImageReady is also useful when you're creating art that you plan to use for Web sites. In this way, you have high-quality artwork in Illustrator that can easily be repurposed for print, and you can add rollovers and interactivity using Photoshop and ImageReady for the Web site.

When exporting a PSD file, you can choose between CMYK, RGB, and Grayscale color models, and you can specify a resolution for your file. If you choose to export a Flat Image, all Illustrator layers are flattened into a single non-transparent layer (what Photoshop calls the Background layer). Alternatively, you can choose the Write Layers option, which preserves Illustrator's layering where possible (**Figure 12.27**). You can also choose to preserve text and other native elements, like compound shapes and Web

 Refer to Chapter 8 for an in-depth analysis on moving files between Illustrator and Photoshop.

slices (see Chapter 8 for a complete list of the attributes that can be preserved between Illustrator and Photoshop).

Figure 12.27 By choosing to write layers, you gain the ability to export a file that preserves live text, layers, transparency and mask effects, and more.

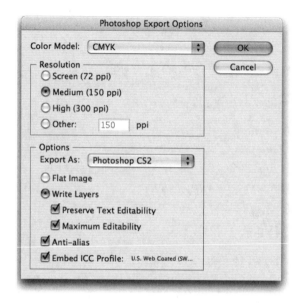

The Tagged Image File Format (.tif)

The TIFF format is widely used in graphics applications. Completely raster-based, a TIFF is a lossless image format. High-resolution files can be quite large, but image integrity is maintained. TIFF files are generally supported by print, video, and 3D rendering applications.

When exporting a TIFF, you can choose from one of three different color models: RGB, CMYK, or Grayscale. Additionally, you can specify the resolution for your image and choose whether or not to antialias the art. Checking the option to use LZW Compression results in a smaller file (the compression is lossless). You can also specify a platform-specific byte order (for better compatibility with Windows systems), and you have the ability to embed color profiles when you're working in a color-managed workflow.

Text Format (.txt)

Sometimes you just need to export the text in a file so that you can use it in another application or for another purpose that Illustrator itself can't handle.

You can export text to be compatible with a specific platform, or you can export text in Unicode, which is platform independent.

CHOOSING FILE FORMATS ON WORKFLOW

There are so many different file formats that it's often difficult to know which one to use for each situation. Of course, every workflow demands special attention and there are always exceptions and special cases. However, for the most part, there are certain rules that you can follow, now that you really understand what each file format is capable of.

Print Workflows

When working in print workflows, designers traditionally use page layout applications like QuarkXPress or InDesign, utilizing file formats such as EPS and PDF.

Traditionally, EPS is used for moving files from Illustrator into page layout applications. However, with the ability to use transparency effects in your Illustrator files, the limitations of EPS become apparent. For example, as a designer, you know that Illustrator creates vector-based files that can be scaled infinitely because they are resolution-independent. You have always been able to save a file as an EPS from Illustrator, place it into an application like QuarkXPress, scale that artwork at will, and never worry about resolution or the quality of the resulting printout.

However, as you learned in Chapter 11, the process of transparency flattening may convert some vector content in your file into raster images, which are resolution-dependent. Because an EPS contains flattened information, you can't assume that an EPS file can be scaled infinitely in a QuarkXPress layout anymore. In fact, you have to think of an EPS file from Illustrator as you would an EPS file saved from Photoshop—you need to limit how much you can enlarge a graphic.

Although this is only a concern when your file contains transparency effects, keep in mind that there are many effects in Illustrator that you can apply that introduce the need for flattening (these are discussed in detail in Chapter 11).

On the other hand, native Illustrator files (which contain PDF 1.4 by default) have the ability to preserve live transparency, and therefore, flattening doesn't occur. When you save your file as a native Illustrator file, you can still scale that file infinitely, after it has been placed into a page layout application. But there's a catch—you need a page layout application that can flatten that transparency when it prints your file. That means Adobe InDesign. Refer to **Table 12.2** for a list of suggested file formats, based on the page layout application that you're using.

Table 12.2 Suggested File Formats

Application	When Transparency Is Present	When Transparency Is Not Present
QuarkXPress	EPS, PDF/X-1a (PDF 1.3)	EPS, PDF/X-1a (PDF 1.3)
InDesign	Native AI, PDF 1.4	EPS, Native AI, PDF 1.4

Web Workflows

Although QuarkXPress can place PDF files, it can't correctly process PDF files that contain transparency within them. To avoid nasty printing issues, always place PDF/X-1a files into Quark, never into native Illustrator or PDF 1.4 files.

Choices are much easier to make for Web designers. Not because there are any fewer file types to choose from, but mainly because the use of file types is usually dictated by the technology that is being used. For example, if you want to create animated content, you know you're using a GIF file or a Flash file. Some sites are restricted as to what kinds of formats are supported (for example, not every Web browser can display SVG files), and so a designer is usually at the mercy of technology when it comes to deciding on a file format.

However, much can be done to a file before a final GIF or JPG is created. Therefore, you may find it beneficial to create your artwork in Illustrator, and then export it as a Photoshop file, which you can then edit and work on in other applications, like Photoshop, ImageReady, or even Adobe GoLive or Macromedia Dreamweaver.

Other Workflows

Of course, there are other workflows, including video, industrial design, architecture and engineering, fashion design, environmental design—the list goes on. With the information you now have about what each file format is used for, you should be able to develop a workflow that works for you.

Automation with Illustrator

With today's "need it now" mentality, we've been thrust into an era where deadlines and delivery dates are shorter than ever—at the same time, we're being asked to perform twice as much work. If you take a moment to read just about every press release and marketing document produced by companies in the high-tech industry, you'll find promises of faster performance and higher productivity with each new software release. Even hardware items, like the TiVo and the Apple iPod, speak of our need for on-demand content.

The good news is that Adobe Illustrator supports several techniques for streamlining workflow through automation—in essence, you can have Illustrator do all of the hard work for you while you take a few moments to grab some lunch (but who takes lunch anymore?).

TAKING ADVANTAGE OF AUTOMATION IN ILLUSTRATOR

Although automation may sound like a scary technical word, it doesn't have to be. Illustrator supports automation via two methods:

- **Actions.** This feature within the Illustrator application contains a set of recorded steps that can you can reproduce by clicking a button. For example, an action may contain the steps necessary to select all text objects in an open document and rasterize them at a specific resolution. Actions are simple to record and don't require any code writing knowledge. However, not every feature in Illustrator is actionable, so there's a limit to what an action can do.

- **Scripting.** Scripting is essentially a programmatic way to interact with an application. Instead of clicking with a mouse or punching a few keys on your keyboard to control Illustrator, you use a script—a set of commands that instructs Illustrator what to do. Because these commands can contain math and logic, a script can create artwork based on variables. For example, a script might draw a graph in which numbers above a certain amount appear in black and lower numbers appear in red. Most of Illustrator's functionality is available through scripting (significantly more so than with Actions), but to use scripting, you do need to know a scripting language. Illustrator supports AppleScript (Mac), Visual Basic (Windows), and JavaScript (cross-platform) languages.

In this appendix, we'll explore these two automation methods as they pertain to Illustrator, and hopefully, this will serve as inspiration for you learn more about automation.

Actions

Recording an action is very simple and straightforward in Illustrator; playing back an action is even easier. To access the list of preset actions via the Actions palette, choose Window > Actions. The 22 actions in Illustrator are grouped within the Default Actions set. In addition, you can also create your own sets and actions.

To create a new set and an action within it, follow these steps:

1. Choose Window > Actions to open the Actions palette (**Figure A.1**).

2. Click the Create New Set icon at the bottom of the Actions palette. Give your set a unique name and click OK.

3. Click the Create New Action icon at the bottom of the Actions palette. When you do, Illustrator prompts you to name the action you're about to record. Choose the set that you just created, and if you'd like, choose a function key so that later you can perform the Action using a keystroke. When you're done, click OK.

4. At this point, you'll notice that the red recording icon at the bottom of the Actions palette is highlighted, indicating that recording has begun. Perform the steps that you want to record in Illustrator.

   You can see each step being added as a line item to your action as you perform it. If a step doesn't appear in your action, it is probably because the function you performed is not actionable.

5. Once you have completed the steps for your action, click the Stop Recording button. At this point, the action is complete.

To play back your action—or any other one—highlight it in the Actions palette and click the Play Current Selection button. If you assigned a keystroke to your Action, you can play it back by pressing the correct key combination on your keyboard.

To apply Actions with a single click, you can activate Button mode in the Actions palette. Choose Button Mode from the Actions palette menu.

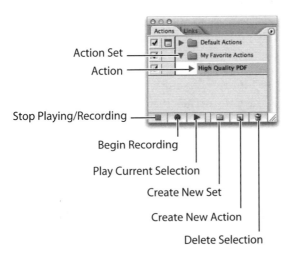

Action Set
Action
Stop Playing/Recording
Begin Recording
Play Current Selection
Create New Set
Create New Action
Delete Selection

Figure A.1 You'll find the Default Actions in the Actions palette. You can create your own sets as well.

Scripting

Illustrator can be scripted using AppleScript, Visual Basic Scripting, or Java-Script. Actually, Illustrator uses a language called ExtendScript, which is an Adobe flavor of JavaScript. You can find resources for this language, such as scripting dictionaries and samples scripts, in the Adobe Illustrator CS2 > Scripting folder.

In general, ExtendScript is used to drive functionality within the application itself. For example, an ExtendScript script might be used to reverse the direction of a selected vector path. In contrast, AppleScript or Visual Basic scripting can be used to drive functionality that uses different applications. For example, an AppleScript script might pull data from an external file or from the Web, use that data to generate a graphic, and then export that graphic in a specified format and email it.

Illustrator includes a PDF entitled "Getting Started with JavaScript," which is a wonderful resource for those of you who want to learn more about scripting in Illustrator.

Each of the sample scripts included with Illustrator either contain separate PDF files describing how the script works or comments embedded directly within the script. You can open and view a script using a script editor or any text editing applications, such as BBEdit, TextEdit, or TextPad.

AUTOMATION AND RELEASING FINAL FILES

Sending a file off to a print service provider for final printing comes with the anxiety of not knowing if everything in the file is okay and if the printed results will come back as you envision them. A good designer knows that sending a file that's free of problems, and that includes all of the necessary support files, is critical to success.

Using some of the automation features we mentioned earlier in this appendix, along with some sample actions and scripts that ship with Illustrator, you can make it a whole lot easier to release final files.

Cleaning Up Messy Files

When you create a new Illustrator file, any swatches, brushes, symbols, and graphic styles that are present in the Illustrator Startup file (located in your

Plugins folder) are added to the new file. Even if you never use these items to create artwork, your file contains this extraneous material. It's also normal for you to add and remove elements as you are working on a design concept. When it comes time to release a final version of your artwork, all of these extra elements are still present.

Although in theory there's nothing wrong with having extra items in a file, experience tells a different story. In such cases, files can become corrupt, or art elements can be accidentally changed. In addition, a file with unused swatches or symbols can add to confusion if a printer needs to edit the file as it goes to press. These extra and unnecessary elements also bloat file size, causing longer save and open times.

Once a file has been deemed final, you can quickly remove all unused items using one of Illustrator's preset Actions. With the Illustrator document open, choose Window > Actions to open the Actions palette. From the Default Actions set, click the one named Delete Unused Palette Items and then click the Play button at the bottom of the palette.

Generating a List of Used Items

It's always helpful to provide your print service provider with as much information as possible about any file that you are sending. Some designers print out a list of all of the files used; others mark up printouts with callouts and swatch chips.

Illustrator can help save time with a script called Analyze Documents, which is installed by default in the Sample Scripts > AppleScript (Sample Scripts > Visual Basic Scripts) folder. You can run the script by simply double-clicking it. The script prompts you with a dialog asking you to identify a folder that contains Illustrator files. The script works on multiple files at one time. The Analyze Documents script then opens each file in the selected folder and generates a new document that lists every font, gradient, spot color, and placed image used in all of the files.

The new file that is created is called DocumentReporter.ai, and it can be formatted to your specification once the script has finished running.

Collecting Necessary Support Files

One of the most requested features for Illustrator is a command that collects all place-linked images and fonts, making it easy to send a file and all necessary support files so that someone else can work on or print the file.

Although Illustrator doesn't have a Collect for Output feature like Quark-XPress or a robust Package command similar to that found in InDesign, Illustrator does ship with a script called Collect for Output, which you can find in the Sample Scripts > AppleScript (Sample Scripts > Visual Basic Scripts) folder. If you think you will use this script often, you might consider placing a copy in the Adobe Illustrator CS2 > Presets > Scripts folder. That way, the script will appear in the File > Scripts submenu within the Illustrator application.

Upon running the Collect for Output script, Illustrator copies the open Illustrator file and all place-linked images into a new folder on your desktop. Unfortunately, the script won't collect fonts, although you can use the Analyze Documents script mentioned earlier to generate a list of fonts that are used in your document to assist in collecting the fonts you need manually.

APPENDIX B

Moving from FreeHand to Illustrator

Believe it or not, this appendix was initiated several weeks prior to the bombshell announcement of Adobe's proposed acquisition of Macromedia. This announcement and possible merger don't change anything. Regardless of what happens with either Macromedia FreeHand or Adobe Illustrator moving forward, you will continue to benefit from your FreeHand expertise. As an already proficient FreeHand user who now desires to get up to speed in Illustrator, you are also about to find yourself ahead of the game when it comes to moving toward program versatility.

Do not look to this appendix for a global pronouncement as to which of the two applications is better. The answer to that question depends upon another: "Better at what?" It would be a wonderful thing to take the best treatment of each feature from each program (and if we did, we would have to include some features from CorelDRAW, Corel Designer, and Deneba Canvas in the mix) and combine them into one ideal vector-based commercial illustration program. Don't count on that happening anytime soon, though.

As a final assurance, before you dive in head first, know that this appendix is written to help you learn a new tool. Its tone is unbiased and your expertise is assumed, and more importantly, respected. This section assumes an intermediate-level proficiency with FreeHand.

GETTING YOUR FEET WET

Despite the initial bewilderment you deal with when faced with a new program, you'll soon find that your FreeHand experience proves advantageous in Illustrator. If you are proficient with FreeHand, you already have a conceptual understanding of the principles of vector drawing.

The key to quickly achieving a matching proficiency in Illustrator is to try to discover the underlying behavioral principles. Don't worry so much about locating each and every specific tool or command. Even if you find the tool you're looking for, you might find that it doesn't seem to work correctly, or that it seems frustratingly backward or illogical. When this is the case, run a mental check on the underlying principle and do a little experiment off to the side to boil down the essential issue; you'll find that you are merely struggling with a different interface layered on a familiar principle. At this point, you will begin to see your "adversary" in its true smaller perspective, and you will feel much less overwhelmed.

This is the strategy we'll employ in the following pages. Rather than memorizing a dizzying catalog of specific commands, you will use the understanding of basic vector path principles that you already possess and then figure out the way Illustrator "thinks" as you go.

The overall goal here is to give you, the already-experienced FreeHand user, a boost over that initial frustration hump so that you can get on with exploring the myriad features found throughout the rest of this book.

Understanding Features vs. Understanding Principles

When trying to adapt to a program that is supposed to be so functionally similar to one we already know, many of us make a basic assumption and commit a basic error: We tend to think it is just a matter of finding corresponding commands and memorizing their locations. We get frustrated when we find out it isn't quite as simple as that.

This naive assumption leads to nasty surprises and confusion, especially when two programs are so similar in purpose—and even general design—as FreeHand and Illustrator.

What we fail to consider is that even if the "equivalent" command we seek is present, it may operate according to a different set of givens—a different set of underlying principles of behavior. In fact, as you shall see in a moment, even the mere *location* of a command may cause it to act quite differently what we'd expected based upon years of experience and habit in another program.

Comparing Underlying Similarities

First, take a deep breath and rest assured that the basic paths, points, and handles that make up Illustrator's vector paths are the same objects as those you are accustomed to creating and manipulating in FreeHand. Both programs draw Bézier paths. As in FreeHand, the following are true for Illustrator:

- Paths are either open or closed and can be filled and/or stroked.

- Paths are connected by, or end at, anchor points.

- All paths have an inherent "direction," and, even if closed, they have a start/end point.

- Points are either corner anchor points or smooth anchor points (there is no Connector Point in Illustrator).

- Smooth anchor points have two direction handles each, which can be individually extended or retracted to affect the shape of their associated segments.

So the basic building blocks of Illustrator vector objects are practically identical to those in FreeHand. It follows, then, that the basic things that you can do with paths are also very similar:

- You can combine multiple paths into *composite paths* (called *compound paths* in Illustrator) to create shapes with holes in them.

- You can group multiple paths (with or without other objects) so that you can manipulate them as a unit.

- You can use paths as masks for other paths (a *clip path* in FreeHand is called a *clipping path* in Illustrator).

- Stacks of paths can be automatically generated to give the appearance of smooth color and/or shape transitions (called *blends* in both programs).

- You can add or subtract paths from each other to create new paths (via Combine operations in FreeHand and Pathfinders in Illustrator).

But even while you are performing the same kinds of operations upon the same kinds of objects, there are some differences. Each command can employ a different method of accomplishing its purpose, can present the user with a different set of parameters, and can exist within a different organizational scheme than those of the more familiar program.

Conceptual Differences: Working with Color

To both illustrate and emphasize the above conceptual gibberish, we'll start with what may be a mildly startling example. What could be more basic than the simple matter of selecting and applying a fill color to a path? Surely this process is practically identical in both programs? Well, let's see.

FreeHand and Illustrator both have the expected Color palette, where colors are mixed, (called the Color Mixer palette in FreeHand) and the Swatches palette, where defined colors are stored. Colors, of course, can be applied to either strokes or fills. So far, so good. But there's a not-so-subtle difference, which makes *all* the difference: In FreeHand, the Fill/Stroke indicator resides in the Swatches palette, whereas in Illustrator, it resides in the Color palette.

This is just an organizational thing, but one with confusing consequences. In FreeHand, because the Fill/Stroke indicators are in the Swatches palette, it doesn't matter if a path is selected while you adjust the mixer sliders; the path is unaffected (**Figure B.1**). But in Illustrator, where the Fill/Stroke icons are right there in the same palette as the mixer, the selected object's color changes as you drag the sliders (**Figure B.2**). You're not just mixing a color; you're mixing a color and applying it to a fill or a stroke at the same time, and you'd better be aware if anything is selected, because whatever is selected will change in color.

Figure B.1 FreeHand: The Fill/Stroke icons are not in the Color Mixer palette. Changing values does not affect the selected objects because you are mixing a color that is not necessarily yet a swatch, fill, or stroke.

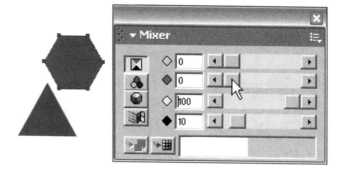

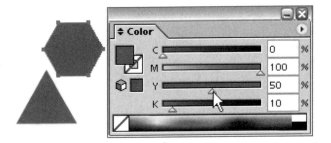

Figure B.2 Illustrator: The Fill/Stroke icons are right there in the Color palette. Changing values affects selected objects because you are adjusting a color that is either a fill or a stroke.

So you see? Just knowing where to find the corresponding Fill/Stroke toggles within the two programs doesn't really help you understand the program. You have to examine the underlying principles—the ramifications—of what that change of location entails before you come to grips with that nagging confusion you feel when you're mixing and applying colors.

Can one method be called right and the other wrong? Probably not. It can be argued that the FreeHand approach encourages you to define color swatches before you actually apply the colors to objects. On the other hand, the Illustrator approach enables something you may not discover even after years of working in the program. Suppose you have two (or more) objects selected. Each has a different fill color, but they both share a particular component value (say, they both have a 10% K component). In such a situation, the slider handle and value appear only for that common component in Illustrator's Color palette. You can adjust that component for all the selected objects in a single move (slide the K slider to 20%, and you have darkened both selected paths by 10%) (**Figure B.3**). If the value of a particular component differs across the selected objects (say one contains 10% C and another contains 5% C), you can equalize them in one move by entering a value for that component. (Enter 15% in the C field; the other components remain unaltered.)

 FreeHand has a similar capability in its Color Control Xtra. But here also, the organization principle is different between two "corresponding" features. The sliders in this dialog start at zero and add the value(s) you enter there to the present values of each selected object.

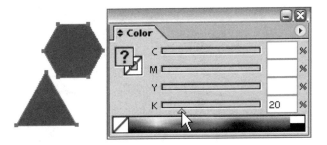

Figure B.3 The treatment in Illustrator means you can adjust a shared component of all selected objects at once without affecting the other components.

A Word of Encouragement

Many years of engrained habit can be difficult to reprogram, but don't sell short that marvelous analog computer between your ears. Many (no, not all) of the difficulties that seem so awfully tedious at first are short-lived. You will undoubtedly find yourself pleasantly surprised that after the initial frustration, somewhere fairly early along the way, the mental bells will go off about the underlying principle involved ("Of course! The selection is affected when I mix colors! The Fill/Swatch selectors are right there in the Color palette!"), and you will stop stumbling over this difference.

FIRST STEPS: LEARNING THE USER INTERFACE

You've just arrived, switched off the ignition, grabbed the suitcase, walked up the porch steps, and swung open the door. Already you can see that the floor plan and decor is rather different than the place from which you came. Go ahead, step inside and flip on the switch.

Multiple Pages, Where Art Thou?

The basic document environments for FreeHand and Illustrator are so similar it hurts. Why this pain? Because the environment in Illustrator is almost identical to FreeHand 3, before the multiple page capability was added. In those days, both programs framed a single page within a very similarly sized (within inches) Pasteboard workspace. FreeHand's page was placed at the lower left and when resized, it grew toward the upper/right (**Figure B.4**). The page in Illustrator was (and still is) placed in the middle of the Pasteboard and when resized, it grew (grows) from the center out (**Figure B.5**).

Both programs conform to the math and engineering convention of having the zero point of its coordinate grid located at the lower left corner of the page. Because the Artboard (page) in Illustrator is always centered in the Pasteboard, be sure to check the alignment of the ruler origin after changing the page size. Do this the same way you do it in FreeHand: double-click the rulers origin—the box where the left and top rulers meet at the upper left of the document window.

Figure B.4 FreeHand's Pasteboard is a little over 224 inches square. The default first page is near the lower left corner. Pages grow upward and toward the right.

Figure B.5 The Pasteboard in Illustrator is a little over 227 inches square. The single artboard is in the center and grows from the center outward.

As for Illustrator's single-page per document limitation, you will occasionally encounter references to workarounds and/or plug-ins that invariably resort to either page tiling or using Layers to imitate multiple pages.

Of course, FreeHand can also tile pages and show/hide layers, and the Free-Hand user will find these workarounds quite unsatisfying substitutes for the real thing. To date, there is no real answer. Illustrator CS2 enhanced the tiling workaround by enabling page tiles to be saved as individual pages in a single PDF file (refer to Chapter 12, *Saving and Exporting Files*).

Working With Rulers, Grids, and Guides

With Illustrator, you can choose between points, picas, inches, millimeters, centimeters, and pixels, and value read-outs in palettes will change accordingly the next time a selection causes them to update. But other scales in FreeHand, such as decimal inches, are not offered, and you cannot create custom scales such as 1"=10' and have value fields reflect the scale accordingly.

The Grid in Illustrator works similarly to FreeHand's, but it offers the option for displaying it as lines of dots like FreeHand, or as lines. A more significant difference is that the Grid in Illustrator rotates with the Constrain angle preference setting.

 Various factors in Illustrator, including the lack of an adjustable pick-distance setting, cause snap to feel less sure in Illustrator, and FreeHand users who rely heavily upon snaps find this a shortcoming. Smart-Guides (see Chapter 7, *3D and Other Live Effects*) goes a long way toward overcoming this problem by providing object snapping behaviors similar to FreeHand's Snap To Object, and also interactive remote object and point alignment while drawing, which Free-Hand lacks.

Guides are also similar to FreeHand's, except that in FreeHand they extend across the page, whereas in Illustrator they extend to the bounds of the entire Pasteboard. As in FreeHand, Illustrator's unlocked guides can be released (View > Guides > Release Guides) to turn them into ordinary paths, and ordinary paths can be turned into Guides (View > Guides > Make Guides). One handy little difference between Illustrator's Guides and FreeHand's is that in Illustrator they snap to your ruler tick marks if you press Shift, whether you have Snap To Grid on or not.

Where's the Inspector?

FreeHand's Object palette (which many FreeHand users still refer to as the Object Inspector) is like a one-stop shop for info on and settings for the current selection. The closest counterpart to this in Illustrator is the Appearance palette, and it is also probably the most important palette to have always handy.

The Appearance palette, like FreeHand's Object palette, is where you find the stack of strokes, fills, and effects that are applied to the current selection. The Appearance palette also displays some of the specific information about the items in that stack; for example, the weight of a stroke appears within its listing.

Beyond that, however, the similarity begins to break down because of this important difference: Although the Appearance palette in Illustrator is where you can *view* the stack of strokes, fills, and effects, it is not where you *edit* them, and in the case of effects, not where you apply them. You can add strokes and fills using the Appearance palette menu, but to adjust their parameters, you still must go to various other palettes. As in FreeHand, you can apply effects to individual strokes or fills, but you select them from the Effects menu, not from the Appearance palette.

For example, consider a simple path with a basic appearance (one stroke, one fill). If this object is selected in FreeHand, the item stack lists the stroke and its weight. Likewise, if an identical object is selected in Illustrator, the stroke and its weight is one of the items listed.

However, in FreeHand, if you then select the stroke listing itself, all of its particular settings and options appear at the bottom of the Object palette. For example, the stroke's type, weight, cap, join, dash, arrowhead, and overprint settings appear, and they are editable right there in the Object palette (**Figure B.6**).

Figure B.6 In FreeHand, the settings for the selected object's attributes are presented in the bottom of the Object Properties palette as contextual screens that display according to which item in the attributes stack is selected. All four of these screens are displayed at the bottom of the single Object palette.

Not so in Illustrator, although the first step is similar. To modify that stroke's options in Illustrator, you first select its listing in the Appearance palette. But to change its weight, dash, caps, and joins, you must still visit the separate Stroke palette. To apply an arrowhead to it, you call up the Add Arrowheads dialog from the Effects menu; to set it to overprint, you visit another separate palette named Attributes; to turn the stroke into a Brush, you visit the Brush palette; and so on (**Figure B.7**).

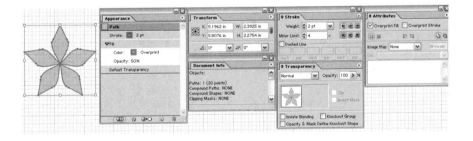

Figure B.7 Although the Appearance palette in Illustrator is similar to the Object palette in that it provides a stack of strokes, fills, and effects and displays some of their settings, and although the detail settings are sensitive to which item is selected in the stack, the actual settings reside in individual separate palettes. Ready access to all of these palettes is necessary in order to make all the settings represented in the previous view of FreeHand's Object palette.

So although the Attributes palette is one that you need to keep upfront and handy as you work, it is not at all the kind of comprehensive centralized object settings palette to which you are accustomed in FreeHand. Hunting around for specific settings is one of the primary causes for disorientation among FreeHand users. You have to get back into the mindset of individual palettes for each type of setting, which was more the nature of FreeHand's early versions prior to the arrival of the Inspector-based interface.

You might logically expect Illustrator CS2's new Control palette to be the centralized counterpart to FreeHand's Object palette. But although it does provide more immediately convenient access to some of the most frequently needed settings, it never presents them all.

By the Numbers

Value fields in FreeHand palettes and dialogs accept and retain numerical values to six decimal places, whereas Illustrator displays four. Under the hood, every measure in Illustrator is converted from its underlying native measure of 72 points per inch. This, combined with the four-decimal display, often leads to what the FreeHand user sees as disconcerting numerical inaccuracies in value fields. For example, if like many users, you've memorized the decimal equivalent of 1/16th as .0625, and then you enter ".0625/2" in a value field, the displayed result will be .0313, not .03125. This does not mean that Illustrator did not make your object .03125 in width. It only rounded the value for the sake of the display in the palette. However (and unfortunately), if you then enter "*2" after the displayed value to double the object's measure, Illustrator recalculates the entire expression, which is now keyed into the field, with a result of .0626 instead of restoring the previous .0625. Does a thousandths of an inch inaccuracy matter? You decide.

Walk This Way: Working with Objects

Differences exist between the way FreeHand and Illustrator let you know what is selected, and this can be quite disorienting. In FreeHand, the edges and points of selected simple paths display. All other objects, such as groups, compound paths, live special shape objects (ellipses, rectangles, etc.), blends, and clip paths display four corner handles of their bounding boxes when selected in their entirety. These handles are usually used to scale the object by dragging.

Illustrator highlights selected simple paths in the same fashion. But that's also how they display regardless of whether they are part of a group, a compound path, or even if they are masked by a clipping path.

This is particularly disconcerting in regard to clipping paths because the edges of the entire clipped contents display, not just the portions inside the clipping paths (**Figure B.8**).

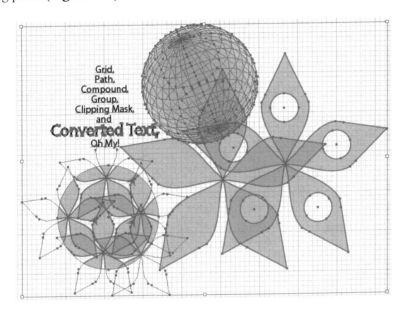

Figure B.8 Complex objects such as compound paths, clipping paths, and groups, highlight the edges of their subparts or contents when selected. It takes a little getting used to.

In Illustrator, you can choose View > Hide Edges when you need to reduce the visual clutter (for example, text objects converted to paths easily become an indistinguishable mass of displayed points). Be aware, however, that if you have Hide Edges on, the selection is not displayed at all if you are working with the Direct Selection tool, because the bounding boxes in Illustrator do not display when working with that tool. Even when you're working with the normal Selection tool, looks can be quite deceiving as to what is actually selected because the bounding box displays around the entire selection, not each object. Therefore, only use the Hide Edges command for momentary toggle on/toggle off purposes, not as a normal working mode.

Using Marquee Selections

Generally speaking, when you drag with FreeHand's pointer, it selects whatever you fully enclose with its dashed-line selection marquee. The Selection tool in Illustrator, on the other hand, selects whatever its selection marquee touches—even objects that partially fall within the marquee area—and this takes considerable getting used to. Which is best? That depends upon the specific circumstances (you could have guessed that).

Actually, upon closer examination, the comparison here is not really all that simple. For example, if you drag a selection marquee using Illustrator's Direct Selection tool (the white-filled pointer), its behavior is very similar to that of FreeHand's Pointer when it is dragged across several simple paths. In both cases, the paths become highlighted, but only the points that were enclosed become selected.

Similar, of course, does not mean identical: Dragging across only segments of simple paths (but enclosing no points) with FreeHand's Pointer selects nothing. The same is true of FreeHand's Subselect tool. In contrast, with Illustrator, the same action of dragging across segments selects the whole path(s) with the Selection tool and selects the crossed-over segments with the Direct Selection or Lasso tool.

So here we have a situation in which *neither* of FreeHand's tools select *anything*; yet *both* of Illustrator's "corresponding" tools select *something*. No wonder users feel like astronauts on a foreign planet when learning the "other" program.

It's best to get this selection behavior mentally nailed down before you progress very far into work with Illustrator. Spend a little time drawing some simple shapes, dragging across them with both selection pointers, and trying to anticipate what will be selected when you release the mouse.

A typical situation in which this difference is particularly bothersome is when you're trying to lasso a few points of paths that overlap other paths. Remember: The selection marquees in Illustrator select whatever they touch. Well, in both Illustrator and FreeHand (these days), a segment is a selectable item. So in FreeHand, you can lasso the cluster of points without also selecting the overlapping path. That is, crossing over segments of the unwanted path does not select them, because the segments are not fully enclosed by the marquee; you just have to be careful not to fully enclose any points of the unwanted path.

This is not the case in Illustrator. If you have to cross over a segment of an unwanted path in order to select points in its interior, doing so selects the unwanted path's segment, which is touched by the marquee. At first, the FreeHand user is inclined to think that Illustrator wants to select segments more than FreeHand does. But the real principle at play here is Illustrator's convention of selecting whatever a selection marquee touches.

Applying Transformations

Illustrator provides a collection of transform tools similar to those in Free-Hand. However, their basic use differs. In FreeHand, the invisible center of transformation is normally set where you first click with the tool. You then drag away from this point to transform the current selection.

In Illustrator, when you select a transform tool, the origin point is at the center of the selection, and it is a visible icon that you can move to where you want it. After you position the origin point, you can click and drag away from it to transform the selection. Initially, the FreeHand user can find this difficult to control for two reasons:

• The FreeHand user wants to habitually mouse down with the transformation tool and immediately start dragging. You can do this in Illustrator, but if you do, the transformation will be centered wherever the origin marker is—at the center of the selection when you first select the tool. Instead, after selecting the desired transform tool, give a full mouse down/mouse up click where you want the transformation centered. Then move the cursor some distance from the marker and begin your drag.

• In Illustrator, the rate at which the transformation occurs is proportional to the nearness of your cursor to the transformation origin when you begin the drag. Therefore, you have finer control over the amount of the transformation if you begin your drag some distance from the position of the origin marker. The principle is similar to FreeHand's Rotation tool, with which a temporary guide appears when you mouse down. If you drag along this guide before beginning your rotation, you have finer control. The difference is that this principle works similarly on all of Illustrator's transformation tools, not just the Rotate tool.

You can use Illustrator's Effect > Distort & Transform > Transform effect to replicate the behavior of FreeHand's Mirror Xtra. Because this is an Effect, the result remains editable until it is nailed down into individual objects by choosing Expand > Appearance. Also, be sure to explore the Transform Each command in Object > Transform > Transform Each, described in Chapter 4, *Advanced Vectors*.

Text Objects

Unlike FreeHand, Illustrator has two separate object types for text objects that auto-expand horizontally and those that wrap. A Point Type object is similar to a FreeHand text object that is set to auto-expand, and you usually create it in the same way—simply click (don't drag) with the Type tool.

An Area Type object is one that is contained within a frame, similar to a FreeHand text object that is not set to auto-expand in either direction. Again, the customary creation routine is the same—drag with the Type tool.

For the full run-down on text handling, see Chapter 6, *Typography*, but here are a few specifics that commonly befuddle FreeHand users:

- In Illustrator, you can't set an Area Type object to auto-expand vertically. You have to become especially careful by looking for the red text overflow icon.

- There is no explicit command for separating Path Type from its path once it has been attached. You can copy the text and paste it into an ordinary text object, or you can use the Direct Selection tool to select and modify the path. However, if you delete it, you will delete the whole Path Type object.

- For type on a path, FreeHand's feature by which a return character wraps the following text to the opposite side of the path is unique to FreeHand. There is no corresponding feature in Illustrator. Creating the common text-around-the-top-and-bottom of a circle treatment requires two type-on-a-path objects (**Figure B.9**).

Combining Paths (Pathfinders)

Be sure to explore carefully and methodically the Pathfinder features in Illustrator. These are analogous to FreeHand's Modify > Combine operations, but you will find many unfamiliar behaviors within them.

In Illustrator, some Pathfinder operations result in compound shapes, which can be non-destructively edited until they are "expanded" into literal new paths. In the Pathfinder palette, these are the four in the top row of icons. Ironically, despite their "live" nature, these are among the functions that will feel most familiar. The behaviors of the first three (Add, Subtract, Intersect) pretty much correspond to FreeHand's Union, Punch,

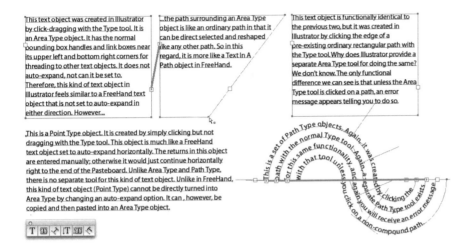

Figure B.9 Illustrator distinguishes between Area Type objects, which do not auto-expand, and Point Type objects, which do. These two cannot be directly turned into one another by changing their auto-expand characteristics as is done in FreeHand. Path Type objects are much like FreeHand Text On A Path objects. There are separate tools for all three (plus the vertically oriented versions of Area and Point). But all three (Point Type, Area Type, and Path Type) can be created with the normal Type tool.

and Intersect commands. The fourth (Exclude) results in something similar to what you achieve in FreeHand when you join several paths into a composite, where overlapping areas become voids.

You will no doubt find some of the other Pathfinders to be less intuitive in the details of their results. Several remove strokes and/or unfilled open paths in the process of performing their shape combinations. For example, Illustrator's Divide behaves similarly to FreeHand's Divide if at least some of the paths are closed. However, Illustrator's Divide creates closed paths around areas surrounded by open paths, whereas FreeHand's Divide is not available to selections of only open paths. This can be an often-advantageous difference (**Figure B.10**).

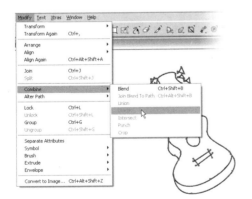
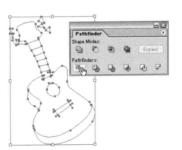

Figure B.10 FreeHand's Combine>Divide command does nothing with this object because there are no closed paths (left). In contrast, Illustrator's Divide creates closed paths around visually enclosed areas resulting in paths you can quickly stroke and fill (right).

The Merge Pathfinder in Illustrator also behaves somewhat similarly to FreeHand's Divide, but it deletes strokes and leaves the selection unaffected if none of the paths are filled (closed or not). But it also does more, and Merge is one of the Pathfinders that gives the FreeHand user new and important capabilities. It removes underlying parts of overlapping fills and simultaneously welds areas of contiguous color (**Figure B.11**).

The bottom line here is for the FreeHand user to just be aware. Pathfinders are indeed intended for the same general purposes as FreeHand's Combine operations, but the devil is in the details. The differences are too numerous and dependent upon specific circumstances for an exhaustive comparison. Be sure to give Chapter 4 a thorough study, and set up simple experiments in which you try to anticipate the results. You'll not only avoid a lot of unexpected confusion, but you'll also find a few "new" gems that you can employ to your advantage with a little ingenuity.

Figure B.11 Illustrator's Merge Pathfinder can remove the overlaps and weld the areas of contiguous color, quickly resulting in paths more suitable for practical purposes such as cutting from sign vinyl.

Working with Composite Paths (Compound Paths)

A FreeHand composite path is functionally the same thing as an Illustrator compound path, with one rather shocking difference: The individual paths of an Illustrator compound path do not have to be closed. That's right. Draw two curved open paths with a stroke, but no fill. Select them both and choose Object > Compound Path > Make. Now use the Direct

Selection tool to select and apply a fill to one of the paths. Both curves receive the same fill, because they are, in fact, one single compound path.

FreeHand users may find it initially distracting and occasionally confusing that Illustrator displays the edges of all the subpaths of a selected compound path. Sometimes this makes it difficult for you to recognize that a selected path is part of a compound path. You see, in FreeHand, you typically click a composite path to select it, and seeing its four corner handles clues you in to the fact that it is a composite or a group. You then deliberately Option (Alt) click to "dig into" the composite and select one of its subpaths. In Illustrator, though, you will more often be using the Direct Selection tool. When you click a compound path, the Direct Selection tool goes ahead and selects the subpath, and therefore you may not realize that it is compounded with other paths.

Another related oddity worth mentioning here is the fact that certain features that FreeHand users would associate only with open paths, such as arrowheads, also apply to closed paths in Illustrator. You are probably aware of the fact that even a closed path still has a direction and a start/end point. But if you apply an arrowhead to a closed path in FreeHand, the arrowhead doesn't appear unless the path is cut or opened. This is not the case in Illustrator; the arrowhead appears at the start/end point of the closed path, and on each subpath of a compound path.

HEALTHY JOGGING: DRAWING AND EDITING PATHS

As in FreeHand, productive and efficient drawing with the Pen tool in Illustrator involves frequent movements of anchor points and direction handles as you proceed. And this is where the FreeHand user stumbles. Surprisingly, the stumbling block is not so much due to Pen tool differences, but more because of Illustrator's fundamentally different approaches toward tools, the simple matter of selection, and the definitions of parts of a path.

Proficient FreeHand users draw paths efficiently by repeatedly switching back and forth between two basic operations: adding segments with the Pen, and adjusting the paths, segments, points, and handles with a selection tool. This oft-repeated process involves the Pen and the Pointer.

Proficient Illustrator users do the same thing—alternately adding segments and selecting subparts of the path—but doing so involves more tools. Depending upon the habits you develop in Illustrator, it can involve the Pen, the Selection, the Direct Selection, the Group Selection, and the Convert Anchor Point tool.

In addition to dealing with the more numerous individual tools in Illustrator, the FreeHand user must simultaneously adapt to a reversal of "selection direction" as he manipulates paths and their subparts. As we'll see, for a number of reasons intrinsic to the principles of its interface, Illustrator's path selection moves generally from deeper to shallower (or, specific to general) as opposed to FreeHand's shallower to deeper (general to specific) approach.

Furthermore, the common selection routines in Illustrator are described as more segment-oriented whereas FreeHand's are more decidedly points-oriented. To the FreeHand-accustomed user, it is much like learning to drive a manual transmission *and* to back a trailer *at the same time*. Understandably, it is at first a very disorienting endeavor, requiring conscious effort with every turn of the wheel, every slip of the clutch. But after a little studied practice at a few narrow boat ramps, it becomes a natural mind shift. Let's examine these underlying differences more closely to help you avoid launching your car into the lake.

Multiple Tools, Not Multiple Clicks

You've heard it said (and probably said it yourself) for years: FreeHand does with one selection tool what Illustrator requires two for. We wish it were that simple. If you take nothing else away from this discussion, be sure to get this one down pat: Illustrator does with *individual tools* what FreeHand does with *consecutive clicks* of a single tool. This deceptively subtle difference is at the very core of much of the frustration and confusion you feel while drawing paths in Illustrator.

In FreeHand, consecutive clicks on the same part of a path with the same selection tool dig deeper, enabling you to manipulate the path's subparts. For example, the first click of the Pointer directly on a segment of an unselected path selects the path. Another click selects the segment (**Figure B.12**).

This does not occur in Illustrator. A tool change—whether you make it by actually picking a different tool or by momentarily invoking it with a modifier key—is required to select at a different "object depth." The net result is that drawing paths with the Pen tool in Illustrator involves more tools (**Figure B.13**).

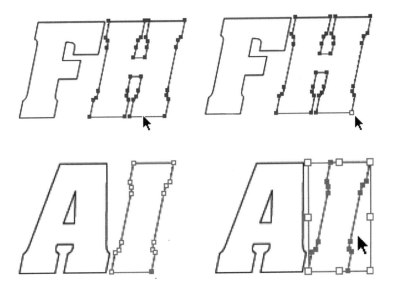

Figure B.12 In FreeHand, click once with the Pointer to select the path; click again to subselect a point.

Figure B.13 In Illustrator, the Direct Selection tool goes right to the point (or segment, depending on where you clicked the path). You can click all day long with the black Selection tool, but it will never direct select a subpart of the path. (Modifier keys can switch you to the other pointer, but we'll get into that later.)

Here's a little history: From its beginning, and for most of its years, Free-Hand had but one selection tool (the black Pointer). To select a path, you clicked it with the Pointer. Then, to select a point on that path, you clicked again on the point. Then, to select a retracted handle "within" that point, you pressed Option (Alt) to tell the pointer to "dig deeper still," and then you simply dragged it out. (If both handles were retracted, the first one dragged out was the outgoing handle; this was followed by the incoming handle if you dragged again).

Meanwhile, Illustrator had its *two* pointers: The "normal" black-filled Selection tool was primarily for selecting whole objects and their bounding boxes. The white filled Direct Selection tool was primarily for selecting the subparts of paths—points and segments.

Then, in version 9, FreeHand acquired its own hollow pointer, the Subselect tool. This was a direct accommodation to the habits and expectations of Illustrator users. But there was a fundamental difference. FreeHand's Sub-select tool did not actually *add* any functionality. Anything that it could select could still be just as easily selected with the original black Pointer, and most experienced FreeHand users simply ignored the new tool (and most still do to this day). In still later versions of FreeHand, certain esoteric responsibilities have been assigned to the Subselect tool to help it earn its keep (having to do with new features, such as the special control handles of the live basic shape objects). This is a quite recent development, and we dare say that all but newcomers to FreeHand still ignore the Subselect tool except for those new feature purposes. And regardless, the fact remains that both the Pointer and the Subselect tool in FreeHand can select all parts of a path—segments, points, or handles.

The salient point here is this: While you are drawing paths in FreeHand, you only need one selection tool working in conjunction with the Pen. In Illustrator, that is not so. This in turn involves the memorization of more (and more complicated) keyboard shortcuts to switch between the more numerous tools.

You will hear some long-time Illustrator users claim to rely entirely upon Illustrator's Direct Selection tool and to absolutely never ever use the "normal" black one. That may or may not be true, but the fact is, if you only use the Direct Selection tool in Illustrator, certain very common selection conveniences (such as those associated with bounding-box related manipulations) will be sacrificed. And if you *do* ever use the black Selection tool, its mere existence can get in the way while you are drawing paths. Further complicating matters, a third "selection" tool is required for accessing retracted handles, as we shall examine momentarily.

"Soft" Mode Change vs. "Hard" Tool Switch

You may remember that when FreeHand acquired its Subselect pointer, the various cursor icons were shuffled, too. The long-established Option (Alt) keyboard modifier of the Pointer now changes the cursor icon to that of the newfangled Subselect pointer. But this is a fairly recent development, and it represents only a visual change, not a functional one. Because the actual behavior is the same as before the extra pointer appeared, many, if not most, FreeHand users still think of the Option (Alt) modifier as a momentary mode change of the current tool (reinforced by the fact that the same key is used to make similar mode changes for other tools), not as a hard switch to an entirely different tool.

In Illustrator, although some of the modifier key presses are indeed momentary, both the general interface and the facts of the matter just discussed result in the opposite sensation. The user impression is more often that of making an actual switch to a different tool. The FreeHand user new to Illustrator struggles with reconciling this difference when a behavior he is trying to understand as a mode change turns out to be an actual change of tools.

"Bottoms Up" Selection

Press the Direct Selection tool in Illustrator's main Toolbox to extend its flyout palette, and you'll see another one with a plus sign (+) next to it. That's the Group Selection tool. As we've seen, pressing Option (Alt) when Illustrator's Direct Selection tool is in hand does not invoke the Convert Anchor Point tool to allow you to dig deeper and drag out a handle. Instead, pressing Option (Alt) momentarily switches to that mysterious third pointer, the Group Selection tool, which digs shallower, not deeper. That is, it selects the whole path.

Note that the same modifier key, Option (Alt), is used in both FreeHand and Illustrator to change the depth of the primary selection tool. But as we've now seen, the depth change is in opposite directions. Add to this what we now know about Illustrator's two pointers. For most FreeHand users, the primary selection pointer is the black one. For most intermediate-to-advanced Illustrator users, the primary selection tool is the hollow one.

This is of much greater significance than merely the color of the pointer. In practice, it translates to this: In FreeHand, the customary selection routine starts with the black pointer in hand, and subsequent clicks, sometimes augmented with modifier keys, generally progress from *general to specific* (object to path to point to handle). In Illustrator, the more common "advanced" selection routine starts with the Direct Pointer in hand. As soon as you make the first click with this tool on a path at which you are already at the deepest level; the point or the segment you clicked is already selected. Sequential clicks using modifier keys, progress from *specific to general* (point or segment to path to group). Note that this is different even from the behavior of Free-Hand's Illustratorish Subselect pointer. The first click of an unselected path with FreeHand's white pointer does not subselect the segment; you click again to do that.

So to review: How do you select a whole path when you have the Direct Selection tool in hand? Press Option (Alt) and click the path. This momentarily invokes the Group Selection tool, telling Illustrator to select up a level to the whole path. In fact, if the path happens to be part of a group or a compound path, another click with the Group Selection tool selects up to the group or compound object level.

Understanding Path Handling Conventions

Here is a list of some of the behavioral differences you'll encounter. Some are conceptually puzzling at first, and these we will explore more fully shortly. Others are merely differences in interface conventions:

- Selected points in Illustrator are displayed as solid; unselected points are displayed as hollow—exactly opposite of the default in FreeHand. However, in both programs, if a whole path is selected, and none of its points are selected, then all points are displayed as solid. (In this detail, Illustrator's convention seems more logically consistent.)

- FreeHand displays selected corner points as hollow squares and selected curve points as hollow circles. Illustrator displays both curve and corner points identically; there is no visual clue as to the type of point selected other than the orientation of its handles.

- A double-click of the Pen does not end a path in Illustrator. To end the current path, you have to deselect it (or click to close the path). Press the Command (Ctrl) key to momentarily invoke a Selection tool and click the page in a non-object location; or press the keyboard shortcut for Deselect, Command-Shift-A (Ctrl-Shift-A).

- In Illustrator, pressing Delete when a point is selected does not merely remove the point; it removes the point *and its associated segment(s)*. Therefore, if you select one point of a closed path and press Delete, you delete the point and the two segments on each side of it, resulting in an open path. If you select a point of an open path and the point is not an endpoint, pressing Delete deletes the point and the two adjacent segments and results in two separate paths. If the point you deleted happened to be only one segment removed from an end point of the path, you still have two separate paths even though the segment next to the endpoint is removed. The endpoint itself is left behind as a "Stray Point"; this behavior is why Illustrator is much more susceptible to the stray point malady than is FreeHand.

- In Illustrator, if you select a point and copy it to the clipboard, not only is the point copied, but also its associated segments. This can be a useful thing. For example, selecting the bottom point of an ellipse is a frequently used method to begin drawing a cylinder. Making this kind of selection, followed by Cut and then Paste In Front, is also a commonly used method for cutting a path.

- When clicked on a segment of an unselected path, the Direct Selection tool selects the segment, not the whole path. (Remember, bottom-up selection.) If the segment has at least one of its associated handles extended, those handles display, letting you know you have selected the segment. However, if the selected segment has both of its associated handles retracted (it is a straight segment) *there is no visual indication* that the segment is selected. Dragging the segment moves it and its associated points, even though the two points are not displayed as selected. If such a selected segment has either of its handles extended, however, dragging it bends the segment. Its associated points do not move, but the extended handle(s) will.

- Subselecting a segment in FreeHand automatically selects its associated points. But in Illustrator, direct selecting a segment selects only that segment's *handles.*

By now it should be abundantly clear that, despite the facts that Illustrator and FreeHand create and manipulate the same kinds of paths and that corresponding tools and commands (often even with the same names) can be found, performing even the most common tasks can require quite different thought processes. Clearly, the conventional wisdom approach of merely searching for and locating corresponding tools is not the path to Illustrator proficiency, but to Illustrator frustration. When commands so basic as pressing the Delete key yields such radically different results, the feature-by-feature details of it all are too numerous to memorize by rote. You have to concentrate on discovering Illustrator's different set of underlying principles and learn to think the way Illustrator does.

Whenever you encounter one of those frustratingly unexpected results, take a moment to move over to the side of the Artboard, draw a simple path, and perform the operation on it until you understand what is going on. Taking a little time to do that pays off big.

Deleting and Adding Points

As we've seen, merely selecting a point and pressing Delete does not delete just the point, but its associated segment(s) as well. Consequently, Illustrator does not provide a way to eliminate a bunch of selected points at once without simultaneously breaking the paths by removing segments.

Similar to FreeHand, Illustrator Pen tool has an auto-add and auto-delete behavior. Unlike Freehand, and in keeping with Illustrator's propensity toward tools, tools, and more tools, the cursor icons that appear when you're using this feature are actual separate tools—the Add Anchor Point tool and the Delete Anchor Point tool live in their own slots in the Pen tool's cluster in the main Toolbox.

When the auto-add and delete setting is on, it only affects selected paths— usually the one you are drawing at the time. If several paths are selected, adding or deleting a point on one deselects the other paths.

Merging Paths

You've drawn an open path with the Pen and deselected it in order to start a new path, which you know will have a different stroke weight, color, or other attribute. You want the new path to snap to and begin at the same place where one of the pre-existing paths starts or ends. When you click, Illustrator assumes that—even though the pre-existing path is not selected—you don't mean to start a new path, but you want to continue adding segments to the existing one.

Illustrator provides a clumsy workaround for this. To prevent this dyslexic mind-reading behavior of the Pen, mouse down somewhere beyond the snap distance of the pre-existing path's end, press the Spacebar, drag the cursor to the endpoint, and only then mouse up. Then continue placing the points of your new path.

Joining and Closing Paths

Inexplicably, after all these years, Illustrator still does not allow you to select a bunch of open paths and issue a Join command to connect them end to end. To join paths in Illustrator, you must direct select the endpoints to tell Illustrator which ends of the paths you want connected, and you must do this two points at a time.

Mentioned in Chapter 4, Rick Johnson's Concatenate plug-in allows you to join multiple paths at once in Illustrator.

This can be very tedious. Often, if the two ends you are trying to join are in close proximity, dragging a selection marquee around the endpoints is easier than Shift-clicking them individually. However, if there are additional points near either of the endpoints, you will direct select them also and the Join command will fail with an annoying dialog. (Check the Don't Show Again button and thereafter you'll just get a system beep when a Join command doesn't work.) Illustrator's Join command is also used to close an open path, but again, it only works on one path at a time.

Selecting Through Objects

Illustrator provides no less than three different ways to select objects underneath others, and unfortunately none of them works as quickly or simply as FreeHand's keyboard modifier that allows you to cycle through the objects under the cursor.

In Illustrator, Ctrl-click (right-click) to invoke the contextual menu and you'll find options for Select Next Item Above/Below. Similar commands are in the Select Menu and are available as keyboard shortcuts. The operative word here is "similar," because the menu and keyboard methods do not select the next/previous object where you clicked, but *in the object stacking order*, regardless of where it appears in the document.

Cutting Paths

Illustrator's Knife tool (it's grouped with the Scissors tool) works much like FreeHand's (drag for freeform cuts; Option (Alt) drag for straight cuts) with one crippling exception: It fails to cut open unfilled paths. This makes it useless for common tasks such as neatly trimming off a bunch of roads at the border of a map. For cutting open unfilled paths, you must resort to other means, such as tediously clicking each path with the Scissors tool.

Note that the failure affects *unfilled* open paths. This is initially confusing to FreeHand users because the Knife will indeed cut across an open path if it is filled, and as we've already noted, Illustrator allows open paths to have fills, contrary to most FreeHand experience.

Also, be careful not to confuse the Knife tool with the Slice tool, which is used for making image slices for optimizing web-based images. The Slice Tool icon looks more like an Xacto knife.

Cloning

There is no explicit clone command in Illustrator. Illustrator users typically use Copy, followed by Command-F (Ctrtl-F) for Paste In Front or Command-B (Ctrl-B) for Paste In Back for this purpose. Doing this by means of the keyboard shortcuts makes it reasonably quick and easy, though, so it's really not as serious an omission.

In Illustrator, you cannot lasso a bunch of points and then issue a Split command to break their paths at those points all in one blow. You can direct select adjacent segments, cut them to the clipboard, and follow this with Paste In Front or Paste In Back as a workaround, just be careful not to leave stray points when you do so.

Reversing

FreeHand users are accustomed to being able to reverse the direction of any path or subpath at any time by choosing the Modify > Alter Path > Reverse Path command. Illustrator has a pair of Reverse Path buttons in the Attributes palette, but these only work on closed subpaths of compound paths. To reverse open paths or subpaths, most users just click the start end with the Pen tool. The auto-join behavior of the Pen thinks you want to start adding segments from that endpoint, and therefore reverses the path. Of course, this means having to reverse each path individually; you can't reverse several paths at once, as FreeHand's command can.

Bungee Jumping: Entering a Sea of New Functionality

If the previous section was "the bad," there is also a middle ground. Some features in Illustrator both delight and disappoint the FreeHand user at the same time. Some are bittersweet and fall short of a FreeHand user's expectations in some ways, and yet also contain certain aspects that are better than what they are accustomed to.

Of course, just as FreeHand has many taken-for-granted "minor" features that make major differences in efficiency and capability, so does Illustrator. These are wonderful surprises that reward the FreeHand user who takes the time to explore their potential.

Aligning and Distributing Objects

In Illustrator, locked objects are not selectable. This means they cannot be used as anchors to which you can align other objects. But when performing alignments in Illustrator, you can designate one of the selected objects as the anchor by simply giving it an extra click before performing the alignment (refer to Chapter 4 for more about defining key objects).

Illustrator's Align palette functions do not work on individually selected points, only on whole objects. That is, if a path's point is included in the current selection, the alignment occurs just as if the whole object were selected in FreeHand. For points, you are limited to the very basic horizontal or vertical options offered in the Object>Path>Average dialog.

The sweet part, though, is the additional functionality of Illustrator's Align palette, especially the Distribute options, which are shown when you select Show Options from the palette flyout. Unlike in FreeHand, you can specify a distance *between* distributed objects. For example, if you want a series of different-sized objects to neatly abut, just enter zero in the Distribute Spacing field.

Employing Round Corners

How often have you performed the goofy positive/negative inset path trick in FreeHand to round the corners of a path? Illustrator has a Round Corners command that you can apply as either a literal Filter (Filter > Stylize > Round Corners) or as a Live Effect (Effect > Stylize > Round Corners). However, it doesn't actually give you corners of the radius you specify; the value you enter is actually the distance from the corner at which the curve is begun. Also, it works on whole paths, not on specific selected points. Still, this should be a welcome feature to FreeHand users.

Expanding Strokes

As in FreeHand, Illustrator provides a means by which you can outline the edges of a stroke with unstroked paths, thereby converting them to closed, filled, and unstroked paths. Illustrator's counterpart to FreeHand's Modify > Alter Path > Expand Stroke command is its Object > Path > Outline Stroke command. (The functionality also resides as a check box in the Object > Expand dialog.)

Illustrator's version of this important command holds a fundamental advantage over FreeHand's: Whereas FreeHand's version invokes a dialog in which you specify the thickness, caps, and joins of the expanded strokes, Illustrator's abides by the already-applied characteristics of each path individually.

Besides just being more intuitive and "sensible" Illustrator's behavior is also more versatile. For example, if you have a line drawing in which several different stroke weights and caps are used, you can turn the entire thing into closed paths in one whack, without giving all the lines the same treatment. An example of where this can be especially useful is in preparing artwork for sign vinyl cutting equipment. Applying Illustrator's Outline Stroke, followed by the Merge Pathfinder, performs much of the necessary preparatory work.

Automation with Illustrator

Appendix A, *Automation with Illustrator*, is devoted entirely to working faster and more efficiently with Illustrator, but it's important to emphasize here that Illustrator supports both AppleScript on the Mac and Visual Basic scripting on Windows. More importantly, there's the cross-platform JavaScript support as well. Adobe has similar built-in scripting support for all of its applications (including Bridge), so what you learn by scripting in one program augments your efforts in the other.

If scripting just isn't for you, you can still create your own custom features by stringing together very simple or quite complex sequences of operations in Illustrator's built-in macro feature, the Actions palette. Many useful examples are provided with the program for common tasks, but you can also build your own specialties; for example, you can perform a series of Expand and Pathfinder operations to prepare artwork for your own sign-cutting workflow, or you can scale and rotate objects to fit the top, left, and right planes of an isometric drawing. Like its JavaScript support, the automation of Illustrator's Actions palette can help make up for some of the features you consider missing relative to FreeHand.

Exploring Illustrator's Live Features

Since version 8, Illustrator has become increasingly centered on more and more elaborate live behavior. These are treatments that remain adjustable until they are nailed down by an Expand command, or by being exported to a format that does not support the effect.

Of course, FreeHand has its share of live behaviors, too. They range all the way from things as mundane as blends to newer Illustratorish features such as transparency. In fact, when you think about it, even something as common as an ordinary stroke weight can be considered a live behavior. But here, we're talking bigger than that. These are major feature sets that the FreeHand user should explore (see Chapter 3, *Objects, Groups, and Layers*, and Chapter 7, *3D and Other Live Effects*) to appreciate their potential.

Working with Brushes

FreeHand has live brushes, but not to the extent of Illustrator's selection. Roughly speaking, Illustrator's Art brush is analogous to FreeHand's

Paint brush, and an Illustrator Scatter brush is similar to a Spray brush in FreeHand.

But FreeHand has nothing like Illustrator's Pattern brush, with its separate tiles for ends, sides, and corners. Pattern brushes can be used for one-time setups of complex objects ranging from border frames with special treatments at the corners, to nuts and bolts with adjustable diameters and lengths (**Figure B.14**).

Figure B.14 Pattern brushes can have ends and corners that are different from the artwork used along their length. You can draw complex objects once and apply them to simple spine paths.

There are some capabilities in FreeHand's brushes that are not replicated in Illustrator. For example, FreeHand's Spray brush lets you apply multiple different symbols within a single brush definition, whereas Illustrator's Scatter brush does not. Both treatments have their advantages. However, we suspect you will come to agree that Illustrator's brushes are, overall, more satisfying in terms of capability and results.

Using Warps

Think of Illustrator's Warp commands (under the Effect menu) as presets of the most commonly needed Envelope shapes, but within a dialog that presents the most commonly needed distortions in the form of sliders. You can use the Warp effect in a blend, as explained in Chapter 9, *Graphs, Distortion, and Blends*, (**Figure B.15**). This feature set is a huge timesaver.

Figure B.15 If you apply the same Warp effect to two copies of the same artwork, you can blend it; the ends of the blends are still live and editable. This is a great technique for export to Flash.

Exploring the Symbolism Toolset

FreeHand's Graphic Hose can be much more down-to-business productive than Illustrator's Symbol Sprayer when you just want to spray a bunch of same objects in a line or within an area. But oh my, the things you can do with the other Symbolism tools after you put the Symbols down! A crowd favorite is the Symbol Stainer tool. To use it, spray a bunch of symbols on the page and then softly and subtly colorize them en mass: very cool and very useful. Be sure to check out Chapter 5, *Brushes, Symbols, and Masks*, for more details.

Adding Dimension With the 3D Effects

FreeHand's Extrude feature is not 3D. It is a 2D construction for simulating 3D objects, much like perspective construction on a drawing board.

Illustrator's 3D Effect is 3D. It renders to a 2D image, of course, as does any 3D program, but it renders as vector paths, rather than pixels. An actual 3D engine is used to generate the model (**Figure B.16**).

Understand, this is not meant to denigrate FreeHand's approach. Both 2D construction and 3D modeling have their purposes and advantages, depending upon what you are trying to do. But the greater realism of

Figure B.16 The simple paths at the top of this figure are all you need to generate the 3D chess piece renderings at the bottom.

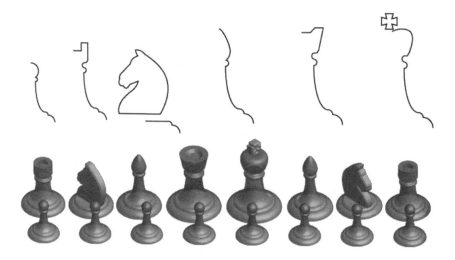

the 3D Effect in Illustrator is plain to see when you first use it. It also offers two major capabilities that FreeHand's does not: Parallel perspective (essential to tech illustrators, online game builders, etc.), and artwork mapping (great for package designs, labeling, and much more).

You can also blend between objects that have the same type of 3D Effect applied. For example, apply a 3D Effect to a path, make a copy, and blend between the two. Then modify the parameters of 3D Effect applied to one. The Blend updates accordingly. Release to layers, export to SWF, and you've got a frame-by-frame animation in much less time than you'd need to build something similar in FreeHand. Be sure to read Chapters 7 and 10 for more information on this subject.

Getting Creative With the Scribble Effect

Scribble is not a single effect; it's a whole feature set. The obvious use, of course, is to make a fill or a stroke look . . . well, scribbled. But you can also use this to quickly render a wide variety of effects from embroidery to television interference. Be sure to read Chapter 7, where this is discussed in more detail and explore this feature set into the wee hours (**Figure B.17**).

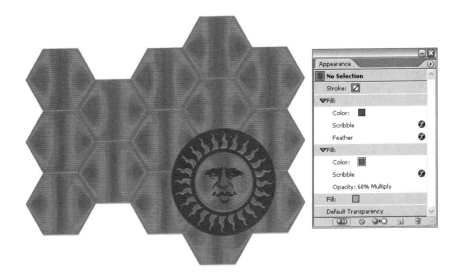

Figure B.17 The shimmer effect used here is based on the Scribble effect applied to two fills. By using two slightly different Scribble angles, you can produce the interference pattern.

Combining Live Effects

Here's where it really hits home: the major Live Effects in Illustrator can often be combined to produce elaborate treatments that would be very time-consuming to replicate in FreeHand; these capabilities are not always evident in a mere surface exploration of the individual features.

For example, you can create a blend between two copies of the same 3D object that have different orientations. This greatly expedites the process of building frame-by-frame animations to use in Flash.

Another example of combining effects involves blending between two symbol instances. To achieve this, drag two instances of a symbol onto the page. Blend them. Now direct select one and use the Symbol Stainer tool to colorize it. The possible combinations go on and on.

TAKING THE LEAP OF FAITH

This appendix is already way over its space budget. It would have to be an entire book to exhaustively compare every feature of FreeHand to Illustrator. But if it functions well as a "leg up" over the initial getting-acquainted curve, it will have served its purpose.

So hop to it FreeHanders. The Illustrator community needs you. Put your noses to the Illustrator grindstone and try to learn its every nuance. Then, when you're up-to-speed (it won't take long), be sure to let Adobe know what you like and don't like about Illustrator; what you've always loved about FreeHand; and that what we're all expecting from them is an absolutely best-ever vector drawing program (Adobe is always happy to hear from its users).

Application Preferences

Adobe Illustrator has many different settings, or *preferences*, that control the program's behavior. There are actually nine different panels of preferences in Illustrator CS2. On Mac OS, you'll find the Preferences dialog by choosing Preferences from the Application menu or by pressing Command-K. On Windows, you'll find the Preferences dialog by choosing Preferences from the Edit menu or by pressing Control-K.

The General Panel

The General panel of Preferences is pretty much a melting pot of settings (**Figure C.1**). These settings are also the ones that alter the behavior of features the most.

Figure C.1 The General Preferences panel offers quick access to settings like Keyboard Increment.

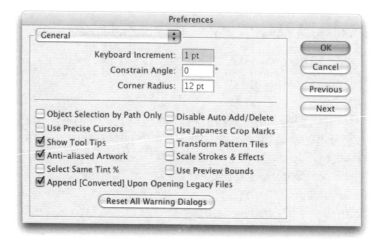

In general, the preferences in Illustrator are application-based, meaning they aren't saved in the file, rather in Illustrator's application preferences file. This also means that if you open a file that was created on another computer, your preferences don't change.

- **Keyboard Increment.** When moving artwork around on your screen, using the mouse or even a pressure-sensitive pen doesn't always give you the control you need. The Keyboard Increment setting determines the distance a selected object moves when you tap any of the four arrow keys on your keyboard. Some call this the *nudge amount*. Don't be fooled into thinking that this setting should always be as small as possible. When you're working with a grid or in scale (designing floor plans, schematics, etc.), it can be extremely helpful to set your keyboard increment to a specific value (like .25 inch). In this way, you can easily tap an arrow two times and know you've moved the object exactly .5 inch. It's no coincidence that when you open the Preferences dialog box, the Keyboard Increment value is highlighted. Power users know they can quickly press Command-K (Control-K), enter a value, press Enter, and then nudge their objects precisely.

- **Constrain Angle.** When you draw objects in Illustrator, they are aligned to the Constrain Angle setting, which is normally set to 0 degrees. However, there are times when you want to draw your document on a specific angle and changing the constrain angle affects all tools and modifier keys in Illustrator.

- **Corner Radius.** When you're creating a shape with the Rounded Rectangle tool, this setting defines the default corner radius for the rounded corners. Note that this preference sets the default behavior, which you can easily override on a per-object basis in the Rounded Rectangle tool dialog box.

- **Object Selection by Path Only.** When working in Preview mode, Illustrator allows you to select an object by clicking its path, or anywhere within its fill area (if it has a fill attribute applied). Although this is convenient, there are times, especially when you're working with complex artwork, when this behavior makes it difficult to select objects. Turning this preference on allows you to select objects only by clicking their paths, not their fills.

- **Use Precise Cursors.** Some of Illustrator's tool icons are cute, like the Symbol Sprayer and the Smudge tools, but they can be hard to position precisely. Even with the Pen tool, it can be hard to know exactly where the real tip of the cursor is. When Use Precise Cursors is active, all cursors are replaced by a simple X icon, which clearly defines the spot you're clicking (**Figure C.2**). You can also toggle this setting by pressing the Caps Lock key on your keyboard.

Figure C.2 The normal Paintbrush cursor (left) can be difficult to use, while the Paintbrush cursor with Precise Cursors turned on (right) is far easier to position.

- **Show Tool Tips.** Illustrator has a lot of icons—tiny chicklet icons, as we like to call them. Sometimes it's hard to know what a tool or button is just by looking at it, so if you hold your cursor over the icon for a second, a little window pops up identifying the name of the feature. These are called tool tips and they are turned on by default. Although they are helpful, some people may think that they get in the way, hence this preference.

- **Anti-aliased Artwork.** Computer screens are low-resolution devices (generally between 72 and 100 ppi), and artwork may appear jagged onscreen. This is especially true with the sharp vector shapes you create with Illustrator. Although the files print fine, looking at jagged artwork all day may cause eyestrain, and doesn't accurately display the way the

 The preferences are saved in a text file called Adobe Illustrator Prefs, and if you're brave, you can edit it in a text editor. If Illustrator's behavior seems odd for any reason, such as tools gone missing from the Toolbox or frequent crashes are occurring, you can try to delete your preferences file (Illustrator automatically creates a new one the next time you quit the application).

 You can delete the preferences files at launch by pressing (Command-Option-Shift) [Ctrl-Alt-Shift] while launching Illustrator. Keep the keys pressed until you see the dialog appear.

graphics will eventually print. This option (on by default) applies antialiasing to Illustrator's Preview mode so your art onscreen appears clean and smooth. Antialiasing is always turned off in Outline view mode. Note that this setting affects how the art appears onscreen only, and does not in any way affect how the art prints.

- **Select Same Tint %.** Illustrator has a feature that allows you to select all objects that are filled or stroked with the same color. When you use this feature, all objects that are filled with tint percentages of that same color are also selected. This preference setting only selects objects that are filled with the same tint percentages of that color (resulting in fewer objects being selected).

- **Append [Converted] Upon Opening Legacy Files.** When you open files that were created in previous versions of Illustrator (what Illustrator refers to as legacy files), you may have to adjust text objects. In order to prevent you from accidentally overwriting your original files, Illustrator tacks on the word [converted] to your file name when it opens legacy files. For more information about text and legacy files, see Chapter 6, *Typography*.

- **Disable Auto Add/Delete.** Illustrator tries its best to help you get your work done, but sometimes its overzealousness gets in the way. By default, when you move your cursor over an existing path with the Pen tool, Illustrator thinks you want to add a point to the existing path and conveniently switches to the Add Anchor Point tool. This is great, unless, of course, you wanted to start drawing a new path with the Pen tool. Turning this preference on politely tells Illustrator, "Thanks, but no thanks."

- **Use Japanese Crop Marks.** Illustrator allows you to create simple crop marks automatically by choosing Object > Crop Area > Make. If you want something more than the standard eight paths, you can turn on this preference. At the very least, people who see your files will know that you're serious about crop marks (**Figure C.3**).

- **Transform Pattern Tiles.** When you apply transformations (such as Scale or Rotate) to objects that are filled with patterns, the default behavior is that only the shape is transformed, not the pattern fill. Turning this preference on changes the default behavior so that pattern fills are transformed as well. Note that this preference sets the default behavior, which you can easily override as you need to using the setting in the Scale tool dialog box or by pressing the tilde key (~) during a transform function.

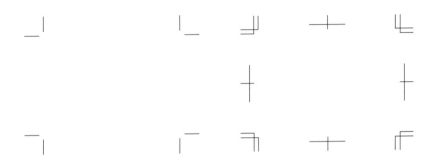

Figure C.3 Regular crop marks (left) use 8 straight lines, while Japanese crop marks (right) are more complex.

- **Scale Strokes & Effects.** Similar to patterns, when you apply transformations to objects that have strokes or effects applied, the default behavior is that only the shape is transformed, not the strokes or the effects. Turning this preference on changes the default behavior so that strokes and effects are transformed as well. Note that this preference sets the default behavior, which you can easily override as you need to using the setting in the Scale tool dialog box.

- **Use Preview Bounds.** One of the benefits of using Illustrator is that you can be extremely precise when drawing objects. Illustrator's Control, Transform, and Info palettes all provide exact feedback on coordinates, positioning, sizing, and more. By default, these palettes use the actual vector path to determine these numbers, not the visual boundaries of the object. For example, you may have a shape that has a thick stroke or a scale effect applied to it, which is not represented in the value you see in the Transform palette. With the Use Preview Bounds preference activated, all palettes use the visual boundary of a file as the value, not the underlying vector path.

- **Reset All Warning Dialogs.** Throughout the daily use of Illustrator, you'll no doubt come to meet a variety of warning dialog boxes. Sometimes these are helpful, and sometimes they can be quite annoying and you'll wish bad things upon them. You'll find that most of these dialog boxes contain a "Don't Show Again" button, which you can use to tell Illustrator that a simple beep would be just fine, thank you. Clicking Reset All Warning Dialogs brings back any warning dialogs that you asked Illustrator not to show again.

The Type Panel

Illustrator has a variety of preference settings that apply specifically to working with type (**Figure C.4**).

Figure C.4 The Type Preferences panel enables you to activate the WYSIWYG font menu.

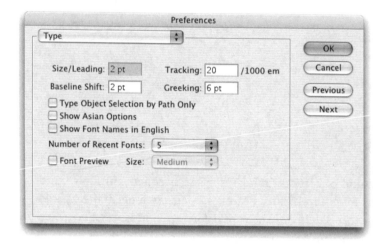

- **Keyboard Shortcut Increments.** Keyboard shortcut junkies know that they can perform a variety of tasks without ever reaching for the mouse. This is never more true than when you are working with type, when your hands are already on the keyboard. Therefore, you can set the keyboard increments for changing Size, Leading, Baseline Shift, and Tracking here. The Greeking setting defines at what point size text is rendered as simple gray blocks in order to enhance redraw performance.

- **Type Object Selection by Path Only.** Similar to the Object Selection by Path Only setting, this one refers to text objects only. With the preference enabled, you can select a text object only by clicking its baseline.

- **Show Asian Options.** Illustrator is extremely popular in Japan and in other Asian countries; therefore it has some features, such as Kinsoku, Mojikumi, Tsume, Aki, and Composite Fonts, that are used specifically in those locales. These features are hidden from view by default, but turning this preference on activates these features and makes them visible.

- **Show Font Names in English.** When working with foreign or non-English fonts, you can use this option to specify that the fonts are listed in the font menu using their English names.

- **Number of Recent Fonts.** As you work, Illustrator takes note of the fonts you use and puts copies of them at the top of your font menu. Especially when you've got hundreds of fonts installed, this can make it easier than scrolling through an entire list to find a particular one. You can have Illustrator track anywhere from 1 to 15 of the most recent fonts you've used. If you need more than 15 recent fonts, you might want to look into taking a course in graphic design.

- **Font Preview.** Illustrator has a WYSIWYG font menu that allows you to preview what each font looks like, directly within the scrolling font menu. You can choose between Small, Medium, and Large preview sizes. There is a slight performance hit that comes with using this feature and this preference setting can enable or disable the preview altogether. One valuable aspect of the Font Preview is that it also displays an icon indicating if a font is TrueType, PostScript, Multiple Master, or OpenType (**Figure C.5**).

Figure C.5 The icons on the left side of the WYSIWYG font menu indicate font type.

The Units & Display Performance Panel

How do you measure performance? You won't find the answer here, but you will find settings for how your rulers appear and how to speed up screen redraw (**Figure C.6**).

Figure C.6 The Units & Display Performance Preferences panel lets you easily switch between a variety of measurements settings.

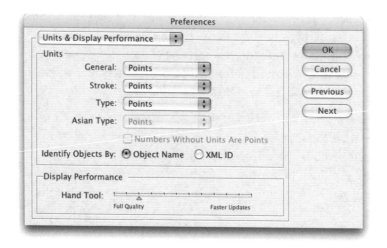

- **Units.** Illustrator can utilize different measurement systems for different uses. These preferences allow you to specify default measurements for General items (rulers and coordinates, sizes and values for objects and drawing tools, etc.), Stroke width and dash settings, and Roman and Asian type specifications (size, leading, etc.). Note that these are all used to set the default measurements in Illustrator, but at any time, you can always enter a value and Illustrator does the conversion for you. So if your document is set to inches, you can still specify a 4p9 rectangle (see next paragraph for information on such measurements).

- **Numbers Without Units Are Points**—When you're using picas and points, the standard notation is to enter the number of picas, the letter "p", and the number of points (i.e., 12p6). If your value is only points, you enter something like p6 to indicate 6 points instead. With this option turned on, simply typing 6 means 6 points (as opposed to 6 picas).

- **Identify Objects By.** Illustrator has the ability to generate templates with XML-based variables, which are useful for generating graphics files automatically using scripts or the Adobe Graphics Server. Some of these templates require that all variables are defined using valid XML names. By default, Illustrator uses the object name to define variables, but you can specify that Illustrator use valid XML IDs instead.

- **Display Performance.** Do you have an ancient video card in your computer? Or are your files so complex that even the fastest of computers begs for mercy when trying to redraw your screen? The Hand Tool slider allows you to dial in the performance that you need when scrolling with the Hand tool. With the slider closer to Full Quality, your graphics do look better while scrolling, at the expense of a slower redraw. You can drag your slider toward Faster Updates for better performance, but you won't get great looking art until you let go of the mouse after scrolling.

The Guides & Grid Panel

Illustrator allows you to define guides, which you drag out from either the horizontal or the vertical rulers (View > Show Rulers). These guides act like magnets, helping you draw or position elements on your page. By default, once you create a guide, that guide is locked and can only be accessed by toggling the View > Guides > Lock Guides setting. In reality, you can turn any vector shape into a guide by selecting it and choosing View > Guides > Make Guides. Additionally, Illustrator has a grid feature that makes your artboard appear almost as if it were a sheet of graph paper. Objects can snap to this grid making it easy to visually align items in a layout.

The appearance of guides and the grid are set using the Guides & Grid Preferences panel (**Figure C.7**). Some people prefer solid lines for guides whereas others prefer dotted lines. You can also choose the color used for the guides. Additionally, you can set the number of gridlines that appear in the grid and how many subdivisions each has. For example, a web designer might specify a gridline at every 10 pixels with 10 subdivisions, which would make it possible to zoom in and see artwork on a pixel-by-pixel basis.

Figure C.7 The Guides & Grid Preferences panel lets you change the color and appearance of grid lines.

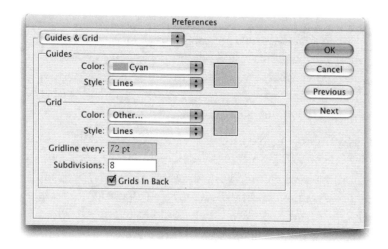

The Smart Guides & Slices Panel

In addition to normal guides, Illustrator has a useful feature called Smart Guides, which performs a variety of cursor feedback options while you work. You can activate this feature by choosing View > Smart Guides. The Smart Guides preferences allow you to control the behavior of this feature (**Figure C.8**).

Figure C.8 The Smart Guides & Slices Preferences panel.

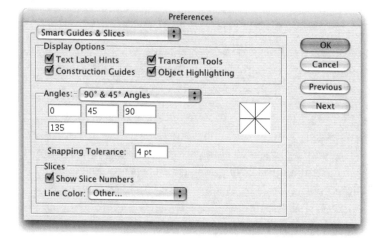

- **Display Options.** Text Label Hints identify items on your screen as you mouse over them (**Figure C.9**); Construction Guides help you align objects by indicating when they are on similar planes or angles as other objects (**Figure C.10**); Transform Tools offer similar functionality to construction guides, but they are specifically for when you are using any of Illustrator's transformation tools (**Figure C.11**); and Object Highlighting identifies the underlying original artwork when you mouse over artwork that has had effects or envelopes applied to it (**Figure C.12**).

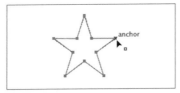

Figure C.9 A Text Label smart guide quickly identifies elements on your screen.

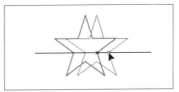

Figure C.10 A Construction Guides smart guide makes it easy to position objects.

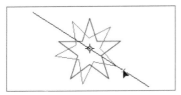

Figure C.11 A Transform Tools smart guide helps when performing transformations.

Figure C.12 An Object Highlighting smart guide makes it easy to quickly find and edit objects.

- **Angles.** The Angles settings allow you to specify at what angles Smart Guides appear when you're using any of the just-mentioned display options.

- **Snapping Tolerance.** The Snapping Tolerance setting specifies the distance to the original pixel from when a Smart Guide is activated.

- **Slices.** Slices are regions that you define to better optimize web graphics. In Preferences, you can define how these slices are indicated on the Illustrator artboard.

The Hyphenation Panel

Straightforward in its implementation, the Hyphenation Preferences panel allows you to choose the default language (which you can override by using the pop-up menu in the Character palette) and hyphenation exceptions and to add new words to the dictionary (**Figure C.13**).

Figure C.13 The Hyphenation Preferences panel lets you add new words to the dictionary in Illustrator for better hyphenation.

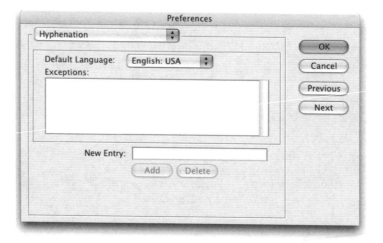

The Plug-ins & Scratch Disks Panel

From an architectural standpoint, Illustrator has a core engine, and the rest of the application is built using plug-ins. Illustrator's Plug-ins folder contains all of these features plus additional files such as startup files (see more about startup files in Chapter 1, *The Illustrator Environment*). Additionally, third party plug-ins like MAPublisher, and CADtools are stored in this folder. The Plug-ins preference simply keeps tabs on where this important folder is (**Figure C.14**).

Just as you did in math class, Illustrator uses a scratch pad to save work while performing normal functions. Sometimes, in really complex files, Illustrator may need a lot of space to work with. You can specify a hard drive or volume that Illustrator should use as a scratch disk to perform these functions. By default, your startup disk is your scratch disk, but you can change to a disk with more free space if you'd like. You can also specify a second scratch disk should Illustrator ever run out of room on the first one.

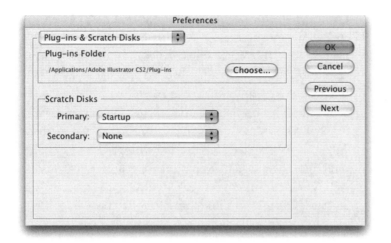

Figure C.14 The Plug-ins & Scratch Disks Preferences panel lets you specify multiple disks for memory-intensive operations.

File Handling & Clipboard Panel

This preference panel covers settings for how Illustrator handles certain files as well as settings for how art is copied to the clipboard for pasting into other applications (**Figure C.15**).

- **Enable Version Cue.** If you own Adobe Creative Suite and are using Version Cue, or if someone in your group owns Version Cue, this option enables you to access a Version Cue Workspace. Version Cue allows you to track historical and alternate versions of files, manage file usage in a multiuser environment, and track PDF review cycles.

 For more information on Version Cue, visit www.adobe.com/ products/creativesuite/ pdfs/understanding_ versioncue_cs2.pdf

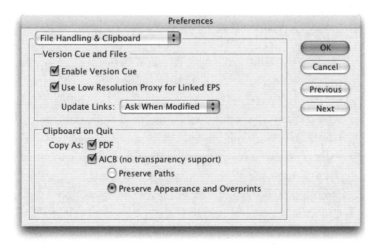

Figure C.15 The File Handling & Clipboard Preferences panel allows you to determine how graphics are copied and pasted into other applications.

- **Use Low Resolution Proxy for Linked EPS.** When you place-link an EPS file into Illustrator, whether it is a Photoshop EPS or any other generic EPS, the preview that's displayed on your screen is the low-resolution preview that's embedded within the EPS file. When you uncheck this setting, Illustrator parses the EPS file and displays the actual file. This results in a much better looking preview on your screen, but it also slows redraw and increases file size. On a separate note, when you're using the Live Trace feature with placed-linked EPS files, the resolution of the image that Live Trace can detect depends on this setting as well. When the option is checked, Live Trace sees the 72 ppi preview file and traces that. By turning this setting off, Live Trace can detect the full resolution of the file and use it to trace the image.

- **Update Links.** When you place-link a file into Illustrator, the Links palette maintains the link information about that file. Because the file is external, you can edit that file easily by using the Edit Original feature, found in either the Links palette or the Control palette. With the default Ask When Modified setting is used, if you edit a linked file outside of Illustrator and return to the Illustrator document, you'll get a dialog box alerting you to the fact that the file was updated, with an option to update the link. Alternatively, you can choose to manually update links yourself through the Links palette, or you can set Illustrator to automatically update all links as they happen.

- **Clipboard on Quit.** Today's modern operating systems use an efficient method to copy and paste data using the system's clipboard, called *promising*. Rather than copy art in a variety of formats to the clipboard (which would take time), applications promise to deliver art when pasted. Then, when you paste the art, the operating system goes back to the application you copied from and gets the data. The problem is, if you've quit the program since you performed the copy function, the operating system can't fulfill its promise. So when you quit an application, it copies whatever was promised to the clipboard (which explains why sometimes it takes a while for an application to actually quit). The Clipboard on Quit preference allows you to determine which file formats are used to copy art to the clipboard when you quit Illustrator. By default, both the PDF and the AICB (Adobe Illustrator Clip Board) options are checked, which gives you the most options. Unless you have a specific reason, we'd suggest that you leave both of these checked at all times. In general, the PDF option supports native transparency and is PDF 1.4 whereas the AICB is flattened data and is PostScript.

The Appearance of Black Panel

In an effort to display graphics on your screen or proofs that closely match what you will see on an actual printed sheet, Illustrator includes a setting specifically for how the color black is displayed or printed (**Figure C.16**). You can choose to have your blacks display accurately, in which case black will appear closer to a dark gray color (closer to what you might see on press), or you can choose to display rich blacks, in which case your blacks will be much darker. Note that these settings are not color management settings and don't affect your final separated output. These settings only affect your screen display or output to an RGB device.

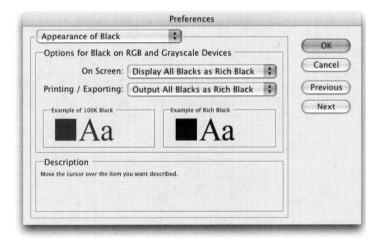

Figure C.16 The Appearance of Black Preferences panel allows you to achieve better color results on your screen.

INDEX

NUT

GODS
&
PHARAOHS
from
EGYPTIAN MYTHOLOGY

TEXT BY GERALDINE HARRIS
COLOUR ILLUSTRATIONS BY DAVID O'CONNOR
LINE DRAWINGS BY JOHN SIBBICK

HATHOR

PETER BEDRICK BOOKS
NEW YORK

SHU

RA-KHEFRI

GEB

WATERS OF CHAOS

Published by
Peter Bedrick Books
156 Fifth Avenue
New York, NY 10010

Printed in Italy

8 7 6 5 4
6 5 4 3   (pbk)

This edition printed in 1998

THE AUTHOR
Geraldine Harris studied Egyptology at Cambridge
University. She lectures on the myths and folklore of
various cultures and is the author of two novels for
children, 'White Cranes Castle' and 'The Prince of the
Godborn'.

Library of Congress Cataloging-in-Publication Data
Harris, Geraldine.
    Gods & pharaohs from Egyptian mythology / text by
Geraldine Harris; colour illustrations by David O'Connor; line
drawings by John Sibbick.
    (The World mythology series)
    Reprint, Originally published: London: P. Lowe, 1982.
    Includes index.
    Summary: Presents the myths of the ancient Egyptians and a
glimpse of the civilization that created them.
    ISBN 0–87226–907–8   ISBN 0–87226–908–6 (pbk.)
    1. Mythology, Egyptian.   2. Gods, Egyptian.   3. Egypt –
Civilization – To 332 B.C.   [1. Mythology. Egyptian.
2. Egypt – Civilization – to 332 B.C.)   I. O'Connor,
David.   II. Sibbick, John. ill.   III. Title.   IV. Title: Gods and
pharaohs from Egyptian Mythology.   V. Series.
[BL2441.2.H37   1991]
299'-31 – dc20   90-23455
                                                  CIP
                                                  AC

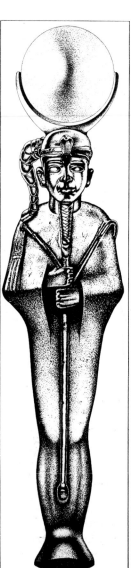

Contents

Red land, black land

For centuries Europeans have been fascinated by ancient Egypt. When the Emperor Napoleon invaded Egypt in 1798 he took with him a team of scholars to examine and record pyramids, obelisks and other ancient monuments. It was one of Napoleon's soldiers who found the famous Rosetta Stone on which the same royal inscription was written once in Greek and twice in Egyptian in two different scripts. In 1822, with the help of the Rosetta Stone, the brilliant young French scholar, Jean Champollion, was able to decipher the ancient Egyptian hieroglyphic script and gave a voice to the past.

Throughout the nineteenth century, scholars travelled all over Egypt to make drawings of temples and tombs and to record inscriptions. These early drawings are often very valuable since so much has been damaged or destroyed in the last hundred years. The early excavators however were little better than treasure hunters; their main concern was to find spectacular objects or well-preserved mummies to take back to European museums. Gradually the importance of methodical excavation was realized and excavators acknowledged that a piece of broken pottery or a scrap of papyrus might be more significant than a gold vase because of the information it could give about ancient Egypt.

In the middle of the nineteenth century the French scholar, Auguste Mariette, entered the service of the Khedive of Egypt and founded the Cairo Museum and The Egyptian Antiquities Service, which still has the task of protecting all ancient sites and carrying out excavations. It was Mariette who in 1881 became suspicious of the large number of ancient royal jewels that were suddenly appearing on the market. He soon discovered that a family from the village of Qurna had found a burial chamber filled with the mummified bodies of some of the greatest rulers of ancient Egypt. In 1898 more royal mummies were found in a tomb in the famous Valley of the Kings and it is now possible to visit the Cairo Museum and gaze on the very faces of the men who ruled Egypt over three thousand years ago.

It was not only the French who excavated in Egypt. The Egypt Exploration Fund, founded in London in 1882, financed numerous expeditions and the British archaeologist W.M.F. Petrie, who worked in Egypt and Palestine for sixty years, set new standards in the excavation and description of ancient sites. It was also a British team who made the most famous archaeological discovery of the twentieth century. In 1922, after many years of work in the Valley of the Kings, Howard Carter found the almost intact burial of a pharaoh of the fourteenth century BC. The treasure of Tutankhamon aroused tremendous popular interest in Egyptology. Since that date expeditions from all over the world have worked to recover Egypt's magnificent past.

Many of the distinctive features of Egyptian civilization can be traced to the country's unusual geography. Egypt is a place of contrasts and the greatest contrast of all is between the 'red land' of the desert and the 'black land' of the lush Nile valley. In very ancient times the Egyptian desert was covered in grass and inhabited by vast herds of animals, like the savannahs of modern Africa. The first Egyptians were hunters, following the herds of game. Then the climate became drier, the savannah shrivelled into desert and the people came down from the uplands to live in the Nile valley and turn its swamps into rich agricultural land.

The skies of ancient Egypt were a clear, brilliant blue and rain was almost unheard of. Only the presence of the river Nile, with its annual flood, made it possible to grow crops. The flood, which brought fertile mud from higher up the river, could be partly controlled by dykes and canals, but there was a limit to what men could do to extend the agricultural land. In the south the habitable land remained a narrow strip on either side of the river; all the rest was desert. In the north the Nile splits up into many branches before reaching the Mediterranean Sea. Much of the fertile land in the Delta was too marshy to be cultivated but it was rich in birds and fish, papyrus plants for paper-making and reeds for hut- and boat-building. The marshes and the numerous waterways made it difficult to travel across the Delta but in the south the single broad river ensured easy communications, especially as boats could sail upstream with the prevailing wind behind them or float downstream with the current. The people of the north sailed the Mediterranean, traded with other Near Eastern countries and were open to

foreign influence. The people of the south, sealed off from the world by the surrounding deserts, were more conservative and had a stronger sense of unity.

To begin with, every small Egyptian settlement or tribal area had its own chieftain, but gradually leaders arose who claimed authority over whole groups of settlements. By the fourth millenium BC some of these leaders were calling themselves kings and their kingdoms grew larger and larger. The ancient Egyptians believed that a man called Menes had once ruled over the south (the Kingdom of Upper Egypt) and had fought a war against the north (the Kingdom of Lower Egypt). In about three thousand BC the south conquered the north and Menes ruled the whole country from his new capital, Memphis.

The Egyptians grouped their rulers into dynasties and counted Menes as the first king of Dynasty One. Modern historians divide the thirty dynasties who ruled over an independent Egypt into seven main periods. The most important of these were the Old Kingdom (c2575–2134 BC), the age of the pyramid builders; the Middle Kingdom (c2040–1640 BC) when the country was reunited by another leader from the south, and the New Kingdom (c1550–1070 BC) when Egypt ruled an empire under pharaohs such as Tutankhamon and Ramesses the Great. In between the 'Kingdoms' came times of political chaos. Foreign invaders occasionally caused havoc and because Upper and Lower Egypt were different in character there was always a danger that under a weak ruler they would split apart again.

Egypt was never able to forget that it had once been two countries. The ruler was always called the Lord of the Two Lands, the King of Upper and Lower Egypt. He wore a double crown made up of the White Crown of Upper Egypt and the Red Crown of Lower Egypt and was often shown protected by The Two Ladies, Nekhbet, the vulture goddess of the south and Wadjet, the cobra goddess of the north.

One thing that did unite all the Egyptians was a reverence for kingship. The king was sacred, the living image of the Sun God himself. Much of a king's time was spent in complex religious

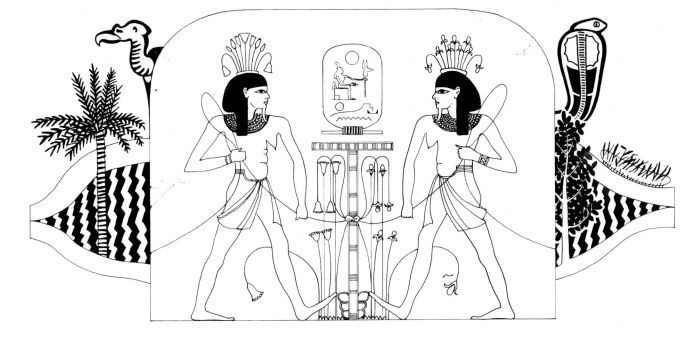

rituals but he was also the active head of government. As absolute ruler his power was enormous but he was meant to use it only for the good of his people. At his coronation an Egyptian king re-enacted the events of creation and promised to conquer chaos and establish *Maat*.

Maat means order and justice and truth and it was personified by a goddess who was the daughter of the Sun God. Kings were supposed to 'live in truth', rule with impartial justice and make Egyptian society reflect the divine order established by the gods. Because kings were thought to be more than human they could stand between mankind and the gods and ask for peace and prosperity for all Egypt.

Some deities were worshipped throughout the country but every part of Egypt had its local god or goddess. Many of these deities embodied the principal characteristics of animals and could be shown in animal or animal-headed form. So the god Khnum, the giver of life, was represented as a vigorous ram or with a ram's head, the goddess Taweret, protector of women in childbirth, had the paws of a lion, the back of a crocodile and the bulky body of a hippopotamus, while the complex nature of the goddess Hathor was expressed in a variety of forms from ferocious lioness to benevolent cow.

A very large number of gods and goddesses were revered in ancient Egypt but behind this diversity lay the idea that all gods were really one. Egyptian texts often simply refer to God but the mysterious power of the Sole Creator was illustrated by giving him numerous divine forms, male and female, beautiful and terrible, fierce and gentle. The ordinary person focused his worship on the forms that were most appropriate to his own life, or on his local god or goddess.

These local deities might achieve national importance if they became the patrons of a dynasty of kings. It was one of the king's chief duties to build temples as houses for the gods and to make daily offerings to them. In return for these offerings the gods were expected to give the king life, health and the power to overcome his enemies. If a king reigned for thirty years he celebrated a *Sed* Festival. During this festival the king went through days of complex rites to win the blessing of renewed life and strength. Everything had to be done twice, once for Upper and once for Lower Egypt and in one of the most important ceremonies the king ran round and round a specially built track. This may have been meant to prove that he was still fit enough to rule as the living image of the Sun God and in very ancient times a king who failed to run the whole course was probably ritually murdered.

For most of Egyptian history, however, the king was allowed to die a natural death. It was thought to be important to the whole country that the dead king was accepted by the gods into an afterlife, to triumph over death just as the sun triumphed over darkness with each new dawn.

Because of this idea the burial rites of an Egyptian king were costly and complex and their most spectacular feature was the erection of a pyramid.

When Egypt was first united, houses, palaces and shrines were built with reeds or in mud-brick, but as early as the Third Dynasty (c2649–2575 BC), Imhotep, the first great architect in history, designed a stone step pyramid for the burial of his master, King Zoser. By the Fourth Dynasty (c2575–2456 BC) the Egyptians were building huge straight-sided pyramids in the desert near Memphis.

The largest of these, the pyramid of King Khufu at Giza, is one-hundred and forty-six metres high and contains about two million, three-hundred-thousand blocks of stone, each weighing between two and fifteen tons. In spite of their vast size the pyramids of Giza are built with extraordinary precision. We cannot be certain how they were constructed but it is clear that simple copper tools and simple methods were used. The Egyptians were not great technical innovators but they had a genius for organization and no shortage of manpower and time.

A king began work on his pyramid as soon as he came to the throne. About four thousand craftsmen were employed to cut and shape blocks of good limestone and fit them together. Getting the blocks from the limestone quarries to the site of the pyramid took up most of the manpower. Once cut, the blocks were loaded onto barges and floated downriver until they were level with Giza. Then they were offloaded, placed on wooden sledges and dragged along a log-causeway to the pyramid site. The final stage was to haul the blocks up the earthen ramps that surrounded a half-built pyramid to the place where they were needed.

It is wrong to think that the pyramids were built by gangs of slaves toiling under the lash. The main workforce was the agricultural population, who had nothing to do for three to four months of every year while the fields were flooded. As many as a hundred-thousand men may have worked together to move vast quantities of stone and build a pyramid for their divine king.

The Great Pyramid is now much the same colour as the desert in which it stands, but when it was first built it was cased in gleaming white limestone and had a gilded capstone. Attached to the pyramid were two temples, linked by a walled causeway, and in a nearby pit a full-size boat was buried for the king's use in the afterlife. After the king's body had been embalmed it was taken to the first temple, The Valley Temple, which contained twenty-three royal statues. The mummy was purified and a ritual was performed to give life to the king's statues so that his spirit could inhabit them as if they were his human body. Then the royal coffin was dragged along the causeway to the second temple where further ceremonies were performed and where priests would continue to make offerings to the king's spirit for centuries after his death. Finally the coffin was taken down a narrow passage into the heart of the pyramid and laid in a stone sarcophagus in the burial chamber.

In the pyramids of the Fifth and Sixth Dynasties (c2465–2152 BC), texts are inscribed on the inner walls and these may be the words recited by the priests during the royal burial. The Pyramid Texts vary in age and character. Some are humble prayers that the king might join the gods as their servant; others are far more arrogant. In the so-called 'Cannibal Hymn' the dead king is said to be so powerful that he can kill and eat the gods to absorb their magic: 'The large gods for his morning meal, the medium ones for his evening meal, the little ones for his supper and the old ones for the fuel under his cooking pot.'

When the rites were over the priests withdrew, lowering a series of huge stones to block the route to the burial chamber. In spite of these precautions, no intact royal burial has been found in the pyramids of the Old Kingdom.

Thieves were able to break in and steal the precious objects buried with the kings, but the pyramids themselves remained to become the greatest of the Seven Wonders of the Ancient World and the only one of those wonders to have survived to our own day.

Archaeologists are not only concerned with gods and kings and a great deal has been discovered about the daily lives of ordinary people in Ancient Egypt. Most of our evidence for daily life comes from the New Kingdom (c1550–1070 BC) and one of the best sources is the village of Deir el-Medina in southern Egypt. During the New Kingdom royalty were buried in large rock-cut tombs in desert valleys close to the city of Thebes, the religious capital of the south. The government built a village for the craftsmen who cut and decorated the royal tombs at nearby Deir el-Medina.

The craftsmen lived with their wives and children in mud-brick houses fronting the narrow streets of a walled village. When the houses were first built they were all identical but the families who lived in them soon changed that by knocking down internal walls, building extensions and decorating the rooms with wall-paintings. In many of the houses the front room was used as a workshop.

The second room was the largest and was raised above the level of the rest of the house on a column made from a palm-tree trunk. It had unglazed windows and a mud-brick platform on which the master and mistress of the house sat. There would have been little other furniture; chairs were for the rich and the important but folding stools and low wooden tables were used. Behind the main room there was often a small bedroom. Egyptian beds had wooden frames, webbing of woven reeds and high footboards. They were made up with linen sheets but a padded wooden headrest was used instead of a pillow. Close to the bed stood chests, painted to look like costly ivory and ebony, which held clothes, jewellery and make-up.

During the New Kingdom, Egyptian clothes were usually made from cunningly draped and pleated linen. Women's clinging dresses and men's long kilts and wide-sleeved shirts were white. Colour was added by brilliant bead collars and bracelets and by the garlands of real flowers worn on festive occasions. Hairstyles could be very elaborate and wigs of dyed wool were sometimes worn. Both men and women used eye make-up and a typical Egyptian cosmetic chest might contain a mirror, razor and tweezers in copper, a pot of rouge, lip-paint, green eye-shadow, black eye-liner and jars of the scented oils that the Egyptians loved to rub on their bodies.

None of the Deir el-Medina houses had the luxury of a bathroom and the passage beside the bedroom led to an open kitchen area. The main items of kitchen equipment were a domed, terracotta oven, a grindstone for the grain which formed a major part of the craftsmen's wages, and cooking pots of every shape and size. Bread and beer made up the bulk of an Egyptian's diet and a small rock-cut cellar behind the kitchen area would have contained jars of beer and perhaps some date wine. Dates or honey were used to make sweet bread and cakes and the Egyptians also enjoyed figs and pomegranates, grapes and water-melons. Beef and roast goose were highly prized but most people only ate meat on special occasions. The protein in their diet was provided by dried fish, lentils and peas. Other common vegetables were leeks, onions, garlic and cucumbers.

A staircase from the kitchen area led up to the roof where vegetables were spread out to dry and animals such as geese or goats might be kept.

The Egyptians were very fond of animals and are often shown with pet dogs, cats or monkeys.

In hot weather people slept on the roof and it was also a place to sit playing a board game or gossiping to the neighbours. From their rooftops the people of Deir el-Medina could look out at their ancestral tombs, built on the slopes above the village and at their local temple. Every house had its own little shrine where daily offerings of wine and bread and flowers were made to the statue of a favourite deity. Some houses had wall-paintings of the goddess Taweret and Bes, the lion-headed dwarf god, who in spite of his fierce and ugly appearance was the much loved protector of women and young children. Bes and Taweret were also carved on beds and headrests to guard sleepers against snakes and scorpions and all dangers of the night, and small images of these deities were often worn as charms, called amulets.

The Egyptians had great faith in the magical power of amulets. Nearly all Egyptian jewellery is made up of amulets and every Egyptian wore them for protection from the cradle to the grave. Hundreds of different shapes were used but the most popular were miniature images of the gods or of divine symbols such as the falcon-eye of the god Horus, the pillar of the god Osiris or the cow-eared human face of Hathor. The gods were not only to be found in the great temples, they were part of daily life and they dominate the stories told and loved by the Egyptians.

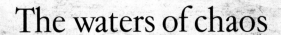

Egyptian religion was richer in symbols than in myths, but some of the gods did have stories attached to them. Unfortunately, because they were so well known, many of these stories were never written down in full. Often a myth has to be pieced together from scattered references to it in hymns and prayers, temple inscriptions, Pyramid Texts and even odder sources such as spells for curing scorpion bites. Many ancient Greek writers were fascinated by the deities of Egypt and recorded myths about them, but it's difficult to know how close these versions are to the original Egyptian stories.

Some myths, such as the murder and resurrection of Osiris, were often re-enacted during royal ceremonials or temple rites. Scholar-priests in great religious centres like the Temple of Ra at Heliopolis, the Temple of Ptah of Memphis or the Temple of Thoth at Hermopolis produced cycles of myths with their own deity as the central figure. All these cycles included creation myths because to the Egyptians, creation was the only important event in history. The whole aim of their society was to preserve the divine order established by the Creator and the idea of progress had no place in Egyptian thought. A dozen different myths were not enough to express the marvel of creation. The Creator had many forms and many names—Ra, Ra-Atum, Amon-Ra, Ra-Horakhty—but all the sources agree that he first arose out of a watery abyss called Nun.

In the beginning were the waters of chaos. Darkness and silence

reigned but in the depths of the watery abyss lay the formless spirit of the Creator, the father and mother of all things. . . . One story tells how a mound of earth slowly rose above the waters of Chaos, just as Egypt seems to rise up as the Nile floods sink in the heat of summer. This mound was the first land and at last there was a place in which the spirit of the Creator could take on a body. In the form of a phoenix with flaming plumage the Creator alighted on the Primeval Mound and his cry shattered the eternal silence with the first sound.

A second story tells how eight creatures with the heads of frogs and serpents moved through the waters of chaos before time began. They were the Ogdoad: Nun and Nunet, deities of the watery abyss, Heh and Hehet, deities of infinite space, Kek and Keket, deities of darkness and Amon and Amonet, deities of invisibility. These mysterious beings swam together to form the great egg that was to hatch the Creator.

Others said that this Primeval Egg was laid on the risen mound by a goose whose cackling was the first of all sounds. The Great Cackler sat on the mound guarding her egg through countless ages until at last it hatched into a shining phoenix. The two halves of the shell separated the waters of chaos and formed a space in which the Creator could make the world.

A third story tells how darkness covered the waters until the Primeval Lotus rose from the Abyss. Slowly the blue lotus opened its petals to reveal a young god sitting in its golden heart. A sweet perfume drifted across the waters and light streamed from the body of the Divine Child to banish universal darkness.

This child was the Creator, the Sun God, the source of all life but every evening a lotus sinks below the surface and does not rise again until dawn. So the Primeval Lotus closed its petals at the end of each day and vanished back into the

waters. Chaos reigned through the night until the god within the lotus returned. The forces of chaos were not conquered for ever at the beginning of time, they surrounded the earth in the form of serpents poised to attack the Sun God. The war between Order and Chaos will never end.

Whatever the form of the Creator, all the stories agree that even when he lay in the watery abyss he knew that he was alone. This solitude became unbearable and he longed for other beings to share the new world with him. In Memphis the priests described how the thoughts of the Creator became the gods and everything else which exists. When his thoughts had shaped them, his tongue gave them life by naming them. Thoughts and words were the power behind creation.

In Heliopolis the priests named the Creator as Ra-Atum and told how after aeons of solitude he spat out Shu, the god of air and Tefenet, the goddess of moisture. For a great span of time Ra-Atum was still alone for Shu and Tefenet were lost to him in the waters of chaos. Then the Creator took an eye from his face and filled it with his power. He called the Eye his daughter, Hathor, and sent her out into the darkness to search for his lost children.

The light of the Eye pierced the forces of chaos and Shu and Tefenet were quickly found and brought back to their father. As a reward, the Sun God set the Eye on his forehead in the form of a great cobra, the uraeus serpent. He promised her that she would have power over his enemies and that in ages to come both gods and men would fear her.

Then Ra-Atum embraced his first children, Shu and Tefenet, with tears of joy. As he held them in his arms, his spirit went into them and they and all the gods to come shared in the divinity of the Creator.

The secret name of Ra

Ra, the Sole Creator was visible to the people of Egypt as the disc of the sun, but they knew him in many other forms. He could appear as a crowned man, a falcon or a man with a falcon's head and, as the scarab beetle pushes a round ball of dung in front of it, the Egyptians pictured Ra as a scarab pushing the sun across the sky. In caverns deep below the earth were hidden another seventy-five forms of Ra; mysterious beings with mummified bodies and heads consisting of birds or snakes, feathers or flowers. The names of Ra were as numerous as his forms; he was the Shining One, The Hidden One, The Renewer of the Earth, The Wind in the Souls, The Exalted One, but there was one name of the Sun God which had not been spoken since time began. To know this secret name of Ra was to have power over him and over the world that he had created.

Isis longed for such a power. She had dreamed that one day she would have a marvellous falcon-headed son called Horus and she wanted the throne of Ra to give to her child. Isis was the Mistress of Magic, wiser than millions of men, but she knew that nothing in creation was powerful enough to harm its creator. Her only chance was to turn the power of Ra against himself and at last Isis thought of a cruel and cunning plan. Every day the Sun God walked through his kingdom, attended by a crowd of spirits and lesser deities, but Ra was growing old. His eyes were dim, his step no longer firm and he had even begun to drivel.

One morning Isis mingled with a group of minor goddesses and followed behind the King of the Gods. She watched the face of Ra until she saw his saliva drip onto a clod of earth. When she was sure that no-one was taking any notice of her, she scooped up the earth and carried it away. Isis mixed the earth with the saliva of Ra to form clay and modelled a wicked-looking serpent. Through the hours of darkness she whispered spells over the clay serpent as it lay lifeless in her hands. Then the cunning goddess carried it to a crossroads on the route which the Sun God always took. She hid the serpent in the long grass and returned to her palace.

The next day Ra came walking through his kingdom with the spirits and lesser deities crowding behind him. When he approached the crossroads, the spells of Isis began to work and the clay serpent quivered into life. As the Sun God passed, it bit him in the ankle and crumbled back into earth. Ra gave a scream that was heard through all creation.

His jaws chattered and his limbs shook as the poison flooded through him like a rising Nile. 'I have been wounded by something deadly,' whispered Ra. 'I know that in my heart, though my eyes cannot see it. Whatever it was, I, the Lord of Creation, did not make it. I am sure that none of you would have done such a terrible thing to me, but I have never felt such pain! How can this have happened to me? I am the Sole Creator, the child of the watery abyss. I am the god with a thousand names, but my secret name was only spoken once, before time began. Then it was hidden in my body so that no-one should ever learn it and be able to work spells against me. Yet as I walked through my kingdom something struck at me and now my heart is on fire and my limbs shake. Send for the Ennead! Send for my children! They are wise in magic and their knowledge pierces heaven.'

Messengers hurried to the great gods and from the four pillars of the world came the Ennead: Shu and Tefenet, Geb and Nut, Seth and Osiris, Isis and Nephthys. Envoys travelled the land and the sky and the watery abyss to summon all the deities created by Ra. From the marshes came frog-headed Heket, Wadjet the cobra goddess and the fearsome god, crocodile-headed Sobek. From the deserts came fiery Selkis, the scorpion goddess, Anubis the jackal, the guardian of the dead and Nekhbet the vulture goddess. From the cities of the north came warlike Neith, gentle cat-headed Bastet, fierce lion-headed Sekhmet and Ptah the god of crafts. From the cities of the south came Onuris, the divine huntsman and ram-headed Khnum with Anukis his wife and Satis his daughter. Cunning Thoth and wise Seshat, goddess of writing; virile Min and snake-headed Renenutet, goddess of the harvest, kindly Meskhenet and monstrous Taweret, goddesses of birth—all of them were summoned to the side of Ra.

The gods and goddesses gathered around the Sun God, weeping and wailing, afraid that he was going to die. Isis stood among them beating her breast and pretending to be as distressed and bewildered as all the other frightened deities. 'Father of All,' she began, 'whatever is the matter? Has some snake bitten you? Has some wretched creature dared to strike at his Creator? Few of the gods can compare with me in wisdom and I am the Mistress of Magic. If you will let me help you, I'm sure that I can cure you.'

Ra was grateful to Isis and told her all that had happened. 'Now I am colder than water and hotter than fire,' complained the Sun God. 'My eyes darken. I cannot see the sky and my body is soaked by the sweat of fever.'

'Tell me your full name,' said cunning Isis. 'Then I can use it in my spells. Without that knowledge the greatest of magicians cannot help you.'

'I am the maker of heaven and earth,' said Ra. 'I made the heights and the depths, I set horizons at east and west and established the gods in their glory. When I open my eyes it is light; when I close them it is dark. The mighty Nile floods at my command. The gods do not know my true name but I am the maker of time, the giver of festivals. I spark the fire of life. At dawn I rise as Khepri, the scarab and sail across the sky in the Boat of Millions of Years. At noon I blaze in the heavens as Ra and at evening I am Ra-atum, the setting sun.'

'We know all that,' said Isis. 'If I am to find a spell to drive out this poison, I will have to use your secret name. Say your name and live.'

'My secret name was given to me so that I could sit at ease,' moaned Ra, 'and fear no living creature. How can I give it away?'

Isis said nothing and knelt beside the Sun God while his pain mounted. When it became unbearable, Ra ordered the other gods to stand back while he whispered his secret name to Isis. 'Now the power of the secret name has passed from my heart to your heart,' said Ra wearily. 'In time you can give it to your son, but warn him never to betray the secret!'

Isis nodded and began to chant a great spell that drove the poison out of the limbs of Ra and he rose up stronger than before. The Sun God returned to the Boat of Millions of Years and Isis shouted for joy at the success of her plan. She knew now that one day Horus her son would sit on the throne of Egypt and wield the power of Ra.

The Eye of the Sun

Hathor, the daughter of Ra had many forms. She could be a cow or a cat and she came to newborn children to foretell their fate in the form of seven beautiful women. Hathor in human form was the most gracious and joyful of goddesses but when she took on the role of the Eye of the Sun, she could also be the fiercest and the cruellest. She was the protector of the gods but when she was angry even the gods feared her. Temple inscriptions and a story written in Egyptian as late as the second century AD tell of a grim time when Hathor left her country and chose to live in Nubia.

The Eye of the Sun was jealous of the other gods and goddesses whom Ra had created. She quarrelled with her father and wandered south to roam the deserts of distant Nubia. The angry goddess abandoned her lovely human form and appeared as a wildcat or a raging lioness. She lived by hunting and butchered every creature who came near her.

Egypt was desolate, for without beautiful Hathor laughter and love withered away and life held no joy. The Sun God hid his face in sorrow and gloom spread across the earth. No-one could console him for the loss of his beloved daughter and worst of all without the power of his Eye, Ra was in danger from his enemies. Darkness tightened its coils around Light and Chaos threatened Order. 'Who will bring Hathor back to me?' asked Ra but the gods were silent. The Eye of the Sun held the power of life or death over all beings and in her furious mood the gods were afraid to approach her. Then Ra summoned Thoth, the wisest of deities, and ordered him to go to Nubia and persuade Hathor to return to Egypt. Thoth obeyed the King of the Gods with a heavy heart. He was sure that if Hathor recognized him she would kill him before he had a chance to speak. With this in mind, Thoth transformed himself into a humble baboon. Then he crept through the Nubian desert, following the bloody trail of the goddess.

When he found her, Hathor was in her wildcat form, sitting on a rock licking her tawny fur. Thoth crawled forward, knocking his head on the ground:

'Hail, daughter of the Sun!' he said humbly.

Hathor arched and spat but when she saw that it was only a baboon she paused and did not spring on him at once. 'Gracious goddess,' faltered Thoth, 'may a humble ape dare to speak to you?'

'Speak and die,' growled the wildcat as she unsheathed her claws. The baboon cringed and kissed the ground, murmuring, 'O, powerful one, if you choose to kill me, I cannot stop you but remember the story of the mother vulture and the mother cat. . . .'

'What story?' demanded Hathor.

'Listen my lady,' said wiley Thoth, 'and I will tell you.'

The wildcat sat down and began to wash herself again. She seemed to take no further notice of the baboon but Thoth knew that if he tried to run away he would feel her claws within seconds. He began his story.

There was once a female vulture, who made a nest in a palm tree and sat on her eggs until four fine chicks were hatched. As soon as they broke through their shells the chicks demanded food, but the vulture was afraid to leave her nest because of a wildcat who lived on a nearby hillside. Now the wildcat had given birth to four kittens and she was just as afraid to leave them, because of the vulture.

The chicks and the kittens were soon crying with hunger so the two mothers came together and arranged a truce. The vulture and the wildcat both swore a mighty oath by Ra that neither of them would attack the other's children. Then the vulture felt safe to fly off and look for carrion and the wildcat felt safe to go hunting.

For some weeks everything went well and the chicks and the kittens thrived. The young vultures were soon trying out their wings and the kittens began to play all over the hillside. One morning while the vulture was circling over the desert, the boldest of her chicks flew out of the nest. His wings were not yet strong and after a short flight he landed on the hillside where the kittens were playing and snatched away a piece of their food.

Quicker than thought, the wildcat struck at the young vulture and wounded him badly. 'Find your own food,' growled the wildcat. The young vulture feebly flapped his wings but he found that he could not fly.

'Now I shall never return to my nest,' he gasped, 'but you have broken your oath and Ra will avenge me.'

When the mother vulture arrived at the nest with a beak full of carrion flesh, she found that one of her chicks was missing and saw him lying dead on the hillside.

'So the cat has broken her oath,' thought the vulture. 'I shan't wait long to have my revenge.'

The next time that the wildcat went off to hunt, the vulture swooped down on the kittens. She killed every one of them and carried them back to her nest to feed her chicks.

When the cat returned with her catch, the kittens were nowhere to be seen. She searched the whole hillside mewing desperately but all she found were a few bloodstained tufts of fur. Then she knew that the vulture had killed her kittens and she cried to Ra for vengeance: 'O great god who judges between the just and the wicked, the vulture has broken her holy oath and murdered my children! Hear me Ra and punish the oath-breaker!'

The Sun God listened to her prayer and was angry that an oath sworn in his name had been broken. Because the vulture had taken her own vengeance and killed all the kittens, Ra ordered a divine messenger to arrange her punishment.

The next day when the vulture was flying over the desert searching for food she saw a lone huntsman cooking a haunch of meat over his campfire. The vulture swooped down, seized the meat in her claws and carried it triumphantly back to her nest. There she dropped it amongst her greedy chicks but a few glowing embers still clung to the underside of the meat. As soon as the embers touched the dry twigs and grass of the nest it burst into flames. The three chicks were burned to cinders while their mother circled helplessly overhead. The wildcat ran to the foot of the blazing tree and called up to the vulture, 'By Ra, you killed my kittens but now your chicks are dead and I am avenged!'

'So my lady,' concluded Thoth, 'both the mothers had broken their oaths and both were punished. Ra hears and sees everything and punishes every crime. Praise to Ra who gives life to all things and whose shining face brings the whole earth joy. The Nile rises to make him a cloak. The north wind and the south wind blow at his command when he crosses the sky above and the sky below. He rules from the heights of heaven to the depths of the ocean. Praise to the Sun God and praise to Hathor his daughter.'

The goddess sat thinking over the story and remembering her just and powerful father. Thoth saw his opportunity and crept closer. 'My lady, I bring you divine food from the palace of the Sun God. Wonderful herbs that give health and joy to whoever tastes them.'

He held out the bunch of herbs in one paw and their sweet scent tempted the wildcat to nibble at them. As she swallowed the divine food, Hathor's mood changed. All her anger melted away and she listened meekly to Thoth. 'These herbs were grown in Egypt,' said Thoth, 'the land that rose from the waters of Nun, the place shaped for gods and men by the Creator, the home of Ra, your beloved father and Shu your dear brother. Is there a single living creature who does not long for the country of their birth?' asked Thoth. 'Even rocks and plants cling to their native soil. Animals live close to the burrows where they were born and as for mankind, Fate allows his favourites to live and die and be buried in the place of their birth. What more could anyone desire and how can anyone live happily or rest in peace in a foreign land?'

While she raged in the desert, Hathor had forgotten her home and her family but the words of Thoth brought back her memory. She thought of her father and her brother and remembered all the temples where men had honoured her as the greatest of goddesses. Suddenly Hathor was overwhelmed by a longing for Egypt and her tears were like a cloudburst.

Thoth watched her cry for a while and then said softly, 'O my lady, now you are grieving for your home but think of the flood of tears that Egypt has shed for you. Without you, the temples are empty and silent. Without you there is no music or dancing, no laughter or drunkenness. Without you, young and old despair but if you come back with me now harps and tambourines, lutes and cymbals will sound again. Egypt will dance, Egypt will sing, the Two Lands will rejoice as never before. Come with me, come home and I will tell you another

story as we travel north. Once upon a time a hawk, a vulture and a cuckoo all met together . . .'

Thoth bounded forward, confident that Hathor would follow, but the goddess suddenly realized that all along the baboon had been trying to lure her back to Egypt. She was furious that he had made her weep and with a terrible roar she turned herself into a huge lioness. Her pelt was the colour of blood and crackled and smoked like a living flame. Her face shone brighter than the disc of the sun and her fiery glance terrified Thoth. He jumped like a grasshopper, he shivered like a frog, he saluted her as if she was the glorious sun itself. 'O, powerful one have mercy! I beg you in the name of Ra to spare me! Gracious goddess, before you strike listen to the story of the two vultures!'

Hathor's anger cooled a little and she was curious to hear the story, so she changed back into a wildcat. Thoth began hastily to speak.

Two vultures once lived amongst the desert hills. One day the first vulture boasted, 'My eyes are sharper than yours and my sight is keener. No other winged creature has a gift like mine.' 'And what is this gift?' asked the second vulture. 'By day or by night I can see to the ends of the

The first vulture lifted his bald head and looked beyond the desert to the shores of the distant sea. 'The falcon has been swallowed by a fish with the snake still caught in its claws. Now the first fish is being eaten by a larger fish.' The vulture was silent for a minute and then spoke again. 'Now the big fish has swum too close to the shore and a lion has scooped it out with his paw. He's making a meal of the fish . . . Ah!' The first vulture ruffled his feathers and sidled along the branch in excitement. 'A griffin! A griffin has just swept down and carried off the lion to its nest!'

'Are you sure? Can it really be true?' asked the second bird.

'If you don't believe me, fly with me to the griffin's nest,' said the first vulture, 'and see for yourself!'

So the two vultures took off from the branch and flew across the desert hills till they were close to the lair of the griffin.

'See,' whispered the first vulture, 'his head is like a falcon's and his eyes like those of a man. He has the body of a lion and his ears are like the fins of a fish and his tail like a serpent.' The two birds watched the griffin tearing the last strips of flesh from the lion's bones and then flew away to a safer place.

'Everything that we have seen shows the power of Ra at work in the world,' began the first vulture. 'Even the death of a fly is noticed by the Sun God and those who kill will be killed, violence is repaid by violence. Yet, strangely, nothing has happened to the griffin, although he ate the lion.'

'That must be because the griffin is the messenger of Ra,' answered the second vulture. 'The Sun God has given him the power of life or death over all creatures. There is nothing stronger than the griffin except the justice of Ra.'

'So my lady, it is your father who repays good with good and evil with evil,' concluded Thoth. 'And he has filled you with his power. You are the Eye of the Sun, his avenger.'

The heart of Hathor beat with a fierce joy and she was proud again to be the daughter of the Sun God.

'Stop trembling. I won't kill you now,' promised the wildcat. 'Your words have bewitched me,

earth,' answered the first bird. 'High in the sky or deep in the ocean, I can see everything that happens.'

'It may be true that your eyes are sharper than mine and that your sight is keener,' agreed the other vulture, 'but my ears are sharper than yours and my hearing is keener. I can listen to every sound from land and sky and sea. I can even hear the voice of Ra as he decrees the fate of all creatures on earth.'

The two birds spent many days arguing over whose gift was the more precious, but one morning as they sat together on the branch of a dead tree the second vulture began to laugh. 'What are you laughing at?' demanded his companion.

'I am laughing at the way the hunter can so quickly become the hunted,' said the second vulture. 'A bird on the other side of the sky is telling me what he's just seen. *You* would never be able to hear him at such a distance. He saw a fly caught and eaten by a lizard. A moment later the lizard was seized and swallowed by a snake and the moment after that the snake was snatched up by a hungry falcon. It proved too heavy and the falcon and the snake have both fallen into the sea. If your sight is so good, tell me what's happened to them.'

yet I know that you mean me no harm. You have driven away my grief and anger.'

'My lady, if you will follow me,' began Thoth timidly, 'I will lead you back to Egypt. It isn't many days journey across these hills.'

'Then let us set out at once, at once,' growled Hathor, 'and no more chattering.'

The baboon began to walk towards Egypt with the wildcat a few paces behind him. Thoth was still afraid that she might change her mind, or lose her temper again so he began another story.

Two jackals lived in the desert and were devoted friends. They hunted as a pair and always ate and drank together and shared the same patch of shade. One day as they rested beneath the branches of a desert tree they saw an angry lion bounding towards them. The two jackals stood quite still and let the lion reach them. He was puzzled by this and roared out, 'Are your limbs stiff with age? Didn't you see me coming? Why haven't you run away?'

'Lord Lion,' answered the jackals, 'We saw you coming in your fury and we decided not to run. You would have overtaken us anyway and why should we tire ourselves out before being eaten?'

Since the powerful are not angry with truth, the lion was amused by this cool answer and he let the two jackals go.

'I have told you nothing but the truth,' said Thoth, 'and now that you have spared my life we can travel to Egypt together and I will protect you.'

'You protect *me*? The Eye of the Sun needs no protection from a baboon.'

'The strong can sometimes be saved by the weak,' answered Thoth. 'Remember the story of the lion and the mouse.'

'What story is that?' asked Hathor and Thoth told it to her as they walked towards Egypt.

Once upon a time there was a lion who lived in the desert hills. He was so huge and strong and fierce that all the other animals feared him. Now one day this lion came across a panther who was lying on the ground more dead than alive. The panther's fur had been torn out and he was bleeding from deep cuts all over his body. The lion was amazed, because he thought that only he was strong enough to get the better of a panther.

'What happened?' he demanded. 'Who has done this to you?'

'It was Man,' sighed the panther. 'There is no-one more cunning than Man. May you never fall into his hands!'

The lion had never heard of a beast called Man but he was angry that any creature should inflict such cruel wounds merely for amusement. He decided to hunt down Man and set off in the direction from which the panther had come. At the end of an hour's walk the lion met a mule and a horse who were yoked together, with metal bits hurting their tender mouths.

'Who has done this to you?' asked the lion.

'It was Man, our master,' said the horse.

'Then is Man stronger than both of you?'

'Lord Lion,' answered the mule, 'there is no-one more cunning than Man, may you never fall into his hands!'

Then the lion was angry again and more determined than ever to find and kill this cruel creature called Man. He walked on and soon met an ox and a cow roped together. Their horns had been sawn off and metal rings pierced their tender noses. When the lion asked who had done such a thing he received the same answer: 'It was Man, our master. There is no-one more cunning than Man, may you never fall into his hands!'

The lion set off again and the next thing he saw was a huge bear lumbering towards him. As he came closer, the lion noticed that the claws and teeth of the bear were missing.

'Who has done this to you?' he asked. 'Surely Man cannot be stronger than you?'

'It is true,' groaned the bear, 'for Man is more cunning. I captured Man and made him serve me, but he said to me "Master, your claws are so long it is difficult for you to pick up food, and your teeth are so long that it is difficult for you to get the food into your mouth. Let me trim your nails and your teeth and then you will be able to eat twice as much food." I believed him and let him do as he asked but he pulled out my claws and filed away my teeth. Then he was no longer afraid of me. He threw sand in my eyes and ran away laughing.'

After hearing this the lion was angrier than ever and ran on until he came across another lion with its paw caught in the trunk of a palm-tree.

'What's happened here?' asked the first lion. 'Who has done this to you?'

'It was Man,' growled the second lion. 'Beware of him, never trust him! Man is evil. I made Man my servant and asked him what work he could do, for he looked such a feeble creature. He claimed that he could make an amulet that would give me immortal life. "Follow me," said Man, "and I will turn this tree into an amulet. Do exactly as I say and you will live forever!" So I went with Man to this palm-tree and he sawed a slit in the trunk and wedged it open. He told me to put my paw inside and I did. The next thing I knew, Man had pulled out the wedge. The cleft closed on my paw and I couldn't get it free. Man threw sand in my eyes and ran away laughing and now I am trapped here till I starve to death.'

Then the first lion roared a challenge: 'Man! I will hunt you down and make you suffer all the pain that you have inflicted on other creatures!'

He bounded on until he noticed a small mouse in his path. He raised one paw to crush it but the mouse squeaked out, 'O Lord Lion, don't crush me! I'd hardly make you a mouthful, you wouldn't even taste me. Give me the breath of life and one day I may be able to return the gift. Spare me now and I will help you when you are in trouble.'

The lion laughed. 'What could a tiny mouse ever do to help the strongest of all beasts? Besides, no-one has the power to harm me.' 'Lord Lion, the weak can sometimes help the strong,' insisted the mouse and he swore a great oath to be the lion's friend. The lion thought this very funny but because it was true that the mouse was not worth eating, he let it go.

Now Man had heard the lion roaring and set traps for him. He dug a pit, spread a strong net of leather thongs across the pit and covered both with grass. That evening the lion came bounding along, looking for Man and he fell in the pit and was caught fast in the net. For hours he struggled to free himself, but in vain. By midnight the great lion lay exhausted, waiting for dawn and for Man to come and kill him. Suddenly a voice close to his ear squeaked, 'Lord Lion, do you remember me? I am the mouse whose life you spared and now I have come to save you. What is more beautiful than a good deed repaid?'

The little mouse began to gnaw at the leather thongs. For hour after hour he worked to set the lion free and just before dawn he bit through the last thong. The lion leaped up and shook himself free of the net. With the mouse clinging to his mane, the lion jumped out of the pit and ran away from Man, back to the desert hills. Fate had taught him that every power will one day

meet its master and that the weak can help the strong.

Hathor understood the moral of Thoth's story and she followed the baboon with new respect but she seemed in no hurry to get back to Egypt. When they reached the edge of the desert she lingered under the date-palms and the sycamore-figs and the carob trees, praising their fruit. The baboon climbed the trees, hoping for a glimpse of Egypt. He tried the fruit and found it good, but he reminded the goddess that the fruit of the trees of Egypt was even better, so they went on together.

When they crossed the border the people of Egypt flocked to honour the returning goddess. At el-Kab she appeared to them as a vulture and in the next town as a gazelle but when they were close to Thebes she turned herself back into a wildcat. Before entering the city they lay down to rest. Hathor fell asleep and Thoth watched over her.

The enemies of Ra were angry that the Eye of the Sun had returned to Egypt. Under cover of night a chaos serpent crept towards the sleeping goddess, hoping to poison her and rob Ra of his protector. Vigilant Thoth saw the serpent poised to strike and woke Hathor. The wildcat leaped on the serpent and broke its back. She was grateful to the baboon for his warning and remembered the story of the mouse who saved the lion.

The next morning they entered Thebes and the city went wild with joy. A great feast was given in the temple of Mut, a feast that went on for seven days with eating and drinking, music and dancing and laughter. Hathor was so pleased that she changed from a wildcat into a lovely and gentle woman. Then she let the baboon lead her north again.

At the holy city of Heliopolis, Ra was reunited with his daughter and when they embraced the whole land leaped for joy. A feast was held in the House of the Sycamore at Memphis and all the gods and goddesses celebrated the return of Hathor. Then Thoth changed back to his usual form and Hathor recognized him at last. He sat down beside her at the feast and Ra gave thanks for the cunning of Thoth who had brought home the Eye of the Sun.

The anger of Ra

On the walls of royal tombs and on the golden shrine that protected the mummy of Tutankhamon, was inscribed 'The Book of the Divine Cow', a book which told the story of how the anger of the Sun God nearly destroyed mankind . . .

Ra was old and his bones were like silver, his skin like burnished gold and his hair like lapis-lazuli. When the people of Egypt saw how old and frail their king had become they murmured against him and the murmurs grew into plots to seize the throne of Ra. The plotters met in secret on the edge of the desert and thought themselves safe but as the Sun God watched over Egypt he saw the traitors and listened to their plotting.

Ra was so sad that he longed to sink back into the watery abyss but he was also more angry than he had ever been before. He spoke to the followers who stood about his throne: 'Summon my daughter, the Eye of Ra; send for mighty Shu and Tefenet; bring their children Geb and Nut; fetch the dark Ogdoad, the Eight who were with me in the watery abyss; raise Nun himself! But let them all come here secretly. If the traitors hear that I have summoned a council of the gods they will guess that they have been discovered and try to escape their punishment.'

The followers of Ra hurried to obey him. The message was taken to the great gods and goddesses and one by one they slipped into the palace. Bowing before the throne of Ra, they begged to know why they had been summoned with such haste and secrecy. Then the King of the Gods spoke to Nun, the Lord of the watery abyss and to the other deities: 'O oldest of living things and all you primeval gods, I wept and men sprang up from my tears. I gave them life but now they are tired of my rule and they plot against me. Tell me, what should I do to them? I will not destroy the children of my tears until I have heard your wise advice.'

Watery Nun spoke first. 'My son, you are older than your father, greater than the god who created you. May you rule forever! Both gods and men fear the terrible power of the Eye of the Sun; send it against the rebels.'

Ra looked out over Egypt and said, 'The plotters have already fled deep into the desert. They are afraid that I will learn about their plans and punish them. How shall I pursue them?'

Then all the gods cried out with one voice: 'Send the Eye of Ra to catch them! Send the Eye of the Sun to slaughter them! All of mankind is guilty, let the Eye go down as Hathor and destroy the children of your tears. Let not one remain alive.'

Hathor, the Eye of the Sun, most beautiful and terrible of goddesses, bowed before the throne and Ra nodded his head. Hathor went down into the desert, raging like a lioness. The plotters scattered this way and that but none of them escaped her. She siezed them and slaughtered them and drank their blood. Then merciless Hathor left the desert and raged through villages and towns, killing every man, woman and child she could find. Ra heard the prayers and screams of the dying and began to feel sorry for the children of his tears, but he remained silent.

When it was dark, Hathor returned triumphantly to her father. 'Welcome in peace,' said Ra. He tried to calm the fury of his daughter but Hathor had tasted the blood of men and found it sweet. She was eager for the morning when she could return to Egypt and complete the slaughter of mankind to avenge their treachery. Soon the power of Ra would be unquestioned, but he would have no subjects to rule.

The Sun God wondered how he could save the rest of mankind from his terrible daughter without going back on his royal word. Soon he had thought of a plan. Ra ordered his followers to run, swifter than shadows, to the city of Abu and bring back all the ochre they could find there. As soon as they had returned with baskets full of red soil he sent them out again to fetch the High Priest of Ra from Heliopolis and all the slave-girls who worked in his temple. Ra ordered the High Priest to pound the ochre to make a red dye and set the slave-girls to brewing beer. The High Priest pounded until his arms ached and the slave-girls worked desperately all through the night to brew seven thousand jars of beer. Just before dawn the red dye was mixed with the beer until it looked like fresh blood. The King of the Gods smiled. 'With this sleeping potion I can save mankind from my daughter,'

he said. 'The people have suffered enough.'

Then Ra had the jars carried to the place where Hathor would begin her killing and ordered the beer to be poured out to flood the fields with crimson.

As soon as it was light, Hathor came down into Egypt to sniff out and slaughter the few who were left alive. The first thing she saw was a great pool of blood. The goddess waded into it and was enchanted by her own reflection in the crimson surface. She stooped to lap up the blood and liked it so much that she drank the pool dry.

The beer was strong and the goddess soon became very happy. Her head whirled and she could not remember why she had been sent down to Egypt. Pleasantly drowsy, Hathor made her unsteady way back to the palace of Ra and sank down at her father's feet to sleep for many days.

'Welcome, gentle Hathor,' said Ra gravely. 'Mankind shall remember their escape from your fury by drinking strong beer at all your festivals.' The men and women who were left did remember and always afterwards Hathor was known as The Lady of Drunkenness. At her festivals the people of Egypt could get as drunk as they liked in honour of the goddess and nobody would blame them.

But Ra was still angry and sad about the rebellion of mankind. Nothing could be the same as it had been in the golden age before their treachery. When Hathor finally woke, she felt as she had never felt before and Ra said, 'Does your head ache? Do your cheeks burn? Do you feel ill?' As he spoke, illness first came into being in Egypt.

Then Ra summoned a second council of the gods and said, 'My heart is too sad and weary for me to remain as King in Egypt. I am weak and old, let me sink back into the watery abyss until it is time for me to be born again.'

Nun said quickly, 'Shu, protect your father, Nut carry him on your back.'

'How can I carry the mighty King of the Gods?' asked gentle Nut, and Nun told her to turn herself into a cow. Then Nut was transformed into a huge cow with golden flanks and long curved horns. Ra mounted the Divine Cow and rode away from Egypt.

The murder of Osiris

When the Sun God decided to leave Egypt the people who had escaped the fury of Hathor were angry and afraid. As the earth darkened everyone blamed his neighbour. Men made the first weapons and attacked anyone who might be an enemy of the Sun God. Ra looked back and knew that from that time onwards, man would always kill man in Egypt. He spoke sadly to the Divine Cow: 'Take me where I can still see mankind, but far out of their reach.'

Then the body of the Divine Cow became the sky, arching over the earth and Ra made the stars and scattered them along the belly of Nut. Next the King of the Gods made the Field of Peace and the Field of Reeds as homes for the blessed dead. By then Nut had begun to tremble because she stood so high above the earth. So Ra created the Heh gods, the Twilight Ones, to support her and he commanded airy Shu to stand between the earth and the sky.

Next Ra summoned Thoth and said to him, 'See, I will shine here in heaven and I will light the sky above and the sky below. You must represent me on earth and record the deeds of men.' Then he created the ibis form of Thoth and made him the keeper of records.

When Ra was lighting the undersky the earth was in darkness and men were afraid and wept for the loss of the Sun God. Ra heard them and also transformed Thoth into the Great White Baboon. Thoth shone with a silvery light and mankind no longer dreaded the sinking of the sun because Ra had created the moon. So ibis-headed Thoth was the wise Scribe of the Gods and Thoth the Baboon shone in the night sky. This was the mercy of Ra to the children of his tears.

Lastly, Ra ordered Nun and Geb to guard the earth from the chaos serpents and he made Osiris King of Egypt and Isis Queen. Osiris proved a wise and kindly ruler who showed the people of Egypt how to grow crops, gave them laws and taught them to know and worship the gods. He even made a long journey through the other countries of the earth to bring them the same gifts. Seth was jealous and would have liked to seize the throne of Egypt while his brother was away, but Isis had stayed behind to rule the kingdom. She had never trusted Seth and she watched him like a mongoose eyeing a deadly snake.

When Osiris returned safely to Egypt there was great rejoicing and even Seth pretended to be pleased. He had already begun to plot against his brother and had found a group of greedy, discontented men to help him. Seth waited patiently until his chance came and at last he was invited to a banquet at his brother's palace on a night when he knew that Isis would be away.

Generous Osiris loved to give splendid banquets to the whole court so Seth's fellow conspirators were there among the guests. As soon as the king's brother arrived he began to talk about a splendid chest that had just been made for him. When the wine had been passed round several times, Seth sent for the chest and all the guests admired the fine wood and the rich gilding. Laughingly, Seth promised to give the chest to any man who could fit it exactly.

The guests crowded round, eager to try their luck, but when they tried to lie down inside the chest some were too short to fit it and others far too tall. Seth knew that only one man there could fit the chest exactly for he had already bribed one of Osiris' servants to find out the king's measurements. When all the other guests had failed, the conspirators gathered round Osiris, pressing him to try.

Trustingly, Osiris allowed himself to be helped into the chest. He lay back and everyone saw that the king fitted comfortably, with his head and heels just touching the ends of the chest. There was laughter among the innocent guests to think that Seth had lost such a prize to his brother. Osiris himself smiled up at Seth and began to speak but his brother signalled to the conspirators. Suddenly the lid of the chest was slammed down and the bolts driven home. While the conspirators held back the innocent guests, Seth sealed the chest with molten lead and Osiris died.

The chest that had become a coffin was carried through the night to the bank of one of the Nile's many branches where the conspirators threw it into the water, hoping that it would drift out to sea and be lost for ever. Then Seth announced the sudden death of his brother and crowned himself as the new king.

When Isis heard the terrible news she was half mad with grief. She cut off a lock of her hair and dressed in the sombre clothes of a widow. Then she set out to look for her husband's body. Wild

rumours were everywhere but for a long time she could learn nothing definite. Isis trudged from village to village, questioning everyone she met and at last she spoke to some children who had actually seen the chest thrown into the Nile and float downstream.

The goddess followed that branch of the Nile until it joined the sea. Every few days she found someone who had glimpsed a gilded chest floating north and she knew that all she could do was follow. Isis left Egypt and wandered along the coastline through strange countries until she came to the kingdom of Byblos. There the people could talk of little but a miraculous tree that had suddenly sprung up on the seashore.

The coffin of Osiris had drifted ashore and into the roots of a sapling. Strengthened by the murdered god, the sapling grew in a single night into a tall and graceful tree. When the King of Byblos heard about this marvel he sent his carpenters to chop down the tree and bring it to his palace to be used as a pillar. The carpenters obeyed and trimmed the felled trunk to make a fine pillar; no-one suspected that the coffin of a god was hidden inside the tree.

When Isis learned about the tree from villagers eager to gossip with a stranger, she made her way into the city of Byblos and sat down by a fountain close to the palace.

When some of the maids of the Queen of Byblos came out to the fountain to draw water, they noticed Isis and asked her who she was. The goddess simply told them that she was an Egyptian and a skilled hairdresser. Then and there Isis cunningly plaited the maids' hair and breathed on their skin so that a divine fragrance clung to them.

As soon as the girls went back into the palace

everyone began to admire their attractive hairstyles and marvellous perfume. The maids told their mistress, Queen Athenais, about the Egyptian woman at the fountain and Isis was sent for. The goddess plaited the Queen's hair and Athenais was so delighted that she asked Isis to stay in the palace. In a short while Queen Athenais came to like and trust the Egyptian stranger and Isis was made nurse to the youngest of the two princes of Byblos.

Every night when the rest of the palace was asleep, Isis crept into the room with the pillar that held her husband's coffin and wept over him. In the daytime she looked after the baby prince.

Isis grew fond of the baby and decided to make him immortal. One night she took him with her to the room where the pillar stood and kindled a fire. She whispered spells over it and laid the sleeping baby in the flames. The fire began to burn away the little prince's humanity but Isis did not watch over him. She turned herself into a swallow and flew round and round the pillar, lamenting her murdered husband with the high, sad voice of a bird.

Queen Athenais, who slept in a nearby room, was woken by the crackling of flames and got up to trace the noise. She opened the door to the pillar room and screamed in horror as she saw her child burning. At once the swallow turned back into a woman and the magic flames died away. Isis told the terrified queen who she was and warned her that the little prince would never now be immortal.

Athenais wept at her mistake and asked how she could serve the goddess. Isis asked for the pillar and took it out from under the roof as easily as plucking a lotus. The goddess cut away the trunk, poured oil on the timbers and wrapped them in linen before giving them to Queen Athenais to be kept and honoured in the temple of Byblos.

Isis was given the best boat in the harbour and a crew to sail it and the coffin was carried aboard. When they reached the Egyptian coast, Isis had the coffin taken ashore in a desolate place. Then she unsealed the lid. The body of Osiris looked as if he was merely asleep and the goddess Isis embraced it lovingly, sobbing wildly in her uncontrollable grief.

The coffin was closed again and Isis journeyed south through the marshes of Lower Egypt. One night when the goddess was asleep, Seth came hunting in the marshes and found the coffin. He recognized it at once and was afraid. Opening the coffin, the cruel god lifted out his brother's corpse and tore it in pieces. Then he scattered the pieces throughout Egypt, certain that Isis would never find them all.

When Isis discovered the empty coffin her cry of anguish reached to the heavens and Nephthys her sister hurried to help her. Though Nephthys was the wife of Seth, she had always loved Isis and Osiris better so together the two daughters of Nut set out to search for the scattered body.

For long, sad years faithful Isis and gentle Nephthys wandered through Egypt and in every place where they found a fragment of Osiris they set up a shrine. At last all the pieces were gathered together and Isis worked the greatest of her spells to make the body whole again. The two goddesses watched over the body in the form of hawks, shading it with their wings, while Isis prayed that Osiris should be restored.

She tried every spell she knew and managed to revive Osiris for one night of love so that her promised child could be conceived. Then the body of Osiris was truly dead but his spirit lived on. Ra-Atum made Osiris King of the Dead in the realm of the Beautiful West and from that time onwards every Egyptian knew that death was nothing to fear, for his spirit would live on in the Kingdom of Osiris.

Horus, the falcon-headed son of Isis and Osiris, was born in the marshes of Chemmis and many stories are told of his perilous childhood there. About two and a half thousand years ago, one of these stories was inscribed on a statue of Horus which shows him strangling snakes and scorpions and trampling on crocodiles. The Egyptians believed that if someone who had been bitten by a snake or a scorpion drank water that had been poured over this statue he might be healed, as Horus once was, by the power of the gods.

The inscription tells how Isis and her baby son were caught by Seth outside the marshes. Pretending that it was all for her own protection,

Seth shut Isis up in a spinning house and forced her to spin flax all day. The goddess was closely guarded and without help she was afraid to try to escape with so young a baby.

It was not long, however, before Thoth discovered where Isis was hidden. The wise god entered the spinning house, unseen by the guards, and spoke to Isis.

'You must leave here quickly and return to the sacred marshes of Chemmis where Seth cannot follow you. Wait there till Horus is old enough to claim his father's throne and then we shall see justice done!'

Thoth told Isis how to plan her escape and left behind him seven magic scorpions who would be her guards on the journey north. That night Isis slipped out of the spinning house with Horus in her arms and the scorpions scuttling in front.

By the time she had walked all night and most of the next day carrying her sleeping child, Isis was exhausted and longed for somewhere to rest. At last she and her scorpions came to a village and Isis paused outside the largest house, hoping to be invited in. When the rich woman who owned the house saw the scorpions she was frightened and slammed the door on the weary mother and child. Isis prepared to trudge on but a poor fisherman's daughter opened the door of

her tiny hut and asked the travellers to share what little she had.

While Isis rested in the poor girl's hut and shared her supper of coarse bread and dried fish, the scorpions muttered together against the rich woman. The magical creatures pooled all their poison in the sting of their leader, Tefen, and the scorpion crawled under the gates of the rich woman's house.

Beside an open window the rich woman's only son was sleeping next to his nurse. Tefen crept onto the bed and stung the child. He woke with a scream and the nurse was roused quickly enough to see a huge scorpion scuttling away. She shouted for her mistress and the whole house was soon in as much uproar as if there had been a fire or a flood. The rich woman snatched up her child and ran from house to house but her neighbours were too afraid now to help her.

When Isis heard what had happened, she looked down at Horus sleeping contentedly in her arms and felt sorry for the rich woman. 'An innocent child shall not die because of me,' said the goddess and she called to the rich woman to bring her the child.

Trembling with fear, the woman carried her son into the poor girl's hut. His skin was already burning with fever and he was panting for breath. Isis stood up and laid her hands on the boy, ordering the poison of Tefen to leave him: 'I am Isis, the Mistress of Magic. Every poisonous creature obeys me. Let the child live and the poison die. Let Horus be well for his mother Isis and let this child be well for his mother!'

At once the fever died away; the child's skin was cool again and he was breathing normally. Now that the rich woman knew who it was that she had turned from her door she was more upset than ever. She took her son away and put him to bed and then carried her richest possessions to the hut of the fisherman's daughter, in the hope of pleasing the goddess.

Isis was glad to see the poor girl rewarded for her kindness and in the morning the goddess and her son continued their journey. They soon reached the marshes of Chemmis in safety and the young god was hidden among the papyrus thickets and lotus pools. Whenever she left the marshes to fetch food, Isis disguised herself as a beggar woman but she did not always leave a guard with Horus. She never imagined that any danger could come to the young god as he played in the mud beside the still waters.

One day when Isis returned to the marshes Horus did not toddle forward as usual to greet her. The golden child was lying on his back in the mud, with water streaming from his eyes and mouth. His body was limp and when Isis laid her head to his chest the heartbeat was very faint.

The goddess chanted spells but as she did not know the name of her son's sickness, she could not drive it out. As her magic failed her, Isis began to cry. Who could she turn to? Her husband was dead, her brother was a deadly enemy and her sister was powerless to help her. The gods were remote, but men were close, in a fishing village on the edge of the marshes. Isis ran there with Horus in her arms.

At her cries of distress the fishermen came out of their huts and they pitied her as they would pity any mother with a sick child. The fishermen tried the simple remedies they knew but Horus only grew weaker. Then one of them fetched a wise woman who was staying in the village. She came to Isis carrying a powerful amulet, the Sign of Life, and took Horus in her arms.
'Don't be afraid, little Horus,' murmured the wise woman. 'Mother of the god, do not despair. Horus is protected from his uncle's malice in the marshes of Chemmis. Seth dare not enter them, but he must have sent a snake or a scorpion to bite and poison Horus.'

Then Isis leaned down to smell the child's breath and knew that the wise woman was right: Horus had been poisoned.

Horus began to moan with pain while the villagers looked on helplessly. Suddenly Nephthys appeared. She had sensed her sister's grief and hastened to Chemmis; with her was Selkis, the scorpion goddess. While Nephthys wept in sympathy, Selkis examined the child. She soon saw that there was nothing she could do for him, the fever was raging through his small body and he would soon be dead.
'Isis, you must cry out to the heavens,' said Selkis. 'Stop the Sun Boat! Then the cosmic wind will cease to blow and time will end, unless Horus is healed. Hurry, or it will be too late.'

Isis looked up to where the gods rowed Ra across the skies in the Boat of Millions of Years and she gave a terrible cry. The whole earth shuddered and the sun stopped, for Isis had power over Ra because she knew his secret name.

When the King of the Gods found that his boat could not move he sent Thoth down to Egypt to find out what had happened.
'What is the matter, Isis?' asked Thoth. 'Surely nothing can have happened to Horus? Why have you stopped the Sun Boat and brought darkness to lands which should be in light?'
'Horus is poisoned,' said Isis bitterly, 'and Seth is to blame. I wish now that I had died with Osiris, I only stayed behind to see Horus avenge his father.'
'Don't be afraid Isis, don't cry Nephthys, I have come from the sky with the breath of life to cure your child.'

Then the wise god began to chant a spell: 'Back, O poison! You are to be vanquished by the power of Ra himself. The King of the Gods commands you to go from this child. The Sun Boat will stand still and half of the world will wither and burn and half will lie in darkness, until Horus is healed. Down to the earth, O poison, so that the sun may journey across the sky again and all hearts rejoice.'

Then the poison began to leave Horus and Thoth sang out, 'The fever is gone, the poison is vanquished! Horus is healed—to his mother's delight!'

Isis said quickly, 'Order the marsh-dwellers to protect Horus.' Thoth agreed and ordered the people and creatures of the marshes to watch over the child until he was old enough to claim his father's throne.
'Ra himself will guard Horus,' promised the wise god, 'and the power of his mother will protect him for she will make everyone love him. I must return to the Sun Boat for they cannot row on without me. I must take the good news to Ra that Horus is alive and well—to his mother's delight.'

Then Thoth returned to the sky and Isis joyfully carried her son back into the marshes, to wait for the time of her vengeance on Seth.

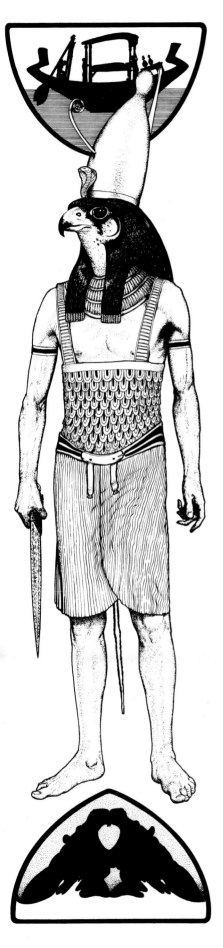

The conflict of Horus and Seth

As soon as Horus was old enough to challenge his uncle Seth he summoned the Ennead, and many of the other gods, to act as judges. With his mother beside him, Horus spoke of the cruel murder of his father Osiris and of how Seth had usurped the throne of Egypt. All the gods were impressed by the eloquence of falcon-headed Horus and when they had listened to the whole of his story they also pitied him.

Shu, the eldest son of the Creator spoke first: 'Right should rule might. Seth had force on his side but Horus has justice. We should do Horus justice by saying "Yes, you shall have the throne of your father." '

Then Thoth said to the Ennead, 'This is right a million times!'

Isis gave a great cry of joy and begged the north wind to change direction and blow westward to whisper the news to Osiris. 'Giving the throne to Horus seems right to the whole Ennead!' declared Shu.

All this time no-one had thought to ask the King of the Gods what he thought about the case.

'What's this?' muttered Ra-Atum. 'Are the Ennead starting to make decisions on their own?'

Shu did not notice that his father's face had darkened and he went on confidently, 'Thoth shall give the royal signet ring to Horus and we will crown him with the White Crown.'

All the gods shouted their approval; all but two. The Sun God was ominously silent and Seth himself suddenly stepped forward and bellowed, 'If there is any dispute about who should rule Egypt, let this puny boy challenge me in person. Then all you gods can watch me overthrow him!'

'We know that would be wrong,' protested Thoth. 'How can we give the throne of Osiris to you when the son of Osiris stands before us? He is the rightful heir, we are all agreed on that.'

'I have not agreed,' said the Sun God coldly.

There was a shocked silence and then Shu wailed, 'What shall we do now?'

The best they could think of was to send for the ancient ram god of Mendes and to ask him to judge between Horus and Seth. So

Banebdjed was hastily sent for and when the ancient god arrived, Ra-Atum said to him, 'Come now, judge between these two young gods, so that they'll stop their wrangling over Egypt and give us some peace.'

Banebdjed knew that Horus was in the right but he was afraid of angering the Sun God so he said, 'We should not decide the matter without the very best advice. Let us send a letter to Neith, the Divine Mother. Let us see what she thinks about it.'

Then the Ennead said to Thoth, 'Write her a letter at once!'
'I will, I will,' promised the scribe of the gods. He blackened the tip of his reed brush, unrolled a piece of papyrus and squatted down to write a flowery letter to Neith. The swiftest of messengers was sent north to deliver the Ennead's letter to the great goddess. Neith read it and soon sent back a letter of her own.

Thoth unrolled the papyrus and read the letter aloud. 'Give the throne of Osiris to Horus his son. To do anything else would be so wicked that the sky would crash down on your heads. As for Seth, double his goods, give him two beautiful goddesses to be his wives and let him leave the throne to Horus.'

Then all the gods shouted, 'This goddess is right!'

The Sun God was very angry and he said contemptuously to Horus, 'How can a feeble boy like you rule Egypt?'

The other gods were angry then and the baboon god Baba stood up and said to Ra-Atum, 'Your shrine is empty; we aren't taking any notice of you!'

The Sun God was so shocked and offended that he covered his face and lay down on his back. The Ennead realized that they had gone too far and shouted at Baba, 'Leave this company at once!' They tried to comfort Ra-Atum but he refused to listen to them. He got up, stalked into his tent and would not come out again.

Nobody could think what to do next and they were all afraid of what might happen to the world if Ra-Atum refused to sail the Sun Boat across the skies. Finally Hathor, the daughter of Ra-Atum, decided on a plan. The beautiful goddess began to dance and as she danced she stripped off all her clothes. The other gods crowded round to get a better view, laughing and applauding. The noise disturbed the Sun God and he thrust his head through his tent flap to find out what was going on. When he saw his lovely daughter dancing, Ra-Atum laughed too and forgot his anger. The King of the Gods returned to sit with the Ennead and said to Horus and Seth, 'We will hear the case again and both of you can put your point of view.'

Seth insisted on speaking first. 'I am Seth, the strongest of the Ennead. When the Sun Boat voyages through the undersky and the serpents of chaos attack, only I can save you. I am the protector of the gods so you should give the throne of Osiris to me!'

Remembering the terrors of the chaos serpents, many of the gods muttered that Seth was right but Shu and Thoth still said, 'How can we give the throne to the uncle when the son and heir is standing here?'

Banebdjed answered, 'How can we give the throne to a youngster when his elder is standing here?'

Then Horus said bitterly, 'Will you rob me of my birthright in front of the Ennead?'

Isis was furious with the Ennead for not speaking up for her son and she complained to them until for the sake of peace they promised that justice should be done to Horus. Then it was Seth's turn to be angry.
'How dare you cowards go back on your word? I shall fetch my great sceptre and strike one of you down with it each day and I swear that I won't argue my case in any court where Isis is present!'

To keep the peace Ra-Atum said, 'We shall cross the river to the Island-in-the Midst and try the case there. I will give orders to Nemty the ferryman not to ferry Isis across, or any woman that might be her.' Then the Ennead and all the other gods and goddesses crossed the river and set up their splendid tents on the island.

Cunning Isis, the Mistress of Magic, changed herself into a bent old woman carrying a jar of flour and honey cakes. She hobbled towards the riverbank where Nemty the ferryman was sitting beside his boat. 'Now young man,' croaked Isis,

'ferry me across at once. In this pot I have food for the young man who is tending cattle on the island. He's been with the herd five days now and his food will have run out.'
'I'm sorry, grandmother,' said Nemty, 'but I have orders not to ferry women across this river.'

Isis delved into her pot. 'I will give you this sweet cake for payment.'

Nemty did not even glance at it. 'I am the ferryman of the gods, what do I need with your cakes?'

Then Isis thrust a skinny finger in front of Nemty's face. 'Do you see this gold ring on my finger? Ferry me across and it's yours.'

The ring was a very fine one and Nemty could not resist such a bribe. 'Alright then, grandmother, give me that ring and I'll ferry you over.' He picked up his pole and they were soon across.
'Hurry back when you've found your cowherd,' shouted Nemty as he tied up his boat.

Isis was already slipping through the trees towards the camp of the Ennead. The gods were holding a feast but Seth was standing apart from the cheerful company. Changing her shape again, Isis walked towards Seth as a beautiful woman, dressed like a widow. Her brother might be the strongest of the gods but she knew that she could always defeat him by cunning. Isis smiled and Seth hurried to greet this attractive stranger, eager to please her.

'Who are you, my pretty?' asked Seth. 'And why have you come here?'

Isis hid her face and pretended to cry. 'O great Lord, I am looking for a champion. I was the happy wife of a herdsman and I gave him a son. Then my dear husband died and the boy began to look after his father's cattle. One day a strange man came and siezed our byre and told my son that he was going to take our cattle and turn us out. My son wanted to protest but the man threatened to beat him. Great Lord, help me and be my son's champion.'

Seth put his arms around her. 'Don't cry my pretty. I'll be your champion and thrash this villain. How dare a stranger take the father's property when the son is still alive!'

Then Isis shrieked with laughter. She turned herself into a kite and flew up into an acacia tree. 'Cry yourself, mighty Seth. You have condemned yourself! You have judged your own case.'

Seth was so angry he wept tears of rage and the other gods demanded to know what had upset him.
'That evil woman has tricked me again,' complained Seth and he told them what had happened.

Then the Sun God said, 'It is true Seth, you have judged yourself, now what will you do?'
'First, I will see that ferryman punished!' growled Seth.

Nemty was brought before the gods and as a

45

punishment for disobeying orders, they cut off his toes. From that day on Nemty never looked at gold again.

Now the Ennead crossed over the river and camped in the Western Mountains while plans were made for the coronation of Horus. Seth still would not admit defeat. He watched the White Crown placed on the feathered head of Horus and said fiercely, 'He may be crowned but he can't rule until he's beaten me. I challenge you Horus; let us turn ourselves into hippopotami and fight deep in the river. Whoever surfaces first will be the loser!' Horus agreed gladly but Isis sat down and wept, afraid that Seth would kill her son.

The two gods were soon transformed into huge, fierce hippopotami and they plunged into the river. Isis quickly took yarn and copper and made them into a magical harpoon. She threw the weapon into the white water churned up by the fighting beasts, but she could not tell which god was which. The copper point stabbed Horus in the flank and he surfaced briefly and roared, 'Mother your spear has pierced me, let me go!'

Isis called to her magic weapon to release Horus and it returned to her hand. She threw it again and this time it stabbed Seth. With a bellow of pain Seth rose up as Isis tugged at the harpoon and cried out, 'O my sister, why must you always be my enemy? What have I done to you? I am your brother, let me go!'

As Isis could not help feeling a little sorry for Seth, she ordered her magic weapon to release him. Horus was furious with his mother for interfering and for pitying Seth. He leaped out of the river with a face like a leopard and cut off his mother's head with one stroke from his copper knife. Then Horus strode towards the Mountains of the West, carrying his mother's head under his arm.

Isis, the Mistress of Magic, calmly turned her body into a statue and walked towards the tent of the Sun God. All the gods and goddesses jumped up in amazement and Ra-Atum said to Thoth, 'Who is this coming with no head?' 'It is Isis,' answered the wisest of the gods, 'and Horus has cut off her head.'

The Sun God was horrified and vowed that Horus should be punished. Isis was soon restored to her usual form and the Ennead went up into the Western Mountains to look for Horus.

The young god had found an oasis and was asleep in the shadow of a palm tree when his uncle discovered him. Seth seized Horus from behind and tore out both his eyes. The young god cried out in terrible agony as Seth strode away and buried the eyes of Horus in the ground. When he returned to the camp of the Ennead, Seth told them that he had found no trace of his nephew.

All through the night poor blind Horus lay in pain and by the morning two beautiful lotuses had grown up where his eyes were buried. Hathor, Lady of the Southern Sycamore, had continued to search for Horus long after the other gods had given up and at last she found him and pitied his agony. Hathor the great huntress caught a gazelle and milked it. Then she knelt beside the young god and said gently, 'Uncover your face.'

Horus did as he was told and Hathor dripped the milk onto his wounds. At once the pain vanished.

'Open your eyes,' commanded Hathor. Horus obeyed and found that the healing magic of the goddess had restored his eyes and he could see again. Hathor hurried back to the Ennead and said, 'Seth has been lying to you. He found Horus yesterday and tore out his eyes, but I have healed him and here he comes!'

Then the Ennead ordered Horus and Seth to stand before the Sun God and hear his judgement. Since both of them had acted wrongly Ra-Atum said, 'For the last time, stop quarrelling and make peace!' Seth pretended to agree and as a gesture of good will even asked Horus to stay with him in his palace. Horus, however, soon found that he could not trust his uncle and he had to ask his mother for help again. Isis willingly forgave her son and whatever trick Seth tried, she managed to turn it against him.

At last, in desperation, Seth demanded one more contest with Horus. Before the whole Ennead he declared, 'Let both of us build a ship of stone and we'll race them down the Nile. Whoever wins the race shall wear the crown of

to stop and he had to obey the great gods.

By this time, Horus despaired of his case ever being settled so he journeyed north to seek the advice of the wise goddess Neith. In the meantime Shu and Thoth persuaded the Ennead to send a letter to Osiris himself in the Beautiful West, the realm of the dead. The journey to that realm was long and perilous but at last a messenger arrived with an angry letter from the King of the Dead. Osiris demanded to know why his son had been robbed of the throne and whether the gods had forgotten that it was Osiris who had given the world the precious gifts of barley and wheat.

When Thoth read this letter aloud to the Ennead the Sun God was annoyed at Osiris for telling him what to do and he wrote back an arrogant letter. After many days another weary messenger returned with a second letter from the King of the Dead and Thoth read it out: 'How good are the deeds of the Ennead!' began Osiris sarcastically. 'Justice has sunk into the underworld. Now listen to me, the land of the dead is full of demons who fear no god or goddess. If I send them out into the world of the living they will bring back the hearts of evildoers to the place of punishment. Who among you is more powerful than I? Even the gods must come at last to the Beautiful West.'

When the Sun God heard this letter, even he was afraid and all the gods agreed that the wish of Osiris should be honoured. Isis herself was sent to bind Seth and bring him in chains before the Ennead.
'Seth, have you stolen the throne from Horus?' demanded the Sun God.

Seth said meekly, 'No, let Horus be brought and given his father's throne.'

The young god was crowned again and placed on the throne of Egypt and Isis gave a joyful shout: 'My son you are King; my heart is glad that the whole earth will be brightened with your glory!'

Then the Sun God had Seth released from his chains and said to him, 'Son of Nut, you shall live with me in the sky as the Lord of Storms and when you thunder the whole earth will tremble!'

Seth was satisfied at last and made his peace with Horus and all the gods rejoiced.

Osiris.' Horus agreed to the contest at once.

Mighty Seth took up his club and struck the top of a nearby mountain. Then he built a huge ship of solid stone and dragged it to the river. Horus' ship was already afloat, for the young god had secretly made a boat of pine and plastered it to make it look like stone. When Seth tried to launch his boat it sank straight to the bottom of the Nile and the Ennead laughed. Seth leaped into the water and turned himself into a hippopotamus once more. He attacked the boat of Horus and because it was only wood it splintered and sank. Horus grabbed his spear and thrust at Seth but the Ennead shouted at him

The journey of the soul

Each dawn Ra the Sun God, in his scarab beetle form, boarded the 'Day Boat' and was rowed across the sky by a crew of gods and the souls of the blessed dead. At noon the youthful sun was strong and blazed down on the earth, but by dusk he had changed into ancient ram-headed Atum. When he reached the western horizon, Ra-Atum boarded the 'Night Boat' and travelled across the sky below the earth and the realm of the dead. Thoth, Hathor, Seth and many other deities surrounded and protected Ra-Atum and the boat of the Night Sun was dragged by jackals and crowned cobras. The dead woke into new life as the Sun God lit up the underworld and Osiris, the ruler of the Beautiful West, saluted Ra-Atum as his twin soul, for they were both images of the Creator.

The Night Sun had to overcome many obstacles on his perilous journey. The terrible demons who guarded the gates of the underworld would not open them unless their mysterious questions were correctly answered and the forces of chaos gathered nightly to attack Ra-Atum. Mighty Seth stood in the prow to fight off Apophis, the greatest of the chaos serpents, for if the sun did not win free of the underworld the waters of chaos would cover the earth and the rule of the gods would end. Every dawn was a hard fought victory of light over darkness, order over chaos.

When an Egyptian king died he was thought to share the ordeal of the Night Sun and his journey through the dangers of the underworld led to a dawn of rebirth and eternal life. The dead king was also identified with Osiris who had suffered death, risen again to rule the underworld and had been avenged by Horus. Every king followed the same pattern of death and rebirth, while his son replaced him on the throne of Egypt as the new Horus.

These ideas, and many others about the afterlife of the king, occur in the spells carved inside some pyramids. At first such spells were only used in royal burials but after the collapse of the Old Kingdom, important commoners began to have the spells painted on their coffins, together with maps of the underworld. By the New Kingdom every dead Egyptian was identified with Osiris and the spells were written on papyrus and buried with the dead. These spells made a book of some one hundred and ninety chapters which the

Egyptians called 'The Spells for Coming Forth by Day' but which is better known now as 'The Book of the Dead'.

All Egyptians went to a great deal of trouble and expense to prepare their tombs and burial equipment. A fine coffin or an illustrated copy of the Book of the Dead were status symbols which showed how wealthy and successful the owner was. The bodies of the dead went through the elaborate and costly process of mummification. In very early times the Egyptians had simply buried their dead wrapped in mats in shallow graves in the desert. The hot, dry sand had preserved the bodies but when the dead began to be buried in wooden coffins inside mudbrick or rock-cut tombs, the bodies decayed. The Egyptians noticed this and tried to develop a method of imitating the effect of the hot sand so that bodies could be preserved and the spirits of the dead could still inhabit them. This art of mummification reached its peak just after the end of the New Kingdom.

When someone died, the grieving relatives would take the body to the embalmers, who lived as a caste apart and wore the jackal mask of their patron, Anubis, the guardian of the dead. When a price for their services had been agreed, the body was laid on a stone slab and the embalmers began their grisly work. A metal hook was used to pull out the brains through the nostrils. The brains were then thrown away since the Egyptians did not recognize their importance and thought of the heart as the centre of intelligence and feeling. Next the stomach was slit open and the vital organs were removed. The inside of the body was rinsed out with wine and packed with herbs and spices. Then the whole body was covered in natron for at least forty days.

Natron is a natural mixture of carbonate, bicarbonate, chloride and sulphate of sodium which absorbs water. The vital organs were also treated with natron and the lungs, liver, stomach and intestines were then packed into four 'Canopic' jars, stone jars with stoppers in the form of the four sons of Horus. After forty days the body itself was completely dry and little but skin and bone remained. The embalmers used bags of myrrh and cinnamon, or humbler

materials such as sand or sawdust to stuff the body, plumping out the limbs and face and making them look more life-like. The heart was replaced in the chest and the stomach was sewn up again. The body was anointed with scented oils and sometimes treated with molten resin before being carefully bandaged with strips of linen. Numerous amulets were hidden in the layers of bandaging and a mask was placed over the head of the completed mummy.

The body was then laid inside a set of painted coffins and taken across the Nile to one of the Cities of the Dead on the West Bank. Loaded onto a sledge, it would be dragged by oxen to the family tomb with the relatives walking behind and professional mourners beating their breasts, tearing their hair and wailing for the dead man as if he was Osiris himself. At the entrance to the tomb a priest performed the 'Opening of the Mouth' ceremony in which he touched the mask of the mummy with a model adze and recited spells to restore the power of sight and speech and hearing to the dead.

The mummy could then be inhabited by the dead man's *ka*. The *ka* appeared as the double of his earthly body but it was the vital force which survived him after death. The *ka* could live in the dead man's mummy or, if that had been destroyed, in a statue of him, but it needed constant nourishment. Every Egyptian was supposed to make food offerings at the tombs of his ancestors but the duty was often neglected or forgotten. Knowing this the Egyptians included pictures of models of food and drink and all the other good things in life in their tombs for the use of the dead. As an extra precaution some tombs were inscribed with a message from the dead promising to reward anyone who would recite a spell to invoke 'bread, beer, oxen, fowl, alabaster, clothing and all good and pure things on which a god lives.'

Though the Egyptians sometimes adopted new ideas, they hardly ever discarded old ones. Because of this their beliefs about death and the afterlife can seen very complicated or plain contradictory. The tomb was the 'house of the *ka*' and the scenes of daily life carved or painted on the walls and the clothes and jewels and furniture buried with the dead make it look as if the Egyptians imagined the afterlife taking place in the tomb and being very like life in Egypt. This is partly true, but it is not the whole story.

As well as a *ka* every Egyptian was thought to have a *ba* or soul, which was shown as a bird with a human head. After death a man or woman's *ba* could take on the form of a swallow or a falcon or a heron and fly wherever it liked on earth with flocks of other souls. Nor was the *ba* confined to earth; it also made a perilous journey through the underworld to win the right to an afterlife of eternal joy.

Most of the spells in the Book of the Dead were designed to help the *ba* as it shared many of the dangers faced by the Night Sun on its voyage. All kinds of terrible things might happen to the *ba* in the underworld and spells were needed to stop him losing his heart, being bitten by snakes, forced to walk upside-down or decapitated.

The *ba* had to endure ordeals of fire and water and might be attacked by monsters such as the Ass-Eating Serpent or the Crocodiles of the Four Quarters, which could only be defeated by using the right spell against them. Before he could get across the Lake of Dawn to the Winding Water, the *ba* had to name the surly ferryman of the gods and every part of his magic boat. Finally he had to face a series of gates guarded by hideous demons who threatened him with their knives. By knowing the secret names of these demons—Faceless One, Wallower in Slime, Clawed One, Feeder on Carrion and Lord of Knives—the *ba* gained power over them.

His goal was the throne room of Osiris, the Hall of the Two Truths, but the *ba* could not enter without speaking the names of every part of the doorway.

Inside the Hall of the Two Truths, the *ba* was met by Thoth and taken to face the forty-two judges of the underworld. He had to greet them by name and swear that he had not committed the crimes that they punished. 'O Long-Strider who comes from Heliopolis; I have done no evil; Flame-Embracer who comes from Kheraha, I have not robbed; O Long-Nosed One who comes from Hermopolis, I have not been envious; Shadow-Eater who comes from the Twin Caverns, I have not been dishonest; O Savage-Faced One who comes from Rostau, I have not murdered . . . O you gods, I know your names and I am not afraid! I have lived in truth and done what gods and men admired. I have given bread to the hungry, water to the thirsty, clothes to the naked and ferried the boatless. I have made offerings to the gods and to the dead, I am pure of mouth and hands!'

To test the innocence of the *ba*, his heart was weighed by Anubis against the feather that symbolized *Maat*, while Thoth stood by to record the verdict. The Egyptians were so afraid of this test that they took to burying a Heart Scarab with most mummies. This was a stone scarab beetle inscribed with a spell to help them in the Hall of the Two Truths: 'O heart of my being, don't witness against me, don't oppose me in the place of judgement, don't rebel against me before the guardian of the scales, don't make my name stink before the judges!'

If the heart was weighed down by the sins and heavier than *Maat*, the *ba* died a second and more terrible death. If the scales were even the victorious *ba* was led by Horus before the throne of Osiris and became an *akh*, a blessed soul. The *akh* might shine among the circumpolar stars or join the crew of the Sun Boat or live in bliss in the peaceful Field of Reeds.

Not every Egyptian believed in a happy afterlife or that spells and offerings and mummification could really help the dead. Some poets pointed to the plundered tombs and empty coffins of long dead kings and nobles and urged their listeners: 'Follow your heart as long as you live! Put myrrh on your head, dress in fine linen and rub yourself with oils fit for a god. Heap up your joys and don't let your heart sink. Wailing saves nobody from the grave. Make holiday, make holiday, never weary of it. No-one can take his goods with him; the dead do not return.'

Others trusted in the goodness of the gods and the promised joys of the land of eternity, 'The right and just which holds no terrors. All our ancestors rest in it from the beginning of time. Those yet to be born, millions upon millions, will all come to it, for no-one can linger in the land of Egypt. Our time on earth is only like a dream and God says "Welcome in peace" to those who reach the Beautiful West.'

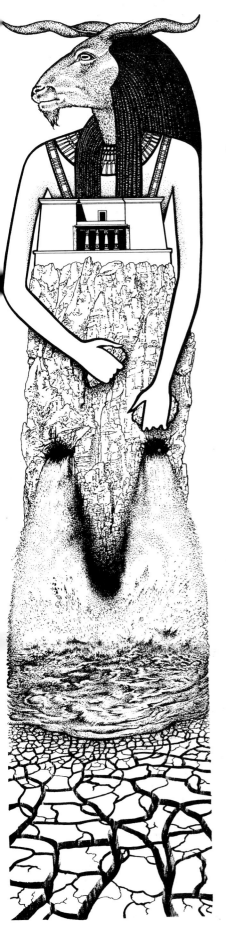

The seven year famine

On an island in the Nile, close to the ancient city of Elephantine, stands a granite rock carved with a story and a scene of a king with three deities: Khnum, Satis and Anukis. The picture and the inscription are about two thousand years old, but the story is set in the reign of King Zoser who ruled Egypt over four and a half thousand years ago.

The story shows how vital the river Nile was to the people of ancient Egypt. The Blue Nile rises in the mountains of Ethiopia and the White Nile in the lakes and marshes of central Africa. The two rivers join near Khartoum, the capital of the Sudan, and flow on towards Egypt. Each year heavy summer rains in Ethiopia and the Sudan swell the Nile. Nowadays the river is controlled by the great Aswan Dam but in ancient times the swollen Nile poured into Egypt and flooded the low-lying land. This inundation covered the Nile valley with a layer of rich mud which was ideal for growing crops when the waters sank low enough for planting to begin. A powerful flood might reach the settlements on the higher ground and do a great deal of damage, but a weak flood, a 'low Nile' was worse. If the flood waters failed to spread out very far, Egypt faced starvation.

In the eighteenth year of Zoser's reign, the Nile failed to rise and flood the land with its life-giving waters. For six years Egypt had suffered low Niles. The floods had only reached half the fields and not enough crops could be grown to feed everyone. Every year the people had prayed for a high Nile and every year the waters had sunk lower. By the seventh year Zoser was in despair.

All kinds of food were scarce. Men robbed their brothers to get enough to eat; children wailed with hunger in their mother's arms; old men squatted in the dust hugging their knees and even the nobles were gaunt and grim. The temples were shut for lack of offerings and the shrines of the gods were deserted.

None of the king's advisers knew what to do until Zoser consulted his vizier, the wise Imhotep.

'Tell me,' said Zoser, 'where is the source of the Nile? Where is the city of the Sinuous One? What god lives there? If I knew that, I could pray to him for help in ending our seven years of famine.'

Imhotep was famous for his skill in architecture and medicine and every other branch of learning, but even he could not answer the king's questions straight away. 'Sovereign, my lord,' said Imhotep, 'I shall go to the temple of Thoth and read his sacred books in the House of Life. If the answers exist, I will find them there.'

Imhotep spent many days studying the sacred writings that only he was wise enough to read. He discovered everything that the king wanted to know and hurried back to court to tell him. 'Sovereign, my lord, far to the south, on an island in the Nile lies the city of Elephantine. It is built on that first mound of land that rose from the dark waters of Nun. The hills that surround the city are of red and black granite and are rich in copper and silver and gold, turquoise, carnelian, emerald and jasper. In the heart of the city stands a temple called 'Joy of Life'. Beneath the temple are two caverns where the Nile sleeps until it is time for the river to rise up and bound towards Egypt in a mighty wall of water. 'Khnum is the god who opens the floodgates. He sits enthroned at Elephantine, with his sandals resting on the Nile and his crown touching the sky. Khnum is the lord of barley and wheat, fruit and flowers, birds and fish and animals. All these good things are offered daily in the temple to the great god Khnum, to Anukis his wife, Satis his daughter and the other deities of Elephantine.'

Zoser was delighted to hear of such a wonderful place on the edge of his realm. He hurriedly unrolled the secret books to learn the rituals that would please Khnum and all the gods of Elephantine. Zoser spent the whole day leading processions of priests to make offerings.

That night, as the king slept, he dreamed that ram-headed Khnum stood beside his bed. In his dream, Zoser leaped up and kissed the ground before the god. Khnum spoke kindly to him.

'I am the maker of mankind. My arms are around you all to hold you steady and keep you safe. I have given you precious stones so that the people of Egypt may build temples and adorn the statues of the gods. I am the master of the flood; when I open the two caverns the Nile gushes out to hug your land and kiss your fields. Mourn no longer; now you have called on me, I shall end the seven years of famine. I will make the Nile gush for you and the great flood will shine again on the fertile shores of Egypt.'

Then glorious Khnum faded from the king's sight but when he woke Zoser remembered his dream. He jumped up full of joy and vigour, certain now that Egypt would be saved. In his gratitude for the god's promises, Zoser decreed that Elephantine should belong to Khnum for ever and that one tenth of all the products of Upper Egypt should be offered in his temple. The farmers were to share their harvest, the hunters, fishermen and bird-trappers were to give up part of every catch and the traders were to heap the altars of Khnum with ivory and ebony and all the produce of Africa. The temple 'Joy of Life' was to be kept in perfect repair and its shrines filled with statues in gold and silver and precious stones. The king's commands were carved on granite, so that they should never be forgotten and Khnum kept his promises. For the rest of Zoser's reign and for many years after, High Niles flooded the land.

The Egyptians came to regard the reign of Zoser as the beginning of a golden age. The wise Imhotep was worshipped as a god and Zoser was remembered as the greatest king of the Third Dynasty. The Fourth Dynasty (2575–2465 BC) marked the start of the Old Kingdom in which Egypt was at the height of its splendour.

The country was divided into districts called Nomes and well governed by a series of strong kings and an efficient civil service headed by the vizier. The government made sure that the natural resources of Egypt were fully exploited. When there were High Niles, barley, emmer (a kind of wheat) and flax for spinning into linen were easily grown. The deserts surrounding Egypt proved to be rich in good stone for building and sculpture and turquoise could be fetched from Sinai. Most important of all were the gold mines of the eastern desert and of Nubia. The kings of Egypt soon conquered and occupied Nubia so that they could work the goldmines and open up trade routes to Africa to barter for ivory and ebony, leopard skins and incense. Encouraged by this new wealth, art flourished. Old Kingdom paintings and carvings are full of a confident delight in life that the Egyptians were never to know again.

King Khufu and the magicians

King Khufu came to the throne of Egypt in about 2500 BC and was the builder of the Great Pyramid at Giza. This story describes how Khufu discovered that a new dynasty of kings was soon to rule Egypt.

One day King Khufu felt bored and he challenged his sons to entertain him with stories of magic. Khaefre, the Crown Prince, at once got up to speak:

'I should like to tell your Majesty about a wonder which happened in the time of your forefather, King Nebka. Close to the temple of Ptah lived a lector-priest called Webaoner. He was a favourite of the king and respected throughout Egypt for his wisdom. Everyone admired him except his own wife. She had fallen in love with a handsome young man from Memphis and one day she packed a sandalwood chest with clothes and fine linen and sent it to the young man as a present. He came to Webaoner's house to thank her and it wasn't long before he had agreed to meet her secretly in a pavilion that stood beside a lake in the garden.

'Webaoner's wife ordered the gardener to take food and wine to the pavilion, to spread its floor with comfortable rugs and cushions and to hang scented torches and garlands of flowers from its columns. Everything was done as she had ordered. The young man joined the lector-priest's wife in the pavilion and they spent the day feasting and kissing and plotting how to get rid of Webaoner.

'Soon whenever her husband was away at court she ordered the pavilion to be made ready and spent days and nights there with the young man. The gardener did not dare to disobey his mistress but when he heard drunken laughter coming from the pavilion or saw the young man bathing in the lake, his heart grieved for his master. At last, when gossip began to spread from the household to the town, he resolved to tell Webaoner the truth about his wife. The gardener asked to speak to his master alone and stammered out his story.

'With a face of stone Webaoner opened an ebony chest and took out some wax. He modelled a crocodile the length of his hand and gave it to the gardener. "When you next see that young man bathing in the lake," said the lector-priest, "throw this crocodile after him." The gardener was puzzled but he promised to obey.

'The next day Webaoner was summoned to court. As soon as he had gone, his wife ordered the pavilion to be prepared and sent a message to her lover. Hidden in a clump of reeds, the gardener waited until the young man waded into the lake to bathe and then tossed the wax crocodile after him. As it hit the water it came alive and began to grow and soon the crocodile was seven cubits long. It swam after the young man and before he could scramble ashore it had seized him in its jaws and dragged him under. On a bed of cushions in the pavilion Webaoner's wife waited in vain for her lover to come back.

'After seven days at court the lector-priest said to King Nebka, "Sovereign, my lord, come back with me to my house and I will show you a great marvel." The king agreed to come and he was soon standing on the edge of the lake surrounded by his pages and fan-bearers. The lector-priest spoke a summoning spell and the smooth waters were broken by the most enormous crocodile that the king and his courtiers had ever seen. From this monster's jaws dangled the young man for the spells of Webaoner had kept him alive under the lake.

'The lector-priest ordered the crocodile to open its jaws and it laid the young man on the shore at the king's feet. Nebka backed away. "Indeed this is a fearful crocodile!" Webaoner bent down and as he touched the crocodile it turned back into wax and shrank to the length of his hand. He presented it to the king, told him the whole story and begged for justice.

'King Nebka ordered the young man to be thrown back into the lake and tossed the crocodile after him, saying, "Take what is yours!" It grew again to a monster of seven cubits and seized the wretched lover and dragged him down to his death. As for the wife of Webaoner, King Nebka ordered her to be burned alive. This your majesty was the wonder which happened in the reign of your ancestor Nebka.'

Khufu was very pleased with this story and ordered that offerings of bread and beer, oxen and incense, be made to the spirits of King Nebka and the lector-priest Webaoner. Then Prince Baufre got up to speak:

'I should like to tell your Majesty about a wonder which happened in the reign of your father Sneferu. One hot day King Sneferu wandered from room to room of his palace looking for some new entertainment but found nothing to please or sooth him. Finally he sent for the wise lector-priest Djadja-emankh and asked him to suggest a diversion.

"Let your Majesty take a boat out on the lake in your gardens," began the lector-priest, "and let the rowers be the most beautiful girls in your harem. Then your Majesty's heart will be refreshed by seeing the birds and flowers of the lake and by watching the rowers."

'Sneferu was delighted with this idea. He ordered a boat to be fitted with oars of ebony and gilded sandalwood. "And fetch me twenty young girls with pretty figures and long braided hair. Take away their clothes, dress them in nets and let them row!"

'Everything was done as the king commanded and Sneferu was soon lounging on a couch on the deck of his pleasure-boat while twenty charming girls, dressed only in glittering nets, rowed him round the lake. The king admired the white lotus flowers and the clusters of papyrus that edged the lake, he admired leaping fish and flights of startled birds but most of all he admired the pretty rowers.

'One of the girls rowing at the stroke oar was wearing a fish-shaped turquoise amulet in her braided hair. She was growing so hot as she rowed that she pushed back the braids that fell across her face. Her hand dislodged the turquoise pendant and it fell into the lake and sank. With a squeak of dismay the girl stopped rowing and first the rowers on her side and then those on the other had to stop too.

"What is the matter? Why have you stoppped rowing?" demanded the king.

"I had a new turquoise amulet shaped like a fish," said the girl at the stroke oar. "But now it's fallen in the lake and I've lost it."

"Row on," ordered the king, "and I will soon find you another amulet."

"But I don't want another amulet," said the girl obstinately, "I want my amulet."

'Then Sneferu persuaded the girls to row him to the shore and he sent for Djadja-emankh. "My brother," sighed the king, "I did as you suggested and my heart was glad to see the girls row but now one of them has dropped her turquoise amulet in the lake and she wants it back . . .''

'The wise lector-priest smiled and then murmured a powerful spell. The waters of the lake rolled back towards either bank leaving a dry place in the middle. There, on a potsherd, lay the turquoise amulet. Djadja-emankh went down to the bed of the lake, picked up the amulet and brought it back to its owner. Then he released the waters with a second spell and they surged back to cover the bed of the lake. King Sneferu gave the lector-priest rich rewards and spent the rest of the day in feasting with the pretty rowers. This, your Majesty, was the wonder which happened in the reign of your father King Sneferu.'

Khufu was much amused by this story and he ordered that offerings of bread and beer, oxen and incense, be made to the spirits of King Sneferu and the lector-priest Djadja-emankh. Then Prince Hardjedef, the wisest of Khufu's sons got up to speak:

'Your Majesty, my brothers have told you about wonders in the past but I can tell you of a living wonder, a great magician.'

'Who is this magician, my son, and where does he live?'

'His name is Djedi and he lives in Djed-Sneferu. He is one hundred and ten years old and still eats five hundred loaves every day and drinks a hundred jugs of beer every night. He knows how to join a severed head to its body; he knows how to make a lion follow meekly behind him and he knows the number of the secret chambers in the Temple of Thoth!'

For a long time Khufu had been trying to discover the number and plan of the secret chambers of Thoth so that he could copy them for his own tomb. He said eagerly to Hardjedef, 'Go and fetch this magician at once; take whatever boats you need!' The prince took three boats and sailed south. When the pyramids of Sneferu were seen on the western horizon the boats moored on the banks of the Nile and Hardjedef was carried in a chair of gilded ebony to the village of Djed-Sneferu.

Djedi the magician was lying on a mat outside the door of his house with one servant massaging his head and another washing his feet. The bearers set down the prince's chair and Hardjedef said, 'Greetings, honoured Djedi. Though you are old you have the vigour of youth. I have come to summon you to the court of my father the king where he will entertain you and all your household and reward you with a fine tomb.'

Hardjedef stretched out his hand to help the old man up and together they walked towards the Nile, the magician leaning on the prince's arm. When they reached the river bank Djedi asked for one boat for his family and one for his books of magic. He himself travelled with Hardjedef in the first boat.

The king received them in the pillared throne-room and when Djedi had kissed the ground before him, Khufu said, 'Well, magician, why have I never seen you before?'

'The one who is summoned is the one who comes,' answered Djedi dryly. 'Now that you have summoned me, I am here. What is your command?'

'Is it true,' asked the king, 'that you know how to reattach a severed head?'

'Sovereign, my lord, it is.'

Khufu beckoned the captain of his guard. 'Go to the prison, choose a criminal and bring him here to be beheaded.'

'No,' said Djedi sternly, 'I may not work my spells on men, the cattle of the gods. It is forbidden.'

The king was furious at this contradiction of his orders but the old magician was not afraid of him and stood firm.

'Go to the kitchens then,' growled Khufu, 'and bring us a goose.'

The captain soon returned holding a struggling goose by both wings. He drew a knife, slit its throat and chopped off the head. The goose's body was placed on the west side of the hall and its head on the east side. Djedi stood between them and murmured a spell. The body jerked to its webbed feet and waddled across the hall towards the twitching head. As the two met, the head sprang back onto the goose's neck and began to cackle. There was no trace of a wound.

Khufu could hardly believe what he had just seen and ordered Djedi to try the spell again on a duck. The old magician murmured the same spell, the duck's severed head joined its body and the bird was caught and carried back to the royal kitchens. Finally Khufu sent for an ox. The great beast was led into the hall and held by three men while its head was severed by an axe. Djedi spoke his spell and the ox stood beside him, alive.

When the ox had been taken back to its stall and all the blood washed from the floor, Khufu ordered the keepers of the royal menagerie to bring in a fierce lion. Muzzled and leashed, the lion was dragged in by two keepers. Djedi ordered them to release it and the keepers scattered as the angry lion tensed to spring. Just in time, Djedi murmured his spell and the lion trotted to his heels and followed him around the throne-room like a dog.

When the docile lion had been taken back to the menagerie, Khufu beckoned to Djedi and whispered to him, 'It is rumoured that you know the number and plan of the secret chambers of Thoth . . .'
'By your favour, Sovereign, my lord,' began Djedi, 'I do not know myself but I do know how to find out. In the temple at Heliopolis is hidden a chest of flint and the plan of the secret chambers of Thoth is hidden in it.'
'Bring me the chest,' commanded Khufu, 'and you shall name your reward!'
'Sovereign, my lord,' answered Djedi, 'the man is not yet born who will bring you the chest of flint. The only person who can find it is the oldest of the three children in the womb of Reddedet.'
'Who is this Reddedet?' demanded Khufu.
'She is the wife of Rawosre, the priest of Ra, Lord of Sakhbu,' replied Djedi. 'She will soon bear three sons to Ra and they will all be kings of Upper and Lower Egypt.'

When the king heard this he was sad and angry and his courtiers trembled but Djedi said calmly, 'What is this mood, my Sovereign? First your son will be king of Egypt and then his son and then the eldest of the children of Reddedet.'

Khufu was still angry to think that his descendants would not rule Egypt for ever but he hid his feelings and ordered that Djedi should live in the house of Prince Hardjedef and be rewarded for his skill with ample rations.

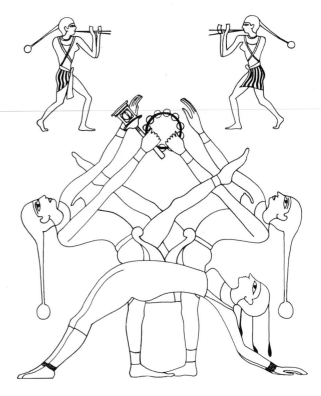

On the fifteenth day of the first month of winter, Reddedet was gripped with the pain of childbirth and lay on her bed for many hours, suffering cruelly. Ra, Lord of Sakhbu heard her cries and moans of agony and sent for Khnum and Isis and Nephthys and for Heket and Meskhenet the goddesses of birth.
'Go down to Egypt,' he said, 'and help Reddedet in her difficult labour for her children will be kings who will build you many temples and make you offerings.' Then the goddesses disguised themselves as a troop of musicians, dressed in gaudy clothes and carrying flutes and rattles and tambourines. Khnum turned himself into their porter and took a birth-stool with him. Then they walked by the house of the priest.

Rawosre stood in the doorway of his house, unshaven and dishevelled. He was desperately anxious about his wife Reddedet for the midwife had not yet arrived from the nearest town. When he saw the musicians and realized that their porter was carrying a birth-stool, Rawosre rushed towards them.
'Ladies, my wife is in childbirth and suffering cruelly . . .'
'We know all about childbirth,' said the goddesses promptly. 'We will help you.'

Rawosre quickly led them to Reddedet's room and was happy to leave them with her. Once the door was locked the deities helped Reddedet onto the birth-stool. Isis stood in front of her and Nephthys behind her while Heket hastened the birth. A golden child was born, already wearing a royal head-dress of lapis-lazuli. When the cord had been cut and the baby had been washed, Meskhenet held him in her arms and promised that he should be a king while Khnum breathed life into him. Two more sons, just like the first, were quickly born, named as kings and given life. Then the goddesses helped Reddedet back to her bed and placed the three children beside her. Reddedet's husband was waiting for them outside.

'May you be happy,' said Isis. 'Your wife has born three fine sons.'

Rawosre was overjoyed. 'Ladies, how can I thank you, what can I do for you? At least take this sack of barley as a small reward.'

Khnum slung the sack across his shoulders and they left the house but before they had gone far, Isis said, 'Should we really return to Ra without having done some marvel to report?'

So the goddesses made three precious royal crowns and hid them in the sack of barley. Then they summoned a heavy rainstorm as an excuse to return to Rawosre's house. Isis knocked on the door and asked one of the servants to store the sack for them or it would be soaked in the rain and the barley would swell and burst before they could get it home. The servant put the sack in a bin in the storeroom and Isis promised that they would call for it the next time they were passing. Then Khnum and the goddesses returned to Ra.

Reddedet kept to her room for two weeks and at the end of that time a feast was planned to celebrate the safe birth of her children. She asked her maidservant whether everything was prepared. The girl said that all the food and drink was ready except the beer, for the only barley in the storeroom was the sack belonging to the musicians.

'Use that to make beer,' ordered Reddedet, 'and Rawosre will give them another sack.'

The maidservant went down and unlocked the storeroom but as she opened the door she heard singing and shouting and cheering as if a king

were passing. She fled back to her mistress and told her what had happened. Reddedet could not believe the girl and went down to the storeroom herself. Sure enough, the room was filled with music and voices acclaiming a king but there was nothing to be seen but jars of wine and lentils and oil and sacks of grain.

Reddedet crept round the room trying to discover where the noises were coming from. She soon realized that they were loudest when she knelt by the bin that held the musicians' barley. Reddedet untied the sack and found the three crowns hidden in the grain. For the first time she understood that her children would be kings. Reddedet put the crowns back into the barley and put the sack in a sealed chest. When Rawosre came home she told him what she knew. He was overjoyed at her news.

A few days later Reddedet quarrelled with her maidservant and gave the girl a slap. She was very angry and said to her fellow servants, 'Why should I stand for this? I've guessed her secret, I know that her children are born to be kings. I shall go and tell King Khufu and see what he will do about it!'

She set out for Memphis but on her way the maidservant passed the threshing floor where her half-brother was binding flax. She told him what she intended to do and he was furious at her disloyalty and gave her a beating with a hank of flax. The girl ran down to the river to bathe her wounds and a crocodile grabbed her and pulled her under.

Her brother returned to the house of Rawosre and found Reddedet sitting crying.

'My lady, why are you so upset?'

'Because the girl I brought up in this house has run away,' answered Reddedet, 'and she means to denounce me to Khufu and I am afraid for my children!'

Then the brother said, 'My lady, the girl came and told me her plan. I gave her a good thrashing and she ran down to the river where a crocodile killed her.'

Reddedet was sorry for the maidservant but her heart rejoiced to think that Ra was watching over his children. She knew then that the god would protect them from the anger of Khufu and that nothing could stop them becoming kings.

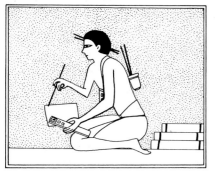

The eloquent peasant

Reddedet's children became the first three kings of the Fifth Dynasty (c2465–2323 BC) and the country prospered under their rule, but during the Sixth Dynasty (c2323–2150 BC) Egypt began to decline.

Many reasons have been suggested for the fall of the Old Kingdom. The climate seems to have continued to get drier and years of low Niles led to famines and weakened the people's faith in their kings. Unwisely, the Old Kingdom rulers gave away many of the royal lands to reward their officials and even allowed them to pass on their jobs to their sons. This made the civil service less efficient and more independent and was particularly dangerous in the case of the officials who governed the Nomes. These governors grew rich and powerful and began to rule their Nomes like petty kings. Wars broke out between them and for the century known as the First Intermediate Period (c2134–2020 BC) Egypt was divided and weak. The story of the eloquent peasant is set in this period when Egypt was full of corrupt officials but the old ideal of impartial justice was still remembered.

In the reign of King Nubkaure a peasant called Khunanup lived with his family by an oasis in the Western Desert. He worked hard all year round to gather foods to trade with in Egypt but he was still a poor man. One day Khunanup said to his wife, 'I'm going down to Egypt to barter for food for our children. Measure out what's left of our grain.'

When she brought the grain from their storeroom, Khunanup divided it into two uneven parts. 'Keep these twenty measures to feed you and the children while I'm away but take these six measures and make them into bread and beer for my journey.'

The peasant loaded his two donkeys with bundles of rushes, sacks of salt and natron, jackal hides and ostrich feathers. When the bread and beer were ready he said goodbye to his wife and children and led the donkeys south towards Heracleopolis.

Some days later, as he was travelling through the district of Perfefi, Khunanup's donkeys were noticed by an official called Nemtynakht. This official was a greedy and ruthless man and when he saw the laden donkeys he decided to take them from the peasant. The house of Nemtynakht stood close to a narrow path which had a corn field on one side and the Nile on the other. The official sent one of his servants to fetch him a sheet and he spread it across the path with its fringe in the corn and its hem hanging over the river.

As Khunanup came along the path Nemtynakht called out, 'Be careful, peasant, don't let your filthy donkeys tread on the sheet I'm drying!'

'Whatever you say,' answered the peasant cheerfully, and he urged his donkeys up into the field to avoid the sheet.

'You wretched peasant!' shouted Nemtynakht. 'Now you're trampling my corn!'

'I can't help trampling the corn if your sheet is blocking the path,' said Khunanup reasonably but at that moment one of his donkeys seized and ate a wisp of corn.

'Thieving beast! I shall take this donkey,' announced the official, 'as payment for my stolen corn.'

'My donkey is worth far more than one wisp of corn!' protested Khunanup. 'I know that this estate belongs to the high steward Rensi. He is an enemy to every thief and he won't let me be robbed on his own land!'

Nemtynakht was furious with the peasant for arguing. 'It is me you have to deal with, not the high steward!'

He beat Khunanup with his staff and seized both the donkeys. The poor peasant sat down on the path and wept.

'Stop wailing,' snapped Nemtynakht, 'or I'll send you to the Lord of Silence!'

'First you rob me, then you beat me and now you forbid me to complain; but you can't stop me asking the gods for justice!'

For ten days Khunanup hung around the house of Nemtynakht, hoping to persuade him to give back the donkeys and their loads. When he saw that it was no use, the peasant walked to Heracleopolis to look for the high steward Rensi. He found Rensi standing on the river bank with a group of other judges, waiting for a barge to take them to the courthouse.

The high steward never refused a plea for justice and he ordered one of his scribes to stay behind and write down the details of the peasant's complaint. As they boarded the barge the other judges said to Rensi, 'Surely there is no need to punish an official for a few skins or a trifle of salt. The peasant probably belongs to him and has been caught trying to sell his master's goods.'

Rensi said nothing, but he was very angry with the judges because he knew that Nemtynakht was dishonest. It also saddened him to think how hard it was for a peasant to get a fair hearing.

The very next day the high steward read the details of Khunanup's case and summoned him before the court. Confident that Rensi was a just man, the peasant knelt down and began to speak: 'O high steward, greatest of the great, when you go down to the Sea of Justice, you shall have fair winds. No storm will strip away your sails and your mast will never snap. Truth will bring you safely to harbour for you are a father to the orphan, a husband to the widow, a brother to the helpless. You are free of greed, an enemy of lies and a friend of truth. You are a lord who hears the voice of the oppressed. Hear my plea, heal my grief, do me justice!'

Rensi, who was used to coaxing a few words out of silent or stammering peasants, was astonished to hear such an eloquent speech. He promised Khunanup that he would hear the case in full next day and hurried to the palace. Rensi bowed before King Nubkaure and said in great excitement, 'Sovereign, my lord, I have discovered a peasant who cannot read or write but who speaks with wonderful eloquence! He is a poor man and one of my officials has robbed him of his donkeys and trade goods so he has come to me asking for justice.'

The king was intrigued. 'As you value my happiness, Rensi, detain this peasant for a while. Be silent when he pleads and have someone write down everything he says. Make sure that he has enough to live on and that his wife and family are provided for. These peasants only come to Egypt to trade when their storerooms are nearly empty. Help them, but in secret!'

Everything was done as the king commanded. Rensi saw that the townspeople offered food to Khunanup and messages were sent to the oasis with orders that the peasant's wife and family were to be cared for. The next time Khunanup came into court, Rensi frowned and spoke coldly to him, but the peasant was not daunted. 'Great lord, justice is the rudder of heaven; you are the rudder of Egypt, the equal of Thoth who keeps the Balance and is the most impartial of judges. If you support the thief, who is there left to punish crime? The desperate can steal without reproach, but you are great and rich and powerful. Lord, be generous, be just!'

Rensi listened with secret pleasure to the peasant's speech and a scribe hidden behind a curtain wrote it all down. When it was over the high steward rose and left the court without a word and Khunanup went away dejected.

The next morning the peasant came back to the court and made a fierce speech attacking judges who were greedy or corrupt. Rensi said nothing but the courthouse guards gave Khunanup a thrashing for his insolence and Nemtynakht looked on and laughed.

For five more days the peasant came to court and pleaded his case but the high steward would not answer him. By the ninth day Khunanup was desperate. He knew that the rations he had left for his family would be used up by now and without him they might starve. The peasant went into the court knowing that if he could not get justice that day he would have to go home.

For the last time, Khunanup knelt before the high steward. 'Great one, do justice for the sake of the Lord of Justice and shun evil. When the just man dies his name is not forgotten on earth and his spirit is blessed in the Realm of the Dead; this is the law of the gods. Speak justice, do justice, for it is mighty and endures for ever!'

The peasant looked up at the high steward but Rensi was silent and gave him no sign.
'A man who once saw has now become blind,' said Khunanup sadly. 'A man who once heard has now become deaf. For nine days I have pleaded in vain, now I shall complain of you to the gods!'

He stood up and strode out of the court but Rensi ordered two guards to bring him back. Khunanup was sure that he was going to be punished for his bold words.
'When death comes,' he said steadily, 'it is like a cup of water to a thirsty man.'

For the first time the high steward smiled at him. 'Good peasant, do not be afraid. Stand there and listen to your pleas for justice.'

Khunanup was astounded when a scribe came forward and read out the nine speeches from a papyrus scroll.
'Come with me now to the palace,' said Rensi and the peasant soon found himself kissing the ground before the throne of King Nubkaure. The king read the speeches and was delighted that a peasant should speak so well and so bravely. He smiled on Khunanup and ordered the high steward to judge his case.

A terrified Nemtynakht was dragged into the throne room and beaten until he confessed his crimes. Then Rensi ordered that all the official's land and goods be given to Khunanup. So the eloquent peasant returned to his oasis a rich man and justice ruled in Egypt.

The shipwrecked sailor

During the turmoil that followed the decline of the Old Kingdom, a warlike dynasty from Thebes struggled to gain control of Upper Egypt. Montuhotpe, the greatest king of this dynasty, united the south and went on to reconquer the north. In about 2040 BC the Two Lands were joined again and the Middle Kingdom began. To renew the country's wealth, large expeditions were sent out by land and sea to mine for gold, turquoise and amethyst. A Middle Kingdom papyrus contains an exotic traveller's tale about one of these expeditions.

On a boat sailing downriver from Nubia to Egypt sat one of the king's most trusted officials, staring dejectedly into space. He was the leader of an expedition which, after a cluster of bad luck, was returning from the Nubian mines without its full quota of gold. He was just imagining what the king would say at the news of this failure when one of the other officials squatted down on the deck beside him.

'May your wishes be granted, commander. Just look at the crew hugging each other and thanking the gods for a safe journey home. At least we've crossed the Nubian border without losing a man. Listen to me! Wash, shave, put on your best clothes. When the king questions you, answer him calmly, without stammering. Then he'll know that you're not to blame. Speech can always save a man.'

The commander was in no mood to be comforted. 'It's no use my friend. Why waste water on a goose that's to be slaughtered in the morning?'

'Let me tell you about my first expedition,' said the kindly official. Settling himself down with his back resting against the commander's chair he related a strange story.

'My first voyage as a poor young sailor was across the Red Sea on a royal ship bound for the turquoise mines. We had a fine crew of one hundred and twenty men; the pick of Egypt. One day a sudden tempest lashed the sea and a giant wave shattered our mast. The crew did everything they could but within minutes the ship was sinking. Every man on board was drowned; except me. I was seized by a wave and thrown up on the shore of a strange island. 'I had just enough strength to crawl out of reach of the surf and into the shelter of a pile of driftwood. I lay there for three days and three long nights, exhausted and wretched, then hunger drove me inland. The centre of that island was like a garden. Birds sang in the branches of date palms and laden fig trees. Cucumbers grew in neat rows beside pools full of fish. Everything was carefully tended but there were no men to be seen.

My arms and my mouth were soon full of food and in my thankfulness I remembered the gods. With the copper knife from my belt I cut off a branch and fashioned a fire drill. When I'd got a fire alight I gathered up the remains of my meal to burn it as an offering to the gods. The moment the food was hissing in the flames I heard a thunderous noise.

'I thought at first that it was the roar of the sea but then the ground began to shake and the trees bowed and broke as if a storm wind was flattening them. When I found the courage to look up, it was not a storm I saw but a huge serpent. He was more than thirty cubits long and his golden scales were inlaid with lapis-lazuli. As he towered above me I fell on my belly and waited for death but the serpent hissed, "Who brought you here, little one? Tell me at once or I will turn you to ashes!"

'But I was too paralysed with fright to speak so the serpent picked me up in his jaws and carried me to his lair. He set me down unharmed and said again, "Who brought you here, little one?"

'I answered him without daring to look up: "I was on a royal ship sailing with a picked crew to the land of the turquoise mines. A storm caught us and wrecked our ship. All my comrades were drowned and I am the only one left. It was the waves who brought me."

'Then the serpent bent over me and said in a gentler voice, "Don't be afraid little one, don't turn pale. You are safe with me. A god has chosen you to live and brought you to this enchanted island. It is full of good things and you shall spend four months here until a ship passes. You will know the crew of that ship and they will take you back to Egypt."

'A deep sigh rippled along the golden coils. "I understand how you have suffered, little one. Seventy-five serpents used to live on this beautiful island. They were my family, my sisters, my brothers, my children and, most beloved of all, the little daughter that the gods

sent to me in answer to my prayers. Then a star fell to earth and my whole family was destroyed in its flames. By chance I was not with them when it fell but when I found the charred heap of their bodies I wished that I had died too."

'I was no longer afraid of the serpent but I kissed the ground before him and said, "When I return to Egypt I will tell the king of your power and generosity. I shall send you scented oils and spices and incense. I shall tell everyone what you have done for me and sacrifice birds and oxen to you in my local temple. I will ask the king to send you a shipload of the finest goods in Egypt."

'The golden coils quivered again, but this time with laughter. "You are not wealthy, little one, and Egypt is not rich in oils or spices or incense, but I am the Lord of Punt, the Master of the Myrrh Groves and this island abounds in oils and spices. As for sending me gifts . . . once you have left this island you will never find it again."

'I was ashamed then of my foolishness but the serpent was kind to me and I lived for four contented months on his island. One day as I sat in the boughs of a tall tree I saw a ship on the horizon and as it sailed closer I recognized many of the crew. I scrambled down and ran to tell the serpent but he already knew my news and was drawing the ship towards the island by his magic. "Farewell little one," he said to me. "You will soon be on your way home to see your family again. Remember me kindly, that is all I ask."

'Then he gave me a cargo of myrrh and oil, spices and perfumes, elephant tusks, giraffe tails, hunting dogs, pet monkeys and all kinds of precious things. I kissed the ground before him and the serpent said, "Within two months you will be home with your family and you will prosper there for the rest of your life."

'Then I went down to the shore and hailed the ship. I embraced the crew and told them my news and we all praised the lord of the island. They helped me to load the precious cargo and we sailed straight back to Egypt, to the palace itself. I presented the myrrh and oil and all the other goods to the king and he was so pleased that he made me one of his officials and gave me land and servants. So, commander, do not despair, for we never know when bad luck will change and what the gods may bring us.'

The prince and the sphinx

The Middle Kingdom was brought to an end in the seventeenth century BC by the rise of foreign rulers in Lower Egypt. For a long time groups of people had been leaving Palestine and settling in the Delta and the biblical story of Joseph and his brothers should probably be set in this period. At first the settlement was peaceful and the foreigners brought with them new skills, such as bronze-making. They also introduced new types of sword and bow and the use of horses and chariots.

In later times the Egyptians called these foreigners the Hyksos and claimed that they had brutally invaded the Delta and oppressed the whole country. Certainly between 1640 and 1532 BC there were foreign kings ruling the north and exacting tribute from the south. The most powerful of these foreign kings were the 'Great Hyksos' who ruled the eastern Delta from the city of Avaris. The Hyksos adopted Egyptian ways and honoured Egyptian gods but before long a Theban family, the Seventeenth Dynasty (c1640–1550 BC) had begun to unite the south against them.

To begin with the Theban kingdom was small. To the south of them, Nubia had broken away from Egypt and had a prince of its own. To the north lay the realm of the Hyksos and the Thebans were forced to pay tribute to King Apophis at Avaris. The struggle against foreign domination lasted for three generations but slowly the Hyksos were pushed back. Avaris fell to the Thebans and the Hyksos king fled to Palestine. The Theban king Amonhotep I (1525–1504 BC) united Egypt again and pursued his enemy to inflict a final defeat, in

the process conquering most of the city states of Palestine. This was the beginning of Egypt's Near Eastern empire and the New Kingdom.

King Amonhotep was followed by his son-in-law, Thutmose I who completed the reconquest of Nubia and took Egyptian armies further north than they had ever been before. Under his grandson Thutmose III, Egypt won control of most of Syria and became the greatest power in the Near East. Thutmose III attributed his victories to Amon, the patron god of the Seventeenth and Eighteenth Dynasties. Amon began his divine career as the obscure 'Hidden God' of invisible forces, but when the Theban family who revered him became kings of all Egypt, Amon's name was linked with that of Ra and he was identified with the Creator, the King of the Gods. Amon-Ra, Mut his wife and Khons his son were worshipped at the vast temple of Karnak in eastern Thebes.

Thutmose III recorded his victories at Karnak and the temple walls are inscribed with lists of gold and silver, chariots, horses and slaves that he took from conquered cities and gave to the god. New Kingdom rulers were expected to be great warriors and Thutmose's son, Amonhotep II (c1427–1401 BC) was renowned for his strength and military skill. He was well over six feet tall, an enormous height for an ancient Egyptian and an inscription close to the great Sphinx at Giza records that Amonhotep excelled at rowing, archery and chariot racing.

The Great Sphinx of Giza is probably the most famous of all Egyptian statues. Carved four and a half thousand years ago from an outcrop of rock two hundred and forty feet long and sixty feet tall, it squats in the desert to the south of the Great Pyramids. The Sphinx has the body of a lion and the head of a king and the Egyptians came to worship it as a form of the Sun God called Harmarchis. The desert sands blow in great drifts around the Sphinx and the statue has often been almost covered by them. In 1818 European visitors to Giza cleared the sand away from the Sphinx and found a granite stela standing between its paws. The inscription on the stela tells of an encounter between the Sphinx and one of the sons of Amonhotep II.

King Amonhotep had many sons but handsome Prince Thutmose was the favourite of the people. Thutmose was stronger than all his brothers and a great sportsman. When the court was at Memphis, the prince liked to slip away from the splendours of the palace with one or two friends and drive his chariot into the lonely western desert. There he would amuse himself with lion hunting or chariot racing or with shooting arrows at a copper target.

One day Thutmose went hunting in the desert near Giza and drove past the Great Sphinx, but only its head was visible, all the rest was buried under drifts of sand. The noonday sun burned down on Thutmose and his companions and made them so hot and tired that they sought shelter in the shadow of the Sphinx. The chariot horses were soon tethered and Thutmose sat down on a patch of cool sand, leaned back on the stone cheek of the Sphinx, and fell asleep.

Immediately he was caught in a vivid dream. The prince found himself standing between giant stone paws and the voice of the Sphinx boomed out across the desert:
'Thutmose, my child, I am your father, I am the Sun God, I am Khepri and Atum and Ra, I am Harmarchis! Listen to me and I will give you my kingdom on earth. You shall stand at the head of the living and wear the White Crown and the Red Crown. You shall rule everything on which the eye of the sun shines. The tribute of all nations will be laid at your feet and you shall live long, because my heart has turned to you.
'All this will happen,' promised the Sphinx, 'if you will serve me. Behold, the sands of the desert are choking me and lie heavy on my limbs. Sweep them away before they overwhelm me and I will treat you as a son!'

When Thutmose woke he remembered his dream and hurried to Memphis to fetch offerings for Harmarchis. Within a few days, he had gathered an army of men to scoop sand into their baskets and carry it away. Gradually the outline of the lion body began to appear and the Sphinx was freed from the desert. Harmarchis kept his promises and Thutmose was soon chosen as Crown Prince. In due time he succeeded his father and throughout his reign Thutmose IV honoured Harmarchis and made offerings to the Great Sphinx.

The capture of Joppa

When King Thutmose III (c1479–1425 BC) came to the throne of Egypt in the fifteenth century BC, he spent season after season fighting in Syria and Palestine to extend the Egyptian Empire. The princes of cities conquered by Egypt were usually allowed to go on ruling as long as they bowed to Thutmose and paid him tribute. A story in a badly preserved manuscript tells how the Canaanite Prince of Joppa, the city we know today as Jaffa, rebelled against Egypt.

The beginning of the story is lost, but it is clear that news of the revolt had reached Thutmose and that he was anxious to crush it before other Palestinian cities were tempted to join in. The king could not leave Egypt straight away, so he sent an army marching north under one of his best generals, a man named Djhuty. To show that Djhuty was to be obeyed by the army as if he was the king himself, Thutmose gave the general his own gold and ebony mace.

Djhuty and his men sailed from the eastern Delta up the coast of Palestine until they reached Joppa. Then the army went ashore and quickly set up camp. Joppa was ringed by massive walls and the only gateway was flanked by towers manned by archers. Djhuty sent a herald to stand before the great gates and shout a challenge: 'Rebel of Joppa, surrender to the Son of Ra, the Golden Horus, the Strong Bull Arisen in Thebes, the Lord of the Two Lands, the King of Upper and Lower Egypt, Thutmose, may he be given life for ever! Surrender at once, or come out of the city and fight.'

The answer soon came back. The Prince of Joppa refused to surrender, but nor would he come out of the city and fight. He was too wise to risk bringing his men out into the open.

Djhuty had no choice but to order an attack on the city. With their shields held above their heads to protect them from the rain of arrows, the Egyptian troops advanced towards Joppa. They pushed tall ladders and wooden siege towers against the walls but the defenders clubbed the men who tried to clamber over the battlements and set the siege towers alight with fire arrows. After three hours of fierce fighting, Djhuty ordered his troops to retreat. Egyptian losses were heavy but the garrison of Joppa had hardly suffered at all.

That night he sat in his tent, wondering what to do next. There was little chance of storming the city and a siege might last for years.

Djhuty knew that he must try cunning.

Early next morning Djhuty sent his herald to the city gates with a letter for the Prince of Joppa. The soldiers on the walls let down a basket on the end of a rope and the letter was quickly drawn up and taken to the palace. The prince read the letter scornfully; it was only another demand for his surrender but then he noticed a message at the bottom scrawled in Djhuty's own writing. In it, the general admitted that he could not capture Joppa and because he was afraid of Thutmose's anger and greedy for bribes, he was prepared to come over to the prince's side. The message ended with an invitation to discuss terms.

A letter was quickly sent to Djhuty agreeing to a temporary truce and a meeting on the open ground between the city and the Egyptian camp. Just after noon the great gates opened to let out the chariots of the Prince of Joppa and twenty of his officers. Then the gates swung shut and were barred again on the inside.

Djhuty and twenty of his officers, all unarmed, met the Prince of Joppa and his men and invited them to sit down and discuss terms over a cup of wine.

Djhuty soon convinced the Prince of Joppa that he was sincere. 'My own wife and children are here in the camp,' began the general, 'but tonight I will send them into the city to stay in your palace as a pledge of my good faith. Tomorrow this army will be at your command, so let us drink to the freedom of Joppa!'

Everyone's cup was filled again and the warriors of Joppa and the Egyptian officers were soon drunk together. Only Djhuty drank less than he appeared to and was still sober. 'Send a messenger to Joppa to tell them the good news,' he suggested to the prince, 'but the rest of us have more to talk about and more wine to get through! Still, it's cruel to leave your horses standing there in this dust and heat. Let them be unyoked and taken into the camp.'

The Prince of Joppa gave the order himself and even agreed to go to Djhuty's tent for a private discussion of the general's reward. As they walked there the prince said, 'I hear that you carry with you the mace of King Thutmose himself. I should very much like to see it.'

Djhuty readily agreed and bowed the prince into his tent. Then he opened a sandalwood box and turned round with the mace in his hand. 'Here is the mace of King Thutmose, the young lion, Sekhmet's son. Rebel of Joppa, you shall feel the King's anger now!' Djhuty brought the mace crashing down on the prince's head, knocking him unconscious. The general quickly bound his prisoner with leather ropes weighted with copper and then sent a messenger to the Prince of Joppa's charioteer.

'My general has prepared gifts for the people of Joppa,' said the messenger, 'to show them that he is now their servant. Your prince orders you to escort the gift-bearers into the city and tell the Princess of Joppa to rejoice because the Egyptians have surrendered and send us tribute.'

The charioteer obeyed at once and drove the prince's golden chariot to the city gates with the gift-bearers marching behind him. Djhuty's gifts were packed in two hundred large baskets, each slung on a pole and carried by two men. The sentries listened to the charioteer's message. They could see that the gift-bearers were unarmed and that the prince's officers were still drinking with the Egyptians. Everything seemed in order, so they sent six men down to unbar the gates.

The gift-bearers marched in through the gateway and the prince's charioteer began to lead them towards the palace. Six men had started to push the gates shut again when the gift-bearers suddenly put down their baskets and tore them open. Egyptian soldiers sprang out, each armed with one sword for himself and two for his bearers. The sentries gave the alarm and fought fiercely but the gates were held open and Djhuty had already captured the prince's drunken officers and was marching his army to Joppa.

Within minutes the city was swarming with Egyptian troops and it was not long before the people of Joppa were forced to surrender or die. Captives were rounded up and the palace was stripped of its treasures. The next day a ship set sail for Egypt carrying rich spoils and the Prince of Joppa and his family as wretched prisoners. When King Thutmose saw them he praised the gods for the cunning of Djhuty and the capture of Joppa.

The doomed prince

There was once a king in Egypt who had no son. He visited all the temples in the land, making offerings to the gods, and begging them for an heir. At last the gods decreed that his wish should be granted. The king hurried back to his queen and nine months later a beautiful son was born to them.

That night as the child slept, rocked by nurses, fanned by pages, guarded by soldiers, the Seven Hathors came to foretell his fate. No-one saw them enter the palace, no-one heard their footsteps, but suddenly the seven goddesses encircled the child and gazed down at his sleeping face.

'He will die through a crocodile, a snake or a dog,' they said in grim chorus, and the Hathors disappeared as mysteriously as they had come.

The nurses fled to tell the king the terrible words of the seven goddesses and he was desolate. But the king was determined to save his son if he could, so he ordered a splendid palace to be built in the middle of the western desert. The baby prince was taken there with all his attendants. He was never allowed to go outside and he was seven years old before he even knew what an animal was.

One day, in his eighth year, the prince managed to find a way up onto the roof of the palace. From there he could look out across the red sands of the desert. The first thing he saw was a man walking along with a dog gambolling at his heels. The prince was fascinated and could not take his eyes off the dog. When one of his attendants scrambled up onto the roof after him, he asked at once, 'What is that following the man along the road?'

At first the man was reluctant to answer, but at last he said 'Highness, it is a greyhound.'

Then the boy said, 'Bring me one just like it,' and he set his heart on a dog; nothing else would please him.

His attendants did not know what to do and they went to tell the king. He was very alarmed but he could not bear his son to be unhappy so after a great deal of thought he said 'Bring the prince the very smallest puppy you can find, and that should keep him happy.'

The prince was enchanted with his puppy and played with it all day long. At first the attendants hovered over them, ready to snatch the puppy away if it tried to bite. But the puppy grew into a gentle and affectionate dog and everyone forgot the danger.

As the years passed, the prince grew more and more restless, and he began to see his palace as a prison. At last his attendants told him what the Seven Hathors had said on the night of his birth. They hoped that this would make him want to stay safely shut up in his desert palace. Instead the prince sent a message to his father saying, 'Why must I be kept here? If I am fated to die, nothing you can do will save me. So let me follow my heart, until the gods decide to take me.'

When the king heard his son's message he was very sad, but he knew that the prince was right. He sent his son a golden chariot, drawn by two white horses, a splendid sword, a bow and a quiver of arrows, and he told him that he could go where he liked. The prince crossed the Nile to the eastern desert, marvelling at all the new things he saw, but he did not notice a huge and ancient crocodile emerging from the river and lumbering after him. He drove his chariot on northwards, with his greyhound crouching at his heels. By day he hunted the desert animals, the ibex and the ostrich, the gazelle and the wild ass; at night he slept under the stars. Day and night the crocodile who was his fate, followed him.

After many weeks, when the prince's feet were sore, from standing up all day long driving his chariot, he reached the land of Naharin. Now the King of Naharin had only one child, a daughter. She had many suitors from the land of Khor and the king did not know how to choose between them. So he ordered a tower to be built, with a single window seventy cubits (about forty metres) above the ground. The king announced that he had shut his daughter up in the tower and that whoever could reach her window in a single leap should marry her. The princes of Khor gathered beneath the tower and day after day, week after week, they tried to leap to the window. None of them could jump so high, but they kept on trying for sometimes they would glimpse the princess standing at her window, and no-one who saw her could fail to love her.

One morning as the princes of Khor were exercising beneath the tower, the Prince of

Egypt rode up and limped down from his chariot. The princes gave a kind welcome to the tired traveller. They bandaged his feet, rubbed scented oils into his wind-burned skin and ordered a meal to be served to him. When he had eaten and was resting in one of the tents that clustered around the tower, they asked him who he was.

The Prince of Egypt did not want anyone to know about the terrible fate hanging over him, so he answered 'I'm the son of an Egyptian officer. My mother died and my father married again. My step-mother hates me and I couldn't endure her cruelty any longer; so I've run away.'

Then the princes of Khor were very sorry for the young man, and urged him to stay with them. The Prince of Egypt gladly agreed and soon he was asking his new friends what they were doing gathered around the tower.
'For three months now,' answered one of the princes, 'we have been trying to leap up to the window of that tower, because whoever reaches the window will marry the King of Naharin's daughter.'
'If my feet weren't so sore,' murmured the Prince of Egypt, 'I would try the leap myself!'

The princes of Khor laughed. None of them thought that the young stranger was serious.

The next morning the princes of Khor tried again to reach the window. The Prince of Egypt stood at a distance watching them as each one ran forward, jumped—and flopped back onto the sand. Suddenly the Princess of Naharin appeared at her window. She could hardly stop herself laughing at the desperate efforts of the princes of Khor. Then she noticed a handsome young stranger standing among the tents. The princess longed for him to look up at her but he pretended not to see her.

For the next few days, the princess came to her window every morning. The princes of Khor were delighted; they did not realize that it was the stranger that drew her. At last, on the seventh morning, when the princess came to her window, the Prince of Egypt looked up and their eyes met. With a single leap he reached the sill. As he stepped through the window, the princess welcomed him with a kiss.

Her attendants rushed to tell the King of

Naharin that a man had reached his daughter's window. 'Which of the princes of Khor is it?' asked the king.

'It is not a prince at all,' said one of the attendants. 'Just the son of an Egyptian officer, who has run away from his stepmother!'

'What?' roared the king. 'Am I to give my only daughter to a fugitive, a nobody? Send him away at once!'

The attendants hurried to the tower and said to the Prince of Egypt, 'Go back where you came from!' They tried to push him out of the room, but the princess clung to him, shouting, 'I swear by Ra-Horakhty that if he is taken from me, I will neither eat nor drink until he is returned to me!' The attendants ran back to the king and told him what his daughter had said. 'Kill the stranger,' ordered the King of Naharin and soldiers broke into the tower, with their spears raised to stab the Prince of Egypt. Then the princess cried out, 'I swear by Ra that if you kill him, I too will be dead by sunset. I will not live an hour longer than he does!'

The soldiers did not dare to kill the prince and they went and told the king. He was very angry, and ordered that the princess and her suitor be brought before him. When the king saw the Prince of Egypt standing proudly before the throne, he was impressed by the young man's dignity and royal appearance. He sighed and gave the prince the kiss of peace.

'Well, if you are to be my son, tell me about yourself.' The prince repeated his story about the cruel stepmother and the marriage was celebrated that very day. The King of Naharin gave his daughter and her husband a splendid palace and they lived there very happily.

In the gardens of the palace was a lake and one night the crocodile who had followed the prince from Egypt slipped into its cool waters, intending to lie in wait for him there. Now a water demon lived in the lake and he did not want to share his home with the crocodile. Every day for three months the demon and the crocodile fought for possession of the lake and so for a time at least the prince was safe from one of his three fates.

It was not very long before the princess wheedled her husband into telling her the true story of his life. When she heard about the prophecy of the Seven Hathors the princess stared in horror at the greyhound sitting at her husband's feet and begged him to have the dog killed. The Prince of Egypt only laughed and said, 'What foolishness! I've raised him from a puppy, and I'm not going to kill him now.'

The princess said no more about it, but from that day she watched over her husband anxiously. One night, after a splendid feast, the Prince of Egypt fell asleep as soon as he lay down on the bed. His wife, however, stayed awake to watch over him. Suddenly a poisonous snake came out of a crack in the wall and glided towards the sleeping prince. His wife snatched up the flagon of wine that stood beside the bed, poured out a bowlful and set it down in the snake's path. The snake dipped its head into the bowl and drank up all the wine. The princess hurriedly poured out a bowl of beer. The snake swallowed that too and was then so drunk that it turned its back and could not move. The princess screamed for the guards and they rushed in and hacked the snake to pieces. The noise woke the prince and he sat up, demanding to know what had happened. His wife showed him the remains of the snake and said, 'Surely Ra will save you from your fates, he has already given one of them into your hands!'

Early one morning the prince got up before his wife and decided to go for a walk around his estates. His greyhound went with him, frisking at his heels. In a remote part of the palace gardens the prince paused to admire a lake fringed with palm-trees and stooped to pat his dog. Suddenly the animal snarled. Its eyes glittered as it began to speak, 'Prince, I am your fate!' It sprang at his throat and the prince fled.

The greyhound followed him, running as only a greyhound can. In desperation the prince waded into the lake and the greyhound, outwitted, paced angrily along the shore. Just as the prince thought he was safe the crocodile came up behind him and seized him in its terrible jaws. The prince almost fainted with horror as the monster dragged him to the bottom of the lake, but he found that could still breathe. The crocodile spoke: 'Prince,' it snarled, 'I am your fate! I followed you from Egypt to kill you, but

for three months now I have been fighting the demon of this lake. Help me to destroy the demon and I will spare your life.' Now when the demon returned . . .

Here, the only existing copy of the original story breaks off. We can never know for certain how the story ended when it was first written down over three thousand years ago, but it may have gone something like this . . .

Now when the demon returned, the waters of the lake seethed but a coldness crept over the Prince and he was unable to escape. Every night the demon left its lake to search for prey; early each morning it returned to the cool waters, for it could not endure the heat of the sun.

As usual when the demon appeared, the crocodile attacked its enemy. The demon gave a bubbling roar as the crocodile's teeth fastened on its leg. Its clawed hands raked the crocodile's back and the two enemies rolled in the slime on the bed of the lake. They fought fiercely but neither could really hurt the other, they were too evenly matched.

With the courage of desperation, the prince drew the bronze dagger that was his only weapon, swam towards the green back of the demon and stabbed at it with all his strength. However, the water slowed his thrust and the scales were too hard for bronze to pierce: the demon seemed to feel the stab no more than an insect bite. It turned its head and the wicked red eyes saw the prince. With the useless dagger still in his hand, the prince kicked out to propel himself upwards. His head broke through the surface of the lake but before he could strike out for the shore, the demon seized him.

All this time the greyhound had been running round the edge of the lake, barking and growling. The Princess of Naharin had missed her husband and she came out into the garden to look for him. When she heard the angry barking she knew that something was wrong. Calling a palace guard, she ran towards the noise.

The first thing they saw was the dog, baring its yellow teeth and growling furiously. At an order from the princess, the guard fitted an arrow to his bowstring and as the dog bounded, slavering, towards them, the guard shot it in the throat. It died instantly. The princess screamed as she saw her husband struggling with a monster in the middle of the lake. Hastily, the guard fitted another arrow but the prince and the demon were too close together to risk a shot.

One clawed hand tore at the prince's hair; the other gripped and pierced his shoulder. The prince stabbed at the scaly chest and pushed with all his strength, but the demon drew him into a fierce embrace. In a few moments he would be dragged down to his death. The prince looked up at the cloudy sky and prayed to Ra.

Suddenly the clouds parted and a brilliant shaft of sunlight struck the lake. Instantly the prince felt his enemy's grip weaken. The red eyes blinked against the dazzling light and the green scales seemed ready to melt in the heat of the sun. With a hiss of dismay, the demon released the prince, intent only on hiding again in the cool water at the bottom of the lake. As the green head sank, the prince raised his dagger and stabbed the demon through the eye. It gave one dying shriek and its flailing limbs knocked the prince backwards, thrusting him down to the bottom of the lake. The princess cried out in agony, certain that her husband was drowning and the guard waded into the turbulent waters to try to rescue him. To their surprise it was the crocodile that caught the prince on its broad back and carried him to the shore. The prince leaped to safety and into his wife's arms.

In spite of all that had happened the prince grieved for his dog and gave it a burial fit for a royal servant. He gave the lake to the crocodile and made sure that rich offerings were thrown into it every day. So the crocodile became fat and sluggish and never returned to Egypt. The princess and her husband invited the King of Naharin to a splendid feast and at last the prince related his true history. The king was delighted to learn that his daughter had married the only son of a ruler far more powerful than any of the princes of Khor.

Soon the prince and his wife travelled to Egypt to tell his father that he had escaped his three fates. The King of Egypt was overjoyed and vowed to build a temple to Ra. The prince and princess lived long and happily together and every day they praised the mercy of Ra, the only power greater than fate.

The two brothers

There were once two loving brothers named Anpu and Bata. Anpu was the elder and he was married and owned a farm. Bata came to live with Anpu and his wife and worked hard and cheerfully for them. He ploughed or reaped, milked the cows, gathered wood and completed a dozen other tasks each day. There was no-one to compare with him for strength and willingness and he was so wise in the ways of animals that he could understand their language. Every morning when he drove the cattle to pasture they would tell him where the lushest grass was to be found and he would take them there. So the cattle became fat and the whole farm prospered because of Bata.

One morning Anpu said to his brother, 'Yoke a team of oxen tomorrow and bring some sacks of seed to the field; it is time to begin ploughing.'

Bata did as Anpu ordered and the two brothers spent the next few days ploughing the fields and sowing barley and wheat. They were pleased with their work but when they came to the last field there was not enough seed left so Anpu sent his brother back to the house to fetch some more. Bata looked for his brother's wife, who was in charge of the storeroom, and found her sitting in the sun braiding her newly washed hair.

'Get up and fetch me some seed,' he said to her. 'Anpu is waiting and I must hurry back.'

Anpu's wife teased out a tangle with her deft fingers and answered without looking up, 'The storeroom's open. Fetch it yourself. Can't you see I'm busy with my hair?'

Bata went off to find a large container and then measured out enough seed to finish the sowing. He came out of the storeroom with a huge load slung across his shoulders, but his back was still straight and his walk sprightly.

Anpu's wife watched him through a curtain of hair and murmured, 'How much are you carrying there?'

'The weight of three sacks of wheat and two of barley,' answered Bata.

'How strong you are!' said Anpu's wife admiringly. 'Strong and handsome.' She got up and stroked the muscles of his arm. 'Come into the house with me, just for an hour. I promise I will be good to

you, and Anpu will never know about it.'

Bata dropped his load and backed away. 'What are you saying? Do you think that I would betray the brother who raised me? He's like a father to me and you should be like a mother. I won't tell anyone about you, but never say such things to me again!' He picked up his load and strode off to the fields.

Anpu's wife was furious with Bata for rejecting her but she was also frightened that he might after all tell someone what she had done. So she ripped her own clothes, worked grease into her skin to make it look as if she was covered with bruises and lay down on her bed to wait.

When the brothers had finished ploughing Bata went to drive the cattle home but Anpu walked straight back to the house. He soon realized that something was wrong. No fire had been lit, no food had been cooked and his wife did not hurry to greet him as she usually did. Instead Anpu found her lying on her bed, moaning and weeping. Her clothes were torn and she seemed to be badly bruised. Anpu knelt by the bed and demanded to know what had happened.

'When your brother came to fetch the seed, he saw me braiding my hair,' she sobbed. 'He tried to kiss me and make love to me but I pushed him away. I told him that you were like a father to him and that he should respect me as his mother. Then he was angry and beat me cruelly and said that he would hurt me even more if I dared to tell you what had happened. O husband, kill him for me,' begged Anpu's wife, 'or I shall never know a moment's peace!'

Anpu believed his wife's story and his anger was as fierce as a leopard's. He sharpened a spear and stood in the shadow behind the door to the cattle byre, waiting to kill his brother. Bata returned with the cattle at dusk and drove them towards the byre but the leading cow turned her head and lowed softly, 'Your brother hides with his spear behind the door. He means to kill you. Run while you can.'

Bata could not believe such a thing. He patted the cow on her rump and sent her into the byre, but when the next cow gave him the same warning he stooped down and saw his brother's feet behind the door. Then Bata was afraid and he began to run. Anpu pursued him, spear in hand, and anger gave him speed and strength. Swiftly as Bata ran, his brother began to gain on him. Dripping with sweat and gasping for breath, Bata prayed to Ra, 'O my good lord, who judges between the wicked and the innocent, save me now!'

Ra heard Bata's plea and caused a river to flow between the two brothers. The river was wide and deep and full of hungry crocodiles so Anpu dared not cross it. He was so furious that he struck his own hand for failing to kill his brother.

Bata paused on the far bank and shouted to Anpu, 'Brother, Ra delivers the wicked to the just, but we must be parted. Why have you tried to kill me without even giving me a chance to explain?'

'Do you deny that you tried to seduce my wife?'

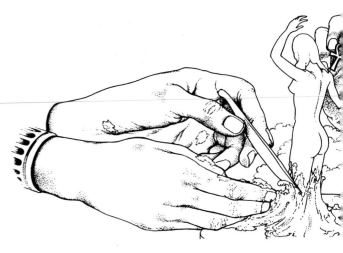

yelled Anpu, full of rage and pain.

'By Ra, it is a lie,' declared Bata. 'You have the story crooked. When I came back from the fields it was your wife who tried to seduce me and I who refused her. You almost murdered your brother for the sake of a worthless liar. By my own blood, I swear that this is the truth!'

In his distress, Bata took a reed knife and wounded himself. When he saw the blood gush out, Anpu believed his brother and was sick at heart. Bata sank to the ground, weak with loss of blood and Anpu longed to help him, but he could not cross the river.

'We must part,' repeated Bata in a feeble voice. 'I shall go to the Valley of the Cedar to find healing. Remember me kindly and listen now. I shall hide my heart in the cedar tree and if that tree is ever cut down I shall be in danger of death. If a jug of beer suddenly ferments in your hand, you will know that the worst has happened. Then you must come to the Valley of the Cedar and search for my heart, even if it takes you seven years. When you find it, place the heart in a bowl of cool water and, though I seem dead, I will revive.'

Anpu promised to obey his brother's words and went sadly home. He killed his wife with the spear he had sharpened for Bata and threw her body to the dogs.

Many days later Bata reached the Valley of the Cedar that lay in the desert hills close to the sea and rested there till his wound was healed. He lived by hunting the desert game and slowly built himself a fine house in the shadow of the great cedar tree that gave the valley its name. Among the branches of the tree he hid his heart.

He soon had everything he wanted; except a companion.

One day the Ennead were walking in the valley and came upon the house of Bata. The nine gods pitied his loneliness and Ra ordered Khnum to make a wife for Bata on his potter's wheel. When the gods had breathed life into her she was the most beautiful woman ever created, but even the Ennead could not give her a loving heart and when the Seven Hathors gathered to declare her fate they said with one voice: 'She will die by the knife!'

Nevertheless the Ennead were pleased with her beauty and they gave her to Bata. 'Your brother has killed his wicked wife,' said Ra, 'and you are avenged. Now, virtuous Bata, here is a wife for you, to be your companion in this lonely place.'

As soon as Bata saw her, he loved her and he knew that whoever met her would desire her. 'Stay in the house while I am out hunting,' he warned his wife, 'or the sea itself may try to carry you off and there would be little I could do to save you.'

Bata's wife nodded meekly but she soon grew bored with being shut up in the house and one day while Bata was hunting she went outside for a walk. As she stood beneath the cedar tree, the sea saw her and surged up the valley to embrace her. Bata's wife screamed and turned to run but the sea bellowed to the cedar tree, 'Catch her for me!' The cedar bowed down and its lowest branch caught in her hair. Bata's wife struggled free and fled into the house, leaving a single lock of her hair tangled in the branch.

The sea tore the lock from the cedar tree and carried it away to the very shores of Egypt, where the Nile seized it. Caressed by the river, the beautiful hair floated to the place where the royal washermen were laundering the clothes of Pharaoh. They dipped his fine linen tunics in the Nile, beat them on the rocks and spread them out to dry but the scent of the lock of hair had filled the river and it perfumed the clothes, too. When Pharaoh next put on a clean tunic he complained that it smelled of a woman's scent. The washermen protested that they had added no perfume but every day the clothes of Pharaoh came out of the river smelling sweetly.

One morning the overseer of the royal washermen paced the riverbank, making sure that everything was done as it should be. Suddenly his eye was caught by a shining lock of hair tangled in a clump of reeds. The overseer waded into the river to fetch it and as soon as he touched it he knew that he had found the source of the mysterious perfume. When the lock was dry it was taken to Pharaoh and he and all his court were sure that they had never seen hair of such a lustrous black, that felt so soft or smelled so sweetly.

'Surely such hair must belong to a daughter of Ra,' said the wise men of the court and Pharaoh longed to make such a woman his queen. 'Let envoys travel to every foreign land to search for her,' suggested the wise men, 'but we have heard that the most beautiful of all women lives in the Valley of the Cedar, so send twenty envoys there.'

Pharaoh was delighted with their advice and eagerly awaited the return of his messengers.

One by one the envoys came back from the foreign lands to say that their search had failed. Last of all a single wounded envoy returned from the Valley of the Cedar. Bata had killed all the rest when he had discovered their errand. The surviving messenger promised Pharaoh that Bata's wife was the woman he sought, so a great army was sent to fetch her. With the army travelled an old woman whom Pharaoh had chosen for her cunning tongue.

When they neared the Valley of the Cedar the old woman went ahead of the army and persuaded Bata's wife to let her into the house while he was away hunting. The old woman took out a casket of precious jewellery that Pharaoh had sent as a gift for Bata's wife. There were golden anklets, bracelets of lapis-lazuli, amulets of silver and turquoise; the old woman told Bata's wife that Pharaoh loved her and waited to make her Queen of all Egypt.

Greedy for the jewels and bored with her life in the lonely valley, Bata's wife agreed to go to Egypt but she was afraid of her husband's vengeance. Long before, Bata had told his beloved wife where his heart was hidden and now she used the secret to destroy him. The Egyptian soldiers were summoned and told to hack down the cedar tree. As it fell, Bata clutched his chest and died and his wife decked herself in Pharaoh's jewels and went with the soldiers. When Pharaoh saw her, his heart leaped with joy and he made her his chief queen.

At the very moment when Bata was killed, Anpu saw the beer in his jug bubble and froth and he knew that something terrible had happened. He put on his sandals, snatched up a staff and a spear and set out for the Valley of the Cedar. There he found his younger brother stretched out on the ground. Bata's limbs were stiff and cold and he no longer breathed. Anpu carried his brother into the house and wept over him, but he did not yet despair. Remembering Bata's words, he began to search for his brother's heart amongst the branches of the fallen cedar.

For three years he searched in vain. By the beginning of the fourth year he was longing to be back in Egypt and he said to himself, 'If I don't find the heart tomorrow, I shall go home.' He spent all the next day bent-backed amongst the fallen branches and, just as he was about to give up, his foot struck against something. Anpu thought at first that it was only a withered cone but when he took it into the house and lit a lamp he saw that he was holding his brother's heart.

Anpu put the heart in a bowl of cool water, placed the bowl beside his brother's body and settled down to wait. All through the night his heart swelled as it absorbed the water and when it reached its true size, Bata's body twitched and his eyes flew open. He stared up at his brother, still too weak to speak. Anpu held the bowl to Bata's lips and he drank the remaining water and

swallowed his heart. Then all his old strength returned to him and Bata leaped up and embraced his brother.

They spent the day talking over the past and planning revenge on Bata's cruel wife. 'Tomorrow, I shall transform myself into a fine bull of a size and colour that no-one has ever seen before,' said Bata. 'Then you must ride on my back to Egypt. When Pharaoh hears about us, he will want me for his own. Take the rewards he will offer you and go home. Then my revenge will begin.'

The next morning Bata changed himself into a huge golden bull with markings as blue as lapis and Anpu mounted on his back. As they travelled through Egypt people flocked to see the marvellous bull and when Pharaoh heard about it he gave thanks to the gods because he was sure that the bull must be their messenger. Anpu rode his brother to the gates of the palace and Pharaoh rewarded him with gold and silver, land and slaves.

Bata was garlanded with flowers and allowed to wander wherever he liked in the palace and its grounds. At first everyone was in awe of him but they soon learned to trust his gentleness. In all his wanderings Bata was only looking for one person and at last he found her.

One morning the queen herself was in the palace kitchens, overseeing the preparation of sweetmeats for Pharaoh. Bata came up behind her and touched the queen with the tip of his horns.
'Look at me; I am alive.'

The queen turned and stared at the bull in amazement. 'Who are you?' she whispered.
'I am Bata,' said the bull. 'I know that it was you who told Pharaoh's soldiers to chop down the cedar tree. You wanted me dead but I am alive.'

Then, as the queen stood trembling with horror, Bata paced slowly out of the kitchen.

In the cool of the evening, Pharaoh sat down to feast with his queen. She wore her filmiest dress and her finest jewels and as she poured out his wine, Pharaoh thought her more beautiful than ever.
'Sovereign, my lord,' murmured the queen, 'will you swear by the gods to grant whatever I desire? Do you love me enough for that?'

Pharaoh kissed her and promised that he would. The queen smiled. 'I desire to eat the liver of the great bull. He does nothing but wander about the palace all day, so why not slaughter him?'

Then Pharaoh was angry and upset at her request but he had given his word and the queen refused to change her mind. The very next morning Pharaoh proclaimed that the marvellous bull was to be sacrificed to the gods. The royal slaughterers seized Bata, roped his legs, threw him to the ground and cut his throat. As the bull died, his blood spattered the pillars on either side of the palace gate. The body was cut up and offered on the altars of the gods but the liver was cooked and given to the queen and she ate it with pleasure.

At dawn the next day the palace gatekeeper ran to Pharaoh's bedchamber and said, 'O, Sovereign, my Lord. A great marvel has happened! Two beautiful persea trees have sprung up in the night in front of the pillars before the great gate!'

Then Pharaoh rejoiced, sure that this was another sign of the favour of the gods; and no-one knew that the trees had sprung from Bata's blood.

A few days later Pharaoh and his queen rode in golden chariots to the palace gate and made

offerings to the marvellous persea trees. Then thrones were brought and Pharaoh sat in the shade of one tree and his queen beneath the other while priestesses sang and danced in honour of the gods.

Pharaoh sat smiling but amongst the rustling of leaves his queen heard a voice: 'False one, you told Pharaoh's soldiers to cut down the cedar tree, you made Pharaoh slaughter the bull, but I am Bata, I am alive!'

Then the queen was very much afraid.

The next time she was alone with her husband the queen used all her womanly arts to please him and made him promise to grant any wish she named.

'Those two persea trees are useless standing at the gate,' she said. 'Have them chopped down and made into furniture for me.'

Pharaoh was uneasy at the thought of cutting down the mysterious trees but the queen sulked and wheedled until he agreed. The following morning she went with Pharaoh to watch the royal carpenters cut down the persea trees. At the first axe stroke, a splinter of wood flew up and entered the queen's lips and the moment she swallowed it she became pregnant.

After many months the queen gave birth to a handsome boy but she did not know that her son was Bata. Pharaoh loved the child and made him crown prince and as the years passed he grew up to be strong and handsome and wise. If the queen found that her son was cold towards her and noticed a growing resemblance to her murdered husband, she dared not speak.

In due time Pharaoh died and rejoined the gods and the crown prince succeeded him. No sooner was the coronation over than the new Pharaoh summoned the queen his mother. In front of the whole court Bata recounted the story of his strange life. He told of his flight from his brother's house, of the woman the gods had given him for a wife and how she had betrayed him.

'Surely such a woman is worthy of death,' said Bata and his courtiers agreed. The queen was led away, weeping, to die by the knife as the Seven Hathors had foreseen. Then Bata sent for his beloved brother and together they ruled Egypt for thirty years.

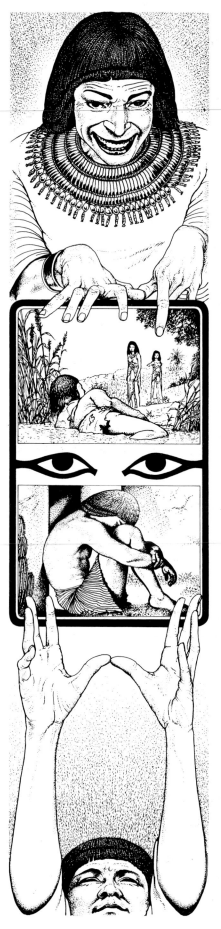

The blinding of Truth

There were once two brothers called Truth and Lies. Truth was noble and honest and his evil brother Lies hated him. One day Lies went to the Ennead and complained that Truth had stolen his dagger. When they asked him to describe this dagger Lies said glibly: 'All the copper in Mount Yal went into its blade and all the timber in Coptos into its haft. Its sheath is the length of a tomb shaft and the hides from all the cattle in Kal make up its belt. There never was such a splendid dagger before,' insisted Lies, 'and Truth has stolen it. If he refuses to give it back, let him be blinded and given to me as a doorkeeper.'

Truth was summoned before the Ennead and protested his innocence. He could not produce the dagger, since it had never existed, and Lies' accusations sounded so plausible that Truth was condemned. The Ennead ordered him to be blinded in both eyes and given to Lies to serve him as a doorkeeper.

Lies soon found that he could not bear the sight of Truth sitting patiently at his door. It reminded him every day of his own wickedness and his brother's innocence. So Lies said to two of Truth's old servants, 'Take your master out into the desert and leave him where a pride of lions is sure to find him. Don't come back until you're sure he's dead!'

The servants were too afraid of Lies to refuse. Sadly, each of them took Truth by the arm and they led him out towards the desert. When Truth felt the hot desert sand under his bare feet, he asked why they had brought him there. The servants wept as they told him about their orders.

'Don't leave me here for the lions,' begged Truth. 'Take me to some distant village and then stain my shirt with the blood of some animal and show it to Lies.'

The servants were glad to do as he suggested. They took Truth to a village half a day's journey away and then hurried back to tell Lies that his brother was dead.

Some days later a lady named Desire was walking in her garden when two of her maids ran up to her. 'Lady,' they panted, 'we have found a blind man lying in the reeds beside the lake. Come and see!'

'Bring him to me here,' said Desire.

The maids soon returned supporting Truth between them. He was exhausted and half-starved but Desire thought that he was the most handsome man she had ever seen. She welcomed him into her house and her bed and a son was born to them, but it was not long before Desire tired of her new lover. Then Truth was banished from the house.

The son of Desire and Truth was no ordinary child. He grew up tall and handsome as a god and by the time he was twelve he surpassed all his companions at school both in reading and writing and in the arts of war. The other boys became jealous, so they jeered at him, 'If you're so clever, tell us who your father is?'

The son of Desire did not know and he stood in miserable silence while the other boys mocked him until he could bear it no longer. Then he ran to his mother and said, 'Please tell me who my father is, so that I can tell the others.'

'Do you see the blind man sitting in the dust by the gate?' asked Desire. 'Well that is your father.'

The boy was shocked by his mother's callousness. 'And you leave him there? You deserve to be condemned to the crocodiles!'

He rushed into the courtyard and embraced his father. Then he brought Truth into the house and made him sit in the best chair. After he had set the choicest food before Truth and helped him to eat and drink, the boy said eagerly, 'Father, who dared to blind you? Tell me and I will avenge you.'

'It was my own brother,' Truth replied.

The boy quickly formed a plan and went to his mother's storeroom to fetch ten loaves, a skin of water, a sword, a staff and a pair of leather sandals. Then he took a handsome dappled ox from his mother's herd and drove it in front of him until he came to the place where Lies pastured his cattle. The boy approached the chief herdsman and said, 'I have to go on a journey. If you will look after my ox while I'm away, you can keep these provisions, this sword, this staff and these fine leather sandals.'

The herdsman readily agreed and the boy pretended to leave the district.

A few weeks later Lies came to inspect his herd. He immediately took a fancy to the handsome ox that belonged to the son of Truth. 'I'll drive that one home and slaughter it as a feast,' said Lies. 'It's easily the finest in the herd.'

The chief herdsman protested that the ox belonged to a boy who would come back soon to reclaim it. Lies shrugged. 'What does that matter? I'll take this ox now and you can give the boy the pick of the herd when he returns.'

So Lies took the ox away and had it slaughtered. The son of Truth soon heard what had happened and visited the herdsman. 'Any beast in the herd is yours,' said the chief herdsman. 'Pick whichever you like.'

'What good is that when none of them can compare with my ox?' asked the boy. 'My ox was so big that if it stood on the island of Amon its chin would be over the Nubian desert and its tail over the marshes of the Delta, with the tip of one horn resting on the Western Mountains and the other on the Eastern Mountains. If it lay down it would cover the Nile.'

The chief herdsman was astounded. 'Is there an ox as big as that?'

The son of Truth pretended to be very angry and he took the chief herdsman and Lies to court to be judged by the Ennead for the theft of his ox. In front of them all the boy described the ox again and Lies exclaimed, 'What nonsense, no-one has seen an ox as big as that!'

'No-one has ever seen a dagger the length of a tomb shaft,' said the son of Truth, 'with all the copper in Mount Yal in its blade, all the timber in Coptos in its haft and all the cattle hides in Kal in its belt.'

Lies turned pale as the boy cried to the Ennead, 'Judge Truth and Lies again. How could you condemn Truth on such a story? I am his son and I am here to avenge his innocence.'

Lies still protested that his original story was true: 'And if Truth is alive and can deny this, then I will confess guilt. Then you can blind me and make me his doorkeeper!'

Lies was confident that his brother was dead but the boy said triumphantly, 'You have judged yourself. Come with me now and I will show you all that Truth is still alive.'

He took the Ennead to his mother's house and showed them his father. When they had heard Truth's story they ordered Lies to be taken out and blinded in both eyes. After that Truth and his son lived happily together and Lies was their doorkeeper.

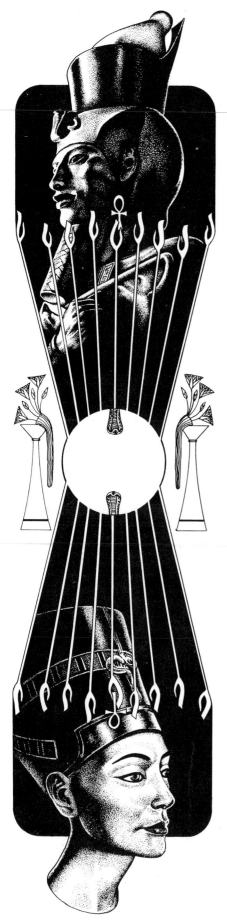

The Sun Pharaoh

In the early fourteenth century BC Egypt's empire seemed secure. Nubia was peaceful and the city states of Palestine and southern Syria had been subdued by five generations of warrior kings. However, when Amonhotep III, the son of Thutmose IV, came to the throne in about 1391 BC, he preferred the luxury of his court to the hardships of campaigning. He concentrated on building palaces and temples and made allies for Egypt by bribing foreign rulers with gold, or by marrying their daughters.

Amonhotep had a vast harem, but he seems to have been devoted to his chief wife, the forceful Queen Tiye. Although Tiye was not of royal blood, it was her son, another Amonhotep, who became Crown Prince. Amonhotep IV (c1353–1335 BC) proved to be the most extraordinary of all Egyptian rulers and he was the first to be called Pharaoh, a title that simply means 'The Palace'. More significantly he changed his name from Amonhotep (Amon is Gracious) to Akhenaten (Beneficial to the Aten).

The Aten was the disc of the sun and the young pharaoh believed that the sun god was the only deity who existed and that it was wrong to worship any other. Akhenaten built temples at Karnak in which the Aten was shown as a sun disc whose rays ended in hands holding out the sign of life to the pharaoh and to his lovely queen, Nefertiti.

Akhenaten soon abandoned Thebes and Memphis and withdrew, with his wife and daughters, to a new capital at el-Amarna called Akhet-Aten (Horizon of the Aten). Built on the edge of the desert, the city was filled with unique art and architecture. In an ordinary Egyptian temple offerings were made to a divine statue enclosed in a shrine inside a dark sanctuary, but in the temples of the Aten offerings were heaped onto altars built in courtyards open to the sun. The complex imagery of the old gods and goddesses was banished and statues and reliefs showed the Aten blessing the royal family. Portraits of Egyptian kings are usually highly stylized and full of remote grandeur but Akhenaten had himself shown as an ugly young man doing ordinary things like eating, drinking, playing with his little daughters and even kissing his wife. Shut up in his remote capital Akhenaten became more and more fanatical in his devotion to the Aten. He forbade the worship of other gods, closed down their temples, and sent gangs of men to hack out the names of deities such as Amon and the plural of the word god wherever they appeared in temple inscriptions. All mankind was to adore the Sole God and to honour Akhenaten as the living image of the Aten.

The events of Akhenaten's strange reign are surrounded in mystery, but it is clear that he made many enemies. The closure of the temples caused economic chaos and most people refused to abandon the old gods and goddesses. Akhenaten seems to have taken little interest in the running of Egypt and in the absence of a strong ruler law and order broke down. The empire was neglected, too, and many of the princes of Palestine and Syria seized the opportunity to free their cities from Egyptian oppression.

Akhenaten probably came to a violent end and his ideals did not survive him long. A ruler called Smenkhara had a brief reign after Akhenaten's death, but the identity and even the sex of this person is uncertain. Some historians think that Smenkhara was a younger brother of Akhenaten, but others believe that 'he' was none other than Queen Nefertiti. Akhenaten's chief wife played a very important part in everything he did and it is possible that he made her his co-ruler. She would not have been the first woman to rule Egypt; Hatsheput, the aunt of Thutmose III, had reigned as king for fifteen years only a few generations before.

Whoever Smenkhara was, he or she was soon succeeded by a new pharaoh, a boy of about nine years old called Tutankhaten. Though Akhenaten and Nefertiti had six daughters, they are never shown with a son. Tutankhaten may have been a much younger brother of Akhenaten or a son by a lesser wife. During most of the boy pharaoh's reign it was his Vizier Ay and the Commander of the Army, General Horemheb, who actually governed Egypt and who reversed all the changes made by Akhenaten. The young pharaoh altered his name from Tutankhaten (Living Image of the Aten) to Tutankhamon (Living Image of Amon). He returned to Thebes and the new capital, Akhet-Aten, was totally deserted, never to be inhabited again. The worship of the old gods and goddesses was restored and their temples were repaired and re-opened. The Amon form of Ra became once more the chief god and gradually Egypt began to return to normal.

Tutankhamon died suddenly at about the age of eighteen. Though he was married to one of Akhenaten's daughters, he had no children. The Vizier Ay took the throne and seems to have married Tutankhamon's widow, though he must have been old enough to be her grandfather. Ay gave his former master a hasty burial in the smallest tomb in the Valley of the Kings and reigned for four years (c1323–1319 BC). He was succeeded by General Horemheb who destroyed the temples that Akhenaten had built for the Aten at Karnak and completed the process of restoring law and order. Horemheb also died childless and left the throne to his elderly Vizier Ramesses, the founder of the Nineteenth Dynasty (c1307–1196 BC). Ramesses' vigorous son, Seti I, reconquered much of the empire and built splendid temples to the old gods.

The pharaohs of the Nineteenth Dynasty called Akhenaten the 'Great Criminal' and tried to destroy even the memory of his reign. The tomb of Akhenaten was desecrated and the names of the 'Great Criminal' and his successors, Smenkhara, Tutankhamon and Ay, were erased from the official list of Egyptian rulers. The treasure of Tutankhamon escaped the grave-robbers just because he was a forgotten pharaoh, buried in an insignificant tomb; and just because Akhet-Aten was abandoned to the desert, it is now the best preserved of all ancient Egyptian cities. When the court returned to Thebes under Tutankhamon, many things were left behind in the houses, palaces and temples of Akhet-Aten. Hundreds of clay tablets found in the remains of the Records Office proved to be copies of letters between the rulers of Egypt and foreign princes and the workshop of a sculptor contained his wonderful portraits of the royal family. Amongst them was a bust of Nefertiti which has made her famous as one of the most beautiful women of the ancient world.

The very people who tried to destroy the memory of the 'Great Criminal' have helped the names of Akhenaten and his family to live forever.

The Princess of Bakhtan

Seti I was followed by his famous son, the Pharaoh Ramesses II, who ruled Egypt for sixty-six years (c 1290–1224 BC). Like his father, Ramesses led his troops in person and he went into battle with his pet lion at his side. He fought hard to control Palestine and southern Syria but though his inscriptions boast of glorious victories, the truth is that the power of Egypt was kept in check by the rival empire of the Hittites. The homeland of the Hittites was the Anatolian plateau, now in Turkey, but during the late fourteenth and early thirteenth centuries BC they won themselves an empire in northern Syria. In the fifth year of his reign, Ramesses fought a great battle against the Hittites and their allies at Kadesh. Accounts of the battle insist that it was only the personal courage of pharaoh that saved the Egyptian forces when they came under surprise attack: 'My Majesty caused the forces of the Hittites to fall on their faces on top of each other, like crocodiles dropping into the river. I was after them like a griffin; I alone attacked all the foreign enemies, because my infantry and chariotry had deserted me. Not one of them looked back as he fled. As Ra loves me and as Atum favours me, everything my majesty says is the truth.'

Though Ramesses II may have fought like 'a raging lion in a valley of goats' both sides claimed Kadesh as a victory. Eventually Pharaoh was forced to make peace with the Hittites and Syria was divided between the two empires. The peace treaty, which still survives in two copies, seems to have been faithfully observed. Ramesses married a Hittite princess and devoted the rest of his long reign to gigantic building projects. He founded a new capital in the eastern Delta on the ancient site of the Hyksos city of Avaris and built many large temples, of which the Ramesseum at Thebes and the rock-cut temple of Abu Simbel are the best known. The quality of workmanship is often low, but in number and size his buildings surpassed those of any other pharaoh. He was worshipped as a god in his own lifetime and the Egyptians never forgot the splendours of Ramesses' rule. A thousand years after his death, a story set in his reign was written down in the temple of the god Khons at Thebes.

One summer Ramesses and his army drove their chariots through the land of Naharin, collecting tribute. The princes of the conquered lands hurried to bow before pharaoh and to bring him gifts of gold and silver, turquoise and lapis-lazuli. The Prince of Bakhtan longed to outdo the others and win the favour of Ramesses, so he offered the most precious thing in all Bakhtan, his oldest daughter. The princess was gracious, wise and lovely and the heart of Pharaoh was more pleased with her than with all the rest of the tribute. He gave the princess an Egyptian name, Neferure, and made her his chief wife. They returned to Egypt together and lived in great joy.

The following summer Ramesses was in Thebes, celebrating the festival of the great god Amon in the splendid temple he had built for him. As the final offerings were made, one of his courtiers whispered to Pharaoh that a messenger from the Prince of Bakhtan had arrived with gifts for Queen Neferure. As soon as he could, Ramesses sent for the messenger. When the gifts had been presented and admired the man kissed the ground before Pharaoh and said, 'Hail, sun who lights the conquered lands! O, Sovereign, my Lord, I have come to beg help for Bentresh, the sister of your Queen. She is ill and no-one in Bakhtan can cure her. Egypt is famous for her wise men's skill in healing. May your Majesty send us such a man to drive out the sickness that has seized our princess!'

Ramesses was eager to help. He consulted with his wisest priests and councillors and chose the royal scribe Djehutyemheb to return with the messenger to Bakhtan. It was a long and difficult journey but as soon as he arrived, Djehutyemheb was taken to the princess. Bentresh lay motionless on her bed. Her eyes were open but she did not seem to recognize her father when he stooped over her. As soon as the royal scribe touched the hand of the princess he sensed the presence of a fever demon of great power and malice. He tried to drive out the demon by chanting his most potent spells and covering her with amulets but with no success. 'Only a god would have the power to drive out such a demon,' said Djehutyemheb. 'Write to Pharaoh and beg him to send you a god from Egypt.'

The Prince of Bakhtan despatched a messenger that very day. After an exhausting journey the man arrived at Thebes during the festival of Amon. Pharaoh was shocked when he read the prince's letter. Such a request had never been made before, but because of his great love for Queen Neferure, Ramesses was anxious to grant it. He hurried to the temple of the great god Khons the Merciful and entering the dark sanctuary, he bowed before the divine image. 'My good lord,' began Pharaoh humbly, 'I have come to tell you about Bentresh, the sister of my queen. A fever demon has seized her and if it is not driven out soon, she will die. Of all your forms, Khons the Determiner is the most famous for healing the sick. Is it your will that an image of Khons the Determiner be sent to Bakhtan?'

The divine image nodded its golden head. Shivering with awe Ramesses asked, 'My good lord, will you strengthen Khons the Determiner with your power before I send him to Bakhtan to save the princess?'

The golden image nodded twice to show divine approval. Ramesses bowed his thanks and left the sanctuary.

Next morning Pharaoh sent four priests to carry the small gilded shrine that held the image of Khons the Determiner to the river bank. The image was wrapped with perfumed mummy bandages and hung with jewelled necklaces. Khon's single plait of hair was carved in lapis-lazuli and a silver crescent glittered on his dark brow. Ramesses gave the god a huge escort of priests, soldiers and servants, with boats for the journey down the Nile and chariots for the journey overland.

A year and five months passed before the stately procession of the god reached distant Bakhtan. At the news of their approach everyone rushed out of the palace to greet them. The Prince of Bakhtan fell on his belly before Khons, crying, 'Great god! Now you have come, be merciful to us as Pharaoh desired!'

Then the prince and his guard escorted the god to the place where Bentresh lay close to death. The priests set down the shrine of Khons the Determiner beside her bed and stepped back. The prince and his soldiers waited anxiously at one side of the room. The air became thick with magic and everyone sensed the unseen conflict as

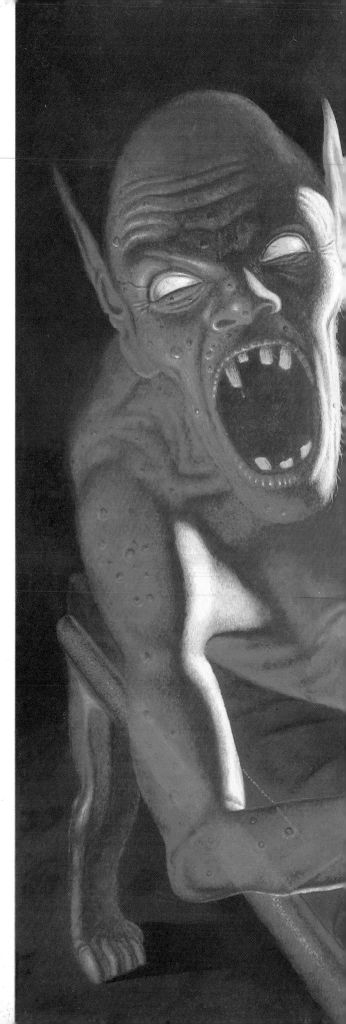

Khons surrounded the princess with his protective power. With a violent convulsion, the fever demon suddenly left the body of Bentresh, hissing with rage and fear. The Prince of Bakhtan trembled when he saw the horrible shape of the fever demon hovering over his daughter, but Bentresh now lay in a peaceful sleep.

'Welcome in peace, great god,' declared the demon. 'Bakhtan is yours. Its people are your slaves and I am your slave too. Have mercy on me. I will leave this place for ever as soon as the prince makes offerings to me.'

The divine image nodded. The priests interpreted the wishes of the god and told the prince what he must do. Rich offerings were sent for and a banquet was spread for the god and the demon. The offerings were accepted and the fever demon left Bakhtan for ever. Then the prince woke his daughter and embraced her and the whole land rejoiced with them.

Bentresh and her father were so grateful to Khons and so impressed by the power of his image that they could not bear to let him be taken back to Egypt. The prince built a shrine for Khons the Determiner and kept him in Bakhtan for three years and nine months.

Then one night the prince dreamed that he saw the god emerge from his shrine in the shape of a golden falcon and fly towards Egypt. Dazzled by the glittering wings, the prince woke shaking with fear. He understood now how dangerous it was to cage a god and that Khons had chosen to return to Egypt.

The next morning the prince sent for the priests of Khons and said, 'Prepare to return to Egypt at once! Return to Thebes and I will send an army to protect you and chariots laden with gifts.'

Many months later the divine image arrived back safely in Thebes and the gifts of the Prince of Bakhtan were offered in the temple of Khons the Merciful. Khons the Determiner was returned to his sanctuary and Ramesses and his queen rejoiced to hear that Bentresh was healed.

The Book of Thoth

Ramesses II had over a hundred sons but his favourite was Prince Khaemwese, whom he made High Priest of Ptah at Memphis. Khaemwese was famous for his learning and for his interest in ancient times. A thousand years after his death the Egyptians were still telling stories which portrayed him as the wisest of magicians. One such story relates how Prince Setna Khaemwese discovered where the Book of Thoth was hidden. The Book of Thoth contained the most powerful of magic spells, and also the most dangerous, but that did not deter the royal magician.

One day, when the court was at Memphis, Setna went to his father and asked his permission to open one of the royal tombs in the City of the Dead. The whole court was shocked at such a request, but Setna explained that the famous Book of Thoth was hidden in the tomb of Prince Neferkaptah. Pharaoh tried hard to make his son give up such a rash idea, but when he saw that the prince was determined, he let him have his way. Ramesses knew that the dead could protect themselves and that Setna would have to learn to respect them.

The prince asked Anhurerau, the bravest of his younger brothers, to go with him and they took a gang of workmen into the City of the Dead. When they reached the ancient tomb of Neferkaptah, the workmen shovelled away the sand that had blown against its entrance. Gradually a wooden door was revealed. Setna broke the seals on the door and ordered the workmen to hack through the wood. Reluctantly, they obeyed. The rotten wood crumbled after a few blows and the tomb stood open. Setna and Anhurerau waited ten, tense minutes to let fresh air seep through the tomb, and then a torch was lit for them. None of the workmen would enter the black doorway, so the two brothers went in alone, Anhurerau holding up the torch and Setna a pace ahead of him.

They walked cautiously down a narrow passageway and through a shadowy hall carved with scenes of Prince Neferkaptah's funeral. Beyond, was a maze of small rooms and twisting passages. As they went deeper into the tomb, the heat and the stale air were suffocating. The light of Anhurerau's torch hardly seemed to penetrate the intense darkness and all around them there were rustlings and scratchings. 'It's only bats.' Setna had meant to reassure his brother, but his whisper echoed through the tomb and above them dozens of bats erupted into flight. As Anhurerau ducked, the whirr of their wings put out his torch and the darkness pounced. Setna froze. They would have to go back—if he could remember the way. It would be no use shouting for help; none of the workmen would enter the tomb. Suddenly Anhurerau gripped his brother's arm: 'Look!' Ahead of them was a faint glow. As the brothers moved towards it, the light grew brighter. Setna and Anhurerau crept round a corner in the passageway and found themselves staring into the burial chamber itself.

The room was crammed with rich furnishings; ebony thrones and vases of alabaster, stools draped with leopard skins and ivory caskets. On a golden couch lay the mummy of Neferkaptah, wrapped in scented linen, his face covered by a glittering mask. Beside the couch sat a beautiful woman, pale as a white lotus, with a little boy huddled at her feet. Light streamed from the scroll of papyrus that lay on a table in front of them, and Setna knew that he was looking at the Book of Thoth. Anhurerau stood trembling in the doorway, but Setna stepped boldly into the burial chamber and saluted the lady. The hand she raised to greet him was almost transparent, but her voice was low and sweet.

'Setna Khaemwese, why do you disturb the rest of the dead?'

'If you give me the Book of Thoth,' said Setna, trying not to sound as frightened as he felt, 'I will leave you in peace.'

The lovely ka shook her head. 'Setna, if you steal the Book of Thoth, it will bring you nothing but disaster. I see from your face that you do not believe me. I will tell you our story, and then you will understand the danger.

'My name is Ahwere. I was the only daughter of the King of Upper and Lower Egypt,' said the ka proudly. She looked down at the silent figure on the couch. 'I loved my brother Neferkaptah more than anything in the world and he loved me. I begged our father the king to let us marry and he agreed. A splendid feast was held to mark our marriage and we lived together very happily. It was not long before a son was born to us and we called him Mrib.' Ahwere reached down to touch the little boy who lay at her feet, and he

smiled up at her as if just waking from a dream. 'My husband was like you, Setna. He loved to wander in the City of the Dead to study the tombs or to visit temple libraries and try to read the ancient scrolls. He was a skilled magician, but he was always seeking more powerful spells. One day my husband attended a festival in the temple of Ptah. As he walked behind a procession, he read the spells written on the shrines of the gods. Suddenly Neferkaptah heard someone laughing at him. In the shadow of a column stood an old priest, amusement doubling the wrinkles on his face.

"Why are you laughing at me?" my husband demanded indignantly.

"I laugh at you reading such paltry spells," answered the priest, "when I could tell you where to find a magic book written by Thoth himself. There are two spells in it. If you read the first spell aloud, you will enchant the sky above and the sky below and the earth itself from the mountains to the seas. You will be able to understand every beast and bird and summon the fishes of the deep, just like a god. If you read the second spell, even if you are in the Land of the Dead, you will take your own form again and see the sun shine and the moon rise and the gods themselves."

'Then my husband flattered the priest. "Oh great one, may you live for ever! Name one wish that I can grant you, but tell me how to find the Book of Thoth." The old man's eyes glittered with greed.

"Give me a hundred silver pieces to pay for my funeral, and when the time comes, two priests to serve my ka." Neferkaptah sent for the silver and when the old priest had counted it he whispered to my husband, "The Book of Thoth is hidden in an iron box at the bottom of the river, near Coptos. Inside the iron box is a box of bronze and inside the box of bronze is a box of sycamore. Inside the sycamore box is a box of ebony and inside that, a box of ivory. In the ivory box is a box of silver and in the silver box, a box of gold and in that box, the Book of Thoth, and there are snakes and scorpions guarding all the boxes."

'Then Neferkaptah was dizzy with excitement. He rushed back to the palace to tell me

everything that had happened and said, "I will sail to Coptos at once and bring back the Book of Thoth!" Then I was afraid and I cursed that old priest. "May the gods smite him for telling you such a secret. I know that Coptos will bring us nothing but sorrow." I begged Neferkaptah not to sail south, but he could think of nothing but the Book of Thoth and he would not listen.'

Ahwere sighed. 'The king gave us a splendid ship. Neferkaptah sailed south and Mrib and I went with him. When we reached Coptos the priests of the temple of Isis and their wives hurried out to meet us and we spent four days feasting with them. On the fifth day my husband sent for pure wax and modelled a boat with all its crew. Then he crouched over it, muttering spells and breathed life into the crew. He launched the wax boat on the river and loaded the royal ship with sand. Then my husband went on board and I sat down on the river bank, determined not to move until he came back.

'Neferkaptah called out to the crew of the wax boat: "Row oarsmen, row to the place where the Book of Thoth is hidden!" The wax men took up their oars and they rowed for three days and three nights and the royal ship followed. On the fourth morning, the wax boat stopped and my husband knew that they must have reached the right place. He threw out the sand on either side of the ship so that the waters divided and there was a strip of dry land in the middle of the river. Neferkaptah went down between the banks of sand, reciting spells, for the iron box crawled with snakes and scorpions.

'The snakes hissed and the scorpions raised their deadly tails but my husband's spells were strong and the snakes froze as they tried to spit poison and the scorpions could not reach him with their stings. Yet around the iron box itself was coiled a serpent too vast for any spell to bind. My husband was not afraid; he stunned it with a blow from his bronze axe and chopped it in half. To his horror the two halves joined up again and within seconds the great serpent was coiling round him.

'Neferkaptah flinched from its poisonous breath. The coils tightened as the serpent tried to crush him, but he just had time to draw his dagger and hack through the glittering scales.

Again my husband cut the serpent in two, but as he staggered backwards the coils rejoined. Neferkaptah snatched up his axe and wearily attacked for the third time. He slashed through its coils and for a moment the serpent lay motionless. Then to my husband's despair the severed coils began to wriggle towards each other. With sudden inspiration, Neferkaptah picked up a handful of sand and threw it between the two halves. The snake struggled to join itself together again but now there was something between the halves the magic wouldn't work. With a frantic hissing the creature quivered and died.

'Neferkaptah kicked the body aside and wrenched open the iron box. Inside was a box of bronze, just as the old priest had said. Impatiently my husband tore open the boxes of bronze and sycamore, ebony, ivory and silver and came to a slender golden box. He lifted the lid and there lay a gleaming scroll—the Book of Thoth.'

Awhere paused. Her pale fingers touched the papyrus on the table in front of her but her eyes lingered on the mask that hid her husband's face. 'Neferkaptah unrolled the Book of Thoth and dared to read the first spell. He enchanted the sky above and the sky below and the whole earth from the mountains to the seas. He understood the speech of every living thing, even the fishes of the deep and the beasts of the desert hills. That was not enough for my husband and he read the second spell. By its terrible power he saw the Sun and the Moon and the stars in their true form and the glory of the gods themselves.

'Then Neferkaptah returned to his ship. He spoke a spell to the river and the waters flooded back over the scattered boxes, but the Book of Thoth was safe in my husband's hand. He ordered the crew of the wax boat to row back to Coptos and they rowed without pausing for three days and three nights.

'Now all this time I had been sitting on the river bank below the temple of Isis. I wouldn't eat or drink until I knew what had happened to my husband and by the seventh morning I looked fit for the embalmers. But at last the royal ship sailed into view and Neferkaptah sprang ashore. When we'd embraced each other, I asked to see the Book of Thoth and he put it in my hand. I read the first spell and the second and shared my husband's power. Then Neferkaptah sent for fresh papyrus and he copied down the words of the Book of Thoth. He soaked the new scroll in beer and then crumbled it into a bowl and dissolved it in water. He swallowed the water and with it drank the power of the two spells. We made thank offerings in the temple of Isis and sailed north again with Mrib our son.

'My husband was delighted with his success but the Wise One knew what Neferkaptah had done and he was very angry. Thoth hurried to Ra the King of the Gods and demanded justice: "Neferkaptah the son of King Mernebptah has discovered the hiding place of my magic book. He has killed the guardian and opened the seven boxes and read the forbidden spells! Such crimes cannot go unpunished." Then Ra gave judgement in favour of Thoth and decreed that we should never come safely home to Memphis. The three of us were sitting on deck beneath a gilded awning. We did not know that from that moment we were doomed.'

Ahwere's dark eyes filled with tears and Mrib covered his ears, as if he could not bear to listen to the next part of the story. 'Our little boy slipped away from the couch where I sat with Neferkaptah. As Mrib leaned over the ship's rail to gaze at the Nile, the curse of Ra struck him and he tumbled into the water. I screamed at the splash and all the sailors shouted. My husband ran out from under the awning and said the second spell of the Book of Thoth. Mrib rose up from the Nile, threw back his sodden hair and spoke. He told us of the anger of Thoth and that Ra had cursed us. No spell could save Mrib, he was already drowned. His lips closed and our son fell dead at my feet. We returned to Coptos and lived through seventy desolate days while Mrib's body was prepared by the embalmers and a princely tomb was made ready.

'After the burial we sailed north to tell our father the king the tragic news of Mrib's death. Neferkaptah watched over me anxiously but I paced the deck, grieving for my son. When we reached the place where Mrib had drowned, the curse of Ra struck me and I fell into the river. The waters closed over my head and I drowned before my husband could reach me. Neferkaptah spoke the second spell and raised up my body. I told him of the anger of Thoth and the curse of Ra, but my ka had already passed into the West. My husband took me back to Coptos and I was buried in Mrib's tomb.

'Neferkaptah boarded the royal ship to sail back to Memphis, but he said to himself, "I cannot bear to stay in Coptos, close to the tomb of my wife and son but how can I go back to Memphis and tell the king 'I took your daughter and your only grandchild to Coptos but I cannot bring them back. I am alive, but they are dead'." My husband knew that he could not bear to live a day longer. He took a strip of linen and bound the Book of Thoth to his body. Then he leaped over the ship's rail and into the Nile. The sailors cried out in horror, but they could not even find my husband's body.

'When the ship reached Memphis, the sailors sent a messenger with the terrible news that both the king's children were dead. The court went into mourning and the king himself came down to the harbour with all the people of Memphis and the priests of Ptah. He saw Neferkaptah's body tangled in the rudders of the royal ship. The body was taken out of the water and all the people wept. The king said, "Let that accursed book be buried with my son." The body of Neferkaptah was taken to the embalmers and after seventy days it was laid to rest in this very tomb. Now I have told you how misery came to us because of the book you want me to give you. The Book of Thoth cost us our lives, it can never be yours.'

Setna was shaken by Ahwere's story but the light of the Book of Thoth dazzled him and he could not bear to give it up. 'Let me have the book,' he repeated, 'or I'll take it by force!' Then the mummy of Prince Neferkaptah slowly sat up and a voice came from behind the mask: 'Setna Khaemwese, if you will not listen to Ahwere's warning, are you a great enough magician to take the Book of Thoth from me? Or will you play four games of draughts? If you win, you shall have the Book of Thoth as your prize.'

At the chilling sound of Neferkaptah's voice, Anhurerau shrank back. What would happen if

Setna lost the games? He whispered to his brother to run but Setna stepped closer to the Book of Thoth. 'I am ready,' he said.

Close to the couch was a draughts board with squares of ebony and ivory, set with pieces of gold and silver. They began the first game, and the pieces moved without being touched. Setna was a skilful player but the dead prince was a better one. Neferkaptah won the first game and murmured a spell. Setna sank into the ground up to his ankles.

Anhurerau tried to pull his brother out, but he was stuck fast. There was nothing that Setna could do but play the second game; he lost that too. Neferkaptah murmured another spell and Setna sank into the ground up to his hips. Setna realized that he had staked his life against the Book of Thoth and the third game began.

There was silence in the burial chamber as the pieces moved across the squares. Setna played cunningly but the dead prince seemed to read his mind and slowly the game was lost. Neferkaptah spoke a third spell and Setna sank into the ground up to his chin. He could move nothing but his eyes and his lips. Setna whispered desperately to Anhurerau: 'Get out of the tomb! Run to Pharaoh and fetch my magic books and the Amulets of Ptah.'

As the fourth and final game began, Anhurerau fled back along the passage. As the light from the burial chamber faded, he felt his way along the walls, praying to Ptah that he would not get lost in the darkness. It seemed a horribly long time before he saw daylight again. Anhurerau burst out of the tomb, terrifying the nervous workmen, and ran to the place where Pharaoh was. When he had gasped out his story Ramesses said, 'Hurry my son, take Setna these books of magic and these amulets of power!' Anhurerau hurried back with magic scrolls under his arm, a torch in one hand and the Amulets of Ptah in the other.

In the burial chamber the silver pieces were already outnumbered by the gold; Setna was losing for the fourth time. It would be his last game; already he could imagine the earth closing over his lips, his nose, his eyes . . . Setna was not playing to win any more, only to delay the dreadful moment. Finally it came. Neferkaptah made the winning move and the words of the fourth spell came from the glittering mask. Setna was opening his mouth to beg for mercy when he heard the sound of running feet.

Anhurerau rushed into the burial chamber, knelt by his brother and placed the Amulets of Ptah on his head. Instantly the power of Ptah freed Setna from the dead prince's spell. He shot out of the ground, swayed for a moment and then grabbed the Book of Thoth. Setna and his brother fled from the burial chamber. There was no need for Anhurerau's torch, light walked in front of them, and darkness behind them. In the gloomy burial chamber Ahwere wept and Mrib clung to her.

'Hail King of Darkness,' she whispered.
'Farewell King of Light! The power that kept us together is gone, and I shall be banished to my lonely tomb.' But Neferkaptah had drunk the words of the Book of Thoth and he was far from helpless.

'Do not be unhappy,' he said. 'I will make Setna return the book himself, with a forked stick in his hand and a dish of incense on his head.'

When the two princes emerged from the tomb, they ordered the workmen to brick up the entrance and pile sand against it. Then Setna hurried before Pharaoh and told him everything that had happened. Ramesses looked grave. 'If you are wise my son, you will return the Book of Thoth at once or Neferkaptah will humiliate you and make you take it back, carrying the stick of a suppliant, with incense burning to protect you.' Setna was not listening; he could not wait to unroll the gleaming papyrus.

For several days he studied the scroll, learning to read the ancient script. One morning Setna paced the courtyard of the temple of Ptah, pondering the words of the first spell. Suddenly he saw a woman walking towards the inner temple with a great crowd of maids and pages. From her dainty sandalled feet to her shining braids of blue-black hair, she was the loveliest creature that Setna had ever seen. For a moment their eyes met and he hardly knew where he was. Then the woman hid her face behind an ostrich-feather fan and walked on.

Setna called to one of his slaves, 'Did you see that woman? Find out who she is!' He waited impatiently in the shadow of the temple gateway until the boy returned.

'My Lord, her maids tell me that she is the Lady Tabube, the daughter of the Prophet of Bastet of Ankhtawy, and she has come here to pray to Ptah.'

'Go back and speak to one of her maids, saying that Setna Khaemwese sends you. Ask her to tell her mistress that she shall have ten gold pieces, or a law case settled in her favour, if she will come and spend some time with me.'

The slave was very surprised at his master's words but he hastened to obey. Tabube was in the next courtyard making offerings of wine and flowers before the statue of Ptah. The slave edged up to one of her maids and whispered his master's offer. The maid was most indignant at such an insult to her mistress and railed at the poor slave. Tabube soon asked what the matter was and, with great embarrassment, the boy repeated the message. Tabube did not seem angry.

'Tell Setna Khaemwese,' she said, 'that I am a priestess and a lady of rank. If he wants to meet me, he must visit my house in Bubastis and I will entertain him there.' The boy hurried back to tell his master and Setna was delighted. He forgot all about his wife and family, he even forgot about the Book of Thoth. He could think of nothing but Tabube and the very next day he sailed north to Bubastis.

He soon found the house of the Prophet of Bastet of Ankhtawy and was asked to wait in the walled garden. Setna walked through a grove of fig trees and sat in a vine arbour, thinking about Tabube. Suddenly, he looked up and she was there. Tabube wore a clinging dress of transparent linen. Her eyelids were green with malachite, her lashes dark with kohl and her hair scented by lotus flowers.

She beckoned to Setna and took him inside the house to an upper chamber. The floor was of polished lapis and the walls were inlaid with turquoise. Ebony couches were draped with soft linen and a table was spread with dishes of pomegranates and vessels of wine. The air was thick with incense. Tabube drew Setna down beside her. She offered him fruit but he was too excited to eat. Tabube poured out the strong red wine and they drank together.

Setna longed to kiss her, but Tabube said, 'I am a priestess, a lady of rank. You ought to marry me and draw up a proper contract.' Setna was too infatuated to think twice about it.

'Send for a scribe,' he said. Almost at once a scribe appeared with a contract drawn up which made over all of Setna's wealth to his new wife. He signed it quickly and as soon as the scribe was gone, Setna tried to kiss Tabube again; but she drew back.

'That contract won't be valid unless your children agree to give up their rights. They are downstairs now, have them sent up so that they can sign our marriage contract.' Setna was too intoxicated by the strong wine and Tabube's beauty to think this odd. His little daughters were brought up and meekly signed the contract

that robbed them of their inheritance. When they had gone, Setna drank another goblet of wine and put his arms around Tabube's waist. She slipped out of his embrace and a tear shone on her rouged cheek.

'If you really love me,' she said, 'you will have your children killed. I am sure they will contest our marriage and make us unhappy.'

When Setna looked into Tabube's eyes, he could deny her nothing. He gave an order for his daughters to be killed and their bodies were thrown from the window into a courtyard. Setna could hear dogs and cats tearing at their bodies as he sat drinking with the beautiful Tabube. Then she put her white arms around his neck and leaned forward to kiss him. Suddenly Tabube's lips opened in a scream and Setna found himself crouching in the middle of a public road, embracing the dust. Tabube and her house had vanished. His head cleared and Setna realized the terrible thing that he had done. He moaned and grovelled in the dust. Passing travellers stared at him, wondering if he was drunk or mad.

Poor Setna did not notice the approach of four Nubians carrying an ebony chair. In the chair sat a man, dressed in splendid robes and wearing royal jewels. He seemed amused by Setna's plight.

'What is Prince Setna Khaemwese doing here in such a state?'

'Neferkaptah has done this to me,' said Setna bitterly. 'he has had his revenge and my children, my lovely daughters . . .'

The royal stranger smiled. 'Go back to Memphis. You will find your daughters safe and sound at Pharaoh's court.'

Setna could hardly believe his ears. Had it all been an illusion? The royal stranger nodded to one of his slaves, who tossed Setna a cloak to cover his filthy clothes. 'Go back to Memphis. Your children are safe,' he repeated. There was something familiar about the stranger's voice but before Setna could thank him, the chair and the Nubians and the stranger himself had vanished.

Setna rushed back to Memphis and his wife and daughters were surprised to be hugged so ardently and asked a dozen times if they were safe and well. That same day, Setna had an uncomfortable audience with Pharaoh. When he had related the whole story, Ramesses said, 'Setna, I tried to warn you but you would not listen. Now will you take back the Book of Thoth before anything worse happens?'

Later that day, workmen reopened the tomb of Neferkaptah. A shamefaced Setna walked through the doorway with a dish of incense balanced on his head, a forked stick in one hand and the Book of Thoth in the other. As he entered the burial chamber, Ahwere whispered, 'Ah Setna, you would never have escaped with your life without the blessing of Ptah!' But her husband laughed. 'So, my prophecy has come true.'

Setna bowed humbly to the dead prince and replaced the Book of Thoth. It lit the tomb like the rising sun.

'Is there anything else I must do?' asked Setna warily. Neferkaptah looked at the pale figures of his wife and son.

'By the strength of my magic,' he said, 'I keep the kas of my family close to me, but the task wearies me. Bring me their bodies from Coptos; then we shall be truly united.'

Setna left the tomb and told Pharaoh about the dead prince's request. Ramesses ordered a ship to be fitted out for the journey south. When Setna reached Coptos he was greeted by the priests of the temple of Isis and he offered oxen, geese and wine to the goddess and to Horus her son. Next day he went with the High Priest of Isis to the City of the Dead to search for the tomb of Mrib and Ahwere. He spent three days wandering among the tombs, turning over the ancient stones and reading the inscriptions, but none of them belonged to the family of Neferkaptah.

From distant Memphis the dead prince watched the search and when he saw that Setna could not find the tomb he turned himself into a very ancient priest and hobbled across the hillside. Setna greeted him courteously. 'You seem the most ancient man I've met in Coptos. Can you remember anything about the resting place of the Princess Ahwere and her son?'

The old man pretended to think for a while and then said, 'The grandfather of the grandfather of my father once said that the grandfather of his father had told him that the tomb of Ahwere lay there, under the southern corner of the house of the High Priest.'

Setna looked doubtful. 'How do I know that you're telling the truth? Perhaps you have a grudge against the High Priest and would like to see his house pulled down?'

'Keep me a prisoner while you pull the house down,' answered the old man with a toothless grin. 'And if you don't find the tomb, put me to death.'

Then Setna ordered his men to tear down the High Priest's house and under the southern corner they found an ancient tomb. At the bottom of a deep shaft were the coffins of Ahwere and Mrib. Setna had them reverently carried on board his ship. He ordered his men to start rebuilding the High Priest's house but when he went to reward the old man, he found the guards in confusion; their prisoner had vanished. Setna understood then who the old man must have been.

Setna sailed north and when they reached Memphis Pharaoh and all his court came to the harbour to honour the royal dead. The coffins of Ahwere and Mrib were carried into the burial chamber of Neferkaptah and the family were reunited. Setna himself saw the entrance bricked up. The tomb of the dead prince was never entered again and no-one else has read the Book of Thoth.

The young magician

Prince Setna Khaemwese and his wife Mehusekhe had two pretty daughters, but they longed for a son. Year after year they heaped the altars of the gods with rich offerings, but their prayers were never answered. Now at many Egyptian temples it was the custom for sick people and barren women to sleep in the sacred precincts. Every night they would lie down hoping that the deity would appear to them in a dream and tell them how they could be cured. In desperation, Setna decided to take his wife to spend the night in the temple of Osiris.

They arrived at dusk to find that the building meant to house the sick was already crowded and that many people were unrolling their bedding in the temple courtyard. Because of her high rank a room was found for Setna's wife, but it was no more than a narrow cubicle with thin walls. The Prince kissed Mehusekhe goodbye and left. She lay down on the strange bed and closed her eyes. The groans of the sick and the tearful prayers of barren women came from every side. Mehusekhe was sure that she would never be able to sleep in such a place, but she murmured a prayer to Isis and Osiris and after three tense hours she finally slept.

Just before dawn, Mehusekhe woke up, knowing that a god had spoken to her in her sleep. She could not remember what form the god had taken but she was sure that a mysterious voice had whispered, 'Wife of Setna, tomorrow you must go to the place where your husband bathes. The pool is overhung by a melon vine. Break off a branch with its fruit. Cut it up; grind it small; mix it with water and drink it down. Then embrace your husband and you will conceive a son.'

Mehusekhe made a thank offering, left the temple and hurried to find the pool and the melon vine. She did everything that the god had commanded and it was not long before she knew that she was pregnant. When she told Setna he was overjoyed and anxious all at once. He hung a powerful amulet around her neck and recited spells over her to keep her and her unborn child safe. One night a god came to Setna in his dreams and said, 'Setna Khaemwese, your wife is carrying a son. When the boy is born you must call him Sa-Osiris and he will do many wonders in Egypt.'

Setna woke from his dream even happier than before and impatient for the months of waiting to be over.

When her time came, Mehusekhe gave birth to a fine boy and Setna named him Sa-Osiris. It soon became clear that this was no ordinary child. When he was a year old, strangers always took him for a boy of two and when he was two everyone thought he was three. Setna watched over his son with pride and loved him dearly and Sa-Osiris was sent to school at an age when other children could hardly talk. He learned to read and write so quickly that within a few months he knew more than the elderly scribe who was his teacher.

Next, the boy was taken to the temple of Ptah, where his father was high priest, and placed in the care of the wise men in the House of Life. It was there that priests studied astronomy and mathematics, medicine and magic and made copies of the sacred books. Sa-Osiris was the most brilliant pupil that they had ever had. He learned the proper ritual for every god in every temple on every day of the year; he learned to name the stars and how to calculate which were lucky and which were unlucky days; he learned spells for driving out all kinds of sickness and for protecting the living and the dead. By the time he was seven he knew each book in the temple library by heart. Everyone who met him was amazed at the boy's cleverness and Setna looked forward to the day when he would present his marvellous son at court.

Late one afternoon Sa-Osiris and his father were together in their house in Memphis, dressing for a banquet. Setna was startled by a sudden wailing and, looking down from his window, he saw the funeral procession of a rich man. A gilded coffin on a sledge was dragged by a pair of oxen and surrounded by weeping women. With their bare feet, unbraided hair and torn clothes, the women were a picture of misery and they had been paid to beat their breasts and wail as loudly as if Osiris himself had just died again. Behind them walked lines of servants carrying ebony chairs, ivory caskets crammed with jewels, ostrich feather fans, chests of fine linen and many other precious things to be buried with the rich man in his splendid tomb.

Following after was another funeral. Wrapped in a mat, a poor man who had died homeless and friendless was being dragged to his shallow grave in the desert sand. He had no mourners to weep for him and not even a pot or a string of beads to be buried with him.

'By Ptah!' exclaimed Setna, 'how much happier the rich man is, even in death, than that poor wretch.'

Sa-Osiris came to the window to stand beside his father and said quietly, 'Do you think so? I only wish that you may share the fate of that poor man.'

Setna was surprised and hurt. 'How can you say such a thing?'

'If you like, father, I will show you what has happened to the rich man whom the mourners wail for and to the poor man who has no mourners. Come with me.'

With a secretive smile, Sa-Osiris gripped Setna's hand and led him out into the street. They took a ferry across the Nile and entered the City of the Dead on the edge of the western desert. As they stood amongst the ancient tombs, Sa-Osiris uttered a spell of grim power to break down the barriers between the realms of the living and the dead. Setna suddenly felt as if the weight of his body had dropped away and

that he could fly. At a dizzying speed the young magician swept his father past the gates of the Underworld. Setna glimpsed the shadowy forms of demons with long knives in their hands but Sa-Osiris knew the proper spells to appease the Guardians of the Gateways. They plunged deeper into the Underworld and when their pace slowed, Setna found himself looking down on a group of men who were squatting on the floor of a gloomy hall trying to plait straw into ropes. Their fingers were raw and their task could never be finished, for a donkey stood at each man's shoulder, eating the straw rope.

There were other men in the hall with jutting bones and faces gaunt with hunger. They were scrabbling to reach the loaves of bread and jugs of water that hung above their heads. Whenever it looked as if they would succeed, demons dug pits at their feet. The wretched men slipped down before they could grasp the food and water and they wept and cursed in their torment and hunger.

The next hall was full of souls pleading for mercy and the pivot of the great door was fixed in the eye of a man who continually wailed and prayed. Setna shuddered as the door swung open and the man screamed in agony, but Sa-Osiris swept them on into another hall. There the

demons of the Underworld were listing the sins of the newly dead in front of the Forty-Two Judges. In the last hall, Setna was dazzled by the mysterious form of the King of the Dead.

Shrouded in white linen, green-skinned Osiris sat beneath a golden canopy holding the crook and the flail, the symbols of kingship. Brave Isis and gentle Nephthys stood behind him and in front of him were jackal-headed Anubis, the guardian of the dead and ibis-headed Thoth, the scribe of the gods. The huge hall was filled with the spirits of the blessed dead and at its centre stood the scales that weighed the hearts of the dead against the feather of Truth. In the shadows squatted a monstrous shape, part lion, part crocodile, part hippopotamus; the shape of the Devourer who gave wicked souls a second death.

Sa-Osiris whispered to his awe-struck father, 'Do you see that blessed spirit who is clothed in golden raiments, who wears the feathers of Truth in his hair and who stands close to the throne of Osiris? That spirit is the poor man, whom you saw carried to a beggar's grave with no-one to mourn for him. His spirit entered the Underworld and was brought to the Place of Judgement. He faced the Forty-Two Judges and his heart was weighed against Truth. His good deeds were found to outweigh his bad deeds in the life that Thoth had allotted to him. Osiris himself ordered that the poor man should be given all the goods buried with the rich man and a place among the blessed spirits.'

Setna gazed in wonder at the shining spirit who only a few hours before had been a beggar on the streets of Memphis. Before he could form his next question, Sa-Osiris began to answer it. 'As for the rich man whose fine funeral you saw . . . in spite of his many chances to be generous to the poor and merciful to the weak, his bad deeds were far greater than his good deeds. Osiris condemned him to imprisonment in the Underworld. He is the wretched soul you saw with the pivot of a door fixed in his eye. By Osiris, the Lord of the Dead, when I said that I wanted you to share the poor man's fate, I knew what would happen to the two souls.'

Then Setna understood that he had misjudged his son and he humbly asked him to explain the other marvels which they had seen.

'The men you saw plaiting ropes that they could never complete and the men striving for food that they could never reach are wicked souls, condemned to torment. Dearest father, take the lesson to heart. If you are kind and gentle on earth, the King of the Dead will be kind and gentle to you. If you are evil, evil will be done to you. This is the law of the gods for all eternity.'

Setna bowed his head and let his son lead him out of the Underworld by strange paths. They passed through fire and water and emerged in the western desert again. As they walked back to Memphis, hand in hand, Setna marvelled at the power and wisdom of Sa-Osiris.
'He is almost like a god and yet when people ask me who he is, I can say "This is my son".'

Under his breath, he muttered spells against the demons of the Underworld, for Setna was afraid. He had seen what no living man had seen before and he knew now that even the son of pharaoh must fear the Judgement of the Dead.

The sealed letter

One day the great Pharaoh Ramesses held court at Memphis. As he sat in his throne-room surrounded by princes, generals, councillors, priests and all the great men of Egypt, a Nubian chieftain was announced. Splendid in leopard skin cloak, nodding plumes and bangles of ivory and gold, the tall Nubian strode towards Pharaoh. He bowed three times before the throne but his words were not humble.

'Is there anyone here who can read the letter I carry without opening it? If there is no priest and scribe of your court who is wise enough to read the contents of the letter without breaking the seal and unrolling the papyrus, I shall carry the shame of Egypt back to Nubia!'

The courtiers were astonished and dismayed. None of them had ever heard of a man wise enough to perform such a feat, but Pharaoh said calmly, 'Send for the most learned of my sons, send for Prince Setna Khaemwese.'

A dozen servants ran to fetch the prince and Setna was soon bowing before his father's throne.

'My son,' began Pharaoh, 'this Nubian chieftain demands to know if there is a wise man in Egypt who can read a letter without opening it.'

Setna tried not to let the Nubian see how startled he was. 'This is a foolish request,' he said, 'but give me ten days and I will see what may be done to stop the shame of Egypt being carried to the land of gum-eaters.'

'The days are yours,' answered Pharaoh and he ordered that the chieftain be given comfortable rooms in the palace and servants to cook him Nubian food. Ramesses left the throne-room with great dignity but he could hardly eat or sleep for fear that his country would be shamed.

Setna was in an even worse condition. He wandered back to his house like a sleepwalker and lay down on his bed, hiding his face in his sleeves. Mehusekhe, his wife, hurried to his bedside and put her arms around him.

'My brother, you are cold and shivering. Are you sick or full of grief?'

'Leave me alone,' whispered Setna. 'My heart is grieving over something a woman cannot help me with.'

Then Sa-Osiris came into the bedchamber and asked what the matter was.

'Leave me alone,' muttered Setna. 'You are only twelve and my heart is grieving over something a child cannot help me with.'

'Only tell me what it is,' pleaded Sa-Osiris, 'and I will drive this grief away.'

Then Setna told his son about the Nubian chieftain and his challenge. 'And if I cannot find an Egyptian to read the sealed letter, I and my country will be shamed for ever.'

Sa-Osiris began to laugh and his parent asked him indignantly what was so funny about that.

'O father, I am laughing because you are lying here in despair over so small a matter. I can easily read this Nubian's letter.'

Setna sat up at once but he still could not believe his good fortune. 'Can you prove what you say my son?'

'Go downstairs, father,' answered Sa-Osiris, 'and take a scroll out of one of your book chests. I will read what's in it from the floor above you.'

Setna ran downstairs. He opened a cedar chest and plucked out a roll of papyrus inscribed with spells for healing fevers. He held it up for a minute and then returned to his bedchamber. Sa-Osiris at once began to recite the spells in the scroll, to the delight and amazement of his parents. Again and again Setna ran down to the lower room and held up random scrolls, but Sa-Osiris always knew their contents. Thoroughly convinced, Setna hurried to the palace to tell his father the good news. Ramesses was overjoyed and he invited Setna and his son to spend the night feasting with him.

The next morning, the Nubian chieftain was brought into the throne-room with the sealed letter tied to the belt at his waist. Sa-Osiris stepped forward.

'You fiend of Nubia, you have come to the beautiful land of Egypt, the garden of Osiris, the footstool of Ra, to bring us shame. May Amon strike you down! I shall now read your letter, so do not dare to lie to Pharaoh about its contents.'

'I shall tell no lies,' said the Nubian haughtily. He was not afraid of the mere child who stood before him but his face changed as Sa-Osiris began to speak in a confident voice.

'This is what is written in the Nubian's letter. Many centuries ago, when Pharaoh Siamun ruled Egypt, Nubia was jealous of his wealth and power. One day the Prince of Nubia was resting in the gardens of a temple of Amon when he overheard three sorcerers talking.

"Were it not that Amon and Pharaoh might punish me," said the first sorcerer, "I would cast a spell on Egypt so that the whole land would like in darkness for three days and nights and the people would tremble."

"Were it not that Amon and Pharaoh might punish me," declared the second sorcerer, "I would cast a spell on Egypt so that the whole land would be barren for three years and nothing would grow."

"Were it not that Amon and Pharaoh might punish me," began the third sorcerer, "I would cast a spell on Egypt and fetch Pharaoh to Nubia. I would have him beaten before our Prince and returned to Egypt, all within six hours."

'The prince sent his servants to fetch the three sorcerers and said to them, "Which of you boasted that you could bring Pharaoh here and have him beaten before me?"

"It was Sa-Neheset," answered the other two sorcerers.

"Cast your spell on Egypt," ordered the prince, "and if you succeed, by Amon, the Bull of Meroe, I will do good things for you."

'Sa-Neheset went away and modelled a litter and four bearers out of the finest wax. He recited spells over them and breathed life into them. Then he ordered the bearers to fly to Egypt, bring back Pharaoh to Nubia and give him five hundred blows. The bearers opened their wax mouths and chorused, "We shall do as you say."

'That night the Nubian sorcerer cast his spell against Egypt and the litter-bearers entered the bedchamber of Pharaoh unseen by the guards. They overpowered Siamun with their magic strength, flung him in the litter and carried him back to Nubia. When they reached the prince's palace, Pharaoh was tumbled out and the litter-bearers beat him with sticks while the Nubian court looked on and laughed. Then they returned him to his bed in Egypt, all within six hours. Then the litter-bearers vanished.'

Sa-Osiris paused and there were angry
murmurs from the Egyptian courtiers.
'May the anger of Amon strike you if you lie,'
threatened the young magician. 'Am I reading
your letter?'
'You are,' muttered the Nubian, 'and every
word is true.'
   Sa-Osiris fixed his eyes on the sealed letter and
began again.
'When Siamun found himself in his own bed
again, he yelled for his guards and attendants.
"How long have I been away," he demanded,
"and what has been happening?"
'There was an embarrassed silence. As far as the
courtiers knew, Pharaoh had been asleep in his
bed all night.
"O Pharaoh, our great lord," began one brave
chamberlain, "May Isis heal you! We do not
understand you, your Majesty has slept in your
Majesty's bed all night."
'Then Siamun turned over and told them to look
at his back. "I tell you I was carried to Nubia last
night and given five hundred blows."
'When the courtiers saw that Pharaoh's back was
dark with bruises they were shocked and
horrified and began to wail. No-one knew what
to do until the wise magician Sa-Paneshe arrived
in the royal bedchamber. He examined Pharaoh
and exclaimed, "This is the work of Nubian
sorcery and I must turn their magic back against
them."
"Hurry," groaned Siamun, "I cannot endure
another night like the last one!"
'Sa-Paneshe fetched his amulets and his books of
magic. He recited spell after spell over Pharaoh
and bound amulets to his brow and neck and
arms. Then he left Siamun in the hands of the
royal doctors and sailed up river to Hermopolis,
to the temple of Thoth. Sa-Paneshe made
offerings to the god and prayed aloud, "O great

one, turn your face to me. Do not let Egypt be shamed by Nubia. You are the creator of magic, you know everything that exists on earth and in the sky above and the sky below. Help me to save Pharaoh and defeat the sorcery of Nubia!"

'Then Sa-Paneshe lay down to sleep in the temple. Thoth came to him in a dream and said, "Tomorrow you must search the temple library until you find a secret chamber. Inside the chamber you will find a locked chest and inside the chest a scroll written in my own hand. Take out the Book of Thoth, copy from it the spells you need and return it to its chest. Tell no-one this secret and you will save Pharaoh."

'Sa-Paneshe woke and remembered his dream. He found the scroll and wrote out a mighty spell for the protection of Siamun. That night in Nubia, Sa-Neheset breathed life into his wax figures again and sent them to Egypt. They entered Pharaoh's room unseen but as they approached the bed they seemed to strike an invisible barrier. Siamun felt the amulets he wore throbbing with power and sensed that the spells of Sa-Paneshe were beating back the spells of Nubia. All night long the wax men marched round and round the bed, trying to find a flaw in the magical defences, while Pharaoh lay motionless, hardly daring to breathe. As morning broke, the litter-bearers were forced to fly back to Nubia and Siamun leaped out of bed.

'He summoned Sa-Paneshe and told him everything that had happened. The Egyptian magician was delighted that his spells had worked but he meant to go one step further and punish the Nubians. Sa-Paneshe sent for the purest wax and modelled a litter and four bearers. He breathed life into them and sent them down to Nubia. In the middle of the night they seized the Prince of Nubia, took him back to Egypt and gave him five hundred blows in front of Pharaoh and his court. Then they returned him to his palace, all within six hours.'

Sa-Osiris stopped to ask, 'Is this the truth?' The Nubian's head was bowed in defeat. 'It is.' 'The next morning,' continued Sa-Osiris, 'the Prince of Nubia woke the whole palace with his moans and curses. The sorcerer Sa-Neheset was dragged into his presence and thrown down on the floor beside the bed.

"May the Bull of Meroe curse you," growled the prince. "It was your idea to cast a spell on Egypt. Now save me from this terrible Egyptian sorcerer!"

'Sa-Neheset recited all the protective spells he knew and covered the prince with amulets but that night the wax men came again and took him to Egypt to be beaten. After three nights of this, the anguished prince sent for Sa-Neheset again and said, "By the Bull of Meroe, you have caused me to be humiliated by Egypt. If you cannot save me from their spells tonight I will have you tortured to death!"

'Then Sa-Neheset begged to be allowed to go to Egypt and challenge his rival to a battle of magic. The prince agreed, but before setting out, Sa-Neheset visited his mother, who had taught him most of his magic. When he had told her everything she said to him, "Beware the magicians of Egypt, my son. If you leave Nubia now, surely you will never come back and when we are parted there is nothing I can do to help you."

"I have no choice," answered Sa-Neheset bitterly.

"Then leave me a token," said his mother, "so I will know when you are in danger and need my help."

"If I am defeated by this Egyptian," began Sa-Neheset, "the water you are drinking will turn to the colour of blood and blood will stain the skies."

'Crammed with magic, the Nubian sorcerer hurried to the court at Memphis. He declared himself before Pharaoh and challenged Sa-Paneshe. The two sorcerers stood outside the palace hurling insults at each other, watched by Siamun and his court. Then Sa-Neheset uttered a fire spell and flames burst out of the ground and swept towards Pharaoh. Quicker than thought, Sa-Paneshe had spoken a water spell and sheets of rain extinguished the fire.

'Then Sa-Neheset muttered a spell of darkness. A black cloud enveloped the palace and no-one could see his hand in front of his face. Sa-Paneshe murmured a spell of light and the rays of the sun melted the darkness. Next the Nubian worked a mighty spell and made a huge vault of stone over Pharaoh and his courtiers. The

Egyptians clung together in terror but Sa-Paneshe conjured a giant ship of papyrus and made it carry away the vault and drop it into the sea.

'When Sa-Neheset saw this, he knew that he could never defeat the Egyptian. His only thought was to escape and he made himself invisible and began to creep away. Instantly Sa-Paneshe spoke a spell that made all invisible things visible and Sa-Neheset was exposed. In desperation the Nubian turned himself into a goose and soared upwards. Sa-Paneshe cast a spell to catch him and brought him down on his back with a fowler standing over him with a knife at his throat.

'At that moment, in Nubia, Sa-Neheset's mother saw the water she was drinking turn red and the sky stained with blood. She knew that her son was in terrible danger and she turned herself into a goose and flew to Memphis. There she hovered over the palace, screaming for her son in the voice of a wild bird. Sa-Paneshe recognized her for a sorceress. He spoke another spell and the Nubian woman was soon lying beside her son with a knife at her throat. As she turned back into a woman she begged the Egyptians for mercy.

"If you are to be forgiven," said Sa-Paneshe, "you must swear by all the gods never to come back to Egypt."

'The Nubian woman swore and her son promised that he would not return to Egypt for fifteen hundred years. Pharaoh was satisfied with these oaths and ordered Sa-Paneshe to let the Nubians go. The Egyptian made them a sky boat and together Sa-Neheset and his mother flew back to Nubia and were never seen again.'

Sa-Osiris bowed before Pharaoh. 'Now you have heard the contents of the letter but you do not yet understand why this Nubian has come here. Revenge is the answer. The sorcerer Sa-Neheset has been born again and now that the fifteen hundred years are over he has come here in the form of a chieftain and stands before you!'

There were gasps of amazement from the courtiers but Sa-Osiris swept on. 'He has never repented of his crimes against Egypt and means to do you harm, but he will not succeed for, by Osiris, I am his ancient enemy. I am Sa-Paneshe.

For fifteen hundred years I have lived among the blessed spirits but when I discovered that this fiend of Nubia meant to return to Egypt I begged Osiris to let me be born again and live just long enough to defeat him. Osiris sent my spirit into the melon-vine and I was born to the wife of Setna. So now I stand here to challenge you once more Sa-Neheset!'

When the evil spirit heard these words he began to cast a terrible spell to destroy Pharaoh and his court. Sa-Paneshe countered with a fire spell and the flames surrounded the Nubian sorcerer. Sa-Neheset struggled with spell after spell to hold them back but at last they reached him and consumed him, body and spirit.

Without a word to his father, Sa-Paneshe whom they had known as Sa-Osiris, vanished like a shadow. His task was over and Osiris had summoned him back to the underworld.

Pharaoh and his courtiers began to speak, praising the wisdom of Sa-Paneshe but Setna wept for the loss of his only son. Ramesses tried to comfort him but Setna went back to his house with a sad heart. He lay down on his bed and Mehusekhe lay beside him and they comforted each other. Nine months later another son was born to them, but Setna never ceased to miss Sa-Osiris or to make offerings to his spirit.

The clever thief

In the fifth century BC a Greek historian called Herodotus visited Egypt. When he came to write about Egypt and its history he included a story about the fabulous treasure of the Pharaoh Rhampsinitus and two thieves who tried to steal it. Rhampsinitus is usually identified with the Pharaoh Ramesses III who ruled Egypt in the twelfth century BC, but no-one is sure how much truth there is in the story. Herodotus is sometimes known as the Father of History, but many people call him the Father of Lies . . .

Rhampsinitus was the richest of all the pharaohs and, to protect his treasure, he ordered the royal architect to build a large room to one side of the palace. This room was to have no windows and only one door and the roof, the floor and the walls were to be built of massive blocks of stone. When the building work was finished Pharaoh filled his new treasury with jars of silver, caskets of jewels and many other precious things. Soldiers were set to guard the door and Rhampsinitus felt quite certain that his treasure was safe.

Several years passed and the royal architect fell ill and soon knew that he was going to die. He called his wife and two sons to his bedside and said to them, 'Pharaoh has never been generous to me and I am not a rich man but I have taken thought for your future. The great stones in the outer wall of the treasury all look the same, but one of them is loose and can easily be moved by two people. I planned this so that my sons could control Pharaoh's treasure.' Then he told them how to find the loose stone but with his last breath warned them not to be too greedy.

Once their father was embalmed and buried, the two brothers lost no time in visiting the treasury. Under cover of darkness, they crept up to the outer wall and quickly found and moved the correct stone. They crept through the gap in the wall and pulled the stone back into place behind them in case anyone came past and raised the alarm. Then they lit the torches they carried with them and gasped at the sight of Pharaoh's treasure.

For an hour the brothers wandered about the treasury, trying on jewelled collars, sniffing rare perfumes and admiring golden statuettes. Finally they remembered the need to get away before dawn. Each of the brothers grabbed two handfuls of silver and they left the treasury by their secret entrance and hurried home.

After this the two brothers visited the treasury night after night. At first they were cautious, taking only small amounts of silver that would hardly be missed and spending their new wealth slowly. Gradually, however, the sight of Pharaoh's glittering treasure inflamed their greed. The brothers forgot their father's warning. They began to take away sackfuls of silver and to steal royal jewels for their mother, jewels that she dared not wear.

One day Rhampsinitus came to his treasury to gloat over his wealth. Pharaoh found the guard alert and the door barred and sealed but when he had broken his own seal and entered the treasury he quickly saw that something was wrong. Some of his favourite jewels were missing and the jars which should have been full to the brim with silver, were half empty. Pharaoh was furiously angry but he was at a loss to know who to blame, since the theft had taken place in a windowless room behind a sealed door.

He ordered that the guard on the treasury should be doubled and resealed the door, but the next morning even more silver had gone from the jars. Pharaoh then had cruel and cunning traps laid in the treasury and waited to see what would happen.

That very night the two brothers moved the stone and crept into the treasury. The elder brother ran eagerly towards the jars of silver and one of the traps closed on him, breaking both his legs. He choked back a shriek of anguish and tried to free himself but the more he struggled the more the teeth of the trap wounded him. His brother tried desperately to free him but with no success. As morning approached, the elder brother knew that he was doomed. 'Brother, either I shall bleed to death before dawn or Pharaoh's guards will find and kill me. If they see my face they will recognize me and our whole family will be punished. Save our mother and yourself and give me a quick death by cutting off my head.'

The younger brother was horrified at being asked to do such a thing but in his heart he knew that he must. He ended his brother's agony with one stroke, severed the head and carried it away

with him, hiding it tenderly under his cloak.

The next morning Pharaoh and his guards entered the treasury and were astounded to find a headless body in one of their traps. There was no sign of how the dead thief had entered the room, so Rhampsinitus was as puzzled as ever. 'The man must have an accomplice,' thought Pharaoh, so he ordered the body to be hung from the outer wall of the palace and set ten men to guard it.

'If you see anyone burst into tears as they pass the body,' said Rhampsinitus, 'arrest them at once!'

The head of the elder brother was lovingly buried by his family but when his mother heard what had happened to the body, she railed at her younger son, 'See where your greed has led us—to misery and disgrace. How can your brother's ka reach the Fields of the Blessed with his head in one place and his body in another?'

She ordered her son to rescue his brother's body and when he refused, threatened to denounce him to Pharaoh as the treasure thief. The younger brother saw that he had no choice and sat down to devise a plan.

The next afternoon he disguised himself and loaded two donkeys with bulging wine-skins. Then he drove the donkeys along the road beside the palace as if he was making for the royal kitchens. He took care not to look up at the pitiful sight of his brother's body hanging on the wall, but when he drew level with the guards he let his donkeys collide, knocking out the stoppers from two of the wine-skins.

The wine gushed out and the younger brother stood dithering in the middle of the road as if he did not know which of the donkeys to cope with first. Seeing good wine going to waste, the soldiers of the guard sprang forward to fill their empty food bowls and flasks. The younger brother swore at them in pretended rage and in a minute or so managed to get the stoppers back into the wine-skins. The guard gathered round him, cracking jokes at his expense, and the younger brother seemed to recover his temper and be so amused that he offered the soldiers one of the half empty wine-skins as a present.

The delighted guards invited him to help them to drink it and they all sat down together in the shadow of the wall. The wine was passed round and the younger brother pretended to drink as much as any of them. Then he got unsteadily to his feet and declared that while they were there, they might as well drink another skinful. The soldiers cheered him and the wine went round again.

It was too much for the guards; first they sang and joked then they quarrelled and cried and finally, one by one, they fell asleep. By this time, dusk had fallen and when the younger brother was sure that all the soldiers were snoring in drunken slumber, he jumped up and cut down his elder brother's body. He slung it over one of the donkeys, covered it with his cloak and took it home. His mother was overjoyed and the body was soon secretly buried in the same tomb as the head.

The next morning the guards woke with terrible headaches; they felt even worse when they saw that the body of the treasure thief had gone. Pharaoh punished them severely and, though he could not help admiring the audacity of the crime, he was more determined than ever to catch the thief.

Rhampsinitus set his daughter up in a house in the city and promised that she would spend the night with any man who could tell her the most wicked and the most clever things that he had ever done. If anyone told her a story about robbing the treasury, the princess had orders to shout for the soldiers who would be hidden nearby.

The princess was soon the talk of the city and the younger brother could not resist a visit to her, but before he went he stole a dead man's arm from the house of the embalmers and hid it under his cloak. He arrived at the house of the princess after nightfall and was shown into her room. Even by the dim light of a single oil lamp, he could see that she was very beautiful but he sat down on the end of her couch nearest to the door.

When she asked him to hold her hand, the younger brother put out the dead man's hand. The princess took it in hers and said invitingly, 'Tell me the wickedest thing you have ever done and the cleverest, too. Speak the truth and I will be yours.'

'The wickedest thing I ever did was to kill my own brother by cutting off his head,' answered the younger brother, 'but he asked me to do it because he was caught in a trap in the treasury. The cleverest thing I have ever done was to steal my brother's body by making the guards drunk.'

Then the princess knew that she had found the man that Pharaoh was looking for. She shouted out that she had the thief by the hand, but when the soldiers rushed into the room they found the princess in a faint with a severed arm lying beside her on the couch. The younger brother had fled into the night and disappeared.

When Pharaoh heard about this last exploit he decided that it would be better to have such a clever young man as a friend rather than as an enemy. He offered a free pardon and a rich reward if the treasure thief would give himself up. The younger brother trusted the word of Pharaoh and presented himself at the palace and told his whole story. Rhampsinitus rewarded the audacious thief by marrying him to the princess and making him one of his chief councillors. After that, the younger brother never needed to steal again and he put all his cleverness at the service of Pharaoh.

The voyage of Wenamon

By the early eleventh century BC Egypt had lost most of her empire
after the mysterious Sea Peoples had invaded from the north and
conquered much of Syria and Palestine. In Egypt itself Pharaoh no
longer ruled unchallenged and the most powerful man in the south
was the high priest of Amon at Thebes. A three-thousand-year-old
manuscript claims to relate what happened when the High Priest
Herihor sent an envoy to the Lebanon.

Every year the great image of Amon-Ra, King of the Gods, was
taken out of the temple and across the Nile to the City of the Dead to
feast with Hathor, Lady of Drunkenness. As the years passed the
sacred boat which carried the divine image became more and more
fragile. The high priest wanted to build a new one but the stunted
trees of Egypt could not produce timber of the right length and
quality. Only the famous cedars of Lebanon were good enough for
such a boat, so Herihor decided to send an envoy to Prince Tjekerbaal
who ruled the Lebanon from the city of Byblos. The high priest
gathered together enough gold and silver to pay for the costly timber
and chose as his envoy a priest called Wenamon. A statuette of Amon
of the Road was placed in a gilded shrine and sent with Wenamon to
protect him on his journey.

After a swift voyage down the Nile, Herihor's envoy arrived at the
city of Tanis and presented himself at the palace of Prince Smendes,
who was more powerful in the north than Pharaoh himself.
Wenamon handed over a letter written by the high priest on behalf of
Amon and a scribe read it aloud to Smendes and his wife, Tentamon.
'We are the servants of the King of the Gods,' said the prince and
princess and they promised to find a ship for Wenamon and the men
of his escort, and to help his mission in every way they could.

It was two months before a suitable ship could be found but in the
fourth month of summer, Wenamon boarded one of Smendes' finest
vessels and greeted its Syrian captain, Mengebet. The next day they
sailed north and hugged the coast of Palestine until they were forced
to put in at the port of Dor to take on fresh supplies. Dor had once
been part of the Egyptian empire. Now it belonged to the Tjeker, one
of the peoples who had invaded Palestine from the north. Wenamon
thought of them as little better than pirates, but he was forced to be

117

polite since he needed their help on his voyage.

Bader, the Tjeker Prince of Dor, sent the Egyptian envoy a gift of fifty loaves, a haunch of roast ox and a jug of strong wine. That night Wenamon and his escort feasted on the deck. The wine was passed round again and again and Wenamon slept where he sat. It was not until morning that anyone noticed that one of the crew had disappeared—and so had all the gold and silver that was to pay for the timber!

Wenamon was distraught. How could he go back to Egypt and confess that the gold and silver had been stolen while he lay drunk on the deck? He hurried to the palace of Beder to see what could be done.

'I have been robbed in your harbour!' began Wenamon. 'You are the ruler here, you are in charge of law and order! Arrest the thief and find my gold and silver. It belongs to Amon-Ra himself and, if it's lost, Smendes and all the nobles of Egypt, the High Priest of Amon and the Prince of Byblos will be angry!'

'Are you joking?' asked Beder coldly. 'What right do you have to come here and give me orders? If the thief had been a Tjeker I would

have replaced your gold and silver from my own treasury. As it is, the thief was one of your own crew, so it's no concern of mine. Nevertheless, as a favour to the King of the Gods, I will order a

thorough search to be made. Stay in harbour for a few days and see if your gold and silver appears.'

Wenamon went back to his ship in a furious temper and waited for nine days. On the tenth day he stormed into the palace and demanded to know if his treasure had been found. Beder simply suggested that he wait a few days longer. Wenamon felt certain that the Tjeker prince had no intention of finding the thief and might even have planned the crime in the first place. He ordered Captain Mengebet to set sail at once.

As they sailed north beyond Dor and past the great port of Tyre, Wenamon brooded on how he could possibly find the price of the timber. Half-way between Tyre and Byblos, they overtook a Tjeker ship. In desperation Wenamon ordered his men to board it and sieze whatever valuables they could find. After a fierce struggle the crew of the smaller ship was overpowered and forced to hand over all the silver they had on board. It came to nearly the same amount that had been stolen in Dor. 'You and your ship are free now,' Wenamon told the outraged Tjeker. 'Go to Beder, your prince and tell him to give you my silver when he finds it.'

Wenamon was feeling very pleased with himself as his ship entered the harbour of Byblos. He set up camp on the sea shore with a special tent for the shrine of Amon of the Road. Captain Mengebet had other commissions from Smendes so the ship sailed on while Wenamon sent a message to Prince Tjekerbaal to say that he had arrived.

It was not long before the master of the harbour approached the Egyptian tents. 'How dare a nobody like you set up camp here?' he demanded. 'The Prince of Byblos orders you to leave his harbour at once.'
'How can I?' asked Wenamon, very taken aback. 'I have no ship, tell your master that.'

The harbour master repeated Wenamon's words to the prince but the curt message came back, 'Get out of my harbour!'

Every day the Egyptian envoy asked to see the prince and every day he was refused.
'Well if you want me to go,' said Wenamon angrily, 'give me a ship.'
'Get out of my harbour!' was the only answer.

After a month of this humiliation, Wenamon was ready to give up. When he discovered that there was a Syrian ship in harbour willing to take passengers for Egypt, he ordered his men to start packing. By the middle of the afternoon only the tent of Amon of the Road was still standing. Wenamon could not bear the thought of foreigners staring at the shrine and mocking the god, so he decided to wait until dusk before carrying Amon of the Road aboard the Syrian ship.

That same afternoon, Prince Tjekerbaal had gone to the chief temple of Byblos. As he approached the altar of the goddess of Byblos, carrying a dish of smouldering incense, one of his pages fell down in a fit. The boy turned white, his limbs shook, his head lolled and he spoke in a deep voice that was not his own. Everyone could see that he had been possessed by some god and they crowded round him to catch his words.
'Bring up Amon of the Road,' gasped the boy. 'Summon the envoy who is with him. The King of the Gods has sent this man. See him, listen to him!'

Then the boy fainted and as priests and courtiers clustered round, trying to revive him, Tjekerbaal began to wonder if he had made a mistake in ignoring Wenamon. He knew that the troublesome envoy was due to leave that night so he sent a messenger racing down to the harbour.

Just as Wenamon was going into the tent to fetch the shrine of Amon of the Road, the Harbour Master ran up to him calling, 'Don't leave! The prince orders you to stay until morning.'
'Are my eyes failing me or are you the same man who has come to me every morning saying, "Go away! Leave my harbour!"' mimicked Wenamon. 'This is just a trick. You want me to miss my only chance of getting home and then tomorrow you'll come again to say "Go away" and blame everything on me.'

However much the harbour master protested that it was not a trick, Wenamon refused to believe him and went on packing. When Tjekerbaal heard this he ordered the Syrian ship to stay in harbour as a token of his good faith to Wenamon. Reluctantly, Wenamon stayed on.

The next morning messengers arrived to escort the Egyptian envoy through the city of Byblos to the palace of Tjekerbaal. Wenamon knelt before the shrine of Amon of the Road to pray for courage and a clever tongue and then let the messengers take him to their prince.

Tjekerbaal received him in an upper room overlooking the great harbour. The prince sat in an ivory chair with his back to the window so that the waves seemed to break against his head. He wore a robe of costly Tyrian purple and golden rings on every plump finger. Wenamon bowed and said grandly, 'I bring you the blessing of Amon-Ra, King of the Gods.'
'And when did you leave the holy place of Amon?' asked the prince.
'Five months ago,' Wenamon answered promptly.
'If this is true,' said Tjekerbaal, 'do you have a letter from the High Priest of Amon to prove that you are who you say you are?'
'I did have a letter,' muttered Wenamon, 'but I gave it to Smendes.'

Tjekerbaal lost his temper. 'I see; so you arrive at my palace with no ship and no letter, expecting me to do what ever you say, and you don't even claim to come from Pharaoh! Smendes probably sent you off in a Syrian ship to get rid of you, hoping the captain would throw you overboard!'

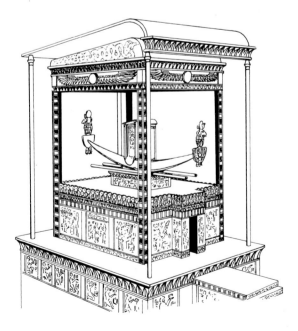

'It was not a Syrian ship,' protested Wenamon. 'It was an Egyptian ship because the crew serve Smendes.'
'Well, well,' said Tjekerbaal irritably, 'what is your business?'

Wenamon came nearer the prince, until there was only the width of an ebony table between them.
'I have come for timber to rebuild the sacred boat of the great god Amon. You know that your father and your father's father sent timber to Egypt. It is your duty to do the same.'
'I'll send timber to Egypt, when Egypt can pay for it,' snapped Tjekerbaal. 'It's true that my ancestors traded with your pharaohs but they didn't cut cedars for them until six Egyptian ships had unloaded their goods onto the quay at Byblos. If you don't believe me, look at the accounts.'

The prince sent for them and three scribes came in, staggering under the weight of piles of yellowing scrolls. Tjekerbaal picked up one that dated to his great-grandfather's day and read out the list of goods supplied by Pharaoh in return for timber for boat-building. Feeling more and more discouraged, Wenamon listened with bowed head.
'If the ruler of Egypt was my overlord,' continued the prince, 'he would simply order me to cut the timber with no talk of payment, but he is not and he cannot. I am not your servant and I am not the servant of the ones who sent you! I am the Lord of the Lebanon. When I speak the cedars fall and the logs lie on the shore. Where is your ship to carry the logs home? Where are the ropes to lash your logs to the deck? Must I do everything for you? It is true that Amon made Egypt before all other lands and that wisdom and skill came to Byblos from Egypt, but that was long ago. Egypt is no-one's master now. You have made a pointless journey.'

Anger lent Wenamon boldness. 'You are wrong. There is no ship that sails on river or sea that doesn't belong to Amon and as for this Lebanon that you call yours, it is nothing but a timber yard for the King of the Gods! How dare you haggle over the price of timber with the envoy of your god? Pharaohs in the past may have sent you shiploads of gold but I can offer you divine gifts. If you say "Yes" to Amon, he will reward you with long life and health.'

Wenamon paused for a moment and then said, 'If you are still doubtful, let me dictate a letter to Smendes and Tentamon, the true servants of Amon. They will repay you for the full expense of cutting and shipping the timber.'

Tjekerbaal was obviously more impressed by the promise of trade goods from Egypt than by divine blessings. One of the scribes stepped forward and the letter was quickly dictated.

Wenamon set up his camp again on the seashore and waited hopefully. After several months, messengers arrived from Egypt. They brought five jars of gold and five of silver, garments woven of the finest linen, five hundred mats, five hundred ropes and five hundred ox-hides for Tjekerbaal. In addition, the Princess Tentamon had sent new clothes, a sack of lentils and five baskets of dried fish for Wenamon.

The prince was delighted with the Egyptian goods and assigned three hundred men to start cutting the timber. The great cedars were felled and left to mature all winter. Then the trunks were stripped of their branches, cut up into logs and dragged by oxen to the seashore.

In the third month of summer, Tjekerbaal sent for the Egyptian envoy. The prince was walking in the palace gardens, protected by a sun-shade and surrounded by fawning courtiers. Many of them were Egyptians who had deserted their own country for the rich court of Byblos and they mocked poor Wenamon until Tjekerbaal said, 'Well, the last of your timber is ready and I have supplied the ships and crews to carry it to Egypt, even though the payment was small. Since you ought to fear my anger more than a storm at sea, set sail at once. I trust that you are grateful. After all, I might have done to you what was done by my father to the envoys of the Vizier Khaemwese. They spent seventeen years waiting in Byblos. Would you like to see their graves?'

'There will be no need,' said Wenamon nervously. 'The vizier was only a man and his envoys were only men. I am the envoy of a god.

You should inscribe on stone, for all men to see, that you welcomed the envoy of Amon, graciously gave him ships and timber and sent him back to Egypt to ask the god for fifty extra years of life for you.'

'These are fine words,' said Tjekerbaal dryly.

'When I get home,' answered Wenamon, 'I shall tell the god and his high priest everything which you have done and they will reward you accordingly.'

The envoy of Egypt bowed to the Prince of Byblos and walked down to the harbour overjoyed that his difficult mission was nearly over. Then he noticed that the harbour was full of Tjeker ships. A Tjeker captain standing on the quay saw Wenamon and shouted, 'That's the man who stole our silver! Arrest him, don't let his ships sail to Egypt!'

Wenamon sat down with his head in his hands and almost wept with frustration. One of Tjekerbaal's scribes hurried up to him to ask what was the matter.

'What is it?'

Wenamon looked up. 'Do you see those birds overhead? They are flying down from Byblos to winter in the warmth of Egypt. They will be there long before me and perhaps I shall never see my home again. Those Tjeker pirates have come to arrest me.'

The scribe ran to the palace to tell his prince what had happened. Tjekerbaal was very annoyed. Now that he had cut the timber for Wenamon he did not want the deal to fall through at the last minute.

'Tell the Tjeker and the Egyptian envoy that I will judge between them in the morning,' said the prince. Secretly, he sent a second message to Wenamon, telling him not to despair. With the message arrived two jugs of the best wine, a whole sheep and a beautiful Egyptian singer who usually waited on Tjekerbaal himself.

Wenamon tried to be cheerful. He had the sheep roasted and shared the wine with the singing girl. Then they sat together on the seashore, the girl playing her harp and singing Egyptian love songs and Wenamon staring at the waves and thinking longingly of home.

In the morning the Tjeker put their case against Wenamon before the Prince of Byblos

and his court. Tjekerbaal pretended to listen with great sympathy.

'And what is it that you want me to do?'

'Arrest him for us,' said the Tjeker captain, 'and let us take him back to Dor to face the punishment for theft.'

'If this Egyptian were only a man, serving an earthly ruler I would hand him to you with pleasure, but alas,' sighed Tjekerbaal, 'he is the envoy of the King of the Gods. As a devout worshipper of Amon, how could I commit the terrible crime of detaining his envoy?'

The Tjeker began to mutter angrily but the prince continued. 'What I shall do is this. The Egyptian will go down to his ships and set sail. As soon as he is out of the harbour of Byblos, I shall release you and your ships so that you can chase him. If you catch him on the open sea that is not my affair and the god cannot blame me.'

The prince was very pleased with this solution, since once Wenamon had left Byblos with the timber, Smendes could not demand the payment back. The Tjeker had to be content with it, too, and Wenamon ran for the harbour. He gathered up the last of his luggage and ordered his captains to sail and put on all the speed they could. Heavily laden with timber, his ships were not as light and swift as those of the Tjeker and Wenamon knelt on the deck and prayed to Amon of the Roads for help.

As soon as they had rowed out of the harbour a strong wind sprang up, blowing them towards Egypt. Wenamon leaned against the mast, limp with relief. Within half an hour they sighted the sails of the Tjeker ships but with such a strong wind behind them there was a good chance that they could keep ahead. Gradually the sky darkened and the wind blew stronger. Lightning flashed, rain sheeted down and the Egyptian ships were soon too busy struggling to survive the storm, to worry about the Tjeker.

The storm raged all through the night but at dawn they sighted land and the weary captains made straight for the shelter of the nearest harbour. The Tjeker had been left far behind, but Wenamon soon had a new worry. His captains assured him that they must have reached the island of Alasiya, the realm of the Princess Hatiba, but the local people seemed far from

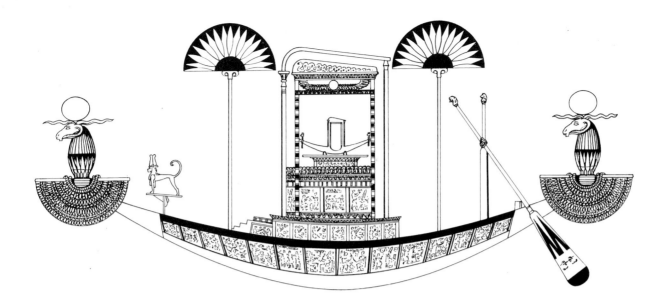

friendly. They were gathering on the quay in an angry crowd and some of them were armed with swords and bows.

Afraid that the townspeople might be about to attack his ships, Wenamon decided to go ashore and look for someone in authority. Surrounded by six of his stoutest men, Wenamon walked down the gangplank into the hostile crowd. At first they were only jostled and jabbered at but then someone threw a stone. Wenamon put up a hand to protect himself but the crowd took it as a threatening gesture and attacked. The Egyptians drew their daggers and prepared to fight for their lives.

Just at that moment, the Princess Hatiba herself came out of a nearby house to see what the commotion was about. Wenamon threw himself at her feet and said desperately, 'Isn't there anyone here who understands Egyptian?' 'I understand it,' said one of Hatiba's attendants. 'Who are you?'
'Tell your lady that I am Wenamon, the envoy of the great god Amon. I come from Thebes, the holy city of Amon and even there we have heard that justice reigns in Alasiya. But is it just to attack someone who has been driven into your harbour by a storm? The crews of my ships belong to the great Prince of Byblos and if anything happened to them here he would be very angry and take his revenge.'

When all this had been translated for the princess she ordered her people to lay down their arms and scolded them for attacking innocent strangers. Then she smiled at the Egyptian envoy and spoke to him in her own language.
'My lady asks you to spend the night in her palace,' said the interpreter and Wenamon accepted gratefully.

For two days and nights Wenamon and his men enjoyed the hospitality of Hatiba. She urged him to stay longer but Wenamon was afraid that the Tjeker might yet catch up with him, so he left Alasiya on the third morning, loaded with gifts for Amon. The captains took a different route from the outward voyage but Wenamon was always nervously watching the horizon for Tjeker sails. He did not feel safe until they reached the coast of Egypt and the timber was taken off and loaded into barges for the long slow journey up the Nile.

Wenamon called at Tanis to thank Smendes and Tentamon for the goods they had sent to Byblos. Then he rejoined the barges and a month later he was back in Thebes. The whole city rejoiced to see the timbers arrive at last. A magnificent boat was built for the image of Amon-Ra, and the high priest rewarded Wenamon and thanked the gods for his safe return to the land of his birth.

Egypt in decline

In spite of the grandiose splendour of Ramesses II's reign, Egypt's power was already waning. The late second millenium BC was a time of turmoil in the Near East; old empires were breaking up and new countries, like Israel, were being formed. At first this turmoil must have seemed remote to Egypt but the successors of Ramesses II soon had to defend their borders against foreign enemies. Libyan tribes, intent on settling in the Delta, attacked from the west and from the north came invasions by the mysterious Sea Peoples who had already swept away the mighty Hittite empire. In the reign of Ramesses III (c1194–1163 BC), the Sea Peoples were defeated in two great battles, one on land and one at sea. Egypt was saved, but most of her empire and with it much of her prosperity, had gone for ever. The story of 'The voyage of Wenamon' shows how low Egypt's prestige had sunk by the eleventh century BC.

Ramesses III was followed by a series of weak pharaohs and the government became corrupt and inefficient. The craftsmen of Deir el-Medina went on strike several times because their wages had not been paid and there was a major scandal when it came out that the authorities in Thebes had been turning a blind eye to the robbery of ancient royal tombs. Nubia slipped out of Egypt's grasp and the leaders of the army and the priesthood became more and more powerful and founded dynasties of their own.

When the line of Ramesses died out, a new dynasty, the Twenty-First (c1070–945 BC), ruled from the city of Tanis in the Delta, but the unity of Egypt was growing frailer. The next dynasty was of Libyan descent and soon split into two rival branches. By the eighth century BC Egypt was divided amongst half a dozen rulers, all claiming to be kings. These petty kings were all defeated in 730 BC by Piye of Napata, the ruler of Nubia. Though Nubia had been independent for centuries, the kings of Napata were in many ways more Egyptian than the Egyptians. They were devoted to the god Amon and still had themselves buried in pyramids, though the custom had died out in Egypt a thousand years before. King Piye's descendants reunited Egypt and ruled as the Twenty-Fifth Dynasty (c712–657 BC). The last of these Nubian kings was driven back to Napata by an Assyrian invasion.

From their capital of Niniveh, the Assyrians had conquered a huge empire and were infamous for the cruelty of their rule. The invasion was a terrible blow to Egyptian pride but the Assyrians did not have enough troops to subdue Egypt completely. They were forced to rule through Egyptian vassals, who were supposed to pay tribute to the Assyrian king. One of these vassals, Psammetichus of Sais, soon led a successful revolt against the Assyrians and claimed the throne of all Egypt. He and his dynasty, the Twenty-Sixth, ruled a united country from 664 to 525 BC.

The Twenty-Sixth Dynasty was a time of comparative peace and prosperity for Egypt. The only threat came from King Nebuchadnezzar of Babylon who had captured Jerusalem and carried the Jews into exile, but his attacks on Egypt were all defeated. In the late sixth century BC, Persia replaced Assyria and Babylon as the greatest power in the Near East and in 525 BC the Persian king, Cambyses, successfully invaded Egypt.

In the fourth century BC Egyptian leaders struggled to make their country independent again. For a time they were successful but the Persians soon reconquered Egypt and ruled more oppressively than ever before. Then the Persian empire itself came under attack from the young King of Macedonia, Alexander the Great. In 332 BC Alexander drove the Persians out of Egypt and was hailed by his new subjects as the son of Amon.

When Alexander died, in 323 BC, his body was brought to Egypt and buried, first at Memphis, and then in a splendid tomb in the new city of Alexandria. His vast empire was divided amongst his generals and Egypt became the share of General Ptolemy, whose descendants ruled the country for the next two hundred and fifty years. Alexandria, with its famous library, became a great centre of Greek learning and Greek law and coinage were introduced, but the Egyptians were allowed to go on building temples to their gods. These acted as strongholds of their ancient culture.

As a family the Ptolemies were cruel and quarrelsome and the women were as ruthless as the men. The most famous of the Ptolemies, Queen Cleopatra VII, had already killed an elder sister and was fighting a war against her younger brother when Julius Caesar arrived in Egypt in 48 BC. To save his throne during a revolt, Cleopatra's father had put Egypt under Roman protection and Rome was only waiting for an excuse to make the country part of her growing empire.

Cleopatra kept Egypt independent by winning Caesar's favour and she bore him his only son. When Julius Caesar was murdered, his power was divided between his friend Mark Antony and his great-nephew Octavian. Antony took charge of the eastern empire and one of his first tasks was to demand the homage of Egypt. However, when Cleopatra came, the Roman general was dazzled by her. Antony and Cleopatra were soon ruling the east together from Alexandria, careless of the disapproval of Rome; but when the inevitable clash with Octavian came they were quickly defeated. Rather than be forced to walk in chains through the streets of Rome, both Antony and Cleopatra killed themselves.

So in 30 BC Egypt became a mere province of the Roman empire. Like the Greeks before them, the new conquerors were fascinated by Egyptian culture. A religion which promised a happy afterlife had a great appeal to the Romans and the cults of Isis and Osiris spread across the empire. A temple of Isis was even built in England, in the Roman city of Londinium. It was not the rule of Rome but the rise of Christianity which was to destroy Egypt's ancient culture. When Christianity became the official religion of the Roman empire, the temples of Egypt were forced to close. Ancient tombs became the homes of Christian hermits, the images of the old gods were defaced and the meaning of the hieroglyphic inscriptions was forgotten. The Egyptians deliberately turned away from their past.

In the seventh century AD Egypt was invaded by the Arabs and became a brilliant centre of Islamic civilization, but a large Christian community remained. The language of this community was Coptic, a mixture of Greek and Egyptian. Still used in the services of the Coptic church, it provides the last living link with the culture of Ancient Egypt.

Writing in Ancient Egypt

Writing was first used in Egypt in about three thousand BC. From that time onwards the country was governed by people who had been trained as scribes and who could read and write the Egyptian language. Reed brushes were used for writing and every scribe carried a palette with cakes of red and black ink, a water pot and a tool for smoothing the surface of paper. Egyptian paper was made from the beaten pith of papyrus stems. It was an expensive material and rough work or school exercises were written on flakes of limestone or potsherds (pieces of broken pottery) instead.

For most of Egyptian history there were two main scripts: hieroglyphic and hieratic. The beautiful hieroglyphic script with its detailed pictures of men, objects and animals was carved or painted on stelae and statues or in tombs or temples but rarely written on papyrus. For everyday use there were simplified or abbreviated hieroglyphs, which made up the flowing hieratic script. Both scripts were usually written from right to left with no breaks between words or sentences and no punctuation marks.

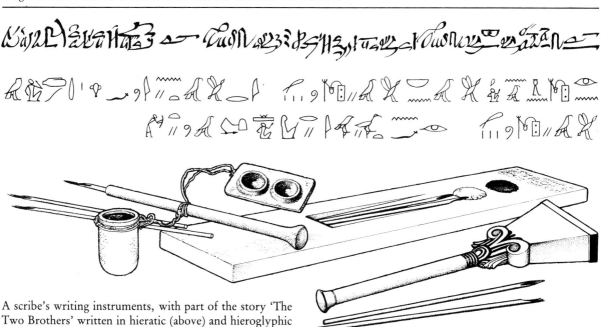

A scribe's writing instruments, with part of the story 'The Two Brothers' written in hieratic (above) and hieroglyphic scripts.

HIEROGLYPHIC SCRIPT

The hieroglyphic script is often referred to as 'picture-writing' but this is misleading. The seven hundred hieroglyphs that were in general use can be divided into two types of sign: phonograms and semograms. Phonograms represent sounds and semograms convey the meaning of whole words. The most common phonograms were twenty-four signs which represent a single consonant or semi-vowel such as:

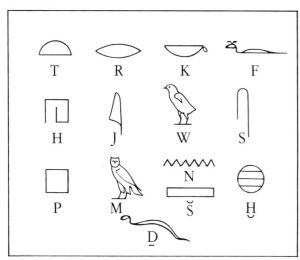

Other signs each represented a combination of between two and four sounds:

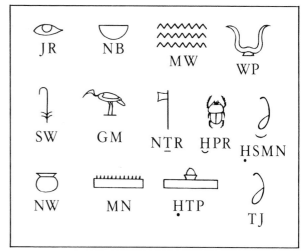

As in many oriental languages, vowels were not written down. This makes it very difficult to decide how an ancient Egyptian word was pronounced or how it should be written out in full. Scholars following different systems often spell the same word in a variety of ways, so that the god of Thebes may be written as Amon, Amun or Amen.

128

To add to the confusion, early Egyptologists frequently used ancient Greek versions of Egyptian words and the Greek names for most Egyptian towns. Names such as Thoth or Hermopolis are now so well known that they have to be preferred to the Egyptian.

In addition to the phonograms two types of semogram were used, logograms and taxograms. Logograms indicate the meaning of a whole word by an appropriate picture:

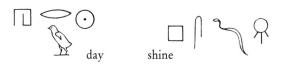

Taxograms were written at the end of a word and they show the general area of meaning to which the word belongs. Verbs of motion, such as to go or to walk, end with a pair of legs:

Words to do with light often end with a picture of the disc or of the sun:

day   shine

Proper names end with a seated male or female figure:

Amonhotep   Tentamon

Most Egyptian words are made up of a mixture of phonograms and taxograms:

 rm (fish) is written with an *r* sign, an *m* sign and a picture of a fish.

 jnr (stone) is written with a *j* sign, an *n* sign, an *r* sign and a block of stone.

In some words a single sound is expressed twice by different types of phonogram:

hnw (praise or rejoicing) is written with an *h* sign, an *n* sign, an *nw* sign, a *w* sign and a taxogram of a man kneeling beating his chest. It should be read as *hnw* not *hnnww*, since the *n* sign and the *w* sign simply reinforce the meaning of the *nw* sign.

To make matters more complicated some signs can act as phonograms, logograms and taxograms:

 spells *pr* in some words.

But because its sign is a simplified house plan it can also be used as a logogram to write house.

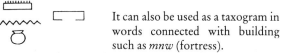 It can also be used as a taxogram in words connected with building such as *mnw* (fortress).

This, together with the Egyptian habit of rearranging the signs to make a word look neater, can make a text from ancient Egypt very hard to decipher. Excavating temples and tombs may be more exciting but it is the dedicated scholars who have struggled to understand the Egyptian language who are the true heroes of Egyptology.

Symbols in the Egyptian myths

At the beginning of each chapter the artist has illustrated some of the objects and symbols identified with the characters and events of the story.

p. 11 RED LAND, BLACK LAND Typical images of ancient Egypt. From the top: the pyramids at Giza, the combined red and white crown of the Two Lands, an early Egyptian community, the outer case of a coffin containing a mummy, the craftsman's village of Deir el-Medina, the River Nile.

p. 21 THE NINE GODS At the top, a stylized representation of the sky goddess Nut and, at the bottom, of the earth god Geb. The central figure is Ra-Atum and the board and pieces are for the Egyptian version of draughts. The birds are ibises, sacred to Thoth.

p. 24 THE SECRET NAME OF RA The Sun God, Ra, is drawn in Egyptian style as a man with a scarab beetle for a head. The magic snake is shown threatening Ra and crumbling into dust after biting him.

p. 26 THE EYE OF THE SUN At the top the sun covered in gloom symbolizes Egypt's depression. Hathor as wildcat looks down on scenes from three of the fables Thoth relates. Below, Thoth as a baboon.

p. 34 THE ANGER OF RA The Sun God shines down on Egypt, shown first as prosperous and then empty of human inhabitants. Nut, in her cow form, wears a sun disc, uraeus serpent and double plume between her horns. At the bottom, Hathor in her lioness form.

p. 36 THE MURDER OF OSIRIS The Nile flowing into the sea forms the background. Isis, as a swallow, circles the tree-pillar which hides the body of Osiris. Below, the infant Horus in the marshes.

p. 41 THE CONFLICT OF HORUS AND SETH Falcon-headed Horus wearing the white crown, with above, the pine boat he used to trick Seth and, below, the two gods fighting as hippopotami.

p. 48 THE JOURNEY OF THE SOUL A wrapped mummy is surrounded by its *ka*. Above is the *ba* or soul, in the form of a heron. Behind is the doorway to the Underworld with, below, the ass-eating serpents and the fire, symbolizing the ordeals through which the *ba* had to pass. At the base, a vessel for embalming fluid in the form of a lotus, a symbol of rebirth.

p. 51 THE SEVEN YEAR FAMINE The ram-headed god Khnum releases the Nile onto a drought-stricken Egypt.

p. 53 KING KHUFU AND THE MAGICIANS At the top, the wax crocodile becomes a real one. In the centre one of King Sneferu's rowers and her fish-shaped pendant. At the bottom, the goose, duck and ox whose severed heads were rejoined to their bodies by the magician Djedi.

p. 60 THE ELOQUENT PEASANT Scenes from daily life based on wall paintings: woman and child gathering grain; the making of bread and beer; peasant and loaded donkey; and scribe with scrolls and writing instruments. In the centre,

the peasant pleading his case against the corrupt official.

p. 64 THE SHIPWRECKED SAILOR The giant serpent looms over the sailor and the fruits of the mysterious island. Below, a fire drill.

p. 69 THE CAPTURE OF JOPPA Egyptian war chariot and arms (bronze scimitar and poleaxe weighted with ball). Below stylized drawing of walled city and symbols of encampment and soldiers carrying a basket.

p. 71 THE DOOMED PRINCE The prince and his fates—crocodile, snake and dog with the water demon and the tower in which the princess was confined.

p. 77 THE TWO BROTHERS The wives of the two brothers are enclosed in stylized hearts. At top and bottom are cedar and persea trees. Between the figures are small sarcophagi, symbolizing the deaths of the two faithless women.

p. 84 THE BLINDING OF TRUTH Lies (top) gloats over Truth's disgrace. Below, Truth is discovered by Desire's maidservants, then slumps in despair at her door. Bottom, Truth reaches up for justice.

p. 86 THE SUN PHARAOH At the top, Akhenaten, wearing the double crown and below, the bust of Nefertiti from el-Amarna. In the centre, the Aten (solar disc) with rays ending in hands holding out the sign of life.

p. 88 THE PRINCESS OF BAKHTAN The god Khons, holding a crook and flail and wearing the sidelock that symbolizes childhood and the disc of the full moon.

p. 92 THE BOOK OF THOTH The prince and his brother approach the inner chamber of the tomb.

p. 103 THE YOUNG MAGICIAN Osiris, in feathered crown, sits beneath a golden canopy with a lotus flower and jackal-headed Anubis and ibis-headed Thoth before him. In the centre, the scales weigh the heart of a dead man against the feather of Truth and the Devourer waits to snatch the damned. Below, father and son fall into the Underworld past the guardian demons.

p. 108 THE SEALED LETTER The Nubian chieftain with his sealed papyrus scroll. Above, the sorcerer's mother in her goose form. Below, the sorcerer returns to Egypt for revenge.

p. 114 THE CLEVER THIEF A thieving hand grasps typical Egyptian gold and silver jewelry. Below, a stylized treasure room, and a wineskin from which wine pours over a sculpture of a severed head. Bottom, the teeth of a man-trap.

p. 117 THE VOYAGE OF WENAMON Wenamon's ships are caught in a storm; below, the cedars of Lebanon.

p. 126 EGYPT IN DECLINE The crumbling majesty of ancient Egypt, based on a statue of Zoser, and coins showing Alexander and Ptolemy I. In the centre, Cleopatra VII, Julius Caesar and Mark Antony. Below, the step-pyramid of Zoser forms the background to the newer influences of Christianity and Islam, symbolized by the cross and the hand. The fingers of the hand represent the five pillars of Islam and the script reads 'God is great'.

Index

Figures in italics refer to
illustrations